ALSO BY LEON F. LITWACK

Black Leaders of the Nineteenth Century (1988)
Editor, with August Meier

Been in the Storm So Long:
The Aftermath of Slavery
(1979)

To Look for America:
From Hiroshima to Woodstock (1971)
Film

The United States
(Seventh Edition, 1991)
With Winthrop Jordan

Reconstruction:
An Anthology of Revisionist Writings (1969)
Editor, with Kenneth Stampp

The American Labor Movement (1962)
Editor

North of Slavery:
The Negro in the Free States, 1790–1860
(1961)

TROUBLE IN MIND

TROUBLE IN MIND

Black Southerners in the Age of Jim Crow

LEON F. LITWACK

8/99

ALFRED A. KNOPF   NEW YORK   1998

"Trouble in Mind," words and music by Richard M. Jones. Copyright © 1926,
1937 by MCA Music Publishing, a division of MCA Inc. Copyright Renewed.
International Copyright Secured. All rights reserved.

Library of Congress Cataloging-in-Publication Data
Litwack, Leon F.
Trouble in mind : Black southerners in the age of Jim Crow /
by Leon F. Litwack.—1st ed.
p.   cm.
Continues: Been in the storm so long.
Includes bibliographical references and index.
ISBN 0-394-52778-x (hc : alk. paper)
1. Afro-Americans—Southern States—History—1877–1964.
2. Afro-Americans—Segregation—Southern States—History.
3. Southern States—History—1865–1951.
4. Southern States—Race relations.
I. Title.
E185.6.L68   1998
975'.00496073—dc21   97-49465
CIP

Manufactured in the United States of America

Published April 6, 1998
Second Printing May 1998

PHOTOGRAPHIC CREDITS

Insert photographs courtesy of:

Doris Ullman Collection, Special Collections, University of Oregon;
Polk Collection, Fisk University; Richard Samuel Roberts Collection,
South Caroliniana Library, University of South Carolina

For Evan and Reva,

Ann, John, and Nadia,

with love

Trouble in mind, I'm blue,
But I won't be always,
For the sun goin' shine in my back door some-day.

Trouble in mind, that's true,
I have almost lost my mind;
Life ain't worth livin'—feel like I could die.

I'm gonna lay my head on some lonesome railroad line,
Let the two nineteen pacify my troubled mind.

Trouble in mind, I'm blue,
My poor heart is beatin' slow,
Never had so much trouble in my life before.

I'm gonna lay my head
On that lonesome railroad track.
But when I hear the whistle,
Lord, I'm gonna pull it back.

I'm goin' down to the river
Take along my rocking chair,
And if the blues don't leave me,
I'll rock on away from there.

Well, trouble, oh, trouble,
Trouble on my worried mind,
When you see me laughin',
I'm laughin' just to keep from cryin'.

CONTENTS

An eight-page insert of photographs follows page 136

PREFACE

Nowhere is the paradox of black life in the United States more graphically revealed than in Ralph Ellison's portrayal of the black odyssey in *Invisible Man*. In the opening scene, the nameless hero is deeply moved by the words of his dying grandfather. After emancipation, his grandparents had stayed on the same place, they had worked hard, and they had brought up their children in the etiquette of accommodation and survival. On his deathbed, however, the grandfather confessed to having lived a more complex life.

> Son, after I'm gone I want you to keep up the good fight. I never told you, but our life is a war and I have been a traitor all my born days, a spy in the enemy's country ever since I give up my gun back in the Reconstruction. Live with your head in the lion's mouth. I want you to overcome 'em with yeses, undermine 'em with grins, agree 'em to death and destruction, let 'em swoller you till they vomit or bust wide open.

The outburst visibly shook the family, some thought he had lost his mind, and the younger children were quickly ushered out of the room. "Learn it to the young uns," the grandfather whispered intensely, and then he died. "My folks were more alarmed over his last words than over his dying," the hero recalled. "It was as though he had not died at all, his words caused so much anxiety. I was warned emphatically to forget what he had said." But he could never put it out of his mind.

The hero had still not sorted out the implications of his grandfather's words when the most prominent whites in town invited him to repeat for them his graduation speech, "in which I showed that humility was the secret, indeed, the very essence of progress." But when summoned to the main ballroom of the leading hotel for this occasion, he found himself in the midst of a noisy, raucous "smoker." Along with some other black youths, he was compelled to participate in a "battle royal"—that is, to undergo a racial baptism. With an audience of whites looking on, the youths—dressed in boxing shorts and boxing gloves—were rushed to the front of the ballroom. The place smelled of cigars and whiskey. "A sea of faces, some hostile, some amused, ringed around us, and in the center, facing us, stood a magnificent blonde—stark naked." The woman danced before them, accentuating the American flag tattooed upon her belly. The whites pretended to be angry if the youths looked at her, insulted if they did not.

The crowd attending the "smoker" was made up of the "better sort," the leading citizens in the community—bankers, lawyers, judges, doctors, merchants, teachers, one of the more prominent pastors, and the school superintendent who had arranged for the hero to give his speech. With sadistic delight, they tormented the black youths in order to humiliate them, to embarrass them sexually, to degrade them, and to underscore the unmistakable limits placed on their aspirations and rewards in a white man's society.

Once the naked woman was removed from the arena, the crowd prepared itself for the climactic scene: the battle royal. The black youths were thrown into the ring, blindfolded, and compelled to fight each other; the last survivor would be designated the winner. By this time, the audience was nearly hysterical, and then, finally, the ordeal ended. Having performed their roles to the amusement and satisfaction of the crowd, the black youths prepared to receive their promised monetary reward, but not until they had fought among themselves for it, scrambling for the coins thrown to them on an electrified rug. The shiny gold coins turned out to be worthless brass pocket tokens advertising a new automobile.

No historian could have improved upon the scene. This is more than a group of sadistic white men having fun at the expense of a group of black boys. It is a racial rite of passage, a necessary initiation into the racial ethics of the white South. "It is a ritual in preservation of caste lines," Ellison explained, "a keeping of taboo to appease the gods and ward off bad luck. It is also the initiation ritual to which all greenhorns are subjected."

The grandfather's dying imperative and the battle royal provide the overture for the extraordinary black odyssey in *Invisible Man*, the struggle of one individual to define himself and maintain his humanity, integrity, and self-respect. Even as the ambitious hero attends col-

lege, even as he is encouraged to believe he is making remarkable
progress, even as he embraces the white man's work ethic and success
credo, even as he accommodates himself to the white man's ways of
thinking and acting, he finds his expectations betrayed and his goals
unreachable. He moves not upward but downward, and he ultimately
leaves the South altogether, moving from a static rural society to an industrializing, urbanizing, and more promising North. But with every
step, he must again perform the rituals expected of him and play the
roles defined by whites, all of them equally dehumanizing, equally degrading, equally unrewarding. For hundreds of thousands of southern
black men and women, this odyssey summed up the entirety of their
lives.

When black Southerners in 1865 staked out their claims to becoming
a free people, they projected a very different vision of the future. They
aspired to a better life than they had known, to a life once thought impossible to contemplate. They wanted what they had seen whites
enjoy—the vote, schools, churches, legal marriages, judicial equity, and
the chance not only to work on their own plots of land but to retain the
rewards of their labor. During Reconstruction, they seized the opportunity to make these goals a reality, to reorder the post-bellum South. It
was a time of unparalleled hope, laden with possibility, when black
men and women acted to shape their own destiny.

But any experiment in biracial democracy was bound to be perilous.
Neither military defeat nor the end of slavery suggested to whites the
need to reexamine racial relationships and assumptions. Confronting a
society "suddenly turned bottom-side up," the white South responded
with massive resistance. The language whites employed to describe Reconstruction, the methods used to subvert the Radical governments
and black voting, and the determination to indoctrinate future generations with the idea of Reconstruction as a "tragic era," betrayed white
fears that this experiment might actually succeed in restructuring the
South and racial relationships. Whites employed terror, intimidation,
and violence to doom Reconstruction, not because blacks had demonstrated incompetence but because they were rapidly learning the uses
of political power, not because of evidence of black failure but the far
more alarming evidence of black success. This was clearly unacceptable to a people who deemed themselves racially superior and who resisted any evidence to the contrary. "There was one thing," W .E. B.
Du Bois would write, "that the white South feared more than Negro
dishonesty, ignorance, and incompetency, and that was Negro honesty,

knowledge, and efficiency." Within a decade, it was all over. The fate of Reconstruction and the betrayal of the promise of a biracial democratic society would affect black Americans and this nation for the next century.

What the white South lost on the battlefields of the Civil War and during Reconstruction, it would largely retake in the late nineteenth and early twentieth century. In what has been called the "nadir" of African American history, a new generation of black Southerners shared with the survivors of enslavement a sharply proscribed and deteriorating position in a South bent on commanding black lives and black labor by any means necessary. The most intense years—the focus of this book—were between 1890 and the Great Migration, but the seeds had been planted in the forcible overthrow of Reconstruction in the 1870s, and the Age of Jim Crow would span more than half a century. This is the story of how the first generations born in freedom, more questioning of their "place" and less inclined to render absolute deference to whites, encountered (and in a certain sense helped to provoke) the most violent and repressive period in the history of race relations in the United States.

The term "Jim Crow," as a way of characterizing black people, had its origins in minstrelsy in the early nineteenth century. Thomas "Daddy" Rice, a white minstrel, popularized the term. Using burned cork to blacken his face, attired in the ill-fitting, tattered garment of a beggar, and grinning broadly, Rice imitated the dancing, singing, and demeanor generally ascribed to Negro character. Calling it "Jump Jim Crow," he based the number on a routine he had seen performed in 1828 by an elderly and crippled Louisville stableman belonging to a Mr. Crow. "Weel about, and turn about / And do jis so; / Eb'ry time I weel about, / I jump Jim Crow." The public responded with enthusiasm to Rice's caricature of black life. By the 1830s, minstrelsy had become one of the most popular forms of mass entertainment, "Jim Crow" had entered the American vocabulary, and many whites, northern and southern, came away from minstrel shows with their distorted images of black life, character, and aspirations reinforced. Less clear is how a dance created by a black stableman and imitated by a white man for the amusement of white audiences became synonymous with a system designed by whites to segregate the races. Abolitionist newspapers employed the term in the 1840s to describe separate railroad cars for blacks and whites in the North. But by the 1890s, "Jim Crow" took on additional force and meaning to denote the subordination and separation of black people in the South, much of it codified, much of it still enforced by custom and habit.

The triumph of Jim Crow in the 1890s and early twentieth century coincided with the coming of age of a new generation of blacks. The veterans who had fought in the abolitionist and Reconstruction struggles were mostly gone, along with their commitment to politics and agitation. Frederick Douglass died in 1895, increasingly disillusioned with the prospects of his people. In his last great public address, "The Lessons of the Hour," he took note of the growing repression, the triumph of disfranchisement, lynching terror, and white indifference. "I have sometimes thought that the American people are too great to be small." But he now doubted that judgment. "I cannot shut my eyes to the ugly facts before me." Many of the achievements of Reconstruction, such as the public schools, were undermined if not devastated altogether. Some of the most promising black leaders, including George White of North Carolina and Ida B. Wells of Tennessee, chose exile in the North over a tortured freedom in the New South. Booker T. Washington would emerge in the 1890s with his program and faith in black progress, but when he died in 1915, not only had his power declined but so, too, had the credibility of his philosophy of uplift through accommodation and hard work.

The vast majority of black Southerners in this period were hardworking men and women, many of them laboring at unrewarding tasks. Only a few managed to enter the small but growing middle class. This book will draw largely from the perspectives and experiences of people who spent their lives in relative obscurity, who never shared the fruits of affluence, who never enjoyed power. This is the story of what they confronted, how they struggled, worked, tried to educate themselves, and found ways to temper their accommodation to the new racial order. And it is the story of what happened to their aspirations and expectations. This is not so much a study of black leadership and ideology as it is a story of daily struggles by black men and women to wrest some meaning and value out of their working lives. It is less a study of the institutional life of blacks than of the experience of being black in the late-nineteenth- and early-twentieth-century South.

This is no easy history to assimilate. It is the story of a people denied the basic rights of citizenship in the land of their birth, yet fully expected to display as much patriotism as their white brethren, who enjoyed the full exercise of such rights. It is the story of a people stamped as inferior, based on the idea of race, yet fully expected to provide the basic labor of the South even as they complied with the perverse etiquette of Jim Crow. It is the story of a people largely invisible (except as caricatures) in the public's mind and consciousness. To suggest that their story is simply another version of the classic struggle of all immigrant groups—Irish, Italians, Germans, Slavs, and Jews, for example—ignores the distinctiveness of the black experience, the unique and overwhelming obstacles blacks faced, and the indignities they were forced to endure. America was founded on white supremacy and the notion of black inferiority and black unfreedom—a notion each new wave of immigrants assimilated as quickly as the epithet "nigger."

Violence and the fear of violence helped to shape black lives and personalities. The intention in these pages is not to depict blacks only as victims or whites only as victimizers. But the extent and quality of the violence unleashed on black men and women in the name of enforcing black deference and subordination cannot be avoided or minimized. The details make for unpleasant reading, sometimes stretching our credulity, numbing the mind to the full extent of the horror, but they must be examined if we are to understand how normal men and women could live with, participate in, defend, even reinterpret such atrocities, so they would not see themselves or be perceived as less than civilized.

Living in largely separate worlds, the two races interacted in conformity to custom, law, and "place." But there were limits. If at times this is a violent history, it is also a study of the extraordinary resourcefulness of black men and women. Under severe constraints, black Southerners created a world of their own "behind the veil," as W. E. B. Du Bois described it, and found ways to respond to their situation. Evidence of this response may be found at all levels, not simply in the actions and words of the most articulate leaders or in the agitation for civil rights. It may be found in the families black Southerners maintained, in the institutions they created, in the schools they worked so hard to sustain, in the businesses they established, in the churches they attended, and in the voluntary associations that afforded them important outlets and support. This interior life, largely unknown and incomprehensible to whites, permitted black Southerners to survive and endure.

Denied access to the political process, limited in what they could acquire in the schools, and dehumanized in popular culture, black Southerners were compelled to find other ways to express their deepest feelings and to demonstrate their individual and collective integrity. What helped to sustain them through bondage and a tortured freedom had been a rich oral expressive tradition, consisting of folk beliefs, proverbs, humor, sermons, spirituals, gospel songs, hollers, work songs, the blues, and jazz. Through a variety of expression, black men and women conveyed not only their disillusionment, alienation, and frustration, but also their joys, aspirations, triumphs, and expectations; they used such expression both to confront their situation and to overcome and transcend it. "How much history can be transmitted by pressure on a guitar string?" Robert Palmer asks in *Deep Blues,* and he answers, "The thought of generations, the history of every human being who's ever felt the blues come down like showers of rain."

The black community was divided over strategies of accommodation and resistance; over aspirations, priorities, and perceptions of whites and themselves; and along lines of class and color. Throughout their history in this country, they were also divided over how to designate themselves as a people. "Africans," "colored Americans," "blacks," "Negroes," and "Afro-Americans" all enjoyed some popularity at various times. The uncertainty over how to define and redefine themselves actually reflected the vicissitudes of race relations and profound shifts in racial consciousness and in the faith blacks placed in the strategies of integration and separation. For the purposes of this work, the terms "Negro" and "black" are both employed, though "Negro" is generally confined to black people as the objects of white concerns, attitudes, and policies. By the 1890s, both Booker T. Washington and W. E. B. Du Bois expressed a strong preference for "Negro," and the term "New Negro" had come into frequent use, evoking for many blacks pride in a new and less submissive generation, and for whites, fearful reminders of Reconstruction. Only with the advent of the civil rights era in the 1960s would "Negro" be discarded by blacks as a term that originated with whites and that had come to be identified with paternalism and subjugation.

Through the first four decades of the twentieth century, the essential mechanisms, attitudes, and assumptions governing race relations and the subordination of black Southerners remained largely intact. The same patterns of discrimination, segregation, unequal justice, and racial violence persisted. Sporadic breakthroughs were made by individual blacks, and the New Deal injected a measure of hope, but the great mass of black men and women in the South still lived out their lives in a severely restricted, isolated, and relatively static world. More than a million black Americans fought in World War II, as they had in World War I, to make the world safe for democracy. After the war, even larger numbers developed new strategies and tactics to make the United States safe for themselves. On some new battlefields—Montgomery, Selma, Birmingham, Jackson, Little Rock, Detroit, Boston, Chicago, Los Angeles—still another struggle would be waged over the meaning of freedom. That struggle persists.

ACKNOWLEDGMENTS

This book passed through a number of stages on the way to completion, and at each stage various institutions and individuals provided indispensable assistance. Teaching both the survey course in American history and an upper-division course in the history of African Americans and race relations, I have tried out much of the material on my students. I am grateful to them for their responses, questions, and encouragement, as I am to the many audiences I have addressed on this subject across the country. The invitation to deliver the Walter Lynwood Fleming Lectures in Southern History at Louisiana State University in 1983 led me to organize some of the preliminary research. Rather than publish those lectures, however, I chose to use them as the nucleus for a larger and more deeply researched book.

The University of California at Berkeley provided initial support with a Humanities Research Fellowship, as did the Rockefeller Foundation. Since 1987, I have been extremely fortunate to enjoy the perquisites of the Alexander F. and May T. Morrison chair in American history at Berkeley. It has provided not only time for research and writing but graduate assistants, travel support, and funds for the acquisition of necessary materials.

My research trips brought me to manuscript libraries in colleges, universities, and foundations, to special collections in public libraries (Yazoo City, Mississippi, and the Schomburg Center in New York), and to state and federal archives. But in addition I was able to explore in some depth the southern landscape, to become more intimately familiar with its physical and human dimensions. Two visiting professorships, one at Louisiana State University in 1985 and the other as the Ford Foundation Professor of Southern Studies at the University of Mississippi in 1989, permitted me to travel the backroads and to explore in particular the Mississippi Delta. I am grateful to William Ferris for the invitation to come to the Center for the Study of Southern Culture at Oxford, and to Keith Dockery for her gracious hospitality at Dockery Farms in the Delta, a place with an extraordinary history of its own.

The quality of any research library rests not only on its collections but on the expertise of its staff. The brief acknowledgment here may seem perfunctory but the debt is enormous. For the invaluable and generous support and assistance extended to me, I am grateful to the staffs of the Alabama, Arkansas, Georgia, Louisiana, Mississippi, and North Carolina state archives; the Special Collections in the Bennett College, Fisk University, Howard University, and the University of Georgia libraries; the Manuscript Division of the Duke University Library; the Southern Historical Collection of the University of North Carolina Library; the Department of Archives and History of the Louisiana State University Library; the South Caroliniana Library at the University of South Carolina; the National Archives and the Manuscripts Division of the Library of Congress; the Schomburg Center for Research in Black Culture of the New York Public Library; the Amistad Research Center and the Manuscripts Division of the Tulane University Library; the Rockefeller Archive Center in Pocantico Hills, New York; and the Yazoo City Public Library, located at the entrance to the Mississippi Delta. For their hospitality and assistance, and for some unusual and rare materials unavailable in many major research libraries, I should also like to acknowledge antiquarian booksellers William French, Philip McBlain, Peter Howard, Glenn Horowitz, John Durham, Daryl Van Fleet, Michael Pincus, Thomas Congalton, Paul Garon, Ralph Sipper, and Thomas Goldwasser, and the staff at Moe's Books in Berkeley. For the depth of their musical knowledge, I am grateful to the staff at Down Home records in El Cerrito, California.

This book builds on the historians who have examined various dimensions of the South and race relations in the Age of Jim Crow, ranging from the early explorations of C. Vann Woodward and Rayford Logan to a group of younger scholars too numerous to acknowledge here but who are well represented in the Notes. I am grateful to them for making my task both easier and more challenging. For sharing ideas and materials on this subject, I am grateful to David Blight, Jeffrey Brand, Randall Burkett, Cita Cook, Pete Daniel, Edmund Lee Drago, Lacy Ford, John Hope Franklin, James Grossman, Darlene Clark Hine, Avon Kirkland, Joseph Logsdon, Patrick Miller, Sydney Nathans, Robert Palmer, Todd Savitt, Virginia Shadron, Clarence Walker,

Graham White, and Shane White. During various stages of the book, I benefited from the work of some diligent and resourceful graduate assistants: Lisa Clark, Paul Harvey, Sarah Jackson, Anne Keary, Charles Postel, Patrick Rael, Marcy Sacks, Nina Silber and Ziaojian Zhao.

To ask friends and colleagues to read and comment on a manuscript, particularly one as large as this, is not easy. It demands from them a considerable commitment in time and effort. I have been most fortunate in this respect. Lawrence Levine not only read the manuscript critically, providing thoughtful and insightful comments, but his own pioneering scholarship in African American folk thought helped to shape my thinking throughout the conceptualization and writing of the book. My colleague Waldo Martin, with whom I share the African American history course at Berkeley, was extremely helpful to me; he noted sections that could be strengthened and he provided needed encouragement about sections I thought might be questionable. Nick Salvatore gave the manuscript the careful and exacting reading I expected from him, prodding and challenging me where necessary. Tony Baragona, a longtime friend, employed his literary and critical skills to help me smooth out some rough sections and clarify what was unclear. For bringing to the galleys and page proofs her extraordinary editorial and literary talents, including a solid command of grammar and syntax, I am grateful to Natalie Reid. My editor at Knopf, Ashbel Green, has been exceptionally patient with a book promised some years earlier. I appreciated his careful reading of the manuscript, and I hope the final product justified his long wait. I want to acknowledge Jennifer Bernstein and Leyla Aker at Knopf for helpful suggestions during the production stage and for prodding me to stay on schedule. I am grateful as well to Carol Carson, the art director, who composed the dust jacket based on some old studio photographs (most of them in Chattanooga) a former student sent me some years ago, having found them in an abandoned shack somewhere in West Virginia or Tennessee.

Finally, this book in its various passages owes much to my wife, Rhoda. The support and understanding, the joys and love she has brought to my work—and to my life—are impossible to describe in a brief acknowledgment but they are deeply felt.

TROUBLE IN MIND

CHAPTER ONE

BAPTISMS

My grandmother and other people that I knowed grew up in slavery time, they wasn't satisfied with their freedom. They felt like motherless children—they wasn't satisfied but they had to live under the impression that they were. Had to act in a way just as though everything was all right. . . . Had to do whatever the white man directed em to do, couldn't voice their heart's desire. That was the way of life that I was born and raised into.

—Ned Cobb[1]

*What did I do
To be so black
and blue?*
—From a song popularized by Louis Armstrong[2]

THE PINE-BOARD SHACK in which Charlie Holcombe spent his childhood in the late nineteenth century rested on top of a red clay hill about a quarter of a mile from the main road in Sampson County, North Carolina. His father, a tenant tobacco farmer, rose each morning at four o'clock, laid the logs for a fire, and roused the children, while Charlie's mother prepared a breakfast consisting of a pot of grits and a slab of salt pork. It was important to be in the field at sunup during the growing season, as the soil was poor and the labor that much more demanding. They worked till sundown.

Grandfather Holcombe did not work in the field; he had "de miseries" in his back and walked with a stick. But he performed other chores, slopping the hogs and feeding the chickens. Charlie Holcombe, considered too young and frail to work in the fields, helped his grandfather with the chores and often accompanied him to the nearby creek to catch "a mess o' catfish" for supper. As they sat there, waiting for the fish to bite, Grandfather would "do a heap o' thinkin'." And sometimes he shared his thoughts with Charlie, his youngest grandson, often imparting practical lessons drawn from his own life on how a black boy might hope to survive in the South less than half a century after emancipation.

Charlie remembered one lesson in particular. After catching a large catfish, Grandfather Holcombe toyed with it for a time, admonishing his grandson to watch him. He carefully lifted the fish out of the creek, let it thrash about, then lowered the line and returned the fish to the water. It would swim again, but not for long. Grandfather suddenly pulled it out on the bank, where it thrashed about until it died. "Son," his grandfather observed, "a catfish is a lot like a nigger. As long as he is in his mudhole he is all right, but when he gits out he is in for a passel of trouble. You 'member dat, and you won't have no trouble wid folks when you grows up."

Neither Charlie's father nor his grandfather had owned the land they worked. But as a young man Charlie Holcombe aspired to improve himself and be independent of whites, and he possessed an abundance of confidence about his ability to succeed. He vowed to break with a bleak past of arduous and mostly unrewarded labor. "I thought I could manage my business better and dat I was gonna be able to own a place o' my own someday. . . . I was a high-minded young nigger and was full of git-up-and-git. Dey wan't nothin' in de world dat I didn't think I could do, and I didn't have no patience wid niggers what didn't look for nothin' but sundown and payday." After his parents died, Charlie moved to Johnston County, North Carolina, took a job on public works, saved some money, and married. In 1909 he settled down on a farm, determined to make it his own. But like so many aspiring young blacks—the children and the grandchildren of slaves—he confronted formidable obstacles in his struggle to be independent. "Dey was always sumpthin' come along and knocked de props from under my plans." That "sumpthin' " might be the worms, rust, or blight consuming the tobacco plants or, more often than not, poor and declining prices and the rigid controls exerted by white men over black income. The only certainty was that by the time the landlord had taken his share and deducted the cost of the fertilizer and the money or credit advances he had made, "dey wan't but jist enough to carry on till de nex' crop."

But Charlie persisted, and one year he seemed primed to break out of this cycle of indebtedness. After selling his tobacco and settling with the landlord, he had something for himself—or so he thought. That was when "the man" called him back and told him he had underestimated the amount Charlie owed him for warehouse charges. The tactic was all too familiar, and Charlie's inability to read the books made any legal protest impossible. "I knowed it wan't right, and it made me so mad I jist hit him in de face as hard as I could. Den I kinda went crazy and might nigh beat him to death." The judge sentenced Charlie to a year's labor on the roads—a lenient sentence for an interracial altercation. His wife and children did what they could to make a crop, but it was not enough to meet expenses. The landlord agreed to carry them over, and it took Charlie three years to pay him back. "By that time I knowed it wan't no use for me to try to ever make anything but jist a livin'."

Although Charlie Holcombe made his accommodation, he wanted something better for his oldest son, Willie. "I was 'termined my oldest chile was gonna hab a chance in dis world, and I sent him all de way through high school." That was more education than any Holcombe had known. But after completing high school, Willie wanted to go to college, arguing that it would enable him to improve his economic prospects significantly. At considerable sacrifice, the Holcombes sent their son to the Agricultural and Technical College of North Carolina in Greensboro. Willie worked hard, made good grades, and in the summer returned to help his parents with the crop. He would take the tobacco to market, carefully scrutinize the accounts, and invariably return with money in his pocket. As Willie progressed in college, however, his horizon widened and he became more ambitious. Increasingly dissatisfied with the tobacco business, he told his father this was no future for a black man with an education. He did not want to return to the farm. "Dat hurt me," Charlie Holcombe confessed, " 'cause I had counted on Willie helpin' me, but I wanted him to do what he thought was best." Willie Holcombe graduated near the top of his class. That, remembered Charlie, "was when de trouble started."

Despite his education, Willie found few opportunities open to him. He returned home from college, disillusioned with his life and bitter over his limited prospects. When he "started settin' around and drinkin' and gittin' mean," Charlie tried to reason with him, but little he could say would alleviate the disappointment and frustration. That fall Willie took a load of tobacco to the warehouse and returned home angry and sullen; the next day he insisted on taking another load to the warehouse. Near dinnertime he had not yet returned. A neighbor finally appeared to inform Charlie that there had been a fight at the warehouse involving Willie. When Charlie reached the scene, he spotted his son lying on the ground, a puddle of blood around his head, and a group of white men standing nearby. "I knowed he was dead de minute I seed him." For a while Charlie just stood there, not knowing what to do. He looked at the crowd and could not find a friendly or sympathetic face. "Right den I knowed dey wan't no use to ax for no he'p and dat I was jist a pore nigger in trouble." Holding Willie in his arms, Charlie could see that his son's head had been bashed in. "Dey was tears runnin' down my cheeks and droppin' on his face and I couldn't he'p it." He placed his son in the wagon, tied the mule behind it, and began his journey down the road. Reaching home, he washed Willie's head and dressed him in his best suit. Charlie and Dillie Holcombe then buried their son at the foot of the big pine tree near the well and planted some grass on the grave.

Charlie Holcombe was never the same again. The spirit he had once shown in his determination to succeed no longer animated him. "For a long time atter dat I couldn't seem to git goin', and dey was a big chunk in de bottom o' my stummick dat jist wouldn't go away. I would go out at night and set under de pine by Willie's grave, and listen to de win' swishin' in de needles, and I'd do a lot o' thinkin'." He knew his son had been killed because of an argument, no doubt over the "settlin' price" for the tobacco Willie had delivered. But Charlie blamed himself for his son's death. He had failed to heed his grandfather's admonition. "I got to thinkin' 'bout what gran'pappy said 'bout de catfish, and I knowed dat was de trouble wid Willie. He had stepped outen his place when he got dat eddycation. If I'd kept him here on de farm he woulda been all right. Niggers has got to l'arn dat dey ain't like white folks, and never will be, and no amount o' eddycation can make 'em be, and dat when dey gits outen dere place dere is gonna be trouble." When in subsequent years Charlie would encounter some "young bucks" dissatisfied with their lives and wanting to "cut loose and change," he would listen to them, then take them out to see Willie's grave.

No other Holcombe child would be sent to college. They all settled down with their families and accommodated to the New South in the same way their father—and grandfather—had accommodated. They went about the business of surviving. "Dey don't hab much, but dey is happy," Charlie Holcombe said of his remaining children, the advice of his grandfather still vivid in his mind. "Niggers is built for service, like a mule, and dey needn't 'spect nothin' else. . . . A nigger's place is in de field and de road and de tunnel and de woods, wid a pick or shovel or ax or hoe or plow. God made a nigger like a mule to be close to na-

ture and git his livin' by de sweat o' his brow like de Good Book says."
Resigned to his "place," Charlie no longer worried that much about the
price his tobacco might bring him. The children came by occasionally
to help him with the crops. He now had ample time to engage in his
own "heap o' thinkin'," and his final years were increasingly reflective.
Sitting by the fireplace, his mind often wandered back to his childhood.
"And I 'member how my gran'pappy used to . . . take me fishin' wid
him. Seems like when a feller thinks back he only 'members de good
parts."[3]

2

THE STORY OF Charlie Holcombe evokes the contradictions of
black life and coming of age in the New South—the initial hopes and
aspirations, the often heightened expectations, as well as the frustrations, the terrors, the tensions, the betrayals, and the necessary accommodations. What came to be impressed on several generations of black
Southerners—the first born in freedom and coming to maturity in the
1890s and the early twentieth century—was the material, political, and
military superiority of white people, the extraordinary power white
men and women wielded over black lives and prospects in virtually all
phases of daily life. "The only thing that you would be thinking of," remembered Ardie Clark Halyard, was "that they were the ones that had
everything." And they maintained their dominance, she sensed, because "all the time . . . they were taking advantage—you could see
that."[4]

The New South into which a new generation of African Americans
would be born had clearly drawn racial boundaries and modes of behavior based on centuries of enforced custom and thought. Every black
child would come to appreciate the terrible unfairness and narrowness
of that world—the limited options, the need to curb ambitions, to contain feelings, and to weigh carefully every word, gesture, and movement
when in the presence of whites. To learn to live with this kind of harsh
reality became no less than a prerequisite for survival. "In this perilous
world," Benjamin Mays recalled of his childhood in rural South Carolina, "if a black boy wanted to live a halfway normal life and die a natural death he had to learn early the art of how to get along with white
folks."[5] Any deviation from white expectations invited instant and often
violent reprisals.

Generations of black youths shared a common training and education based on their early racial experiences. The initial revelation of the meaning and force of race might be triggered by a physical altercation, an abusive epithet, a telling glance, or an exchange of words. For the black child, the encounter or incident was at times shocking and traumatic, at other times too subtle to be fully grasped, as in the way white people insisted on calling their father "boy" and their mother "girl" (or "uncle" and "auntie" if they were advanced in age).

As children, blacks and whites sometimes crossed the racial divide, playing together and sharing stories, experiences, games, even plans (and fantasies) about their future lives. The innocence of the relationship might encourage them to think of it as a genuine, even an enduring friendship, that color differences (even if acknowledged) mattered less than the personal qualities that drew them to each other. But the suddenness with which those relationships were dissolved suggested how quickly the outer world intruded—and prevailed. Parents, both white and black, often interceded to break off the fraternization, and when the shared play stopped, usually in adolescence, so did the friendship. Even before parents acted to sever the relationship, white youths might seize upon a disagreement to turn unexpectedly on their black playmates.

The suddenness with which life came to be defined on the basis of perceived racial differences, and how little one could do in response, made an indelible impression on young blacks. "The white children I knew," a black woman recalled, "grew meaner as they grew older— more capable of saying things that cut and wound." Often the break entailed no words at all, only a quiet but devastating snub. Robert Russa Moton would always remember the day his white playmate returned home from boarding school for the Christmas holiday. Having eagerly awaited his arrival, Robert rushed forward to greet him. But his childhood friend rejected his advances and treated him coldly, refusing even to shake his hand. "I went into the kitchen with Aunt Viny, the cook. I was feeling bad." While Robert sat there, the white youth burst into the room and enthusiastically returned Aunt Viny's embrace. "I sat unhappy, puzzled, thinking," young Moton recalled. "Sometimes I wonder if I ever thought quite as seriously on life as I did that night."[6]

If interracial companionship and play persisted into adolescence, it did so according to the terms laid down by white playmates and at their toleration. "[W]e kep' our places," Sam Bowers recalled of his association with white boys in the 1880s. "We always remembered dere wuz a

diffrunce. We didn't furgit we wuz black." That difference was made
perfectly clear in the games a Virginia black remembered of a childhood spent both in slavery and freedom. When they had played "Injuns
an' soldiers," the white boys had been the soldiers and the black boys
the Indians. When they later played "Yankee an' 'Federates," the actual
outcome of the Civil War was irrelevant. " 'Course de whites was always de 'Federates. Take us black boys prisoners an' make b'lieve dey
was gonna cut our necks off. Guess dey got dat idea f'om dere fathers."[7]

When white and black youths worked together on the same job,
racial differences might erupt with little or no warning. While employed in a logging camp, Jacob Reddix shared some tasks with a white
youth of the same age. The two said little to each other, but at one
point Reddix casually questioned a statement made by his coworker.
After cursing Reddix for daring to dispute his word, the white youth
grabbed a club, screaming at the same time, "You goddamn black nigger, I'll teach you how to talk to a white man!" The intervention of the
white superintendent ended the threat, but Reddix thought it best to
quit the job.[8]

The first encounter with racial insult tended to hurt the most, as it
often came with neither provocation nor explanation. Mary Church,
born in Memphis near the end of the Civil War, simply could not understand why a railroad conductor had summarily ordered her out of a
railroad coach. After inquiring of other passengers, "Whose little nigger is this?" he had resolved to remove her from the car reserved for
whites. "I could think of nothing that I had done wrong. I could get no
satisfaction from Father, however, for he refused to talk about the affair
and forbade me to do so." Nor did five-year-old Louis Armstrong obtain a satisfactory response when a friend of his mother dragged him to
the rear of the Tulane Avenue trolley in New Orleans in 1905. Noticing
the sign "For Colored Passengers Only," behind which he had been
compelled to sit, he asked what it meant. The response provided neither information nor reassurance. "Don't ask so many questions!" the
woman scolded him. "Shut your mouth, you little fool." For the impressionable young Richard Wright, the experience of traveling by train
to Arkansas with his mother and waiting in line at the "Colored"
ticket window forced him to contemplate the kind of world he was
entering—"a sense of the two races had been born in me with a sharp
concreteness that would never die until I died."[9]

The humiliation is what so many remembered. The incidents involving public transportation almost always occurred in full public view,

and the scenarios that were acted out became all too familiar. White passengers and spectators would cheer the conductors enforcing the racial codes, while any black witnesses needed to maintain a discreet silence. James Weldon Johnson never forgot his racial initiation, not only his forcible ejection from a railroad coach reserved for whites but also, even more vividly, the smug satisfaction on the faces of the white passengers. Reflecting over the incident some years later, Johnson insisted the passengers had entirely misread his reaction. "If their satisfaction rose from any idea that I was having a sense of my inferiority impressed upon me, they were sadly in error; indeed, my sensation was the direct opposite; I felt that I was being humiliated." When Ida B. Wells was forcibly removed from the ladies' coach, she, too, remembered in particular how the "white ladies and gentlemen" vigorously applauded the action of the conductor.[10]

For many black youths, early racial encounters became nothing less than defining moments in their lives. When James Robinson, born in 1907, attempted to board a bus in Knoxville, Tennessee, a white man cursed him and roughly pulled him off the steps of the vehicle. "You damn little darkey, didn't anybody learn you to stay in your place?" he shouted at Robinson. "You get the hell back there and wait till the white people get on the bus." With a glance to the approving spectators, the white man exclaimed, "Give the nigger an inch and he'll take a mile." When Robinson looked appealingly to several black spectators for sympathy, they turned their heads. Finally, when all the whites had boarded, the driver slammed the door in Robinson's face and drove off. "Inwardly I boiled. It hurt inside, all the way down. . . . I wanted to cry but hate wouldn't let me. . . . What hurt me most of all was that grown-up Negro men had not dared to speak in behalf of a helpless child."[11]

The indignities visited on black youths were meant to impress on a new generation the solidity of racial lines and the unchallengeable authority and superiority of the dominant race. Harassment played invariably on racial stereotypes, forcing blacks from the earliest age to act out roles for the amusement of whites, to cater to their whims and desires. That was reason enough, Ed Brown recalled of his childhood in Georgia before World War I, to avoid whites altogether, to make every effort to stay out of their sight. "My motto was, when I was a boy, Don't Meet Nobody. When I seen somebody comin or heard a horse, I'd step outside the road and they'd pass on by. . . . Because nine times out of ten you'd be made to dance, or to drink some whiskey."[12]

To be forced to dance or imbibe some alcohol, or to be compelled to fight each other, all for the entertainment of white spectators, were familiar acts of public submission. Nor were whites averse to exploiting for their own amusement the alleged sexual prowess of black males. In the optical company in Memphis where he worked, young Richard Wright found himself confronted by two white employees, one of whom questioned him about the size of his penis. "I heard that a nigger can stick his prick in the ground and spin around on it like a top," he remarked, laughing. "I'd like to see you do that. I'd give you a dime, if you did it." Wright chose to ignore them, but only after he had been compelled to deny in their presence that their questions and comments had in any way offended him. His face and demeanor, however, must have suggested otherwise, as the two white men warned him to watch his step. In reflecting over this incident, Wright wondered if there were any way a black youth could maintain his dignity in the presence of whites. "I had been humble, and now I was reaping the wages of humility."[13]

While racial harassment forced on young blacks a recognition of limits, it also awakened in many of them a new sense of themselves, a capacity for rage, and, not infrequently, the rationale and the willingness to destroy white lives—all of which needed to be contained if they were to survive. Elaborate scenarios came to be plotted in their imaginations, however, sometimes shared with close friends, more often harbored individually. Few whites, especially those who claimed to know the Negro best, were capable of comprehending the accumulation of black resentment or the degree to which black men and women, whatever their age or outward appearance, were willing to avenge the indignities heaped on them. After being thrown off the bus in Knoxville, James Robinson did not adapt easily to the lesson he had been forcibly taught in racial etiquette. "Revenge was my only thought. I considered setting Lang's grocery on fire. He had done nothing to me but he was white; Lang and every other white man was my natural enemy. I was a Negro and in their eyes this was my crime." Benjamin Mays overheard talk about a black woman living with a white man; both came down with a lingering illness and suffered for years before they died. Many blacks, Mays recalled, thought it God's punishment, and some of them found comfort in the belief "that God would mete out the punishment that Negroes were powerless to inflict."[14]

The talk and reported incidents of white violence became for Richard Wright a critical part of his childhood "education." When he was scarcely ten years old, "a dread of white people" lodged itself "per-

manently" in his feelings and imagination. "Nothing challenged the totality of my personality so much as this pressure of hate and threat that
stemmed from the invisible whites. I would stand for hours on the
doorsteps of neighbors' houses listening to their talk, learning how a
white woman had slapped a black woman, how a white man had killed
a black man. It filled me with awe, wonder, and fear." He asked countless questions for which he received no satisfactory responses, and he
imagined scores of scenarios involving resistance and vengeance that
he lacked the power or the opportunity to act out. The presence of
whites informed every action, every thought, his very demeanor. "Tension would set in at the mere mention of whites and a vast complex of
emotions, involving the whole of my personality, would be aroused. It
was as though I was continuously reacting to the threat of some natural force whose hostile behavior could not be predicted." Young
Wright had not yet been subjected to the abuse of white men or women,
neither verbally nor physically, "but I had already become as conditioned to their existence as though I had been the victim of a thousand
lynchings."[15]

All too often, thoughts of revenge against whites found an outlet
only in violence against blacks. In the South Carolina countryside in
which he grew up, Benjamin Mays believed his people fought each
other "because they were taking out on other blacks what they really
wanted but feared to take out on whites." The need he felt as a young
man to reconcile his blackness, his manhood, and his rage, Mays confessed, drained him emotionally. "To exercise manhood, as white men
displayed it, was to invite disaster." Mays had seen his father cringe in
the presence of whites, and yet his father relished telling the story of
how as a youth he had outwitted and outfought two white men. Every
time his father related the story, Mays recalled, "he would laugh, and
laugh, and laugh. It was his prize story."[16]

Young blacks underwent the rites of racial passage in a variety of
ways. But the specter and threat of physical violence—"the white
death"—loomed over nearly every encounter. If they themselves were
not the victims, the violence fell on members of the family, friends, and
neighbors, almost always with the same intent—to remind black men
and women of their "place," to impose severe restraints on their ambitions, and to punish any perceived signs of "impudence," "impertinence," or independence. Benjamin Mays looked on helplessly in 1898
as a crowd of armed white men rode up to his father, cursed him, drew
their guns, and forced him to remove his hat and bow down to them. "I

was not yet five years old, but I have never forgotten them. . . . That mob is my earliest memory." Martin Luther King, Sr., born in 1899, spent his youth in rural Georgia, where he witnessed drunken white men beat a black man to death for being "sassy," a term commonly used by whites to identify troublemaking, "uppity," and "impudent" blacks. In this instance, the victim's "sassiness" consisted of refusing the demand of the white men that he hand over his paycheck. He had been murdered not for violating the racial code but for being successful at his mill job and pocketing his pay. Shocked by what he had seen, King asked the familiar question "*Why*, I thought, *why did they do that?*" He had no answers, and he could find comfort only in hating whites. "My way to protect myself, I thought, was to build around myself an armor made of my hatred of whites. It was needed. It was valuable. And it helped me to deal with the memories, the terrible dreams and recollections. To hate those responsible made it bearable, and so I indulged myself, and began to despise every white face I saw." Six-year-old Pauli Murray would never forget the sight of John Henry Corniggins's body lying out in the field, where he had been shot to death for walking across a white man's watermelon patch. Rushing home, a distraught Murray pleaded with her Aunt Paulin for some explanation. But there was no easy way to explain the South's racial mores. "I can't tell you, child," Aunt Paulin replied, trying to calm her niece. "There are some things you'll understand better when you get older." That obviously pained response only reinforced the terror Pauli had experienced that day. The sight of John Henry's body, his little brother crying as he knelt by his side, the mother's ear-shattering screams as she approached the scene—these memories could not be easily erased.[17]

Struggling to understand the limits imposed on their behavior, young blacks came to appreciate the frequency and random nature of much of the racial violence. It seemed designed not only to punish the alleged offenders but also to send a message to the entire community. Eight-year-old Lucy Miller stood in her front yard in Daytona Beach in 1907, watching white residents parade through the black community the body of a black man they had just lynched. The victim, Lucy learned, "had dared to stand up for his rights," and whites were now using his corpse, placed on the back of a wagon, as an example "so that there would not be any effort on the part of blacks to get out of their place." Benjamin J. Davis, born in 1903, spent his childhood in Dawson, a rural town in southwestern Georgia. Among his earliest memories was the day the sheriff and his deputies came across the railroad tracks with a wagon to arrest a black man accused of having "sassed" a white man in the downtown area. News of the incident had already spread to the black neighborhood, and the delegation of law enforcement officials had been expected. The black residents lined the road leading to the victim's home. "The wagon passed right in front of my house," Davis recalled, "and I stood in front of the picket fence watching the proceedings. It looked like a parade, on the one hand, and a funeral, on the other. Men, women, and children were sobbing." His mother offered a simple explanation of the arrest: "They say he didn't behave himself downtown." Davis knew, too, that the victim would probably be sentenced to a long term on the county chain gang and that many blacks never survived that ordeal.[18]

It was impossible to dismiss examples of white violence and terrorism as aberrations; they were too much a part of everyday life. But to make sense of the violence, to comprehend its meaning and implications, provoked questions that defied any easy answers. Born in 1878 and reared in Georgia, Richard R. Wright, Jr. (a prominent educator unrelated to the Richard Wright who grew up in Mississippi and became a noted writer) made every effort to avoid white people. He could not recall the face of a single white child before he was ten years old. His notions of racial differences and relations with whites were based on conversations with boys older than himself. From them he learned to fear whites and to accommodate to the prevailing etiquette. His racial baptism came "with great suddenness and tragedy" during his teenage years in Augusta. On Christmas Day he saw a crowd of whites chasing a large black man; they caught him near Bethel church and when he turned on them swinging a heavy stick, they shot him. The mob then jumped on the prostrate body, smashing his face and torso with the heels of their shoes. No policeman appeared, and no one tried to assist or defend the victim. Young Richard, who had stood only a few feet away from the attack, fled with his companion. The tragedy he had just witnessed became, as he said, "indelibly imprinted" upon his memory. Although he would subsequently observe other black men shot, hunted, and beaten, none made as much of an impression. "I have not seen anything that stunned me like that incident." Nor could Audley Moore, born before the turn of the century in New Iberia, Louisiana, easily put out of her mind the first sight of a lynching victim. "I remember Grandma allowing us to look through the shutter and be careful not to open it too much, so they wouldn't see us." The victim was being drawn by a wagon. "He was tied and his head was bumping up and down on the clay, the hard, crusty road . . . and the men hollering behind; white men, like wolves, were behind this man. Well, you know that's a terrible thing for a child to see, and you grow up that way. . . ."[19]

The perceived absence of legal redress compounded the impact of these initial encounters with white violence. From the very outset of their lives, young blacks came to learn that in the New South the differences between justice and injustice, the law and lawlessness, were at best ambiguous, at worst senseless, so blurred as to be indistinct. The ways in which they experienced the courts and police power were hardly calculated to enhance their respect for the law or for the white man's sense of fair play. The very relationship black people bore to protective agencies contrasted sharply with that of whites. Even as white children were inculcated with the image of the policeman as a friend and protector, black children learned to fear him as the enemy. As a child in Durham, North Carolina, Pauli Murray viewed the local police as "heavily armed, invariably mountainous red-faced [men] who to me seemed more a signal of calamity than of protection." Based on conversations with other boys and adults, Richard R. Wright, Jr., recalled, "I was convinced early that policemen were my enemies. I never approached a policeman with a question until I had been in Chicago for nearly a year." That same negative image always dominated Albon Holsey's perception of law enforcement. Growing up in Georgia at the turn of the century, he and his friends always lived in "mortal fear" of the police, "for they were arch-tormenters and persecutors of Negroes. . . . I ran from policemen so often when I was a boy that even now [in 1929], though I am past forty, if one walks upon me unexpectedly my first impulse is to take to my heels."[20]

If the sight of law enforcement officials in the towns and cities made blacks nervous, the not uncommon sound in the countryside of bloodhounds and posses tracking down black fugitives—many of them escapees from a peonage farm, a prison-labor camp, or a chain gang— brought a chilling terror and a renewed sense of vulnerability to black homes. The warning sounded by older residents echoed in the minds of young blacks: that white men with hounds and guns were not always overly particular about whom they caught in their manhunts. The object was to bring back a black body, not necessarily the guilty party.[21]

The subject of the police often dominated conversations among young blacks. The stories invariably revolved around chases, harassment, clubbings, illegal arrests, and coerced confessions. But other tales also made the rounds, tales that did wonders for black pride and soon became legendary. With particular relish, some blacks recounted their success in outwitting law enforcement officers. Still others took delight in their exploits, even if caught. Richard R. Wright, Jr., vividly recalled the fate of a boy in his neighborhood in Augusta, Georgia. Sentenced to the chain gang, the boy seemed proud of his notoriety and enhanced standing in the community. "Some of the boys," Wright remembered, "talked about him as though he were a hero." Several days later, however, they spotted their friend with chains around his ankles working on the local roads. It was a sobering sight. "Several of us went out to see if it were really true," Wright recalled; "the sight put fear in me."[22]

For black youths, as for their parents, the daily reminders of "place" and inequality were nearly everywhere. The degrading racial etiquette, the places they were forbidden to enter (parks, libraries, restaurants, even some churches) or where they were rigidly separated from whites (public transportation and theaters), the dehumanizing caricatures, the ritualized subservience, the verbal and physical harassment, the savage public murders, and the quiet murders—all of these, the dramatic and the mundane, became part of their lives and elevated their racial awareness to new levels. Albon Holsey sensed as a teenager in the first decade of the twentieth century that the odds were stacked against him, no matter what he did.

> At fifteen, I was fully conscious of the racial difference, and while I was sullen and resentful in my soul, I was beaten and knew it. I knew then that I could never aspire to be President of the United States, nor Governor of my State, nor mayor of my city; I knew that the front doors of white homes in my town were not for me to enter, except as a servant; I knew that I could only sit in the peanut gallery at our theatre, and could only ride on the back seat of the electric car and in the Jim Crow car on the train. I had bumped into the color line and knew that so far as white people were concerned, I was just another nigger.

By adolescence, then, most black youths had already experienced in a variety of ways the racial mores and etiquette of the New South. Margaret Walker, whose childhood was spent in Mississippi, recalled that by age ten, she had run the entire gauntlet of racial baptisms. Black adults had looked on helplessly while white boys had thrashed her. She had sat in the Negro section on the streetcar, marked off by iron bars that could not be moved. She had climbed a fire escape to enter a segregated theater that did not have a regular Negro entrance. She had attended school in a one-room wooden shack. And etched deeply in her memory was the night her father, who taught in a local college, was chased home at gunpoint by a drunken policeman who resented the sight of a "nigger" carrying books and a fountain pen.[23]

Race consciousness came early. The initial lessons in race relations invariably revolved around the difficulty of effecting any changes and the permanency of the position of inferiority assigned blacks. "The boys talked about it constantly as something fixed," Richard R. Wright, Jr., recalled of the many conversations he had with friends. What he learned in school about the Dred Scott decision, Wright came to discover, was not simply history. The U.S. Supreme Court's idea that "a black man has no rights which a white man is bound to respect" remained a defining principle in southern life half a century later, and Negroes who accepted that principle were thought to be "good Negroes," while those who wanted rights were "bad Negroes." Many older persons, Wright remembered, seemed resigned to the notion that God had cursed the Negro race, that the white man was created to rule, the black man to serve. And to a large degree that notion simply mirrored harsh day-to-day realities. Such expressions as "white is right, black is wrong" or "that's a white man's job!" conveyed meanings readily understood by young blacks. Some parents went so far as to tell their children, "It's a white man's world, and you just happen to be here, nigger."[24]

If black youths sought answers or comfort from their ministers or churches, they often came away disappointed with the results. When Margaret Walker began to wonder about her circumscribed place, she looked to religion for an explanation. Why, she asked, would an almighty God permit such repression and exploitation? "Why were there segregated churches and segregated hospitals and cemeteries and schools? Why must I ride behind a Jim-Crow sign? Why did a full-grown colored man sit meekly behind a Jim-Crow sign and do nothing about it? What could he do?" The more she thought about it, the more convinced she became that God sided with whites because God was white, and she simply resigned herself to that truth. "The world was white, and I was black." While in hiding to avoid whites threatening to lynch his uncle, James Yates heard his mother's whispered and anguished prayers, "Oh my Lord, save us!" The next day, he asked her, "Mama, you say the Lord loves everybody. Why does he let white folks treat us Blacks like this?" Not satisfied with her response, he persisted, "Mama, why didn't the Lord create some Black angels? In all the Sunday School books and the bible all you see are white folks." This time, his mother's response quieted him. "Boy," she replied, "stop questioning the Lord's will." That ended the session. "Whenever Mama came out with 'boy!' I knew to stop whatever I was doing or saying."[25]

That they faced insuperable obstacles, with or without God's active consent and participation, found additional reinforcement in an economic order that made the fear and violence of poverty as pervasive in the lives of young blacks as the fear and violence of white people. The equation of hard work and material well-being, as they could easily see, had little relevance to their lives. Observing their parents and other black adults, children knew how much arduous labor they performed, how six days a week they wasted their bodies in the fields, trying without success to make crops that would meet the expenses of subsistence living. If too young to go out into the fields, children performed a variety of household chores, not all of them to their liking. Asked to write a composition in school, Leona, a thirteen-year-old girl in Wilmington, North Carolina, expressed her thoughts about the responsibilities thrust on her at home. Called "My Hate," the essay mostly detailed her daily routine.

> I going to rite about the thing I hates. I has a lot of hate but the thing I hates the most is little childern, dogs and turkys. The childern is my Mother childern and she go out and leav them on me all day. I has to keep them dry and I has to iron they close. The dog is my Father dog. They is houn dog and they has to be kep home . . . The turky is my Grandmother turky and they is the hatfullest of all. If they gets wet they dies. Seem like it all the time rain and turky don't wants to live. What I wants I wants to get reddy to teach school and then I will not have to do none of this Hatfull stuff.[26]

For some black children, their introduction to the ways of white folks came from being exposed to white homes, either through stories told by their parents who worked in the homes or in some instances by themselves working there. That was bound to expose them to a very different world, to stark differences in lifestyles and expectations, to houses in which one usually found handsome furnishings, an abundance of good food, and the impressive dress and decorum of the white elite and middle class. Children working in white homes learned at the same time important rules of class and race: They must confine themselves to the kitchen (unless assigned tasks in other parts of the house), they must use a separate toilet set aside for them, and they must eat out of separate dishes and cups reserved for their use.

Few black Southerners, young or old, experienced the inside of a white home. The vast majority of working families needed to grapple with the results of economic subordination and diminishing returns for their labor. In the black South, hard times were a way of life, not a sudden jolt in the nation's or the region's business cycle. And the precarious economic position of the family came home to most black children in what William Henry Holtzclaw remembered as a particularly "excruciating kind of pain—the pain of hunger." On some nights, he recalled, "we would often cry for food until falling here and there on the floor we would sob ourselves to sleep." Raised by his grandmother in rural Alabama, William J. Edwards recalled mostly "hard times in the way of getting something to eat," trying to survive on a subsistence less than that of many blacks in the vicinity. By eating alone during school recess, he tried to conceal from his fellow pupils a lunch consisting of bread and water, but the children discovered his secret and laughed and poked fun at him.[27]

What created the most frustration, and remained particularly vivid in the minds of young blacks, was the feeling of helplessness, the inability to do anything about their predicament. And that feeling often applied to the very essentials of life. There was "nowhere to go [for food] and nowhere to turn to get it," Esther Mae Scott recalled of her upbringing in Warren County, Mississippi. Richard Wright's mother tried to stifle his hunger by pouring him a cup of tea, "but a little later," he recalled, "I would feel hunger nudging my ribs, twisting my empty guts until they ached. I would grow dizzy and my vision would dim. I became less active in my play, and for the first time in my life I had to pause and think of what was happening to me." If a child's mother cooked for a white family, it was customary to wait until she returned from work late at night to share the scraps she had managed to remove from the white folks' table and kitchen. Families also found ways to make their food last longer, as, for example, by adding water to the milk. "[B]read and half-water-and-milk constituted supper for many months," William J. Edwards recalled. Even if the bare essentials were available, the regular diet in many families of fatback, cornmeal, and molasses left children badly deficient in protein and chronically anemic—a condition they shared with many of their poor white neighbors.[28]

Not only poverty but also the physical environment—the neighborhood and dwellings in which they were reared, along with the schools some of them attended—reinforced feelings of separateness and inferiority. Black Southerners had only to look around them and compare what they had with what most whites possessed. The location of the black section of town, the condition of the streets, the state of sanitation, the quality of the housing, and the sharply limited access to what lay outside their neighborhood all attested dramatically to their "place" in the larger society. "We could look out the holes in the roof at the stars," one youth recalled of the cabin in which he lived.[29]

Whatever the relative isolation of blacks in the countryside and the cities, and despite legal and extralegal segregation, the two races came into frequent contact—on the country roads and city streets and sidewalks, at the workplace and warehouse (where the cotton would be weighed and sold), and in the stores, public buildings, and public vehicles. Memories of racial encounters, often punctuated with offensive epithets, helped to shape black lives and outlooks. Ten-year-old Albon Holsey, in running an errand to the grocery store, passed the home of a young white man who was playing with his child on the front porch. Pointing at Holsey, the man stood the child on his lap and taught her an important lesson, "Look—[a] nigger. Say 'nigger.' " For as long as they could see young Holsey, the father kept repeating those words to his child. The first time Margaret Walker was addressed as "nigger," she listened to her parents' belabored explanation. It made no sense to her, neither the encounter, the epithet, nor the explanation; she knew only that the term made her an object of scorn and ridicule. Even if her parents had been able to offer a reasonable explanation, she later recalled, it would have made little difference, as they could never have erased the pain she suffered.

> I could not understand my overwhelming sense of shame, as if I had been guilty of some unknown crime. I did not know why I was suffering, what brought this vague unease, this clutching for understanding. . . . [T]here is a difference in knowing you are black and in understanding what it means to be black in America. Before I was ten I knew what it was to step off the sidewalk to let a white man pass; otherwise he might knock me off.[30]

The term "nigger" might be used among blacks, often in jest or friendship, sometimes in derision, but both in intonation and intent it took on a totally different meaning when invoked by whites. After a white clerk in a drugstore called him a "nigger" and refused to serve him at the soda fountain, a nine-year-old Tennessee youth pleaded with his foster mother for an explanation. "Why should I be called a nigger? It must be very bad to be a nigger." Receiving no satisfactory response ("[t]his was the first time she refused to explain something to me"), he could not sleep that night thinking about what it meant. "What could a nigger be and why should God make a nigger?" Nor did his mother help matters when she threatened to whip him if he persisted in asking such questions of her and others. "We are all nigger and there is nothing wrong about it," she finally told him. That response only heightened his initial bewilderment.[31]

Whether used by a white or a black person, the term "nigger" sometimes suggested a class rather than a racial identification. When a white man whom she knew and respected implored her, "[D]on't be a nigger. . . . Niggers lie and lie!" Zora Neale Hurston did not believe it to be a racial insult but a well-intended admonition. "The word Nigger used in this sense does not mean race," she explained. "It means a weak, contemptible person of any race. . . . I knew without being told that he was not talking about my race when he advised me not to be a nigger. He was talking about class rather than race."[32]

Even as the term "nigger" entered in various ways their vocabulary and the conversations to which they were exposed, young blacks learned to use white terms of contempt for Jews and newly arrived immigrants, in particular Chinese and Italians. "Our first talk about the word 'Nigger,' " a schoolteacher recalled, "came about because their lips were so careless with 'Sheeney,' 'Chink,' and 'Dago.' "[33] Black youths also learned the epithets by which poor whites were described— "trash," "rednecks," "peckerwoods," "crackers," "buckrah"—and viewed them with contempt, very much as their elders did, as the bitterest and most lethal enemies of black people.

If the ability to diminish others by invective made them feel more American, young blacks made the most of it. As a youth in Atlanta, Horace Bond recalled that the first time he was called "nigger," the word had been hurled at him by a Jewish youth whose father owned a store in the neighborhood. Without hesitation, Bond responded by shouting, "Christ-killer." He came away from the incident shaken both by the virulence and instinctiveness of his response and by the shocked reaction of the Jewish boy. Richard Wright claimed not to have seen a Jew until he moved to Elaine, Arkansas, where a Jew owned a store in his neighborhood. Everyone he knew hated Jews, Wright recalled, not as economic exploiters but as "Christ killers," reflecting what they had learned at home and in Sunday school. Once having identified the Jew as "fair game for ridicule," and not fearing any violation of the prevailing racial etiquette, Wright and his playmates would dance around outside the store and sing:

> *Jew, Jew,*
> *Two for five*
> *That's what keeps*
> *Jew alive*

or they would chant in unison,

> *Bloody Christ killers*
> *Never trust a Jew*
> *Bloody Christ killers*
> *What won't a Jew do?*

To a large Jewish woman, they would add for good measure,

> *Red, white, and blue*
> *Your pa was a Jew*
> *Your ma a dirty Dago*
> *What the hell is you?*

And there were still more, "some mean, others filthy, all of them cruel." No one in the black community, Wright recalled, thought to question their right to use such language; if anything, their parents approved, whether actively or passively. "To hold an attitude of antagonism or distrust toward Jews was bred in us from childhood; it was not merely racial prejudice, it was a part of our cultural heritage."[34]

As they grew older, reaching adolescence, learning more about the world outside their neighborhoods, the questions black youths asked about their condition and prospects became increasingly insistent, particularly when they began to compare their circumstances and prospects with those of white youths. Could life be lived any differently? To what could a black youth reasonably aspire? Was America, in its racial attitudes and practices, larger than the South? After hearing from her maternal grandparents about the way it had been during slavery and emancipation, Rosa Louise McCauley (Parks), born in

Tuskegee, Alabama, in 1913, found it difficult to understand why "if we were a free people . . . we had to be deprived of the better things"— such as a decent building for a school. By the time fifteen-year-old Richard Wright entered the eighth grade, he could find no reason to be encouraged about his life or his prospects. The bleakness with which he viewed the future affected everything he did, including his schoolwork. "What was it that made the hate of whites for blacks so steady, seemingly so woven into the texture of things?" he wondered. "What kind of life was possible under that hate? How had this hate come to be?" Neither his family nor the schools he attended offered any reassurances. James Robinson, who realized he was beginning to hate whites, insisted on knowing why whites hated him, but he, too, found no ready answers. "I wanted answers but no answers came. My father was never at home to talk to me, my mother was too tired or too sick. When I asked older people, they simply said, 'shut up'—little children were to be seen and not heard. . . . I thought many things but kept them to myself. A strange war of my own was going on within me."[35]

The more insistent the questions became, the more troublesome were the answers, evasions, or silences. Ardie Clark, who grew up in Covington, Georgia, was shocked to learn that the mother of one of her classmates had been lynched. The details were hazy, and no one would explain what had happened or why she had been lynched. "It was very frightful to all of the students who knew the girl in school," she recalled. But to Clark's dismay, no explanation was forthcoming, and for some reason the affair remained "a great secret" among the adults. At the turn of the century, when she was about eight years old, Esther Mae Scott came upon the charred bodies of several black men in a Vicksburg street, all of them burned beyond recognition. "We dare not to talk about it, we dare not to say anything. It was just there. . . ." And the more relentlessly Richard Wright questioned his mother about what he had heard in the streets or seen with his own eyes ("I saw more than I could understand and heard more than I could remember"), the more she refused to discuss any of these matters with him. Whenever she did respond to his queries, he sensed her answers were incomplete. "She was not concealing facts," he thought, "but feelings, attitudes, convictions which she did not want me to know; and she became angry when I prodded her."[36]

The search for explanations all too often yielded results that were less than reassuring. Parents and relatives seemed irritated when asked questions about racial matters, and many sought to avoid them. To the obvious query about why they could not do certain things came the ready response, "because you're colored," as if that were self-explanatory. But a Decatur, Mississippi, father answered the same question in a way his son was not likely to forget: "Well, son, that's the way it is. I don't know what we can do about it. There ain't nothin' we can do about it. Because if we do anything about it, they kill you." For some parents, no doubt, the burden of providing answers was too much to bear. (More than a century after the Emancipation Proclamation, a black leader recalled with difficulty the moment "when you suddenly find your tongue twisted and your speech stammering as you seek to explain to your six-year-old daughter why she can't go to the public amusement park.")[37]

The often ambiguous and tortured responses weighed heavily on black children, reinforcing the shock and bewilderment they felt over their initial racial encounters. Upon experiencing the inability of family members to provide satisfactory answers—or any answers—young blacks began to sense how powerless they were in dealings with whites, how little control they or their parents were able to exercise over their lives and destinies, and where the real power resided in southern society. Audley Moore's mother, a devout Catholic in Iberia Parish, Louisiana, had for some years proudly sat in a pew with her name engraved on a silver plaque. She had paid for this privilege. But in the early years of the twentieth century, even these privileges fell victim to the ravages of enforced segregation. One Sunday, as Audley and her mother entered the church, they found a screen had been installed in the rear bearing the words "For Colored Only." That was where they were ushered, after trying unsuccessfully to sit in their purchased pew. To be forced to undergo this insult in an avowedly Christian establishment took a heavy toll on both mother and daughter. "I saw my mother cry. I saw my mother, who had taught me never to show your feeling, I saw the tears roll down my mother's cheek, and she stayed back of that pew, knelt down." In time, blacks in Iberia Parish erected their own church, but Audley Moore would never forgive or forget her mother's humiliation that Sunday morning. "I can remember as though it was yesterday, you know?" And she recalled how her mother's reaction to the insult had in many ways been as inexplicable as the insult itself. "Now my spirit was, I'd walk out, but she stayed there."[38]

For some black youths, an abrupt, often traumatic awakening to the impotence of their parents in a white world became in itself a racial baptism. When Chester Himes thought back to his life in the South, "one moment" stood out as having hurt him "as much as all the others put together." His brother had been critically injured in an accident, and Chester accompanied his parents as they rushed him to the nearest hospital—"a white people's hospital." Sitting with his brother in the backseat, Chester would be forced to watch "the pantomime" acted out at the emergency entrance. His father, "crying like a baby," was pleading without success that this white hospital admit a seriously injured black boy. Young Himes looked on, trying to contain his rage. His mother at one point fumbled in her handbag for a handkerchief, and Chester Himes found himself thinking, "I hoped it was for a pistol."[39]

Hostile encounters between white and black youths underscored the inability of parents to afford protection to their children. When black adults warned children to be careful to stay out of trouble, the thrust of that advice was "Stay out of trouble with white people." That included the stern warning to avoid picking a fight with any white person, young or old, and not to retaliate if struck. But situations arose that made those admonitions impossible to heed, and parents did not necessarily agree among themselves on what kind of disciplinary action, if any, they should take. During slavery, parents were helpless to protect their children from a whipping, and they were sometimes compelled to inflict the punishment themselves in the presence of whites to teach the disobedient child a lesson—and to avert even harsher punishment if meted out by the overseer or owner. The same mode of punishment, often for the same reasons, persisted into freedom. The problem with hitting a white youth, even in self-defense, was the likelihood of retribution. The white boy, Ed Brown recalled, thought "he had the ups on you. And he did. If you hit him back he'd run and tell his parents. Then here would come his father to your parents. This would scare them bad. They couldn't protect you. They would have to whup you in front of this man to keep down a lot of stirment."[40]

Not all parents submitted easily or unconditionally to white expectations, and many chose to withhold nothing from their children about the facts of black life. To communicate to their children the overwhelming power wielded by white people, however, was not necessarily to concede to whites innate or moral superiority. "You are as good as anybody!" Benjamin Mays's mother kept reassuring him. Generations of young blacks, like Charles Evers in the 1920s, would hear the same admonition. "The white people weren't any better than we were," his mother informed him, "but they sure thought they were."[41] Parents might also make clear to their children that although they needed to condition themselves to comply with the racial status quo, this was not the way it had to be or should be.

If some parents found it difficult to explain the facts of black life and race relations to their children, or if they were unreliable and selective informants, the community provided alternative sources of information upon which black youths might draw. In Knoxville, Tennessee, life in the black community revolved around the water spigot, where James Robinson as a child overheard conversations about nearly every matter pertaining to whites and blacks, including the strong sexual attraction of white women to black men. To Zora Neale Hurston, growing up in the all-black town of Eatonville, Florida, Joe Clark's store, even more than the local church, was "the heart and spring of the town." Sitting on boxes and benches, men exchanged information and judgments, Hurston recalled, passing "this world and the next one through their mouths. The right and the wrong, the who, when and why was passed on and nobody doubted the conclusions." The women tended to gather every Saturday night, invariably to discuss their men as providers (sometimes as lovers) and to speculate on recent gossip. "There was open kindnesses, anger, hate, love, envy and its kinfolks," Hurston remembered, "but all emotions were naked, and nakedly arrived at." Although children were barred from these discussions, she remembered dragging her feet upon entering and leaving the store, picking up scraps of gossip and trying afterward to decipher "adult double talk." The tales of illicit love affairs and the boasts of male sexual potency fascinated her, but nothing she heard matched the "lying" sessions. On those occasions, the men related folktales involving God, Devil, Br'er Rabbit, Br'er Fox, Sis Cat, Br'er Bear, Lion, Tiger, and Buzzard—extraordinary tales in which "all the wood folk walked and talked like natural men."[42]

Based on work experiences, the testimony of family members, conversations overheard, and day-to-day interaction, young blacks formed lasting impressions of white people, which they eagerly shared with each other. Among black teenage schoolboys in Jackson, Mississippi, Richard Wright recalled, conversations invariably revolved around the subject of white folks. The verbal play was in many respects a test of racial loyalty. "The touchstone of fraternity was my feeling toward white people, how much hostility I held toward them, what degrees of value and honor I assigned to race. None of this was premeditated, but sprang spontaneously out of the talk of black boys who met at the crossroads." Often with no specific focus, the talk would roam over "vast areas" of black life and race relations. Through these conversations, Wright recalled, "[o]ur attitudes were made, defined, set, or corrected; our ideas were discovered, discarded, enlarged, torn apart, and accepted." Typically, he and his friends regaled each other with tales of the strange antics and foibles of white people, mimicking white manners and speech and sharing experiences based on a special, sometimes intimate, knowledge of "white folks."

> "My mama says that old white woman where she works talked 'bout slapping her and Ma said: 'Miz Green, if you slaps me, I'll kill you and go to hell and pay for it!'"
> "Hell, I woulda just killed her if she hada said that to me."
>
> "The first white sonofabitch that bothers me is gonna get a hole knocked in his head!"
> "That ain't gonna do you no good. Hell, they'll catch you."
> "Ha-ha-ha. . . . Yeah, goddammit, they really catch you, now."
> "Yeah, white folks set on their white asses day and night, but leta nigger do something, and they get every bloodhound that was ever born and put 'em on his trail."
>
> "Man, you reckon these white folks is ever gonna change?"
> "Hell, no! They just born that way."
>
> "Man, what makes white folks so mean?"
> "Whenever I see one I spit."
> "Man, ain't they ugly?"
> "Man, you ever get right close to a white man, close enough to smell 'im?"
> "They say we stink. But my ma says white folks smell like dead folks."
> "Niggers smell from sweat. But white folk smell *all* the time."

Some years later, when Wright was working in Memphis, lunch conversations with his fellow black workers invariably revolved around "the ways of white folks toward Negroes." If during these conversations a white person happened to come upon them, Wright recalled, "we would have assumed silent, obedient smiles."[43]

The aspirations and ambitions of black youths were almost certain to have been deflated by the time they reached maturity. Growing up in the late nineteenth and early twentieth centuries, they were exposed to the popular self-help messages and the dominant success creed, but they knew from personal observation and from stories they had over-heard that successful blacks existed mostly at the toleration of whites and within rigidly circumscribed limits. They knew, too, that evidence of black success all too often provoked white resentment rather than re-spect. If the poverty of their parents induced taunts and derision from white children, the demonstrated success of their parents might pro-voke angry and violent responses. A black woman recalled being told by a white playmate, "You think you are white because your folks own their own home, but you ain't, you're a nigger just the same, and my pa says if he had his rights he would own niggers like you, and your home, too."[44]

Trying to make sense of the world around them required young blacks to learn to control their instincts and ambitions. When her father once angrily shouted, "Lemme tell you something right now, my young lady; you ain't white," Zora Neale Hurston thought she knew why he had reprimanded her: "That is a Negro saying that means 'Don't be too ambitious. You are a Negro and they are not meant to have but so much.' " Not only did young blacks need to consider realistic limits to their aspirations but also, like their parents, they risked provoking whites if in any way they flaunted their possessions or achievements. While in high school, Benjamin Mays experienced his "most embar-rassing" interracial encounter ("as vivid in my mind today as if it hap-pened yesterday"). His mother always made certain he dressed cleanly and neatly when he went out. On this day, as he waited for his mail at the local post office, a well-known young white doctor, Wallace Payne, entered, struck Mays in the face, and exclaimed, "Get out of my way, you black rascal. You're trying to look too good anyway." Stunned and momentarily blinded by the blow, young Mays was speechless. "My greatest sin, of course, was that I was 'trying to look too good.' . . . [A] Negro was not supposed to look neat or intelligent, or to stand erect around Dr. Payne." Mays also recalled the questions that went through his mind. "Why did I take it? Why didn't I hit back? . . . Maybe I had already been conditioned by Mother's admonition, 'Stay out of trou-ble.' " He also knew that if he had retaliated in any manner, verbal or otherwise, he would most likely have been "shot dead on the spot," and nothing would have been done about it. No white person would have testified on his behalf, and the few blacks in the store would have been too frightened to testify against any white man, particularly one as prominent as Dr. Payne.[45]

Tales of self-made men, making it from rags to riches, inspired young Americans in the late nineteenth century. But the way many young blacks heard them, tales of black ambition somehow seemed to end in disaster. If the stories served any purpose, they helped to explain some of the violence that otherwise seemed so senseless. When white men came to Eunice Rivers's home and beat her father, she could think of no reason. There had been no provocation. The more she reflected over the attack, however, the more she came to believe that by supplementing his farm work with paid labor at the sawmill, her father "was just living a little bit too well to be a Negro. . . . A Negro's s'posed to be in a little cabin, and the white man tell him when to go and when to come." Her father, however, had opted to own his own small home and be independent, and that obviously did not sit well with some local white residents. The attacks persisted. Finally, after night riders shot into their house one night, her father gave in and moved the family back into one of the rental cabins. The harassment ceased, Eunice Rivers recalled, "and we stayed there."[46]

The perils of success came to be forcibly impressed upon Richard Wright, who spent his childhood and adolescence in Mississippi, Tennessee, and Arkansas. In what he would call his "baptism of racial emotion," Richard was eight years old when white men murdered his Uncle Hoskins in the saloon he owned in Elaine, Arkansas. Local whites had long resented and coveted his uncle's flourishing business, and he had been warned a number of times to leave the community. The entire episode drained young Wright, not simply his uncle's murder but the almost eerie aftermath. There was no funeral, no mourning. Aunt Maggie was not even permitted to view her husband's body or to claim his assets, and Richard had no idea when or where he was buried. "There were only silence, quiet weeping, whispers, and fear," Wright recalled. "Uncle Hoskins had simply been plucked from our midst and we, figuratively, had fallen on our faces to avoid looking into that white-hot face of terror that we knew loomed somewhere above us. This was as close as white terror had ever come to me and my mind reeled." Bewildered by the incident, he asked his mother why the family had not resisted. He would not ask that question again, as "the fear that was in her made her slap me into silence."[47]

Fear underscored the "place" of blacks, young and old alike, conditioned their relations with white people, and forced them to hedge their words and actions. It affected posture and speech, gestures and demeanor in the presence of whites. Richard R. Wright, Jr., at an early age acted on his sense of how the community felt about white people. "I began to fear white people, to go out of my way rather than confront them." Thinking back to the awakening of their racial consciousness, many black Southerners associated it less with a specific incident in their childhood than with a perceived way of life in which fear of whites played a dominant role. "You know you're black from the day you're born. . . . Being black is part of the air you breathe," Charles Evers recalled, and though he grew up in Mississippi in the 1920s his observation would have seemed all too familiar to earlier generations. Like many young blacks, Benjamin J. Davis tried to avoid whites altogether. But he would never forget his earliest impressions. "White people were a strange lot to me. The only contact I had with them was hateful. I regarded them as colorless—especially physically—somewhat inferior, wicked and authoritarian."[48]

If the actions of white folks seemed at times bewildering and inexplicable, the answers came soon enough. With increasing forcefulness, race, color, and class assumed an overwhelming immediacy for black youths, the principal ways in which the world was interpreted for them. Pauli Murray spent her childhood in Durham, North Carolina, in the years preceding World War I. The lessons she imbibed in the significance of race, color, and class, not only for one's standing in the larger society but also in the black community, had already been taught to generations of black southern youths.

It seemed as if there were only two kinds of people in the world—*They* and *We*—*White* and *Colored*. The world revolved on color and variations in color. It pervaded the air I breathed. I learned it in hundreds of ways. I picked it up from grown folks around me. I heard it in the house, on the playground, in the streets, everywhere. The tide of color beat upon me ceaselessly, relentlessly. . . .

It was color, color, color all the time, color, features and hair. Folks were never just folks. They were white folks! Black folks! Poor white crackers! No count niggers! Red necks! Darkies! Peckerwoods! Coons!

Two shades lighter! Two shades darker! Dead white! Coal black! High Yaller! Mariny! Good hair! Bad hair! Stringy hair! Nappy hair! Thin lips! Thick lips! Red lips! Liver lips! Blue veined! Blue gummed! Straight nosed! Flat nosed! . . .

To hear people talk, color, features and hair were the most important things to know about a person, a yardstick by which everyone
measured everybody else.[49]

The black child quickly learned these lessons. Not only whites placed
a premium on shades of color, on class, and on education. Growing up
in North Carolina during Reconstruction, Charles W. Chesnutt felt
himself to be a virtual exile because of his light complexion and education. "I am neither fish[,] flesh, nor fowl," he noted in the journal he
kept, "neither 'nigger', white, nor 'buckrah.' Too 'stuck-up' for the colored folks, and, of course, not recognized by the whites." No less con-
fused about his identity, four-year-old Ely Green came to realize on
Chistmas Day 1897 that his stepfather was not his father. And, as he recalled, he was constantly reminded of that fact. "I was looked on as a
half-white bastard, and called that by almost everyone that knew me."[50]

When Lucy Ann Potts, the daughter of a prominent black landowner in Alabama, agreed to marry John Hurston, an "over-the-creek
nigger," she disgraced herself in the eyes of her family and earned their
enduring anger. Her principal offense lay in crossing class, not color
lines. "Over-the-creek niggers," her daughter recalled, "lived from one
white man's plantation to the other. Regular hand-to-mouth folks.
Didn't own pots to pee in, nor beds to push 'em under. Didn't have no
more pride than to let themselves be hired by poor-white trash." To escape the family tensions, John Hurston moved his new bride to the all-
black town of Eatonville, Florida, where he would be elected mayor
three terms and write the local laws, and where their daughter, Zora,
would be born.[51]

The emphasis on color often raised deep rifts within families and
communities. Alice Allison Dunnigan remembered vividly the day her
maternal grandmother expressed contempt for "yellow niggers," making it clear that this made Alice inferior to her darker-complexioned
older brother. The incident, Dunnigan recalled, "planted a seed of inferiority in my mind which I have never been able to weed out completely." Audley Moore, on the other hand, growing up in Louisiana,
resented the ways in which light-skinned people of color felt themselves
superior to those with a darker complexion. "[T]his was taught to us,"
she recalled, "it was taught. Everything that happened in your life was
to demean the original people, the African complexion." She thought it
"a terrible scourge" that those with a mixed heritage should somehow
flaunt their superiority. It "added insult to the injury" inflicted by

whites, she insisted, "raping us, then teaching us that we were better than the black ones that had escaped the rape."[52]

Reinforcing the bewilderment of many young blacks, the pull within the community was toward white standards of beauty. Not only did color count but hair as well, "good hair" deemed preferable to "bad hair." Some black families tried valiantly to minimize these differences. "Oh, all hair is good," Abna Aggrey's father reassured her, after someone had noted that she did not have her mother's "good hair." Susie Williams's father forbade anyone in the family to describe persons by the color of their skin. But despite the reassurances and attempts to evade the subject altogether, color invariably entered into the daily conversations and arguments of adults and children; indeed, as James Robinson recollected of his childhood in Knoxville, Tennessee, the "worst taunt" black children could use in addressing each other was "old black nigger." That was because, he explained, "no one wanted to be black if he could help it," and although many sought escape through skin lighteners, these creams never worked as they were advertised. "We called each other black with a sting which no white boy's insults could equal."[53]

The children of mixed parentage quickly learned that possession of a light complexion still defined them as black in the eyes of white people—and in the eyes of the law. That reality had to be assimilated along with the initial acknowledgment of white parentage. It seldom came easily. To be told that their father (or much less frequently, their mother) was white could be a startling revelation, capable of provoking a variety of emotions, as it did for Augusta Swanson, who grew up in a family in which her two sisters and brother all had different fathers. She knew the identity of her father, a prominent white grocer in town, and his proximity made inevitably for additional complications and tensions. When he chose to visit the family, as he did on occasion, his daughter refused to have anything to do with him. "I wouldn't even come out to see him," she recalled. "I didn't want to see no white man." She would not place any of the blame on her mother. "Because, see, in the country, they didn't have no money, and the only way they could get it was to go with these white men to get a little change." Caddy Gordon, on the other hand, who had two children by slaveowners, expressed a certain pride in her children's mixed heritage and she passed that pride on to her grandchildren as well. "There ain't no poor white blood running through your veins," she told them. "That's one thing we can say with pride. There is no trash in our blood. It's good aristocratic blood."[54]

If many young blacks took refuge in their blackness, and in their relative isolation from whites, some experienced self-hatred and self-deprecation and came to resent their color, physiognomy, and dialect. It induced some even to imagine the unthinkable, to fantasize a life outside of color. The attraction to whiteness was neither new nor difficult to understand. After the Civil War, some blacks entertained the fantasy that emancipation might have changed their lives and destinies in more substantive ways had it also turned them white. To a black girl growing up in Mississippi more than half a century after emancipation, the advantage of being white was quite obvious. "The reason was that we worked every day, hard work, and we never did have food. The people that wasn't working, which was the white folks, they had food and they had clothes and everything. So I wanted to be white."[55] The images of blacks they encountered in school, moreover, were not calculated to inspire them about their race or history; their parents, teachers, and newspapers, consciously or not, often held up white values, behavior, and racial features for emulation, and the popularity of skin whiteners and bleaching creams, and the ways in which many blacks of all ages attacked their "nappy" hair with hard brushes, combs, and creams attested to the pervasiveness of white standards. They were impossible to escape.

> *Oh!*
>> *Stan' back, black man,*
>> *You cain't shine;*
>> *Yo' lips is too thick,*
>> *An' you hain't my kin'.*
> *Aw!*
>> *Git 'way, black man,*
>> *You jes hain't fine;*
>> *I'se done quit foolin'*
>> *Wid de nappy-headed kind.*

But black women in Auburn, Alabama, on the eve of World War I, sounded a different note,

> *Ain't crazy 'bout no high yellow, worried about no brown,*
> *Come to picking my choice, gimme*
> *The blackest man in town.*

as did this street minstrel in North Carolina in 1911:

> *Brown gal she dress like Paris,*
> *Yellow gal she do de same;*
> *Old black gal wears a burlap sack,*
> *But that's dressin' jus' de same.*[56]

3

SINCE EMANCIPATION, many black families had equated freedom with the need to test boundaries, to respond less obsequiously to every white whim and gesture. To mark the difference between slavery and freedom, some made a point of dropping the old social usages, though this might risk a confrontation with the unwritten white racial code. One black-authored etiquette manual advised blacks in 1899 to address whites as equals, not as inferiors. Pauline Fitzgerald learned as a small girl in North Carolina never to address a white person as "marse," for it implied the old slave-master relationship. "You can call him 'Mr. Smith' or 'Mr. Frank,' " Pauline's father admonished her, "but if I ever catch you saying 'Marse' again, I'll whale the daylights out of you." With equal firmness, Caddy Gordon, who had once been enslaved, taught her children and grandchildren not to say "Yas suh" and "No suh" and "Yas 'um" and "No mum" to white folks.[57]

But the old habits were not so easily discarded. The language and demeanor of blacks helped to define their "place" in southern society, and emancipation and Reconstruction made white men and women even more anxious, even more sensitive to any deviation from expectations. For most blacks, then, personal security required them to learn how to accommodate to daily indignities and to repress any impulses toward individuality or assertiveness in the presence of whites. "[T]he safety of my life in the South depended upon how well I concealed from all whites what I felt," Richard Wright remembered. That same need to conceal thoughts and feelings pervaded countless childhoods well into the twentieth century. "My problems started when I began to comment on what I saw," recalled a woman born into an impoverished family in Durham, North Carolina. "I insisted on being accurate. But the world I was born into didn't want that. Indeed, its very survival depended on not knowing, not seeing—and, certainly, not saying anything at all about what it was really like."[58]

The imperative in each black family—educating their children in survival—seemed clear enough, even if some families chose to inculcate the racial etiquette with less forcefulness than others. In raising their children, black parents assumed an awesome responsibility. They needed, as Ralph Ellison would observe, "to adjust the child to the Southern milieu . . . to protect him from those unknown forces *within himself* which might urge him to reach out for that social and human equality which the white South says he cannot have. Rather than throw himself against the charged wires of his prison, he annihilates the impulses within him."[59]

The initial shocks of racial awareness laid the groundwork for learning the necessary rituals of subservience and subordination. Some of them were prescribed in law; most of them existed by habits and customs that were enforced no less ruthlessly than the law. The etiquette of race relations in many instances perpetuated the social usages that had prevailed during slavery. Every child had to be instructed carefully—or learned often more dramatically outside the home—how to interact linguistically with white people. During his high school years in Orangeburg, South Carolina, Benjamin Mays applied for a house job newly vacated by his friend Isaiah Kearse. When he knocked at the front door of the prospective employer and asked about the position held by "Mr. Kearse," Mays quickly came to realize he had already made "two grave mistakes": knocking at the front door and referring to his friend as "Mr." After the white man angrily called him a "black s.o.b.," he made it perfectly clear that no one by the name of *"Mister* Kearse" had worked for him. "Isaiah worked here; and if you want to see me go to the back door." Mays chose to look for employment elsewhere.[60]

For some black youths the most difficult part of this lesson in racial etiquette was to learn that they should never expect whites to reciprocate with similar terms of deference and respect. That double standard deeply disturbed young James Robinson. "No white man ever took off his [hat] when he came in our house; not even the school supervisors who visited our school did that." But like other demands made on black Southerners, the terminology and deferential gestures and posture, along with the sensitivity of whites to any deviations, entered into their daily lives, and there was little they could do about it. "Son, it's like this in the South," an older relative explained to Ely Green. "A Negro is a 'boy' until he is a man. Then, he is a 'Dad' or an 'Uncle.' Women are 'Aunts' or 'Mamys.' This is the white man and his law. 'Uncles' and

'Mamys' they carry around with them. They try to square themselves with God for the way they have worked them half to death."[61]

Not only would black men and women of any age find themselves in serious difficulty if they failed to extend every social courtesy to white people, young and old, and regardless of class, but black males needed to exercise the utmost vigilance in their relations with white females. This was, they were warned, a particularly dangerous species, capable of precipitating potentially explosive situations in which black life might be arbitrarily terminated. If at all possible, black males were to avoid situations in which they might be alone in their presence. When that was not possible and they encountered white females, they were to give them "space and the time of day"—and nothing else. "Avoid white women, show them respect, *leave them alone*" came to be often repeated words of caution. Whatever the provocation, they were never to raise their voice to white women, and on all occasions they needed to look down or away in conversations with them or when passing them on the street, being careful to avert any eye contact. "Look a white folks in de eye you askin' for trouble" was a common form of advice communicated by black parents to sons and daughters alike. The urgency of such advice rested on the many examples of black men, including boys, grabbed by a mob and brutally lynched for having allegedly leered at a white woman. "You couldn't smile at a white woman," a Jones County, Mississippi, black man thought. "If you did you'd be hung from a limb."[62] And of course black males were warned to avoid any physical contact with white females, such as brushing up against them when passing them on the streets or in stores and crowded situations.

With equal urgency, but with only mixed success, black parents sought to protect their daughters from white men. That meant, if possible, keeping them out of white homes. "The only thing that I can remember that my parents talked about, when it came to race," Ardie Clark recalled, "is that they never wanted a girl of theirs to have to work in the home of a white person. . . . [T]hey felt that the white man would take advantage. That was the principal idea." Septima Clark's father never permitted his daughter to work in a hotel or in domestic service, and her mother insisted that none of their daughters be permitted to nurse a white baby. "They might mark your legs," her mother warned. That was her "unique" way of telling her daughters that white men might offer gifts or otherwise tempt them into a sexual relationship. Hezekiah and Louvenia Mays forbade their daughters to work in the fields for white farmers unless one or more of their sons worked along with them, and one of the sons always accompanied his sister to the store. Nor did the father, as a rule, permit any of his daughters to cook for white families. (He made an exception in the case of a white doctor who had befriended the Mays family during a typhoid fever epidemic and had saved several of their lives.)[63]

Employing whatever resources they could command, young black women also learned to protect themselves. When they needed to obtain water at the neighborhood well, a South Carolina black woman recalled, she and her sister armed themselves with a two-by-four with a nail in it. "We slashed fellows' shoulders several times when they tried to attack us. They were never successful. My sister shot a white guy once when he broke into our house and tried to rape her." If black males had undertaken such actions, they would no doubt have paid a terrible price. Every black person, young or old, male or female, had to weigh the possibility that self-defense would provoke an even more violent white response. The family of a beautiful young black woman in Smithville, Georgia, came to realize there was no way they could provide her with proper protection in the community. Not only did white men seek her company but also they told her she was "just too good-looking for a nigger man." Finally the young woman's mother sent her away to ensure her safety. "It was a hard place to raise daughters," one resident recalled, "especially the pretty ones."[64]

The felt urgency to acculturate black children into the difficult process of "getting along" infused much of the advice parents gave their daughters and sons: the admonitions to be alert and cautious, to act with the utmost restraint and deference, to contain their rage and resentment over insults, to do nothing that might bring into question the veracity of whites or contradict their expectations, and, most important, to have as little as possible to do with whites. "[L]et those white folks alone," Willie Thomas's father warned his son. "Honor the white folks, honor 'em, yassuh an' nosuh. You have to do that." Willie Thomas learned his lesson, and years later as a bluesman he sang his own tribute to racial etiquette, "Yassuh an' Nosuh Blues":

> *Well, on my way a-goin' along, I got no success at all,*
> *I go to my bossman' house, walkin' in, forget to reach for my hat;*
> *When I forget, leave it on my head,*
> *'Cause he likely to get him a club an' knock it off my head.*

Oh, if you forget, tell you, "Nigger, what's wrong with you?"
"What you mean, boss?" "I want you to get that hat off yo' head!"

Yassuh an' nosuh, all over there's no good place,
Oh, yassuh an' nosuh, an' all over this earth there's no place;
He may be young, he don't have to be no more than sixteen or seventeen years,
You got to honor him at the groun'.[65]

It was the black person who had to make the adaptation and accommodation, who had to acquire the proper demeanor and know the proper responses. "It was always the Negro's responsibility to find ways and means to get along with white people," Benjamin Mays came to realize; "never need white people concern themselves with getting along with Negroes." In his youth, Richard Wright, too, came to resent the one-sided nature of learning racial etiquette, that only blacks needed to learn and heed these lessons. "In my dealing with whites I was conscious of the entirety of my relations with them, and they were conscious only of what was happening at a given moment. I had to keep remembering what others took for granted; I had to think out what others felt."[66]

Young blacks learned still another difficult lesson. Acquiescence by itself was not always sufficient; it had to be cheerfully and convincingly given. Even as whites employed a variety of techniques to keep black people in their place, they insisted on more than a forced obedience; they demanded a ritualized compliance, not only deference but a demonstrated, grinning deference—acquiescence by inflection, gesture, and demeanor.[67] It had been no less required of enslaved blacks. In the antebellum South, particularly when a visitor happened upon the plantation, the owner had often put his favorite slaves on display. And to the inevitable question of whether they preferred freedom to slavery, they would—as they knew all too well—be expected not only to respond in the negative but also to grin and shuffle as they did so.

In freedom, no less than during slavery, the brooding, sullen, unsmiling black person alarmed whites, made them feel anxious and insecure. The grinning, laughing, obsequious black person comforted whites, reinforcing both their racial assumptions and their self-esteem. When responding to a white person, as blacks learned early in life, they were expected to say "Yassuh!" with as much meaning and cheer as they could muster. The black minstrel went so far as to paint the grin on his face. Richard Wright, among others, came to be deeply impressed with the premium whites placed on black deceit, how they encouraged irresponsibility. "[T]heir rewards were bestowed upon us blacks," Wright recalled, "in the degree that we could make them feel safe and superior."[68]

During slavery, black men and women had acquired considerable experience in the uses of obsequiousness, duplicity, humility, flattery, and evasion. The ability to anticipate the moods, whims, and expectations of the white families for whom they worked, the knowledge of how to massage the egos and feed the self-esteem of whites, and that almost instinctive sense of when to feign stupidity, even to "act the nigger," had enabled scores of enslaved black men and women to resist without seeming to resist their condition. After emancipation, the "darkey act" and "mother wit" and guile remained critical strategies for survival. Even as the children and grandchildren inherited the tales of their parents' enslavement, they also came to learn the arts of survival and accommodation, the posture and demeanor of deference by which generations of African Americans had managed to mask their feelings and emotions in the presence of whites: the hat in hand, the downcast eyes, the shuffle and scrape, the fumbling words, the head-scratching and grin suggesting incomprehension. And many blacks learned to manipulate these qualities to their own advantage.

Within black families, conflicts were bound to emerge over how to reconcile the harsh demands of white domination with the desire to instill in their children individual self-worth and racial pride. Lucy Ann Hurston had no desire to "squinch" the spirit in her daughter, Zora, and watch her become "a mealy-mouthed rag doll"; on the contrary, as Zora recalled, "Mama exhorted her children at every opportunity to 'jump at de sun.' We might not land on the sun, but at least we would get off the ground." But John Hurston demurred. "Papa did not feel so hopeful. Let well enough alone. It did not do for Negroes to have too much spirit. He was always threatening to break mine or kill me in the attempt." Resigned to a rebellious daughter, he predicted the worst and envisaged "posses with ropes and guns" ready to make her pay the price for her uppityness and impudence. "The white folks were not going to stand for it," Zora remembered him saying. "I was going to be hung before I got grown. Somebody was going to blow me down for my sassy tongue. Mama was going to suck sorrow for not beating my temper out of me before it was too late." Her sister, on the other hand, heeded her father's warnings, and she was "meek and mild" and knew how to get along with white folks. "Why couldn't I be like her?" Zora wondered, but she no doubt sensed the answer.[69]

To prevent their children from becoming "white men's niggers," black elders might admonish them not to compromise their self-respect and personal dignity. Caddy Gordon, who had been a troublesome and often whipped slave, confided to her children and grandchildren that she had nothing but contempt for black people "who simpered around white folks." She told them they did not need to love white people, that she neither loved nor hated them but simply respected those who respected her. She counseled her children and grandchildren never to think or to act out of fear, no matter how frightened they might be. "You could only die once. Better die for something than nothing. You have to fight every inch of the way to be free, every inch of the way. . . ."[70]

Delivering the clothes their mother had washed for a white family, James Robinson and his brother confronted a "gang" made up mostly of poor whites. After charging the brothers with entering "a white man's neighborhood," the youths mocked them for carrying clothes to "those damn uppity white people who can afford to have darkies do their dirty work and flunkey for them." It was not the first time James and William Robinson had confronted the group. "We couldn't buy them off; they didn't want our money. They wanted merely the pleasure of beating us until we cried for mercy." This time the brothers fought back, precipitating a vigorous argument in the Robinson family. Hearing of the fight, Henry Robinson prepared to whip his son, but Willie Belle Robinson intervened, declaring that the boys had done nothing wrong. "They did right; they defended themselves against a gang of damn crackers," she exclaimed. "They've got to learn what to expect. They're black and they'll be black until they die. And as long as they're black, they're going to be hated, scorned, cheated and persecuted. At least they can have the satisfaction of acting like men." Later that night, the questions raised by this family dispute made it impossible for James to sleep. "Would it be like this all my life?" he asked himself. "Was there no escape from the tyranny of a Negro's existence? I had no answer; I was sure there was none. . . ." He wondered why his father and other blacks had not organized and stood up for their rights. He wondered why they did not bother to fix up their homes, learn to read, and improve themselves. When he raised these questions with others, however, he was told not to concern himself about such matters. He came to realize, with additional exposure, that he had underestimated "the viselike hold" of the white South on its black residents. "No wonder the whites encouraged our preachers, it later occurred to me. They were a cheap and useful tool with their soothing talk—'They that wait on the Lord'; 'You may have all this world but give me Jesus. '"[71]

While not wanting to provoke whites to retaliation, blacks found ways to adapt to the racial code without submitting totally to it, and children learned these lessons, too. Confronted with separate drinking fountains for blacks and whites ("there was white water and there was colored water"), Abna Aggrey obeyed her mother's instruction not to drink from any fountain. "Come home," she told her. "We've got water at home." In the absence of any alternatives, she did ride the Jim Crow (racially segregated) car and obey some other regulations, "but there were certain things that we just did not accept." Her mother also set an example by refusing to purchase goods in stores in which the clerks addressed her by her first name. She would inform the clerk that she was honorably married and they should address her either as "Mrs. Aggrey" or nothing at all. "We were just taught that we must do whatever we do to the best of our ability," Abna Aggrey recalled. "And when we had done that, then we had no reason to feel inferior."[72]

The shock of being beaten for forgetting to say "sir" to a white man forced Richard Wright to watch white people carefully, "to observe their every move, every fleeting expression, how to interpret what was said and what left unsaid." He listened carefully when his boyhood friend in Jackson, Mississippi, admonished him to contain his independent manner. "Dick, look, you're black, black, *black*, see? Can't you understand that? . . . When you're in front of white people, *think* before you act, *think* before you speak. Your way of doing things is all right among *our* people, but not for *white* people. They won't stand for it." And when as a teenager, Wright applied for a job, he heeded his friend's advice and played by the rules. "I was very careful to pronounce my *sirs* distinctly, in order that he might know that I was polite, that I knew where I was, and that I knew that he was a *white* man." And yet, although Wright agreed with the essential wisdom of his friend's counsel, he could not submit totally to the demands made on him. His senses had "reeled in protest" when his uncle tried to teach him to grin, hang his head, and mumble apologetically. "I could not make subservience an automatic part of my behavior. I had to feel and think out each tiny item of racial experience in the light of the whole race problem, and to each item I brought the whole of my life. While standing before a white man I had to figure out how to perform each act and how to say each word."[73]

Within the family, children learned that white folks were not the only source of violence and abuse, that it could come from loved ones and kinfolk as well. Men asserted their authority over women, and parents asserted their authority over children. Ned Cobb endured a number of harsh beatings by his father, some for failing to obey his instructions at work, some for what Cobb regarded as no reason at all. "I never did forget none of his treatments toward me. You forever remember the wrongs done to you as long as you live." Richard Wright sustained brutal beatings from his mother, grandmother, and schoolteacher aunt, often for trying to stake out his own independence, sometimes for what were regarded as acts of impudence.[74]

When black parents sought to discipline their children, they were often preparing them for encounters with white people, for the harsh and inhospitable world that lay outside. Many a mother and father administered a whipping in the hope of protecting their children from far worse punishment at the hands of whites. But other considerations also loomed large. The code of behavior that parents instilled in the young was in most instances also a guide to how they should behave within the family and black community. Children were taught to demonstrate proper respect and deference in the presence of adults, particularly the elderly, and they were expected to adhere to certain moral values and standards of behavior. Many of the same demands made of them in the presence of whites applied equally in the presence of blacks, and "mind yo' manners, child" became a familiar refrain in black childhoods. In enforcing discipline in the family, Georgia Gordon's mother, for example, did not hesitate to administer a whipping because, her daughter thought, "she didn't want to see us work on the chain gang." On occasion she would expose her children to the sight of such a gang working on the roads and dragging their chains, to underscore her warning, "That's what you get for being disobedient."[75]

In the household in which William Henry Holtzclaw grew up, his mother assumed responsibility for teaching proper conduct and morality. The Census taker in 1880, he recalled, classified his parents as illiterate because they could neither read nor write. But they possessed, Holtzclaw insisted, "a very clear understanding of right and wrong; in their own way they were moral teachers, and they knew how to make their lessons impressive." When his mother admonished him not to

steal from white people, she also taught him something about the workings of the white mind. White folks, she explained, expected Negroes to
steal from them, even wanted them to steal, because it reinforced in
their minds the intrinsic moral and racial superiority of the white race.
Since that was their expectation, she concluded, "we must show them
that we would not."[76] Not only did she impress her son with the immorality of theft but, more important, she taught him how to maintain
his dignity by refusing to play into the expectations of whites and reinforce their views about the "natural" predilections of black people.

While parents and grandparents imparted lessons in morality, accommodation, and survival, they transmitted at the same time a culture
and a heritage. For scores of young blacks, their elders became revealed
texts, conveying through story and song a history of practical value.
The tales related during slavery had often underscored the skills of
trickery and deception as critical survival tactics. In the stories that revolved around the character of Br'er Rabbit, for example, weaker animals (like black men and women during slavery) devised ingenious
schemes that usually ended in outwitting and humiliating the stronger
animals. After emancipation, animal and human trickster tales, along
with songs, proverbs, jokes, anecdotes, storytelling, and verbal games,
remained significant survival mechanisms. With few of the normal outlets for expression available to them, black men and women found alternative ways to impart their innermost feelings, beliefs, and history.

No child's education was complete without hearing family stories of
what life had been like under slavery—"how dey couldn' never do
nothin' . . . but what de white folks say dey could do." The tales of brutality made a vivid impression, as did the stories of survival, resistance,
and trickery, how they had stood up to their owners and overseers in
some instances, and how they had found ways to protect families and
friends. Born the same year as the Emancipation Proclamation, Daniel
Goddard overheard numerous discussions among parents and family
friends of the Nat Turner and Denmark Vesey insurrections and the
slave revolts in the Caribbean. He was impressed with the network of
communication maintained by the slaves. He learned that these uprisings "were known all over the South" and that enslaved blacks had
been "as well aware of what was going on, as their masters were."[77]

The stories of enslavement and emancipation would find a special
place in the folk history of African Americans. In relating the incidents
in her life, Caddy Gordon, like many others, enabled her children and
grandchildren to confront the full horror of enslavement. Finding it

impossible to accommodate to her condition, she had been a source of constant torment to her owners. Sold and whipped many times in her life, she had remained strong-willed and defiant. Long after emancipation, the "Caddy" stories became an integral part of the family tradition. And with each retelling, they took on a more dramatic intensity: how Caddy had been sold on the block when only eight years old; how Caddy located her mother after emancipation; and, in the story that became the family favorite, how on being informed of her freedom Caddy had dashed into the Big House, confronted her mistress, flipped up her dress, "and told her to do something. She said it mean and ugly. . . . 'Kiss my ass!' " To dramatize to her children and grandchildren "what slavery was like," she also showed them the thumb-deep scars that the whip had left on her back. Only when Caddy Gordon described how it had felt as a slave to be raped were the children ordered out of the room.[78]

If children in the late nineteenth and early twentieth centuries understood the reluctance of their elders to violate the prevailing racial code, many could take pride in those who in the past had found ways to confront, overcome, or undermine the repressive apparatus of whites. Ely Green's grandfather used the stories of his enslavement to teach his children and grandchildren not to cringe in the presence of whites or display a fear of them. "That's what is wrong with the niggers," he would observe. "They are too afraid. . . . When I was a boy your age I was . . . put on the block and sold with five other brothers and sisters." Benjamin Davis's grandmother, born in slavery, described beatings that permanently crippled her, most of them inflicted when she interceded on behalf of her family. "I wasn't going to let 'em kill my children," she explained as she related her story. And she talked with both pride and sorrow about her husband, a recalcitrant slave who had always aspired to be "somebody." When Benjamin questioned his grandmother about what that meant, she replied, "I don't know. I guess he wanted to be a man." But when her husband intervened to defend her from a whipping, he was beaten and sold, "and neither I nor the children ever saw him again."[79]

When former slaves shared their life histories with children and grandchildren, the telling itself might prove to be—for the narrator as for the young audience—a traumatic and unforgettable experience, stirring memories and evoking feelings of both anger and compassion. The tales of brutality Mary Church heard from her grandmother affected both of them deeply. "She was rarely able to finish what she began," Mary remembered. "I tried to keep the tears back and the sobs suppressed, so that Grandmother would carry the story to the bitter end, but I seldom succeeded." It was as a young girl in Baltimore in the early 1920s, entrusted with the care of her great-grandmother, a former Virginia slave, that Billie Holiday came to learn of her slave heritage. "She had been a slave on a big plantation in Virginia and she used to tell me all about it," Holiday recalled. "We used to talk about life. And she used to tell me how it felt to be a slave, to be owned body and soul by a white man who was the father of her children."[80]

For many young blacks in the late nineteenth century, the descriptions of enslavement and the betrayal of expectations after emancipation served to reinforce the bitterness they felt over their present condition. When he told his grandchildren about slavery, Bessie Jones's grandfather wanted to impress on them the difficulties blacks encountered both in surviving and in overcoming enslavement. "They didn't know which way to go," he declared, and he would "moan" an old song to make his point:

> *I done done all I could do*
> *What more could I do, Lord*
> *Lord I done done all I could do*
> *And I can't hold out.*

"That is real," he would add, "and something to think about. They meant that; they didn't know what to do. Looked like they did everything to get along, and nothing they did done any good." The songs, he thought, "and the meanings of those songs," had helped them to deal with the hardships. God, he insisted, had given those songs to enslaved blacks as a way of communicating their feelings and aspirations. "It was handed down to them without any schooling."[81]

The tales of bondage, escape, resistance, and adaptation all entered the black folk tradition. Not only did these tales provide a history to working people with few traditional kinds of documents, but the stories became a shared oral experience as well. When Janet Johnson compiled a family history for her elementary school in Bentonia, Mississippi, some 115 years after the Civil War, she was able to trace her slave ancestors back to 1700 and the birth of Sarah Martha Coleman, who was captured and enslaved at age thirty. She learned, too, that her "great-great-grandmother" had played a role in the Underground Railroad and that still another ancestor had been killed trying to escape

to the North. All of this information, she revealed, had been handed
down generation by generation, usually when a child turned twelve.
"And I'm supposed to pass it on to the generation when I get older."[82]

The stories provided communal admiration for the men and women
who had survived enslavement. Contrary to what they sometimes read
in their school textbooks, young blacks learned at home about their
past in ways calculated to instill pride rather than shame. "My grandmother always said that she was *Somebody* and she came from being
Somebody," Frances Albrier recalled. "My grandmother knew more of
her history than she told us. . . . She had a feeling of pride in her background that gave her life meaning. Many people lost that pride because
they didn't know their history." Children learned not only how their
parents and grandparents had survived enslavement but also how the
labor of the slaves had helped to create the wealth of the South. Bessie
Jones's grandfather made that clear through a song that included this
verse:

I've never seen the likes since I've been born
The bull cow kicking off the milk cow's horn.

In the pasture, he noted, no bull was likely to kick off the milk cow's
horns. "We talking about the white man, see," he explained. The
Negro was the milk cow, the white man the bull cow. "He kept him
hewed down in every respect. His voice was even kicked off to where he
couldn't speak up for himself or nothing." The Negro had performed
all the hard work, the necessary labor to start and build a home on this
land. But after he had "put all that down," the white man had insisted,
"You get outa the way, nigger; I'm going to decorate it." And, he soon
insisted, "I built it." But the Negro had done all the hard work, he had
laid the foundation, and the white man knew it, and "that's what that
song meant." Bessie Jones thought to ask her grandfather if white people understood that the song was about them. "No," he would reply,
"they ain't got sense enough. . . . All a white man's brain is up in the top
of his head. You see where he gets bald quick? To keep that colored
man down he just has to scratch it all out."[83]

Young blacks not only listened to the stories of slavery and passed
them on to still another generation but also honored the survivors of
enslavement. More than two hundred former slaves came to the First
Baptist Church in Hampton, Virginia, on December 4, 1893, to hear a
tribute from their children. Punctuated by shouts from the audience of

"Thank God, it's come," "I thank you, my Jesus!," and "Dats so, sister," the youthful speakers talked of the sacrifices their parents had made. They reminded them of the furtive prayer meetings, the war and the coming of freedom, and how as slaves they had been denied an education now available to their children. Catherine W. Fields, a Hampton graduate of the Class of '78, noted that black people had sometimes said to her, "We can't sing 'My country 'tis of thee'—this is not our country but the white people's." But she reassured them, "The soil of this land has been watered by the Negro's tears and blood. If it is not our country, whose is it?"[84]

4

THE "SHOCKS OF CHILDHOOD" shaped lives, personalities, outlooks, prospects, and modes of accommodation. To learn to live with racial fear could be debilitating and devastating. The New South for a new generation of blacks had all the markings of a closed society, one that was prepared ruthlessly to impose and maintain its authority in all phases of daily life and to undermine black achievement and dignity. It was for many a bleak and cheerless world. But even as whites rigidly controlled black lives and behavior, they could seldom fathom the workings of the black mind. And even as young blacks made the required accommodations to the prevailing racial code, they contemplated alternatives and developed a variety of responses and strategies.[85]

Benjamin Mays, born in 1895, spent the first twenty-two years of his life in South Carolina. "There wasn't much going for the Negro in the world in which I was born," he remembered. A time of learning and questioning, his childhood taught him certain fundamental truths. He knew that southern whites were his enemy—"not only my enemy but the enemy of all Negroes." And he sensed, along with many others of his generation, the formidable obstacles he faced. "Long before I could visualize them, I knew within my body, my mind, and my spirit that I faced galling restrictions, seemingly insurmountable barriers, dangers and pitfalls." How, he wondered, could he aspire to "be somebody" in a society that frowned upon blacks aspiring to be anybody? How could he unlearn the accommodationist patterns he had imbibed since infancy? How, in fact, could any black person avoid trouble when his "place" in the South "was whatever any white man's whim dictated at any given time"? He knew that those who "grinned, cringed, and kow-

towed" to whites faced the same dangers as the few who refused to do
so. He knew, too, that whites were superior to him only in their ability
to wreak violence on his people. Although he lived "in constant fear"
that he would be a victim—that he, too, might be lynched—young
Mays refused to believe that God had willed such a fate. "I came to the
conclusion that I could never do what I hoped to do or be what I aspired to be if I remained in the state of my birth."[86]

As a schoolboy in Florence, Alabama, W. C. Handy, born in 1873, listened to a diatribe by a gubernatorial candidate. This was his baptism
in racist oratory. Alarmed at the virulence of the speaker's argument,
he ran home, buried his head under a pillow, and wept. Later he wandered off into the woods across the road from the cabin in which he had
been born. There, with no one within hearing distance, he began,
"slowly" and "deliberately," to respond to the arguments of the politician he had heard earlier. "At the top of my voice I . . . hurled the lie
into his teeth. The woodland took up my shouts. The words of my defiance echoed and reechoed. That pleased me. I went home and slept
well, a great burden removed."[87]

When Richard Wright turned twelve, shortly after the end of World
War I, he looked back at his childhood. He had read the pulp literature.
He knew the Horatio Alger rags-to-riches stories. He knew "from cover
to cover" the Get-Rich-Quick Wallingford series. But he realized, too,
that he lived in a country that placed clear limits on black aspirations.
"Yet I felt that I had to go somewhere and do something to redeem my
being alive." Earlier, he had formed in his mind, as he would later recall, "a conception of life that no experience would ever erase, a
predilection for what was real that no argument could ever gainsay, a
sense of the world that was mine and mine alone, a notion as to what
life meant that no education could ever alter, a conviction that the
meaning of living came only when one was struggling to wring a meaning out of meaningless suffering." He would learn to live with the terrors. He would learn to live with the tensions and the anxieties, and
with the still unanswered questions. He wondered, however, how long
he could bear it, how much longer he could maintain his composure
and demeanor. What he had learned and experienced, he could never
put out of his mind. And that made for sleepless nights. "I no longer *felt*
that the world about me was hostile, killing; I *knew* it."[88]

Charles W. Chesnutt, twenty years old in 1878, a teacher in Fayetteville, North Carolina, found his thoughts turning increasingly to the
North, where, as he realized, racial prejudice also thrived, "yet a man

may enjoy . . . privileges if he has the money to pay for them." Confiding his thoughts to his journal, young Chesnutt struck at the same time a note of defiance: "I will live down the prejudice, I will crush it out. I will show to the world that a man may spring from a race of slaves, and yet far excel many of the boasted ruling race." To "exalt" his race came to be a principal mission in his life. Two years later, as he thought over his life in the South and the prospects of his race, he became even more ambitious. He vowed to seek through his writings "not so much the elevation of the Colored people as the elevation of the Whites." He understood the formidable barriers, that "subtle almost indefinable feeling of repulsion toward the negro, which is common to most Americans." He sensed that white prejudices could not be taken by storm, by an open assault. "[T]heir position must be mined," he concluded, "and we will find ourselves in their midst before they think it."[89]

Mary Tuck, born in 1893, grew up in Yazoo County, Mississippi. The stories she heard from her grandmother all revolved around the "hell" called slavery. "My grandmother used to sit down and tell us everything. That's all she used to tell everybody, slavery. And she worried that we were gonna be in the same shape like it was in slave times. You worked for nothing, they didn't pay you nothing to work. You'd just be half dead." At a very early age, Mary learned the demands placed on black families who worked the cotton fields. She worked in the house, while the others went to the field. "I had to cook, I had to wash, iron, milk the cows and keep the house clean." The labor was arduous, and she would have preferred working in the fields with her parents and siblings. At age seven, to supplement the income, she began to work for a white family. "I . . . had to get up in a chair to get to the stove." She and her mother also took in washing and ironing for the twenty children who stayed at dormitories at the nearby white high school. When she married at age sixteen, Mary Tuck recalled, nothing really changed in her day-to-day duties. In relating the stories of slavery, Mary Tuck's grandmother had expressed the hope that it would be different for her children and grandchildren. But life as Mary Tuck experienced it had its own compulsions. "Seems like there's slavery on us since we've been big enough to have clothes and things and food. . . . I know what us had, we had a hard time coming up and you know what they did back here before we was born, you know it was worser."[90]

Each black family, each individual, was forced to make some kind of accommodation to the demands of the racial code. Like many children of former slaves, Ned Cobb, born in Alabama in 1885, learned to obey whites and to avoid trouble. That was the legacy he inherited. He began plowing at age nine, and his father hired him out ten years later. Early on he sensed the need to confront and cast off the lingering vestiges of enslavement. "I wasn't over ten or twelve years old until I begin to come into the knowledge of more different things wrong than I can really tell." His father, Ned thought, although legally free, remained "in his acts" and in his fears of whites a slave. "Just throwin' his money in a dead hog's ass and takin' shit. No forethought about it. . . . He wasn't a slave but he lived like one. Because he had to take what the white people gived to get along. That much of slavery ways was still hangin' on." Young Cobb endured his father's scoldings—and his beatings. But he could not endure his father's "weakness toward white folks," the way he cringed in their presence and yielded to their demands. That was where Ned chose to draw the line. Over his father's protests, Ned warned a white neighbor to keep his cow out of their corn crop. Not yet twenty years old, he reveled in his triumph, sensing the critical importance of this occasion—a true coming of age. "I felt right then that I was a man and I begin to take on man ways, man acts, so far as right. . . . I wasn't sassy and impudent to nobody, but I done got to the wrong age on me then to feel like it was right for folks to run over me or run over my folks."[91]

Bill Patton, a hardworking farmer near the end of the Civil War, chose to move with his family between 1901 and 1904 to a newly opened plantation called Dockery Farms, in the upper Mississippi Delta. Combining the roles of farmer and part-time preacher, Patton tried to support his large family. He reprimanded his son, Charlie, for his childhood obsession with playing the guitar—"the devil's music"—and tried to force him to mend his ways. But Charlie kept on playing, learning to perform a new musical form that had already achieved considerable popularity in the Delta. Like other bluesmen, Charlie made music about what he saw around him. Offering up his own set of values, judgments, and experiences, Charlie helped to counsel and baptize a new generation in the ways of black folks and white folks in the New South.[92]

Benjamin Mays, W. C. Handy, Richard Wright, Charles Chesnutt, Mary Tuck, Ned Cobb, Charlie Patton—a mere handful of the hundreds of thousands of black Southerners coming of age in the New South between the end of Reconstruction and the 1920s. In the spirit they often showed, in the modes of accommodation they adopted and reshaped, and in the ways in which they experienced and chose to confront and condition the mechanisms of race control, they reflected the growing restlessness and tensions of the first postemancipation generations, the first generations to be born outside the discipline of slavery. They did not go unnoticed. In the perceptions of white men and women, they symbolized not the promise but the threat of a New Negro.

CHAPTER TWO

LESSONS

Geo'ge Washin'ton I hate to say you nevah tole a lie,
I wish there wuz no Washin'ton, I do, I hope I die.
When I wuz a little boy some white man felt o' my haid,
Said, "Some day you may be president,"—some day I nevah see.
Somebody lie, dat's sho as you born, somebody lie on me.[1]
        —A song heard in Texas after World War I

COMPARING THE EXPERIENCE of his people with other immigrants, a former Tennessee slave thought "every nationality" in the United States had been given a distinct advantage over African Americans. "Sometimes when I am on my wagon," he reflected, "I look at the children coming from school, and I say, 'If I had had that opportunity when I was coming up I would be "sons of thunder." ' "[2] No wonder the slave South had thought it critical to prevent black men and women from acquiring even the bare essentials of learning. Knowledge encouraged independence and free thought. Knowledge opened up new vistas, introduced people to a larger world than the local town and county. Knowledge permitted workers to calculate their earnings and expenditures. These were sufficient incentives for whites to maintain black illiteracy—or to place clear limits on how much knowledge blacks should acquire and to make certain it was the right kind of knowledge imparted by the right kind of teachers.

Forbidden by antebellum laws and custom from learning to read or write, enslaved black men and women sensed the importance of these skills by the very vehemence with which whites enforced the prohibition, the extraordinary measures whites adopted to criminalize black literacy and to insulate blacks from intellectual contamination. "The white folks never would let me pick up a picture and look at it," a Tennessee woman recalled of a childhood spent in slavery. "I would be looking at pictures, you know, and I would get a whipping." After emancipation, her brother and uncle urged her to go to school, but by this time, she later reflected, "the white folks had beat all the learning out of me." On the Louisiana plantation where she was enslaved, Sarah Benjamin recalled, any black man, woman, or child who managed to acquire a competence in reading or writing was well advised to keep that talent hidden. "If yer learned ter write dey would cut yer thumb er finger off."[3]

Slaveholders, legislatures, and the courts deemed black illiteracy essential to the internal security of the white South. But lapses in enforcement did occur, sometimes in the very ranks of slaveholding families, more often in the slave quarters and fields, outside of white scrutiny. Larger numbers of free blacks managed through their own initiative to acquire a rudimentary education, some in clandestine schools, others in the schools for the freeborn tolerated in a few communities. Whenever opportunities existed, some blacks tried to make the most of them. "The ignorant whites had every chance to learn, but didn't," a black preacher observed in 1865; "we had every chance to remain ignorant, and many of us learned in spite of them."[4]

White vigilance, however, mostly succeeded. On the eve of emancipation, the vast majority of southern blacks were illiterate—a condition most southern whites preferred to perpetuate. Economic self-interest alone dictated continuing vigilance, as it had before the war. "They didn't want us to learn nothin'," Annie Perry recalled. "The only thing we had to learn was how to work." Robert Russa Moton, born in 1867, recalled how his mother devoted an hour each night to teaching him the blue-backed primer, but did so clandestinely, not wanting the Virginia family for whom they worked to know she was teaching him to read or that she could read. "For several years she had kept from them the fact that she even knew one letter of the alphabet from another."[5]

If black people needed to be persuaded of the compelling importance of learning, they had only to look around them. Power, influence, and wealth were associated with literacy and monopolized by the better-educated class of southern whites. "My Lord, ma'am, what a great thing larning is!" a freed slave exclaimed to a white teacher in South Carolina. "White folks can do what they likes, for they know so much more'na we." Like most young slaves, Booker T. Washington had viewed the mysteries of reading and writing from a distance, as when he escorted his owner's son to a schoolhouse he was forbidden to enter. But that prohibition only excited his curiosity, and when his mother explained to him that whites considered reading too dangerous for black people, he was even more anxious to acquire this skill. "From the moment that it was made clear to me that I was not to go to school, that it was dangerous for me to learn to read, from that moment, I resolved that I should never be satisfied until I learned what this dangerous practice was like." No less impressed, Mary Jane McLeod (Bethune), the fifteenth child of former slaves and one of the first born free, managed to obtain some early schooling and reveled in the opportunity afforded her. "The whole world opened to me when I learned to read."[6]

After emancipation, employers, landlords, and storekeepers, among others, seized every opportunity to exploit black illiteracy for personal gain. The value of "book-larnin' " was at no time more dramatically impressed on blacks than at "settling up" time and when it came to signing a labor contract. To know how to read, write, and cipher, to calculate rates of interest, to command a knowledge of prices, to be familiar with the most fundamental methods of accounting—these skills were deemed increasingly essential if blacks were to carve out for themselves a larger degree of independence in the workplace, if they were to cast off the remaining vestiges of slavery that made them economically dependent on whites. To an elderly Louisiana freedman, that was reason enough to send his children to school, even if their absence from the fields deprived the family of additional earnings. "Leaving learning to your children was better than leaving them a fortune, because if you left them even five hundred dollars, some man having more education than they had would come along and cheat them out of it all."[7]

Common sense alone persuaded parents to obtain some kind of education for their children. "Education only hurts a fool," Thomas Doyle decided, as he sent his children to school. He wanted them to know enough to look after their own interests, "to 'figger' and keep accounts so nobody can take advantage of them." Despairing of the poor schools and limited education available in Early County, Georgia, and seeking an alternative to the mission school, where white teachers predominated, Eunice Rivers's father sent her to Tuskegee Institute, where black teachers would train his daughter in the elementary through high school grades. Each time she returned home, he examined her thoroughly on what she had learned, and invariably this strong-minded farmer demanded that she be able to translate her newly acquired skills into matters of practical value. "That bale of cotton weighs 700 and something and it's twenty cents a pound, how much money do I get out of it?" With equal determination, Mack Parker sent his son, Will, to school, and some years later when he thought the plantation manager might be cheating on the settlement, he asked his son to examine the books. "*That's* what I sent you to school for," he insisted.[8]

Nearly every black political convention during Reconstruction proclaimed the critical importance of education, seeking to drive home to black families the obvious truth that "knowledge is power." Accordingly, from the earliest days of emancipation, many blacks sought to condition their future employment on the availability of a schoolhouse and a teacher, insisting that the details be written into the labor contract. Timothy Smith, a former house servant and farmhand, chose to remain on the same plantation after his former master agreed to give Smith one-fourth of everything he made, feed the Smith family, *and* provide time for attending school at night. "I seen that education was a great thing and something that I badly needed," Smith remarked, "especially in keeping my accounts." Hired out to local farmers in rural Georgia, William H. Heard signed a contract that stipulated both his wages and his right to a lesson at night.[9]

Not only did the ability to read and write provide some protection to blacks from exploitative whites, but it also might improve their prospects for different kinds of work. When Charles W. Chesnutt taught in a country school in North Carolina, he encountered parents reluctant to support a teacher; most of them were poor, working other people's land, and they felt despondent about their prospects. "You preachers and teachers are too hard on us," a black man told Chesnutt, expressing skepticism about the need to pay a teacher's salary. "You want us to pay you thirty or forty dollars a month for sitting in the shade, and that is as much as we can make in 2 or 3 months. . . . We all of [us] work on other people's, white people's, land, and sometimes get cheated out of all we make; we can't get the money." To persuade them, Chesnutt stressed education as the only way to escape the condition of dependency. "You say you are all renters, and get cheated out of your labor," he pleaded. "Why don't you send your children to school, and qualify them to look out for themselves, to own property, to figure and think about what they are doing, so that they may do better than you?"[10]

The practicality of Chesnutt's admonition came to be appreciated by blacks able to use their literacy to advance themselves on a job. "I can read and I can write and I can figure," boasted Lee Lincoln, born in 1886, the son of sharecroppers who, as he recalled, "didn't have time to fool with schooling for themselves or any of us children." After his mother's death, he gave up working on the farm for a job on the Louisville and Nashville Railroad in Memphis, trucking outbound freight. "That was the job that learned me a man's got to have schooling to get anywheres." He needed to be able to read the signs posted on freight cars indicating the town for which the car was headed. "You had to know how to read to know what to load up." His employer taught him some of the basics, and Lincoln acquired the rest on his own, studying every night and during lunch breaks, until he was able to read the signs without assistance. "My, I was one proud Negro!" He would later be made a regular officer on the L. & N. line, working the Nashville yards, and he knew the promotion would never have come his way "if I hadn't picked up what little education I had." He continued his studies in night school; at the same time, he paid a white man fifty cents a session to teach him, "and there wasn't a night that I didn't learn more than a dollar's worth."[11]

From the moment schools were available after the war and during Reconstruction, blacks flocked to them in impressive numbers, often exceeding whites in their enthusiasm and in their attendance rates. Visiting the cotton mills near Atlanta, a northern journalist thought it highly ironic that a family of white mill employees hired a black woman to cook for them while they sent their children to the mill to work; the cook, on the other hand, sent her children to the public schools. Outside of land, education ranked highest in the priorities of freed slaves, widely perceived as the proven way to free themselves from mental and physical dependency on whites. To be educated was to be respected. To be educated was to be somebody. To be educated, Johanna Bowen assured her granddaughter, Frances, was "to have a good life and to become something worthwhile in life." To be educated, many came to believe, was to be like the whites they had seen using education to their advantage. Anxious to send her child to school, a Virginia mother implored her daughter "to try to be like Miss Mary Anne, mistess' daughter, an' all de other spectable white folks' girls." When Charles Whiteside's master informed him that he was legally free, that same master also told him that his freedom was essentially meaningless, that he would always remain a slave, "cause you got no education, and education is what makes a man free." Whiteside was impressed. He worked hard and sent each of his thirteen children to school—"to make them free," as he said.[12]

To afford their children an opportunity for schooling, or to improve on the schools they now attended, black parents were often willing to make significant sacrifices. Since emancipation, such sacrifices had included migrating to the cities, to the next county, or to other regions where schools were available and an improvement over what they had left behind. "[T]hat's how we got moving around," Bazoline Usher recalled of her childhood, "to find schools, to try to find some place where [her father] could have better schools for his children." Refusing to accommodate to a skimpy school term lasting only six weeks, the Davis family left Dawson County, Georgia, choosing to migrate "north" to Atlanta so their son, Benjamin, could attend city schools for a nine-month term. When Henry Hugh Proctor's family abandoned the countryside for Fayetteville, North Carolina, they did so to afford their twelve-year-old son an opportunity they as slaves had been denied. "My mother said to my father that they had spent all their lives working for other people; now they should spend the rest of it working for their children."[13]

Not all black parents eagerly shared the same passion for education. Some gave contradictory advice, wanting their children to make something of themselves but doubting the relevance of a formal education. Ely Green was eager to begin school so that he could help his grandfather with the accounts. "School don't mean anything to a nigger," his grandfather responded. "What do they have to do except work like hell from morning till night year in and year out, and do what the white man tells them to do, and it don't take no education to do that." He suggested, instead, that his grandson emulate his grandfather, who had never been inside of a schoolhouse but had managed to become economically independent. "Make your own job. Get something of your own. Don't have no boss. Be on your own. When we niggers come to learn that, then we will be somebody."[14]

Many black parents simply found it impossible to dispense with the labor of their school-age children, whether in the fields or in the house. Edward Sugg worked during the day and attended night school at Hampton Institute, where one of his teachers, Booker T. Washington, called him "the most faithful and earnest" of his students. But whenever Sugg returned home to rural North Carolina, he was reminded of his exceptional status. "Som of the colored peoples in my nabor-hood if you talk to them a bout sending their childrens to school the[y] will tell you that they are going to send them to the cotton patch and corn-field school. The[y] say that they are not got the money to send their childrens to school like the white peoples are."[15]

For scores of blacks coming of age in the late nineteenth and early twentieth centuries, schooling occupied a very small part of their lives, if any at all. Not so much a rejection of education as an adaptation to economic realities, black youths found they had few choices once their age made them part of the labor pool. "Soon as one gits old enough he's put in de field," Mary Matthews recalled. "Dey ain't no time to go to school. . . . My schoolin' was so pieced up I don't know how far I got. Like dese chil'en now, I had to go when de crop was housed and quit when work started." Throughout the South, that experience became commonplace in the lives of young blacks. Recalling her childhood in Yazoo, Mississippi, Mary Tuck told how her father permitted the children to go to school "when we could," usually for a month, "then he come and took us out, let Mama go to the field and we stayed at the house and worked. Didn't get no schooling. None of the children didn't get no schooling to amount to nothing."[16] To send a child to school also entailed additional expense and work; parents needed to feed and prepare the children before sending them off in the morning, make and mend their clothes, and provide them with books and slates—a drain on incomes that at best provided only bare subsistence.

For some children, the amount of education they received depended on how much was available. Sam Gadsden, born in 1882, completed his education in the fifth grade. "That was the top grade for us here in those years," he recalled. West T. Jones, born in 1872, managed to complete six years, trying "to get all the learnin anybody would give me. . . . I understands a heap of things I wouldn't but for that little schoolhouse out there in the country." Few high schools were available for blacks, and what little education they did receive hardly prepared them for the advanced grades. Following the lead of other southern cities, Augusta, Georgia, in 1911 chose to reduce schoolwork for black children and stipulated that only industrial training would be offered them in the eighth grade and largely in the seventh. That would make it almost impossible for any black child to prepare for high school work in the public schools.[17]

For many black parents, the early grades provided sufficient time for their children to learn to read and write. "I didn't get much schuling," Emma Grisham recalled, "mah daddy wuz lak mos' ole folks, he thought ef'n you knowed yo a,b,c's en could read a line, dat wuz 'nuff." The acquisition of more advanced learning came to be perceived by many parents as simply a luxury they could ill afford. James Bowers

wanted his children to have "a fair eddication." That meant, his son recalled, "a colored chile otta go to work an' quit school atter dey learned
to read an' write an' figger enough so people couldn't beat 'em out of
what dey made." Such advice proved to be popular, as it made practical
sense. "Ain't figures enough?" asked John Montgomery, Jr., a chimney
sweep in New Orleans. He went as far as the third grade ("[t]hat was
enough fo' me") before his father took him out of school and sent him
to work. "Sho', school is all right fo' them who wants it," the chimney
sweep thought, "but I figures all you got to know is how to read and
write, then nobody can cheat you out of nothin'! Ain't figures
enough?"[18]

To proceed beyond a rudimentary education, as parents and employers recognized, was to invite higher aspirations and ambitions than
agricultural labor. "I don't see where schoolin' could git a nigger like
me," a laborer reflected. "Niggers ain't got enough money for more
than a half-way education. When they git it, it jest messes them up to
where they won't have the jobs they can git once they's out of school."
If some parents discouraged children from being overly ambitious, they
did so out of an appreciation of the limits whites imposed on black aspirations. "What's the use of learnin' how to be a bookkeeper if you
ain't gonna never have no books to keep?" a father in Bolivar County,
Mississippi, pointedly asked. After learning everything he could in the
local school, Benjamin Mays aspired to continue his education elsewhere. But his father objected, believing that too much education
spoiled blacks and that there were only two "honest occupations" for
black men: preaching and farming. "My father must have repeated this
dictum a thousand times." He thought schooling had little if anything
to do with farming. "Would reading all the books in the world teach a
man how to plow, to plant cotton and corn, gather the grain, and harvest the crop?" As for the ministry, he deemed an education equally unnecessary. "God 'called' men to preach; and when He called them, He
would tell them what to say!"[19]

If some parents chose to hold their children out of school or to limit
the amount of education they received, the decision often reflected a
sensitivity to the volatile nature of race relations. Knowing the deep resentment many whites felt toward educated blacks, keeping a child out
of school kept that child out of trouble. A black businessman in Mississippi went so far as to oppose compulsory education as "a dangerous
thing" for his race.

Because as soon as you take a country boy and teach him something about the world and give him new ideas, you ruin him for the farm. And you make a Negro dissatisfied with his position. As long as you keep him ignorant, he's satisfied to work for some white man on the plantation; but as soon as he learns to want other things, he comes to the city to try to get them. When he gets here, he finds the white man has everything, and he can't get the kind of work or job he wants, and he is dissatisfied. And then you have a dangerous situation.

Articulating the same position, a black Mississippi teacher who once considered himself "a great believer in Negro education" came to doubt the wisdom and practicality of that belief. "You educate your children—then whatcha gonna do?" he asked. "You got any jobs for 'em? You got any business for 'em to go into?" Once they had acquired an education and heightened expectations, they would hardly be content to return to their old way of life. "[E]ducation changed their tastes; they gotta have better things than you got—an' why? Jes' 'cause they got education and learned about things—got themselves usta things you don't even know about. Yeah, that's what education does!"[20]

In the experiences of black Southerners, the possession of knowledge would at times work to their detriment. Charles Holcombe would always believe that if he had kept his son away from school, he would never have been killed by whites in a dispute over crop payments. "He had stepped outen his place when he got dat eddycation." Henry Kirkland, an Alabama farmer, worked for Jasper Clay; his son, Emmet, acquired "a pretty good book learnin" and kept his father's books, an account of everything received from Clay. When it came to "settlin' up" time, Clay, as usual, informed Kirkland of the amount he still owed him. This time, however, the black farmer thought to question the results. Breaking with custom, by which no one challenged the white man's accounts or truthfulness, Henry Kirkland told his son to check the figures against his own account book. That act by itself infuriated Clay, who "flew in a passion over that book business," fatally shot the black farmer, and seriously wounded the son. Emmet Kirkland soon departed for the North—hoping for a more hospitable area in which to practice his "book learnin."[21]

But for many black Southerners, the acquisition of some kind of education remained a high priority. In the black community it was a mark of accomplishment, and some who had rejected schooling when they had been afforded the opportunity deeply regretted their failure. As a child, Robert Pete Williams had rebelled against the insistence of his mother that he attend school. In time, however, he came to appreciate what he had missed, if measured only by his standing in the community. His inability to read or write, he felt, had cast him in an unfavorable light among his contemporaries. Although Williams became a well-known bluesman, he still thought about the consequences of his early truancy:

> *You know I'm all down an' worried, because I broke my mother's rule, . . .*
> *Been out on the solid highway, keep from goin' to school. . . .*
>
> *Woh, in this town, the people call me a fool, . . .*
> *The people all call me a fool, darlin', because I didn't go to school at all.*[22]

By contrast, a schoolteacher in North Carolina recounted the story of a sick black woman preparing for death. She gave the teacher her will, plans for a funeral and a grave, and insurance policies, requesting that she look after them. When the teacher asked her if she wanted to see her husband, who had deserted her, she replied, "No, and if you ever hear from him, tell him I don't leave him even a good wish." She then displayed an envelope, containing what she called her most prized possession, and handed it to the teacher for safekeeping. "When I am gone, no one will care about this envelope. Will you promise to keep it, so I will know I am not all gone so soon?" The envelope contained college credits she had accumulated after attending night school while working all day.[23]

2

WHEN IN THE AFTERMATH of emancipation the Freedmen's Bureau (a federal agency) and various northern missionary societies moved to meet the educational needs of the newly freed slaves, they found not only a ready and anxious audience but also a flurry of activity already undertaken by blacks themselves to secure and administer schools for their people. The almost unbounded enthusiasm for learning stimulated blacks to take the initiative and in many instances to covet independence from white authority of any kind. The development of a system of tax-supported public education in the South was largely an achievement of the governments established under Radical

Reconstruction, with black legislators leading the way in enacting the necessary legislation. But with the end of Reconstruction, the vision of an educated black South rapidly eroded, along with the commitment to solidify the achievements of the previous governments. Educational opportunities for blacks varied considerably from state to state and within each state. In much of the rural South, where most blacks lived, educational facilities remained primitive, if they existed at all. The loss of political power and influence quickly translated into reduced funding for schools, leaving blacks to make the most of what little they had.

After emancipation, the very location of the schools attested dramatically to the enthusiasm and resourcefulness of blacks seeking an education. Until the state or locality could afford to build permanent structures, or more frequently in the absence of any such structures or commitment to build them, classes might be held almost anywhere—in abandoned cabins converted into instant schoolhouses, mule stables, billiard rooms, plantation cotton houses, warehouses and storerooms, discarded white schools, buildings owned by black fraternal orders, and, most commonly, in black churches. As late as 1910, in the Georgia Black Belt, some three-fourths of the black schools still met in churches and private homes, and the only way to build new schoolhouses was to close down the schools for three months and use the teachers' salaries to buy the materials.[24]

Where buildings could not be located, often because of white hostility, classes might alternate from day to day, or at night, in the cabins of black families eager to secure an education for their children—and themselves. Among Robert Moton's earliest memories was his mother rushing through the evening meal after a day's labor in the fields to prepare their cabin for night school, mostly for adults. (No schools had yet been established in the region for white or black children.) "I recall now the eagerness with which some twenty-five or thirty men and women struggled with their lessons, trying to learn to read and write while I was supposed to be asleep in my trundle bed, to which I had been hurried to make room for this little band of anxious, aspiring ex-slaves." The demand for a school was so great in Portsmouth, Virginia, that after Mary Jane Wilson graduated from Hampton Institute in 1874, her father built a school for her in the backyard of their home. "I had as many as seventy-five pupils at one time. Many of them became teachers. I had my graduation exercises in the Emanuel A.M.E. Church. Those were my happiest days."[25]

In the urban South, the number of schools available to blacks did not come close to meeting the demand. Even as schools were established for whites, the needs of blacks were usually neglected, as in Atlanta. The black schools there became so crowded that they were forced to hold two sessions. In 1903, to accommodate a school population of 14,465 whites and 8,118 blacks, there were 20 white schools and 5 black schools, 200 white teachers and 49 black teachers. Even with the double sessions, nearly half of the black children in Atlanta were barred from the public schools because of insufficient room. In Charleston, early in the twentieth century, one public school was expected to meet the needs of black residents, and pupils were "virtually herded" into what local blacks called "the ABC galleries." Describing the opening of the public schools in Savannah in 1911, the local black newspaper called it "the same pitiable sight for Negro children as has been the case for years." Hundreds of prospective pupils had clamored for cards of admittance on the preceding Saturday, only to be rejected because of the inability to accommodate them; they "besieged" the school on opening day, hoping somehow to be admitted, but the seats were all occupied and they were sent home. The statistics were little better in the rural regions. All too typical was Clayton County, Georgia, where in 1902 a total of 32 schools accommodated a population of 5,572 whites, while 17 schools served 4,026 blacks.[26]

With public schools unable to meet the demand for teaching black children, parents might voluntarily tax themselves to establish additional educational opportunities. Nearly every religious denomination also had one or more schools. In some areas, especially in the cities, private schools were available, and sufficient numbers of black families were able to afford the tuition to sustain the institutions. In Charleston, where white teachers dominated the faculty of the black public school, many of the more "intelligent and respectable colored" sent their children to the private schools. Although acknowledging that the public schools provided better textbook training, these parents chose to weigh that advantage against the ability of the private schools, staffed mostly by black teachers, to instill "self-respect" and impart "very desirable historical information." The sorry state of public schools in Florida initially induced Mary McLeod Bethune to found her school for girls in Daytona Beach. The black colleges also helped to meet the demand by offering instruction in the lower grades. In Atlanta, the large private educational institutions, including Atlanta University, Clark University, and Spelman College, helped to make up for the absence of any black public high school. While white parents, then, could send their children to a public high school at the taxpayers' expense, blacks were forced to pay additional fees to provide advanced training.[27]

The schools blacks attended, especially in the rural South, looked very much alike. Few of the pupils could ever forget the conditions under which they tried to acquire the rudiments of an education: the makeshift, primitive, unpainted one-room board structures, with shaky floors and cracks in the walls and roof, and the potbellied, wood-burning stove in the center of the room. The students sat on crude, hard, backless benches made of split logs. The teacher sat at a table, sometimes fenced in with a railing. The only light came from small, glassless window openings. The front door also acted as the exit. Plank blackboards might be available, but teachers were expected to furnish the chalk and eraser. Whatever furnishings adorned the room were found by scouring through dumps or trash piles in the neighborhood.[28]

In the absence of the most basic school supplies and furnishings, teachers and students improvised as best they could. A baseball "did duty" in one schoolroom to explain to students the motions of the earth; sand spread on the floor served as a relief map for geography classes; and pebbles retrieved from the school grounds were used as "the basis of a talk on common sense." Mary McLeod Bethune, when she established her school in Daytona Beach, Florida, needed from the outset to demonstrate her resourcefulness: She used charred splinters from burned logs as pencils and mashed elderberries for ink. With no primers available, Robert Fitzgerald, a schoolteacher in Amelia County, Virginia, used primarily the Bible and the *Farmer's Almanac*.[29]

The length of the school term varied with labor demands, the growing schedule of cotton, and the weather. If the children were sufficiently grown (eight years old), they did not come to class until after the cotton had been picked, often in November, sometimes as late as January, and they would have to leave school in the early spring to prepare fields for the new crop. In the experience of most rural youths, the school year consisted of two to five months, compressed between harvest and spring planting time. In Mississippi, as a general rule, boys between ages eight and ten were permitted to attend school only two months of the four-month term because they were needed in the fields. "I ain't went to school a hundred days in my life," Kelly Jackson said of his life in Bentonia, Mississippi, where he was born in 1894. "See, we had three months to go to school. And the only time I could go would be when it rained, and I couldn't plow. . . . I went to plowing when I was eight years, and then the only time I could go to school was when it rained." While the crops were being harvested, classes consisted largely of children too young to work in the fields. On rainy days, when there was no work, older students might swell the numbers, but the bad weather often rendered the ramshackle schoolhouses inoperable, even if students could find their way to them through the mud and slush of backwoods roads and fields.[30]

Attendance, then, varied sharply, usually defying prediction. No sooner had some students settled down to schoolwork than a parent or employer would appear at the door and order them to the fields. On rainy days, if the sun came out by noon, the employer or overseer would invariably ride up to the school and call out the tenants' children. Labor demands simply translated into irregular attendance—or no attendance at all—and it was the reason cited by most black youths who failed to obtain any kind of real education. The average student dropped out of school in the fifth or sixth grade, having acquired the bare rudiments. "That's all. Three months," exclaimed Hughsey Childs, who grew up in North Carolina, "well, you could barely learn the alphabet in three months." When Henry Baker's employer told him he had no work for him until they would begin gathering the crops, Henry decided to attend school. He lasted five days. "Muh landlord he'rd dat I wuz gwine tuh school so he sent fer me en tole me he had a job right away en he put me back tuh work."[31]

The disruptions in their schooling, the impossibility of reconciling an education with the demands made on their labor, became for many black youths a source of continuing disappointment and frustration. It came as a severe blow to Booker T. Washington when the need to supplement the meager family income forced him to discontinue his studies at the day school. Although Benjamin Mays managed to overcome early setbacks in his determination to be educated, he would never forgive his father's employer for trying to keep him out of school. "From that moment on, I put him down as being against me. In fact, I considered anyone my enemy who was not in sympathy with my aspiration to get an education." By age nineteen, Mays recalled, not once in his life had he been able to remain in school more than four months in any year. For some parents, however, the determination to see their children educated took precedence over labor demands. When the landlord came to the workers' quarters to "stir up" cotton pickers, William Henry Holtzclaw's mother hid her son, then slipped him off to school. At age nine, when he began to work as a regular field hand, his mother devised still another plan to educate her children: William alternated in the fields each day with his brother. "[O]ne day I plowed and he went to school, the next day he plowed and I went to school; what he learned on his school day he taught me at night and I did the same for him. In this way we each got a month of schooling during the year."[32]

The obstacles teachers faced ranged from inferior facilities, irregular attendance, and white harassment and suspicion to the difficulties encountered in gaining the confidence of the black students and the black community. For many a teacher, the introduction to the classroom was a rude awakening. Entering the school in which he would teach in rural Tennessee, eighteen-year-old W. E. B. Du Bois, educated in New England, found "a windowless log cabin" with none of the usual classroom amenities. The cabin had been used by the previous owner—a Colonel Wheeler—as a place to store his corn.

> There was an entrance where a door once was, and within, a massive rickety fireplace; great chinks between the logs served as windows. Furniture was scarce. A pale blackboard crouched in the corner. My desk was made of three boards, reinforced at critical points, and my chair, borrowed from the landlady, had to be returned every night. Seats for the children—these puzzled me much. I was haunted by a New England vision of neat little desks and chairs, but, alas! the reality was rough plank benches without backs, and at times without legs.

Neither his experience as the only black student in Great Barrington High School in Massachusetts nor his first-year studies at Fisk University had prepared Du Bois for his first days in this rural outpost.[33]

Not only would teachers need to improvise necessary materials, but they also would often have to teach two sessions a day to accommodate the number of students. That problem plagued the urban schools in particular. In Atlanta, in 1903, teachers had to perform double duty, instructing two sets of pupils, each set for half of the school day, at less than two-thirds the salary paid white teachers. On Johns Island, near Charleston, newly graduated Septima Clark persuaded the school trustees to employ an Avery College schoolmate to assist her in teaching 132 children. Even with the additional help, she confronted an awesome task.

> Here I was, a high-school graduate, eighteen years old, principal in a two-teacher school with 132 pupils ranging from beginners to eighth

graders, with no teaching experience, a schoolhouse constructed of boards running up and down, with no slats on the cracks, and a fireplace at one end of the room that cooked the pupils immediately in front of it but allowed those in the rear to shiver and freeze on their uncomfortable, hard, back-breaking benches. And with no equipment. . . .

Three white teachers in the same community each taught from 3 to 18 students. The salaries of the overworked black teachers amounted to $35 a month; the white teachers, on the other hand, earned $85 a month.[34]

The experience of Septima Clark typified teaching in the rural schools. More often than not, one person taught, or at least attempted to teach, all classes and subjects. In Jesse Thomas's one-room school in Pike County, Mississippi, the teacher had to "hear" all the classes from the first to the seventh grade. The term "hear" was commonly used, Thomas recalled, "because it was about all any teacher could do with seventy-five or one hundred students all in one room and comprising seven different grades. How she was able to classify the students I do not know. Most of the time, most of the teachers themselves had not gone beyond the seventh or eighth grade. . . ."[35]

Teaching in the city had some compensations. Although salaries were poor, they tended to be paid, and the teacher had ready access to a vibrant black community. Most black teachers, however, found themselves in isolated backwoods settlements, where life was far more arduous and economic survival a continuing challenge. Earning perhaps $15 to $20 a month for five months in the year, they would need to board and feed themselves. In Burke County, Georgia, where teachers were paid from $18 to $30 a month (only one teacher received $30), few were able to realize the full value of their salary, as they had been forced to contract to trade at the store owned by the chairman of the board of education. One teacher recalled a number of black public schools in the Black Belt in the early twentieth century that received $37 for the school term of four months, and he wondered how a teacher could survive on $9.25 a month.[36]

If some teachers chose to make the best of a bad situation, they often found encouragement in the support they received from black parents. That support could not always be measured in dollars and cents. When William Holtzclaw established an industrial training school in Utica, Mississippi, in 1902, a grateful mother wrote him, "[D]ear fessor,

Please cept dis 18 cents it is all I has I saved it out n my washin dis week
god will bless yo will send some more next week." Similar letters accompanied baskets of eggs and other commodities—all of this, Holtzclaw recalled, helping to breathe "fervent hope" into his project.
Teaching in Cuthbert, Georgia, Richard R. Wright, Jr., received a
small salary from the American Missionary Association, but parents
promised to pay him 25 cents' tuition (a considerable sum for most of
them) for each pupil; many made their payments with chickens, eggs,
potatoes, and "anything else that could be bartered for education." Still
another way to support a school became a custom in many rural sections: The teacher would move from home to home, boarding for a
portion of the school year with each family.[37]

Not only did teachers need to accommodate to insufficient resources, irregular attendance, and a skeptical if not outright hostile
public, but they often had to endure insufferable or overly paternalistic
white supervisors and educational officials. Already overworked and
underpaid, Atlanta teachers, for example, had to deal with a white
superintendent of schools whose behavior and abuses were "common
talk" among local blacks. On entering a classroom, he always addressed the black teacher by his or her first name; if any teacher had
reciprocated, of course, his or her teaching career would have abruptly
ended. In addition, the superintendent had been known to use his
position to make "indecent proposals" to young female teachers.[38]

The educational preparation of a black teacher varied considerably.
In much of the rural South, teachers had not been educated past the
seventh or eighth grades. William Holtzclaw, who grew up in Alabama
and later taught in Mississippi, recalled that when a pupil got as far as
the word "abasement" in the Webster blue-back speller, he or she was
made an assistant teacher and shortly thereafter relieved the white
teachers. The best of the black teachers, he thought, had advanced no
further than the fourth grade. Holtzclaw would find himself in the
same situation, asked to teach with the barest of preparations but needing to support the family after the death of his father. "Of course I
knew little, but I taught what I did know—and I suppose some things
that I did not." The "common talk" among blacks, a rural Georgia
teacher reported, was that authorities preferred incompetent teachers
in the black schools. That was perfectly consistent with white fears of
the effects of black learning.[39]

By the end of the nineteenth century, more blacks opted for high schools and colleges, believing such advanced training necessary if they were to pursue careers as teachers. But some whites, fearing the consequences of overeducated blacks, chose to encourage blacks to enter teaching without becoming scholars. That is, authorities framed examinations that black applicants could easily pass without a high school education. In Beaufort County, South Carolina, a teacher complained that a number of black graduates had failed to pass the qualifying examination and suggested that the questions be made simpler. Agreeing with her suggestion, the white superintendent drew up a list of questions—"too trifling to bear the name," one resident wrote—with the word "Negroes" at the top, while preparing a different and more demanding qualifying examination for whites. Protesting this double standard, a black teacher warned against permitting whites "with their feigned sympathy" to enlist her people in a scheme calculated to promote ignorance. "Like Joab of old they come to us in a friendly manner and at the same time pierce us through with a dart. We must not suffer ourselves to be betrayed with a kiss."[40]

3

WHAT THE BLACK child learned in school was expected to underscore a moral, productive, and accommodative life. The same lessons communicated to freedmen after emancipation were embellished for their sons and daughters. Self-improvement manuals, biographies of self-made men, and inspiring success stories abounded in the black communities, as in the white. Most black youths, like generations of whites, imbibed the moral and patriotic lessons taught in nearly every school and from every pulpit, the virtues and work ethic esteemed by mid-nineteenth-century Americans and propagated in *McGuffey's Readers* and the Webster blue-back speller.[41]

While teaching children how to write and read, the primers set down a simple code, a common set of moral and patriotic precepts instilled through brief moral tales, uplifting aphorisms, religious admonitions, and childlike rhymes. America was defined for them as a democracy of economic equality, in which success came ultimately to the hardworking, the sober, the honest, and the educated—to those who adopted a work ethic of diligence, perseverance, and punctuality; served their employers faithfully and respected authority, property, and the sanctity of contract; cultivated habits of thrift, cleanliness, and temperance; and led moral, virtuous, Christian lives.

For black children to "make it" in the larger society, school administrators and teachers assumed that their pupils needed to learn to communicate in proper English. To discard the slave past, many believed, was to discard the still common slave dialect. But black children, even adults, needed to weigh the obvious advantages of learning standard English pronunciation against the desire for acceptance among their peers. In speaking "correctly," Richard R. Wright, Jr., recalled of the Georgia community in which he was raised, any black person might be ridiculed as "proper" or "white folksy." Moving to Savannah some years later, Wright encountered the same problem. When his friends misused or mispronounced certain words, he hesitated to correct them or to pronounce them correctly in their presence for fear of embarrassing them. "Speaking correctly seemed to be a sort of betrayal of the community which so innocently rolled off phrases of their slave inheritance, in vivacious and sometimes elegant and eloquent speech. Some of the influential 'leaders' never learned to speak correctly." Teaching in a rural school in North Carolina, Charles Chesnutt thought himself compelled to "unteach" the English spoken by his students. "I shall try and do the best I can, for it is my duty. . . ."[42]

Along with the acquisition of proper English, students began to learn something about their society. But even as teachers and administrators appreciated the need to familiarize students with contemporary issues, they also recognized the overriding need to be cautious and circumspect. "Every wide-awake teacher," advised *Southern Workman,* the organ of Hampton Institute, "wishes to see his children alive to what is going on in the world about them, to make them realize that life is not confined to the narrow limits of their school district. . . ." But the journal warned teachers to avoid controversial subjects, such as accounts of lynchings and murders, "and in general all things of a sensational nature, and such as are likely to encourage race antagonism."[43]

Not all teachers followed that advice, and black students in some schools were kept informed of current events, particularly those affecting their race. An English visitor to a black school in Montgomery, Alabama, found a pupil writing on the blackboard a quotation from a recent speech in the U.S. Senate on the Brownsville affair, involving President Theodore Roosevelt's harsh treatment of a black regiment in Texas. The quotation read "We ask no favor for them because they are negroes, but justice for them because they are men." The visitor was impressed. "Evidently," he concluded, teachers suffered no consequences in exposing their students to "the all-absorbing problem."[44]

Nothing Richard Wright learned in school, as he recalled, helped him to answer the questions he kept asking about his condition as a Negro and the prospects of his race. The subject of race relations and the place of blacks in America was not even addressed. When he raised these questions with his friends, moreover, they would either remain silent or turn the questions into jokes. "They were vocal about the petty individual wrongs they suffered," Wright recalled, "but they possessed no desire for a knowledge of the picture as a whole. Then why was I worried about it?"[45]

The history to which black children were exposed in the classroom and the primers made a virtual gospel of the superiority of Anglo-Saxon institutions and ways of thinking and acting. They imbibed the same lessons taught in the white schools, essentially a sanitized history of Anglo-Saxons and northern Europeans: Pilgrims, Puritans, and Founding Fathers. It was not their history, nor had it much relevance to their lives or to the lives of their parents and neighbors. What little they learned of their own history consisted often of disparaging caricatures of black people as the least civilized of the races—irresponsible, thoughtless, foolish, childlike people, satisfied with their lowly place in American life, incapable of self-control and self-direction. The history of black people was a history of submission gladly endured and of services faithfully rendered. Transported from the darkness of heathen Africa to the civilized and Christian New World, grateful slaves found contentment and happiness. Illustrations of blacks, if they appeared at all, depicted well-fed, carefree laborers frolicking in the fields: amiable, deferential Uncle Toms greeting their patronizing and loving masters, hat in hand, evincing a demeanor of contentment, docility, and faithfulness. The occasional malcontent, like a Nat Turner, was said only to have launched a "horrible massacre" that killed many innocent white people. The treatment of emancipation depicted blacks passively waiting for Massa' Lincoln to strike off their shackles. And Reconstruction saw the enthronement of black ignorance and inexperience, with the Ku Klux Klan in some accounts redeeming Anglo-Saxon civilization from alien rule.[46]

The history lessons taught in public schools were calculated to produce patriotic citizens, albeit with a distinctive white southern bias. Visiting a Charleston school, an observer was somewhat taken aback to hear some five hundred black children sing,

In Dixie Land
I take my stand,
To live and die in Dixie.

If black children were to learn of their own past, or if they had a past, it would need to be found elsewhere. Mamie Garvin Fields, born in Charleston in 1888, contrasted the lessons she learned in the public school with what her cousin Lala taught in the informal neighborhood school Lala's father had constructed in the rear of the house. In the public school, where most of the teachers were white, young Mamie found herself drilled in "the Rebel tradition"; she learned to sing "Dixie" in Negro dialect, along with Stephen Foster favorites. "This was what they wanted to instill in us." But at Lala's, as Mamie Fields recalled, she learned "things that you didn't get at public school," such as how her people came to be enslaved. "I learned about slavery as our relatives had experienced it and what it meant. She taught us how strong our ancestors back in slavery were and what fine people they were. I guess today people would say she was teaching us 'black history.' "[47]

Through stories passed down from generation to generation, and in the black-authored histories that appeared in the late nineteenth and early twentieth centuries, blacks fashioned their own history. "In all the books that you have studied you never have studied Negro history, have you?" an elderly Tennessee black inquired of a Fisk University interviewer in the 1930s. "You studied about the Indians and white folks, what did they tell you about the Negro? If you want Negro history you will have to get [it] from somebody who wore the shoe, and by and by from one to the other you will get a book." From the mouths of grandparents and parents, as the first freeborn generations heard them, the stories of enslavement, the Civil War, and emancipation bore no resemblance to the popular histories and schoolbooks. To Joseph Sutton, born in 1885, the son of former slaves, the simple version of the Civil War he imbibed subverted both white southern and northern interpretations. "The North couldn't whip the South, that's the way the slaves got free. And then, after that, they got the slaves in there, that made thousands and thousands of more help for the North, and then the North could whip the South." Learning from his family what the schools he attended failed to teach, Richard Wright, too, came to be exposed to some strikingly different versions of the Civil War and Reconstruction. Conversations with his grandmother, "year after year," gradually revealed the details of his grandfather's life, and young Richard took pride in hearing of his achievements. Resentful of slavery, he managed to escape when the Civil War broke out, enlisted in the Union Army "to kill southern whites," and guarded ballot boxes during Reconstruction. Even the return of whites to political dominance had not crushed his spirit. "He was convinced that the war had not really ended, that it would start again."[48]

Growing up in rural South Carolina, Benjamin Mays learned enough of the history of his people at home to remember that his earliest heroes were exclusively black. Not only his parents instructed him but also periodically someone would come to the house selling pictures of black leaders or pamphlets about their lives and exploits. Portraits of Frederick Douglass, Booker T. Washington, and Paul Laurence Dunbar occupied a prominent place in the home. "In my high school days, Booker T. Washington meant more to me than George Washington; Frederick Douglass was more of a hero than William Lloyd Garrison; Dunbar inspired me more than Longfellow. I heard about Crispus Attucks and was thrilled." And in the high school he attended, Mays was fortunate enough to be taught to admire the black legislators during Reconstruction, not the white racial demagogues who succeeded them. "I had identity."[49]

Sensing a profound contradiction between their formal education and what they learned and experienced outside the classroom, black youths often reacted with some indifference, skepticism, or outright hostility to the history and patriotic values with which they were inculcated. The familiar phrase "the land of the free and the home of the brave" had a different ring in black schools. By the time she was six years old, Pauli Murray recalled, she had become disillusioned with her country. "I hated George Washington, mumbled the oath of allegiance to the American flag which we children were taught in the second grade and was reluctant to stand up when we sang 'The Star-Spangled Banner'. . . . My folks would have been horrified at my private seditious thoughts if they had known of them." A white teacher in a black school in North Carolina recalled that her class wanted to stamp their feet whenever they sang "Marching Through Georgia," and were unwilling to hear "Dixie." She also knew better than to ask some of her students to sing "America." As one of them explained, "I'm going to be a man [and] can't vote; when I can vote I'll sing, 'My country, 'tis of thee.' "[50]

Attending school in Knoxville, Tennessee, James A. Atkins took some pleasure in thinking of himself as a dissenter. In his history class he found it difficult to appreciate the standard version of the struggle between the first white settlers and the Indians. "I could not understand why every victory by the encroaching trappers and settlers was glorious, while that of the Indians, as rare as it was, could only be described as low and sneaking or a bloody massacre. . . . What was skilful and crafty on the part of the invading settlers became something very low, when practiced by the defending Indians." He began to suspect that it all came down to ways of interpreting historical information, to a point of view. And the point of view that predominated in the classroom reflected the perspective that dominated the community in which he lived. In the same class, he studied the Civil War, and that, too, became in his estimation the expression of a singular and distorted view. "Neither the Union soldiers nor the Negro people were treated fairly, so I thought, by the historian." To the delight of William Holtzclaw, he found a book that provided a different and extraordinary insight into his people—*The Life of Ignatius Sancho,* the account of an educated black West Indian. He had never seen the memoirs of a black man, "and I cannot express the inspiration I received from learning for the first time that a colored man could really make history."[51]

Although often hedged by cautious administrators, some black teachers endeavored to redeem the black past even as they projected hope about the future. In the class James Yates attended in rural Mississippi, the teacher was uniquely outspoken. "[N]ot only did he say things we didn't understand but things we almost didn't dare to relate to." Within one hundred years, the teacher told them ("with so much conviction," Yates recalled, "I wanted to look over my shoulder to see if the sheriff was listening"), the United States would have a black president and "[a] great day is coming when Blacks will be voting all over Mississippi!" The class did not know quite what to make of these bold if not reckless and foolhardy predictions. "We couldn't help laughing at him. How could we think of a Black man as president, when all we saw of Blacks was in the fields or in the white folks' kitchen, or as an occasional tradesman getting low pay like my father?"[52]

To redeem their history was to get beyond their slave past and discover their cultural roots. Such knowledge could also dispose of white claims of superiority in civilization and intelligence. More than one black leader and educator made the point that until a people knew and faced up to its past, it had no real future. "Do you ever think of the fact that we have no record?" a North Carolina educator asked a school principal in 1907. "That we have no history to which we can appeal?

That we are going on from day to day living, and moving, and having our being among men without making any authentic record of what we are doing or who we are? Does it not occur to you that, until we can tell who we are and what we have done we can have no standing among the other races of men?" That such a record could be found seemed clear enough, but obviously white chroniclers and textbook writers had no intention of acknowledging its existence. "There is enough history of the Negro race to make a Negro proud of his race," insisted David A. Straker, a black activist, teacher, and lawyer who left South Carolina for the North in 1887. "Why not then teach the Negro child more of himself and less of others, more of his elevation and less of his degradation. This only can produce true pride of race, which begets mutual confidence and unity."[53]

To counter the prevailing belief that black people had no record of human struggle and achievement, early black chroniclers delved into a past that preceded the actual arrival of Africans in the New World. Targeting "the blind prejudice of negrophobists," William H. Ferris, a black academic, told a statewide meeting of the North Carolina Negro State Teachers' Association in 1903 that students needed to study Negro history and the social customs of their ancestors. In a historical sketch prepared for the conference, Ferris compared the Negro race to the ancient Greeks "in poetic insight, richness of imagination, love of the mystical in religion, and the gift of speech, qualities not found in the practical Roman and deficient in the still more practical Anglo-Saxon."[54]

To use the past to redeem the race, black teachers and educators drew heavily for inspiration on the African heritage, seeking to offset the stereotypes that dominated most textbooks. Richard Robert Wright, Sr., a graduate of Atlanta University, founded in 1880 the first public high school for blacks in Georgia, located in Augusta. When asked three years later to testify before a U.S. Senate committee, he drew on his training in classics and history at Atlanta to answer a query about the relative intellectual achievements of whites and blacks.

I think that about all the great religions which have blest this world have come from the colored races—all. In other words, what is called the Aryan race has not originated a single great religion. I believe too, that our methods of alphabetic writing all came from the colored race, and I think the majority of the sciences in their origin have come from the colored races. . . . Now I take the testimony of those people who know, and who, I feel are capable of instructing me on this point, and I find them saying that the Egyptians were actually woolly-haired negroes. . . . Now, if that is true, the idea that this negro race is inherently inferior, seems to me to be at least a little limping.[55]

Whatever the merits of Wright's sources (he cited Humboldt and Herodotus, among others), he had made an important point. For blacks to be fully exposed to their past—indeed, to the entire history of civilization—need not reinforce feelings of inferiority; on the contrary, it might suggest the provinciality of white Americans who clung to beliefs and stereotypes long discredited elsewhere in the world.

What a teacher could accomplish was often limited by textbooks carefully selected to reflect a white southern point of view. "We have been grossly neglected by most all historians," a school principal in North Carolina wrote Booker T. Washington in 1891, "and if you teach some of the text books that we use in N.C., the pupils will learn from them that they belong to the most inferior race on the earth and also fail to learn one single great thing done by a negro." The letter writer, Edward A. Johnson, who was born in slavery, had recently authored *A School History of the Negro Race in America* and wanted Washington's endorsement for a textbook that "contains information that every colored child should know." But black leaders and educators sympathetic to such productions had a difficult time getting them into the school curriculum. Robert Smalls, a black leader in Beaufort, South Carolina, informed John E. Bruce, a black journalist who had just published a volume of biographical sketches of eminent black men and women, that he would make every effort to introduce the book into the public schools but held out little hope for success. All textbooks, he warned Bruce, had to be approved by the state's board of education, and nearly all of the approved books were "either the productions of the Southerner, or those with Southern leanings."[56] And Smalls in this instance clearly made "Southerner" and "Southern" synonymous with white people.

Differences over what kind of history and English should be taught sometimes reflected different attitudes toward black culture itself—the degree to which it needed to be nourished or whitened in the classroom. Although W. C. Handy was permitted to take charge of the band and orchestra at Alabama State Agricultural and Mechanical College for Negroes, he found it difficult to pursue his interest in ragtime music. The ultraconservative black president, William H. Councill, insisted on music steeped in the European classical tradition. "In this school, like many others," recalled Handy, "there seemed to be an unwritten law against American music and any inferior song of foreign origin was considered 'classical.' " But one night, in a band recital, Handy overcame the problem, sneaking into the program a ragtime number, "My Ragtime Baby," renaming it "Greetings to Toussaint L'Ouverture" while retaining the vigorous tempo. "It did the trick. The students couldn't sit still, nor could the teachers. The president himself patted his feet." Unlike Councill, the president of Fisk, a white man with a northern missionary background, had no problem in encouraging "negro music," claiming it would be a powerful factor in the elevation of the race. After all, he wrote to the General Education Board, in requesting funds for a music building, "They are born musicians. They are bound to sing. The Devil is already trying to get a mortgage on this divine gift. No surer way of toning up the pulpit end of the church can be found than by elevating the music end."[57]

When Robert Russa Moton entered Hampton Institute as a student in 1885, he would no doubt have preferred Councill's stance. His first night proved to be memorable. The entire student body of some six hundred students gathered, along with the faculty and a large number of white visitors, to listen to a white chaplain offer prayer, after which the students sang "plantation songs, the religious folk songs of the Negro." The songs were familiar to Moton, and the singing "almost carried me into a new world," but he found himself discomfited if not embarrassed by the experience. To hear such songs "sung by educated people and in an educational institution" was not what he had expected at Hampton. "I had expected to hear regular church music such as would be sung by white people mostly, and such as was written as I supposed by white people also. I had come to school to learn to do things differently; to sing, to speak, and to use the language, and of course, the music, not of coloured people but of white people." He had enrolled in Hampton, he explained to a classmate, because he had wanted "to learn something better." And thinking of the numerous whites who had attended the performance, he resented exhibiting "the religious and emotional side of our people to white folks," most of whom, he thought, listened "simply for entertainment and perhaps amusement." When several weeks later, also on a Sunday evening, the white headmaster whom he greatly admired talked about the songs as "a priceless legacy" of the race, Moton came away impressed but "not entirely convinced."[58]

The curriculum offered in the black schools sought to accommodate varying expectations, even as it reflected both a shortage of resources and the need to placate white authorities and a suspicious white public. At Georgia State Industrial College near Savannah, the white commissioners decided that neither Latin, Greek, nor higher mathematics would be taught—a decision that a number of the students found humiliating and unacceptable. Some students threatened to leave the college until the president agreed to permit teachers to provide lessons in "the forbidden courses" at night and in the afternoon as an extracurricular activity. Surprised by the agitation and threatened departures, the commissioners agreed to restore classics to the regular curriculum. Charles Chesnutt was much less fortunate in acquiring the instruction he wanted in Latin, French, German, and music. "First class teachers would not teach a 'nigger' and I would have no other sort." As long as he remained in the South, Chesnutt concluded, his opportunity to be educated in advanced subjects would be frustrated.[59]

The conflict in the curriculum between an industrial and a classical liberal education was as old as the first efforts to educate black youths, in both the North and the South. After the Civil War, the acknowledged model was Hampton Institute in Virginia under founder and headmaster Samuel Armstrong, a white man. The idea was simple enough: Teach black youths the essential virtues of frugality, sobriety, and hard work, the same virtues many of them imbibed from *McGuffey's Readers*. A son of missionaries, the headstrong and paternalistic Armstrong came to be convinced that black aspirations to a higher civilization rested on the acquisition of a proper work and moral ethic. Through industrial and vocational training, blacks would acquire the necessary skills and discipline to make their own way in life and provide inspiration and models for others to emulate. At the same time, they would need to shun politics as counterproductive and classical education as unproductive if not frivolous.[60]

Most visitors to Hampton came away impressed with the results, but Henry McNeal Turner, an outspoken black clergyman who visited in 1878, expressed considerable disdain. Hampton, he concluded, taught Negro inferiority. Three years earlier, Booker T. Washington had graduated from Hampton, certain he had received a unique and inspiring education that had no equal anywhere. "At Hampton, I found an opportunity for class-room education and for practical training in industrial life, opportunity to learn thrift, economy, and push. Amid

Christian influences, I was surrounded by an atmosphere of business, and a spirit of self-help that seemed to awaken every faculty in me and cause me for the first time to realize what it means to be a man instead of a piece of property." And when Washington was asked to head a new black school in Tuskegee in 1881, he chose to make it a virtual replica of Hampton. Through industrial training, black youths would not only acquire skills as bricklayers, blacksmiths, and printers, but they would also acquire those essential middle-class virtues: thrift, cleanliness, work, and self-help. Even as Washington upheld the right of blacks to acquire a classical education, he thought too many had been "taught about everything except that which he depends upon for daily bread." At the same time, however, Tuskegee taught young blacks to curb their ambitions and aspirations, to adapt themselves to the limitations placed on them. That made the institution particularly palatable to whites, North and South, winning the highest praise from President William McKinley when the presidential train stopped in Tuskegee in 1898. "An evidence of the soundness of the purpose of this institution," the president told a gathering, "is that those in charge of its management evidently do not believe in attempting the unattainable. . . ."[61]

By World War I, the Hampton-Tuskegee idea had spread throughout the black South, supported in large part by northern philanthropy filtered through Booker T. Washington. Few whites played a more critical role in that support than William H. Baldwin, Jr., a railroad entrepreneur and educational reformer. Holding important positions in the Southern Education Board and the General Education Board, he helped both to provide funding for and to propagandize the Hampton-Tuskegee gospel.

> Face the music; avoid social questions; leave politics alone; continue to be patient; live moral lives; live simply; learn to work and to work intelligently; learn to work faithfully; learn to work hard; learn that any work, however menial, if well done, is dignified; learn that the world will give full credit for labor and success, even though the skin is black; learn that it is a mistake to be educated out of your necessary environment; know that it is a crime for any teacher, white or black, to educate the Negro for positions which are not open to him; know that the greatest opportunity for a successful life lies in the Southland where you were born, where the people know you and need you, and will treat you far better than in any other section of the country.[62]

Each new black school in the South, with few exceptions, articulated the same educational philosophy, not only because the administrators believed it but also because they knew their future funding depended on it. If these schools did not produce the anticipated army of skilled craftsmen, they did send out teachers who would proselytize future generations in the virtues of the industrial work ethic and in the critical need to acquire mental discipline and self-control. When Henry Davidson established an industrial school in Centerville, Alabama, he claimed he wanted to reach the "great masses" in the rural South. Although not a Tuskegee graduate, he modeled his school on the same principles: to teach black youths "the dignity of labor" and how "to be of better service to themselves, to their employers, and to the community in which they lived." In extolling the virtues of manual training, he embraced Washington's warning against "educating away from work." Too many black youths had left school "with mere book learning," and that hardly prepared them for the world they entered. "The time is fast approaching, is verily upon us, when the standard of a man must be measured by what he does, not what he knows."[63]

That same Washingtonian ideal would be reiterated by scores of black educators, teachers, and valedictorians in the late nineteenth and early twentieth centuries, with some of them adding an emphatic religious dimension. "Jesus Christ is our Model, and the Bible our chief text-book," the administrators of Samuel Houston College in Austin, Texas, affirmed, along with the customary promises to provide industrial training and "safe leaders for the race." A graduate of Georgia State Industrial College urged students to acquire skills in business. All too often, he complained, blacks looked to a college education only to prepare them for "the so-called higher callings" of lawyer, doctor, preacher, and teacher, neglecting the prospects of a business career. "Why," he asked, "should you be a teacher and live by man's ignorance; a minister and live by his sins; a lawyer and live by his quarrels; a doctor and live by his diseases; rather than a merchant and live by honest gain?" Studying at Clark University in the 1880s, Elias B. Holloway remembered a popular teacher who extolled the financial success of men such as Jay Gould and Cornelius Vanderbilt. But even as students were urged to emulate these industrial heroes, they listened to a visiting speaker, Dr. J. C. Price, president of a black college in North Carolina, advise them always to be in some debt to the white man, because the white man was likely to be more interested in the welfare of a debtor.[64]

Befitting an aspiring new black middle class, Hampton and Tuskegee sought to inculcate their students not only with industrial education but also with the social graces, dress, demeanor, and gentility esteemed in late-nineteenth-century American society. To be an efficient farmer, artisan, cook, or dressmaker would be to little avail if young blacks did not also acquire a proper demeanor, refined cultural tastes, and an appreciation for cleanliness and sanitation. As in white society, etiquette manuals appeared to instruct black youths and to supplement school texts. Elias M. Woods, in his published lecture *The Gospel of Civility* and subsequently in a fuller text, *The Negro in Etiquette,* addressed in particular social usages among blacks and the need to ferret out some of the remaining vestiges of enslavement, whether in "sidewalk etiquette" or in forms of address and greeting. "Thank you, Boss," he advised, "is more 'nigger' which the negro has got to shake off himself. . . . Of all men, the truckler is the most despised. How much easier it would be to say, 'Thank you, sir.' " Still another "slave mannerism" involved the ways in which blacks walked on public thoroughfares. Woods suggested "an easy, graceful gait," not the more prevalent "shuffling, awkward walk—a kind of dragging the feet along, allowing the front part of the heels to strike first, and wabbling or moving staggeringly from side to side." The advice such manuals offered black youths often repeated and embellished what parents sought to impart to their children, as in how they should conduct themselves in the presence of whites, particularly white women. But *The Negro in Etiquette,* even as it taught proper respect for white women, demanded the same consideration for black women and deplored black men who failed to show it.[65]

Even as they promised to inculcate proper manners, morals, and discipline, black educators made a point of reaffirming their faith in southern whites and in racial harmony. It seemed to Joseph Winthrop Holley, founder of Albany State College, as it had to Washington, that southern whites in fact possessed "a feeling for the Negro of a kind simply unknown to the Northern white man." More than 250 years of slavery, he thought, had "bred" into southern whites an interest in the Negro race "found nowhere else in the world." When in 1902 William J. Edwards, founder of Snow Hill Normal and Industrial Institute, summed up its first seven years, he chose to emphasize those features that would continue to attract philanthropic support. The school had confirmed for most people the fact that the South was "the best place for the Negro"; it had fostered among blacks "a love for country life" and the belief that "intensive farming" afforded them the "opportunity of the age"; and finally, but of critical importance, it had diminished crime, along with black political participation, and had improved relations between the races.[66]

Neither the Washingtonian model, the rhetoric of uplift through industrial training, nor prescriptive prophecies focusing on service to the white man went unchallenged. Even before W. E. B. Du Bois questioned the primacy of industrial over traditional classical training, black parents and teachers had made their objections and skepticism known, often to the exasperation of black educators. Joseph Booker, the president of Arkansas Baptist College, thought his students understood that education was simply "to make them better fitted for work," but "the race at large," he feared, "expected education to do for them what Lincoln could not do—Emancipate them from work." Only among "the intelligent Negroes" and "the best and wisest white people" did he find strong sympathy for industrial education, the nearly unanimous white support based on the desire to see the Negro "fitted for his natural and logical calling."[67]

When William J. Edwards established an industrial institute in "the blackest of the Black Belts," he thought industrial and agricultural training would be viewed as the most appropriate for this poor region. But many parents nonetheless opposed his curriculum, even removed their children from the school when Edwards made them work as part of their training. The objection parents offered was simple enough: "their children had been working all their lives and they did not mean to send them to school to learn to work." Attributing the opposition to "illiterate preachers and incompetent teachers," Edwards resolved to keep the "Industrial Plank" in the institute's platform.[68]

Even the proponents of industrial training had their limits. The idea, some insisted, was to produce skilled workers, not a new black service class. In that spirit, the principal of a school in Lowndes County, Alabama, rejected an appeal from the director of the Detroit League on Urban Conditions Among Negroes in 1918 that he send his graduates there to work in domestic service. Although he thought his students would make "excellent servants," he preferred they be "care-takers" in their own homes and "enter into the life of the community."[69]

After visiting Atlanta University in 1902, an agent for the General Education Board, which dispensed funds among black schools, claimed to find "no great enthusiasm" for industrial work. Nor did he come away entirely impressed with how the more traditional subjects were taught. Visiting the political science class taught by W. E. B. Du Bois, for example, he acknowledged the professor's command of the subject matter but thought his questions called for "abstract reasoning beyond the ability of the students, either from the standpoint of their own experience in life, or from their limited historic information." Du Bois, he felt, should have used questions to elicit from the students information they had acquired in their courses in Greek, Roman, and English history. In concluding his confidential report, the agent thought Du Bois had simply failed to recognize "elementary principles of Psychology which underlie scientific methods of teaching."[70]

If white philanthropic foundations sometimes viewed Atlanta University with suspicion, Tuskegee Institute could be expected to command the most enthusiastic support. But even Tuskegee came under the sharp examination of its Committee on Investment of the Endowment Fund, staffed by white men who made regular reports on what pleased and displeased them about Washington's school. After conversing with "leading citizens" in Montgomery and Birmingham about Tuskegee, one committee member found indifference rather than hostility, as if the school had little relevance to Alabama. To remedy that perception, he proposed a program at Tuskegee to train domestic servants and children's nurses. When he sounded out prominent whites about his idea, he was warmly received. Such a program, they told him, would go far to bridge "the gap now unfortunately existing between the two races in the South." Still another observer reported to the Committee on Investment his concern about the Bible school at Tuskegee. It seemed to encourage too much of the religious emotionalism that underscored the "backward" or "primitive" nature of black people. What bothered him in particular was the degree to which "the singing and the talking" he had heard were "the same kind as I heard in negro churches many years ago, and appeared to be lacking in that good sense and simplicity which Dr. Washington has infused into most of his work."[71]

Under steady scrutiny by white visitors and largely dependent on philanthropic agencies for survival, black schools and colleges found it impossible to fulfill the vast array of expectations imposed on them. Seeking to balance the survival of the school, the expectations of students and parents, and white public sentiment, the black principals and college officials had to play a difficult and often precarious game. Administrators of the Slater Industrial and State Normal School in Salem, North Carolina, suffered acute embarrassment over a class motto in Latin adopted by the graduating class. The objection was not to the motto but to the use of Latin. After investigating the incident, the president of the Board of Trustees thought the school should not have to suffer because of the "smart-Alex" act of one class or "foolish advisor." After all, he noted, the trustees had discarded from the curriculum all of the "ornamental and useless branches," and the heavy preponderance of manual training classes should be sufficiently reassuring. The male students had built many of the campus buildings and were performing all the farm work; the female students worked in and around the school, and they also took in laundry, "so as to learn how to do the work and at the same time turn an honest penny into our limited treasury." The president of the faculty admitted "the error in allowing the class to select a motto in Latin" but reassured critics that Slater aimed only at "increasing the Negro's industrial efficiency" and that the school offered no advanced studies, Latin, or higher mathematics "and only the simplest elements of some of the natural sciences."[72]

Based on the understanding that blacks would be trained in agriculture and the trades, South Carolina State College opened in 1896 in Orangeburg. As a student there, Benjamin Mays recalled how everyone was compelled to learn a trade; one day each week was set aside for this purpose, and a student could work at his trade on Saturdays and in the afternoons. (Mays started out in harness making and shoe repairing but, failing to distinguish himself in either trade, he turned after a year to painting.) Students could opt for more traditional subjects, but the college needed to maintain the pretense if not the reality of being exclusively concerned with training blacks to be mechanics and farmers. Mays once heard a teacher claim that the college was able to teach Latin only because they called it "agricultural Latin." ("The spirit if not the letter of this allegation was true," Mays insisted.) The Mississippi state legislature, in 1878, made perfectly clear its expectations of "higher education" among blacks when it changed the name of Alcorn University to Alcorn Agricultural and Mechanical College.[73]

Mindful of public hostility, administrators and faculty at Samuel Houston College, in the heart of Austin, made every effort to placate local whites. Adopting as the school motto "Strive always to treat others better than they treat you," students were reminded that the survival of the college depended on their behavior. If they worked in the homes of whites, they should go out of their way to be "honest, industrious and reliable." And whenever students encountered whites in public, they were admonished to be "polite and kind to everyone" and "to give all the side walk if necessary." The college claimed to have won the sympathy of the white community. While a student at Alabama Agricultural and Mechanical College, W. C. Handy came to understand the strategy worked out by the president, William H. Councill, to keep his school solvent and tolerated. Backed by the motto on the chapel wall, "Work is the Measure of Worth," the president, Handy observed, made every effort to demonstrate to southern whites "that the aim was not so much to lift the Negroes socially but to make better cooks, nurse maids, mechanics and share farmers of them. Thus the real benefit would come to the whites." When Councill in 1901 applied to the governor for funding, he emphasized the fact that the college was placing into the rural districts and towns "teachers who are not only competent to teach, but who are in harmony with the institutions and customs of the South." The prominent white citizen who endorsed Councill's request pronounced him "a good man and fine manager" and "politically all right."[74]

It was a spectacle Gustavus A. Steward learned to detest. Employed at St. Paul Normal and Industrial School in Lawrenceville, Virginia, he looked on with suppressed disdain as the black administrators prepared for the visit of a prominent white donor. The "desire to please him," Steward wrote in his journal that night, "almost degenerated into toadyism." Evening prayer service was held in a special place, and the donor called upon the students to impart the lessons they learned at St. Paul's to others. Throughout the service and speech, Steward noted, the school's principal beamed in approval—"all for this white man who had given the school some money." At the close of the donor's talk, Steward added, "we (the congregation) tickled his ear with plantation melodies." Steward described the school's director as preoccupied with putting on airs, making it appear as if he were achieving something important. "He has the Tuskegee bragging spirit," a quality Steward found in most of the Tuskegee graduates. And yet, he observed, "the most conspicuous failures I have known here at St. Paul's have been men from Tuskegee."[75]

The caution with which black administrators and teachers acted no doubt reflected fears for their tenure, as well as for future funding. But the "toadyism" noted by Steward at St. Paul's had a way of taking on a life of its own, and the price paid in self-pride and dignity could be substantial. To an exasperated black Texan, the "pity" of the educational system was that it taught blacks subservience rather than independence. Although the children he observed were eager for the opportunity to learn, "the greatest lesson they seem to be learning is cowardice. . . . The children used to fight back, but now I see so much cringing, such fear in their faces when a white man thunders at them, that you wonder what sort of slavery this is and where it is to end." He openly expressed his concerns but he wondered if his words had any effect. "The principal told me that the things I said to them were what they needed to hear, but that no man here dared speak that way."[76]

The environment in which black schools tried to survive helps to explain some of the "toadyism" of administrators and the fears and self-doubts of teachers and students. To survive financially and politically, it was necessary to be aware of and to meet the expectations of whites, to allay their deep concerns about the subversive effects of black education. Laurence Jones, for example, wanted to convince the public that his Piney Woods School in Mississippi would make more efficient laborers of his students. The argument found ready acceptance among local whites. "He says he ain't gwine to teach 'em so much book larnin'," a much-relieved sawmill operator remarked, "but he wants to learn 'em to do more and better work, so when we wants good work done we can git it. That nigger seems like a good nigger. I like him."[77]

After the death of Booker T. Washington, Tuskegee Institute inaugurated a special commemoration of his life and influence and called it Founder's Day. It was an opportunity for the trustees and the public to come to Tuskegee to praise Washington and to hear alumni tell of their achievements since graduation. In 1922, on Founder's Day, the Booker T. Washington monument was unveiled; the large sculpture revealed Washington lifting the veil of ignorance from the face of a black slave. Some years later, the hero in Ralph Ellison's *Invisible Man* finds himself gazing at the monument. "I am standing puzzled, unable to decide whether the veil is really being lifted, or lowered more firmly in place; whether I am witnessing a revelation or a more efficient blinding."[78]

4

SINCE EMANCIPATION, Blacks had to overcome formidable obstacles to their education, ranging from organized white resistance to authorized white neglect. The very reasons that encouraged so many blacks to acquire an education after the Civil War were no less com-

pelling in driving many whites to oppose black schools. Even as the debate persisted over the merits of such schooling, the opposition
mounted in some areas made it a moot question. Speaking with "an intelligent business man," a visiting journalist was startled by the virulence of his reaction to an important black school in the vicinity. The
school should be dynamited, he insisted, and the principal run out of
the state. That, he explained, would force blacks to understand that ignorance, hard labor, and white domination constituted their permanent destiny. Although the visitor found the hostility contained in these
remarks "incomprehensible," he did not find it exceptional.[79]

That kind of hostility manifested itself all too frequently in violence
directed selectively at black schools, teachers, and administrators. The
deliberate burning of schoolhouses, along with the harassment and
murder of teachers after emancipation and during Reconstruction, developed into a wave of terror directed at efforts to educate black children. The fate of Alonzo B. Corliss in Alamance County, North
Carolina, typified the violence Klansmen visited on white teachers of
black schools during Reconstruction. Employed by the Friends Freedman's Association, the lame teacher was dragged out of his bed and
house without his crutches. The attackers flogged his body with raw
cowhide and green hickory sticks, after which they cut off the hair from
one side of his head and painted half of his face and shorn head black.
For three hours on a cold November night, Corliss lay where they had
left him in the woods before he regained consciousness. When found,
he was attempting to crawl home. He had asked his attackers what
offenses he had committed against them, and they had responded,
"Teaching niggers." Nimrod Porter, a farmer and sheriff in Maury
County, Tennessee, tersely recorded in his diary the fate of the local
black school in 1868: "The Ku, Kluck, Klan ordered the School Mistress to stop her School. She done so and told the children to go home,
so the School is broken up."[80]

The sight of blacks carrying books often had the same effect on
whites as the sight of armed blacks, and many would have found no
real distinction between the two threats. After the Civil War, in
Charleston, South Carolina, black children hid their books in market
baskets until they reached the schoolhouse, fearing they would be harassed or turned back if whites thought they were going to school. Caroline Smith, who lived in Walton County, Georgia, told how Klansmen
were determined to keep black schools out of the area. "They went to a
colored man there, whose son had been teaching school, and they took

every book they [the family] had and threw them into the fire; and they said they would just dare any other nigger to have a book in his house." When whites burned down the first black school in Selma, Alabama, in the 1890s, a black resident thought it resulted from white resentment over the effects of education, particularly overhearing blacks called "Mr." and "Mrs."[81]

The experience of white teachers in the black schools depended on whether they were native whites or Northerners. While an often grudging accommodation was made to native white teachers, those who had come from the North were seldom fully accepted in the community. Accused of indoctrinating and overeducating black children, some found themselves ostracized in the community and subject to violence. Unable to find lodgings among whites, they often had to depend on black hospitality, and that in turn only increased white resentment over race mixing. Black teachers, whether native-born or not, found themselves labeled "dangerous niggers" and had to be particularly careful in what and how they taught. If not humiliated, beaten, murdered, or forced into exile, some teachers, white and black, found it nearly impossible to obtain credit in local stores.[82]

When Lura Beam, a new graduate of Barnard College in New York, chose to teach in a black school in Wilmington, North Carolina, in 1908, she was warned the white community would ostracize her. Upon arriving at the train station and requesting that a hack driver take her to the school, she was told, "Lady, that's a nigger school, you don't want to go there." Memories of the recent race riot were still fresh, and Beam found an atmosphere demanding caution when dealing with both races. If black parents and pupils ignored her on the street, even crossing to the other side to avoid her, that was done, she learned, "to protect us both." If they were to retain her, blacks needed to show her the same deference afforded all whites, even if local whites refused such deference. For Beam, however, there had been no way to prepare for this extraordinary situation. "I was told to get used to the fact that a Negro does nothing with me unless he is waiting on me. He walks behind me. He stands while I sit. He knows better than to eat in my presence."[83]

The ambivalence whites felt about black schools extended to native whites who assumed teaching positions in such schools. "The Negro is docile if approached properly," the school superintendent of Charleston explained, and native white teachers had acquired the "knack" of handling black students properly. The social stigma once attached to native whites teaching in a black school had diminished. Economic need induced some to accept such positions, while others embraced the notion that if blacks were to be taught at all, whites should control what and how they were taught. But native white teachers, like those born in the North, were expected to abide by a rigid protocol. If pupils encountered their white teachers outside the classroom, it would be a breach of decorum to speak to them. Until 1920, white teachers dominated the Charleston black schools. When local blacks began to agitate for employment as public school pedagogues, launching a massive petition drive, whites initially resisted, claiming that only mulattoes wanted black teachers while the cooks and laundresses desired white teachers. The decision of one black woman to send her child to a private school rested on her preference for "the patient 'New England schoolmarm' " over the poor white public schoolteacher who thought it beneath herself to teach black children and refused to speak with them on the streets.[84]

Along with their teachers, black students were always vulnerable, likely to encounter hostility and suspicion for the simple act of attending school. Increasingly, the students found themselves thrust into the political arena as a volatile issue, the objects of race-baiting politicians who hoped to exploit for their own benefit white fears of educated blacks. W. C. Handy recalled the number of times his band was hired to provide music for white political rallies. That would invariably subject them to a "passel" of political oratory and demagoguery. He remembered in particular the gubernatorial candidate who vowed, if elected, not to spend one dollar for "nigger education," because "education unfits the nigger." After employing the traditional tribute to those faithful blacks who had stood by their masters and mistresses during the Civil War, the candidate asked the audience, "Now what kind of nigger did we leave them with? It was the uneducated nigger." In the event of another war, however, he asked the audience if they felt they could leave their families with "the nigger of today." The crowd responded with a chorus of "No's." That was why he would refuse to spend one dollar "for nigger education," the candidate concluded, his voice quavering, mist coming over his eyes as he extended one arm while resting the other dramatically over his heart. After the candidate's final words, Handy's band played "Dixie." When they were safely removed from the crowd, members of the band recalled the speech, exchanged "amazed" glances, and nudged each other with their elbows. "Then we all laughed—laughed." Recalling that incident,

Handy reflected over the effects of the speech on his fellow band members. "We could laugh and we could make rhythm. What better armor could you ask?"[85]

The white South was never of one mind on the question of whether to educate blacks and, if so, to what degree and under whose auspices. Confronted with the establishment of schools and the apparent determination of blacks to utilize them, some white Southerners relented. But the accommodation they made varied considerably in enthusiasm and tolerance. Under control of "the best white people of the community," and with the right kind of teachers, realistic goals, and an appreciation of limits, black schools could be geared to a productive and stable labor force. The idea was simple enough, and no one expressed it more coherently than Major Peter W. Meldrim of Savannah when he addressed a commencement at a black college. "I believe in education for you people," he declared. "The state of Georgia needs intelligent Negroes [which he pronounced as "Niggras"] but I do not believe in educating you people to want things you can never get. We must educate the Negro to be the best possible Negro and not a bad imitation of a white man." The applause that greeted these remarks reflected the feeling of the mostly black audience that the speaker, in supporting black schools, was far in advance of local white opinion.[86]

Since emancipation, numerous "leading" whites had embraced a similar argument: Teach the newly freed slaves a proper deference for their superiors, fidelity to contracts, respect for property, the rewards of industriousness, and other virtues calculated to ensure a compliant and efficient labor force. By the early twentieth century, that frame of mind could induce southern whites to encourage black education even as they discouraged any schooling calculated to inflate black expectations. And it could encourage certain northern philanthropists to devote their efforts and resources to develop in the South an education for blacks that in no way threatened white supremacy. The idea was to make black education compatible with the prevailing racial hierarchy—indeed, to use the classroom to preserve and reinforce that hierarchy. "The more intelligent the negro becomes," a Maryland newspaper editorialized, "the more he sees his dependence upon the republic that made his advancement possible, and the more he respects and treats with deference the dominant race, and the less boisterous, clamorous and abusive he becomes." Considering itself a friend of black education, the same newspaper, in responding to those less friendly, thought the entire society benefited from teaching blacks "a greater respect for toil—manual toil." It envisaged blacks building houses, paving streets, making clothes, and painting and plastering, as well as farming. "What the negro needs is to be taught and shown that labor is his salvation—not books. The state appropriation is intended to encourage that teaching."[87]

What underlay the movement for black education among some whites was clearly the pressing need to inculcate a new generation of blacks with proper moral and religious values. That overriding concern persuaded a white bishop in Mississippi to insist that black education was too important to be left entirely or primarily to black teachers. The ideal school, he thought, would be under the supervision of a white clergyman, where "carefully selected" portions of the Bible would become a part of the curriculum, and "where the race should be taught that race integrity is obedience to God's own creation and appointment, and that race intercourse, kindly and cordial, is not race equality."[88]

Not only must blacks be given the right kind of education, but also they should not be overeducated. The woman Richard Wright worked for expressed surprise when he told her he was in the seventh grade. "Then why are you going to school?" she asked. Her surprise turned to shock when he told her of his ambition to be a writer. "A what?" she exclaimed, needing confirmation. "You'll never be a writer," she told Wright. "Who on earth put such ideas into your nigger head?" Benjamin Mays recalled the alienation he felt in his native county in South Carolina: "The chasm was so wide between black and white in my day that I never felt that any white person in Greenwood County or in South Carolina would be interested in anything I did." Actually, some whites were acutely interested in what blacks did and feared the consequences. The problem with northern-imported education and educators, many whites concurred, had been the attempt to make Negroes "ambitious" by training them as doctors, lawyers, and preachers. "They acquire uppishness; they begin to swell, and to fancy that they are equal to the whites." And some chose to abandon the countryside. "After a fellow has learned to wear a clean shirt at college," a white South Carolinian lamented, "he is not going into the cotton patch."[89]

The inferior mental capacity of Negroes had long been a staple in the arsenal of white racism. Under the cover of ethnological science, some whites argued with absolute certainty that the Negro's brain could only be educated within clear limits. "There's no bringing him past a certain point—and that's a low one" repeated a popular axiom about the intellectual limits of blacks. Dating back to slavery, this belief confirmed the inability of black people to look after themselves and their need to defer to the superior judgment and wisdom of whites. While some thought the race could be improved through education over a long period of time, many felt the defects were irremediable, citing as evidence the relative mental capacity of white and black children, in particular the "imitative" qualities of the black race. "The black child has a good word-memory and a good eye-memory," the superintendent of the Birmingham public schools explained to a visitor in 1909, laying down the classic argument. "He will often learn by rote quicker than a white child—but it is a different thing when it comes to understanding what he learns."[90]

Of course, if blacks had natural intellectual limits that consigned them permanently to an inferior position, whites had nothing to fear. That was one way advocates of black education could justify expenditures for black schools. "You need not be afraid of the negro boy," a North Carolina legislator assured a joint session of the General Assembly. "It will take him a thousand years to get where your boy is." Even if black children competed favorably with whites, a southern white leader argued, the growth and development of black intelligence had its limits. "The Negro's skull is thicker," he explained, "his brain is smaller than the white man's," and he cited scientific testimony that the sutures of the skull, which permit growth and expansion, develop earlier for blacks, usually at the age of fourteen. "This accounts for the fact that while Negro children at school often compare favorably with whites, adults do not."[91]

No matter how fervently whites embraced these beliefs in black inferiority, no matter what controls were placed on the quality and extent of black education, the fears and skepticism never really subsided. The principal concern remained readily apparent—the danger in teaching blacks until, in the words of one fearful educator, they had the same "instincts and drives" as whites. That would be a certain invitation to trouble. That would be "worse than foolhardy," a prominent white editor affirmed. "It was not unlike placing a loaded magazine rifle in the arms of a chimpanzee." If taught the same lessons as the white child, would not the black child be encouraged to develop the same instincts, the same interests, and the same ambitions? Would that child not then aspire to the same goals and insist upon achieving them in the same way? No one summed up white fears more succinctly than the Mississippi politician who warned, "Ambition in the negro is concreted in lust."[92]

That was reason enough for many elected public officials to rigidly control and minimize black educational opportunities, even to oppose expending funds altogether for the education of Negroes. "It is money thrown away," a Mississippi politician argued in 1899, alleging that education simply implanted in blacks aspirations and ambitions whites would never permit them to gratify. Deploring any efforts to encourage black education, J. Thomas Heflin warned the Alabama Constitutional Convention of 1902 that "as soon as you elevate him you ruin him." And that could prove disastrous to both races. "The negroes are being educated very rapidly, and I say in the light of all the history of the past, some day when the two separate and distinct races are thrown together, some day the clash will come and the survival of the fittest, and I do not believe it is incumbent upon us to lift him up and educate him on an equal footing that he may be armed and equipped when the combat comes."[93]

No matter what blacks learned in the classroom, white critics suggested, it could not really improve or elevate the race. To the argument that educating blacks equipped them for citizenship, the governor of Georgia responded in 1901, "We have failed. They are worse citizens today and more dangerous to the State than they were thirty years ago. Education has had no more effect on them morally and intellectually than it has physically. God made them negroes and we cannot by education make them white folks. We are on the wrong track. We must turn back." A Presbyterian clergyman in South Carolina reached the same conclusion in 1889, dismissing as absurd the notion that education might be a panacea for blacks. "[A]n 'educated' negro," he noted, "is just as much negro as before, just the same raw hide volume with the incongruous addition of a gilt edge; he is only a little more aggressively offensive than his less ornate brother."[94]

For blacks to overcome ignorance and illiteracy after two centuries of deliberate exclusion from schooling was challenging enough. But to be forced to deal at the same time with such deeply rooted white bigotry and ignorance, often at the very highest levels of government and education, could be an exasperating and exhausting experience. Charles Chesnutt, teaching in rural North Carolina and aspiring to a different kind of life, rapidly discovered he had to confront far more than the intellectual deficiencies of his pupils. A friend informed him of a recent conversation with a white store clerk about the new schoolteacher in town.

"Bob, what kind of a fellow is this Chesnutt[?]"

"Well, sir, he's a perfect gentleman in every respect; I don't know his superior."

"Why! he's a nigger, ain't he?"

"He's classed with the colored people, but . . ."

"Well, what kind of an education has he?"

"He's not a college bred man, but he has been a hard student all his life. You can't ask him a question he cannot answer."

"He's this shorthand writer?"

"Yes, sir."

"Does he think he's as good as a white man[?]"

"Every bit of it, sir . . ."

"Well he's a nigger; and with me a nigger is a nigger, and nothing in the world can make him anything else but a nigger."

After being informed of the details of the conversation, Chesnutt noted in his journal that the store clerk "embodies the opinion of the South on the 'Negro Question.' "[95]

When the Southern Educational Association met in Houston in 1911, the delegates found it impossible to separate the question of black education from perceptions of a new generation of blacks. If nothing else, the welfare of southern whites demanded the proper education and training of a generation of blacks undisciplined by slavery. "He must be trained for his environment—must be taught how to live morally and hygienically." And that education "should be industrial and not literary and cultural," providing practical lessons for young blacks in subjects most relevant to their welfare, "such as agriculture, stock and poultry raising, cooking and the arts and thrift and economy."[96]

The assumptions of whites about the intellectual capacity of blacks all too often betrayed the fear that they might be proven wrong. In much of the white South, the belief grew—with additional evidence of expressive if not aggressive black behavior—that the danger of black education still lay in the distinct possibility that it would succeed in elevating blacks to the same level as whites. "Let us be frank and honest," the Charleston *News and Observer* editorialized in 1904. "The great mass of the white people of the South have no idea of educating the Negro to be a citizen—their equal, either social or political. They want him to be the white man's help, and if he is not willing to occupy a subordinate position in this country, the sooner he leaves it, or the southern part of it at least, the better for all concerned." No doubt many whites would have seriously heeded the warning sounded by a Raleigh newspaper, though it was meant to mock opponents of black education: "Reading and writing still bear watching. When a negro learns to articulate correctly and say 'they' instead of 'dey' and 'that' instead of 'dat' we are prepared to expect the worst."[97]

Whatever the safeguards, then, the specter of an educated Negro continued to haunt much of the New South. He was an affront to white sensibilities, a challenge to white expectations. It had long been an article of faith that an educated black person was subversive of good race relations. Education, like the ownership of land, spoiled the Negro as a laborer, developed in him wants that could never be satisfied, expectations that could never be realized. Education, like the ballot, inflated black aspirations toward full equality. Education, a South Carolina "gentleman" bluntly affirmed, "spoils him [the Negro] as a nigger, and it doesn't turn him into a man." Still worse, a Memphis newspaper insisted, blacks obtain "just enough of learning to make them realize how hopelessly their race is behind the other in everything that makes a great people, and they attempt to 'get even' by insolence, which is ever the resentment of inferiors."[98]

The problem for many whites finally came down to perceptions of the effects of black schooling in a society that depended on blacks to perform most of its menial tasks. "It's a question," a Montgomery, Alabama, lawyer argued, "who will do the dirty work. In this country the white man won't; the Negro must. There's got to be a mudsill somewhere. If you educate the Negroes they won't stay where they belong; and you must consider them as a race, because if you let a few rise it makes the others discontented." Rather than fit blacks for daily life, then, education made them increasingly useless and provocative. It raised as many if not more problems than it resolved. "It tends to make the negro unwilling to work where he is wanted," a white "gentleman" explained to an English visitor in 1909, "and desirous of working where he is not wanted. . . ."[99]

The educational opportunities already extended to blacks had, in the estimation of many white observers, unsettled labor relations and exacerbated race relations. "It has taken him out of his true sphere and has not qualified him for any other," a prominent Virginian wrote in 1888. "Have you known one of these so-called educated negroes, who depends for support on the labor of his hands?"[100] The consequences of educated blacks unable to make full use of their education went to the very heart of white concerns. Access to schools would mislead Negroes and falsely raise their expectations. Had not the experience of Reconstruction demonstrated to whites the disastrous consequences of elevating black aspirations? Bennet Puryear, a Baptist educator at Richmond College and former slaveholder, in a blistering published attack on black education, advanced the popular notion that the very qualities—docility, unthinking obedience, and improvidence—that "fit" the Negro for menial offices and a subordinate position disqualified him for "the higher walks of life." If black ambitions were heightened, Professor Puryear asked, how could blacks be expected to be satisfied with their low economic, social, and political position? To educate a laborer beyond his calling was to unfit him for that kind of labor. "If a man is engaged in work below his education, he feels degraded by it, and that sense of degradation compels him to do inferior work." The results of black schooling, then, would soon be apparent. "The bootblack is not a better bootblack, but a worse one, the ditcher is not a better ditcher, but a worse one, if he can also calculate a solar eclipse or read with a critic's ken the choral odes of the Greek dramatists. . . . The cook, that must read the daily newspaper will spoil your beef and your bread; the sable pickaninny, that has to do his grammar and arithmetic, will leave your boots unblacked and your horse uncurried." By its very nature, Puryear noted, a public school system legitimized the doctrine of Negro equality, as it tried to prepare blacks for the highest functions of life. But if the Negro was "by congenital inferiority" unfit for such functions, as Puryear insisted, to attempt to educate him had to be "a manifest absurdity." And it would be of lasting disservice to the black race. "To invite the negro from those pursuits which require firm muscles and little intelligence to those callings which demand less muscle and higher intelligence, is to invite him to his sure extermination."[101]

The argument advanced by Puryear would be repeated in various forms for the next half century. For many whites it was nothing less than practical good sense. Appraising public sentiment, a black educator suggested in 1904 that "the mass of the whites" thought educating the Negro would make him of less material advantage to them. The Negro could be more easily exploited when ignorant. "[I]t really seems hard to be rid of the notion that the negro is to be 'used' without regard to his success and advantage." When two years earlier Alice May penned an essay, "What A Southern Woman Has To Say On The Negro Question," the practical consequences of elevating blacks through education was uppermost in her mind. "Why, education is ruination to [the] nigger, he does not want to work any longer after he learns to say A B C." That was bound to unsettle white families accustomed to black servants but finding none in whom they could any longer place much confidence. Fretting over his sister's inability to find a decent cook, Nathan C. Munroe, Jr., blamed it directly on the schools open to blacks. Clearly, he wrote her, "too much learning drives them mad."[102]

To talk of a "good ole nigger," as did a white preacher in Tuskegee, Alabama, was to talk of an uneducated and satisfied Negro. "He never had any education and never wanted any. You take some of these young niggers that get a little learnin' and thar ain't no gittin' along with 'em." The clergyman did, however, have some good words to say for the black school in Tuskegee. "I'll say one thing . . . for this nigger school of [Booker T.] Washington's hyar—they won't let 'em be too uppity thar." He recited the story of a black student coming to Tuskegee on a crowded train who refused to give up his seat to a white "lady." Washington happened to be on the train and demanded to know the youth's destination. When he responded, "To the school," Washington retorted, "No, you ain't. We don't want your sort hyar. You can turn aroun' and go home." In telling the story, the preacher placed his seal of approval on Tuskegee Institute. "Yes, Booker's got some good ideas, if he is a nigger."[103]

Education and economics interacted in various ways to force whites to pay closer attention to the amount and quality of education offered to blacks. Employers discovered, for example, that paying higher wages to their black workers might be counterproductive. Families who managed to save their earnings often opted for a different way of life and managed to purchase a small farm or business. Once they improved their economic position, they immediately took their wives and daughters out of the white people's kitchens and sent their children from the fields to the schools. With the development of ambition and a higher standard of living," one observer noted, "the Negro follows the steps of the rising Irishman or Italian: he has a better home, he wants his wife to take care of it, and he insists upon the education of his children." Seeking to explain the often "blind and bitter hostility" of whites to black education, this same observer attributed it to ways in which education enabled "the better sort of Negro" to rise above unskilled employment and domestic service—precisely those areas in which laborers were sorely needed.[104]

Whites found it possible to express a sympathy for black education as long as it did not affect the blacks on whom they depended. Seeking to establish a school for blacks in the Mississippi Delta, William Holtzclaw discussed his plans with white planters in the region. One of them applauded Holtzclaw's scheme as "a good work" and thought blacks should be educated—but, he quickly added, not in the Delta, where it would be harmful. "What I want here is Negroes who can make cotton, and they don't need education to help them make cotton." The majority of planters Holtzclaw interviewed, all of them "men of culture and wealth," doubted the wisdom of black education; some thought it might be possible to improve the older blacks "but you will never do anything with some of these young 'niggers,' and it is a waste of time to try." In Thomas Dixon's popular novel *The Leopard's Spots,* Charles Gaston, the governor-elect of North Carolina, proclaims his support of agricultural education for blacks. But the Reverend Durham, the hero of the novel who articulates Dixon's creed, strongly dissents. "Make the Negro a scientific and successful farmer, and let him plant his feet deep in your soil, and it will mean a race war." That kind of thinking may help to explain why the principal state-supported black school in Virginia had no objections to an extensive curriculum in Latin and Greek, presumably because it would qualify blacks for nothing, but refused to permit "the science of agriculture" to be taught.[105]

The education of blacks had somehow to be reconciled with their political and economic subordination, and in the eyes of many whites the contradiction could simply not be successfully resolved. "If education makes him discontented and diverts him from his true place is it not an injury to the whites?" asked one newspaper. And if educating blacks injured whites, was not the state acting contrary to its best interests? "Our civilization and safety require the social bar to be forever preserved between the races. Education of negroes tends to throw down that bar. It is preparing the way for social equality. Enfranchisement was a step in that direction. Equal education is a tremendous stride."[106]

The only way to make certain that the Negro never again became a factor in southern politics, as a voter or as an officeholder, was to curtail

his educational opportunities. A Mississippi editor talked of the benefits—"quiet, good order and perfect security"—the elimination of
black voting in 1890 had brought to the state. But in 1898 he expressed
alarm—"folly bordering on to crime"—over the future, if blacks
should take advantage of educational opportunities to qualify to vote.
That concern alone prompted whites in some regions to oppose black
schools. Since many whites readily agreed that the Negro as a voter was
"a menace," why should the South provide the education that would
enable him to vote and hold office? To uplift the black man politically,
to place him on an equal basis with whites, was to uplift him socially,
and that was reason enough for whites to be alarmed. "Equality is
equality," an educator emphasized. "If the negro is fit . . . to make laws
for the control of our conduct and property . . . he is certainly fit to eat
with us at our tables, to sleep in our beds, to be invited into our parlors,
and to do all acts and things which a white man may do."[107]

White opinion could run deep on this question, tapping the very
core of white racial fears. To educate the Negro was to inflict on him
cruel and unusual punishment, and to inflict on society a potential
monster. Inflated with ideas of his own importance and capability, the
educated Negro was bound to become discontented, resentful, and
dangerous. "When a negro boy or girl is taught to regard himself or
herself as the social equal of white children," a white psychologist
warned in 1904, "a state of feeling is engendered in the breast of that
pupil that is to curse his or her life for all time." No matter what was
taught in the classroom, education fed the propensity of blacks to think
themselves the equals of whites, potentially if not now, and such perceptions, warned John Temple Graves, who replaced Henry Grady as
editor of the *Atlanta Constitution,* inflicted serious damage on the black
psyche, with far-reaching consequences for the entire society. "[T]he
negro's criminality has increased as his illiteracy has decreased, and his
race antagonism has grown with his intelligence." And Graves suggested the reasons were sufficiently obvious.

> Education brings light, and light perception, and with quickened fac-
> ulties the negro sees the difference between his real and his constitu-
> tional status in the republic. He sees that neither worth nor merit nor
> attainment can overcome the world-wide repulsion of type and color;
> and, seeing this, he is moved to rebellious protest and sometimes to vi-
> olent revenge.

Thwarted in his ambitions, marked by public sentiment as an inferior, denied a social elevation commensurate with his intellectual training, the educated Negro was likely to visit his resentment on the most prized possession of white men—their women.[108]

To protect "the chastity of white women," to preserve southern white civilization, was to reduce black expectations and ambitions. And since education did more than anything else to elevate those expectations and ambitions, common sense—if not the internal security of the white South and the sanctity of white womanhood—demanded a reconsideration of the issue. Was it not possible, a prominent white politician wrote to President Theodore Roosevelt, that educating blacks armed them with a weapon they might use to combat whites? That argument, he thought, was gaining credence in the South "by the disposition on the part of the negro everywhere apparent to declare himself independent of the white man." In her crusade to awaken the nation to the nature of the black menace, Rebecca Felton noted that in her state of Georgia the number of crimes committed by blacks increased proportionally to the amount of money spent on black education. In expressing support of Felton's crusade, a northern woman offered advice Felton had already embraced: "When the people of the South I mean the *white* people learn to *curb the education* of the Negro then will they learn the value of the purity of our sex."[109]

The association of crime and education gained in popularity in proportion to the increased publicity given to aggressive behavior by literate blacks. "Book learning has not proved to be a blessing to them as a rule," a North Carolinian affirmed, citing the growth in court cases and blacks in prisons and on chain gangs. "You do not find many in these places that are unable to read." The president of North Carolina Agricultural College, after estimating that blacks were "three times as criminal" as whites, found that literate blacks committed the majority of the crimes. Unpersuaded by these arguments, a Raleigh newspaper defended black education. Comparing the number of crimes committed by "educated" whites and uneducated blacks, it questioned the growing inclination to view the educated black criminal "as a victim of his ill-advised opportunities."[110]

For black Southerners, this proved to be a frustrating, an exasperating, an impossible situation. Even as whites scorned black incompetence, they feared evidence of black competence. Even as whites mocked the intellectual pretensions of blacks, they feared intelligent blacks. Even as whites derided blacks for their ignorance, they resented educated, literate, and ambitious blacks. "We, the Southern people, entertain no prejudice toward the ignorant per se inoffensive Negro," an Alabama editor explained. "It is because we know him and for him we entertain a compassion. But our blood boils when the educated Negro asserts himself politically. We regard each assertion as an unfriendly encroachment upon our native superior rights, and a dare-devil menace to our control of the affairs of the state." After insisting that the South had given the Negro "the best education fitted for the life he was to live," a Georgia editor and publisher threw up her hands in exasperation over the effects of black schools. "The more education the negro receives the more ungrateful he becomes for the blessings that have made this education possible."[111]

For blacks to acquire an education threatened many whites, including those who argued that blacks were mentally unfit to be educated. For blacks to remain ignorant and illiterate, on the other hand, invited toleration, even as whites used that ignorance and illiteracy to exploit blacks and to justify white superiority. What fed white apprehension and talk of race war were not so much perceptions of a race regressing but rather of one that was progressing. How were black Southerners to resolve this kind of paradox? What could they do for themselves that would not be construed as a threat to the internal security of the dominant society? W. E. B. Du Bois came to appreciate the depth of white fears and how those fears were directed less at the vagabond or the criminal black as at the educated black "who is coming forward":

> If my own city of Atlanta had offered it to-day the choice between 500 Negro college graduates—forceful, busy, ambitious men of property and self-respect, and 500 black cringing vagrants and criminals, the popular vote in favor of the criminals would be simply overwhelming. Why? because they want Negro crime? No, not that they fear Negro crime less, but that they fear Negro ambition and success more. They can deal with crime by chain-gang and lynch law, or at least they think they can, but the South can conceive neither machinery nor place for the educated, self-reliant, self-assertive black man.[112]

Curtailing the educational opportunities of blacks, along with segregation and disfranchisement, were important mechanisms of racial control. In the white mind, these were all ways to resolve racial ten-

sions. Not only would limited schooling contain black political and social ambitions, but it also would help whites to maintain an adequate
source of cheap labor. And, consistent with white perceptions of a new
generation of blacks, it would discourage black independence, advancement, and achievement. Reflecting over why whites should be
so "unsettled" over "a few inefficient, grotesquely inefficient negro
schools," a University of Mississippi professor provided a response that
went to the very heart of the issue: "Because the white people want to
'keep the negro in his place,' and educated people have a way of making their own places and their own terms." If whites feared "liberated
minds," he suggested, it was because such minds contemplated rights
and demands that, in the case of black people, would result in racial
strife and endanger the entire community. "So thinks the average white
man."[113]

Black Southerners readily understood the professor's observation.
They understood, too, that in the estimation of many fearful whites
what separated the New Negro from the old Negro was access to
schools and the acquisition of literacy. A story that would make the
rounds among blacks, no doubt spanning several generations, revealed
once again a marvelous insight into the workings of the white mind. As
he was leaving the railroad depot with a northern visitor, a southern
white man saw two Negroes, one asleep and the other reading a newspaper. He kicked the Negro reading a newspaper. "Would you please
explain that?" the Northerner asked. "I don't understand it. I would
think that if you were going to kick one you would kick the lazy one
who's sleeping." The white Southerner replied, "That's not the one
we're worried about."[114]

5

WHATEVER TOLERATION and public support whites afforded
black schools assumed a rigid segregation between white and black
pupils. During Reconstruction, short-lived experiments in biracial education had occurred, mostly in New Orleans, but it quickly became
clear even to black legislators that they would have to abandon the goal
of racially integrated public schools. The light-skinned black lieutenant
governor of Louisiana managed to send his children to a school with
whites, but it did not last long; the white children harassed them until
they were withdrawn. "They're good enough niggers," one of the

white boys observed, "but still they're niggers; you can't teach 'em not to be black."[115]

By the end of Reconstruction, the issue had been settled. "The only condition under which the two races can co-exist peacefully," declared a New Orleans newspaper in 1874, "is that in which the superior race shall control and the inferior race shall obey." That editorial observation came in response to raids conducted by mobs of whites, expelling students "visibly Negro" from the city schools and questioning those who appeared to be white but were suspected of having Negro blood. Some years later, New Orleans public schools dispatched their finest white pupils to a "spelling bee" in Cleveland, only to find that they would be forced to compete with some black children. The superintendent of schools in New Orleans accepted responsibility, made a public apology for his error, and promised that in the future no race mixing would ever occur in any school function, lecture, or ceremony.[116]

The insistence on segregated schools sometimes extended to any contact by whites with those institutions, even as visitors. In Orangeburg, South Carolina, "a well-to-do white citizen" made a public apology in the local newspaper for accepting an invitation by a black school to make some remarks to the children. "I am heartily sorry for what I did, and I hope after this humble confession and expression of regret that all whom I have offended will forgive me." Accompanying the letter was an affidavit signed by various citizens claiming they were "as anxious to see the coloured race elevated as any people," but they insisted that this be done "inside the colour line." Even for some southern whites, however, the incident made a mockery of their region. Condemning the apology, the *Charlotte Observer* thought it betrayed white "narrowness and malignity. . . . Few people have conceived that race prejudice went so far, even in South Carolina."[117]

During Reconstruction, the controversy over racial integration had caused considerable turmoil in higher education. Rather than admit blacks, some universities closed their doors altogether or tried to survive without state funding. In those states where blacks wielded political power, opportunities might actually expand for black students. The University of South Carolina admitted blacks, and the legislature appointed blacks to the board of regents. By 1875 most whites had withdrawn from the university, some 90 percent of the students were black, and more than a third of these were on state scholarships. The overthrow of the Reconstruction governments, however, fully restored segregation throughout the southern educational system. James H.

Johnson entered the University of South Carolina in 1874; the end of Reconstruction in that state in 1876 also terminated his college education. "I was in my junior year, when I left." Once having ousted the blacks, college authorities tried to bring back teachers and students who had earlier abandoned the institution. In seeking the return of one former professor, a trustee assured him, "Nothing could be farther from my thoughts than suggesting, in the remotest manner possible, that you should return here to teach negroes, or to connect yourself with any educational institution in which they are present or are likely to be present in social or other equality with our race."[118]

Where maintaining a dual system proved impossible, black schools might be nonexistent or located at considerable distance from each other. The Bluffton school district in South Carolina chose to settle this matter in a unique—and no doubt exceptional—manner. The white teacher agreed to divide the school day into two sessions, morning and afternoon, one for whites and one for blacks, and he would teach both sessions.[119]

To black parents and students, the opportunity to be educated assumed a greater importance than whether they would share the same classrooms with whites. Many took pride, in fact, in their own institutions, and in the camaraderie and relaxation of racial tensions that separation made possible. As a student at Georgia State Industrial College near Savannah, Richard R. Wright, Jr., recalled how he and his companions boasted of their prowess relative to their white counterparts. "If they think they are better than we are . . . why don't they meet us on equal terms? We are ready to meet any white students in debate, in baseball, football or in foot races." Of course, Wright and his friends knew whites would reject such an offer, and the reason was readily apparent to them. "They are afraid we will beat them."[120]

Some black leaders and newspapers, by the 1890s, had launched campaigns to replace all white teachers in black schools ("mixed schools," they sometimes called them) with black teachers. "If we are to have separate schools," declared the *Baltimore Afro-American* in 1895, "and we are perfectly satisfied and contented to have them thus, they ought to be wholly so, as much as are the schools provided for white pupils." If it be deemed "right in principle" for white teachers to instruct black children, the paper argued, it was "equally right" for black teachers to instruct white children. "Why should one class of citizens enjoy more privileges in this matter than other citizens?"[121]

On the eve of World War I, schools remained rigidly segregated. Few Southerners, black or white, made much of an issue of the separation. Although blacks continued to agitate for full and equal access to public facilities, many were willing to accept segregation in education provided the schools were equal in quality, comfort, and the allocation of funds. That would remain for nearly half a century the principal issue, not so much the separation as the equalization of educational opportunities and resources. Most often, however, blacks were hard-pressed to maintain what little they had gained since Reconstruction.

This had to be a far cry from what the pioneers of black education had envisaged. Back in 1870, Frederick Douglass's newspaper predicted that the day would come "when people will smile at the fact that this question could have been discussed with so much acrimony of spirit." Half a century later, the "acrimony of spirit" had, if anything, been heightened, and the prospects for improving the conditions under which black children attended school were not encouraging. It proved easier to attribute black ignorance to racial inferiority, to a limited intellectual capacity. That argument not only had a way of quieting critics but was also far less costly to taxpayers. "Expenditures of time, energy and money must be per capacity of the negro instead of per capita," a prominent white editor insisted, and he suggested at the same time that those Negroes who had been "miseducated" be returned "to the proper starting point before it is too late."[122]

6

RAISING HER FAMILY near Stonewall, Mississippi, Ida Yates told her son about the school she had attended in her youth. "We young ex-slaves were all in this room, classes were conducted in shifts. Those who had to wait their turn sat by the creek or waded in the cool, running water." When six-year-old James Yates prepared to enter first grade in 1912, he walked some ten miles to reach the same log cabin school his grandmother and mother had once attended. "Things hadn't changed much since then," he recalled. "There was still the same schoolhouse and the same teacher. We played in the same creek. One thing new was added—baseball, with balls made from rags, and broomsticks used as bats."[123]

In *Plessy* v. *Ferguson,* the Supreme Court of the United States in 1896 recognized and validated the principle of "separate but equal" facilities for blacks and whites. But in practice, if schools for blacks were to be tolerated in the South, they were not only to be separate but unequal, inferior in every way to opportunities afforded white students. The separate and unequal school system stood as one of the principal legacies and cornerstones of white supremacy.

Throughout the South, then, with few exceptions, the story of black schools became a case study in deliberate and criminal neglect. W. E. B. Du Bois did not exaggerate when he described the history of black education in the New South as "enforced ignorance." To attend school in a building that resembled "a tobacco barn" was not conducive to a genuine education, one teacher in a black school observed, but it did not necessarily hurt the child. "It does hurt, though," she added, "to have the largest classes, the poorest paid teacher, the shortest school year, and an acute shortage of books, paper, pencils, blackboards, and maps." [124]

And it hurt to know that states often used funds appropriated for black schools to improve and sustain the education of whites. In opting for racial segregation, the white South chose a dual school system it could not afford to support. With white and black schools competing for available funds, black schools were certain to be the principal victims. In Lowndes County, Alabama, a school for blacks operated for three months, but some years it never opened. Authorities explained that the money for school purposes had been depleted to vaccinate local residents. The white school, however, operated as usual. Ned Cobb insisted that in Alabama the state often used funds appropriated for black schools to maintain the education of whites ("[w]hite schools was runnin on part of the colored schools' money"); any financial shortage was sufficient reason to shut down the black schools. "Mighty little we got from the state government. That money was comin here through white hands and they was half-concerned with keepin colored children *out* of school. . . . Sometimes, school wouldn't run over a month and a half or two months and they'd send out word from Beaufort, 'Close the schools down, close the schools down. Money's out.' Colored had to close their schools down, white folks' schools was runnin right on till May."[125]

To little avail, blacks reacted with anger to the neglect of their educational needs, and the degree to which their own tax money might be used to help finance the white schools. In Mississippi, blacks asked the state legislature in 1918 "by what process of reasoning" it could take the common funds of both races "and use it to the glory of your children and leave ours in ignorance, squalor and shame." But whites remained essentially unmoved. In the early twentieth century, popular campaigns in the South to improve the educational level of whites often came at the expense of blacks. By 1901, W. E. B. Du Bois reported, the black school system had not cost white taxpayers "a cent." Between 1880 and 1910, in fact, in most of the South, black taxpayers actually helped to subsidize the white school systems.[126]

Statistics of black education in the late nineteenth century describe a dreary ending to the commitment made during Reconstruction to equal public education. In cutting the costs of government, the state legislatures of the New South sacrificed the public school system on the altar of "economy." After viewing the schools in Suwanee River country, a visitor claimed to find what he had seen elsewhere in the South in the early 1900s. "The negroes are semi-outcasts. They get only the dregs." A white state school official in North Carolina concurred. He found in 1913 the average black rural schoolhouse "a disgrace" to any civilized people. "To one who does not know our history, these school-houses, though mute, would tell in unmistaken terms a story of injustice, inhumanity and neglect on the part of our white people." Even "the most tolerant minded" whites, he noted, looked upon black schools "as a liability rather than an asset," based on the commonly accepted theory "that the poorer the school supplied to the Negroes, the better it would be for society and the state."[127]

No matter how it was measured—by the quality of the facilities, the length of the school term, financial appropriations, student-teacher ratio, curriculum, teachers' preparation and salaries—the education available to black children in the New South was vastly inferior to that available to white children. At least twice as much was spent on white students as on black students, and in many states the ratio was far more lopsided. The minimum salary for white teachers was nearly twice as high as the maximum salary paid black teachers. Few books or supplies were available in black schools, placing an even greater burden on the already underpaid teachers. When Benjamin Mays entered school at age six in 1900, South Carolina spent $6.51 annually on each white child in school, $1.55 on each black child. Fifteen years later, Mays entered high school. The state in 1915 spent $23.76 on each white child in school, $2.91 on each black child. That same year, the superintendent of education in South Carolina thought to ask, "Is it too much to hope for a minimum of $25 per white child and $5 per Negro child?"[128]

The same patterns, the same statistics of neglect, prevailed elsewhere in the South. Although blacks comprised a majority of the population of Mississippi, no state gave less to black education between 1890
and World War II. At the turn of the century, blacks in Mississippi
made up 60 percent of school-age children, but they received only 19
percent of the state's school funds; the state superintendent of education acknowledged in 1899 that the public school system had been designed "primarily for the welfare of the white children of the state, and
incidentally for the negro children." After reporting that in Alabama
some $22.96 was spent annually for each white child's education, but
only 98 cents for each black child, a northern black newspaper could
only agree with Booker T. Washington's sarcastic comment on the
enormous comparative advantage enjoyed by white schools over
black schools: "This is too high a compliment to pay to our natural
intelligence."[129]

The consequences were readily apparent. When Pauli Murray entered school in Durham, North Carolina, in the 1920s, she inherited
nearly half a century of separate and unequal education in the South.
The schoolhouse, located in the West End, resembled a warehouse
more than a school. The dilapidated two-story wooden structure
creaked and swayed in the wind as if it might collapse. The exterior
showed the effects of some hard winters. The interior featured bare
and splintery floors, leaky plumbing, broken drinking fountains, and
smelly toilets that were usually out of order. "It was never the hardship
which hurt so much," Murray remembered, "as the contrast between
what we had and what the white children had." The new books white
children used ("we got the greasy, torn, dog-eared books"), the field
days in the city park white children enjoyed ("we had it on a furrowed
stubby hillside"), the prominent mention white children received in the
newspapers ("we got a paragraph at the bottom"), the attention bestowed on public displays in white schools by city officials, including the
mayor ("we got a solitary official")—all served to set the white schools
apart from the black schools. No one pretended to take seriously the
Supreme Court decision commanding separate but equal schools. To
Murray, the school she attended defined her very being. "Our seedy
run-down school told us that if we had any place at all in the scheme of
things it was a separate place, marked off, proscribed and unwanted by
the white people." The lesson imparted was absolutely clear. Whatever
else Murray learned in school, she came to understand that her color
marked her as an inferior in the eyes of whites, regardless of how she

conducted herself, regardless of how well she did in school, regardless of her social class.[130]

If students, parents, and teachers accommodated themselves to a separate and unequal school system, they did so from an absence of alternatives. But accommodation never came easily, nor did it necessarily imply acquiescence. Leona McCauley taught in a one-room, one-teacher rural school that "was just a little shack," and she made the best of the situation. But she also impressed on her daughter, Rosa, born in 1913 and growing up near Montgomery, Alabama, that this was not "the way it was supposed to be."[131] Some forty years later, when Rosa McCauley Parks refused to give up her seat on a Montgomery bus, her mother's admonition became an impetus to action.

7

FOR THOSE WHO completed their schooling, whether at the high school or college level, commencement exercises were a special event, a time to recognize and celebrate their academic achievement and to contemplate future prospects. If a special occasion for the students, graduation was a critical time for administrators, as the festivities were open to the public and attended by various white dignitaries and trustees. Since administrators regularly walked a fine line between satisfying their benefactors and meeting the needs of faculty and students, an event that brought all these groups together took on added importance. Wishing to impress outsiders, administrators feared any action or appearance that might prove embarrassing or disruptive.

The adult commencement speaker was often white, perhaps a trustee, a city or state official, a professor from a nearby college, a donor, or a prominent local citizen. In a message that conveyed hope and encouragement to the graduates, the speaker would invariably invoke images of self-reliance, the traditional work ethic, and moral values embraced by most Americans in the late nineteenth century. The speaker could also be expected to maintain a proper distance, "blessing the graduates," as one teacher recalled, "without going near them and saying what adults always say to youth as if they believed what they were speaking."[132]

If a black dignitary addressed the graduates, he usually repeated the same platitudes, proclaiming, as did Norris W. Cuney in addressing commencement exercises in Milam County, Texas, that the race that demonstrated the most energy and thrift was bound to succeed. And like others, he seized the occasion to extol the virtues of industrial training. "It is cruel to drive the mechanical genius of your boy into an early grave by having his head crammed with Latin and Greek, when he is born with the soul of invention and the deftness of the machinists." The black speaker, often a self-made merchant, landowner, or minister, might also be expected to appear as an exemplar to the graduates. As they had succeeded, others could also succeed, provided they possessed the necessary character, shrewdness, and fortitude to take advantage of the opportunities afforded them. In a graduation address at Hampton Institute, Congressman George White of North Carolina warned in 1899 that a diploma by itself did not ensure success. "[Y]our success in life will depend, not on that piece of paper, but on your self, on your own manhood and womanhood." But within a year, addressing his colleagues in the House of Representatives, White sounded a different note:

> It is easy . . . to taunt us with our inferiority, at the same time not mentioning the causes of this inferiority. It is rather hard to be accused of shiftlessness and idleness when the accuser . . . closes the avenues for labor and industrial pursuits to us. It is hardly fair to accuse us of ignorance when it was made a crime under the former order of things to learn enough about letters to even read the Word of God.

After completing his term, White chose exile in the North to continued repression and denial in the South.[133]

The valedictorians assumed an important responsibility in commencements, as they would represent the students before the larger public. Admonished to avoid anything that smacked of politics, racial grievances, or controversy, they were expected to extol the virtues and moral principles on which their education had been based, as well as the administrators and benefactors who had made their education possible. The valedictorian of the Class of 1875 at Hampton Institute (the same class in which Booker T. Washington graduated) talked about the need for intelligence and racial harmony, and, in the view of one observer, "showed a comprehension of the ignorance and superstition of the black race."[134]

Of critical importance, the valedictorian was expected to allay any apprehensions of whites in the audience about the content of the edu-

cation he had received. At the state college he attended in South Carolina, Benjamin Mays recalled that if the valedictorian had majored in
English or history, the school's president made certain that some student also gave a speech extolling the glories of agriculture and the
trades. When W. E. B. Du Bois completed his work at Fisk University in
1888, each of the five graduates gave a commencement oration, all of
which stayed well within the accepted guidelines: "Anglo-Saxon Influence," "Women in Public Life," "Feudalism," and "Thought as the
Prime Condition of Progress." Du Bois opted to address the audience
on his boyhood hero, Otto von Bismarck. Graduating from Austin
High School in Knoxville in 1907, James A. Atkins wrote the class song
and as valedictorian chose to lecture on "Knowledge Is Power." A "red-
letter event" in the Knoxville black community, the graduation exercises were held at a local theater—an elegant establishment that once a
year permitted blacks to sit in any seat.[135]

To make certain their admonitions were heeded, and to avoid any
public embarrassment, the principal or college president might be expected to hear or scrutinize the address before it was given—or he
might choose to write it himself. Selected as the class valedictorian,
Richard Wright contemplated what he would tell the audience, only to
have a speech handed to him written by the principal. He told the principal he had prepared his own speech. The principal was not impressed. "Listen, boy," he admonished Wright, "you're going to speak
to both *white* and colored people that night. What can you alone think
of saying to them?" Wright insisted that people were coming to the ceremony to hear the students, and he would make his own speech. The
principal's impatience turned to exasperation: "You can't afford to just
say *anything* before those white people that night," and he noted that the
superintendent of schools would be present and that Wright was in a
position to make a good impression on him. "I've been a principal for
more years than you are old, boy. I've seen many a boy and girl graduate from this school, and none of them was too proud to recite a speech
I wrote for them." When Wright remained determined to deliver his
own speech, the principal called him "a young, hotheaded fool,"
threatened to hold back his graduation, and then suggested that his cooperation might be rewarded with a teaching position in the school system or a scholarship for college. Rejecting the offer, Wright responded,
"I want to learn, professor. But there are some things I don't want to
know." And with those words he left the office. "I went home," Wright

recalled, "hurt but determined. I had been talking to a 'bought' man and he had tried to 'buy' me. I felt that I had been dealing with something unclean." His classmates and his uncle pleaded with him to deliver the principal's speech, suggesting that his future prospects were at stake. Upon reading what the principal had given him, Wright conceded that it was "simpler and cleaner" than his address, "but it did not say anything; mine was cloudy, but it said what I wanted to say." In the end, the principal relented, fearing Wright might cause an uproar that would be even more damaging to the school. On graduation night, Richard Wright presented the speech he had written. "When my voice stopped there was some applause. I did not care if they liked it or not; I was through. Immediately, even before I left the platform, I tried to shunt all memory of the event from me. A few of my classmates managed to shake my hand as I pushed toward the door, seeking the street."[136]

The mottoes selected by graduating classes—"By Example We Lift As We Climb," "There Is Room at the Top," "Deeds, Not Words"—exemplified the success ethic embraced by students, faculty, and administrators and anticipated much of the content of the commencement addresses. But if most graduation speeches and class mottoes suggested limitless horizons, black graduates faced, in fact, rigidly limited prospects. The Class of 1886 at Tuskegee Institute, for example, felt sufficiently optimistic about their prospects to adopt as their motto "There Is Room at the Top." No doubt the school's principal, Booker T. Washington, encouraged the class in embracing such lofty aspirations. But in the town of Tuskegee, experience taught many blacks the dangers of success, that white people were apt to resent successful blacks as vehemently as they feared educated blacks. "I know men who won't keep a horse," one Tuskegee resident declared. "If they get one they will sell it. If you ask such a one why he sold his horse he very likely will say: 'A white man see me in dat 'ere horse, he look hard at me. I make [up] my min' a mule good 'nugh for a ole nigger like me.'"[137]

The black graduates would need to temper their expectations. They would need to learn to play by a different set of rules. They would need to know how to accommodate to white expectations. Having already confronted white skepticism about their education, they would need now to face white fears over any evidence of their success. Obviously not the stuff of which commencement speeches were made, this was nonetheless the real world the "educated" young black man and woman entered in the late nineteenth and early twentieth centuries.

Formal schooling could do only so much to prepare them for that world. "You see, schoolin helps a heap of folks," Josh Horn reflected, "and I is glad the children is got some. But I been thinkin—it ain't always book learnin that counts the most; sometimes it's learnin what you gets just studyin what other folks *does,* that lets in the light."[138]

CHAPTER THREE

WORKING

*They meet with darkness in the daytime. And they grope at noonday as in the
night.*

—Book of Job, 5:14

She was thinking of nothing now; her hands followed a lifelong ritual of toil.

—Richard Wright

Ain't it hard, ain't it hard,
Ain't it hard, to be a nigger, nigger, nigger?
Ain't it hard, ain't it hard?
For you can't git yo' money when it's due.

—Heard in Newton County, Georgia, 1909[1]

WHEN W. E. B. DU BOIS traveled by "Jim Crow Car" through the
Black Belt of Georgia, some thirty-five years had passed since the end
of slavery. But its "dark heritage" and many of its vestiges were everywhere to be seen, along with its survivors and their memories. "This
land was a little Hell," a black farmer told Du Bois. "I've seen niggers
drop dead in the furrow, but they were kicked aside, and the plough
never stopped. Down in the guardhouse, there's where the blood ran."
The bleakness of the countryside, with its rows of old, dismal one-
room cabins, resembled the bleak and cheerless renters and laborers
who inhabited them and toiled in the adjacent fields. It was here in the
heart of the Black Belt, with the people he met acting as a kind of
tragic chorus, that Du Bois sensed he had rediscovered the past and
come face-to-face with his cultural and racial heritage. It was here, he
thought, in this "land of rapid contrasts and of curiously mingled hope
and pain," that he had found "the Negro problem in its naked dirt and
penury."

The once-flourishing farms and plantations that made up the Cotton Kingdom had fallen on hard times, along with the residences of the "slave barons," reduced now to "phantom gates" and fading recollections of a "merry past." The happy, carefree "darkies" had become what they had always been—necessary figments of a vivid white imagination, found now mostly in the images and artifacts of popular culture, in renditions of a history whites wanted so desperately to believe. "They are not happy," Du Bois observed, "these black men whom we meet throughout this region. There is little of the joyous abandon and playfulness which we are wont to associate with the plantation Negro. At best, the natural good-nature is edged with complaint or has changed into sullenness and gloom, and now and then it blazes forth in veiled but hot anger."

Many of the young blacks in the region filled the prison farm (or "stockade," as some called it), sentenced there, local blacks claimed, not because they had committed a crime but to provide the forced labor on which the state depended for much of its income. Occasionally Du Bois would encounter a relatively prospering and independent black farmer who had somehow managed to retain his land and make a living out of it. "I says, 'Look up! If you don't look up you can't get up,' " one black farmer declared, attributing his success to persistence. But most of the laborers Du Bois met had fallen victim to a system that crushed hopes and stifled ambition.

The problem lay not in the willingness of blacks to work the land they knew so intimately but in the betrayal of their expectations, in the failure to reap rewards that were in any way commensurate with their labor. Du Bois listened to story after story from hardworking blacks cheated of their earnings, turned off their lands, or refused land they could afford to purchase. When Luke Black spoke "hopelessly" of his prospects, Du Bois wondered, "Why should he strive? Every year finds him deeper in debt." From the meager yield of cotton, black tenants needed to pay a quarter to a third of the crop in rent and most of the rest in interest on the food and supplies they had purchased on credit. No wonder so many of them had been reduced from tenants to day laborers, trying to subsist on the dollar-and-half-a-week salary when work was available. Still another black farmer related his life history: He had labored for forty-five years, "beginning with nothing and still having nothing." Discouraged, resentful, "hopelessly in debt," he stopped Du Bois along the roadside to inquire about a black youth in nearby Albany, reportedly shot and killed by a policeman for talking too loud on the sidewalk. "Let a man touch me, and he dies," he told

Du Bois, speaking slowly and with added emphasis. "I don't boast this,—I don't say it around loud, or before the children,—but I mean it. I've seen them whip my father and my old mother in them cotton-rows till the blood ran. . . ."

The economics of the black South seemed fairly elementary. The "keynote" of the Black Belt, Du Bois found, was the persistence of debt—the inability of most people to make income cover expenses. "The country is rich, yet the people are poor," Du Bois wrote, and "a pall of debt hangs over the beautiful land; the merchants are in debt to the wholesalers, the planters are in debt to the merchants, the tenants owe the planters, and laborers bow and bend beneath the burden of it all." Few incentives existed to make the tenant farmer or laborer become a better farmer; if anything, the unambitious enjoyed a greater degree of toleration, as they threatened no one and reinforced the racial assumptions of whites. It was this lack of incentive, Du Bois insisted, that took its inevitable toll on the work ethic. "They are careless because they have not found that it pays to be careful; they are improvident because the improvident ones of their acquaintance get on about as well as the provident. Above all, they cannot see why they should take unusual pains to make the white man's land better, or to fatten his mule, or save his corn." The white employer, on the other hand, showed the northern visitor the worn-out land, the ruined mansions, and the seemingly "sulky, dissatisfied, and careless" workforce and exclaimed, "This is Negro freedom!" A white merchant in Albany, Georgia, told a black customer, "Why, you niggers have an easier time than I do," to which the black man replied, "Yes, and so does yo' hogs."

Even as blacks came to learn soon after emancipation the limited content of their freedom and prospects, whites eager to retain their laborers found that a "slavery of debt" worked almost as effectively as the old slavery of legal ownership. That was the reality Du Bois immediately grasped on this trip through the Black Belt. And the consequences were readily apparent in the people's faces, movements, and expressions. A ragged black man sitting on a log, aimlessly whittling a stick, spoke softly and indistinctly as he captured for his visitor the essence of black economics in the New South: "White man sit down whole year; Nigger work day and night and make crop; Nigger hardly gits bread and meat; white man sittin' down gits all. *It's wrong.*"[2]

Field hands translated those sentiments into song, articulating the same distinct message in various versions:

Niggers plant the cotton,
Niggers pick it out,
White man pockets money,
Niggers does without.[3]

De big bee suck de blossom,
De little bee make de honey,
De black man makes de cotton and corn,
And de white man totes de money.[4]

2

WITH "THE SURRENDER," as blacks called it, the War for Southern Independence and the enslavement of black men and women both came to an end. It remained for the vanquished—white Southerners—to accept the reality of defeat, their continuing dependence on black labor, and the need to make a settlement with nearly four million black men and women who had their own ideas about freedom and work. The possibilities were suddenly enormous for a fundamental reorganization of southern life. No wonder that for many freed blacks it was an exhilarating time, not so much a "jubilee" as a moment of intense hope and heightened expectations. Much of the hope and many of the expectations came to be focused on the opportunity to achieve some semblance of economic independence, to be free of the arbitrary power of white people to determine every aspect of their working lives.

But black Southerners badly underestimated the staying power of those men and women accustomed to ruling their lives. Whites had their own ideas about black freedom and moved quickly to dictate the terms of that freedom. No sooner had slavery ended than former masters and mistresses talked confidently of how the newly freed slaves would remain dependent on them for guidance and support. But whether in the house or in the fields, the same class that had thought blacks to be tied to them by feelings of dependence soon came to discover how painfully dependent they were on their black laborers, how helpless they were to look after themselves. "They don't like 'em and yit they cain't git along without 'em," a Georgia black observed in summing up white sentiment.[5]

The testimony of white women forced to assume responsibility for the daily chores once undertaken by their help was virtually unanimous on their continued preference for blacks, and it remained so long after the war ended. "My wife says she would not have felt so bad about the results of the war," an Alabama mill owner declared, "if it had only left her her negro servants." Few white "ladies" with whom she was familiar, a Virginia woman noted, could even contemplate trusting the care of their babies to white nurses. Nor, in the estimation of another woman, could whites replace blacks in the kitchen. "If I have white help in my kitchen, I feel as if I'd got to work with them and be careful what I asked them to do; but I have no hesitation in ordering a nigger just as I please, and never think of needing to do anything myself."[6]

If few white families cared to acknowledge their helplessness in the absence of blacks, the women and men who worked for them knew only too well. "They need us all the time," a black domestic said of the white family she served. "They don't want no food unless a nigger cooks it. They want niggers to do all their washing and ironing. They want niggers to do their sweeping and cleaning and everything around their houses. The niggers handle everything they wears and hands them everything they eat and drink. Ain't nobody can get closer to a white person than a colored person. If we'd a wanted to kill 'em, they'd a all done been dead."[7]

Nor could the white planter and farmer accustomed to black labor in the fields contemplate any other way of life or work; the attempts after the war to utilize immigrants, native whites, even Chinese laborers in some places simply confirmed the preference for blacks. "I must have niggers to work for me," a Virginia planter conceded some years after emancipation. "I can't do nothin' on my place without 'em. If they send all the niggers to Africa, I'll have to go thar, too." If some whites occasionally fantasized about ridding themselves of the "Negro problem" by ridding themselves of the Negro, few seriously considered it. To contemplate a South without blacks was simply impossible. "Deport them and the South would be ruined," a Charleston man conceded. "We must have their labor, and wherever the niggers go, I go too. If I had to work my land with whites, I'd quit. I couldn't manage or depend on them." And still another white resident posed the alternatives all too starkly. "If to-day they were all to take ship for Africa, who would chop the wood to-morrow morning? Who would make the fire, who cook the breakfast, who serve it, who would dress the baby, who would hitch up the horse, ply the hoe, and guide the plough?"[8]

The dependence of whites on black labor reversed the often

expounded theories about black helplessness and black dependence. The irony of such talk was never lost on black men and women. A story that made the rounds in the early twentieth century responded to growing discussion in the white South of how to replace black labor with white immigrants from Europe. In a small southern town, an elderly black man noted whites coming out of the courthouse, where a meeting had been held. He stopped one of the whites and asked him, "Whut you white fokes doin' in dar? Whut you plottin' 'bout now?" When told they were planning to bring more white people into the South, the black man looked very dubious. "Well, don't you like that, uncle?" the white man asked him. "Don't you think it will be a good thing to have more white people here?" The black man shook his head in obvious disapproval. "No, Ah don't like dat!" The white man insisted on knowing why he objected to more white people. "Cause we Negroes is got all de white fokes hyeah now *dat we kin support!*" the black man responded.⁹

The preference for black labor rested on stereotypes and expectations as old as the southern labor system. The Negro as the workhorse or mule of the South, easily adaptable to the climate and every demand of labor, "naturally cheerful and contented" (as contrasted with northern workers), took on additional force after emancipation, as if whites desperately needed to believe it. "The mule and the nigger, you know, was made the same day, and they're just suited to each other," an Alabama planter explained. "The mule is rough and so is the nigger." The notion persisted that blacks would perform labor and submit to treatment self-respecting whites would refuse to tolerate. A Virginian in need of a man to help him at first asked for either a white or a black but on second thought said he preferred the black "to do my principal hard and drudge farm work." In that same spirit, an Alabama planter made absolutely clear his partiality toward blacks. "Give me Negroes every time. I wouldn't have a low-down white tenant on my place. You can get work out of any Negro if you know how to handle him; but there are some white men who won't work and can't be driven, because they are white."¹⁰

Nothing in the experience of the planter class had prepared them to deal with blacks as free workers, and in many respects they were far less equipped to make the transition to freedom than the former slaves. Few seemed capable of learning new ways and shaking off old attitudes. "They were against your staying free," observed Sam Gadsden, who was born in 1882 and lived and worked on Edisto Island, South Car-

olina. "It was not easy for them. It is as though you had raised some cattle and then the cattle all ran away and were gone. But then they didn't
even stay gone, but came back and hung around the place you thought
was *your* place and you couldn't control them any more. It's easy to see
how you're going to feel. That's the way the white people felt who came
back after the war and found the Colored people living here all about
the place, running free."[11]

Even as they acknowledged emancipation, white families rarely sur-
rendered the convictions with which they had held black men and
women as slaves, and they fully expected those men and women to
maintain the same demeanor and level of obedience. Not only did
whites expect blacks to remain the principal working class, but they also
demanded willing workers who understood and resigned themselves to
their "place." "The white man he thought we ought to still work for
them like we did during slavery time," a former Texas slave recalled. "It
is still that way. . . . They still thinks the negro ought to work for them
for nothing and like it. Well, we do, and they make us like it too."[12] The
kinds of questions whites chose to ask about the future revealed only a
grim determination to recover the past, to find new ways of exploiting
black labor and commanding black lives. "Can not freedmen be organized and disciplined as well as slaves?" a white South Carolinian asked
in 1871. "Is not the dollar as potent as the lash? The belly as tender as
the back?" The three questions posed by this former slaveholder said it
all, as the answers could easily be anticipated. And more than thirty
years later, whites continued to act in that spirit. "When there's trouble," a South Carolina planter told a visitor in the early 1900s, showing
him a hickory wagon spoke, "I just go down with that and lay one or
two of 'em out. That ends the trouble. We've got to do it; they're like
children and once in a while they simply have to be punished. It's far
better for them to take it this way, from a white man, who is their friend,
than to be arrested and taken to court and sent to the chain-gang."[13]

The aspirations of black men and women came into sharp conflict
with the perceived needs of the planter class. What nearly every field
hand aspired to after emancipation was the chance to work for himself
on his own plot of land, to become the proprietor of a small farm. That
was the way to give substance to their freedom, to undergird their political rights with an essential economic independence, and gain a more
certain entrance into the mainstream of an agricultural society. But
such aspirations were not to be realized, at least not on any significant

scale, as whites found unacceptable, even intolerable, black landownership or the prospect of an independent landed black yeomanry. No sooner had the Civil War ended than a Florida planter made perfectly clear his priorities and the priorities of most of his class, at the same time embracing the new business creed of the nation: "There is now nothing between me and the nigger but the dollar—the almighty dollar, and I shall make out of him the most I can at the least expense."[14]

That overriding objective—to "make out of him the most I can at the least expense"—became the guiding principle of labor relations in the New South, and it prevailed no matter who enjoyed political power. What the planter class wanted was an abundant supply of cheap, docile, hungry, and subordinate laborers—the only productive workforce conceivable to them. Recognizing that former slaves possessed neither land nor money for rent or supplies, planters exploited their poverty to exact black labor and to control black lives. "The Idea of a Southerner," a Tennessee man wrote to his sister in Massachusetts in 1904, "is to keep the negroes as nere th line of pauperism as is compatibel with self support." For blacks to succeed in acquiring and working their own land posed dangers as great as those raised by the specter of blacks succeeding as students, voters, or legislators. "As long as they are poor they are all right, but as soon as they get some money they get uppity."[15] For many in the white South, that observation became an article of faith.

Statistics of black landownership mostly confirmed the success of whites in maintaining blacks as a subservient workforce. Blacks worked the land, whites owned the land. Since emancipation, freedmen and freedwomen had coveted land of their own, but even blacks able to pay for such land had often encountered unwilling sellers. "[W]hites will not sell," an observer noted in 1878, "thinking the possession of land a sort of patent of nobility, to which blacks should not be admitted." For most blacks, however, obtaining the necessary means frustrated any thought of independent proprietorship. Even where wartime experiments in leasing lands to freed blacks had proven so promising, as in Mississippi and South Carolina, their abandonment testified all the more dramatically to the betrayal of that promise. "We thought we was goin' to get rich like the white folks," recalled Felix Haywood, who had been a slave in Texas. "We thought we was goin' to be richer than the white folks, 'cause we was stronger and knowed how to work, and the whites didn't and they didn't have us to work for them anymore. But it didn't turn out that way. We soon found out that freedom could make folks proud but it didn't make 'em rich."[16]

Overcoming extraordinary obstacles, some blacks managed to acquire land and make the most of their opportunity. Sufficient numbers did so between the 1880s and 1920 to comprise an emerging rural middle class. Such advances were most pronounced in the upper South, where whites were less resistant to black landownership. But in the areas of heavy black concentration, as in the Black Belt, the advances were far less impressive. The Census of 1880 revealed that in thirty-three counties of Georgia where blacks lived in substantial numbers "not more than one in one hundred" black farmers owned land; twenty years later, only 14 percent of black Georgian farmers owned their farms, and in 1910 only 13 percent. In 1900 an estimated 75.3 percent of black farmers in the South were sharecroppers or tenants.[17]

Attracted by newly opened opportunities, thousands of blacks found themselves lured to the Mississippi Delta in the late nineteenth century. The quality of the lands being cultivated justified the rapid settlement of the region, but for blacks the opportunities seldom evolved into economic independence. From 1890 to World War II, in Mississippi, more than half of the farms and the vast majority of tenant farms were worked by blacks. But three of every four farm owners were white; an estimated 85 percent of all black operators in any given decade did not own the land they farmed. By the 1920s, in the Delta, where the overwhelming majority of the people (some 74 percent) and most farm tenants (86 percent) were black, black owners comprised only slightly more than 2 percent of the farm operators and worked about the same percentage of the cultivated land.[18]

The attention lavished by black editors and leaders on stories of "successful" black farm owners in the late nineteenth and early twentieth centuries masked the fact that such farmers often barely survived. The small units of land they acquired were of questionable quality and not suited to productive crops. Organized and resentful whites were often prepared to drive blacks off more productive lands. Ownership of land, then, gave some black farmers the pretense but not always the substance of economic independence, and many would be forced back into dependence on whites. In most of the South, farm tenantry continued to outstrip ownership (even in the decades in which farm ownership showed increases), and the mass of black agricultural laborers in any of the decades between emancipation and World War II were desperately poor, dependent, and impoverished.

3

BASED ON THEIR perception of the critical economic role they expected to occupy in the newly reconstructed South, blacks had anticipated a different scenario. Even without land of their own, newly freed blacks and the first generations born in freedom hoped to translate white dependence into a modicum of economic success, to have a meaningful voice in determining the conditions under which they would offer their labor. Ned Cobb, an Alabama sharecropper, articulated with particular cogency the quality of the new labor relations. Born in 1885, the son of former slaves, he spent a lifetime seeking the economic independence denied his father. Recalling that struggle, he raised questions and imparted impressions that generations of black Southerners could easily share:

> In my condition, and the way I see it for everybody, if you don't make enough to have some left you aint done nothin, except given the other fellow your labor. That crop out there goin to prosper enough for him to get his and get what I owe him; he's making his profit but he aint going to let me rise. . . . That white man gettin all he lookin for, all he put out in the spring, gettin it all back in the fall. But what am I gettin for my labor? I aint gettin nothin. I learnt that right quick; it's easy to understand if a man will look at it. . . . You want some cash above your debts; if you don't get it you lost, because you gived that man your labor and you can't get it back.
>
> Now it's right for me to pay you for usin what's yours—your land, stock, plow tools, fertilizer. But how much should I pay? The answer ought to be closely seeked. How much is a man due to pay out? Half his crop? A third part of his crop? And how much is he due to keep for hisself? You got a right to your part—rent; and I got a right to mine. But who's the man ought to decide how much? The one that owns the property or the one that works it?[19]

How these questions came to be answered would have a lasting impact on the quality of black lives and the prospects for improving those lives. And for nearly a century, the consequences would profoundly affect race relations. Whether expressed collectively, as in tough bargaining sessions and plantation strikes and walkouts, or individually, as in the personal struggles waged by a Ned Cobb, the efforts of former slaves and the first generations born in freedom to use their labor to force concessions from white employers marked a dramatic break with the past.

Although winning far less than they coveted, black Southerners did not respond passively to perceived limitations placed on their working lives and opportunities. Wherever possible, they rejected working in gangs under white supervisors, believing it to be a relic of enslavement. They chose to break up the slave quarters, if only to underscore their quest for independence. In securing farms of their own and moving onto those farms, whether as purchasers or (more often) as renters, they achieved a certain sense of personal autonomy and forced on the old planter class a reorganization of the labor system. Many of the women who continued to work in white homes no longer lived there, equating the new arrangement with emancipation from the constant surveillance of the white family. Where men and women hired themselves out, they often resisted long-term arrangements, preferring to maintain as much freedom of movement as possible. "[T]he colored people of this vicinity are so proud," a white Virginian noted, "that they think it is somewhat a 2nd slavery to hire by the month or year." And if they returned to work on the old places where they had labored as slaves, they tried to wrest whatever concessions they could. "I am anxious to get the 'Butts Place,' " William White wrote his "Old Master" in Alabama in 1870. "Please let me know whether I can get it or not, and on what terms. . . . I have been doing tolerably well since my freedom, better than most of my old fellow servants. I hope a better day for both black and white is coming in the future."[20]

To dramatize their independence of whites, some black families experimented with new arrangements. In removing themselves from the fields and the white family's house, black women evinced a desire to spend more time tending to the needs of the family and to escape the abuse that often accompanied close proximity to white men. In removing their wives, daughters, and mothers from domestic and field work, many black men sought to assert their position at the head of the family and provide family members with a protection denied them as slaves. From the early days of emancipation, whites registered continual complaints not only over the decline in the quality of domestic labor but also over the number of women who had withdrawn from the kitchens and fields. "The domestics trained in slavery," an observer noted in 1893, "have all either died or scornfully left the boss's house. The fat old colored mammy that presided with such severity in the kitchen is now only a reminiscence."[21] With a new generation of blacks, the complaints of whites turned to the refusal of young black women to perform domestic chores of any kind and the insistence of black parents on sending children to school rather than to the field or having daughters help in the fields rather than cook in the white family's kitchen. "[I]t is not like it used to be when you owned the negroes," a Louisianian confessed, exasperated over his efforts to hire blacks, "it is very difficult to get one to wait on you."[22]

While still a child, Ned Cobb remembered watching his mother toil in the fields, doing "anything my daddy told her to do as far as cultivatin a crop out there . . . that a man ought to done. She'd plow, she'd hoe. . . . She'd be out there with her dress rolled up nearly to her knees, just so she could have a clear stroke walkin." Memories of his mother's toil and her early death no doubt influenced Cobb to arrange things differently in his family. The woman he married had as a teenager worked in the field, chopping and picking cotton and milking the cows. "When we married," Cobb recalled, "that was all off. . . . She worked at the house. Of course, she worked some in the field but she didn't make me no sort of regular hand in the field. When I married her I cut her loose from the field to a great extent. I didn't try to take her teetotally out, but the work she done in the field weren't enough to wear her down." With considerable pride, Cobb noted how he always refused to permit his wife to wash clothes for white families. "I didn't want any money comin into my house from that. My wife didn't wait on white folks for their dirty laundry. There was plenty of em would ask her and there'd be a answer ready for em."[23]

But many black women and children had no choice but to work outside the home. That was clear soon after emancipation. By 1870, in the Cotton Belt, nearly all white wives (98 percent) defined their occupation as "keeping house"; many black wives (40 percent), however, listed their job as "field laborer." Some years later, the percentage of black working women approached 90 percent in the poorest sharecropping households.[24] On some places, white employers threatened to turn a family out of their rented place and confiscate their possessions if every member did not work in the fields. That frustrated many a child's education and sometimes compromised the man's place at the head of the family. Even if landlords made no such demands, most black families found they simply could not survive without every member contributing to the income, and in some instances wives thought it important to share the work to reduce the physical burden on the husband and to enable the children to attend school. "My husband never did like for me to work," Martha Harrison recalled, and he would ask her why she continued to work when he was doing everything in his power to provide for her needs. "Looks like you don't 'preciate what I'm trying to do for you," he would say. "Yes, I do, honey," she would reply, "I jest help you 'cause I don't want you to break down. If you put a load on one horse it will pull him down, but two horses can pull it jest as easy."[25]

Both in the field and in the house, the labor of women proved indispensable. "They do double duty," a Mississippi woman observed, "a man's share in the field, and a woman's part at home." Zora Neale Hurston recalled her father's boast that "he had never allowed his wife to go out and hit a lick of work for anybody a day in her life," but the expectations imposed on her in caring for the eight children and performing the many household tasks would hardly have permitted her to labor elsewhere. The notion of a woman's work as never done was grounded in experience. And the experience varied only slightly from household to household. Up at dawn, she cooked breakfast for the family, after which she joined her husband and the grown children in the fields, plowing or chopping cotton. She would return to the cabin in midmorning to cook dinner, clean up, and return to the fields in the early afternoon and work until sundown. In the evening, she might also be expected to milk the cows and feed the chickens before preparing supper, after which she performed household chores, such as mending, making, washing, and ironing clothes and scrubbing floors. "Plenty of times," a North Carolina woman recalled, "I've been to bed at three and four o'clock and get up at five the first one in the morning. Just with the Lord's help, that's all." It was not as though alternatives were readily available, if at all. Rosina Hoard, born in 1859, bore the double burden as a price of survival. "I had my house work and de cookin' to do and to look after de chillun, but I'd go out and still pick my two hunnert pounds ob cotton a day." Crippled with rheumatism after the birth of one of her sons, she still needed to work in the fields. "I couldn't bend on my knees and pick cotton, 'cause I couldn't git up again." After her husband's death, she added washing clothes to picking cotton. "Since we've been free," she said of her life, "I'se been through de toughs. After I got married, I went through de toughs."[26]

Although young blacks aspired to something else in their lives, including an education, the primary classroom for most of them remained the fields, and the lessons they learned were of hard work, few rewards, and poor prospects. "Don't know much about education," re-marked a former slave who had served in the Civil War. "All I got I got it out in the field. That was my fountain pen and pencil, the blade of the hoe, and my slate was the ground." That same imagery was em-ployed by Richard Manuel Amerson, born in rural Alabama between 1885 and 1890, to describe his lifetime. "I is educated, yassum, to hard work and graderated, yassum, in lies. I write with a hoe and reads with a plow." Amerson had been eager for schooling but after a "two day ed-ucation" he went to work, and he would stay at work in a variety of ca-pacities: farmer, lumberjack, track liner, storm pit builder, well taster, lay preacher. "Anything at all that man has to do to keep on living, I can do it. I can preach the gospel, I can moan and groan, I can counteract conjure stuff, and I can play my mouth harp. And I can look and I can see—that's the biggest part of it all. . . . In the ordinary sense I can't neither read *nor* write. But the sense God gave you don't depend alto-gether on schooling. I was schooled in hard work. . . ."[27]

Even as they labored in the fields and kitchens, many black men and women dwelled on the thought that such labor was necessary if they were to release their children from the same compulsions. It was a way to sustain them as they performed their daily tasks, a way of making some sense out of their labor, particularly the amount of work they performed to enrich other people's lives. "My main object of working was wanting the children to have a better way of living," Maude Lee Bryant said of her labor in Chatham County, North Carolina, "that the world might be just a little better because the Lord had me here for something, and I tried to make good out of it, that was my aim. And I always looked down on nothing being hard, really."[28]

4

THE STORY SURFACED in the 1930s, but the realities it depicted mirrored the experiences of scores of black men and women, probably a sizable majority, in the late-nineteenth-century South. A white man and a black man happened upon two boxes at a rural crossroads (where so much seems to happen in southern black lore). Having spotted the boxes first, the black man ran ahead and opted for the larger box. Upon opening it, he found picks, shovels, and hoes. He then turned around to see how the white man had fared. "Well de Wite man he got de little box and when he open hit dar war pens an pencils an paper an er big count book wat he keeps wat de niggars owes em in. And dats de way hits been eber since. De Nigger just caint outfigger de Wite man for he sure ter cut yer down."[29]

The pens and pencils simply put the finishing touches on the complex arrangements between agricultural labor and capital that emerged after emancipation and persisted until World War II. The system evolved fitfully, and the arrangements varied from place to place, but a recognizable pattern soon emerged. Most plantations were subdivided into individual "farms," ranging usually from ten to thirty acres. The planter rented these "farms" or plots to black families; in many cases, he also furnished the necessary tools, work animals, and seed, and shared the cost of fertilizer. Establishing themselves on their plots, the tenant families worked on "halves," paying the planter one-half of the crop they raised; if the family supplied their own tools and animals, they paid one-fourth to one-third of the crop. In either case, they might have to pledge another portion of the prospective crop to the supply merchant (often the landowner serving in that capacity) for the food and clothing he "furnished" them. In place of plantations, then, a new system of agricultural labor settled into place in which some blacks worked as share-tenants, paying a share of the crop as rent, and some as individual sharecroppers, exchanging their labor for a share of the profits on the crop they produced, less the deductions for the housing, the provisions, the tools, the seed, and the farm animals advanced ("furnished") to them during the year. Substantial numbers of blacks worked under neither tenantry nor sharecropping but as hired wage hands.

The move toward tenant farming, sharecropping, and wage labor reflected the inability of blacks to acquire land of their own after emancipation, whether because they lacked the necessary funds or were barred by local custom. Whites continued to associate black landownership with an independence they did not welcome, as it threatened to undermine their control of a cheap labor force, but they desperately needed black workers. Planters aspired to be laborlords and landlords; blacks aspired to be owners rather than laborers. The sharecropping system came to be perceived by both sides, at least in its initial stages, as a compromise, enabling black families to escape gang labor, work for themselves on their own plots, and achieve a measure of autonomy in their daily lives. The landlord maintained control of the land, drew from a pool of black labor, and still exerted considerable supervisory power over that labor. With a share of the crop acting as an incentive, black families were encouraged to work in the fields, with the head of the family acting out the role of the overseer, meting out punishments to lagging family members if necessary. "[W]here the Negro works for wages, he tries to keep his wife at home," a traveler noted in 1875. "If he rents land, or plants on shares, the wife and children help him in the field."[30]

The preference for renting over sharecropping reflected the amount of economic autonomy a renter could enjoy. The tenant or renter owned the crop he made; the sharecropper did not. Renters had more at stake at harvest time: A poor crop could cost them everything, but they would enjoy higher profits from a good crop than sharecroppers, and they often had more acreage at their disposal. Freer of the landlords' controls, the renters could also raise their own provisions and sell any surplus. Benjamin Mays's father was a renter, owning his own mules and paying a rent of two bales of cotton weighing five hundred pounds each for every twenty acres he rented; the entire family worked on the farm, and some of them supplemented their earnings by working as day hands for white farmers in the neighborhood. Bessie Jones liked the independence renting gave the family. "You see, a sharecropper don't ever have nothing. Before you know it, the man done took it all. But a renter always have something, and then he go to work when he want to go to work. He ain't got to go to work on the man's time. If he didn't make it, he didn't get it." Henry Baker both sharecropped and rented, and clearly preferred to rent. "'Coase when I wuz rentin' lan' I know'd whut I had tuh pay de white folks but when I wuz sharecropper dey paid demselves en let me have de balance. Dat's one reason I say a man ought tuh have a little home uv his own 'cause ef he workin' on somebody else's place, somebody is goin' tuh take 'vantage uv him, don't care who he is."[31]

The vast majority of black Southerners worked as tenants (renters), sharecroppers, or wage hands. Even within the same place, however, different arrangements were possible. As early as 1867, a North Carolina planter reported that most of his workers labored for a share of the crop "but I also have about fifteen good men at wages." On some plantations, workers insisted on working for pay; on others, they insisted on shares. "I am no hireling, Sir," a North Carolina laborer responded in 1874 to the request that he work for wages rather than "halves." The manager of a Louisiana sugar plantation noted in 1887 in the journal he kept that the "hands" were ready to work, all of them "at wages fixed at 65 cts 1st class women 50 cts per day." A nearby planter paid the same wage but chose to retain five cents a day until the crop had been completed. Sam Gadsden made an arrangement in 1906 in which he worked directly for the landlord on the plantation as his rent for using some of the land. He agreed to work one work day a week during growing season for every three acres of land he used; the remaining time he spent working on his own crop. In another unusual arrangement, Bill Patton in the Mississippi Delta rented land from Will Dockery for one-fourth of his crop (supplying his own tools and provisions); he then subrented the land to eight sharecroppers, whom he also "furnished," for half of their crop. The enterprising Patton also owned four logging wagons and teams and ran a profitable business hauling timber. On Saturdays he cooked and sold fish next to the store on the Dockery plantation. "He didn't do no kind of work," his granddaughter recalled, "but he just see to the work being done." His grandson recalled him as "a big farmer on Dockery's."[32]

In opting to become a tenant farmer, sharecropper, or wage hand, the black laborer had hoped to escape the arbitrary economic power exercised by whites and find a rewarding alternative to the dependence and supervised gang labor associated with slavery. Although it fell far short of providing blacks with land they could call their own, the system provided a certain degree of psychic compensation, imparting the feeling if not the actuality of independence. Even as it made more difficult any collective resistance to white depredations, the dispersal of the tenants on the plantation gave each family a much-welcomed distance from whites and hence more personal freedom. By their own hard labor and diligence, moreover, black families expected ultimately to own the land they were working. For most of them, however, such triumphs would be rare in number, expectations were mostly disappointed, and hopes rapidly faded. Almost in proportion to the fall in cotton prices, black indebtedness increased, as did the controls wielded by laborlords and landlords. By 1880 a grateful South Carolina planter could insist, "Our People made no greater mistake, after the war, than the assumption that the abolition of Slavery, annihilated entirely the white man's control over the negro."[33] If sharecropping and tenantry represented a compromise between tenant and landlord, it proved in practice to be a one-sided compromise in which almost all the advantages rested with the planters eager to gain and control black labor. What came to be compromised was not so much the prevailing labor system as the very quality of freedom black Southerners could enjoy.

The cycle of work and debt became as routinized as the labor performed. Having agreed to a contractual arrangement, the black family worked the land allotted to them until the fall, when the cotton was picked, ginned, and baled. The "settlin' time" became "the moment of truth." The tenant or cropper learned the amount his cotton had earned and what he owed for the supplies and interest charged to his account. The disadvantage lay in the fact that the planter sold the crop and the storekeeper kept the books. Time after time, the black laborer came away owing more than he had made, forcing him to deal with the same merchant and landlord for still another year. It was the same every year, Manda Walker recalled, "After de last bale was sold . . . him come home wid de same sick smile and de same sad tale: 'Well, Mandy, as usual, I settled up and it was "Naught is naught and figger is a figger, all for de white man and none for de nigger." ' "[34] No wonder "settlin' time" would become a much-repeated theme in blues songs.

Well, it makes no difference
How you make out your time
White man sho' to bring a
Nigger out behin'.

Chorus:
Ain't it hard? ain't it hard?
Ain't it hard to be a nigger? nigger? nigger?
Ain't it hard? ain't it hard?
For you cain't get yo' money when it's due.

Lemme tell you, white man,
Lemme tell you, honey,
Nigger makes de cotton,
White folks gets de money.

Ef you work all de week
An' work all de time,
White man sho' to bring a
Nigger out behin'.[35]

The settlement placed the black tenant and sharecropper in a vulnerable position. If illiterate, he could not challenge the figures or the contractual arrangement. "Well, you had to take their word for it," Kelly Jackson recalled. "What they said. You couldn't argue with them. You better not 'spute them. They would tell you at the end of the year you just have to take what they say. You couldn't ask no questions." If literate, the laborer still dared not question the settlement, if he valued his job or his life. "I have been living in this Delta thirty years," a Mississippi sharecropper revealed, "and I know that I have been robbed every year; but there is no use jumping out of the frying pan into the fire. If we ask any questions we are cussed, and if we raise up we are shot, and that ends it." The black educator to whom he told the story called his case "a typical one."[36]

For most black tenants and croppers, the settlements simply defied both analysis and questioning.

> *You may work on the railroad*
> *You may work on the freight,*
> *You may get up in the morning*
> *And work till late,*
> *You may work around the house*
> *Till the big settling time—*
> *It makes no difference—*
> *You are coming out behind.*[37]

Not only did planters and storekeepers exploit the credit system to their advantage, but they also resisted every challenge to their authority, deeming it a bad example for other blacks and subversive of the social and economic order. Aaron and Mary Matthews moved onto Lem Jones's farm in 1919 and spent nearly two decades with him. "We never had a fair deal while we was wid Mr. Jones," Mary Matthews recalled. "Every time he settled wid us he took de inside track and 'lowed us what he pleased. We knowed it, but twa'n't no use to complain. . . . We knowed we wouldn't git nothin' dat way but cussin'." Both toiled in the fields and had nothing to show for it. "He charged us wid stuff we didn't know what 'twas for and wouldn't explain nothin'." One year, when the crops were good and prices high, they managed to deposit $600 in the bank and purchase five mules. The idea was to accumulate enough to buy their own piece of land. But when Lem Jones discovered the Matthews family had banked the money (his brother worked in the bank), he refused to furnish them necessary provisions until they had spent everything they had deposited. "What can you do wid sech as dat?" Aaron Matthews asked. "Den next he got busy and worked us out'n de mules, one at a time. At de end o' de year he'd take 'em for debt, claimed we didn't pay out or owed him stuff we didn't know what for." Mary Matthews then purchased a five-cent notebook and asked Jones to write down what he was charging them. "He cussed at me, said I didn't have no sense, I was a fool," and, as Aaron Matthews recalled, "He said nobody should keep no dam' books on his place, and if we didn't like it, Goddam' it, git out!" The recollection still infuriated Aaron Matthews years later. "If I had had justice, we'd be livin' on a farm o' our own right now. I tell you one thing: hell's gettin' het up right now for some folks. De devil's waitin' for 'em; dey're goin' jus' as straight," at which point his wife interrupted him, "Hush talkin' so bad 'bout de man, Aaron. Everybody's got some good in 'em if you can find it."[38]

What the labor system did, along with the laws used to enforce it, was to stifle black ambition and enterprise and make a mockery of the work ethic. When John Hurston left Macon County, Alabama, he did so because sharecropping devastated his prospects for improvement. "There was no rise to the thing," his daughter observed. That was how an Arkansas black woman recalled her family's situation. Every time they made a crop they had little to show for it. "Why didn't you work harder?" the white folks would say, after telling her the seed and provisions advanced had wiped out their profit. "Then they take all the cotton we raise, all the hogs, corn, everything. We was just about where we was in slave days." Sam Gadsden discovered in South Carolina that it was best to divide his cotton among a number of brokers to get the best price, as they cheated him if he appeared overly ambitious or flaunted his success. "They had an allotment there for any Colored farmer, and if you brought in any more than that allotment, they would play a bad trick on you." After dividing his crop, however, "each one thought I had just an ordinary, little crop and he paid me for it." He still paid only half of what the white farmer received but "it was a lot better than no pay at all." Ned Cobb discovered, too, that whites paid less for cotton delivered by black farmers than by white farmers. "Colored man's cotton weren't worth as much as white man's cotton less'n it come to the buyer in the white man's hands. But the colored man's labor—that was worth more to the white man than the labor of his own color because it cost him less and he got just as much for his money."[39]

Landlords and storekeepers, individually or in combination, exploited the poverty, the illiteracy, and the helplessness of their tenants, croppers, and laborers to maintain them in subordination. And the consequences were apparent on the faces of scores of beaten-down workers. William Pickens recalled all too vividly the day in 1888 when his father settled with the landlord on the plantation in Arkansas to which the family had been lured from South Carolina. "Father came home with sad, far-away eyes, having been told that we were deeper in debt than on the day of our arrival. And who could deny it? The white man did all the reckoning. The Negro did all the work." The second year, the entire family worked and made a much larger crop. "But at reckoning time history repeated itself; there was still enough debt to continue the slavery." Whites succeeded, Pickens added, in robbing black people of everything but their humor. In the bottomlands of Arkansas, as elsewhere in the South, blacks depicted the planter on set-tlement day sitting down, taking out his pen, and reckoning the final settlement.

> A nought's a nought, and a figger's a figger—
> All fer de white man—none fer de nigger![40]

Every year, Moses Burse's father thought he would emerge from debt, and every year the landlord told him how much he owed. "What the hell could you do? You living on his place, you couldn't walk off." Some did walk off, but they might not get very far before being re-turned to the workplace. What Robert Curtis Smith observed some years later captured the experiences of many beleaguered black farm-ers at the turn of the century:

> [I]f you make a crop and don't clear nothin' and you still wound up owin' on your sharecrop and on your furnish' and you try to move, well the police be after you then all right. But if you're clear well mostly, you can't go too far because of the money. If you move, or if you try to move, they know if they like the way you work they make you pay somethin' just for holdin' the house up. If, after you pay that you want to move, well you cain't go too far because . . . you gonna need money to carry you on to the place where you can get work. And if you cain't get work at one place you go on to the next place, but you cain't go too far, because you ain't got enough in hand to go that far.

If a tenant or cropper wanted to move, the debts he had accumulated would follow him. The landlord might permit him to leave, however, if the new employer agreed to pay the laborer's debts.[41]

Sensing the discouragement of the workforce, and fearing they might lose their labor, some planters tried to make certain each of their workers received something at the settlement, if only to pacify them. "The niggers ain't contented if they have nothing to show for their year's labor," one planter explained. He tried to ensure a modest surplus for the workers by placing limits on how much they could purchase during the year. "But treat 'em as I do, and your niggers 'll stay with you for years."[42]

When in 1879 thousands of black Southerners left rural Texas, Louisiana, Mississippi, and Tennessee, in what came to be known as the Exodus, many of them cited the need to escape the cycle of indebtedness. After years of "tireless diligence and the nastiest labor," Orange Pucket of Tensas Parish, Louisiana, explained, he still had nothing to show for his efforts. Pucket managed to escape to St. Louis, but many of his fellow Exodusters were far less successful or encountered heavy resistance. In "a fit of madness," John Lewis recalled, he told his landlord, "It's no use, I works hard and raises big crops and you sells it and keeps the money, and brings me more and more in debt, so I will go somewhere else and try to make headway like white workingmen." The landlord turned angrily on his tenant and warned him, "If you try that job, you will get your head shot away." The violence visited upon "Delta runaways," as they came to be called, testified to the seriousness of the threat.[43]

To avoid trouble, if not to preserve their lives, many tenants and croppers had few options but to accept the settlement and stay on for at least another year. A protest was an act of impudence, and few blacks chose to chance it; still fewer could risk or afford taking their case to the courts. Landlords and merchants always had ready explanations for settlements the workers found unfathomable. When a sharecropper in Tunica County, Mississippi, charged that he had been shortchanged in the settlement, the planter's response went right to the heart of the matter: "This plantation is a place for *me* to make the profit, not you." The response summed up more than two centuries of black-white relations in the South, as did the black response that Frederick Douglass recalled hearing before the war.

> *We raise de wheat,*
> *Dey gib us de corn;*
> *We bake de bread,*
> *Dey gib us de cruss;*
> *We sif de meal,*
> *Dey gib us de huss;*

We peal de meat,
Dey gib us de skin,
And dat's de way
Dey takes us in.
We skim de pot,
Dey gib us the liquor,
And say dat's good enough for nigger.[44]

The economics of the New South rested essentially on the servitude of tenantry, sharecropping, and the crop lien. To survive, the tenant or cropper needed credit. Landless, the only security he could offer was the crop he would grow. The local storekeeper or supply merchant provided the credit and secured it by placing a lien on the crop. The tenant had to plant cotton, the only crop with substantial cash value. He had to trade with the same storekeeper until he had paid off his debt; the law forbade him to trade elsewhere. And that forced him to pay exorbitant prices and interest charges ("from 25 percent to grand larceny") for his goods.[45] Written into the statute books, the crop lien underwrote the arrangement by which the tenant mortgaged his crops to purchase his food and supplies; the crop thus became the security for the cash or provisions advanced to plant it. Year after year, the position of the tenant or sharecropper deteriorated; the price he received for his crops did not even come close to paying off his debt, and he was forced to commit himself to still another year to obtain credit. It proved to be an ingenious way for whites to assure themselves of a cheap and bound labor force; it kept blacks in perpetual debt, poverty, and exhaustion from which there was little likelihood of escape or relief.

It was not quite slavery, as many tenants, sharecroppers, and wage hands found ways to move to new places, and some defied the odds and achieved a measure of economic success. But the resemblance to the old compulsions still dismayed southern blacks. Archie Booker, a Virginia black man who had experienced both slavery and freedom, shook his head when he thought about the new labor system that had evolved after emancipation. "Dem sharecroppuhs is jes like slaves," he observed. "Dey don' know slavery is ovuh."[46] As a business proposition, some whites thought the new labor system a distinct improvement over slavery. "The niggers work them [the plantations] just the same," one observer wrote, "and the white men get all the niggers make without the responsibility of caring for the black workers." And to listen to some white observers, black laborers remained as content in poverty

Black Southerners in the Age of Jim Crow

and indebtedness as they had been in slavery. "No other laborer [than the Negro] of whom I have any knowledge," an Alabama planter declared in 1888, "would be as cheerful, or so contented on four pounds of meat and a peck of meal a week, in a little log cabin 14 × 16 feet, with cracks in it large enough to afford free passage to a large sized cat."[47]

Neither the illusion of autonomy imparted by renting nor hard work and frugality could overcome the hopeless cycle of work, debt, and poverty that so sharply circumscribed the economic freedom of black Southerners. Nor could it obscure for very long the fact that most black farmers, although nominally free, worked in a system of coercive labor, enjoying neither ownership of the land nor the full rewards of their work. For black Southerners, the promise of the new organization of labor had been their ability to work for themselves and ultimately achieve independence of whites. But in reality most of them worked the white man's land, planted with the white man's seeds, plowed with the white man's plow and mules, and harvested a crop they owed largely to the white man for the land, the seeds, the plow, and the mules, as well as the clothes they wore and the food they consumed.

Examples of black economic success and landownership existed but failed to proliferate. The great mass of laboring black families, whether they rented lands or worked for wages or shares, remained farmers without land, agricultural workers who comprised a rural proletariat. And the prospects for improving their position were not especially encouraging, as opportunities to escape the system contracted rather than expanded. The bargaining power blacks wielded proved less formidable in practice than in theory. Rather than escaping the arbitrary power of whites, blacks found themselves firmly in their clutches. Rather than achieving independence from whites, black farmers and laborers found themselves plunged ever deeper into dependency and debt, unable to clear themselves of that debt, pledging their future crops to obtain credit and sustain themselves during the current crop.

Until after World War II, each new generation of black Southerners had to face this reality. Born in 1885 (the same year as Ned Cobb), Jesse O. Thomas experienced "shock and frustration" when his father told him that one of the neighbors had offered the owner a larger rental for their land than the Thomas family could afford to pay. They had lived for more than two decades on the land, complying with their contractual agreement, fulfilling their obligations to the owner at the end of each year but retaining little after the debts had been paid. "How can a neighbor cause us to move off our own land and out of our own home?" Jesse asked his father. He would never forget the reply. "We do not own this land. We are sharecroppers."[48]

5

THE FEW BLACKS who succeeded in the New South often held themselves up as models for emulation: If they made it, others could do so by adopting the same work ethic. But some readily acknowledged how difficult a task it would be for others to make it as they had. The annual conferences called in Mississippi to celebrate black economic achievement and hear from successful farmers spent much of the time endorsing the prevailing Gospel of Wealth. At one such meeting, in 1907, speaker after speaker extolled the work ethic and detailed his own achievements. But a member of the audience suddenly interrupted the parade of success stories. He warned the audience not to be misled by the rags-to-riches tales they had heard or read. It would not be that easy, and they should expect unremitting struggle to achieve their ends. "It takes a long sight longer to buy a home and pay for it than it does to tell about it after you get it," he declared, and he enumerated the obstacles he had faced:

> I want to tell you, brother, it took me fifteen years to pay for my home, and during that time I had to undergo all sorts of hardships; getting a home and getting it paid for means to get up before day and stay up late at night; it means you have got to hide yourself on Sunday and to keep folks from seeing your rags while they are going to church with their fine slick clothes on; it means that you have got to see the mouths of your wife and daughters stuck out day by day, while they accuse you of mistreating them; it means that your neighbors will put the devil in your children's heads every time your back is turned; it means that you must eat corn bread and salt meat mixed with cowpeas, and leave off sugar and coffee, and rice, and biscuit, and a whole lot of other things. Brethren, I am telling you what I knows, and if you ain't prepared to stand these things, you better stay like you is.

The interruption had not been welcomed by the organizers of this conference on economic uplift. His remarks created an uproar, in fact, as many members of the audience punctuated the speaker's words with responsive shouts of "Yes, Lord," "Tell it, brother," and "That sho am the Gospel-truth." After one respondent loudly exclaimed, "If that is the case, I believe I'll stay like I is," the president of the conference thought matters had gotten out of hand. Returning to the theme of the meeting, he tried to reassure the audience that times were different now. But the member of the audience who had precipitated the disturbance scoffed at the president's reassurance, exclaiming, "Times don't never get no different with a man that ain't got nothing."[49]

The warning was more than prophetic. If some blacks still refused to resign themselves to the permanent status of landless agricultural workers, the attempts to escape the cycle of indebtedness proved to be exceedingly difficult. Any attempt by black laborers to organize to improve their position encountered an instant and ruthless white response, with the "ringleaders" generally beaten or lynched. Both law and custom were designed to ensure a permanent and tractable black labor force. Failure to fulfill the terms of a contract subjected blacks to civil and even criminal penalties. Replacing the discipline of slavery, vagrancy laws, contract labor laws, and a variety of local ordinances reinforced the power of employers to procure, maintain, and exploit black workers. In many communities, blacks found without "lawful employment or business" were subject to arrest. Almost exclusively aimed at blacks, the vagrancy laws were enforced sporadically, often at harvest time in the event of a labor shortage. Few blacks understood the intricacies of the law as a potent weapon in the hands of landlords and merchants. "Because the colored man wasn't educated to the laws for his use; they was a great, dark secret to him," Ned Cobb explained.[50]

Emigrant agent and enticement laws placed harsh restrictions on labor recruiters and prohibited employers from offering higher wages to attract laborers who were employed elsewhere in the region. Informed that one of his workers had moved onto a neighboring plantation, a North Carolina employer wrote "to say that he [the worker] is under contract to stay and work with me until 1st Feb next and that he is in my debt and to request you to make him leave your place at once."[51] Labor recruiters or employers who attempted to entice a black laborer to leave his or her place of employment ran the risk of imprisonment and heavy fines and vigilante retaliation.

The failure of tenants to maintain their contractual or verbal obligations might result in their expulsion, often with devastating consequences. When Ned Cobb's father suffered a bad crop, he could not pay the landowner his rent in full. Rather than carry him over to the next settlement, the landlord threw him off the plantation, but only after stripping him of his possessions. "They come out there and took that horse and wagon and even went in the pen and got the fattenin hog," Ned Cobb recalled. "They claimed they had a note against him and they took all he had. In those days, it was out of the knowledge of the colored man to understand that if you gived a man a note on everything you had, exactly how you was subject to the laws. . . . I was big enough and old enough to stretch my eyes at conditions and abominate what I seed."[52]

But on many plantations, tenants unable to settle their debts were compelled to stay. Perpetual indebtedness might translate into perpetual confinement to the same workplace. By the end of the nineteenth century, many black workers—the precise number proved elusive— thus found themselves enmeshed in a new form of unfree labor. Peonage was the name applied to involuntary servitude based on indebtedness, and it thrived in the lumber, cotton, and railroad industries, mostly in the Deep South. A Department of Justice investigator estimated in 1907 that some one-third of the larger planters (operating from five to a hundred plows) in Alabama, Georgia, and Mississippi were holding their black workers to "a condition of peonage," arranging for the arrest and forcible return of those who left their workplace before settling their indebtedness.[53]

Once the landlord or supply merchant advanced goods to a sharecropper or tenant, he had him within his grasp. When the crop failed to cover expenses, many workers agreed to contract for another year, and some chose to move on. When the landlord or supply merchant compelled the worker to remain on the place until the debt had been paid in full, that worker had entered into a condition of involuntary servitude for debt—or peonage. Employers might elect to dispatch such a tenant, along with his family, to another employer willing to assume the debt. A Rankin County, Mississippi, farmer did precisely that, selling Dan January and his family to another white farmer. When January refused to be sold, the employer and others beat him brutally. After the worker's children removed their unconscious father to his home, the white men returned with a rope and threatened to lynch him unless he agreed to work for the purchaser of the debt.[54]

Although Congress had prohibited peonage in 1867, enforcement proved exceedingly difficult, whether because of official indifference, the powerlessness and illiteracy of the victims, or the blurred distinction between peonage and tenantry. All too often, peonage operated with the full connivance and encouragement of state and local authorities. Convicted of a crime, the black offender would have to pay both a fine and court costs, more than he or she could afford. But an employer would then intercede to pay the fine, requiring the offender to work for him until the debt had been settled. The McRee Brothers, a firm composed of four brothers, owned a substantial farm near Valdosta, Georgia. To procure labor, they made arrangements with city officials to arrest "strange negroes" on petty charges; the brothers would then pay the fines and court costs and contract with the blacks for reimbursement through their labor. Having settled the terms, they would handcuff the released blacks, remove them to their place, put them to work under a guard, and keep them locked in a stockade at night. If laborers should try to escape, the employers would use dogs to hunt them down. Lula Frazier and Henry Wilson, although acquitted of the charges against them, could not pay the lawyer's fee and were sold to the McRee Brothers and held in "involuntary servitude" for several months. David Smith and David Brimmage, both sentenced to thirty days on the chain gang (Smith for stealing a watermelon), had to work seven months for the McRee Brothers. After an investigation, a federal grand jury indicted the McRee brothers on peonage charges, and they were found guilty and fined $2,000. The brothers paid their fine, returned to their homes, and extended an invitation to the presiding judge, court officials, and representatives of the press to come down to their plantation and "enjoy a season of shooting."[55]

Although the federal government sought to prosecute offenders for violating peonage codes, white juries and witnesses usually proved to be uncooperative. Fears of retaliation made many black witnesses reluctant to testify, and investigators encountered a host of difficulties in procuring evidence. Responding to reports of peonage in the railroad camp of a construction company, a federal agent proceeded to the scene. Downriver from the camp, he spoke with a resident about the prospects for catching fish in the river. The man told him the fish were plentiful but no one was prepared to eat them. "I asked him why and he said the river was full of dead negroes," and they had clearly come from the railroad camp upstream. The evidence collected by the agent suggested a case of peonage, but the indictment resulted in a mistrial.[56]

"Nigger got caught in the spokes of the wheel any way it rolled," Ned Cobb observed. Peonage was but one of the spokes, and it operated with ruthless efficiency, permitting a substantial number of employers to exert absolute authority over their workers. "Why are they tolerated?" the foreman of a grand jury in Jackson, Alabama, asked.

"Because the negro is about the only sufferer and few whites in the South will take a stand against the white man . . . in favor of the negro, not perhaps that they endorse the conduct of the white man but because to do so would spoil the negro, who regards any defense in his behalf as an effort to license him to do wrong."[57]

6

TO ESCAPE AGRICULTURAL labor for more rewarding occupations became increasingly difficult. The position occupied by skilled black craftsmen and artisans during slavery deteriorated under freedom. The fears and resentments of their white counterparts translated into a fierce and losing struggle by black artisans to retain their position. "No matter how good a Negro wuz," a bricklayer and plasterer said of his experience in Athens and Atlanta, Georgia, "he wuz the last to be hired and then he wuz given some minor job. I saw that even if a Negro wuz a better brick layer, all the white workers wuz given the first jobs and after they wuz all supplied, then the Negro workers got what wuz left." In many skilled trades, blacks encountered difficulties in acquiring the necessary training and faced opposition from the trade unions. "[W]ith the growth of the Labor Union," a black Texan observed, "the black man has been crowded out."[58]

Blacks seeking alternatives to field labor in the towns and cities of the New South invariably found themselves confronted with the familiar reply, "This is white man's work," when they sought to improve their situation. That was precisely the response Richard Wright encountered in Memphis when he sought to improve his skills in an optical company. "What are you trying to do, get smart, nigger?" one of the white employees almost immediately demanded to know. Frustrated in his search for employment, an aspiring black youth in Portsmouth, Virginia, described to Booker T. Washington the opportunities available to him: "There are so many people around here and such a little work; there are four or five candidates for the cleaning of every spittoon."[59]

Black barbers still dominated that profession, and a number of them were quite successful. The savings accumulated by Alonzo Herndon, who came to Atlanta in 1882 as a journeyman barber, would ultimately lay the foundations for the highly successful Atlanta Life Insurance Company. The only way for barbers to retain a white clientele was to serve them exclusively, as many did. Protesting their exclusion, a black delegation demanded shaves at the shop of a black barber in Chattanooga, only to be turned away. When they demanded to know if their money was not as good as a white man's, the barber replied, "Yes just as good, but there is not enough of it."[60] For the most part, however, blacks dominated jobs that few whites wanted and that paid the least wages for often grueling work. The bulk of black workers could be found in personal or domestic service.

Formidable obstacles kept at a minimum blacks in the legal and medical professions. Not only did prospective lawyers face the difficult task of obtaining college training, but also the extent to which they could practice their profession might be seriously compromised by local customs and attitudes. Opportunities in the medical profession were equally bleak, and the doctors who graduated from black medical schools encountered difficulties in both practicing their profession and improving their skills.[61]

Between Reconstruction and World War I, white promoters of the New South prescribed their own brand of uplift. Through industrialization and cheap labor, the South would pull itself up by its bootstraps and gain the respect, recognition, and investment capital of a rapidly industrializing America. But the New South envisioned by its boosters, while dotting the countryside and towns with textile mills, deepened rather than eradicated poverty, distributing its effects among both whites and blacks. Low wages prevailed in industrial jobs, some of which were open to blacks. The least segregated industry, iron and steel, paid wages comparable to those of skilled laborers, but it was confined largely to the Birmingham area and in its early stages was something less than an economic success. The more extensive lumber and timber industries employed blacks almost exclusively but for poor-paying jobs that often proved fleeting, and many of the workers were forced back into agricultural labor. The textile mills, the most successful economic enterprises, rested on the exploitation of white women and children, who were compensated for their low pay and terrible conditions by a company policy of not hiring blacks to work alongside them.[62]

Finding it difficult to pursue industrial labor, blacks struggled to escape sharecropping by moving up the agricultural ladder, first becoming a tenant paying a fixed rent and ultimately becoming a landowner. Successful black farmers, however, attracted attention. For them to be tolerated, they needed to remain deferential to whites and refrain from any displays or expressions of success that suggested impudence. But the rules by which this game was played might change at the slightest whim of whites. Even if successful blacks abided by the rules, many whites considered signs of black success sufficient evidence of impudence.

7

FEW PEOPLE, wrote W. E. B. Du Bois, "ever worshipped Freedom with half such unquestioning faith as did the American Negro for two centuries."[63] But the expectations raised by emancipation and Reconstruction proved to be short-lived, perhaps nowhere more dramatically or with more far-reaching consequences than in the workplace. In less than two decades, black Southerners went from slave labor to various forms of forced labor, from euphoric optimism about their prospects to a condition of despair in which the betrayal of expectations became a way of life—a far cry from the quality of freedom many blacks had envisioned for themselves and their families.

If their expectations had been raised, that was because they had listened to their leaders, teachers, ministers, and professed white friends. They had been encouraged by hopeful messages of uplift and self-help. They had taken seriously the moral and economic injunctions and the promised rewards for hard labor. Through their industry, skill, and enterprise, they were told, they would gain a place in American society commensurate with their numbers and weight in the economy. It was simply a matter of blacks assuming individual responsibility for their condition and future. "The negro must do for himself," one newspaper advised, "just what other people worthy of emulation have done for themselves, no more, no less, and then he will become similarly appreciated, but not till then."[64]

Everywhere blacks turned, or so it seemed, these assurances were imparted and embellished. By no means confined to black America, the dominant economic, religious, political, and educational institutions in the late nineteenth and early twentieth centuries emphasized those qualities of character deemed suitable to economic success: diligence, loyalty, and punctuality in the workplace, and respect for property and authority. The school primers, much like the literature of self-help, imparted through various moral and success tales the rewards of faithful labor. "Let the Negro acquire intelligence, integrity and industry," a black college monthly proclaimed in 1901, "and the Negro problem will vanish as mists before the fiery rays of the sun." A textbook designed to instill racial pride in young blacks confidently predicted that when the majority of the race demonstrated "high character," public sentiment would change, "and we will no longer be measured by the vices of the vicious, but by the virtues of the majority. Nothing tells for progress like self-respect. Money without it will not solve the problem, let there be both."[65]

The church taught that material success was outward evidence of an inward moral and religious character, that God rewards the industrious, the thrifty, and the virtuous. "Wealth, intelligence and godliness combined, make their possessors indispensable members of a community," the bishops of the African Methodist Episcopal Church advised newly freed slaves in 1866. That same year the A.M.E. Church suggested that the only way to win over the hearts and minds of white Americans was to exercise their economic power: "If free black labor affects the pocket in any way, it will affect the heart." And if any doubts remained as to the extraordinary rewards of materialism, the advice offered by the Reverend Henry Highland Garnet, a veteran black leader, resonated with blacks in 1865 as it did half a century later: "The more money you make, the lighter your skin will be. The more land and houses you get, the straighter your hair will be."[66]

The growing literature of racial uplift, along with the black press, focused on the few blacks who were forming the nucleus of a propertied and entrepreneurial class in the South. Celebrating them as models of self-help for aspiring blacks, race promoters enumerated their wealth and celebrated the virtues and resourcefulness these men had embraced to achieve their lofty position. Few summed up the black imperative more succinctly than a black newspaper in Richmond, which used a motto that would find a ready home in black self-help advice and oratory: "We cannot reach the top of the ladder at one bound. Bow low, and work! 'Stoop to conquer.' You do the stooping, and your children will do the conquering." Editorial admonitions in the same newspaper amplified that advice: "Colored men, educate your children, buy property, be religious and all will be well. Cultivate tidiness. Show to the world what twenty-five years of freedom has done for you."[67]

That advice would be expanded on in economic-uplift conferences in which successful blacks related their experiences and imparted the lessons that if heeded might produce the same results. The semicenten-

nial celebrations of emancipation in 1913 repeated many of these stories to demonstrate the progress blacks had made in fifty years, invariably by embracing the middle-class virtues esteemed by most
Americans. At one such celebration, a black educator urged an overflowing audience to heed his advice, choosing the words that had by
now become clichés in the self-help literature:

> Foster the spirit of industry. Seek honorable employment and render
> faithful and efficient service. Keep out of the court house. Frown upon
> idleness and give no place to the idler. Be polite to everybody and
> teach your children politeness. Make it a purpose of your life to have a
> clean, well-ordered home. Save a part of all the money you make. Be
> decent in manner. Be clean in person. Respect yourself and you will
> respect others and others will respect you. Attend your Sunday school
> and churches. Make the Bible the rule of your every-day life. Trust in
> God and do right. Remember that no agency outside of yourself can
> raise you to respectability and honor among your fellows.[68]

Although the advice to blacks relied on clichés, it served a very specific purpose. The same qualities and work ethic deemed vital to economic success were also designed to ease the accommodation of blacks
(and whites) to the dominant economic order. The notion of "room at
the top," one black educator suggested, had to be rethought. Every
black worker, no matter what occupation he held, needed to be content
with his place. The washerwoman, for example, should aspire to be the
best possible washerwoman, to reach "the top of her art, for washing is
an art as much as music or mathematics." The same could be said of
the carpenter, the mason, the hod carrier, and the common laborer.
White employers, of course, welcomed the educator's advice as an accommodation to reality, particularly when he suggested that workers
should consider themselves the property of the employer, faithfully
obeying his instructions and requests. He need hardly have added that
such workers were expected to reject agrarian radicalism, along with
communism, socialism, labor unions, and strikes.[69]

No matter how they divided on other issues, black leaders exhorted
their people to adopt the work ethic and lift themselves up by their
bootstraps. "If you would be prosperous," declared Frederick Douglass, "you must be industrious." More conspicuously than any other
black leader, Booker T. Washington, the principal of Tuskegee Institute
and the most powerful black leader of his time, seized on the theme

that material success would elevate blacks in the eyes of whites. He liked to tell the story of two white men passing on the street an educated black man who owned several houses and lots and had a substantial bank account. One of the white men turned to the other and said, "By Gosh! It is all I can do to keep from calling that nigger 'Mister.' " To Washington, the moral of the story needed no amplification. "That's the point we want to get to."[70]

The sentiment was hardly new, but Washington formulated it neatly and effectively in aphorisms that would find their way—along with his portrait—into tens of thousands of black homes. "No race can prosper till it learns that there is as much dignity in tilling a field as in writing a poem." "The trouble with the Negro is that he is all the time trying to get recognition, whereas what he should do is to get something to recognize." "An inch of progress is worth more than a yard of complaint." "In the future let us emphasize our opportunities more and our difficulties less. Let us talk more about our white friends, and about our white enemies less. . . . Let us . . . spend less time talking about the part of the city that we cannot live in, and more time in making the part of the city that we can live in beautiful and attractive." "We call too many meetings to resent something, and not enough to construct something." And when Washington proclaimed, "There is little race prejudice in the American dollar," he proposed in effect to replace the color line with the dollar line.[71]

The challenge, then, could hardly be clearer: Black people must assume responsibility for their own destiny. If they transformed themselves, embraced the work ethic, acquired property, improved their homes and home life, educated their children, and practiced the classic moral virtues, the legal and extralegal disabilities now imposed on them would disappear. "Prosperity, brains, and character will settle the question of civil rights." Of what use was the ballot, Washington asked, when economic dependence translated so easily into political dependence? "If a white man has upon his plantation in the South 500 Negro voters the majority of whom depend upon him for houses, for land, for food and clothing, this white man is going to control the franchise of the majority of those people. No law passed by congress or any state can prevent it."[72]

Whatever prejudices and resentments divided blacks and whites in the South would vanish, Washington insisted, when "the black man, by reason of his intelligence and skill, can create something that the white man wants or respects." That would be standard Tuskegee gospel, the underpinning of Washington's formula for racial progress and harmony. Not only did Washington always speak and act in the expectation of white recognition of black advancement, but few articulated it with as much confidence. "It is not within the province of human nature," he assured his people, "that the man who is intelligent and virtuous, and owns and cultivates the best farm in his county, shall very long be denied the proper respect and consideration. . . . The Negro merchant who owns the largest store in town will not be lynched."[73]

Even some who would become Washington's staunchest critics embraced his message of redemption through economic uplift. W. E. B. Du Bois, among others, advised his people, "The day the Negro race courts and marries the savings-bank will be the day of its salvation."[74] Black educators and "spokesmen," Emancipation Day commemorations, black industrial fairs, the National Negro Business League, and the black press mostly endorsed and embellished Washington's gospel of work, providing a sufficient number of worthy models of success to keep the dream alive.

But Washington, Du Bois, and the various prophets of Negro progress through economic and educational uplift were badly mistaken. The advice they offered in the 1890s was no more credible than it had been in the 1860s, perhaps even less so, and the assumption on which that advice rested would prove to be as naive as it was persistent. The literature and rhetoric of uplift and self-help proliferated almost in direct proportion to its irrelevance to the working lives of most black Southerners. It was not as though blacks were averse to the virtues deemed essential to success. But acquisition of those virtues appeared to make little or no difference. The experience of most black men and women in the New South directly contradicted the assurances and mocked that fundamental assumption of the American Dream that material success is the direct result of hard work. Without any urging from others, and usually because they had no choice, black Southerners applied themselves to the tasks at hand and practiced the virtues thought necessary for economic well-being. But faithful adherence to the work ethic brought most of them nothing. A lifetime of hard work, honesty, diligence, frugality, and punctuality might, in fact, leave them worse off than when they began.

For most black men and women, despite Washington's optimism, the bootstraps approach simply did not work. No matter how hard they labored, no matter how they conducted themselves, no matter how fervently they prayed, the chances for making it were less than encouraging; the basic rules and controls remained in place.

> *Our father, who is in heaven,*
> *White man owe me eleven and pay me seven,*
> *Thy kingdom come, thy will be done,*
> *And if I hadn't took that, I wouldn't had none.*[75]

Some decades later, as if to suggest how little had changed, a native Mississippian described the people with whom he grew up as "hard-working, God-fearing, church-going folk who prayed trustingly to an Almighty God. Six days a week most of them toiled like beasts of burden—but to little avail. Their lives did not change materially; they simply got older, grew weary, took sick and died."[76]

8

AS EARLY AS the Civil War, a North Carolina black captured the uniqueness of the black experience in white America. "It is not enough to tell us that we will be respected accordingly as we show ourselves worthy of it, when we know there are some worthy ones whose fate is just the same."[77] The worthy, along with the unworthy, often found themselves victimized and disrespected. After all, the real danger posed by Negroes, in the eyes of many whites, lay in the possibility that they might actually succeed, and that any such success would be at the expense of whites and subversive of southern society.

Even if some whites preferred to think otherwise, they came to recognize the forcefulness and pragmatic truth of such views. Speaking to that "truth," a former governor of North Carolina observed in 1903 that some philanthropists believed Booker T. Washington's program to be "the right one," that industrial education was all that blacks required "to get them in harmony with their environment." He found such an assumption highly questionable if not downright naive:

Never was there a greater mistake. The truth is the negro is going to fare best and be happiest when his position is most subordinate. Financial and industrial equality is as bad in the eyes of the whites as social

equality. The negro who gets very prosperous is to be pitied, for
straightway he is in a situation where danger confronts him. Let him
own a fine farm, blooded horses and cattle, and dare to ride in a carriage, and if I were an insurance agent I would not make out a policy
on his life. In plain English, to get above his ordained situation in life is,
generally speaking, to invite assassination. The Anglo-Saxon element
North and South is not going to brook much elevation of an inferior
race.[78]

Although some blacks responded to this candid observation with outrage and incredulity, the former governor demonstrated a more realistic grasp of black prospects and less confidence in Anglo-Saxons than a
number of his critics.

The advent of a New Negro, unschooled in the ways of slavery and
subordination, no doubt aggravated white fears of black success, but
those fears were, in fact, deeply rooted and had long been felt and articulated. For whites accustomed to blacks only as servants and slaves, successful or ambitious blacks were quite simply an anomaly, difficult to
imagine and entirely "out of place." From their first days of freedom,
black men and women had been forcibly reminded that lofty ambitions
and evidence of advancement might be resented rather than welcomed
by whites. Typical of the complaints registered by the Freedmen's Bureau after the Civil War were violent attacks on blacks who were making something of themselves. The case of Perry Jeffrey was all too
typical. Unable to find him in their raid on his home, a band of whites
killed his son and burned the furniture and clothing. "Perry had a good
crop, some 25 bags of cotton, but dare not stay to gather it," the local
Freedmen's Bureau agent reported, "he and his family leave for Augusta today; he has made the Sheriff his Agent to sell his crop. Perry is a
good old man, industrious, and he has a good character from his old
Master."[79] A memory of the Ku Klux Klan that persisted long after
emancipation was that they "didn't 'low de niggers ter have nuthin' "
and that they singled out for robbery and murder enterprising blacks
suspected of having saved their earnings. "If you got so you made good
money an' had a good farm," Pierce Harper, a former North Carolina
slave, recalled, "de Klu Klux'd come an' murder you," as they did his
neighbor Jim Freeman. "Dey taken him an' destroyed his stuff an' him
'cause he was making some money. Hung him on a tree in his front
yard, right in front of his cabin."[80]

The paradox seemed perfectly clear. While black leaders, preachers, and the success manuals admonished black men and women to embrace self-help and the work ethic, whites consciously withheld from blacks the tools and opportunities available to other Americans to lift themselves up economically. Even as Washington preached his self-improvement creed, evidence of blacks making good on that creed often provoked white resentment and violence rather than respect and acceptance. Neither individual worth, intelligence, nor achievement seemed capable of bridging racial barriers and easing the prevailing tensions; on the contrary, those very qualities in black people might inflame tensions.

The violence inflicted on black people was often selective, aimed at educated and successful blacks, those in positions of leadership, those determined to improve themselves, those who owned the best farm in the county and the largest store in town, those suspected of having saved their earnings, those who had just made a crop—that is, black men and women perceived by whites as having stepped out of their place. Sam Gadsden of Edisto Island, South Carolina, recalled the fate of Jim Hutchinson, a grassroots leader who organized local blacks and helped them to establish clear titles to their land. "He was a good man for what he knew. He didn't know much, but he did all he could for anybody in need. He helped them get straightened out and get their own homes. And his work has endured. . . . Then one day they killed him. . . . He was leading the Colored people too much."[81]

No wonder many young blacks in particular came to believe that education and ambition would bring them only frustration and disappointment. The belief grew as well that it was futile to work hard and obtain money and property because the "man" will somehow find a way to deprive them of their gains, whether by fraud, violence, or intimidation. A black man sentenced to seven years of hard labor for stealing a turkey had no difficulty explaining to a white visitor why whites inflicted such injustices on blacks. "[D]e white folks don't like to see de black folks git on; jess so soon as one ob us am 'dustrious an' like to git up a little in de worl', dey git up some false sw'arin' ag'in him an' git him inter de chain-gang, like dey done me. It was false sw'arin' as done it. I neber stole no turkey; I neber stole nuffin in all my life."[82]

Booker T. Washington had only to read his mail to gain some sense of what was happening around him, to know that evidence of black success all too often provoked white resentment and retaliation. Few letters conveyed more revealing and disturbing news than the one he received from his friend Isaiah Montgomery. Back in 1890, as the only black delegate to the Mississippi Constitutional Convention, Montgomery had approved property qualifications for voting, convinced that blacks would be encouraged to obtain property and thus gain acceptance by whites. Some years later, in 1901, he advised black people that they may successfully conduct almost any kind of business in an average town, and "just as they adapt themselves to sound business principles, more and more will come to them the recognition that is due to every useful and upright citizen."[83]

But only three years later, in 1904, an obviously shaken Montgomery wrote to Washington about some recent incidents in Clay County, citing them only as examples of "the depths to which Mississippi has descended."

> Rev. Buchanan has the best appointed printing establishment of any colored man in the State, and conducts a Baptist Newspaper . . . and was no doubt prospering, his daughter was his cashier and Bookkeeper, they kept a Horse and Buggy, which the young woman used frequently in going to and from work; they kept a decent house and a Piano; a mass meeting of whites decided that the mode of living practiced by the Buchanan family had a bad effect on the cooks and washerwomen, who aspired to do likewise, and became less disposed to work for the whites. [A mob forced Buchanan and his family from the town, not even permitting them to remove their possessions.]

> Thomas Harvey runs a neat little Grocery, he kept a Buggy and frequently rode to his place of business, he was warned to sell his Buggy and walk. Mr. Chandler keeps a Grocery, he was ordered to leave, but was finally allowed to remain on good behavior. Mr. Meacham ran a business and had a Pool table in connection therewith, he was ordered to close up and don overalls for manual labor. Mr. Cook conducted a Hack business between the Depots and about town, using two Vehicles, he was notified that he would be allowed to run only one and was ordered to sell the other.[84]

While trying to maintain some struggling churches as a missionary in the late nineteenth century, Simon Peter Smith, who had been born into slavery in Columbia, South Carolina, lived in a number of communities in which he observed race relations on a day-to-day basis. His letters echoed Montgomery's sobering observations. From Marietta,

Georgia, for example, he wrote of whites who came to town to "have some fun with the niggers," and threatened several black citizens, including the barber, who owned substantial property. It was the third time the barber's life had been placed in jeopardy, and Smith suspected he knew why this particular black man had been singled out. "He is the most respectable and wealthy colored man in this town." From Whiteville, North Carolina, Smith noted the difficulties blacks encountered throughout much of the state. "The prejudice against those who are getting education, and property . . . is greater than ever." If any black person owned much land, he noted, whites sought to "get him [into] trouble so as to get what he has." In one instance, a black property owner, to defend his legal title, "had to give three lawyers half of his land to save him the other half."[85]

The fears of black success and assertiveness that had provoked much of the white violence directed at Reconstruction proved equally pervasive in the late nineteenth and early twentieth centuries, when blacks no longer posed a political threat. "It is getting to be a dangerous thing," a Savannah black newspaper observed, "to acquire property, to get an education, to own an automobile, to dress well, and to build a respectable home." The newspaper then cited a number of incidents in which "prosperous and industrious Negroes" had been singled out for slaughter. Similarly, a black newspaper in Louisville voiced despair over "daily examples" of white men singling out for harassment "the black man who has something, who knows something and who stands for something." Not infrequently, the newspaper reported, successful blacks found themselves accused of improper relations with a white woman and were forced to sell their property at a loss and leave town. Appeals for protection to leading whites had proved futile, "for they are aiding and abetting the whole thing." A black newspaper in New Orleans, in repeating these observations, provided its own view of "The White Man's Burden":

> In this country the white man considers that Negro the burden who wants to be somebody. For his benefit state constitutions are recast and separate car laws enacted. For him white-cap notices are posted and bands of armed men ride at dead of night. He is counted "too smart" when he contends for his rights, and in many communities ordered to leave his property or crop when he seems too prosperous. This is "the white man's burden."[86]

Contradicting the lessons taught in their primers, blacks came to learn early in their lives not only the limit but also the potential danger of the aspirations they harbored. Eunice Rivers witnessed her father intimidated into submission because "he was just living a little bit too well to be a Negro." Richard Wright understood that his Uncle Hoskins had been murdered by whites who had long desired his flourishing liquor business. Audley Moore understood that her grandfather had been lynched for "standing up to some white people" who desired his land. "This was all it amounted to, because after he was lynched they ran my grandmother off the land, and she had to take her five little children and flee for her life with the things they had on their back, nothing else. . . ." Zelma George's grandfather had some education, established a thriving business, constructed a house "better than most of the houses lived in by white people," and sent his children to college. But the family was "*constantly* in trouble" in the Texas town in which they resided, until finally their refusal to take insults "plus their lifestyle and college training" became more than the white community could tolerate. Warned to leave the town, her grandfather had to take whatever he could get for the property, and the family hastily departed. The daughter of a Mississippi sharecropper recalled how her father kept cropping until he had saved enough to purchase some wagons, plow tools, and mules. But a white man came to her father's lot and poisoned the mules. "It killed everything we had. . . . That poisoning knocked us right back down flat. We never did get back up again. The whites did it just because we were getting somewhere. White people never like to see Negroes get a little success."[87]

Evidence of success, no matter how it was achieved or displayed, made every black man and woman vulnerable. To convey an air of independence or prosperity was to invite trouble. The simple fact was that many whites equated black success with "uppityness," "impudence," "getting out of place," and pretensions toward racial equality. "He think he white" was the expression whites sometimes used to convey that suspicion, or "He is too smart," "He wants to be white and act like white people," and "He think he somebody." It became almost routine for a black newspaper to report that the unexplained attack on a local black "looks more like the old story of a Negro's being too prosperous or independent."[88] Whatever the models of success highlighted in the literature of race promotion, tales of black aspirations and ambition all too often ended in disaster, as more than one bluesman would suggest in the early twentieth century.

Well a nigger an' a white man, playin' seven up,
The nigger beat the white man, scared to pick it up.[89]

The ability of a farmer to "pay out" (settle his debts and pay off his mortgage) marked the end of his dependence on the landlord and merchant. Both white and black tenant farmers aspired to achieve such independence, but most failed to break out of the cycle of indebtedness that came to characterize the southern labor system. Precisely because of the success it suggested, however, in the face of overwhelming odds, a black farmer's ability to "pay out" invited both incredulity and resentment, and sometimes ended in violence. Henry Baker, a hardworking, enterprising, and shrewd Alabama farmer, remembered the way a white neighbor greeted the news that he had "paid out" his debts. "Aftuh I settled fer hit an evahthing, he wuz de sickest man yuh evah seed 'cause he wuz a renter hisself en he jes couldn't stan' tuh see a 'nigger' git ahead uv him." Magnolia Gates recalled how her father had purchased some mules and worked on halves until he was able to clear his debts, including what he owed for the mules. He then revealed his intention to move to another place. "If I had known this," the proprietor angrily responded, "you never would have got those mules." Ned Cobb spent five years, from 1914 to 1919, trying to get out of debt to his landlord, only to be told every year, "Well, you lackin so much and so much of comin out. . . ." It was a common experience for black farm laborers. But Cobb persisted and managed to pay off his note to a much-chagrined landlord, and he would never forget that moment of triumph—and resolve. "Right there and then it struck my heart and mind: 'You'll never get another note on me, never under Christ's kingdom.'"[90]

Enterprising blacks who were perceived as overly ambitious or as potential competitors of white professionals and businessmen found that they could not always enjoy the fruits of their achievements. Not only were they excluded from living in white residential districts, but also they sometimes found it impossible to operate their businesses and to practice their professional skills. In a number of places, black physicians were beaten and forced to leave town when they took black patients away from white doctors or for no other reason than the fact that they were black doctors. In a number of Mississippi communities, white mobs simply expelled black physicians thought to be "prosperous" or otherwise troublesome.[91] Few individual cases, however, attracted as much notoriety as that of Thomas Moss of Memphis. He had saved his money as a letter carrier, and with two other black men—Calvin McDowell and Henry Stewart—opened the People's Grocery Company in the thickly populated black suburb, where it competed with a white-owned grocery. Moss and his partners were murdered by a mob because they had armed and defended themselves against white marauders threatening their property and because, as one of Moss's close friends surmised, "they were succeeding too well. They were guilty of no crime but that." After the murder of the three men, a mob looted the grocery, creditors closed the place, and what remained of the stock was sold at auction.[92]

> *Tom Moss was an innocent man*
> *He was at home in bed*
> *Teacher of a class in Sunday School*
> *Was shot through the head*
>
> *Oh me, oh my, Lord have mercy on me.*
> *Oh me, oh my, Lord have mercy on me.*
>
> *They are roaming the streets with guns*
> *Looking for us to shoot*
> *All we can do is pray to the Lord*
> *There is nothing else we can do.*[93]

The murder of Thomas Moss shocked his good friend Ida B. Wells. "A finer, cleaner man than he never walked the streets of Memphis," she recalled. "He was well liked, a favorite with everybody, yet he was murdered with no more consideration than if he had been a dog, because he as a man defended his property from attack." The brutal murder prompted Wells to question an assumption even she had once accepted: that white lynch mobs wreaked extralegal justice on deserving criminal rapists. But Moss, McDowell, and Stewart had committed no crime against white women. "This is what opened my eyes to what lynching really was." The more she examined the causes of individual lynchings, the more convinced she became "that the Southerner had never gotten over his resentment that the Negro was no longer his plaything, his servant, and his source of income" and masked this resentment behind the charge of rape. The Moss lynching, like so many others, she concluded, was "[a]n excuse to get rid of Negroes who were acquiring wealth and property and thus keep the race terrorized and 'keep the nigger down.' "[94]

In the absence of legislation barring blacks from improving themselves and purchasing land, white raiding parties or sometimes entire communities imposed their own sentences, ranging from forced dispossession to expulsion, and often both. In Warrenton, Georgia, notices were sent to four black residents who had managed to make money "in some kind of business enterprise," ordering them to leave. "No charge has been presented against them," a witness reported. "They have simply offended their white neighbors, because they have become too prosperous."[95] Near Savannah, Tennessee, white tenants objected to blacks operating successfully on land they owned. Ben Pettigrew, accompanied by his two young daughters, was driving a load of cotton from his farm to town. Several miles from his place, four white men appeared on the road, shot the black farmer to death as he sat in the seat of his wagon, and dragged his two daughters from the top of the load and hanged them from a nearby tree. While their bodies dangled from a limb, the mob drove the wagon loaded with cotton under them and set fire to it. The message sent to enterprising black farmers in the region could not have been clearer.[96]

Organized white farmers (often known as "whitecaps"), most of them fearful of black success and competition, many of them desperate to provide for their families, terrorized black farmers who worked on, rented, or acquired land coveted by whites. "There is a good deal of excitement here about what is called "the White Caps," a Mississippian wrote from Pike County in 1893. "They are running all the darkeys off from . . . mills and farms at a dreadful rate." Signs appearing on lands desired by whites and worked by blacks warned "If you have not moved away from here by sundown tomorrow, we will shoot you like rabbits." When "de white caps" called on Ebenezer Brown in Amite County, Mississippi, his wife met them as he hid; they warned him to quit his present job and not trade "wid de Jews" anymore. Warnings posted in Hominy, Oklahoma, in 1911, as in a number of Georgia counties in 1916, targeted blacks who had purchased land they intended to work as cotton farms or who worked on rented plots.[97]

Whether they assumed the title "whitecaps" or operated anonymously, white farmers since the end of the Civil War had chosen to take out many of their racial and economic frustrations on black farmers. The testimony of beleaguered black families, much of it collected by Congress during Reconstruction and in the late nineteenth century by the Department of Justice, is strikingly similar. White terrorist bands, mostly operating at night, were wreaking a deadly violence on

"quiet, industrious, law-abiding" blacks whose only offense was renting, owning, residing on, and cultivating farms. Such blacks were said
to be a bad example of enterprise and ambition for other blacks,
threatening the supremacy and even the livelihood of whites. "[T]hey
wanted to run me off . . . on account of my crop," a Mississippi farmer
testified. "They took everything I had, and all my wife had, and broke
us teetotally up."[98] Incidents of white violence, in fact, had a way of increasing in the summer months after blacks had planted their crops.
"Now is the season," explained a Georgia editor, "when the tenant with
the best crop gets run off the place."[99]

Not confining themselves to farm lands, barns, and homes, night-
riding whitecaps also destroyed the institutions that helped to sustain a
black community—churches and schools—and assassinated "leading"
or "troublesome" blacks. The total effect of white terrorism and intimidation was to discourage blacks from accumulating enough to arouse
white resentment, while forcing the more enterprising to abandon their
homes and occupations and leave the county without any protection or
any compensation for their property. "If we own a good farm or horse,
or cow, or bird-dog, or yoke of oxen," a black Mississippian testified in
1913, "we are harassed until we are bound to sell, give away, or run
away, before we can have any peace in our lives." The flagrant disregard for law and order and the growing fear expressed by local whites
of losing business as well as valuable black laborers ultimately quashed
the whitecaps, but groups and individuals continued to act in their
spirit and with similar ruthlessness.[100]

Few understood better than Ned Cobb of Tallapoosa County, Alabama, the limits placed on black advancement and how evidence of
black success aggravated white fears and anxieties. Through perseverance, hard work, and extraordinary resourcefulness, aided by a literate
wife who kept the accounts, Cobb managed to accumulate some property, to move from a cropper to a tenant to a small landowner. But to
keep the mules, equipment, and property proved to be a continual
struggle, demanding far more calculation, resourcefulness, and energy
than he had expended to acquire it.

> I had men to turn me down, wouldn't let me have the land I needed to
> work, wouldn't sell me guano, didn't want to see me with anything.
> Soon as I got to where I could have somethin for sure and was makin
> somethin of myself, then they commenced a runnin at me, wantin to
> make trades with me.

Nor did Ned Cobb's white neighbors appreciate his resourcefulness in stocking up an impressive supply of meat on his place. "They looked hard, didn't stop lookin. . . . They didn't like to see a nigger with too much; they didn't like it one bit and it caused 'em to throw a slang word about a 'nigger' havin all this, that, and the other. I didn't make no noise about it. I didn't like that word, but then that word didn't hurt me; it was some action had to be taken to hurt me."[101]

Whether based on the possessions he acquired or his ability to "pay out," Cobb attracted attention and resentment. That was because, he explained, white people "hated to see niggers livin like people." For blacks to accumulate property or money was to make them independent, and whites feared the consequences.

> Afraid a nigger might do somethin if he got the money in his own hands, do as he please; might hold on to it if he wanted to hold it, might spend it accordin to his pleasure. The white people was afraid— I'll say this: they was afraid the money would make the nigger act too much like his own man. Nigger has a mind to do what's best for hisself, same as a white man. If he had some money, he just might do it.[102]

For some blacks, the way to survive in the South was not to accumulate enough to arouse white resentment. The unsuccessful black man posed no threat; he knew his place. Cobb described his own father as such a man.

> He had money but—whenever the colored man prospered too fast in this country under the old rulins, they worked every figure to cut you down, cut your britches off you. So, it might have been to his way of thinkin that it weren't no use in climbin too fast; weren't no use in climbin slow, neither, if they was goin to take everything you worked for when you got too high.

Ned Cobb's brother seemed to have adopted that lesson as a way of life, working precisely in that spirit. "He made up his mind that he weren't goin to have anything and after that, why, nothin could hurt him."[103]

The experience of Ned Cobb spoke to the experiences of countless black families in the late-nineteenth- and early twentieth-century South. To fail was to confirm white expectations; to succeed was to provoke white fears and hostility, antagonizing whites who deemed such success impossible for an inferior race and who feared and resented any proof to the contrary. "The more rapid the progress," one observer noted, "the more frightful the mortality." That suggested the magnitude of the problem. Nothing so contradicted and undermined Booker T. Washington's assumptions about the rewards of material progress as the number of respectable and successful blacks victimized by lynch mobs and rioters. For black leaders, as for the great mass of black men and women, this paradox could not be easily overcome. "Thirty years ago," a black lawyer in Louisville told an English visitor in 1909, "the prejudice was against the ignorant, shiftless and thriftless black; now it is against the thrifty and industrious, the refined and the cultured—against those, in a word, who come into competition with the middle-class white."[104]

Although designed to calm racial tensions, the Washington success formula, it appeared, was a double-edged sword. By making blacks more ambitious and less content with staying in their "place," by encouraging them to acquire the property and wealth said to be necessary to secure white recognition, the success ethic in many instances only exacerbated white fears and hostility. Perhaps Washington never fully grasped the tragic flaw in his success creed. Even if he did, he no doubt would have defended his position as the only alternative to racial suicide. But Americans, white or black, have not easily accepted defeat, especially if perceived as betrayal. That feeling of alienation pervaded the appeal made in 1910 to President William Howard Taft by a group of black ministers. Citing a recent case near Palestine, Texas, in which some twenty "innocent, unarmed men" were murdered, the ministers articulated an appeal for justice that turned Booker T. Washington on his head without naming him.

> We sought strength thru education, but the more we advance along this line, the greater the discrimination. We have bought land, built homes and established Churches, but those states as desire to do so go on disfranchising us, lynching our men on frivolous charges and unproved allegations, and widening the chasm which race differentiation has made broad enough. When progress does not promise to save a people, that people is near unto desperation. [105]

Two years later, a Louisiana blacksmith who had exiled himself to Detroit in 1903 to escape a condition *"far worse* than *death* to me and to our people" tried to explain to Washington the basis for white hostility: the ability of the black man to prove to his former owners that he was not "the 'thing' they supposed him to be,"and the fact that "the 'Negro' has proven himself to be the 'white mans' equal, if not his superior."[106]

After reporting various incidents in which white mobs had singled out prospering blacks for harassment or murder, the editor of a Louisville newspaper thought the lessons to be derived from these examples were patently obvious: The "shiftless, worthless, ignorant, and vicious Negro" was precisely the kind of Negro white men preferred.[107] John Smallwood, a black preacher, drove home the same point, underscoring the difficulty black people faced if they aspired to anything that violated white expectations. "So long as negroes will drink common whisky, dance jigs, and make apes of themselves, the mass of white men in the Southern States applaud them as good fellows; but so soon as one becomes a bank president, a property owner, and a gentleman, he becomes offensive to society."[108]

Not surprisingly, then, when blacks vied for or managed to secure federal appointments in the post office, whites responded instantly and angrily. As postmaster, he or she would be placed on a level equal to if not above many whites. That was reason enough for an employee in the Atlanta post office to resign in 1889, after a black had been appointed. "My father used to own 200 negroes," he explained, "and I used to have two negroes wait upon me when I was a school boy and of course, I can't work in the same office with a negro." Not only would such an official interact daily with whites, including white women, but the post office might become a meeting place for local blacks, making it impossible for white women to enter. The black postmaster, like any black official, was out of his or her place, symbolizing political ambition and an assertiveness that could only raise the specter of social equality and mongrelization. "If the Administration deliberately sought to insult our people, it could not better succeed than by making these [postal] appointments," a Democratic attorney wrote, protesting a pending black appointment in North Carolina, "and if it was the purpose to create race prejudice and set back the Negro it could not better succeed than by placing him where he is regarded as an insult to our people." From the same town, a Populist Party activist got right to the point in a letter to one of the state's senators: "I have no charges to make against the applicant—he is a good man—but the people here do not want a colored P.M."[109]

That feeling persisted whenever blacks held positions of responsibility that might intrude on white lives. After the removal of a black sheriff

in South Carolina, for example, no one objected to his competence—
"He was capable enough, and did his duty"—but residents thought it
"terribly galling to see a 'nigger' in the courthouse handling white
men's money." Even the move to replace white with black messengers
at the Atlanta telegraph office elicited objections, as it not only deprived whites of jobs but also made blacks "custodians of the private
correspondence of white people."[110]

When James K. Vardaman campaigned in Indianola, Mississippi, in
1903, he chided the people for "receiving mail from the hands of a
coon." He had in mind Minnie W. Cox, a black businesswoman who
had been appointed postmistress. Although inspectors and townspeople had found her to be efficient and polite, she was unacceptable as a
propertied black woman. Some thought her a "menace to white civilization"; others felt the prominent position she held would be a "constant incitement" to the rape of white women. Angry protest meetings
and talk of violence prompted the postmistress to resign and leave the
state. John Harris claimed to be the first man to carry rural mail in
Georgia directly to homes, and he took considerable pride in that fact.
But when the position was upgraded and the salary rose from $30 to
$75 a month, it suddenly became more than a menial job, and whites
coveted it. A congressional candidate promised that if elected he would
give the job to a white man, and he made good on the promise. After
fifteen years of service, Harris lost his job. "There wasn't nothin' ever
charged against my service record or my character. Even the congressman that got me fired, testified to that and said I'd served faithful and
well, but he thought a white man should have the job."[111]

In these and other instances where whites resisted appointments of
blacks to prominent or upgraded positions, the essential point remained the same, even if the rhetoric supporting it varied: The objection was to a black person holding any other than a servile job. The
qualifications or competence of the individual counted far less than
race; indeed, as during Reconstruction, the possibility that a black man
or woman might perform the job as competently as a white person only
made the concern and hostility that much more urgent and compelling.
The danger lay in the probability, moreover, that such appointments
would encourage other blacks to aspire to higher places. Responding to
the report in 1910 that a black Bostonian might be named an assistant
attorney general of the United States, a Charleston, South Carolina,
newspaper found such appointments not only "highly injudicious" but
particularly harmful to black people. "It were better for the race were

the policy of baiting them with false hopes abandoned definitely and finally."[112]

Even white "friends" and benefactors used such condescending phrases as "very good for colored people" or "good enough for a Negro" to define the limits of black progress.[113] The assumption prevailed well into the twentieth century that blacks were incapable of competing equally with whites. But no matter how often whites repeated that belief, the fear persisted that blacks might prove them wrong. Evidence of black achievements only increased white anxieties. That such achievements often demanded extraordinary skill and ingenuity, as well as perseverance and hard work, made them all the more threatening. In the white South, the successful black, like the poverty-stricken, often paid a heavy price, whether physical or psychological.

No matter what strategies they adopted, black leaders could never resolve or surmount such contradictions. The World's Columbian Exposition in Chicago in 1893 celebrated American ingenuity and the extraordinary progress made by this nation over four centuries. Progress, in fact, came to be perceived as almost uniquely American; progress explained America and validated the American Dream. But for the vast majority of black men and women, working out their individual lives in the rural and urban South, that dream was both elusive and potentially dangerous. Progress could be an enemy, detrimental to health and personal safety.

9

AFTER HEARING THE Emancipation Proclamation read on his plantation in mid-1865, an elderly black man remarked to his coworkers, "They have taken off the bridle but left the halter." Half a century later, the halter remained very much in place, restraining black aspirations and securing black subordination. "He is kept in debt so that he can never get out," a traveler in Georgia in 1919 said of the black farm laborer, "and so lives with a halter 'round his neck." The sights and sounds of the working South had changed but little, as if time had passed over the landscape. Generations of blacks inherited the same routines, the same provisions, the same houses, the same obligations, the same compensation. "Their isolated life," a Hampton graduate wrote from Arkansas and Mississippi in 1899, "has rendered it impossible for them to know of a better way of living, and having known no other they are content to exist in this miserable way with no effort at improvement." Some two decades later, Richard Wright helped an insurance agent sell his wares among sharecroppers in Mississippi, and he came away appalled. "I saw a bare, bleak pool of black life and I hated it; the people were alike, their homes were alike, and their farms were alike."[114]

Men, women, and children still worked "from can to cain't," stooping before the cotton plants, picking the white seedy cotton from the bolls, and placing their harvest in long white sacks strapped over a shoulder. Few observers failed to be impressed by the rhythmic movements of the workers. Some visitors came to record their songs, some to describe the picturesque scene, as if a Stephen Foster ballad or a Currier & Ives engraving had come to life. But for the subjects of their gaze, it was another day of work. "I'm talking about hard work," Carrie Millender recalled of her days working the family farm in Alabama. "They didn't have tractors. You plowed the mule. You hoed grass. . . . Picked cotton. . . . See that was hard." And it remained as unrewarding as it had been fifty years earlier. The experience of Bernie Morris in Mississippi in the 1930s testified dramatically to how little had changed, to how sensitive landlords and planters remained to any challenge to their authority. A tenant on a plantation where there were "200 nigguhs an' not one had evuh axed whut dey owed," Morris kept his own books and insisted on a proper accounting at settlement time. But after being paid off, he was dismissed from the plantation. "It wuzn' on'y whut he wuz keepin' dem frum stealin' frum *him*," another tenant recalled, "it wuz dat he wuz showin' de uthuh nigguhs de wrong idea, see? 'Cordin' to de white man, he wuz spoilin' his nigguhs!" That he was regarded as an efficient worker made no difference; his conduct could not be tolerated. "Dey tole Bernie, 'Well, Bernie, you uh good farmer, but you got tuh fine yo'self a new place fuh nex' year. You got de wrong attitude. You bettuh go somewheah wheah you kin use yo' pencil!'"[115]

Having vowed to maintain control of black labor, whites half a century after emancipation could take a certain pride in their achievement. The landlord and merchant class had succeeded in using ownership of the land, control of credit, fraud, vagrancy laws, blacklists, the courts, the police, and vigilante groups ready to destroy crops, livestock, barns, homes, schools, and churches to keep aspiring black farmers mostly landless, dependent agricultural laborers. Not only had they managed to keep most blacks at the bottom of the agricultural ladder, but they also had reduced many landowning farmers to the status of tenants, sharecroppers, and wage hands.

Having succeeded in keeping black laborers down, whites insisted blacks lacked the capacity to improve their lives, that their condition was proof of their unfitness and incapacity, their cultural and racial inferiority. The purpose of the labor system, a black newspaper suggested in 1899, was "to degrade a man as low as possible and then kick him for being a hog." Although the signs of a grinning acquiescence were less visible, whites still insisted that blacks happily endure their daily lives. White families liked to regale visitors from the North and abroad with tales of contented black folk, such as the black Georgian who when faced with the choice of a term in the state penitentiary or having to live in Massachusetts gratefully opted for the penitentiary. And like the mayor of Savannah in 1916, whites loved to contrast black laborers in the South with those on whom northern employers were forced to depend.[116]

The economics of repression produced a black workforce mostly dependent on whites for their daily sustenance. But it did not necessarily produce the docile, contented, easily controlled workforce whites had envisioned. Whatever the talk about a new slavery—and there was much in the labor system and peonage to support such notions—landlords and laborlords were not able to exert the control over the black workforce that had existed before emancipation. With few if any prospects for improving their lives, workers were bound to be unpredictable, restless, and troublesome. Although plantation strikes were rare, usually spontaneous, and seldom well organized, they occurred often enough to occasion considerable grief and concern to the affected proprietors. A Louisiana rice planter complained in 1882 of having only fifteen acres planted when "the trouble with his hands began," and they were "now on a strike." A Louisiana sugar planter in 1887 boasted of having "effectually squelched" a strike, though it had been necessary "to apply a strong remedy—and it was done"; he expected no further trouble from the workers, most of whom had returned. The planter intended to make a profitable crop, as he told his son, and he would "use every exertion" to maintain him at school as a gentleman. "Extravagance and waste are reprehensible evils in rich people—but persons . . . have to keep up a certain appearance and respectability which requires some outlay of money." In some instances, as on Bluff Place in Beaufort County, labor disturbances seemed almost routine. "The Negroes are all on a strike wont pick the cotton and are sassy as can be," Alice Louisa Fripp noted in her diary. That state of affairs continued for at least another month, with workers striking some days, working other days.[117]

The troublesome aspects of black labor surfaced all too frequently. Enraged, frustrated, continually disappointed over a year's labor that yielded nothing but additional indebtedness, blacks found ways to strike back, sometimes destroying property belonging to the landlord, more often using their mobility and whatever education they had acquired to strike a better deal. As during slavery, they also maintained subtle forms of resistance, seizing advantages where they could find them, maneuvering their way around white expectations without necessarily violating them, testing the limits of white tolerance and endurance. Having tried to manage a plantation in Pointe Coupee Parish, Louisiana, Jack Chalaron confessed defeat, complaining of "a sudden, a marked change in the Conduct of the hands towards me and a spirit to mutiny against my authority." A. T. Montgomery, a Mississippi cotton grower, found himself in 1908 "so disgusted with negro labor that I have resolved not to plant cotton again." The previous year, a South Carolina planter had entered into his diary a complaint that appeared in a variety of journals: "Not a dog gone Niger worked today." And to a planter in North Carolina, the same complaint took on more menacing proportions. "Croppers have not struck a lick and it does not look like they are going to do any . . . they are worse than I ever saw them about going to work. They are all up to something, but I can't tell you what it is." A week earlier, he had accused his croppers of "playing their same old game."[118]

Organized protest, while rare, occurred with sufficient frequency to alarm white industrial boosters who liked to compare the stable and docile labor force in the New South, free of strikes and unions, to the turbulent workers of the North. The Knights of Labor conducted some successful organizing drives among blacks in the industrial sector and sugarcane fields, the United Mine Workers made headway among white and black workers, and the Industrial Workers of the World enjoyed some momentary successes among black and white stevedores and turpentine and lumber workers. On the docks of New Orleans, black and white workers achieved some impressive organizing successes. But there were limits to labor solidarity across racial lines, even in the unions that tolerated a black presence, and both blacks and whites sometimes opted for independent action and organizing. At best, as in Montgomery, Alabama, a separate-but-equal approach prevailed, at least momentarily. Both a white and a black union had been organized in the building trades, both were represented on a labor council, and on Labor Day they paraded together until they came to a certain point, whereupon one body turned to the right and the other to the left to finish the celebration in its own park.[119]

All too often, however, tensions between black and white workers, as well as violent hostility of state and local authorities, frustrated strike and organizing activity. Not only would black strikers be instantly replaced, but also strike leaders were subjected to beatings, arrest, and forced exile. Although blacks and whites glimpsed the possibilities of organizing around common grievances, both economically and politically, the attempts to substitute class consciousness for race consciousness in the New South was largely a history of futility, failure, and betrayal. For black Southerners, there was no exclusively economic or political way out. Hence that old black folk wisdom: "Even after a revolution the country will be full of crackers."[120]

10

NOWHERE DID THE growing tensions between black laborers and white employers seem more pronounced than in domestic service, as these tensions reached deep into the family circle and involved the closest contact between blacks and whites. Since emancipation, the difficulty in finding "good help" had been a constant source of annoyance to whites accustomed to black servants. The expression "they don't work like they used to" became a virtual cliché. Comparing her experience as a young woman with servants to her daughter's "trials," a Virginia woman could only testify in 1891 to the "changed nature of domestic service," and found it to be "altogether evil." Hearing of the difficulties of others, some thought themselves "comparatively blessed," as did a Georgia newspaper publisher, if they still retained "an old time darkey" for a cook.[121]

But the term "trouble with Negroes" soon came to be synonymous with troubles in the household and punctuated the correspondence, diaries, and conversations of white women and men. "Wherever one goes, the question of servants seems sure to come up," a Virginia white woman observed, and the litany of complaints, she thought, sounded familiar in most southern communities: how rare it was to find "a good and satisfactory servant"; dependency on "the 'new issue' Negroes, who have grown up in freedom, utterly untrained as cooks, house-maids, or nurses"; and the ways in which these Negroes "plunder us, carrying home with them at night all they can lay their hands on to feed trifling husbands or children growing up in idleness." And finally, and no doubt most aggravating, "We wear ourselves out in efforts to teach them," only to lose them.[122]

Whatever the "troubles" with black servants, however, the dependency on them half a century after emancipation had in no way abated. The fear of losing their cooks and maids plagued households, as the search for replacements and the need to train newly hired blacks proved to be a constant source of exasperation. "[T]his past summer," an observer wrote in 1905 of a Black Belt town, "nearly every woman in town who has a cook was shivering with fear lest she would 'quit.' " In Athens, Georgia, housewives feared that the black lodges kept "a blacklist" and that "the servants keep 'tabs' in this way on their employer." No doubt such "a blacklist," if kept, might have noted the compensation as well as the treatment accorded employees. Sensing his wife's exasperation over how to keep the family cook, Colonel William R. Pope, on active duty in France in World War I, came up with a novel inspiration: "Can't you pay a little more for a cook so as to keep one when you get her? I know all your servants have always bled you and I know the negroes are worthless but maybe more pay will solve the question."[123]

Accustomed to "help," white families rarely paid much attention to the demands placed on the blacks who worked for them. Perhaps they had persuaded themselves that black men and women, like the mules they worked, were constructed for service and could withstand the routine that few whites might endure. Of course, the "help" had their own sense of the burden they carried and their own way of expressing it.

> *Missus in de big house,*
> *Mammy in de yard.*
> *Missus holdin' her white hands,*
> *Mammy workin' hard,*
> *Mammy workin' hard,*
> *Mammy workin' hard.*
> *Missus holdin' her white hands,*
> *Mammy workin' hard.*[124]

Up at dawn to prepare breakfast for the white family, cleaning the house in the morning, preparing lunch, washing clothes, making dinner, and tidying up afterward, most black women worked a long day, often until ten o'clock at night. "You might as well say that I'm on duty all the time—from sunrise to sunrise, every day in the week," a middle-aged house worker and mother in Georgia testified in 1912. "I am the slave, body and soul, of this family." For thirty years, she had worked for four different families, occupying the positions of "house-girl," chambermaid, cook, and nurse, "frequently" working from fourteen to sixteen hours a day. "I am not permitted to rest. It's 'Mammy, do this,' or 'Mammy, do that,' or 'Mammy, do the other,' from my mistress all the time. . . . I live a treadmill life."[125]

Women and men employed in the house also had to learn the etiquette of household labor. They would sit at their own table, eat from separate plates, drink out of separate buckets and dippers, use their own toilets, and enter the house only by the back door. They would abide by the same rules of etiquette in how they addressed members of the family, and of course they would not expect such courtesies to be reciprocated—an unquestioned assumption for whites, "an indignity" in the estimation of an Alabama house worker. "The women are called 'Cook,' or 'Nurse,' or 'Mammy,' or 'Mary Jane,' or 'Lou,' or 'Dilcey,' as the case might be, and the men are called 'Bob,' or 'Boy,' or 'Old Man,' or 'Uncle Bill,' or 'Pete.' In many cases our white employers refer to us, and in our presence, too, as their 'niggers.'" And to maintain their jobs, she added, "we must tamely submit, and answer when we are called."[126]

Violations of work rules or house etiquette invited instant recrimination, whether verbal or physical. Like many of her contemporaries, Magnolia Le Guin, a Georgia farm woman born after slavery, found her black "help" mostly unnerving. "The greatest trials I believe of my life is to be obliged to have on our home place impudent, disrespectful, saucy negroes." One servant "unsettled" her when she put off for a day doing the ironing, another for talking "sass." It was more than Le Guin could bear. "Oh, what physical and mental suffering it has caused," she confided to her diary, and she implored the Lord for assistance. "Lord help me to be right in Thy sight when the negroes are provoking me." On another occasion, her need to scold a servant for his "impudent" behavior seemed to have unhinged her altogether, and she regretted afterward the emotions and temperament she had displayed. "It excited me to deal with an impudent negro and I feel as if I had been sick all day. Oh, how excited I become over any impudence from darkies. . . . God forgive me for all I said today that I ought to have left unsaid and give me courage and preserve me calmly to say to the impudent ones what I ought to say." The servant's "impudence" had consisted of drinking out of the same water dipper used by the white family.[127]

Black houseworkers might also find themselves working within the homes of middle-class black families. Instructions in black-authored etiquette manuals on how to treat servants, although not differing sharply from the rules in white homes, did reveal a far greater sensitivity to the rights and feelings of servants. "Ladies," one manual admonished employers, "the sooner you begin to consider the fact that your help is flesh and blood the better service will they give you. Every command, request, rather, should savor of leniency and be tempered with sympathy." The employing black family should also bear in mind that a servant's "aversion to intense heat, cold, over-work, and loss of rest is about the same as that of the employer's"—an insight that would have been lost on most white employers. Mistreatment or indifference, the manual insisted, would most likely produce poor and indifferent service. That did not mean, however, that black employers had to endure insolence or vulgarity from their servants. "The sooner that grade of help is started off the premises the better." But the manual promised black employers faithful and reliable service if they treated their household labor "as nearly as practicable as members of your own family."[128]

Whatever the persistent mythology about the submissive, obsequious household faithful, domestic workers by the early twentieth century impressed whites as a different and far more obstreperous workforce, less willing to subject themselves to the whims and demands of their employers, less willing to compromise their self-respect and independence. Ella Thomas, a domestic worker, made a point of informing the families for whom she worked about the household tasks she was willing and unwilling to perform. "I only gets on my knees to pray," she would tell them.

> A maid suppose to say how she can work. If you don't never open your mouth for yourself, who going to talk for you? . . . I didn't have the advantage of education, but I could look and see that if I didn't change something about my life, I'd be living just like my aunt lived—fearing the whites, doing everything they say. Some people say, oh, you're just independent, but I say I just figured how to get along the best I could.[129]

Dissatisfied houseworkers had long found ways to even the score in bouts with their white supervisors, whether slaveowners or employers. "How many times I spit in the biscuits and peed in the coffee just to get back at them mean white folks," Aunt Delia, the cook in a North Carolina family, recalled. Few white families ever knew how many within their household evinced the same spirit as Aunt Delia, but the suspicion grew that many of their servants, including the most "faithful," might qualify. Even a black-written book of etiquette thought it important to remind prospective employers of servants that treating them well might make them less indifferent to their work. "[T]he cook that's in a good humor when she is preparing a meal is more careful that her hands are kept clean, and into what she slings the sweat which runs in ringlets down her glossy cheeks, and where the nose drips fall, than she who's in ill humor. Landladies, one and all! 'What goes on in the kitchen is a sealed book.' "[130]

What one observer called an "incipient strike" characterized white-black relations and tensions in many households—perhaps in most, if one believed the frequency and quantity of the complaints. Not only had the quality of service rapidly deteriorated, but also there appeared to be some deliberateness in the behavior and movements of the black workers. "No matter how much they may be needed in the house, no matter how important the occasion may be, or how urgent the need for their services," a white housewife complained, "whether you have a wedding in the house, or sickness, or whatever you may have, they will just leave the cooking-stove and the housework and everything else and go off. . . ." And she began to suspect a certain degree of spitefulness in their actions, as if to underscore their independence. "I have known them to leave when they knew that invitations were out for a dining in the house; they would just leave without any particular reason at all, but simply from some foolish desire for change."[131]

Domestic workers had already asserted a growing independence. Most of them now lived outside the white household, a significant postemancipation development comparable to the breaking up of the old slave quarters. Some chose to slow the pace of labor, to reduce the amount of tasks they were willing to perform, and to take their own holidays. "The negro women young and old are willing to work in kitchens in their way," a Tennessee man informed his sister, "they come in the morning if they come at all when they are ready, and leave when they choose." A Mobile man informed a friend that his servants made "the most fantastic conditions."

For instance, they won't do a stroke of work after three o'clock. If you want a meal after that hour, you must prepare and serve it yourself. As for the abstraction of household stuff from the kitchen, it is carried on openly and systematically—they call it "Cook's excursion." In the case of domestic service, in fact, the difficult conditions which are being felt all over the world are intensified by—what shall I call it?—the race pride, or the race resentment, of the black. Domestic service was one of the badges of slavery; and now, if he or she will undertake it at all, it must be on such terms as shall remove from it all taint of servility.

He could appreciate the reasons for this development, but he deemed it likely to intensify "friction between the races."[132]

Reflecting the labor they performed and the meager pay they received, domestic workers learned to protest (and supplement) their income by taking full advantage of the "service pan." The term applied to food (usually left over from meals) and commodities that the cook or servant might smuggle out for consumption by her family. "[I]f it were not for the service pan," one such worker noted, "I don't know what the majority of our Southern colored families would do. The service pan is the mainstay in many a home." Many white families had come to expect such "theft," and some almost welcomed it as a way to diminish their own sense of guilt and confirm their moral superiority. For domestics, however, it was simply another way to survive: "I indignantly deny that we are thieves," a houseworker testified. "We don't steal; we just 'take' things—they are a part of the oral contract, exprest or implied. We understand it, and most of the white folks understand it." Although tolerating the "service pan," a white Alabama woman deemed it childlike behavior and a "race defect." One day she chided her cook about "stealing" and asked her why she did so. "Hit's dis way, Miss Sarah," she replied, *"we* all thinks we is got the right to take from *you* all dis as much as our daddies and mammies was worth endurin' slavery times!" But the advice given in a black-written book of etiquette to employers of servants sounded a different note: "No one should keep servants about the house who cannot afford to give them to eat just such as the family has."[133]

Thought by many whites to be childlike, lazy, slow-moving, sloppy workers, with a propensity for theft and absenteeism, black servants found ways to exploit the stereotype to their own advantage. If that was what whites expected of them, some blacks might be happy to oblige them. If it reinforced white views of black inferiority, it provided blacks with enhanced feelings of independence and perhaps additional time for themselves and their families. After all, black Southerners never expected to win the debate over the work ethic, as some blacks in Texas made clear in 1905.

> *Well, they call me a rounder if I stay in town, and they say*
>   *I'm a rounder if I roam aroun';*
> *I got it writ on the tail of my shirt: "I'm a nachel-bo'n*
>   *rounder and don't need to work."*
> *And so I ain't bothered; no, I ain't bothered.*

Whether blacks worked efficiently and zealously or not, they could not escape the stereotypes white Southerners held of them. If blacks performed hard labor to the satisfaction of whites, that quality would be expressed in the aphorism "work like a nigger." If blacks failed to work to the satisfaction of whites, that quality would be expressed in the aphorism "lazy as a nigger."[134]

In time, the accumulation of hard labor, indignities, and verbal and physical violence would have its effect on the bodies and minds of women and men performing the tasks demanded of them. July Ann Halfen, ten years old at the end of the Civil War, worked in Mississippi for the same woman for some fifty years, scrubbing, washing, ironing, and nursing the children. But when the old mistress died, the daughters Halfen had nursed accused her of stealing too much and dismissed her. All that remained were July Halfen's memories, as she thought about her life. "O, I is bin treated mi'ty bad in my life. No mam, I neber had any good thing happen to me in my life. All I eber kno'd wus hard wurk an' got mi'ty lil'l fur dat. No mam, I neber sing now; dar is nuffin in my life to make me sing. When I wus young I cud sing but all dem songs is gone frum me now. All I kno' is sufferin' an' dis misery is got a good hold on to me."[135]

Perhaps the difficulty encountered within white households should have been sufficient warning. Women who worked for whites outside of their homes could be no less recalcitrant. Laundry workers were a particularly active group, and their protests knew no color line. Booker T. Washington had to contend with a petition from twenty-eight laundry workers at Tuskegee Institute in 1911, expressing dissatisfaction with their pay and the workload. "You know the laundry is the hardest work done by female hands on the grounds," they asserted. "We believe all honest laborers should receive fair payment for their labor, as long as

they render conscientious services—regardless of sex." A faculty committee recommended a 20 percent increase, up to a maximum of 72
cents a day; the average student worker was earning 50 cents a day.[136]

The female workers at Tuskegee gave voice to a tradition of protest
and agitation among washerwomen. Perhaps the most audacious of
these protests was the strike staged in Atlanta, the pride of the New
South. Having already established a reputation as a troublesome workforce, washerwomen in Atlanta faced a hostile white community when
an estimated three thousand of them staged a strike for higher wages in
1881. The association they formed had been organized in a black
church, preachers in the other black churches had joined in announcing a mass meeting, and during the strike itself strikers held their
nightly meetings in the churches. "They passed resolutions informing
all women not members of the society to quit work or stand the consequences," an alarmed reporter wrote. "I tell you, this strike is a big
thing." When the *Atlanta Constitution* noted that the strike had inconve-
nienced many citizens, it sounded an even more ominous note that demanded white attention and vigilance: "Not only washerwomen, but
the cooks, house servants and nurses are asking an increase. The com-
binations are being managed by the laundry ladies." That was more
than enough to mobilize the power and resources available to white Atlantans. Landlords threatened to raise house rents of washerwomen to
prohibitive levels, and the city council prepared to require all washerwomen belonging to any "association" or "society" to pay a business
tax or buy a license—the same tax levied against local merchants. "We
mean business this week or no washing," the strikers replied, warning
that they would settle for nothing less than "full control of the city's
washing at our own prices," much as the city controlled their husbands'
work at their prices. It was bold talk, but the back of the strike had been
broken by the intimidation, the arrests of strike leaders for disorderly
conduct, and the threat to place more offenders on chain gangs.[137]

11

THE RESPONSE OF white Atlanta simply reminded blacks, if they
needed reminders, that whites wielded overwhelming power over their
working lives and destinies. Organized black activity that seemed to
challenge white authority and control of labor always assured a quick
and ruthless response, including the full power of the state, the courts,

and the police. The same force brought to bear on trade unions and "associations" in the cities could be wielded to crush organized activity in the countryside.

The Colored Farmers' National Alliance, for one, threatened to organize hundreds of thousands of black farmers and laborers. At one point, Richard Manning Humphrey, the white Baptist minister who headed the alliance, claimed 1.2 million members, and in 1891 many of these joined in a strike of cotton pickers demanding $1 a day instead of the prevailing rate of 50 cents a day. But the failure of the white Farmers' Alliance to provide support, and the determination of authorities to quell the "uprising," quickly doomed the strike and the black organization.[138]

As if man-made obstacles were not sufficiently daunting, black farmers faced natural hazards, not only some disastrous floods but also the boll weevil, an insect pest that destroyed cotton fields in the early twentieth century. In the summer of 1903, the boll weevil hit Texas with devastating force. "I saw hundreds of farms lying out," an agricultural reformer wrote. "I saw wretched people facing starvation; I saw whole towns deserted." And it rapidly spread eastward. When Richard Wright's parents moved from Natchez to Memphis, young Richard remembered only talk of "the eevel boll weevil." Ned Cobb chose not to move. He could long remember how the pest had come to Tallapoosa County, Alabama, between 1910 and 1920 and how it had devastated both cotton fields and farmers' lives and livelihood. "Couldn't nobody pay on his debts when the weevil et up his crop."[139]

> *"Well," the farmer told the merchant,*
> *"I want some meat and meal";*
> *"Well," the merchant told the farmer,*
> *"Boll weevil's in yo'r field."*[140]

The weevil—barely a quarter of an inch long—laid its eggs in the cotton bolls, and in a very short time the bolls, which were to have yielded a harvest of cotton, had been reduced to empty shells. Efforts to combat the insect proved unavailing, and Ned Cobb confessed that the "little sneakin devil" frightened him with its resiliency and "creepin" ways.

When the boll weevil starts in our cotton and go to depositin his eggs in them squares, that's when he'll kill you. Them eggs hatch out there in so many days, up come a young boll weevil. It don't take em but a short period of time to raise up enough out there in your field, in the spring after your cotton gets up—in a few days, one weevil's got a court of young uns hatchin.[141]

The boll weevil made no distinctions based on race or class, destroying white and black farmers, large and small. Ned Cobb's fascination with the insect suggested a certain admiration, as "everything God created He created for a purpose." And if that purpose included the destruction of white fortunes, some black farmers felt a grudging sympathy for an insect that could render white men powerless, that could exert controls over white men that they could not. "They were a proud and selfish people, those plantation owners," Mahalia Jackson recalled, "and I believe . . . that God finally send the boll weevil to jumble them. . . . Thanks to the boll weevil, a lot of those thieving plantation people died out, too."[142]

> Boll weevil said to the merchant,
> "Better drink yo cold lemonade;
> When I git thru with you
> Gwine drag you out o' the shade—
> I have a home! I have a home!"
>
> Boll weevil said to the doctor,
> "Better po' out all them pills;
> When I get through with the farmer
> He can't pay no doctor's bills—
> I have a home! I have a home!"
>
> Boll weevil said to the preacher,
> "Better shet your church house door;
> When I get thru with the farmer
> He can't pay the preacher no more—
> I have a home! I have a home!"
>
> Boll weevil said to the farmer,
> "Better sell yo' old machine;
> When I get thru with you
> You can't buy no gasoline—
> I have a home! I have a home!"
>
> Boll weevil said to his wife,
> "Better stan' up on yo' feet

> *N' look way down here in Georgy*
> *At all the cotton we got to eat—*
> *All night long, and all day too!"*
>
> *Boll weevil said to the farmer,*
> *"I wisht that you wuz well."*
> *Farmer said to the boll weevil,*
> *"I wisht you wuz in hell!"*
> *Boll weevil blues! Boll weevil blues!*[143]

Even the cries of dismay often took the form of a respectful conversation between the black man and his uninvited cotton-consuming guest, with the black farmer wondering why the insect should wipe out people already overburdened and victimized.

> *Now Mister Boll-Weevil, if you can talk why don't you tell?*
> *Now Mister Boll-Weevil, if you can talk why don't you tell?*
> *Say, you got poor Kokomo down here in Georgia catchin' a lot of hell.*[144]

The exploits of the boll weevil affected black farmers in a number of ways. Planters reduced their cotton acreage and chose to give up cotton altogether in favor of livestock or food crops. That in turn reduced the demand for black labor, and many field hands, sharecroppers, and tenants found themselves forced off the plantations to seek work elsewhere.

When Ned Cobb recalled that "all God's dangers ain't a white man," he had the boll weevil in mind. Actually, both antagonists displayed aggressive appetites and the capacity to destroy black aspirations and to cheat blacks out of the products of their labor.

> *Don't you see how them creeturs*
> *Now have done me wrong?*
> *Boll weevil's got my cotton*
> *And the merchant's got my corn.*
> *What shall I do? What shall I do?*[145]

But the boll weevil was no match for the white man's rapaciousness. "[W]hat the boll weevil can do to me," Cobb reflected, "aint half so bad to what a man might do. I can go to my field and shake a poison dust on my crop and the boll weevil will sail away. But how can I sling a man off my back?" That question took on a real urgency in the 1890s

and the early twentieth century, when white Southerners, faced with
the specter of a New Negro, moved on every front to make certain that
their assumptions about black inferiority went unchallenged.

> *Boll-weevil in de cotten,*
> *Cut wurm in de cawn,*
> *Debil in de white man*
> *Wah's goin' on.*[146]

CHAPTER FOUR

WHITE FOLKS: SCRIPTURES

Southern whites cannot walk, talk, sing, conceive of laws or justice, think of sex, love, the family or freedom without responding to the presence of Negroes.
—*Ralph Ellison*[1]

"What do they talk about when they're eating?"
"Mostly they discusses us culled folks."
—*A butler's assistant in the home of a prominent Atlanta family*[2]

We venture to say that fully ninety per cent of all the race troubles in the South are the result of the Negro forgetting his place. If the black man will stay where he belongs, act like a Negro should act, work like a Negro should work, talk like a Negro should talk, and study like a Negro should study, there will be very few riots, fights, or clashes.
—*Shreveport (Louisiana) Times, 1919*[3]

SOME SEVENTY-FIVE YEARS after the Civil War, two white women approached a small house on Camp Street in New Orleans. They had been told it was the home of Mary Harris, an elderly black woman who had once been a slave on a sugar plantation in Louisiana and who might be willing to share her memories of those days for an oral history project. "Sure I remember slavery times," she told them. "I was a big girl, turned eleven. I used to pull the fan that kep' off the flies while the white folks was eatin'. It wasn't hard work but my arms used to get tired—'specially at dinner when they set so long at the table." She had never been whipped, she said, because she had performed her tasks and knew never to talk back to white people. Her mother, how-ever, had felt the lash more than once, and the experience had left a lasting impact. "My ma tol' me she was brutally beaten an' she was bitter all her life."

The two white women returned the next day to resume the interview. This time they found Mary Harris's son barring their way. "Slavery!" he exclaimed. "Why are you concerned about such stuff? It's bad enough for it to have existed and when we can't forget it there is no need of rehashing it." The women tried to explain to him that they only wished to preserve the reminiscences of former slaves about the Old South, slavery, and the Civil War and that his mother possessed a "marvelous memory" of those times. That same "marvelous memory," the son retorted, had filled him with bitterness and anger. He reminded them of the stories of brutality and abuse he had heard from his mother. The visitors replied that all slaveholders had not behaved in such ways. Slavery had its "unfortunate" side, they agreed, and they had conceded as much to his mother the previous day, but the two women took pride in the fact that "old slaves still tell of their love for 'ole Miss' and 'ole Marse,' and the loyalty and love existing between them could never have been created in raucous hearts."

The son remained unmoved, and he did not hesitate to reveal his own feelings about the past and the legacy he had inherited. "Yes'm, I'm bitter and the more I think about it the madder I get. Look at me. They say I could pass for white. My mother is bright too. And why? Because the man who owned and sold my mother was her father. But that's not all. That man I hate with every fiber of my body and why? A brute like that who could sell his own child into unprincipled hands is a beast—the power, just because he had the power, and the thirst for money."

Having made his point, the son relented and agreed to let the two women see his mother again. But they had heard enough. The son's remarks had badly shaken them, and they preferred to leave rather than resume the interview. "After such a tirade we were afraid, deciding that 'discretion was the better part of valor.' It was our first experience with a madman."[4]

2

FIFTY YEARS AFTER the Emancipation Proclamation, white Southerners reached a consensus on the need to resolve growing racial tensions. Some 90 percent of black Americans still lived in the South, and the dominant racial attitudes, in the estimation of Thomas Bailey, a southern educator, were nothing less than "a creed of a people—a part of their morality and of their religion." That racial creed, as he heard it expressed by "a group of representative Southerners," had become for most whites an orthodoxy—"practically the *common opinion* of the South"—and Bailey in 1913 enumerated its major premises:

1. "Blood will tell."
2. The white race must dominate.
3. The Teutonic peoples stand for race purity.
4. The negro is inferior and will remain so.
5. "This is a white man's country."
6. No social equality.
7. No political equality.
8. In matters of civil rights and legal adjustments give the white man, as opposed to the colored man, the benefit of the doubt; and under no circumstances interfere with the prestige of the white man.
9. In educational policy let the negro have the crumbs that fall from the white man's table.
10. Let there be such industrial education of the negro as will best fit him to serve the white man.
11. Only [white] Southerners understand the negro question.
12. Let the [white] South settle the negro question.
13. The status of peasantry is all the negro may hope for, if the races are to live together in peace.
14. Let the lowest white man count for more than the highest negro.
15. The above statements indicate the leadings of Providence.[5]

With varying degrees of intensity, and regardless of social class, the overwhelming majority of southern whites subscribed to this racial creed and passed it on to a new generation of whites born in the late nineteenth century who had no memory of slavery. Seeking the views of this generation on race relations, a professor at Southwestern Presbyterian College in Memphis asked his class in 1909 to submit essays on the question "What will become of the American negro?" Ranging in age from eighteen to thirty-seven, the forty-eight students came from "well-known and influential" southern families; nearly half of them were candidates for the ministry.

Although a small minority in the class pleaded for patience and tolerance and contemplated a Negro capable of improvement (but not so-

cial or political assimilation), most of the students embraced the prevailing racial orthodoxy. Expressing none of the nostalgia or sympathy
of some of their elders, they articulated in their essays a gloomy assessment of southern blacks, including that "thoroughly untrustworthy"
new generation, perceiving them as a subversive and potentially dangerous force capable of plunging the entire section into racial warfare.
("The negro of today is insolent, ungrateful and even brutish in his attitude toward the white people.") Measured against the standard of the
Anglo-Saxon ("the most pure, proud, noble race that ever walked the
earth"), southern blacks were inferior in both character and capacity
("the most vile, degraded, and filthy race living") and seldom able to
rise above "the plane of indecency, immorality, and crime." Race, not
class or schooling, made any fraternization impossible. That seemed
obvious. ("No man with a drop of Southern blood in his veins will
stoop so low as to associate with the black man, no matter how highly
educated he may be.")

Believing that the right to vote filled Negroes with "absurd and dangerous aspirations," none of the students would countenance either social or political equality, and only a few placed much confidence in
education to improve the prospects of blacks. Many already judged
schooling an abject failure, likely to transform the black man "from a
humble servant into a ferocious and obnoxious disturber and breeder
of race equality." Some repeated the old shibboleths ("[w]hen you educate a negro, right there and then you ruin him"), and still others
blamed the high crime rate on educated blacks.

Even those not ready to abandon educational efforts on behalf of
blacks thought these should be limited in content and objectives. Teach
the Negro to read and write "but only that he may labor more efficiently for the white man." Higher education, on the other hand, unfit
the Negro for work and made him "unbearably impudent." After all, as
one student asked, "What good does it do to teach a negro Shake-
speare, Latin, or Greek when all that he will ever be is a day laborer and
a field hand?" Still another student articulated an underlying fear that
many whites tried to mask: Education might actually succeed. ("If we
educate him, we fear he will become our equal, and in time amalgamation would be the result of education.")

Perceiving the races as "drifting farther and farther apart," students
anticipated a bleak future. Remedies ranged from creating "a black
man's State" (but whites would obviously need to make the laws) to
rigid controls that would keep blacks in the cotton fields (where they

would be free from "whiskey, cocaine, and consumption"). Many of the students, however, despaired in their essays of any solution, and predicted that black efforts to achieve education, social equality, and civil rights would in time precipitate a race war blacks would surely lose. The most optimistic of the students based their hopes on blacks' recognizing their incapacities and remaining in their place. ("A negro can succeed in the South if he is content to be a negro and remain in a negro's place.") Not only had God condemned the sons of Ham to be hewers of wood and drawers of water, but also "it is up to the white man of today to see that this prophecy is fulfilled."

Perhaps the most disturbing revelation was the degree to which these young southern whites not only demonized, but dehumanized black Southerners. "The negro and the mule are born to go together," one student wrote, repeating a familiar refrain. But in making that same comparison, another student was much less sanguine about the ultimate outcome. "The negro is more like a mule than anything I can think of. . . . It is said of a mule that he will carry you ninety-nine times to kill you the hundredth. So it is with the negro: he will prove faithful for many years and at the last kill you and all your family. You cannot get the brute out of the negro; therefore he must be kept under subjection."

After reading the essays, the professor found little room for optimism. "I am simply placing before readers the signs of the times, without theories, without apology, without defence. These are not theories that *might be*, but tendencies that *are.*" He expected this group of students to occupy positions of influence in their communities; they were tomorrow's leaders and shapers of public opinion. "Are not the indications plain," the professor concluded, choosing to underline his words for emphasis, *"that the black man is to be restrained, hampered, brow-beaten, discouraged within the next quarter of a century as never before in all the bitter years of his existence on this continent?"*[6]

3

THE YOUNG BLACKS who came of age in the late nineteenth and early twentieth centuries impressed W. E. B. Du Bois as a generation "to whom War, Hell, and Slavery were but childhood tales" and "whose young appetites had been whetted to an edge by school and story and half-awakened thought." Understandably, the white South carefully monitored this generation, the first born outside the discipline of slavery, and many whites—including a new generation who enjoyed fewer relations with blacks—did not like what they saw and heard. A Mississippi clergyman found in 1904 "great unrest and growing discontent" among blacks. "They are beginning to feel friendless and hopeless." In the absence of those "peculiar attachments" and "common memories and sentiments" that had once bound the races, numerous observers testified, new generations of whites and blacks were growing up "in unmitigated mutual antipathy." The races, many agreed, had never been farther apart, and the consequences were readily apparent. "The white people seem to have forgotten that all the old Uncles and Aunties are gone," a Georgian warned, "and do not know how to figure on the possibilities of the new issue."[7]

Unfamiliarity, W. E. B. Du Bois explained to a visitor to Atlanta University in 1908, bred mutual suspicion and hostility. Whereas blacks once had friends among whites of the same age, that occurred now with much less frequency. "The younger white people," Du Bois observed, "have no feeling towards the negro but dislike, founded on utter lack of comprehension." The schools, Du Bois insisted, helped to encourage such antipathy. "The progressive negro is held up as a bugbear to the white child, who is told to 'Look out, or he will get ahead of you!' Fear, jealousy, and hatred are actively taught to the rising generation of whites."[8]

When whites talked about a New Negro, and they did so with increasing regularity, more often than not they were acknowledging problems in containing the ambitions and controlling the behavior of a new generation of black Southerners. Although whites and even older blacks took pains to remind this generation of the restraints placed on their freedom, the admonitions often went unheeded, along with the old customs and racial etiquette—or so it seemed. Between the end of Reconstruction and World War I, the problem created growing concern and heightened tensions. "The new negro," warned a Georgia editor, "is killing the relation established by the old negro."[9]

The contrast encouraged white Southerners to seek comfort in an idealized version of the past. To flatter their egos, as well as to assuage their doubts and apprehensions, whites during slavery had invented the figure of Sambo, the simple, faithful, cheerful, unresentful, deferential Negro menial who was always eager and willing to serve, even to give his life for his owners. The model slave, Sambo evinced the characteristics, mannerisms, body movements, and demeanor whites expected of an inferior and childlike race. If whites embraced this image during slavery, they became downright ardent in their reverence for it after emancipation. They needed Sambo more than ever before. Even as many whites embraced the New South, they chose to romanticize "the old Negro," the rapidly disappearing Negro. Between 1890 and World War I, white Southerners went to extraordinary lengths to mythologize the past, to fantasize an Old South, a Civil War, a Reconstruction, and a Negro that conformed to the images they preferred to cherish, images that both comforted and reassured them. They wanted to remind themselves of black loyalty and service in the past, to honor "the old slavery-time Negro," the unemancipated, unreconstructed Sambos, with their "dignified humility" and "unfailing devotion to duty," who remained committed to the lessons and traits they had acquired as slaves. "Paradoxical as it may seem," a white Georgian explained to a northern audience, "the South loves the negro—not the new negro, but the old."[10]

The qualities attributed to the "old Negro" permitted whites to speak fondly of the civilizing and restraining influences of slavery and fearfully of the consequences of emancipation. In a glowing public tribute in 1899, Judge James M. Greer told an audience in Memphis of how he had known the Negro as both "a trusted, loyal slave" and "as my friend and my inferior." Employing a rhetoric familiar everywhere in the South, he defined the "old Negro" as most whites wanted to remember him and as they insisted on memorializing him:

> If he was wanting in settled purpose and determined mental effort, he was also without malicious hatred or puling complaint. If he had the thoughtlessness of childhood, he had also its faith. If he was religious without reason, he was devout without hypocrisy. . . . If he was without fixed principles in his life, he was kind in his impulse. If he was without the knowledge of books, he had gained much from observation. If he never originated, he readily imitated. . . . If he was without profound wisdom, he was also without deep sorrow.

In concluding his portrait, Judge Greer underscored still another quality of the Negro for which he no doubt thought the white South should be forever grateful: "If his courage was small, his rebellions were few."[11]

For their own self-esteem and place in history, southern whites who had owned slaves and defended slavery needed to persuade themselves and pass on to a new generation the paternalistic notion that they had always acted in good faith, meeting their obligations to a race possessing neither the physical nor the mental resources to care for themselves. "We know and remember, as our children cannot, the brighter side of Negro character," an Alabamian observed.[12] To keep those memories alive, whites became obsessed with the need to revise the past to serve the present. That revision, by the turn of the century, had taken on the dimensions of an extraordinarily popular and ritualistic white nostalgia, featuring merchandised caricatures of grinning, carefree darkies and popular literary and artistic embellishments of the slaves and the racial utopia in which they had lived and worked and allegedly thrived.

When she dedicated her published memoirs of the old plantation to "my dear black Mammy," a Florida white woman sounded the prevailing theme of the literature of nostalgia: "Her skin was black, but her heart was white." In tributes to the former slaves, whites might assign to them some of the best qualities ordinarily reserved for the superior race. Even so, no one doubted the proper relations between whites and blacks, and whites found it difficult to think of former slaves as mature adults possessing mature feelings. Told of the death of a former slave, an Atlanta lawyer heaped on Sam Bell (known to him as Uncle Sam) the most extravagant praise—indeed, the ultimate compliment—but there was no doubt he was talking about an inferior. Despite the color of Uncle Sam's skin, the attorney declared his old slave to be " 'a South Carolina gentleman,' instinctively refined, spontaneously courteous and polite, in speech truthful, in conduct without guile, in simplicity and humility, a little child."[13]

By the turn of the century, the "old plantation Negro," whose behavior was said to be as easily explicable as it was quaint and picturesque, had provided sufficient material for a literary industry. Thomas Nelson Page, in many best-selling books and in articles in popular journals, eulogized the venerable old-time uncles and aunties, endearing them not only to native whites but also to a national audience. Like many white interpreters of black behavior, Page evoked the merits of paternalism and permitted his carefully selected or imagined ex-slaves to revel in nostalgia about the past. "Dem wuz good ole times, marster, de bes' Sam ever see!" one of his characters exclaimed. "Dey wuz, in fac'! Niggers didn't hed nothing 'tall to do." As filtered through Page's translation and predilections, the reader had no way of knowing the circumstances under which "Sam" memorialized slavery or the extent of his duplicity, the degree to which he might be masking his genuine feelings. What Page wanted to remember and celebrate in his dialect stories was that "relation of warm friendship and tender sympathy" between the races. And he wanted to memorialize that relationship in the early twentieth century because it was being undermined by "Afro-Americans" with their "veneer of a so-called education."[14]

The even more popular Joel Chandler Harris elaborated on familiar stereotypes of blacks, regaling generations of Americans with the stories told to white children by an Uncle Remus, a kind, aged storyteller who blended wisdom, deference, and humility. Through the characters of Br'er Rabbit, Br'er Wolf, and Br'er Bear, among others, Harris related Negro folktales, many of them suggesting the duplicity, guile, and cunning black men and women employed to survive in slavery. Through some of these same stories, and in others he invented and embellished, Harris perpetuated myths about the character and contentment of blacks and their enduring love of the white folks they served. And like many of the popular caricatures, Harris's black characters not only lavished praise on their owners but also mocked the postemancipation aspirations of their own people, particularly their enthusiasm for education. "Hit's de ruinashun er dis country. . . . Put a spellin'-book in a nigger's han's, en right den en dar' you loozes a plow-hand."[15]

The literature of nostalgia rested in large part on the stories told in dialect by favorite mammies, aunties, and uncles, most of them collected, edited, and published by former mistresses and masters. In one such work, *Mammy's Reminiscences*, published in 1898, Martha S. Gielow of Alabama wanted to capture the genuine folk wisdom of "the old-time Mammy and Daddy, the devoted foster parents to the children of the South." In her view, minstrel performers had distorted and exaggerated the old Negroes, making them "almost unrecognizable by those who knew and loved them." The sketches in *Mammy's Reminiscences* were presented as "drawing-room monologues," and they featured not only "Mammy" but also "Sambo," a "pickaninny," and the plantation preacher. Dedicated to her own "mammy," pictured on the title page, the stories described and glamorized life in the slave quarters and the Big House. Inscribing a copy of the book to a friend, Gielow lamented the end of the way of life she had sought to capture:

> *For the old plantation days*
> *they are no more,*
> *And the "Mammy," & the "Daddy,"*
> *once so dear,*

We will never know again
Except in soft refrain
Of the quaint plantation lore,
Sweet & queer.[16]

Nostalgic tributes to the "loyal slave" became a stock-in-trade of political oratory, finding their way into the speeches of even the most vitriolic and demagogic Negrophobes. Addressing a "spellbound"
audience, Senator James K. Vardaman placed the black mammy only
slightly lower on the pedestal of the "lost cause" than the southern
belle and the Rebel soldier:

> Ah! how well I remember the old negro mammy who took the place of
> the one who bore me, how well I remember that type of the faithful
> old slave who looked after me and other boys of my time with a faith-
> fulness and tender care of a mother.

But even as Vardaman brought tears to the eyes of his audience by
reciting the virtues of the "old southern mammy," he aroused their indignation when he contrasted that venerable figure to a new breed of
lustful, assertive, and ambitious Negroes. "[T]his grand old type of the
darky is passing," he warned. "It is supplanted by the Afro-American,
which means a good servant girl or a good farmhand spoiled—the result of a faulty and sentimental educational system."[17]

That same combination of paternalism and intense Negrophobia
characterized much of the rhetoric of the New South. A prominent
North Carolinian, in a letter to a northern critic of the South's racial
policies, reflected the felt need of some whites to single out the old slave
generation for special consideration. In this instance, the "special consideration" took a curious turn. After proposing that the United States
acquire a separate territory for blacks, he proposed to send there the
restless, discontented blacks. The "docile kindly old negro," satisfied
with his place in the South, would obviously wish to remain among
those whites who still loved and understood him. That assumption permitted the writer to lecture his northern critic on an often repeated
central theme in the rhetoric of white nostalgia—how southern whites,
and only southern whites, truly know the Negro.

> You know little of the true feelings between the old-fashioned negro
> and ourselves, Mr. Storey. You have not suckled at the breast of a

negro Mammy, as I have. You have never had your old negro nurse to throw her loving arms about you, when you return to your old home, as I sometimes do now, at 59 years of age.[18]

Few white politicians were more relentless in their exploitation of the race issue than Ben "Pitchfork" Tillman of South Carolina. But like Vardaman and other white leaders, he alternated his rabid racist rhetoric, often in the same speeches, with effusive tributes to the many "good" Negroes who accepted their subordinate place with equanimity, cheerful compliance, and faithful labor, and who rejected agitation for social and political equality. In his own servant, Joe Gibson, Tillman professed to have the utmost confidence. "A more loyal friend, no man ever had," he told his colleagues in Congress. "Every child that I have would share his last crust with that negro tomorrow." And in the ultimate tribute, he confessed, "I do not know whether I belong to Joe or Joe belongs to me. . . . [W]e have agreed to live together until one or both of us die, and when I go away, if I go first, I know he will shed as sincere tears as anybody." Joe Gibson died first, and Tillman kept his word, arranging the funeral and erecting a monument over Gibson's grave. But like others, Tillman extolled the virtues of "the old Negro" to warn the South of the threat of the New Negro. While the former slaves had benefited from the discipline of slavery, their sons and daughters—"inoculated with the virus of equality"—were responsible for "all the devilment of which we read every day."[19]

The rituals of white nostalgia in the late nineteenth century featured much-publicized reunions of former slaves with the families they had once served. In describing such a reunion in Palmetto, Georgia, the reporter used the occasion to pay tribute to the "faithful" Negroes and to the whites who had assumed responsibility for civilizing and Christianizing them. Fifteen former slaves gathered at the Menefee plantation, where they had once worked. Each of those attending the reunion— the reporter attached the title "Uncle" or "Aunt" to their names— fondly recalled "in their quaint negro dialect" the antebellum and war years, comforting and regaling a crowd of whites with songs and stories of the good times and the kind treatment they remembered. The musical entertainment they provided impressed the reporter as an example "of that quaint, perfectly harmonious kind such as only negroes can make." When the black men and women were ushered into the Big House and shown the portrait of their former master, they were said to have stood with bowed heads, many of them weeping, each of them

offering unrestrained praise. Perceived generational differences influenced how newspapers reported such events, and this reunion was no
exception. As if to underscore the contrast between the former slaves
who assembled for the reunion and the new breed of Negro, the reporter suggested that race relations in Palmetto were not entirely harmonious. Only recently, a white mob had shot down three young black
men after they had been arrested on charges of attempting to burn the
town to the ground.[20]

The opportunity to honor aging former slaves was not left entirely to
whites. Partially with an eye toward white patronage, black organizers
of "colored fairs" invited former slaves to participate in ceremonies recalling the old times. The meetings of the ex-slaves associations often
coincided with these fairs and became highly publicized rituals that fed
white nostalgia. On both sides, selective memories prevailed, most of
the recollections dwelling on the kindly relations said to have characterized blacks and whites during slavery. "There were no bitter memories," a black participant said of these meetings. "There were no harsh
criticisms. There were no unpleasant allusions. The object of our gatherings was to recall and keep in mind delightful days and the many joy-
ful events of the past." On the fiftieth anniversary of the Emancipation
Proclamation, the Ex-Slaves Association of North Carolina gathered at
the Great Negro State Fair. Former owners and their descendants were
invited to partake of the festivities, they provided transportation to the
ex-slaves, and in an exceptional gesture they helped to prepare and
serve the dinner. "There are no differences between us," a member of
the association exulted. "We have no problems to solve. We understand
our relations. We love each other still."[21] During the twenty years
since he founded the Georgia Ex-Slaves Association, the Reverend
B. R. Holmes observed, he had never heard at their meetings any ex-
slave speak of bondage with bitterness; on the contrary, they rejoiced in
recalling the old times—"all of us wukin' dar in de fiel' togedder chop-
pin' cotton and singin'."[22]

No less spectacular than the reunions and associations, old slaveholding families and their descendants tried to keep alive the paternalism that, in their view, had in the past characterized the relations
between whites and enslaved blacks. The letters written by ex-slaves to
their former owners generally fed that paternalism, with the black
writer longing to see them ("I am very anxious to see you and Miss Fannie and all of My other friends both White and (Col)"); often needing
financial aid or prepared to return to the old plantation ("I never feel

like I am at home untill I get to your house. When I come again I exspect to Stay as long as I live if agreeble with you"); and invariably bestowing his or her gratitude on the old master ("[W]hen you exit this world if I am living I am come pell to say like one of old. A great man this day has falling in israel. [N]ot only me but many more will cry the same. [F]or your fame is spread a brod in this world").[23] The visits of former slaves also encouraged whites to reflect on the beneficence of the old regime. After one such visit, a white woman explained to her grandson how the reunion testified to "the loving feelings" the "old slaves" still retained for their former owners.[24]

Even with the passing of the slaveholding class, many of their children tried to perpetuate the memories and attachments. Half a century after the end of slavery, in Marshallville, Georgia, the sons of a former slaveowner donned aprons and acted as waiters at a dinner in honor of eleven former slaves. The elderly Negroes made speeches to commemorate the affair. Although the hosts acted as the waiters, they were not about to leave the preparation of the dinner to whites; they found "the best cook" in South Georgia. Both southern and northern newspapers reported these social affairs, helping to cement the gradual rapprochement of the two sections and the tacit understanding that southern whites had always known what was best for their Negroes and had their best interests in mind.[25]

Having evoked warm and sentimental memories of "the faithful darkey" and the "devoted mammy," the white South lamented and ritualized their passing. "I always called him 'uncle,' " explained a saddened South Carolina farmer as he tried to reconcile himself in 1893 to the loss of a former slave. "He came as near being a christian as any negro I know." When in 1903 a physician in Sumter County, South Carolina, wrote of the deaths of "old man Jack" and "old Jim and his son Jim," he added mournfully, "The old darkies are thinning out fast." By the early twentieth century, effusive tributes to the "old darkies" knew few bounds. Most of them repeated the familiar themes of unwavering fidelity and service: "She was like a member of the family." "She never realized what her freedom meant and used to tell us in a tone of genuine regret of the good old days 'befo' de wah.' " "Aunt Ann is dead! Those black wrinkled old hands that used to rock us in the cradle all the day long are quietly folded for an eternal rest."[26]

Obituaries and memories of former slaves figured prominently in the local press, making all the more explicit in the impressionable minds of native whites the degree to which emancipation and a new generation of blacks had destroyed the best qualities of the Negro. Under the heading "Death of a Good Negro," an Atlanta newspaper lamented the passing of a local hotel porter, describing him affectionately as a "faithful, good negro, who won the esteem and confidence of all who knew him by his unfailing devotion to duty. He was punctual as a clock, always reliable and trusty." The death of Archibald Thomas in 1910 permitted a Baltimore newspaper to reminisce about a time "when black men really loved their masters and the masters regarded their black men as members of their families." Under the heading "Archie Laid To Rest," the obituary identified the deceased as a "survival of the 'old South' "—a former Virginia slave who came to Baltimore after the war and rose to the position of doorman at the Merchants Club. Always displaying a "quiet, obliging, yet self-respecting manner," he helped to link the present to "a picturesque past."[27]

Tales of the sorrow evinced by former slaves at the deaths of members of the white family they had served also became part of the folklore of nostalgia. In Jefferson County, Mississippi, whites would long recall how at the death of her former mistress in 1914, Betsy Durrell ("Aunt Betsy") ran to the open grave, threw in a sprig of evergreen, and cried, "Farewell, Ole Missus, I'll meet you over there." It had never been easy to separate feigned from genuine black grief over the deaths of former owners; in some instances, at least, during and after slavery, blacks simply did what was expected of them when one of the "white folks" died and reserved to themselves in the privacy of their homes their actual judgment of the deceased. With great relish, a former Tennessee slave remembered the death of a particularly cruel mistress. The slaves on the plantation solemnly filed into the Big House to pay their final respects, covering their faces with their hands as if to hide their tears and stifle their sobs. Once they were outside, however, one of them murmured, "Old God damn son-of-a-bitch, she gone on down to hell." That same theme could be heard nearly a century later, in Coahoma County, Mississippi, where field hands still sang a version of an old slave song:

> *My ole mistress promised me*
> *Before she died she would set me free. . . .*
> *Now she's dead and gone to hell*
> *I hope the devil will burn her well.*[28]

In a scene acted out with elaborate fanfare in 1897, whites and blacks alike comprised a funeral procession bearing to her grave a servant who had obviously commanded considerable admiration in the community. "[S]he had a grand funeral," wrote a grateful relative. He described in detail the flowers sent by prominent local citizens to honor this "beloved mammy" and the elaborate funeral these citizens had helped to provide. Nothing impressed him more than the presence of so many whites and so much whiteness.

> [S]he had a white coffin white hurse drawn by white horses driven by a white driver [S]he had 12 Paul Bearers, 6 young ladies in all white bearing wreaths of white roses. Young gentlemen in white handled the coffins [O]ver 600 people viewed her face at the church.

This was the first time, he noted, that anyone could recall a Negro being accorded such a lavish burial, particularly the white hearse and driver. "[T]hey dont let colored folks have it but these people have surely been kind & showed me every respect possible, white & colored."[29]

Some of the old faithfuls even enjoyed the rare distinction of burial in or near the plot of the family they had served rather than in the Negro burial ground. In a cemetery in Lexington, Virginia, a former slave and his former owner lay side by side, and the stone above the black man's grave read "To the memory of **SAMUEL HAYS** in loving remembrance for faithful service this stone is erected by the desire of his master." Some churches, as in Greensboro, North Carolina, chose to erect a monument to honor the slaves—designated by the local newspaper as "the more humble residents of the fields"—who were buried there with their masters. What had inspired this monument, one resident explained, was the felt need to depict "the spirit of the better class of white people in the south" and to counter the efforts "to misrepresent this spirit."[30]

The persistent notion of "the faithful slave," whose loyalty had been tested during the war and who had stood by the beleaguered family of his or her owner to the very end, revised, distorted, and grossly simplified the actual behavior of scores of enslaved black men and women. When Preston H. Turner extolled in 1906 the virtues of a former slave and body servant during the Civil War, calling him a "brave faithful hero" and "a life long friend," he contrasted his behavior with that of "many servants" who had "deserted to the enemy."[31] The white South knew perfectly well that the record of black "loyalty" during and after the war had been mixed. Tens of thousands of black Southerners— men and women—had found individual ways to undermine the Confederate war effort, whether as spies, informants, or guides, or by the withdrawal of their labor, and nearly every white family history contained examples of slave "desertion," "betrayal," "impudence," and "ingratitude."

With the passage of time, however, such reminders were rarely heard. By ignoring the complex history of black behavior during the Civil War, whites distorted generational differences, reducing the former slaves—and a new generation of black men and women—to one-dimensional caricatures. To think of slaves who had betrayed their masters was to think of slaves who had not been themselves, who had been misled, who had lost their minds. It seemed inconceivable that the Negroes they thought they knew so well might have developed their own norms of behavior and evolved their own concepts of freedom, and their own sense of individual autonomy and self-worth.

Whether in published histories, school textbooks, or public displays, the revision of history in the late nineteenth century came to accord with the selective memory of white Southerners. Even as whites honored the memory of the black "faithful," they made every effort to obliterate lingering reminders of the "unfaithful" and the "troublesome." In 1900, the Mississippi legislature, by a vote of 94 to 0, authorized the Ladies Auxiliary Cemetery Association, an organization of white women, to remove the remains of James D. Lynch and the monument memorializing him from the white to the black cemetery in Jackson, Mississippi. He had been secretary of state during Reconstruction, and he had served in that position with particular distinction—all the more reason to sentence this black leader to historical oblivion.[32]

But if the legislature felt compelled to downgrade James Lynch's burial site, they had no wish to diminish evidence of slave fidelity. When a young legislator proposed to stop the pensions paid to old Negro servants who had served with their owners in the Confederate Army, "every old Soldier in the house rose up in his Manhood and put themselves on record against it." After all, asked a southern writer nearly a half century after the war, "Is there in the drama of humanity a figure more picturesque or more pathetic than the figure of the

African slave, as he followed his master to the battlefield, marched and hungered and thirsted with him, served and cheered and nursed him— that master who was fighting to keep him in slavery?" Virtually the same language, replete with examples, dominated reactions in North Carolina in 1907 to a proposal that it be the first state formally to recognize and reward through a pension "the true, faithful negroes of the Confederate Army."[33]

In the proliferating literature of the War for Southern Independence, the "unfaithful" Negro would be accorded only passing notice if any at all. To blot out the memory of black resistance, intransigence, and flight, the slaves who would be commemorated in song, verse, and bronze were those who had fulfilled white expectations, who had stood steadfastly by their masters and mistresses, who had shared with them the wartime privations and tragedies, and who had extended no welcome to the Yankee invaders. And since the white South could always find examples of blacks who conformed to the stereotype, they chose to celebrate them as the genuine articles—as the true representatives of the slave past. "Could any people have expected more of a so-called servile race?" asked one grateful white woman in 1925, recalling the war years. "Do you wonder that we of the Old South hold them in loving memory? Do you not think the loyalty and devotion they showed deserve all the praise we can render? Is it strange that we should wish to erect monuments to the Slaves of the South and to the memory of the dear 'Old Black Mammy'?" It was comforting, as well, to reflect over the "indifference" of blacks to their emancipation and how they had been "too timid" to assist their Yankee emancipators.[34]

In the name of the "lost cause," nearly every community in the South had some kind of statue honoring the Confederate soldier. It occurred to some whites to offer comparable recognition of the faithful Negro, to honor with an appropriate public monument the wartime "faithfulness and affection" of the enslaved population. Thirty years after the end of the war, in a park dedicated to the Confederate war dead, the citizens of Fort Mill, South Carolina, placed an unusual statue, with the names of ten slaves engraved on it. The stone carvings on each side depicted a black man seated at the edge of a field of grain and grasping a scythe in his hand, and an elderly black woman seated on the steps of a plantation house and holding in her arms a white child. The inscription depicted the war as it would be relived in the mind of the white South.

Dedicated to
The Faithful Slaves
Who, Loyal to a Sacred Trust,
Toiled for the Support
Of the Army, with Matchless
Devotion, and with Sterling
Fidelity Guarded Our Defenseless
Homes, Women and Children, During
The Struggle for the Principles
Of Our Confederate States of America[35]

After the 1890s, meetings of Confederate veterans' associations often featured elaborate tributes to black wartime loyalty and acknowledged the need for formal recognition of their service. The United Confederate Veterans' Association, meeting in Jacksonville, Florida, typified this growing sentiment, unanimously adopting a resolution urging the erection of a memorial to honor "a loyalty never before exampled in the history of the world."[36] By the 1920s, local and state efforts to honor the former slave culminated in proposals for some kind of national recognition. The United Confederate Veterans and the United Daughters of the Confederacy took the initiative, and in 1922 a bill was introduced into both houses of Congress to authorize a monument in Washington, D.C., "in memory of the faithful colored mammies of the South." Defending the bill, Congressman Charles M. Stedman of North Carolina noted that the custom of erecting monuments dated back to the ancient past. "But you will search the history of all ages in vain," he declared, "for the record of any people who have erected a monument to an inferior race or to any class of that race dwelling amongst them to perpetuate the memory of qualities which entitle them to remembrance and gratitude. . . . The fidelity of these colored mammies has scarcely a parallel in history." After Stedman completed his oratorical tribute, his colleagues in the House—Democrats and Republicans, Southerners and Northerners alike—gave him a standing ovation. Black Washingtonians, however, were less moved, and one black citizens' group declared their opposition to the proposed statue, calling it "propaganda" aimed at diverting attention from "the wrongs done colored women during the Civil War and Reconstruction." Nothing came of the legislation, but the agitation continued, and as late as 1939 still another proposal was made for a statue that would both honor and express the "humility and meekness" of the "old negro mammy."[37]

The fantasies of whites knew few if any restraints. For the World's Columbian Exposition of 1893 in Chicago, Rebecca Felton, an outspoken Georgia political activist, proposed a southern exhibit "illustrating the slave period," with a cabin and "real colored folks making mats, shuck collars, and baskets—a woman to spin and card cotton—and another to play banjo and show the actual life of [the] slave—not the Uncle Tom sort." The idea, she explained, was to display "the *ignorant, contented darkey*—as distinguished from Mrs. Stowe's monstrosities." And she had in mind two particular Negroes, Aunt Ginny and Uncle Jack, "two darkies of the old regime that didn't know a letter in the book." Her friends, along with exposition officials, warmly embraced the idea, and Felton could think of no more dramatic way to display before the northern public the finest qualities of the South. "Every body says it will be splendid," she wrote, and again she underscored the importance of the Negroes selected for the exhibit. "They don't want any educated negroes—simply the old ones who were real slaves—and contented. I told them I could depend on those two [Aunt Ginny and Uncle Jack] to be sober and well behaved." If "Uncle Remus" (Joel Chandler Harris) could be induced to raise the money for the exhibit, Felton added, "it should be called 'Uncle Remus' Cabin.'"[38]

The ideal of the "faithful" Negro came to be embraced with greater fervency as it became less credible. Whatever nostalgia it continued to evoke about the past, whites sensed that it bore no relationship to the present. "It is idle to talk of the fineness of the old-time negro who was illiterate," an impatient Edgar Gardner Murphy wrote in 1909. "He, and the paternalistic conditions which created him, are gone forever."[39] What had replaced that "old-time negro," however, created in the white South an alarm that rivaled even the horrors associated with Reconstruction.

4

THE COMPELLING NEED to immortalize the "old Negro" reinforced fears of the "New Negro." When whites raised the specter of a new generation of blacks, they did so out of growing apprehension, not admiration. If the image of a New Negro brought pride to many blacks as a sign of the race's regeneration, that same image frightened whites into thoughts of racial degeneration, suggesting a Negro who had cast off those endearing and comforting qualities associated with the old

Negro. Worst of all, the New Negro violated white expectations of black people, confounded their feelings of superiority, and violated stereotypes long assimilated into the white psyche.

To listen to white Southerners in the late nineteenth century, the New Negro, born in freedom and undisciplined by slavery, was devoid of the habits of diligence, order, faithfulness, and morality that had been taught their elders; young blacks possessed neither the temperament, demeanor, nor humility of the former slaves, and they were said to be more restless, less deferential, and, still worse, less fearful of whites. "The generation of Negroes which have grown up since the war," a Memphis newspaper charged, "have lost in large measure the traditional and wholesome awe of the white race which kept the Negroes in subjection." In the absence of restraints placed upon "the horrible and beastial propensities of the Negro race," this new generation threatened to become a subversive force in southern society.[40]

The ways in which whites chose to characterize "these newfangled Niggers" suggested both the disdain and the fear in which they were held. Although whites might differ over which quality in the New Negro they found most offensive and threatening, they could readily agree that the descendants of the slaves had become a troubling presence: "irrepressible," "a great pest and nuisance," "lazy and thriftless," and not "half so good" or "half so industrious" as the old Negroes.[41] "[M]any of them are getting too bold and reckless in their behavior," one woman wrote, "and need a good lesson occasionally." A white farmer in Georgia, more realistic and tolerant in his appraisal, found the behavior of young blacks disconcerting but understandable. "The old-time darky shows more politeness than the younger ones do," he observed. "The old-time darky is very courteous to everybody; the present-day young darky is a good deal like us white folks."[42]

For many whites, the critical factor in evaluating a new generation of blacks was the degree of control they could exercise over them. That went to the heart of matters, whether in employing blacks as workers or coexisting with them socially and politically. And many whites were unsettled by the refusal of young blacks to submit to the old discipline. "There's no managing the neegahs now, they's got so biggety," a Georgia woman complained. Even those whites who professed a sympathy for black advancement and education found themselves disheartened by the presence of large numbers of blacks whose behavior knew few restraints. The black population, in the estimation of a Virginia woman, had fallen into two distinct classes: the "best class," who were quite "amiable" and acquiring property, and a larger class, "a most ig-norant and degraded class, consisting, alas, chiefly of young people who are almost savages, ever on the verge of crime if not already crim-inals, a constant danger to the land." [43]

The white South demanded not only acquiescence, but a demon-strated, grinning acquiescence. "They now constitute our labor system," Henry Watterson, editor of the influential *Louisville Courier-Journal*, declared in 1908. "We want them and they want us. But we don't want them if they are sullen and discontent. We want them as they are industrious and happy." The failure of young blacks to display those reassuring qualities unsettled native whites in the late nineteenth and early twentieth centuries. If most young blacks conformed to the prevailing racial etiquette, they did not do so with the same conviction as their elders; they did not laugh or smile as often, they did not play their roles with the same cheerfulness.

> They don't sing as they used to [an Atlanta white woman told a north-ern visitor]. You should have known the old darkeys of the plantation. Every year, it seems to me, they have been losing more and more of their carefree good humour. I sometimes feel that I don't know them any more. Since the riot [1906] they have grown so glum and serious that I'm free to say I'm scared of them!

Still another observer, attributing the end of the Negro's "singing habit" to the diminished influence of "the old-time darkey," found the New Negro to be increasingly "serious, self-conscious, less optimistic and less mirthful." That opinion was confirmed in his mind when a group of Negro laborers responded with obvious indifference to his re-quest for a song. "Dese niggers can't sing," the foreman on the job ex-plained. "Dey don't sing no more like dey used to. Niggers quit singing so much."[44]

Clinging to their selective admiration for a passing generation of for-mer slaves, whites used the New Negro to sharpen and embellish the contrasts and to suggest the ways in which emancipation had destroyed the best qualities of the Negro. Myrta Lockett Avary, daughter of a Virginia slaveholder, conceded in 1906 that she reserved her deep affec-tion for a rapidly diminishing breed—"the happy, soft-voiced, light-footed servitor" who exemplified "the old order." Her memories of the past rested on a firm belief in the enduring strength of the traditional ties binding the white family and their former slaves. The new generation, however, "in reaching out for higher and better things than the old attained," unsettled her. "The negro who is a half-cut white man is not a negro, and it can be no offense to the race to say that he is unattractive when compared with the dear old darkey of Dixie who was worth a million of him!"[45]

The Negro who strayed from the path of white expectations stretched the limits of white tolerance. If blacks adhered to the prevailing etiquette, if they played by the white man's rules, if they maintained the deference associated with the "faithful slave," they would be tolerated, even feted. The superintendent of schools in Fulton County, Georgia, explained to a visiting northern journalist, Ray Stannard Baker, how racial etiquette worked in the South—when it worked properly—to reward black deference to their superiors. He told the story of a Negro who had come to him for a job. His name seemed familiar. "Yas, sah," the Negro acknowledged. "Ah'm the son of yo' ol' mammy." That association and the manner in which the Negro had solicited the job proved sufficient. "The Negro who makes his appeal on the basis of this old relationship," Baker explained, "finds no more indulgent or generous friend than the Southern white man, indulgent to the point of excusing thievery and other petty offenses, but the moment he assumes or demands any other relationship or stands up as an independent citizen, the white men—at least some white men—turn upon him with the fiercest hostility."[46]

Even as many whites pretended not to recognize the new breed of blacks, they still claimed a unique, intimate knowledge of black behavior and culture. "I know the Negroes like a book," one white man boasted. "I was brought up with them. I know what they'll do and what they won't do. I have had Negroes in my house all my life."[47] But as the boasts grew louder, the confidence on which they rested diminished. Fewer whites were as certain. That very uncertainty compelled them to cling all the more fiercely to the old distinctions, even as they moved to reaffirm in every possible way the absolute subordination of black men and women.

5

THE "CORNERSTONE" of the Confederate States of America, declared its vice president, Alexander H. Stephens, "rests upon the great truth that the negro is not equal to the white man; that slavery, subordination to the superior race, is his natural and moral condition." With the abolition of slavery and the overthrow of Reconstruction, white supremacy became the cornerstone of the New South, based on the same assumption "that the negro is not equal to the white man" and that "subordination to the superior race is his natural and moral condition."

Although that view commanded a broad consensus, its attainment remained elusive and troublesome. For native whites, no matter what they did, the "eternal, insoluble Negro question" continued "to vex, perplex, and demoralize" them. It had become, a South Carolinian noted in 1889, "the all absorbing topic of the day," and a decade later an English traveler pronounced it "the skeleton at the feast of Southern life."[48] The appearance of a New Negro simply added a new dimension to the "race problem," as it came to be called. But in the minds of many, it aggravated an old problem, elevating the presence of the Negro and the exercise of his constitutional rights to the level of a crisis. Reconstruction had long been over, white rule had been almost fully restored, and few blacks managed any effective challenge to that rule. And yet in the late nineteenth century the "problem" still tended to dominate the conversations of whites, and for some it became an obsession, fed constantly by rumored as well as confirmed reports of "aggressive" and unpredictable black behavior. "White people among themselves talked an incredible lot about colored people," a white teacher in a black school noted. "The colored, in turn, spread the word about whites all over town."[49]

Despair over resolving "the race problem" increased almost in direct proportion to the perceived deterioration of race relations. Not only did the problem persist in the white mind, but also pessimism over ever resolving it deepened. Writing to his son in 1885, nearly a decade after the end of Reconstruction, Jabez Curry, a prominent Virginia educator, found no grounds for optimism. Sooner or later, he feared, "there must be a terrible collision or a fatal amalgamation, or both." Five years later, he told his son he had finished his manuscript on the Negro problem but it had brought him no relief. "It so alarmed me and has such a sad, pessimistic tinge that I have quietly put it in my drawer." He could find no remedy that would be feasible. It is not so much "the *civil status* of the negro as his *presence*, that makes the outlook so gloomy." No less troubled by the Negro's presence, Paul H. Hayne, in 1886, the last year of his life, held out little hope for his native South. "The accursed

negro Race, fickle, unfaithful, half-savage, released from every wholesome restraint, shows itself more intractable and hostile to the Whites
every year."[50]

More than thirty years later, in the immediate aftermath of a war to
make the world safe for democracy, white assessments of the racial crisis had in no way abated. Robert Winston, a North Carolina superior
court judge and Durham lawyer, confided his concerns to Moorfield
Storey, a white reformer who in 1909 became the first president of the
newly established National Association for the Advancement of Colored People (NAACP). He was no less despondent than Curry and
Hayne had been three decades earlier. Winston, like Curry, considered
himself a racial moderate, and, like Curry, he had actively supported
efforts to educate blacks. He considered Storey a representative northern activist on behalf of civil rights for blacks. Both of their positions,
he now concluded, were badly mistaken. "Your efforts are as blind as
Samson's in the fall of the temple and the worst of it is, my efforts are
equally blind and futile, indeed harmful." If either one of them should
be successful—in advancing black rights or in educating blacks and
thereby opening their eyes to their subordinate condition—the end result could only be a race war blacks were certain to lose. "You can not
understand what it is all about. Indeed you think that the trouble is lack
of education and refinement on the part of the negro. You are wide
very wide of the mark. The trouble is fundamental and elemental."[51]

Whatever the ideology or incidents on which Winston based these
views, his belief that the racial troubles in the South were so "fundamental and elemental" as to defy remedy enjoyed considerable white
support. "Even the good people of the South," W. E. B. Du Bois
thought, "are taking their hands off, saying, 'We can't do anything.' "
That pessimism was based, too, on a popular notion that enjoyed academic standing: that the race had demonstrated throughout its long existence an incapacity for improvement, except under the immediate
tutelage of whites. "If we blot out the achievements of the American
Negro who has passed through slavery," a paternalistic Mississippi
planter and scholar asked, "what has the race left to boast of?" No
amount of education, he believed, no external influences, could possibly elevate the Negro to the same level as the white man.[52]

But if some whites despaired of any solution to the "race problem,"
many did not. Confronting an increasingly unfamiliar Negro, they
turned to familiar remedies. Understandably anxious, fearful, and frustrated, they embraced time-tested arguments. "I don't believe in slav-

ery," a white woman remarked a half century after its abolition, "but I do believe in holding the negroes down!" The South Carolina newspaper editor to whom she made her observation chose to record it in his diary as "a spontaneous and perfectly natural avowal of the almost unanimous Southern opinion, white, about the negroes."[53]

Although variations of that view existed, it remained the guiding principle of a considerable amount of legislation and extralegal activity in the late-nineteenth- and early-twentieth-century South. At the core of the "race problem," an Atlanta newspaper editor suggested, only one question needed to be asked and answered: "Will the white man permit the Negro to have an equal part in the industrial, political, social and civil advantages of the United States?" The answer was no less obvious than the question, and he had no difficulty in articulating it:

> The answer to it is in every white man's heart, even if it does not lie openly on every white man's lips. It may be expressed in diplomacy; it may be veiled in indirection; it may be softened in philanthropy; it may be guarded in politic utterance, and oftenest of all it is restrained by ultra conservatism and personal timidity. But wherever the answer to this vital question comes, stripped of verbiage and indirection, it rings like a martial bugle in the single syllabus—NO!
>
> This may not be right, but it is honest. It may not be just, but it is evident. It may not be politic, but it is a great, glaring, indisputable, indestructible fact. I do not stop to defend it. I do not justify it. I do not argue it at all, but I state it as a truth that we may as well in the beginning look frankly and fearlessly in the face. North and South, the answer, wherever it is honest, is the same.[54]

No less than the integrity and preservation of the white race was at stake. That explains why the maintenance of white domination dwarfed any other political issue. This was the litmus test for any aspiring politician, and it could make or break a person's standing in the community. "The white who does not believe in it above all else is regarded as a traitor and an outcast," an English visitor observed in 1890. "The race question is, in the South, the sole question of burning interest. If you be sound on that question you are one of the elect; if you be unsound, you take rank as a pariah or as a lunatic."[55]

To ensure the subordination of black men and women, whites proposed to treat them as essentially a "peasant class" serving the labor needs of the dominant population. If blacks aspired to something better and succeeded in improving their economic lot, some whites were willing to tolerate their gains provided they kept to their place and maintained a proper deference; they became in effect "white men's negroes," dependent on white protection and toleration. "As soon as these negroes begin to 'put on style,' and express their social *dignity,*" a white Mississippian observed, "even if this exhibition is confined strictly to their own race, mutterings and murmurings begin. Let these favored negroes take the mildest interest in politics or any decided personal stand against the dominant whites, then the trouble begins in good earnest."[56]

The notion that black men and women were doomed to provide labor and service to whites, while otherwise keeping to their separate and inferior place, had come to be so deeply rooted as to defy any challenge or doubts. Assumptions about black character and destiny had changed little since slavery, and these cast the Negro as a "helpless subject" and "child of nature" requiring the guidance and restraint of whites; black people needed to be protected from themselves, and only white Southerners knew them well enough to provide that guidance and restraint. "The white man is not cruel in this," one observer insisted; "he wants to protect the negro and to be kind, but he can allow him no will of his own. He has accustomed himself to the slavish obedience of the negro, as the opium-eater is accustomed to his opium. And to give up the paralyzing drug is intolerable to his nervous system."[57]

Even as whites expressed alarm over signs of black aggressiveness and discontent, they insisted with even greater vehemence that most blacks were perfectly happy and "content with their inferiority." That had always been an integral part of white racial ideology. To think otherwise was to entertain terrible thoughts that could drive whites over the edge. "You would be greatly surprised and delighted to find how comfortable and contented, I might almost say happy is the negro race, infinitely more so than you or me," a North Carolina judge wrote a northern critic. "They have a genius for comradeship, they love their 'white-folks,' as a rule." The necessary corollary to this familiar argument was that most black discontent stemmed from blacks who were not themselves, who had been most likely misled by white agitators alien to the South. Such views of the true nature and contentment of blacks, however, did not go unchallenged. No matter how attractive and useful this argument may have been in the past, some whites thought it no longer bore any relevance to reality. From his study of race relations and history, Charles P. Moncure of Virginia came away in 1883 with a clear assessment of black attitudes: "[I]n their hearts, they *hate all white people.*"[58]

But if whites harbored reservations about the real feelings of blacks, they remained resolute in the conviction that only whites could resolve the "race problem." The ideology of white supremacy always rested on the arrogant assumption that white people owned the country, that this was essentially their domain. "This is our country," John Temple Graves, an Atlanta editor, told a University of Chicago audience. "We made it. We molded it. We control it, and we always will. We have done great things. We have mighty things yet to do. The negro is an accident—an unwilling, a blameless, but an unwholesome, unwelcome, helpless, unassimilable element in our civilization. He is not made for our times." On that basis, the white South could appeal to the entire nation for support of its racial policies, as Graves was doing on this occasion. "Put yourself, men of Illinois, in the place of the people you would condemn," he asked his audience, after which he enumerated the political and social challenge blacks posed to the dominant white population in the South. And he did not hesitate to predict that they would react to such a danger precisely as southern whites had been compelled to react.

> Never, never in a thousand years will the negro, North or South, be allowed to govern in this republic, even where his majorities are plain. We might as well fix this fact in our minds to stay. No statute can eradicate, no public opinion can remove, no armed force can overthrow, the inherent, invincible, indestructible, and if you will, the unscrupulous capacity and determination of the Anglo-Saxon race to rule.[59]

Even as men like Graves appealed for a national resolution of the "race problem," hopefully by ridding the nation of the Negro's presence, the South reacted to critics or potential critics with an ongoing denunciation of northern hypocrisy. Having undertaken the mission of educating the entire nation on "the Negro Question," Thomas Dixon, the popular novelist, excoriated the North for the reception accorded Booker T. Washington on his visits there, calling it "the most loathsome and disgusting worship of a Negro." But the most frequently heard condemnation of northern racial attitudes focused on their alleged dishonesty—that none but the "basest and most degraded" whites admit blacks to social equality, and yet the North would force social equality on the South even if it shook the very foundations of government and plunged the region into "rapine and blood."[60]

Increasingly, however, southern whites acknowledged evidence that the North had come to its senses, understood the "peculiar" problems the South confronted, and supported them in their racial solutions and practices. By the turn of the century, the white South could articulate and implement its racist feelings without much fear of northern or federal intervention. Nor was there any need to apologize for the heightened rhetoric and actions. "We took the government away," Ben Tillman boasted to his Senate colleagues. "We stuffed the ballot boxes. We shot them. We are not ashamed of it. The Senator from Wisconsin would have done the same thing. I see it in his eye right now. He would have done it." And when Senator Tillman toured the North, he was greeted by enthusiastic and appreciative audiences. If anyone dared challenge him, he had only to hold up to the North its own racial record: "The brotherhood of man exists no longer because you shoot Negroes in Illinois, when they come in competition with your labor, as we shoot them in South Carolina when they come in competition with us in the matter of elections. You do not love them any better than we do. You used to pretend that you did, but you no longer pretend it, except to get their votes."[61] On the eve of World War I, a South Carolina editor confided to his diary the state of public sentiment, without necessarily sharing it: "Truth is the people of the South—and of the United States—have no idea of conceding to the negroes the full rights of American freedmen in this year of our Lord 1917."[62]

6

THE VOCABULARY WHITES used to describe race relations in the late nineteenth and early twentieth centuries became increasingly apocalyptic. The term "race war" took on a life of its own. Any attempts by blacks to achieve political or social equality, whites warned, would trigger a violent showdown, and both moderate and extremist whites expressed confidence in the outcome. "The black race would be wiped out," a former Confederate officer predicted. Attempts to improve the condition of blacks would be counterproductive; educating them, in fact, might speed their demise, not their elevation. The logic seemed unassailable: Once blacks gained "a smattering of education," a Virginian wrote in 1910, responding to an optimistic article on the Negro by Andrew Carnegie, they would naturally aspire to public office and the possession of land. To achieve those objectives, they would no doubt organize and resort to violence. That, he predicted, "would be an end of the negro, and the solution of the problem would be crimsoned with more blood than was required to break the bonds of slavery."[63]

Not only would blacks be routed in a race war, but "moderates" and "conservatives" who professed a sympathy for the Negro's cause acknowledged they would be helpless to defy public sentiment. The threatened use of overwhelming force, a Georgian insisted, simply revealed the depth of white feelings on the question of race. Under no circumstances, he insisted, would white supremacy be in any way compromised: "Before we submit we will kill every Negro in the South. This is not idle boasting or fire-eating, but the cold hard facts stated in all calmness."[64]

Apprehension over the deterioration of race relations reflected growing concern over a generation of blacks who manifested a restlessness, an unease, a quiet, grinless compliance that made them increasingly unrecognizable. "It is the new generation that brings this trouble," insisted a prominent Presbyterian minister in New Orleans. And the consequences of their presence were readily apparent. "The alienation is going on, widening, deepening, and intensifying," a white Southerner wrote in a national magazine. "The white man is losing his sympathy and the negro his feeling of dependence."[65] If the evidence of such behavior seemed overwhelming in the early twentieth century, some whites detected it much earlier. After traveling through Louisiana in 1890, a prominent white educator expressed deep concern over the future of his people, describing conditions as "almost volcanic." Fourteen years later, a former Alabama congressman and cabinet officer found mutual antagonism and "sullen and angry discontent" everywhere, particularly among a new generation of blacks who had grown up in an atmosphere of alienation and distrust of whites. "[T]he two races seem almost ready to separate themselves into hostile camps. . . ." Comparing race relations in the early twentieth century to what they had been like after Reconstruction, a North Carolinian lamented the extent to which blacks showed disdain for the old customs, monopolizing, for example, the inner side of the sidewalks once deemed the white man's "right of way." This was no small matter. Such "assertions of independence" and "racial equality," if tolerated, were bound to have disastrous consequences. "[W]hen the whites yield in what would be usually called 'trifles,' they may some day discover that little by little these trifles have grown into 'thunder-bolts.'"[66]

Fewer whites found themselves able to talk with any confidence about the future of race relations. Doubts and apprehensions surfaced with every perceived change in the demeanor of blacks, with every reported incident of "sassiness" or "impudence," with every example of black assertiveness, with every story of a black person who had forgotten his or her place, who had permitted more of the old customs to slip by. And those stories by the late nineteenth century were assuming an alarming regularity. Two young black women at a school in Raleigh, North Carolina, read essays in which they predicted that the French Revolution would be nothing compared to "the storm that will break if the negroes do not get all their rights." An "impudent" sleeping car porter was dragged from a train in Mississippi after he had "sassed" a white telegrapher; he was promptly flogged and "badly disfigured." A woman in Aiken, South Carolina, who did not regard herself as hysterical, still shuddered whenever she recalled having to walk down the main street "under the eyes of those hundreds of great hulking blacks" staring at her "with half-suppressed insolence." A rural white family in North Carolina would not permit their daughters to walk unescorted to the schoolhouse a mile and a half away.[67] From the trivial to the serious, from the rumored to the confirmed incident, from a state of anxiety to outright hysteria, white fears mounted between the 1880s and World War I, as did their mobilization to deal with the crisis. The few whites still supportive of black rights were almost powerless to allay those fears. "For several years," a white churchman in Birmingham observed in 1905, "I have beheld the spirit of intolerance, of race-contempt and race-hatred, growing, and it is emphatically more vigorous and venomous than it was half a decade ago."[68]

For some, this problem was not distant but readily discernible in their own households. When middle-class white men and women talked about "trouble with Negroes," as they did incessantly in these years, they were often describing the death or departure of an old servant or laborer, the impossible task of replacing them with equally compliant and competent workers, and a resulting breakdown of labor relations and the old domestic relationship. Although many employers placed the blame on young Negroes unwilling to work, the problem was, in fact, not as new as some whites preferred to believe. Emancipa-

tion had worked hardships on white employers by the steady "desertion" of blacks (including old "faithfuls") and by the refusal of those
who remained to work under the same conditions. That refusal became
even more rampant as a new generation of blacks emerged, many of
whom chose to escape from the constraints under which their parents
labored. "The negro youth," noted one observer, "will no longer cheerfully spend half a day doing a white man's small jobs for a ham bone or
a drink of whiskey."[69]

By the end of the century, as immediately after the Civil War, the
"servant problem" had taken on the proportions of a crisis. White
women accustomed to black help spent countless hours, in conversation and in correspondence, discoursing on the incompetence, impertinence, and unreliability of their black domestic workers. This included
disastrous experiences not only with young black women and men who
had never known slavery but even with those "mammies" who once
seemed to take such pleasure in performing the household tasks. The
most frequent complaints came at the expense of newly hired servants
("the incompetent, everchanging and worthless") whose "rude and
boisterous manners" contrasted sharply with the "pleasant and respectful manners" of those who had been raised in slavery. "You used to
could tell a nigger something and they'd listen to you, but that time's
gone by," a white Virginian exclaimed in exasperation, directing his
anger at a young black woman who had ignored his instructions. "She
as much as said she knew more than I did, and I'd rather be called the
meanest name there is than have a nigger tell me that."[70]

Accustomed to implicit obedience and incapable of fathoming the
reasons for black disaffection, white employers fell back on familiar
stereotypes and assumptions to explain the problem. After Nathan
Munroe heard that his sister in Georgia had lost her cook, he wrote to
express his sympathy: "I know that being 'cookless' makes a great deal
of trouble, annoyance and inconvenience; but as you say 'niggers' are
perfectly worthless, unreliable and of no manner of account, especially
when schools are open to them." After extolling the virtues of the old
Negro servants, a Virginia woman confessed to "absolute despair" in
her efforts to train a new generation of blacks. "[W]hat a trial they are!
What uphill work it is to teach them manners!" But what more might
be expected, this embittered woman concluded, from "a creature that
has grown up in a half-savage state" since the end of the Civil War.
"They have a faculty for learning by rote, and so has a parrot. They
have a faculty for imitation, and so has a monkey. The wonderful

progress of the negro race, so vaunted by the supporters of the Hampton Institute, begins and ends there."[71]

Evidence of black assertiveness ("insolence" in the white lexicon) was by no means confined to the workplace. Whites found such behavior rampant among young blacks in public places, manifested in the refusal to step aside when white people (including women) approached them on the sidewalks, in their willingness to initiate conversations with whites or to address them without being first addressed, in the conspicuous ways they sometimes attired themselves or improved their furnishings and homes, and in their growing inclination to defend themselves when attacked, even to initiate combat. "The negro children of the city are usually the aggressors when trouble occurs between them and white children," a Chattanooga newspaper complained.[72]

If any doubts remained about the dangers the New Negro posed, whites had only to cite the increase in crime and the degree to which young blacks figured prominently in arrests. To the former attorney for the Commonwealth of Virginia, the new breed of black lawbreaker revealed nothing less than a generational transition. "[M]y experience with the negro," he testified, "was that it rarely happened that any of the old order of negroes were brought to court upon criminal charges." More often that not, he noted, those he prosecuted in recent years tended increasingly to be young Negroes, "not our home negroes, but masterless men who had drifted into the neighborhood."[73]

Having sharply curtailed the lives and prospects of black agricultural laborers through sharecropping and tenantry, whites complained when growing numbers of young blacks chose to give up a losing struggle on the land and move to the towns and cities. Reports of "worthless" young Negroes crowding the streets and urban dives and saloons increased, along with the acknowledgment that such blacks had little or no respect for the old rules of racial etiquette.

The menacing behavior that whites perceived in the young Negroes coming to adulthood confirmed their worst fears about the ultimate results of emancipation. If some whites thought young blacks were expressing resentment over "the excessive dullness of their lives," most preferred to believe that they were reverting to their origins and basic instincts, to savagery and African primitivism. It was nothing less than a postemancipation retreat into bestiality. Frustrated in their ambitions, freed from the necessary restraints and compulsions of enslavement, blacks had become little more than fiends and wild beasts, prepared to devour defenseless whites in their steady retrogression. "The time has come for honest, manly effort," Bishop T. U. Dudley of the Protestant Episcopal Church of Kentucky warned in 1885 in a national magazine. "Separated from us, their neighbors and their friends," the Negroes "must retrograde toward the barbarism whence they are sprung, and then, alas, we might be compelled to wage relentless war against them for our own preservation."[74]

The notion that black Southerners, no longer confined to the paternalisic custody of slavery and doomed to compete with whites, were destined for racial extinction enjoyed immense popularity in the late nineteenth century. The Census of 1880, however, revealed a substantial and unexpected increase of blacks, causing the "experts" to reconsider predictions of racial demise. Philip A. Bruce, a Virginia aristocrat and historian, argued in 1889 that increasing numbers of black laborers might precipitate a racial apocalypse. Young blacks coming to maturity after Reconstruction, he warned, resembled not their slave fathers but "the original African type." The development of African traits marked the Negro's regression and a "further departure" from Anglo-Saxon standards. Less accustomed to restraint than their parents, this new generation, Bruce warned, was "more inclined to act upon their natural impulses. They are more headstrong than their immediate ancestors, and to that degree, have a more decided tendency to retrograde." For Bruce, then, the very presence of the Negro was an invitation to ultimate disaster, and he thought deportation to be the only solution. "The South cannot remain permanently half black and half white."[75]

To listen to white alarmists, who enjoyed a popular following, Negroes of all classes and conditions threatened the very foundations of white civilization. But having agreed on the source of the "problem," whites could not quite make up their minds about which Negro posed the largest menace: the educated man, frustrated in his ambitions and trying to be white, or the ignorant "brute," unable to restrain his savage and barbaric instincts and propensities. A white manager in charge of a gang of black railroad workers in the black town of Mound Bayou, Mississippi, extolled the older leaders of the community (including Isaiah Montgomery, the town's founder) as "hard-working, trustworthy, [and] moral." But the young people "were the reverse," many of them "spoiled by book education," disdainful of farming, and eager only to drift to the cities. The increasing "immorality" of the young and the tendency among them to commit crimes he attributed to an education that had "awakened a keener appetite for pleasure."[76]

No more compelling evidence existed, in the minds of whites, for the need to confront the dangers of this new generation than the perceived increase in black crimes against white women. "Strangely enough," a former Alabama congressman and cabinet officer declared in 1904, "some fifteen years or more ago, after this new generation had arisen, a new crime began to appear in the South—the rape of white women by negroes." He had no explanation for this phenomenon, but he was not alone in his recognition of its association with a new generation, and for most observers that was sufficient explanation. Thomas Nelson Page, even as he memorialized the "old negroes" in his dialect stories, conceded that with the appearance of a "New Issue" Negro, rape had become a critical problem. The new generation, he feared, had imbibed the lessons of racial equality taught during Reconstruction, and whites were reaping the consequences.[77]

Frustrated in his ambitions, circumscribed in his movements and in the exercise of his rights, the New Negro purportedly took revenge on whites by preying on their women. That argument was articulated repeatedly in the many conferences on race problems at the turn of the century and in the highest academic circles. "The crime of assault," a prominent psychologist told a symposium in 1904, "is the crime of the 'New Negro'—not of the slave nor of the ex-slave." Whatever his education or training, his black skin and public sentiment marked him as an inferior, and his resentment over this revelation led him to employ force to achieve his ends. The psychologist was simply parroting remarks made on previous occasions, as when Alexander C. King of Atlanta, a prominent attorney, told the conference on "Race Conditions and Problems" in Montgomery, Alabama, in 1900, that the Negro felt a "growing estrangement" and as "an emotional race" resented what he considered a denial of his rights.

> In the lawless this incites a tendency to strike to damage, in order to show their power for revenge. To criminal tendency is added race animosity, and this in the brute with passions of the lowest order, incites to the assault on women of the other race. He will triumph over the other race in the person of a woman of that race.[78]

The disposition toward rape allegedly increased as the Negro's respect for and fear of whites declined—a trait clearly manifested in the new generation of blacks. That was the conclusion reached by Philip A. Bruce. Like Page, he extolled the virtues of the "old" Negroes. But with their passing, he feared, the race was reverting to its original African type. A new generation of young black males, impatient with restraints, acting on their natural impulses, and giving full vent to their lascivious nature, had targeted white women.

> There is something strangely alluring and seductive to them in the appearance of a white woman; they are aroused and stimulated by its foreignness to their experience of sexual pleasures, and it moves them to gratify their lust at any cost and in spite of every obstacle.

This was not, Bruce suggested, an ordinary case of sexual attack. Always "beastly and loathsome," rape when committed by a Negro on a white woman was marked by "a diabolical persistence and a malignant atrocity of detail" unique even in "the natural history of the most bestial and ferocious animals." And, Bruce suspected, the black rapist was acting out a desire to strike at whites where it would hurt the most.

> He is not content merely with the consummation of his purpose, but takes that fiendish delight in the degradation of his victim which he always shows when he can reek his vengeance upon one whom he has hitherto been compelled to fear; and, here, the white woman in his power is, for the time being, the representative of that race which has always overawed him.

Nor did Bruce think the young Negro even understood the enormity of his crime, as he was "so accustomed to the wantonness of the women of his own race."[79]

The situation, in the estimation of growing numbers of southern whites, demanded that they not simply preach but also practice white supremacy. The fiery Georgia politico Rebecca Felton made it virtually a one-person crusade to arouse the public to the dangers the New Negro posed to white womanhood. It was no longer possible for young white women to walk alone or be left at home without male protection. "The brutal lust of these half-civilized gorillas seems to be inflamed to madness." These criminal assaults, Felton hastened to add, were not the work of the "old time" Negroes, whose "loyalty and fidelity" had been tested during the war and who remained to this day "remarkable for their orderly and law-abiding conduct." The blame rested squarely on "the youngest class" of blacks, who aspire "to level all distinctions between the African and Anglo-Saxon races."[80]

The contrast between the "old-time darkies" and the New Negro
suggested to many whites a graver threat to white supremacy than Reconstruction itself: the compelling need to impress on a new generation
of blacks—who had never known the discipline and the civilizing and
restraining influences of slavery, who refused to permit whites to define
them, who had not learned to curb their ambitions—that there were
substantial restraints on their freedom, clear limits to their aspirations,
and lines they dared not cross if they valued their lives. "[L]et Southern people recognize in the 'New Negro' a person far removed from
the darkey of other days," one prominent white warned.[81]

By the 1890s, when that first freeborn generation reached maturity,
the need to control blacks took on a new urgency. Custom and etiquette
no longer provided whites with adequate feelings of protection; they
were no longer deemed reliable mainstays of racial supremacy. With
increasing regularity, or so it seemed, especially in the towns and cities
to which they were flocking, young blacks ignored the etiquette and violated the customs. "They are the worst elements in Southern society,"
a Nashville newspaper charged, "and if something is not done soon to
put a check to their depreciations [sic], life in towns and cities will grow
unbearable."[82]

The situation demanded vigilance, both legal and extralegal, and the
remedies ranged widely, including lynching and expulsion. "There is
absolutely no place in this land for the arrogant, aggressive, school-
spoilt Afro-American," vowed Thomas Watson, and he advocated virtually any means necessary to make certain that the black person who
remained in the South be one who accommodated to white expectations. "We know Sambo, and we like him first rate, in his place. And he
must stay there, too." One of Watson's fellow Georgians, Mary C.
Bryan, wondered if that "place" needed to be the South. "Since our
old-time friend, the negro, who as a slave was trustworthy and gentle,
seems to have retrograded through freedom into a dangerous beast, it is
surely necessary that he be removed from among us." Endorsing that
sentiment, and discarding any traces of sentimental paternalism, a
Georgia banker confided that he found it "strange that the White manhood of the country does not arouse and do these brutes as was done
with the Indians—get them away."[83]

Proposals to remove blacks from the South gained in popularity, but
few wanted their total disappearance. A North Carolina judge called
on the federal government to acquire a body of land—"fertile and fair
to life"—in the South that would be the exclusive domain of blacks.

They would be encouraged, not coerced, to move there, and he expected the settlement to attract those ambitious and restless blacks who desired political rights and social equality. "The docile kindly old negro, and his descendants, who are satisfied with things as they are, would remain among us a blessing to themselves and to us." A South Carolina editor made a very similar proposal, in which blacks would be placed in a separate state near the southern border, where they would enjoy political rights under the protection of the federal government. "Those of them who might prefer to remain among us as laborers and in other occupations, would no longer be a source of political irritation and a dark menace in the future."[84]

If not removed altogether, Negroes needed to be rigidly monitored and regulated. The very language employed to describe the growing Negro menace suggested that the problem be treated like any other epidemic or virus threatening the health and security of the community. To assess the results of emancipation was to raise the specter of blacks "inoculated with the virus of equality." To talk about black political participation was to talk about "the cancer on the body-politic which, if not cured, will make of it a carcass." To consider the social danger posed by blacks was to contemplate the need to avoid and reduce contamination, to dilute the black poison in the body of the South (as Atlanta's chief health officer expressed it) to the point where it lost its toxicity. The white people of the South, a Memphis merchant explained to an English visitor in 1909, had little choice but to practice pest control. "[W]e whites have learnt to protect ourselves against the negro, just as we do against the yellow fever and the malaria—the work of noxious insects."[85]

The disease demanded extraordinary measures, and whites went about applying them systematically to the "New Negro" and the "old Negro," to both accommodationists and the troublesome. Race and skin color, not demeanor or behavior, defined who would be affected. For many white Southerners, in fact, the distinction between the old Negro and the New Negro had always been an unreliable predictor of black behavior; the older blacks may simply have been more adroit and experienced in masking their feelings. Although James K. Vardaman, a firebrand Mississippi politician, praised the "good Negroes" of the South, he adamantly defended the right to slaughter "every Ethiop on the earth to preserve unsullied the honor of one Caucasian home." Although the "good Negroes" may occasionally be victimized, he reminded whites that "the good are few, the bad are many, and it is impossible to tell what ones are . . . dangerous to the honor of the dominant race until the damage is done." Mistakes were bound to be made, Vardaman conceded, but that was unavoidable, as racial self-preservation took precedence over legal and moral niceties. "We do not stop when we see a wolf to find if it will kill sheep before disposing of it, but assume that it will."[86]

Although radical solutions to the "race problem" abounded, ranging from "extermination" to "colonization," most white Southerners settled on containment—not education or even gradual uplift but submission and permanent subordination, what one white frankly described as "back into slavery, without the name."[87] If black people had become a source of social danger and contamination, the need to control, contain, and quarantine them in every conceivable fashion could no longer be questioned.

CHAPTER FIVE

WHITE FOLKS: ACTS

We were bottled up and labeled and set aside—sent to the Jim Crow car, the back of the bus, the side door of the theater, the side window of a restaurant. We came to know that whatever we had was always inferior. We came to understand that no matter how neat and clean, how law abiding, submissive and polite, how studious in school, how churchgoing and moral, how scrupulous in paying our bills and taxes we were, it made no essential difference in our place.

—Pauli Murray[1]

Got me accused of peepin'—I can't even see a thing,
Got me accused of beggin'—I can't even raise my hand.
Bad luck, bad luck is killin' me,
I just can't stand no more of this third degree.
Got me accused of taxes, I don't have a lousy dime,
Got me accused of children an' nary one of them is mine.
Got me accused of murder, I never harmed a man,
Got me accused of forgery, I can't even write my name.[2]

ON BOARDING THE STREETCAR, the woman took the most convenient seat available. "What do you mean?" the conductor shouted at her. "Niggers don't sit with white folks down here. You must have come from 'way up yonder." The woman replied that she was a visitor and had no knowledge of the new law. "Well, no back talk now," the conductor loudly admonished her, playing very much to his audience; "that's what I'm here [for]—to tell niggers their places when they don't know them." The whites in the car laughed over her discomfort. "Not one of them thought that I was embarrassed, wounded, and outraged by the loud, brutal talk of the conductor and the sneering, contemptuous expressions on their own faces." Rather than move to the Jim Crow section she left the car, prompting one of the passengers to remark,

"These niggers get more impudent every day; she doesn't want to sit where she belongs."

After walking downtown, the woman attempted to use an elevator in a public building, only to be told to heed the sign posted at the entrance. "I guess you can't read," the elevator operator told her, "but niggers don't ride in this elevator; we're white folks here, we are. Go to the back and you'll find an elevator for freight and niggers." The whites who then occupied the elevator appeared to enjoy her dismay.

The day's events in this Alabama city had left their mark on the woman. As a native Southerner, the daughter of a former slave, it had not been her first experience with the ways of white folks, only a different manifestation of the same phenomenon. "I have been humiliated and insulted often," she declared, "but I never get used to it; it is new each time, and stings and hurts more and more." Her children, she knew, would be better educated than her generation, and she expected the accumulation of insults and humiliations to add to their dislike of whites. "I dread to see my children grow. I know not their fate. . . . It does not matter how good or wise my children may be, they are colored. When I have said that, all is said. Everything is forgiven in the South but color."[3]

2

BETWEEN 1890 AND 1915, in the face of racial tensions heightened by disturbing evidence of black independence and assertiveness, whites acted to ensure the permanent political, economic, and social subordination and powerlessness of the black population. This was the work not only of racial demagogues but also of the "best people," the most educated, the most refined, the most respected. None other than Henry W. Grady, editor of the influential *Atlanta Constitution* and a "founding father" of the New South movement, made absolutely clear his adherence to the racial creed. "The supremacy of the white race of the South," he declared in 1887, "must be maintained forever, and the domination of the negro race resisted at all points and at all hazards—because the white race is the superior race. This is the declaration of no new truth. It has abided forever in the marrow of our bones, and shall run forever with the blood that feeds Anglo-Saxon hearts."[4]

To maintain and underscore its absolute supremacy, the white South systematically disfranchised black men, imposed rigid patterns of racial segregation, manipulated the judicial system, and sustained extraordinary levels of violence and brutality. At the same time, the findings of "science" and the learned professions and the dissemination of dehumanizing caricatures reinforced and comforted whites in their racial beliefs and practices. Historians for their part rummaged in the past to find a history that would best serve the needs of the present, and professors and teachers went on to miseducate the next several generations in a prescribed version of reality.

When the white South acted on its racial creed, it sought to impress on black men and women their political and economic powerlessness and vulnerability—and, most critically, to diminish both their self-esteem and their social aspirations. The idea of social equality was so abhorrent, so weighted with fears of racial impurity and degeneration, that the very suggestion of such equality had to be rigorously rejected and punished. That meant refusing to sit next to a black person in a public vehicle or in a restaurant or theater or public place, not because the blackness would rub off but because whites could not permit any appearance of equality. Alfred H. Stone, a white Mississippian and former slaveholder, claimed that southern whites had no objection to personal association with Negroes, "provided it be upon terms which contain no suggestion of equality of personal status."[5]

As an inferior, the Negro was expected to keep to his prescribed place in southern society. It had always been a central tenet of white racist ideology, one Virginia white woman testified, "that whenever the two races come into contact, the white man must rule, and the black man must serve." That was the imperative, as any relationship that encouraged Negroes to think themselves the equal of whites would elevate the inferior and degrade the superior race. Nowhere was this more dramatically evident than at the polling place, where under the law both black and white men cast their ballots, and in any public office in which black men interacted with whites as equals or superiors. The Fifteenth Amendment, in making this possible, violated the overriding assumption of Negro inferiority and threatened whites by inflating black ambitions.[6]

With the end of Reconstruction, blacks had not ceased to vote, but their ability to influence the outcome of an election had been severely diminished. Many withdrew from politics altogether, persuaded that it offered no solution to the daily problems of economic survival. If blacks should choose to exercise the ballot and in doing so threaten white supremacy, whites quickly resolved the matter through intimidation and violence. The economic dependence of most blacks on white landlords also worked to reduce or coerce the black vote. "He got most of our tenants to vote right, or if not to stay at home and not vote at all," Jane Bobo Springs said of her husband's "campaigning" on the eve of the 1880 election. She did acknowledge a lone dissenter. "John Anderson the only one to vote with the Rads! (good for nothing thing). He will not be on the place next year."[7]

As long as blacks gave any evidence of participating as voters, candidates, or officeholders, as long as they aspired to exercise political influence and power, the issue would remain a major irritant. The specter of Reconstruction, as embellished and distorted by politicians, academicians, and publicists, rapidly became the white Southerner's version of "waving the bloody shirt." For some years northern Republicans had reminded voters of traitorous Confederates, but that rhetoric paled in volume and duration to the ways white Southerners used Reconstruction as a reminder of military defeat and racial humiliation.

Disfranchisement, mostly through state constitutional amendments, came to the South in the 1890s because the issue of political participation remained linked in the white mind with black assertiveness and social equality. "Shut the door of political equality," Senator James K. Vardaman of Mississippi promised, "and you close the door of social equality in the face of the black man; shut the door of social equality and you smother in his native savage breast the fury of his passion, which is but the blind craving of his soul to be equal of the white man, and the partner of the white man."[8]

Nearly every newspaper editorial on the "race problem," nearly every speech by candidates for public office, nearly every constitutional convention and state legislature insisted on the linkage of social and political equality. "Political equality breeds ambition for social equality," one observer insisted, in explaining the causes of lynching. "The negro thus asserts himself, and his sense of his own importance, which was quiescent and pacific so long as he was kept in political and social subordination, becomes often offensively and insolently inflated." White Southerners, in the estimation of an Augusta, Georgia, newspaper, could perform no greater service to the black man than to eliminate him from politics, "making him know that the white man is of the superior race, always has been and always will be and that social equality, in the sleeping car or elsewhere, is an impossibility, absolutely so, and in perpetuity."[9]

That clear message resounded throughout the South. As long as blacks remained participants in the political process, they would aspire to social equality. Underscoring the importance of this issue, an Atlanta newspaper in 1906 conveyed the message in an exaggerated typeface and capital letters.

POLITICAL EQUALITY BEING THUS PREACHED TO THE NEGRO IN THE RING PAPERS AND ON THE STUMP, WHAT WONDER THAT HE MAKES NO DISTINCTION BETWEEN POLITICAL AND SOCIAL EQUALITY? HE GROWS MORE BUMPTIOUS ON THE STREET, MORE IMPUDENT IN HIS DEALINGS WITH WHITE MEN, AND THEN, WHEN HE CANNOT ACHIEVE SOCIAL EQUALITY AS HE WISHES, WITH THE INSTINCT OF THE BARBARIAN TO DESTROY WHAT HE CANNOT ATTAIN TO, HE LIES IN WAIT, AS THAT DASTARDLY BRUTE DID YESTERDAY NEAR THIS CITY, AND ASSAULTS THE FAIR YOUNG GIRLHOOD OF THE SOUTH. . . .[10]

To bar the black man from the polling place was to bar him from the bedroom. If blacks voted with whites as equals, they would insist on living and sleeping with whites as equals, and no white Southerner could contemplate such degradation. "To the ignorant and brutal young Negro," novelist Thomas Nelson Page reminded his fellow whites in 1904, social equality "signifies but one thing: the opportunity to enjoy, equally with white men, the privilege of cohabiting with white women." To Georgia feminist Rebecca Felton, overwhelming evidence suggested that the number of rapes had increased "by reason of the corruption and debasement of the right of suffrage," and it would continue to grow "with every election where white men equalized themselves at the polls with an inferior race," making the black man think he is "a man and a brother." Black voting, then, constituted a clear and present danger to white womanhood. The black voter, "debased by bribery and political trickery," Felton warned, had no hesitation in following his instincts "wherever they led him—in revenge or bestiality."[11]

The issue was not black political power. Only in a few isolated places, as in North Carolina, did that continue to pose any serious threat to whites. Nor was there any persuasive evidence to suggest that white and black farmers or workers might choose to collaborate politically to resolve common economic grievances. Whenever such collaboration did take place, whites found themselves unable to substitute class for race consciousness. Always ambivalent about their commitment to biracial politics, white "reformers" (like the Populists in the 1890s) proved to be unstable, unreliable, unpredictable, and not infrequently downright treacherous political allies. If they were willing at certain times in certain places to make expedient alliances with blacks, they did so without abandoning their belief in white supremacy. It was possible to claim allegiance to Populist principles, for example, while denouncing black voting as a "heinous outrage" and opposing educational qualifications for the suffrage that would disfranchise "the poorer classes of the toiling masses."[12]

Middle- and upper-class whites, as in the constitutional conventions and in the numerous conferences on race relations, expressed a growing concern over poor whites. But the problem lay less in the possibility that poor whites might align themselves with blacks than in their propensity for terrorizing blacks and destabilizing the social order. Some way had to be found to establish a peaceful coexistence in which blacks could be secure in their subordination and whites of all classes secure in their supremacy. If the white laboring classes responded favorably to the racist demagoguery of this period, that was because the rhetoric reflected their feelings of insecurity and perceived loss of power and status. Alexander C. King, a Georgia corporate lawyer who would later be elevated to a judgeship by President Woodrow Wilson, made perfectly clear to a prestigious conference on race relations the principal source of fear among the white masses—"the degradation of the white through the existence in the South of the Negro."

> With the lower classes and the lower order of the whites, the prospect of having Negroes better educated, richer and better equipped for the struggle of life, menaces their social standing, while Negro suffrage obliterates that distinction which, before the war, made the poorest white man a citizen in the sense that the richest free Negro could never become his political equal, and placed him where the Roman citizen stood to the provincial in the days when Roman citizenship was the heritage only of the Roman.[13]

The last bastions of anything resembling black political power fell before the onslaught of racial demagoguery and white supremacy, including those places where for a time whites and blacks had found it expedient to combine forces for political ends. In North Carolina, long after the South had been "redeemed," blacks continued to wield impressive political power in the ten eastern counties comprising the Second Congressional District, largely through a coalition of Republicans and Populists. But it was at best an uneasy alliance, as a Populist leader confided after the "fusion" victory of 1896: "The Negros [sic] are fussing for rule and power and must be put into subjection, and any course we may persue [sic] that does not lead in that direction consistently will divide the majority of Pops, or make democrats of them." Two years later, "the growing assertiveness and impudence" of black political leadership made even more urgent the cry of white supremacy. Democratic candidates and the press aroused the white electorate through a recital of "exasperating" incidents of black "insolence" and violations of racial etiquette. None were more offensive in their conduct, charged one newspaper, than the educated blacks. "When you educate a negroe [sic], thereafter there are only three avenues he looks to—teaching school, preaching and politics. Give them a smattering of education and they are then ready for one or the other or all three of these roles." The appeals to racial fears were more than sufficient to crush the coalition, culminating in a massacre of blacks in Wilmington in 1898 and the disfranchisement and depoliticization of blacks in 1900.[14]

The issue in the 1890s throughout the South was how racial coexistence could be reconciled with the unquestioning domination of whites. Although U.S. citizens, black Southerners would no longer be permitted to exercise significant political power or influence. That was the clear intent of disfranchisement. It made no difference what class of blacks exercised the vote; indeed, the more literate and intelligent the black voter, the greater the danger he posed and the more apt he was to seek to transform political into social equality. "I am just as much opposed to Booker Washington as a voter, with all his Anglo-Saxon reenforcements," James K. Vardaman of Mississippi insisted, "as I am to the cocoanut-headed, chocolate-colored, typical little coon, Andy Dotson, who blacks my shoes every morning. Neither is fit to perform the supreme function of citizenship." The year Mississippi disfranchised blacks, a Jackson newspaper underscored Vardaman's argument. "If every negro in Mississippi was a graduate of Harvard, and had been elected as class orator . . . he would not be as well fitted to exercise the right of suffrage as the Anglo-Saxon farm laborer, *adscriptus glebae* of the South and West. Whose cross "X" mark, like the broad arrow of Locksley, means force and intellect, and manhood—*virtus*."[15]

The thoroughness of disfranchisement shocked even blacks who had anticipated the worst. By virtue of their race, not their intelligence or economic class, black men would be disqualified from participation as voters or as officeholders. That effectively disposed of the arguments advanced by black accommodationists that once black people educated themselves and improved their economic standing, they would win their way back into the political arena. No matter what strides blacks made in education, one newspaper insisted, whites would never again permit blacks to participate in the political process. "They do not object to negroes voting on account of ignorance, but on account of color."[16]

The various mechanisms used to disfranchise blacks differed from state to state, as did the timing and most compelling motives. Mississippi set the pattern in 1890. Although whites had employed intimidation and force to reduce black voting, fears remained that an expanding black population might challenge white supremacy, particularly with the advent of a new generation of blacks who were perceived as less susceptible to white control and more prepared to discard old customs and understandings. "The plan," then, a Democratic leader asserted, "is to invest permanently the powers of government in the hands of the people who ought to have them—the white people." The constitutional convention proceeded to adopt a measure that made no mention of race—thereby blunting federal intervention or legal challenges based on the Fourteenth and Fifteenth Amendments—but accomplished the proclaimed objectives of the disfranchisers. The key provision required voters to be able to read or provide "a reasonable interpretation" of any section of the state constitution. That provided a convenient loophole for illiterate whites. The dominant race would prevail, largely through the ways in which white registrars used their powers and examined potential black and white voters.[17]

If any doubts lingered as to how the enforcers would employ the discretion given them in the new constitution, the results were soon in. "The political map of Mississippi no longer contains a black belt," a Jackson newspaper exulted in 1892. Even if blacks acquired literacy, it did them little good at the polls, as the registrars crafted questions ("How old was Christ when he was born?") impossible to answer. Some years later, a popular story making the rounds in the black community told of a black man trying to register to vote. His ability to pass the literacy requirement momentarily flustered the registrars. After conferring, they showed him a headline in a Chinese newspaper and asked him if he knew what it meant. "Yeah, I know what it means," he replied. "It means that niggers don't vote in Mississippi again this year."[18]

The state of Mississippi provided a model, and in less than two decades the rest of the South in various ways followed its example. William J. Montgomery, a newspaper publisher, lawyer, and business-man, served as a delegate to the South Carolina Constitutional Convention of 1895. Thinking his colleagues might profit from the experience of Mississippi, he wrote to some nineteen prominent citizens of that state, requesting their evaluation of the results of disfranchisement. The responses differed only in the degree of enthusiasm expressed over the elimination of the Negro from politics. Disfranchisement, they all agreed, had worked "admirably," "charmingly," and effectively, removing the Negro from politics "as absolutely as if the negroes had been deported to Liberia." What had been a black majority of 75,000, one correspondent wrote, had become "a *safe legal* white man's majority." A Yazoo City man exulted in the fact that in his county of 40,000 people, two-thirds of them black, only 50 Negroes qualified to vote. Not only would disfranchisement save South Carolina from "the dominion of the negro," one correspondent promised, but it need not discriminate against illiterate whites. "The poor ignorant white people do not care about it and when they do vote no point is made on them." An Oxford, Mississippi, correspondent thought blacks had already been "practically" eliminated from politics, "so really we have not had the opportunity of seeing how the thing would work because there has been no need to use it." No writer suggested that disfranchisement had thwarted a possible coalition of blacks and poor whites; on the contrary, whites could more easily divide among themselves on political issues, and the Populist Party "has developed great strength."[19]

In much of the South, the story was the same. Disfranchisement produced instant changes in the composition of the electorate. In Louisiana, as late as 1896, there were 130,000 registered black voters; eight years later, the number had been reduced to 1,342. Residential, literacy, and tax requirements had almost depleted the electorate. In Alabama, five years after the constitutional convention of 1901, there were 205,278 whites registered to vote, 83 percent of the male whites of voting age, compared to 3,654 blacks, 2 percent of the adult men. That ratio would persist for the next half century. By 1910, black men had been practically disfranchised in almost every southern state, using one

or a combination of different mechanisms: a poll tax; property ownership; a literacy, educational, or understanding test; residency requirements; and the notorious grandfather clause, which exempted from the
literacy and property tests those entitled to vote on January 1, 1867,
along with their sons and grandsons. Of course, by virtue of their previous exclusion from voting, blacks could not qualify under that
clause.[20]

Whatever devices individual states adopted, the implementation of
the laws determined who would rule. Lawyers and justices of the peace
found the proper legal language, the precedents, and the procedures
that would effectively circumvent the Fifteenth Amendment, underscoring the prominent role played by the legal profession in the South
in perverting the democratic process. Many years later, Roger T.
Stevenson, who presided as a magistrate for a quarter of a century in
Seaboard, North Carolina, spoke with pride about how the township
had never gone against a candidate he supported. In conducting elections, he recalled, if intimidation did not always succeed in dissuading
blacks from registering to vote, the power he wielded as a registrar to
judge the qualifications of voters never failed. "Some wrote the Constitution, I reckon, as good as a lot o' white men, but I'd find somethin'
unsatisfactory, maybe an *i* not dotted or a *t* not crossed, enough for me
to disqualify 'em. The law said 'satisfactory to the registrar.' " In using
his powers, Stevenson felt he had fulfilled his responsibilities to his race.
"We're bound to keep the nigger down; it's all that saves us."[21]

Certain black Southerners, often businessmen, clergymen, and professionals who enjoyed through their deferential behavior a reputation
in the community as "good negroes," along with some "trusted" blacks
of lesser economic stature, were permitted to register and vote. Ike
Pringle—"Uncle Ike"—of Lincoln County, Mississippi, had voted
since Reconstruction without being challenged; he was said to be "totally unreconstructed, a true negro of the Old South" who "always
sided with his white folks." Questioned about his allegiance, "Uncle
Ike," as whites affectionately addressed him, did not hesitate to capsu-
late his political history: "I always voted for our side de house."[22]

In much of the South, the absence of significant white resistance to
black disfranchisement made any extensive rationalizations unnecessary. Vardaman had not tried to hide the motive for calling a convention in Mississippi. "There is no use to equivocate or lie about the
matter. . . . Mississippi's constitutional convention of 1890 was held for
no other purpose than to eliminate the nigger from politics; not the 'ig-

norant and vicious,' as some of those apologists would have you believe, but the nigger. . . . Let the world know it just as it is." Nor did this
delegate to the Alabama convention of 1901 find any reason to be circumspect: "Our purpose is plain. It is not denied by any man upon the
floor of this convention or in this State." The debates revolved not
around the issue of whether blacks ought to be disfranchised but what
device might prove most effective and least costly and yet not be inconsistent with the language of the Fifteenth Amendment. When asked
how Alabama had eliminated the black vote, a former state official provided an explanation that would have been heartily shared—and
cheered—in much of the white South. "At first, we used to kill them to
keep them from voting; when we got sick of doing that we began to
steal their ballots; and when stealing their ballots got to troubling our
consciences we decided to handle the matter legally, fixing it so they
couldn't vote."[23]

Caught up in the age of Progressive reform, some whites preferred
to view the new restrictions on blacks as reform, not repression, as a
way to use the law to contain both races, resolve racial tensions, and
maintain the social order. They could avoid the rhetorical extremes of
a Vardaman or a Tillman and maintain their "respectability" while
achieving the same desirable results. "It was not a desire to get rid of
Negro domination that prompted the new constitution of Mississippi,
or the new constitution of Louisiana," a former Alabama congressman
told a gathering of "moderate" whites in 1900. "The white men already were dominant in both States; they were simply taking steps in
the direction of pure elections." Disfranchisement was a way to reform
and purify the electoral process, to root out fraud and bribery. The
logic seemed unassailable. To curb the purchase of votes, reduce the
number of people eligible to vote. To suppress once and for all the cry
of "Negro domination," eliminate the Negro voter, no longer making it
necessary to abuse the democratic process. "They don't love to soil
their clothes," a white resident of the Alabama Black Belt said of
"moderate" proponents of disfranchisement, "they want the black
cloud lifted somehow, anyway, but surely and finally." The black newspaper in New Orleans mocked the white rationale for disfranchisement
in Louisiana: "How can we perpetrate one big steal . . . so that we may
have no more fraudulent work to do hereafter? . . . We want to be honest, hence we shall steal all we wish at once and then stop. We want to
raise our children right."[24]

The problem with a political system based on fraud and violence was that it required constant vigilance. And some whites, like this delegate to the Alabama constitutional convention of 1901, doubted if the current system, although "magnificent," could be perpetuated indefinitely without legal intervention. "It is Christianity, but not orthodox. . . . It is wrong but right. It is justice but injustice. It is life instead of death. That this subordination will continue, we do not believe." That is, unless the delegates chose to write it into the constitution, as they did in 1901, to replace "this revolutionary method by legal machinery."[25]

Perhaps to reassure themselves, perhaps for northern consumption, white leaders, editors, and publicists did offer a variety of explanations, some more subtle than others, for the actions taken to depoliticize blacks. For some, invoking the old paternalism conveniently explained disfranchisement while at the same time affording a semblance of hope for the future of race relations. "The negro race is under us," ex-governor of Alabama Thomas G. Jones told the disfranchisement convention, "we have shorn him of all political power. . . . In return for that, we should extend to him . . . all the civil rights that will fit him to be a decent and self-respecting, law-abiding and intelligent citizen of this state."[26] But that hope was naive if not downright duplicitous. To deprive blacks of political power was to deny them the very means by which they might become "self-respecting, law-abiding and intelligent" citizens.

The white South succeeded in eliminating most blacks as participants in the democratic process. Although constitutional provisions were often sufficient to dissuade blacks from voting, whites continued to resort to violence whenever necessary. Even if they could qualify to vote, blacks realized the consequences of exercising that right. James Plunkett, a Virginia black, understood the meaning of democracy when left to white Southerners to define it: "Man from Georgia said, 'we dont stop colored from voting if he want to vote, but a bullet would follow him out the door.' " A Mississippi newspaper made the same point when it reported that the body of Marsh Cook, a black candidate for the constitutional convention of 1890 who was denouncing white people in his campaign speeches, had been found riddled with bullets. "The *Clarion-Ledger* regrets the manner of his killing, as assassination cannot be condoned at any time. Yet the people of Jasper are to be congratulated that they will not be further annoyed by Marsh Cook."[27]

Whatever the promises, disfranchisement failed to bring racial peace to the South. To some whites, of course, legal disfranchisement was a beginning, not an end, and a way had to be found to make absolutely certain that blacks would never again exert political influence. Dependence on the whims of the registrar still left some unsatisfied, including the implication that poorer whites were no better than blacks, that they were no more qualified to vote except for the special allowances made on their behalf and the ability of registrars to waive or ignore the literacy and understanding clauses. Recognizing the need to go further than the new constitutional provisions, some in the South thought it a "folly bordering on to crime" to provide educational facilities for blacks. That money ought to be used to educate ignorant whites. The disfranchisement provision had worked well in Mississippi, a newspaper noted six years after its adoption, but the literacy qualification for voting had ceased to be an efficient guarantee of white supremacy as long as blacks had access to schools.[28]

Even as the states restricted the vote, affecting most blacks and some whites, they acted to reassure whites of all classes of their racial superiority. "The quarter of a century that has passed since the war," a New Orleans newspaper editorialized, "has not diminished in the slightest degree the determination of the whites to prevent any such dangerous doctrine as social equality, even in the mildest form. . . . We cannot afford to surrender anything in this case." Even as a resident of Biloxi, Mississippi, voiced his satisfaction with the results of disfranchisement, he noted that it had "solved the race problem [only] so far as politics is concerned."[29] Based on such sentiments, deeply rooted in the white psyche, the efforts to separate the races, to quarantine and marginalize black Southerners, extended beyond the polling places to every aspect of day-to-day life where blacks and whites came into contact with each other.

3

RACIAL SEGREGATION WAS hardly a new phenomenon. Before the Civil War, when slavery had fixed the status of most blacks, no need was felt for statutory measures segregating the races.[30] The restrictive Black Codes, along with the few segregation laws passed by the first postwar governments, did not survive Reconstruction. What replaced them, however, was not racial integration but an informal code of exclusion and discrimination. Even the Radical legislatures in which blacks played a prominent role made no concerted effort to force integration on unwilling and resisting whites, especially in the public schools; constitutional or legislative provisions mandating integration were almost impossible to enforce. The determination of blacks to improve their position during and after Reconstruction revolved largely around efforts to secure accommodations that equaled those afforded whites. Custom, habit, and etiquette, then, defined the social relations between the races and enforced separation in many areas of southern life. Whatever the Negro's legal rights, an English traveler noted in Richmond in 1866, he knows "how far he may go, and where he must stop" and that "habits are not changed by paper laws."[31]

But in the 1890s whites perceived in the behavior of "uppity" (and invariably younger) blacks a growing threat or indifference to the prevailing customs, habits, and etiquette. Over the next two decades, white Southerners would construct in response an imposing and extensive system of legal mechanisms designed to institutionalize the already familiar and customary subordination of black men and women. Between 1890 and 1915, state after state wrote the prevailing racial customs and habits into the statute books. Jim Crow came to the South in an expanded and more rigid form, partly in response to fears of a new generation of blacks unschooled in racial etiquette and to growing doubts that this generation could be trusted to stay in its place without legal force. If the old Negro knew his "place," the New Negro evidently did not. "The white people began to begrudge these niggers their running around and doing just as they chose," recalled Sam Gadsden, a black South Carolinian born in 1882. "That's all there is to segregation, that caused the whole thing. The white people couldn't master these niggers any more so they took up the task of intimidating them."[32]

What made the laws increasingly urgent was the refusal of blacks to keep to their place. In the late nineteenth century, economic and social changes swept through the South, introducing new sites and sources of potential racial contact and conflict; at the same time, white women in increasing numbers moved into the public arena and workplace. Both races availed themselves of the expanding means of rail transportation, with middle-class blacks in particular asserting their independence and social position. Refusing to be confined to the second-class or "smoking" car, they purchased tickets in the first-class or "ladies" car, much to the consternation of whites who resented these "impudent" assertions of social equality. In response to white complaints, conductors expelled blacks from the first-class seats they had purchased, resulting in disruptive incidents and litigation.

Segregation, even more than disfranchisement, came to be linked to white fears of social equality. The railroad and the streetcar became early arenas of confrontation, precisely because in no other area of public life (except the polling place) did blacks and whites come together on such an equal footing. "In their homes and in ordinary employment," as one observer noted, "they meet as master and servant; but in the street cars they touch as free citizens, each paying for the right to ride, the white not in a place of command, the Negro without an obligation of servitude. Street car relationships are, therefore, symbolic of the new conditions." In daily travel, the proximity of the races was likely to be much closer, more intimate, more productive of cvil, as a New Orleans newspaper suggested: "A man that would be horrified at the idea of his wife or daughter seated by the side of a burly negro in the parlor of a hotel or at a restaurant cannot see her occupying a crowded seat in a car next to a negro without the same feeling of disgust." An English visitor heard the Jim Crow car defended not only as a necessary means to keep the peace but "on the ground of the special aversion which . . . the negro male excites in the white woman."[33]

In South Carolina, where legislation segregating public transportation had been previously defeated, the question took on a new urgency in the late 1890s. Explaining that urgency and why it no longer opposed such legislation, a Columbia newspaper referred to the "many" and "constant" complaints over racial intermingling on the railway trains.

> The seeming humiliation put upon respectable colored people is to be regretted, but they suffer from the conduct of those of their race who have not appreciated the privileges which they were accorded on the railroads of this state. The obtrusiveness and hardly-veiled insolence of many negroes constantly offends ladies traveling and this settles it.

Legislators and editors voiced support of segregation while lamenting the passage of the "old Negro." The linkage seemed obvious. The new laws, explained a state senator, were not needed to protect whites from "good old farm hands and respectable negroes" but from "that insolent class who desired to force themselves into first class coaches."[34]

To resolve this growing problem, state after state, beginning in the 1880s, responded by designating cars for whites and blacks, in many instances making the "smoking" or second-class car the only car available to black passengers. The same assertiveness by blacks on the urban streetcars and trolleys, including the refusal to sit in separate sections or to give up seats to whites, prompted municipalities to take similar action. In Jacksonville, Florida, for example, the city council enacted a separate streetcar ordinance after reports of disturbances on the cars and growing complaints from whites about "the attitude" of black passengers.[35]

Some municipalities prescribed separate cars; most settled on partitions that separated the races on the same car, with blacks relegated to the rear seats. On boarding a streetcar in Atlanta, for example, the passenger would see over each door a sign reading

>White People Will Seat From Front of Car Toward
>the Back and Colored People from Rear Toward Front

With some exceptions, that became the standard arrangement. In Birmingham, blacks sat in the front section, and attempts to reverse the order clashed with custom. "After all," one white resident noted, "it is not important which end of the car is given to the nigger. The main point is that he must sit where he is told."[36]

Variations appeared in the way municipalities chose to define and enforce the restrictions. In the absence of clear demarcations within the car, it might be left to the discretion of the conductor. "Heh, you nigger, get back there," an Atlanta conductor shouted, and the black man, who had taken a seat too far forward, complied with the demand. But in most places, as in New Orleans, screens clearly defined where blacks could sit, and if whites filled their section, the screen could be moved farther to the rear. To listen to black passengers, the restrictions were often enforced arbitrarily, almost always to their discomfort and disadvantage. In responding to the complaint of a black woman, who objected to a white man smoking in a car assigned black passengers, the conductor placed the entire Jim Crow apparatus in its proper context: "The law was made to keep you in your place, not the white people."[37]

The new railway stations in Birmingham, Atlanta, Charleston, and Jacksonville impressed visitors with their spaciousness and impressive architecture. Each station also had its separate entrances, waiting rooms, and ticket offices marked "For White Passengers" and "For Colored Passengers." The rod separating the white section from the black section, unlike the screens in streetcars, as one visitor noted, was neither provisional nor movable "but fixed as the foundations of the building." Throughout the South, segregation was extended to waiting rooms, most often confining blacks to smaller and cramped quarters. In one station, the waiting rooms were designated "White Men," "White

Women," "Black Men," and "Black Women," but some of the local whites became alarmed at the limited scope of the term "Black" and authorities substituted "Colored."[38]

Although blacks had previously experienced segregation in various forms, the thoroughness of Jim Crow made it strikingly different. What the white South did was to segregate the races by law and enforced custom in practically every conceivable situation in which whites and blacks might come into social contact: from public transportation to public parks, from the workplace to hospitals, asylums, and orphanages, from the homes for the aged, the blind, deaf, and dumb, to the prisons, from saloons to churches. Not only were the races to be kept apart in hospitals (including a special section for black infants requiring medical attention), but some denied admission to blacks altogether. Laws or custom also required that black and white nurses tend only the sick of their own race. By 1885, most states had already legally mandated separate schools. Where intermarriage and cohabitation had not been outlawed, states quickly moved to place such restrictions in law.

The signs "White Only" and "Colored" (or "Negroes") would henceforth punctuate the southern landscape, appearing over the entrances to parks, theaters, boardinghouses, waiting rooms, toilets, and water fountains. Movie houses were becoming increasingly popular, and Jim Crow demanded not only separate ticket windows and entrances but also separate seating, usually in the balcony—what came to be known as the "buzzard roost" or "nigger heaven." And blacks came to learn that in places where they were permitted to mix with whites—stores, post offices, and banks, for example—they would need to wait until all the whites had been served. Special rules also restricted blacks when shopping in white stores, forbidding women, for example, from trying on dresses, hats, and shoes before purchasing them.[39]

The rapid industrialization of the South introduced another set of problems, increasing racial tensions in places employing both races. Where whites and blacks worked in the same factories, the law would now mandate segregation wherever feasible. The code adopted in South Carolina, for example, prohibited textile factories from permitting black and white laborers to work together in the same room, or to use the same entrances, pay windows, exits, doorways, or stairways at the same time, or the same "lavatories, toilets, drinking water buckets, pails, cups, dippers or glasses" at any time. Under certain conditions, such as an emergency, the code permitted black firemen, floor scrubbers, and repairmen to associate with white laborers.[40]

Separation of the races often meant the total exclusion of black men and women from certain facilities. The expansion of recreation in the late nineteenth century mandated exclusion of blacks from most amusement parks, roller skating rinks, bowling alleys, swimming pools, and tennis courts. It was not uncommon to find a sign at the entrance to a public park reading "Negroes and Dogs Not Allowed." Excluding blacks from parks deprived them not only of a recreational area but of free public entertainment. "Think of it," a black visitor to Atlanta informed a friend in New York, "Negroes not allowed in some of the parks here, to listen to [a] band which plays here on Sundays." Some communities admitted blacks to parks on certain days, designated a portion for their use, or made arrangements for separate parks.[41]

With few exceptions, municipal libraries were reserved for the exclusive use of whites. Between 1900 and 1910, some public libraries extended limited service—that is, blacks were still denied access to the reading room or the privilege of browsing in the stacks, but they might in some instances borrow books for home use. Rather than make any such provisions in the main library, some cities chose to establish separate branches to serve black patrons.[42] But for whites who feared educated blacks, barring them from libraries altogether made eminently good sense. "[T]he libraries in the Southern States are closed to the low down negro eyes . . . because he is not worthy of an education," a Florida white man wrote to a northern critic. "All the mean crimes, that are done are committed by some educated negro. . . ." In one community, the librarian had a ready answer to a question about why blacks could not be permitted to check out books: "[T]he southern people do not believe in 'social equality.' "[43]

Although most business establishments welcomed black customers, there were exceptions and restrictions. Many laundries, for example, posted signs reading "We Wash For White People Only"; in Nashville, a laundry declared on the sides of its delivery wagons and on advertisements in streetcars "No Negro Washing Taken."[44] Where custom had largely governed which if any restaurants blacks could patronize, laws in some states mandated separate accommodations, often a small room with a separate entrance, and many restaurants barred blacks altogether.[45]

In the early twentieth century, the growing availability of automobiles to both races precipitated a variety of measures. While some communities limited the access of black motorists to the public streets, others placed restrictions on where they might park. In much of the

South, racial etiquette dictated that black drivers should make no effort to overtake buggies and wagons driven by whites on unpaved roads. Not only could such behavior be construed as "impudence," but also the white passengers might be enveloped by a cloud of dust. "As a rule," Benjamin Mays recalled, "Negroes did not pass white people on either a dusty or a muddy road. . . . I have been with my father when he apologized for passing a white driver by saying, 'Excuse me, Boss, I'm in a hurry.' Did this mean that my father mentally accepted or emotionally approved this cringing behavior? I doubt it. . . . It was a technique of survival."[46]

If the use of roads could be legislated, so could a town's sidewalks, where custom had always dictated that blacks step aside to provide ample room for whites. In Danville, Virginia, after hearing complaints about black children occupying the entire sidewalk on their way to and from school, a new police rule limited their use of those sidewalks when white children were coming or going in the other direction.[47] Of course, whether by law or custom, blacks of any age were expected to step aside when white adults approached.

In the towns and cities, segregated residential patterns were now legally sanctioned, making it difficult for blacks of any class to move into a white block and accelerating the appearance or growth of a distinct district designated as "darktown" or "niggertown." Whether by custom or ordinance, the newer and most rapidly growing cities tended to be the most segregated; by the mid-1890s, for example, racially exclusive sections characterized Atlanta, Richmond, and Montgomery.[48] In some of the older antebellum communities, where house slaves and free blacks had lived near their white employers, black housing tended to be more widely scattered. Some whites thought laws or ordinances restricting where blacks could live were unnecessary, that public sentiment would expeditiously settle the issue. "[T]here is no use to make a law that says one set of men can do this or do that," a resident of Greensboro, North Carolina, argued. "In this white man's town when an African proposed to 'move into' a white section, he was given to understand that it wouldn't do. And if he had moved in he would have moved out a great deal quicker—and a pile of ashes would have marked the house. That is what the White Man will do, law or no law, and that is understood." In a small community south of Clinton, Mississippi, as in Forsyth County, Georgia, public sentiment and night riders imposed their own version of exclusivity by driving out all the black residents.[49]

The legislation of Jim Crow affected all classes and ages, and it tended to be thorough, far-reaching, even imaginative: from separate public school textbooks for black and white children and Jim Crow Bibles on which to swear in black witnesses in court, to separate telephone booths, separate windows in the banks for black and white depositors, and Jim Crow elevators in office buildings, one for whites and one for blacks and freight. New Orleans went so far as to adopt an ordinance segregating black and white prostitutes; Atlanta confined them to separate blocks, while a Nashville brothel settled for a plan by which black prostitutes were placed in the basement and white prostitutes on the ground and upper floors. In Atlanta, the art school that had used black models needed no law to dispense with their employment.[50]

Even as the laws decreed that black babies would enter the world in separate facilities, so blacks would occupy separate places at the end of their lives. The ways in which Jim Crow made its mark on the ritual of death could assume bizarre dimensions. Will Mathis, a convicted white felon, appealed to a judge that he be hanged at a different hour than Orlando Lester, a black man, and from a different set of gallows. The same plea was made by a white Tennessean convicted of the brutal murder of his wife. After he objected to going to the gallows with three black men, the authorities agreed to hang them first.[51] Custom, if not ordinances, dictated that blacks and whites be buried in separate cemeteries. "If a colored person was to be buried among the whites," one observer noted sarcastically in Alabama, "the latter would all rise from their graves in indignation. How they tolerate the 'niggers' in heaven is a mystery, unless the mansions there are provided with kitchens and stables." On the edge of Little Rock, Arkansas, in still another unique expression of white supremacy, a section of the cemetery once reserved for blacks was converted into an exclusively white cemetery. "There are a lot of colored folks buried there and white folks on top of them," a black resident observed. "They didn't move the colored because there wasn't nobody to pay for moving. They just buried the whites on top of them."[52]

Enforcement of the Jim Crow laws could be as harsh and vigorous as the spirit and rhetoric that had demanded them. Had these laws not been adopted, an English visitor thought, "the South would have been a nation of saints, not of men. It is in the methods of its enforcement that they sometimes show themselves not only human but inhuman." The often savage beatings and expulsions on railroads and streetcars attested not only to white determination to enforce the law but also to black resistance to its implementation. Calling the Jim Crow car an "unmixed blessing," a Richmond newspaper noted that those "ill-advised" blacks who had protested it "only accentuated its need and its usefulness." Law and custom interacted to keep blacks in their place, and it would be the responsibility of blacks to learn how to adapt to these conditions as a way of life. That required a knowledge not only of local customs and laws but also of the way these might differ from place to place. "Every town had its own mores, its own unwritten restrictions," a black educator recalled. "The trick was to find out from local [black] people what the 'rules' were."⁵³

Perhaps the most revealing aspects of Jim Crow were the exceptions made for black domestic workers. If a black servant, for example, accompanied a white child into a railroad coach or into a park reserved for whites, that was perfectly acceptable, since the association did not imply an equal relationship. "Everything was all right," a Georgia house servant revealed, "so long as I was in the white man's part of the street car or in the white man's coach as a servant—a slave—but as soon as I did not present myself as a menial, and the relationship of master and servant was abolished by my not having the white children with me, I would be forthwith assigned to the 'nigger' seats or the 'colored people's coach.' " The same exception applied to black servants overseeing white children in public parks that barred blacks. Some of the parks bore signs reading "No Negroes Allowed on These Grounds Except as Servants." A black teacher ventured into a restricted park in Charleston in the company of a white friend and fellow teacher and precipitated no objections. "Of course," she noted, "every one thought I was her maid."⁵⁴

Whether in the exceptions made for black employees or in the quality of the facilities afforded blacks, the position of superior and inferior had to be absolutely clear. "The black nurse with a white baby in her arms, the black valet looking after the comfort of a white invalid," an Episcopal minister in Napoleonville, Louisiana, explained, "have the label of their inferiority conspicuously upon them; they understand themselves, and everybody understands them, to be servants, enjoying certain privileges for the sake of the person served. Almost anything the Negro may do in the South, and anywhere he may go, provided the manner of his doing and his going is that of an inferior. Such is the premium put upon his inferiority; such his inducement to maintain it."⁵⁵ On this basis, the poorest illiterate white could claim a standing in society denied to the wealthiest and most intelligent and educated black.

4

THE DEMANDS MADE by Jim Crow worked their way into the daily
routines of black men and women. Pauli Murray remembered all too
vividly the signs and how they had "screamed" at her from every direction: "For White Only," "For Colored Only," "White Ladies," "Colored Women," "White," "Colored."[56] The signs instructed blacks as to
where they could legally walk, sit, rest, eat, drink, and entertain themselves. But if the signs were new to the South, the custom of segregating the races was not, only its legalization and the intensity with which
the old customs were now enforced and expanded. Experiencing these
strictures on movement and presence constituted the initiation of a
new generation into the meaning of blackness and freedom in the post-
Reconstruction South.

For all blacks, whatever their age, education, or social class, Jim
Crow was a daily affront, a reminder of the distinctive place "white
folks" had marked out for them—a confirmation of their inferiority
and baseness in the eyes of the dominant population. What the white
South insisted on was not so much separation as subordination, a system of controls in which whites prescribed the rules of racial conduct
and contact and meted out the punishments, and much of the impetus
for the legislation had stemmed from how whites perceived a new generation of blacks. When asked about the rigidity of the Jim Crow laws
and why they had been passed, a black domestic worker in Mobile cited
two reasons: "There were low-class blacks coming in from the country,"
and, she added, "White people, they want everything their way."[57]

Travel and movement, no matter the distance, exposed blacks to a
variety of risks and humiliations. Whether on the streetcars or railroads, at the ticket offices or in the baggage and waiting rooms, they
faced Jim Crow restrictions and the insults and violence that often accompanied their enforcement. The laws made no exceptions among
blacks based on class or education; indeed, the laws functioned on one
level to remind black people that no matter how educated, wealthy, or
respectable they might be, they were still not entitled to equal treatment
with the poorest and most degraded whites. "The blackest hands can
cook the food for prejudiced throats," a black newspaper in South Carolina observed in 1889; "the blackest, dirtiest arms can hold the whitest,

cleanest baby; the blackest, most illiterate man can sit on the same seat, even with a lady, as a driver; but the angry passions rise when a well-dressed, educated, refined negro pays his own fare and seats himself quietly in a public conveyance."[58]

Black Southerners were left to brood over the message imparted by the Jim Crow laws and the spirit in which they were enforced. "There is no wonder that we die," an Alabama woman sighed; "the wonder is that we persist in living." A black newspaper in Alabama thought the Jim Crow laws on streetcars and railroads "infamous enough," but those in power seemed determined to add additional restrictions with no thought as to how they insulted and degraded black men and women. "The Negro is as docile as he can be," the newspaper noted, "and day after day he is reminded through the daily papers . . . that some additional project is on foot, or is about to be promulgated to stand as a menace to his development, or a curb to his ambitious manhood . . . and we wonder what the harvest will be."[59] Lacking any political power, blacks were helpless to check white repression. And, reminiscent of slavery, parents and children were forced to watch family members humiliated and abused, with no opportunity to afford them protection or to retaliate.

If blacks ventured into unfamiliar territory, they needed to be doubly cautious about their movements and always sensitive to local customs. The "unwritten law" in the rural South dictated that a white resident must be able to vouch for the character of all Negroes unknown to the mass of the community. That meant that a black stranger could be stopped anywhere at any time and forced to state his business to the satisfaction of any white questioner; if the stranger provided the wrong answer or replied in a manner less than deferential, he or she was likely to be arrested or forcibly removed. After sunset, entire communities and the surrounding area might be off-limits, and every black person assumed responsibility for being able to assess the racial terrain and where his or her presence invited trouble. "A Negro with a bundle on his shoulders at the dead hour of the night," an Atlanta newspaper warned, "is always an object of suspicion." Unfamiliar with southern racial folkways, a northern black visitor gazed with astonishment at the signs displayed conspicuously along the rail route to New Orleans, ranging from "Nigger—Read and Run" to "Niggers and Dogs Not Allowed." W. C. Handy, in his frequent sojourns through the South, recalled more than once passing through towns with signs warning

"Nigger don't let the sun go down on you here." In the all-black town of Mound Bayou, in the Mississippi Delta, however, "the boot was on the other foot," as Handy noted, and "sentiment" among the townspeople applied the same exclusionist rule to "rednecks" and "peckerwoods."[60]

The workings of Jim Crow often seemed downright ludicrous. But blacks had no choice but to tolerate it, even as they mocked—among themselves—its absurdities, contradictions, and obscenities. It took little time for Jim Crow practices to become a standard item in black folklore and humor. Perhaps the only way to fathom the depths of white desperation and absurdity in keeping themselves apart from blacks was to subject white actions and rationales to the ridicule they deserved. One story told of a white deacon in Mississippi entering his church only to find a Negro. "Boy," he called out, "what you doin' in here? Don't you know this is a white church?" The black quickly explained, "Boss, I only just got sent here to mop up the floor." The response— and more importantly the manner in which it was rendered—reassured the deacon. "Well, that's all right then. But don't let me catch you prayin'." Still another story involved the elderly black man who managed to talk his way out of a traffic citation by telling the judge, "Lord, boss. I sho' thought them green lights was for the white folks and the red lights was for us cullud folks." The absurdities of race etiquette also became a target in black humor. A white woman, referring to her black servant, told her son, "I and John will look after the chickens." Her son, in the sixth grade, corrected her, "Mother, the grammar says it must be *John and I,*" to which his mother immediately responded, "Grammar or no grammar, boy, I won't put any Negro ahead of me."[61]

The restrictions might also force blacks to reverse their natural instincts. A black college president related a story about descending from a train at the railroad station in Atlanta. He heard a woman scream behind him; she had caught her heel and was falling headfirst down the steps. Instinctively he raised his arms to catch her when he suddenly remembered where he was and dropped them to his sides, allowing the white woman to fall and suffer injuries, a victim of the very customs she no doubt embraced. The black audience to which the college president related the story howled with laughter.[62] It was a rare opportunity to exact some satisfaction for the humiliations black men and women were forced to endure every day.

5

THE CONSENSUS IN the white South over the need to establish a rigid color line and maintain racial supremacy allowed for little dissent. And since whites were prepared to punish dissent, most blacks might have been expected to accept quietly and passively the restraints imposed on their lives. A black newspaper in New Orleans phrased the troubling questions black communities were asking of themselves, if only to maintain some degree of self-pride: "[H]ow should Negroes face existing conditions? Should they submit tamely and uncomplainingly with the feeling that time will bring the remedy, or should they contend bravely and unceasingly for what they believe right and what they believe themselves justly entitled?"[63] The questions could not be easily answered. Black Southerners possessed no political leverage, and the legal and military apparatus made protest risky and possibly disastrous. The ways in which blacks chose to deal with the Jim Crow transportation laws provided a model of pragmatic dissent—that is, dissent that stopped short of becoming a confrontation.

With the imposition of rigid new laws restricting black travel, trains and streetcars were for a time arenas of racial conflict. In demanding the laws, white editors and legislators, among others, had aroused the public with stories of dirty, slovenly blacks commingling with whites. But much of the violence was actually directed at middle-class blacks who could afford to ride in first-class or parlor cars—well-dressed, polite, respectable black "gentlemen" and "ladies" getting out of "place" and thrusting their unwanted presence on whites. It became all too common for a black man—such as the president-elect of a small college in Louisiana—to find himself surrounded by angry white passengers shouting, "Get out of this coach. We don't allow niggers in first-class coaches." When a black delegation traveled by train from Savannah to Indianapolis to attend a convention, the railroad company guaranteed them first-class accommodations. But after news of this delegation had been dispatched by telegraph, a mob of some fifty armed men met the train at a station and assaulted the "well-dressed" delegates. Some quickly fled, some defended themselves. When a young schoolteacher and graduate of Atlanta University screamed in fear, a white man put a pistol to her breast and told her, "You

G-d d——d heffer, if you don't hush your mouth and get out of here, I will blow your G-d d——d brains out."[64]

Between 1890 and World War I, blacks responded to the new Jim Crow laws by organizing boycotts of streetcar lines in more than twenty-five cities in every state of the former Confederacy. The boycotts varied in effectiveness, ranging in length from a few weeks to as long as two or three years, and in a few places resulted in "crippling" losses for the transit companies and even a temporary suspension of the Jim Crow ordinance. Blacks walked, they mobilized private carriages, drays, and hacks, and in several cities protesters developed informal transit systems and companies. The protest organizers were primarily prominent business and professional blacks who made an important distinction between confrontations with whites and organizing boycotts and black transit companies. No concerted attempt was made to defy the Jim Crow laws; that is, only in rare instances did blacks challenge the laws by violating them, sitting and refusing to leave their seats in the white-only compartment. Some ministers participated in the boycotts as leaders and supporters, while others counseled compliance with the new legislation. Most black newspapers offered enthusiastic support of the protests. "Do not trample on our pride by being 'jim crowed,' Walk!" the *Savannah Tribune* implored its readers. In supporting a boycott, a group of Lynchburg, Virginia, blacks asked their people to respond to "a gratuitous insult" by affecting "the white man's pocket. 'Tis there his conscience often lies."[65]

Although the boycotts and independent transit companies energized black communities, they altered neither white attitudes nor the "gratuitous insult" of Jim Crow. Few of the boycotts could be sustained for very long, and blacks lacked the financial resources necessary to run competing lines. In the absence of community-organized protests, individuals needed to make their own response, and most chose for practical reasons to comply with the new laws. Some blacks took the matter to the courts, and a few risked forcible ejection, injuries, jail, and a fine by refusing to move to the Jim Crow cars. Lucy Rucker recalled a childhood in Atlanta in which she walked to school every day rather than ride on the segregated streetcar. "If you can't get the same accommodations," her father told her, "you're going to walk." Noncompliance with Jim Crow in this family became a matter of self-pride. "We didn't ride the streetcar; we did not go to the theater. And any place where it was segregated, we didn't go."[66]

Few of the black protests between 1890 and World War I had any staying power. Some were organized, some spontaneous, but seldom did any of the protests evolve into a mass demonstration or a sizable movement, and few if any of them addressed the economic plight of blacks. The driving force was often the effort to improve segregated facilities, to make them the equal of their white counterparts. A number of black spokesmen made it clear they did not wish to impose their presence where it was unwanted by whites, but they resented paying first-class fares for second-class accommodations. The idea was not so much to end racial separation as to eradicate inequality. Although short-lived and limited in focus, the protests did suggest a black population prepared to chip away at the foundations of white supremacy. But nearly half a century would have to pass before those foundations were confronted directly by an organized mass movement.

6

LIKE SO MANY of the segregation statutes enacted in the 1890s and the early twentieth century, a law enacted by Louisiana in 1890 forbade any railroad passenger to enter "a coach or compartment to which by race he does not belong." Homer Plessy, a light-skinned black, claiming the statute violated his rights under the Thirteenth and Fourteenth Amendments, chose to challenge it in court. After purchasing a first-class ticket on the East Louisiana Railway from New Orleans to Covington, he took a vacant seat in a whites-only car. Not heeding the demand that he leave that car, Plessy was forcibly ejected and placed in the parish jail of New Orleans.

In *Plessy* v. *Ferguson,* the U.S. Supreme Court in 1896, by an overwhelming 8 to 1 vote, rejected Plessy's appeal and found no problem with accommodations that were "equal but separate." The majority opinion embraced popular views on race. "Social prejudices," wrote Justice Henry B. Brown for the majority, may not be "overcome by legislation," and legislative bodies were "powerless to eradicate racial instincts." Rejecting the idea that "the enforced separation of the two races stamps the colored race with a badge of inferiority," Justice Brown observed, "If this be so, it is not by reason of anything found in the act, but solely because the colored race chooses to put that construction upon it." Equal rights, in any event, did not require "an enforced commingling of the two races," and any effort to force such commingling would only exacerbate race relations. "If one race be inferior to the other socially, the Constitution of the United States cannot put them upon the same plane." The doctrine of white supremacy could not have been enunciated more clearly. Ironically, the lone dissent came from John Marshall Harlan, a southern justice and son of a slaveowner. By permitting the states to regulate civil rights "solely upon the basis of race," he argued, the Court had deprived black men and women of equal protection before the law. It would require another fifty-eight years for a majority of the Supreme Court to agree.[67]

The decision in *Plessy* v. *Ferguson* was less than dramatic in its impact. For most black Southerners, it simply underscored what they already knew from personal experience—that the quality of their lives and freedom depended on the whims, will, and toleration of a majority of whites in their locality or state. The Court's decision, along with the elaborate structure of Jim Crow, remained in force for more than half a century, as did the reality of separate and unequal treatment. The train compartment reserved for blacks came to symbolize that reality. "[I]n every instance and without recourse," a white southern critic observed, it was "the most uncomfortable, uncleanest, and unsafest place."[68]

In defending the "reasonableness" of the Louisiana statute, the Supreme Court affirmed the right of the state "to act with reference to the established usages, customs and traditions of the people, and with a view to the promotion of their comfort, and the preservation of the public peace and good order." That judgment accorded perfectly with what had become standard gospel in the movement to disfranchise and segregate southern blacks. Not only "rednecks" and "extremists" but also the "best people" helped to institute and implement these "reforms." As "friends" of the Negro, they assured themselves and the country that they were acting for "the protection of both races" and for "peace between the races." "Each race must develop its own civilization," a Knoxville, Tennessee, newspaper editorialized. "The South understands the colored man and treats him better than does any other section."[69]

To repress the Negro, then, was to act in his best interests. "If we can eliminate the negro from politics," a North Carolinian told a newly elected state legislator in 1898, "it ought to be done for *his sake,* as well as ours." The argument permitted whites to coat their racial practices in the language of paternalism. Conferring the vote on blacks had "retarded and injured them," a North Carolina governor advised a black teacher, creating "unfriendliness" by whites "that it will take years to get over." In giving the Negro "false ideas," an Alabamian affirmed, the suffrage "antagonizes the man who should be his best friend." An Atlanta judge and former slaveholder suggested that segregation would protect blacks from, among others, whites like himself. "If a big black man got into the streetcar and pressed up against my wife," he told an English visitor, "I would brain him."[70]

The notion that disfranchisement and segregation benefited both races, that placing restraints on blacks actually protected them, resembled the antebellum argument that enslavement had been the best possible condition for black people, that it had conferred incalculable benefits on a race incapable of caring for itself. In that same spirit, an educator who considered himself "the friend of the negro" could argue after Reconstruction that keeping black people in their place simply affirmed their unique value and virtue. "The same quality that fits them for subordinate positions unfits them to be voters." The same "remarkable sweating capacity of the negro" that makes him "objectionable" in the streetcars, jury box, legislative halls, and public places "wonderfully fits him for his proper functions as a laborer," enables him, in fact, to perform work "which suits him as it suits no other race, and in doing which he is incomparably superior to any other race."[71]

Whether racial "moderates" or "extremists" prevailed in the ongoing debate over the destiny of black Southerners, the "Negro question" for most whites was no question at all but a matter of racial self-preservation in the face of perceived threats and challenges. Nor did most whites require elaborate explanations for their actions or feel any need to ease their consciences. After all, in reinforcing the powerlessness and inferiority of blacks, they were not acting in bad faith, only abiding by a community morality based on decades of habit and custom. "If anything would make me kill my children," a white woman confided to a northern visitor, "it would be the possibility that niggers might sometime eat at the same table and associate with them as equals. That's the way we feel about it, and you might as well root up that big tree in front of the house and stand it the other way up and expect it to grow as to think we can feel any different."[72]

Whatever the language whites employed to clothe their actions, the net effect remained the same: the dehumanization of black men and women. Not only did many whites invoke the language of disease to explain the need to quarantine blacks, but even those "moderates" who claimed to be the best friends of the Negro succumbed to talk about the regressive nature and bestial appetites of blacks that had to be restrained. The patrician historian Philip A. Bruce thought the mass of blacks were as incapable of voting intelligently "as the mules and oxen that draw the plows and wagons." In his view, it had been as essential to suppress the black vote "as it would have been to suppress the votes of all the Southern mules and oxen, had a Republican Congress, in the spirit of Caligula . . . seen proper to confer the suffrage on these animals." That view of blacks as "mules and oxen," articulated by a "moderate," echoed more extremist notions, as expressed by James K. Vardaman, of the Negro as "a lazy, lying, lustful animal" whose nature "resembles the hog's." Neither the Fifteenth Amendment nor the Declaration of Independence, he declared, applied to "wild animals and niggers."[73] Whether described by a "moderate" or an "extremist," by political rhetoric or by popular culture, black people had been reduced to something less than human.

If black men and women were little more than animals, they needed to be restrained in every sphere of activity. The entire legal—and extralegal—apparatus of the South helped to impose and maintain those restraints. What happened in the courts of law only underscored and reinforced the actions of legislators and public officials.

7

DURING A TRIAL in Wake County Superior Court in Raleigh in 1906, the deputy sheriff handed a character witness the Bible used for administering oaths. But the presiding judge, believing the light-colored witness, E. A. Johnson, to be a white man, reprimanded the deputy for giving him the wrong Bible. "That one over there is the one for the use of white people," he declared. "Not that I am a stickler about such matters, but if there are to be different Bibles kept for the races then you must not get them mixed that way. Have a different place for them, and keep them apart." Once Johnson's racial identity was revealed, the story made the rounds as a "good joke" on the presiding judge.[74]

Although seemingly a trivial matter, what the Jim Crow Bible symbolized about the double standard of justice in southern courts had far-reaching and deeply serious implications. Twenty years after the abolition of slavery, equal justice under the law remained an elusive goal for black Southerners. "Pears to me dar hain't no justice for a man ob my color down yere," a black convict reflected in 1885. "Long time ago, when I was a little chile, I yered dat de good Mas'r Linkum had sot all de brack folks free; but 'tain't so, boss. We hain't no more free dan de hoss or de mule dat you drives 'bout and beats like you hab a mind." Some years later, Benjamin Mays came to understand that the law as enforced against black Southerners was essentially lawless. "Negroes always got the worst of it. Guilt and innocence were meaningless words: the Negro was always blamed, always punished. . . . Whenever a white man was involved, the Negro was automatically guilty." Among themselves, Mays recalled, Negroes talked incessantly about the unfairness of the law, but they were "impotent" to do anything about their grievances and "dared not even mention them to whites."[75]

In the antebellum South, the law and the courts had sanctioned the unquestioned authority of the owner to deal with his slaves. "The power of the master must be absolute," a southern judge affirmed, "to render the submission of the slave perfect." Actually, some black men and women who experienced both slavery and freedom compared the quality of postemancipation justice unfavorably to the plantation justice most of them had known as slaves—if only to suggest how self-interest, sometimes the paternal instincts of owners, had afforded blacks as chattels and investments a unique if minimal protection. "Before the war, you belonged to somebody," Henry Banner reflected. "After the war you weren't nothin' but a nigger. The laws of the country were made for the white man."[76]

The Fourteenth Amendment and Reconstruction momentarily raised black expectations. When Congress wrote the equal-protection and due-process clauses into the Constitution, black Southerners achieved a semblance of equal justice, particularly in those regions where they exercised political power. They could file formal complaints, obtain legal counsel, and testify in court. In some states and cities, they occupied judicial posts and served as sheriffs, chiefs of police, and policemen. Racially integrated juries meted out justice to white and black defendants. (South Carolina went so far as to stipulate that a jury be constituted racially in proportion to the number of black voters in the county.)[77]

But these triumphs proved short-lived. Economic dependence, political setbacks, and unpunished white violence took their toll. When whites after Reconstruction moved on every front to solidify their supremacy, nowhere was the reassertion of power over black lives more evident than in the machinery of the police and the criminal justice sys-

tem. In most states, the changes occurred almost simultaneously with
the end of Republican rule. Black jurors, for example, almost immediately disappeared. "They got votes," a Richmond white man explained, "and we cannot give them everything." Although blacks
remained by law entitled to due process and equal protection under the
law, whites had no intention of acceding to a color-blind society,
whether inside or outside the courtroom. It left a bitter legacy for a new
generation who had never known slavery. By 1891, in the estimation of
Jane and Minnie Evans, two black women who resided in Waynesboro,
Mississippi, it had become impossible to obtain even minimal protection in the courts. "A colored man cannot get any charge made against
a white man here. They take the colored man and send him to the penitentiary and the law is not executed on the white man at all. We will
have to have some protection or else go away from here."[78]

By the late nineteenth century, the criminal justice system operated
with particular efficiency in upholding the absolute power of white
people to demand and obtain the submission and labor of black men
and women. Verdicts were based less on evidence of guilt than on the
race of the defendant and the deeply rooted assumption that black
men and women were by nature more prone to criminality and impul-
sive violence than whites and required more rigid control and restraint.
The judgment pronounced by a South Carolina planter in the aftermath of emancipation enjoyed widespread acceptance in the late nineteenth century and influenced scores of decisions in the courtroom:
"All the men are thieves, and all the women are prostitutes. It's their
natur' to be that way, and they never'll be no other way."[79] And since it
was "their natur' to be that way," whites chose to punish some infractions and to ignore others, depending on the nature of the offense and
the color of the victim.

Where sufficient evidence was lacking, white juries were known to
convict black defendants on little more than paranoia. To maintain
racial control was to check any potential black challenge, and that
translated into policing the black community for any signs of subversive activity or expression. A former justice of the peace in North Carolina recalled with considerable satisfaction how a judge found ways to
convict a local black leader after news had spread about meetings he
had organized in the woods, and talk of insurrection. "Henley [the
black leader] was arrested, but they couldn' seem to get enough evidence to convict him. The judge twisted the law around some way so

Henley could be convicted of tryin' to interfere with the law, and he got five years in the pen. I never heard no more o' Henley round here."[80]

The imperatives, then, were clear. To extinguish the memories of black jurors, judges, police, and legislators during Reconstruction was to make clear the undisputed and permanent authority of whites. To impress upon the first generations of freeborn blacks the constraints and discipline once associated with slavery was to remind them constantly of their circumscribed place in southern society. To enforce labor contracts and vagrancy laws was to control black labor, and to control black labor was to control black lives. The entire machinery of justice—the lawyers, the judges, the juries, the legal profession, the police—was assigned a pivotal role in enforcing these imperatives, in exercising social control, in underscoring in every possible way the subordination of black men and women of all classes and ages. Few thought to question that role; indeed, most whites expected nothing less.

In administering justice, the courts regularly excluded blacks from juries, disregarded black testimony, sometimes denied counsel to the accused, and meted out disproportionately severe sentences to black defendants. Not only did whites assume black guilt in most cases, but they also often held the entire race responsible. When a white man commits a crime, an Alabama black woman reflected, "that is simply one white man gone wrong." But if a black man commits a crime, "[a]ll of us must bear his guilt. A young white boy's badness is simply the overflowing of young animal spirits; the black boy's badness is badness, pure and simple."[81]

If accused of a crime, the black defendant faced at the very outset the difficulty of securing competent legal counsel. Skilled white lawyers could find little time for black defendants unable to pay legal costs and, fearing the loss of their white clients, little reason to defend them at all. If assigned by the court to defend a black accused of a crime against a white person, even the most conscientious white lawyer faced formidable obstacles in his attempt to mount a serious defense. He had to think not only about his own livelihood but in some instances about his life as well.

Denied the opportunity for formal college training, black lawyers were scarce in the South. Most of them were self-taught, and where and under what circumstances they could practice often depended on local custom and attitudes. At the very outset of their careers, they en-

countered skepticism about their ability to succeed in a profession demanding intellectual acumen. "We have met unreasoning prejudice
which denied us excellence of any kind," a Mississippi black attorney
and former state legislator testified at the turn of the century. "In many
instances we have commenced our trial before a jury whose pre-formed
judgment would disqualify them from sitting in any other case. We
have found, not our clients, but ourselves on trial, and not ourselves
alone, but the whole race with us."[82]

The "unreasoning prejudice" to which this black lawyer alluded varied from petty harassment to total exclusion from the legal process.
When James Weldon Johnson applied for admission to the bar in
Florida in 1898, he faced a grueling examination from three white attorneys. After several hours, two of the examiners agreed he had
passed "a good examination." The other, however, was unable to accept the result. "Well, I can't forget he's a nigger," he told the others,
"and I'll be damned if I'll stay here to see him admitted."[83]

To practice their profession, lawyers might be required to appear in
a number of counties and judicial circuits. But black attorneys never
knew for certain how they might be treated in different regions, or even
in the next county. Samuel A. Beadle, a graduate of Atlanta University
and Tougaloo College, obtained his legal training in the law offices of
two prominent white Mississippi lawyers and politicians. He had no
difficulty practicing law in the state's major urban centers, Jackson,
Natchez, and Vicksburg. But in several other areas he ran the gauntlet
of white harassment and exclusion. In the Yazoo City courtroom, he
was barred from entering inside the railing where the court's officers
and attorneys sat. In Columbus, in the northeastern part of the state,
he could not even enter the courtroom, his life was threatened, and the
court remained adjourned until he had left the city.[84]

Beadle's experience would be shared in varying degrees by other
black attorneys in the South, regardless of their legal training or the
deference they showed court officers. Local custom invariably prevailed, and that often excluded blacks from courtrooms except as spectators, custodians, and defendants. Many communities, then, simply
denied blacks the right to practice in the courts, refusing to permit
them to approach the bench, to swear them in as attorneys, or to recognize them as officers of the court. In some courtrooms, as in several
Mississippi towns, blacks were compelled to sit in and argue their cases
from the gallery, the place to which black spectators were relegated.

When an attorney insisted on the right to practice in West Point, Mississippi, he was almost thrown in jail. More than one black attorney arrived in a community to argue a case, only to be told the trial had been completed and he should board the first train leaving the town.[85]

Persuaded that they would be unable to practice law with any expectation of success or toleration, numbers of black lawyers abandoned their communities or took lesser jobs that were not threatening to whites. P. F. Williams tried to practice in Brookhaven, Mississippi, only to find his potential black clients too intimidated to request his services. Buck Colbert Franklin was expelled from court by a white judge who insisted that no black person would represent anyone in his court; Franklin then moved to the all-Negro town of Rentiesville, Oklahoma.[86]

The ability to practice in a court in no way ensured a black attorney equal or decent treatment. Willis E. Mollison agreed to defend a black man in Vicksburg who had violated the statute against enticing away laborers. In response to one of Mollison's questions during cross-examination, a witness replied, "None of your business." When Mollison asked him to repeat the remark, the judge quickly interrupted, "Mollison, your man is convicted and sentenced for thirty days. Court is adjourned." The judge told Mollison privately that he acted to save him from a beating. Obtaining the respect of the presiding judge and opposing attorneys, not to mention the jury, challenged black lawyers at every turn. Some courts objected if a black attorney or witness was addressed as "Mister" and struck such references from the record.[87]

Treatment of black lawyers varied considerably from state to state and within states. Some courts accorded them the same recognition and courtesies accorded white attorneys. Even in the most repressive regions, as in Mississippi, a judge might intercede to permit a black attorney to disregard local custom, though such tolerance might be costly to the judge's career. The principal problem facing a black attorney, once he had won the right to practice his profession in a community, was how he could defend his clients without violating the prevailing racial etiquette that dictated a Negro's "place." "The profession of law," a black attorney in Durham, North Carolina, wrote in 1909, "is the most difficult one for a colored man to follow in the South because he must deal with white judges, white jurors, white lawyers, white witnesses and a public sentiment created by whites." The black lawyer faced as well the prospect of impoverished clients and the task of building a clientele among blacks who perceived—for good reason—that any chance of success in the courts might be significantly enhanced with representation by a white attorney. And like most "successful" blacks, lawyers needed to be careful of their reputation in the white community, avoiding controversial issues that might compromise their acceptance and toleration. When Samuel J. Lee, a black attorney in Charleston, died in 1895, the local newspaper praised him as "beyond criticism, extremely courteous and never presuming."[88] That was the very least expected of any black lawyer practicing in the South.

Black defendants in the criminal justice system confronted obstacles that few were able to overcome. Upon entering the courtroom, often without a lawyer, they faced a white judge and a white jury already convinced of their guilt on the basis of their race and unwilling to grant much if any credibility to their testimony. And they confronted a familiar double standard based on race. Not only did the courts treat black "crimes" such as theft, vagrancy, drunkenness, and impudence with extraordinary severity, but they also often ignored the same offenses when committed by whites or treated white offenders with leniency, particularly if the victims were black. In Augusta, Georgia, William A. Pledger, a black Republican politician, observed in 1876 that nothing serious happened in the municipal courts to white men arrested for theft but "a leading colored man" who defended himself after being assaulted by a white was sentenced to the chain gang. "It is lawful for a white man to repel force by force either with white or black men," Pledger observed. *"It is unlawful* for a colored man to repel force with force save with a negro, a dog or a white Republican."[89]

Although arrested for the same offense, a black person could expect to serve far more time and pay a much heavier fine than a white person. It was commonly said that many more black men spent years in prison for stealing a farm animal than white men did for murdering blacks. For conviction on a petty theft charge, a black might have to stay several years in the penitentiary, often because he was unable to pay the fine and court costs; a white would most likely serve no more than ninety days in the county jail or pay a small fine and be reprimanded. A study of Georgia's state convicts in 1882 revealed gross disparities in sentencing, with blacks serving twice as long as whites for burglary and some five times as long for larceny. Among them may have been "old man Campbell," an eighty-year-old black preacher sent to the penitentiary, according to a black leader in Georgia, "for what a white man was fined five dollars." A black newspaper in New Orleans once said of an unfortunate black defendant, who had been sentenced to ninety days in jail for petty theft, that he was given "three days for stealing and eighty-seven days for being colored."[90]

The courts granted virtual immunity to whites accused of crimes against black men and women. An Augusta, Georgia, newspaper in 1890 made clear the prevailing unwritten law of the region: "If a negro kills a white man, he is pretty sure either to be lynched or hung. But if a white man slays a negro, he is in no danger of being lynched, and as to his being hung for the crime there is not much probability." That dictum was acted out in 1911 when an all-white jury acquitted some young white men of murdering a local black preacher who had tried to defend his wife from assault. The white defendants had belonged to prominent families, and that was no doubt sufficient to excuse their offense. This black song, heard around 1915, said it briefly and plainly:

> *If a white man kills a negro, they hardly carry it to court,*
> *If a negro kills a white man, they hang him like a goat.*[91]

With emancipation, black Southerners welcomed the right to testify in court cases, believing that it finally granted them a constitutional protection whites had long enjoyed. But even that precious right amounted to little if whites intimidated witnesses and refused to grant black testimony any credibility. Incidents in which blacks who testified against whites were threatened, murdered, or beaten were commonplace, making many black witnesses to a crime reluctant to become involved in a legal proceeding. When Ned Cobb talked about how black Southerners had long been "disrecognized," that "the white man in the country had everything fixed and mapped out," he aptly summed up the entire judicial system, but he focused his attention on the treatment accorded black testimony. As Cobb observed, the circumstances surrounding black testimony were critical, whether the person testifying was a witness, the plaintiff, or the defendant, and whether the case involved a white man or woman.

[N]ow a nigger could go in court and testify against his own color in favor of the white man, and his word was took. But when it come to speakin out in his own defense, nigger weren't heard in court. White folks is white folks, niggers is niggers, and a nigger's word never has went worth a penny unless some white man backed it up and told the same thing that the nigger told and was willin to stand up for the nigger. But if another white man spoke against the nigger and against the white man that was supportin him, why, they'd call that first white man "nigger-lover" and they wouldn't believe a word he said.[92]

Of course, if black testimony was less than reliable, whites often had only themselves to blame, as blacks for good reason perceived the need to tell white people what they thought white people wanted to hear, whether an employer, a judge, or a jury.

The virtual exclusion of blacks from juries after Reconstruction made a mockery of any pretense toward equal justice. Not only were black defendants deprived of a jury of their peers, but also the infrequency with which whites were apprehended, tried, and convicted of crimes against blacks had much to do with the reluctance of white witnesses to testify and the even greater reluctance of white juries to convict. Alexander M. Salley, a conscientious white sheriff, could only express his exasperation over what took place in the courtroom in 1889 in his native South Carolina. "I never have heard of a clearer case in my life . . . but it is the height of folly to try to convict a white man for killing a poor negro. A certain class think it is something to be proud of. It was perfectly disgusting to me to see men running after these self declared murderers. They had a perfect ovation. . . ." A judge in Georgia, Henry C. Hammond, was involved in "the solemn farce of trying a white man for the atrocious murder of a negro." A similar trial had just been concluded in his court, he wrote his mother, and when the jury returned its verdict "the giant butcher who had been 'vindicated' by *his* peers arose and said 'I want to thank the Jury for their kindness to me and I want to thank the judge too.'" But the gratitude was wasted on this particular judge. "You have nothing to thank me for," he told the defendant. Privately, Judge Hammond acknowledged that he had become "deeply depressed by the depraved condition of the people of this county," and he feared that it might be deemed "illustrative of a general condition prevailing throughout the South." Equally exasperated, Judge Emory Speer, in a peonage case argued in Georgia, practically ordered the jury to return a guilty verdict, as the evidence was both substantial and overwhelming. The jury required only five minutes to acquit the defendants. During the trial, Speer had to reprimand the attorney general several times for using the term "nigger," and finally ordered him to desist if he wanted to argue his case.[93]

The exclusion of blacks from juries reached the U.S. Supreme Court, but some initial triumphs for blacks only raised expectations that would soon be dashed. In *Strauder* v. *West Virginia,* the Supreme Court in 1880 held that a state statute restricting jury service to "white male persons" violated the rights of blacks under the equal-protection clause of the Fourteenth Amendment. But that same year, in *Virginia* v. *Rives,* the Court upheld the conviction of two blacks by an all-white jury in Virginia, as the statute on jury selection made no mention of race. The mere absence of blacks on juries, no matter how complete and systematic, the Court held, did not prove conclusively "that any civil right was denied, or that there had been any discrimination against the defendants because of their color or race." It had to be shown that state officials consciously and purposely excluded blacks from juries because of their race or color. By finding no such proven discrimination, the Court effectively denied the plaintiffs' desire to remove the case to a federal court, where they stood a better chance of obtaining some semblance of justice.[94]

The Supreme Court clarified still another critical point: The constitutional right to a jury of one's peers did not require a jury of one's peers in a specific case, as, for example, when blacks might be plaintiffs or defendants. "A mixed jury in a particular case is not essential to the equal protection of the laws," the Court held. The finding ignored substantial and increasing evidence that a black person could not obtain equal justice from an all-white jury in the South. In some states, the name of a black person might inadvertently be drawn for jury service, but such mistakes were rare. When in 1900, court clerks in those counties in the South where blacks constituted a majority were asked about blacks on juries, most reported that few if any blacks served in that capacity and that most whites would find them incompetent if not "farcical" if they did. In one Alabama county, a black man whose name was drawn by mistake for service on a grand jury and who insisted on being impaneled, served but two days. After being taken out at night and badly beaten, he asked to be discharged from his duty. "This will convey to your mind," the county clerk reported, "that Negro jurors are not very wholesomely regarded and tolerated in this county. The fact is, Negroes have never been or never will be allowed to sit on juries in this county." With some exceptions, this clerk had summed up the reactions of local officials throughout the South.[95]

The Supreme Court decisions on jury service imparted an important lesson to white southern legislators that they would not soon forget. Rather than bar blacks directly, they would have to find other means to keep them off juries. That lesson would subsequently be applied to vot-

ing, as legislators searched for ways to disfranchise blacks without violating the Fifteenth Amendment. The same lesson would be used to
affirm the constitutionality of racial segregation in an equally ingenious if devious fashion, as whites eagerly embraced their own version
of the separate-but-equal doctrine.

The courts, along with the police, played a critical role as the enforcers of Jim Crow. Once previous customs became lodged in the
statute books, it was imperative that any breaches be swiftly punished
as examples to others of how the new order would be implemented.
That included upholding the authority of conductors in public transportation to mete out their own brand of justice to passengers who did
not know their "place." When a black Alabamian resisted a conductor
who unnecessarily cursed and struck him, the question of self-defense
had to be subordinated to the larger issue. The judge fined the black
man $10 and made clear his reason: "I fine you that much to teach you
that you must respect white folks."[96]

To bring charges against a white person could by itself be interpreted as disrespect or impudence and invite harassment, violence, and
ridicule. All too typical was the case in Hinds County, Mississippi, in
1897, in which a black woman charged a white man with having beaten
her with an ax handle. The presiding justice of the peace told her he
could find "no law to punish a white man for beating a negro woman."
After a police court in Jackson also rejected her complaint, the local
press treated the case as "a very funny incident."[97]

The courts treated quite seriously cases in which black males were
accused of any offenses against white women. If such a case reached
the courts rather than be settled by a mob, it might suggest something
less than a capital crime. Evidence of undue attention paid to a white
woman or any kind of physical contact, no matter how inadvertent, resulted in judgments disproportionate to what a white man might receive in a similar case. In sentencing a black man to fifteen years in the
penitentiary for snatching a white woman's purse, the presiding judge
made clear that this was not a simple case of theft. He would not tolerate a black man laying his hands on a white woman.[98]

Since the courts were expected to control black labor, they treated
with equal seriousness cases in which black men and women challenged the authority of their employers. After being cursed furiously, a
black worker in Montgomery, Alabama, decided to quit his job. The
employer responded by hitting him over the head with a crowbar and
knocking him unconscious. The worker brought charges, only to be

told by the magistrate that he should feel fortunate to have escaped with his life and that if he appeared in the court again he would be heavily fined and sent to the state work farm. A black domestic servant in Granville County, North Carolina, fared no better. When the wife of her employer struck her with a stick, the servant retaliated. That unexpected behavior provoked the white woman to shoot and wound her. Still "bathed in her own blood," the servant was arrested and convicted for assaulting a white woman and sent to the county jail.[99]

Even as the courts acted to enforce Jim Crow and control black workers, they demanded compliance with the nonstatutory laws of racial etiquette. Not only black attorneys but also black plaintiffs, defendants, and witnesses had to be cautious about their behavior in the courtroom. In the municipal court in Wilmington, North Carolina, a judge fined and reprimanded a black witness who persisted in referring to Negroes with the prefix "Mr.," "Mrs.," and "Miss." Unable to pay the fine, he was committed to the workhouse until a superior court finally discharged him. No less sensitive to the need to uphold the unwritten rules of racial etiquette, a Baltimore judge summarily dismissed charges against two white men for assault and battery. The victim of the beating, a black man, had demanded that the two men apologize to a black woman they had insulted. "It makes no difference whether it is in North Carolina, Virginia, or Maryland," the judge affirmed, "it is an insult to ask a white man to apologize to a 'nigger' and I, myself would never do it to a nigger unless my conscience led me."[100]

Unequal justice often translated into hasty or summary justice, permitting black defendants few if any legal safeguards. The judge who presided over Richmond's police court in the early twentieth century acquired such a reputation, imposing fines and imprisonment after hearing only a brief statement of the charges and often before black defendants had an opportunity to respond. "Judge Crutchfield, you can't tell him nothin'," one of his victims testified, and if a black defendant employed legal counsel, the cost might be compounded. " 'Tain't no use to have a lawyer, nuther. Judge Crutchfield don't want no lawyers in his co't. Like's not he cha'ge you *mo' fo' havin'* lawyer. Then you got pay lawyer, too."[101]

To forestall lynch mobs, courts often speeded the conviction and execution of black defendants, distorting whatever semblance of constitutional protection remained for them. The ordinary legal procedures designed to ensure a fair trial found little toleration when an offense was deemed serious enough to justify mob action. In 1911, Lawson

Davis faced an almost certain lynching after he had allegedly attempted to enter the bedroom of a white woman. He was persuaded, however, to plead guilty to sexual assault. No doubt to appease any potential lynch mob, a jury was quickly impaneled, the evidence presented, and the sentence—ninety-nine years in prison—handed down. The entire procedure took only seven minutes. Trials in which black defendants pleaded their innocence might consume less than one hour, and few trials exceeded four to six hours.[102]

In the unlikely event a black defendant should be acquitted in a case involving a white person, it often proved to be something less than a triumph of justice. After an acquittal in a murder case, in which the evidence of innocence had been overwhelming, the successful attorney advised his client that local whites might not accept the verdict with equanimity. "[T]he thing for you to do is sell what you got and get away from here. Stay a while, then come back when it blow over." The man heeded the advice and waited twenty years before he returned to the community, at which point two white men caught and castrated him "and then went off laughin about it."[103]

Established customs in race relations prescribed in some regions of the South a selective enforcement of the law. The statute books were of little use in spelling out the details. Any aspiring lawyer in Mississippi, Sidney Fant Davis insisted in 1914, needed to be familiar not only with the common law, the civil law, and the statutory laws but also with "negro law." This law, "one of the most complicated" branches of jurisprudence, untaught in law school, "about which no book on earth, so far as I know, sheds the faintest ray of light," had to be learned by "experience and observation." Anyone who studied the common law and the statutory laws of the state in preparation for the bar examination, as Davis had, might have assumed that these applied to all persons regardless of race, color, or previous condition of servitude. "Nothing is farther from the truth," Davis discovered. "The judges, lawyers and jurors all know that some of our laws are to be enforced against everybody, while others are to be enforced against the white people, and others are to be enforced only against the negroes. . . ."[104]

Only native-born Mississippians, Davis suggested, had an almost instinctive feeling for the intricacies of "negro law." But the novice would soon discover that it rested largely on custom, racial assumptions, the unquestioned authority of whites, and a heavy dose of paternalism. Some crimes committed by one race might not be punishable when committed by the other race. If a white man were found guilty of adultery or bigamy, for example, he might have to serve from three to ten years in the penitentiary, but authorities were apt to ignore such a crime when committed by blacks, dismissing it as a racial defect. Nor would it be likely for a black or a white man to be tried for raping a black woman, in view of the lascivious nature of such women. If a black person were found guilty of larceny, the likelihood of a trial and the length of the sentence depended "on what he has stolen and from whom he has stolen it" and on the wishes of his employer. Rather than bring such a person to trial, the accused might be given "an ex-parte hearing" in the barn or gin house, in which the employer handed down the verdict "with a piece of gin belting, or about three feet of the butt end of an old buggy trace."

The double standard in "negro law" for judging racial behavior extended to a variety of areas. Authorities might be hesitant, for example, to arrest blacks for playing "craps," since that game of chance with dice was recognized as a Negro game exclusively. But with poker, the roles were reversed, and blacks were advised to avoid a white man's game. For obvious reasons, carrying arms was "white folks' business." While it was permissible, even expected in some regions, for able-bodied white males above age sixteen to tote pistols, an armed black might be dealt with severely "to protect the lives of both the white people and the negroes themselves."

If a black person killed a white man, according to "negro law," he would suffer death "in some form or other, the time, place and manner of his execution depending altogether on who caught him, the sheriff's posse or the friends of the deceased." But if a black person killed a black person, the "usual practice" was to appoint "some young inexperienced attorney" to take his case, allow the defendant to plead guilty, and sentence him to life imprisonment. The community thereby saved the expense of a drawn-out trial, the defendant escaped hanging, and the state secured still another convict whose labor could be sold to augment the annual revenue.

The degree to which "negro law" prevailed in the South is very much open to question. The fact remains that tens of thousands of black Southerners spent considerable time in jails and state penitentiaries for violations that "negro law" might have mitigated. More likely, "negro law" depended on the severity of the crime and operated mostly where employers meted out punishments in the hope of retaining the labor of the accused. Not only did it strengthen the employer's authority, but it also suggested the extent to which the "best sort" in the white South operated under their own sets of laws and regulations. The frustrating experience of federal agents seeking to prosecute prominent whites for peonage and the abuse of convict laborers underscored the degree to which upper-class whites deemed themselves above the law.

Whether "negro law," the common law, or statutory law prevailed, the consequences for black men and women were pretty much the same. No wonder the criminal justice system (some called it "legal lynching") figured so prominently in black song and folklore.

> *White folks and nigger in great Co't house*
> *Like Cat down Cellar wit' no-hole mouse.*[105]

When blues singers emerged in the late nineteenth and early twentieth centuries, they focused on subjects that were part of the day-to-day lives of black Southerners. If most of them avoided disfranchisement and segregation, if few of them addressed directly the issue of lynching, they commented in a variety of ways on an experience they could share with everyone in the audience, and that was the blatant unfairness of the judicial and law enforcement systems—the bigoted police, judge, and jury; the coerced confessions; the petty prosecutions; the leniency shown white offenders; the impossibility of securing a fair trial; the disparate sentences; and the terrors of imprisonment, the chain gang, and convict labor.

> *Tied in a hundred feet of chain,*
> *Every link of the chain was initial to his name.*
> *Warden come early that morning for him to be hung*
> *On account of something he hadn't done.*[106]

The song "Pore Red" told the story of a black man unable to pay his bail or fine—an altogether familiar experience. "Some Got Six Months" and "I Got Mine" told similar versions of an unfair trial and a judge who habitually reserved the harshest sentences for black defendants. In the earlier version, "Some o' them got six months, / Some o' them paid their fine. / With balls and chains all 'round their legs, I got mine." In the later version, the singer had more to say about the unfairness of the sentence:

Some got six months, some got a solid year,
But me and my buddy, we got lifetime here.
Some got six months, some got a solid (year).
But me and my buddy, we got lifetime here.

You know that ole judge must been mad,
Yeah, that ole judge must been mad, darlin'.
When he gave me my sentence, he throwed the book at (me).

First time in trouble, I done got no fair trial at all, oh Lord,
Seem like to me, baby, they locked the poor boy in jail.

Despairing of any possibility of achieving justice, "Penitentiary Blues" mocked the judge's sentence as a way of mocking the entire system: "Six months ain't no sentence, two years ain't no time, / I got a friend in prison here, doin' ninety-nine." In other versions, as in black folklore, the length of the sentence became a matter of pride, even of superiority. Sentenced to ninety-nine years in prison, Stagolee told the judge, "Judge, ninety-nine ain't no goddam time. / My father's in Sing Sing doing two-ninety-nine." Even executions became a subject for speculation. "Wonder why they electrocute a man at the one o'clock hour at night?" one bluesman asked. The answer he provided would have made perfect sense to his audience. "The current much stronger, people turn out all the light."[107]

Apocryphal or not, a story that resonated with truth in the black community told of a judge who tried to stop a lynch mob by pleading with them, "We've always been considered a progressive community and I think we're progressive enough so's we can give this boy a fair trial and then lynch him." Nearly every black person suspected such judges were common. One popular story in the black community involved a black man brought into court for kicking a white man. The judge asked him why he had kicked the white man. The black replied, "Well, Capum, what would you do if someone called you a black son of a bitch?" "That," the judge answered, "would hardly be likely to happen." "Well, Capum," the black defendant persisted, "spose they call you the kind of a son of a bitch you is?" Some years later, black cynicism about the judicial system was summed up in the story of the white man driving a convertible in Mississippi and running into two blacks, hitting them so hard they flew up into the air. One landed in the backseat of the convertible (he was charged with illegal entry); the other landed about 150 feet down the road (he was charged with leaving the scene of a crime).[108]

Even as they affirmed their belief in white supremacy, some whites believed blacks deserved the same legal protection as whites and tried to afford them such protection. But such whites were exceptional, and they often acknowledged their helplessness even in cases where evidence of black innocence or white guilt might be overwhelming. In Colleton County, South Carolina, six white men severely beat a young black man, his wife, and his mother; only the wife escaped death, though she was described as "more dead than alive." The white men had accused them of stealing a Bible from a church. Brought to trial, all the men were acquitted. No attempt was made to prove them innocent, although, in the estimation of a white resident of Beaufort, "the evidence was overwhelming against them." The incident in Colleton County only underscored the observation made by a white resident of Augusta, Georgia, in 1890. This man, a Democrat, had little regard for blacks, but he feared that whites might someday pay a heavy price for the abuses of white supremacy. "Why, you can't convict a white man of the murder of a negro, nor even of a white friend of the negro." He could conceive of a time when several southern states might have to be abandoned to blacks "if we would avoid terrible consequences from the wrongs we are heaping on them."[109]

Sensitive to the indictment of their legal system, some whites pleaded for fair treatment of black defendants, finding no necessary conflict between equal justice and white supremacy. A Mississippi judge in 1910 prefaced his plea for equal justice with an avowal of his "well-known" political opinions. But he insisted that these opinions were in no way inconsistent with his belief in judicial fairness. "The Negroes in Mississippi do not vote, and should not; they do not sit upon our juries, and they should not; but they do come into this court asking for the white man's justice, which has been the boast and pride of our race, and they are entitled to it." That blacks deprived of the vote and barred from the jury box might be at a disadvantage in the state and municipal courts did not appear to disturb him. In reporting the judge's remarks, *Crisis Magazine*, edited by W. E. B. Du Bois, thought them "remarkable" for the liberal spirit they expressed. When a jury in Shreveport, Louisiana, in 1898 found a white man guilty of murdering a Negro, and the judge sentenced him to the penitentiary for five years, a black newspaper in New Orleans focused not on the light sentence but on the first known case in Caddo Parish in which a white man had been sent to the penitentiary for murdering a Negro. "Hence we say all honor to the presiding judge . . . the D[istrict] A[ttorney] . . . and the jury." It was deemed a rare triumph.[110]

Occasionally, conscientious judges would seek to mitigate some of the more glaring abuses of the judicial system, as in the authority of municipal courts to sentence violators of municipal ordinances— "men, women, and children"—to chain gangs. In a federal district court in Georgia in 1904, Judge Emory Speer questioned that authority in no uncertain terms, finding it in conflict with constitutional protections. "Under the American system the chain gang has no place in the jurisdiction and procedure of police courts, where trial by jury is not a right of the accused." The judge, in rendering this decision, chose to reject the argument advanced by a state official that while a sentence to the chain gang would permanently ruin the reputation of a white man, it would have no such effect on blacks.[111]

The bleakness of the criminal justice system was dramatized when some whites hailed as a substantial triumph those instances in which a black accused of a serious crime received a trial rather than a lynching. The editor of the leading newspaper in Columbia, South Carolina, called such moments "an immense gain." Although acknowledging that southern courts were "imperfect," he insisted blacks could obtain justice. But that insistence might have seemed of doubtful value to black Southerners, as it still condemned them to a different standard of judgment. "While it may be and is true," the editor explained, "that sometimes a white man who kills a negro escapes just punishment at the hands of the jury, it is equally true that seldom is a negro who kills a white man unjustly punished. In a word, while the white man gets too much mercy, the negro does get justice. It is a simple fact that invariably our judges are disposed to protect negroes from oppression."[112] How judges were able to provide such protection, when white crimes against blacks went mostly unpunished, was left unexplained.

As the enforcers of white supremacy, the police assumed a pivotal role. During Reconstruction, blacks had been employed in some places as sheriffs and police—a traumatic experience for local whites. But the experiment proved short-lived, not because black police were inefficient or dishonest but because by their very presence they undermined the foundations of white supremacy. By the late nineteenth century, most black police had been removed, and white officers assumed primary responsibility for maintaining the color line and detecting any breaches or suspicious black behavior. Operating in the spirit of the antebellum slave patrols, they kept an eye on black movement and group meetings and enforced an unofficial curfew on black strangers and residents alike. Not only did they enforce vagrancy laws to solidify control of black labor, but also by virtue of their arrests they helped to swell the black labor force exploited by local and state governments; in Talladega, Alabama, for example, police arrested a weekly quota of blacks to fill out the chain gangs.[113]

The use of excessive force by the police underscored the determination to remind blacks at every opportunity of their vulnerability and helplessness. If the police sometimes singled out young blacks for punishment, it was a way to check their tendency toward "impudence," to restrain their restlessness, and keep them in their place. When police in a Georgia town asked a group of black youths for their names, one of them replied, "Ulysses." The policeman asked his colleague for assistance in spelling the name, at which point the black youth offered his services: "I know how to spell it. Let me write it for you." Enraged over such insolence, the officer struck the boy with his fist, knocking him to the ground; in court the next morning the young black was fined $25 for "using disrespectful and insulting remarks to an officer while in the discharge of his duty." This "crime" was deemed so serious that the white man for whom the youth's father worked was unable to "straighten" it out with authorities. The parents, in the meantime, were unable to pay the fine. "Ulysses went to the chain-gang," his boyhood friend recalled, "and I never saw him again."[114]

The violence meted out by the police and sheriffs was no aberration but stemmed from ideological conviction—the still commonly accepted antebellum belief that blacks understood only force, that they worked and behaved best under the threat of the lash, and that their uncontrolled impulses required a special quality of discipline. Atlanta's police force, among others, acted on such assumptions. "We have lived in Atlanta twenty-seven years," a local black newspaper observed, "and we have heard the lash resounding from the cabins of the slaves . . . but we have never seen a meaner set of low down cut throats, scrapes, and murderers than the city of Atlanta has to protect the peace." A Richmond, Virginia, black newspaper suggested that blacks regarded the local police "with a distrust bordering on hatred," and that police officers reciprocated such feelings "with compound interest."[115]

Not only did the police deal severely with blacks accused of crimes against white persons or property, but they also often chose to ignore black violence against blacks. The cynicism blacks manifested toward the police and the courts was captured in this observation attributed to a white chief of police: "If a nigger kills a white man, that's murder. If a white man kills a nigger, that's justifiable homicide. If a nigger kills another nigger, that's one less nigger."[116] When a black was arrested for killing another black, some prosecutors offered the defendant a lenient plea bargain, or, in the event of a conviction, some judges chose to hand down a less severe sentence.

The unwritten southern code often reduced the punishment of blacks who enjoyed good relationships with influential whites. It seemed to David L. Cohn, a native of the Mississippi Delta, that for every black unjustly sent to prison, another was saved through white influence and protection. "Every plantation Negro—and many Negroes of the towns—has his 'white folks' to whom he looks for protection when he violates the law." Brought into court, he might first be asked by the magistrate, "Whose nigger are you?" If he named an important person in the community, he could escape with a light sentence or no sentence at all. If he named a white of no importance, he would receive harsher treatment, and if he had no white folks at all to intervene on his behalf, "his fate is in the lap of the gods."[117]

If an accused or convicted black man was valued for his labor, that was all the more reason to listen to the appeal of a white employer that his life be preserved. A Vicksburg, Mississippi, black woman watched helplessly as an influential white man intervened on behalf of her husband's black murderer and helped to secure his acquittal. After all, she bitterly noted, to whites in need of good field hands "the live nigger is worth more than the dead one."[118] That sentiment accorded perfectly with the argument advanced by Governor Cole Blease of South Carolina when he commuted the death sentence of Stake Morris to life imprisonment at hard labor in the state penitentiary.

> This defendant was convicted of killing another negro. I am naturally against electrocuting or hanging one negro for killing another, because, if a man had two fine mules running loose in a lot and one went mad and kicked and killed the other he certainly would not take his gun and shoot the other mule, but would take that mule and work it and try to get another mule; therefore, I believe that when one negro kills another, that he should be put in the Penitentiary and made to work for the State.[119]

Bluesman Memphis Slim recalled that the reputation of a black defendant as a good worker could easily mitigate a crime if his victim was black. "If you were a good worker, you could kill anybody down there, so long as he's colored. [Just] don't kill a good worker."[120]

Intervention by whites seldom came without a price. By helping to reduce or vacate the punishment of a black defendant, an employer or "patron" enjoyed an even greater degree of authority over the person whose life had been saved or whose sentence had been lessened or set aside. That might prove to be a permanent indebtedness, virtually binding blacks to their patrons and exacting that much more labor from them. It was understood, Sarah Fitzpatrick recalled, that "when white fo'ks kill darkies nothin' wuz dun 'bout it." But when a black person killed another black person, "de white fo'ks . . . make 'im wurk dat much harder." When Henney Moton appealed for her son, who had been sentenced to death for murder, she directed her letter not through legal channels but to a prominent white man, perhaps her former owner. And she understood the price she and her son would need to pay if the appeal proved successful. "[H]e Says if you will come & do it fore him [save him from hanging] he will Stay with you the balance of his days. . . . Aunt Henney says if you ever did any thing fore her now is the time & says if you wan to own her you can do it by buying her & Milton both." Whatever the price, she suggested, "Save my childs Neck from the galos if you can."[121]

But there were limits to the tolerance afforded blacks accused of killing other blacks. Punishment was apt to be severe in the event of a particularly brutal black-on-black crime or if the black victim had a good reputation among whites. When a jury sentenced to death a black man in Sharkey County, Mississippi, it essentially adopted the thinking of the prosecutor: "This bad nigger killed a good nigger. The dead nigger was a white man's nigger, and these bad niggers like to kill that kind. The only way you can break up this pistol toting among niggers is to have a neck-tie party." The black attorney for the defendant, Willis E. Mollison, had no problem in understanding the verdict and sentence: "The average white jury would take it for granted that the killing of a white man's nigger is a more serious offense than the killing of a plain, every-day black man." On appeal, however, the Mississippi Supreme Court reversed the decision, ruling that the remarks of the prosecuting attorney had been improper and prejudicial to Mollison's client. "Those who are at all familiar with the favor, indeed, we may say affection, that the white man entertains for a 'white man's nigger,' can well and justly appreciate the effect that such an unwarrantable statement, made by an officer of the law, will have before the ordinary jury of the land."[122]

The murder of a black woman by a black man often qualified under "negro law" as less than a capital crime. Fearing that a jury might think otherwise, Henry Hammond, a white attorney in Thomson, Georgia, prepared to intervene. "I must give attention for I don't want the fool jury to hang the nigger." The details of this case were not revealed. Ordinarily, such crimes were greeted with a certain indifference in the white community, believing it characteristic of black behavior. But the courts might choose to deal severely with such cases, not out of solicitude for the black victim but if the murder revealed something in the character of the accused black man that posed potential dangers for white women. That was clearly the thinking of the state's attorney in a Mississippi trial in 1906 when he prosecuted David Sykes for murdering another black man, charging that the defendant had committed the crime because he coveted the victim's wife. "You ought to convict him," the prosecutor told the jury, "because he might rape some of the white women of the country." Sykes was sentenced to death.[123]

Much like mob lynchings, legal lynchings became public rituals in which a holiday atmosphere more often than not prevailed. Legal or extralegal, a hanging provided a welcome diversion. The public's curiosity over the rites of death had to be satisfied, the "crime" had to be avenged, and since many public hangings required two or three attempts, speculation over the level and duration of the victim's agony replaced the obsession with torture that characterized mob lynchings. Vendors selling ice cream and lemonade made their way through the large crowd in Oxford, Mississippi, that had come to witness the hanging of George Walton, a "one-legged darkey." Only on the third attempt did the hanging succeed, with Walton "kicking in the air and suffering untold agony." A public execution in Beaufort, South Carolina, attracted people from the countryside and the Sea Islands. "The hanging was done in the jail yard," a young white resident noted in his diary, "but the scaffold was built up so that it could be seen from the street. The rope broke the first time the criminal fell so they had to hang him a second time. The man showed a great deal of nerve and self possession. Not even losing his head when he went up the second time."[124]

Public executions, like lynchings, made lasting impressions on those who witnessed them. In Rockingham County, North Carolina, Tildy

Carter went to her death, along with the two men convicted of being accomplices in the murder of her husband. For this midday hanging, the entire countryside was invited. Because there had been talk of "an attempted rescue on the part of the negroes," the local militia also had to be called out. The three blacks were dressed in their white shrouds and placed on the coffins with the ropes around their necks. Nine-year-old John Morehead, a white youth, observed it all, and years later he could still distinctly recall "how the bodies turned round and round due to the twist in the ropes." As no one claimed the body of one of the men, a doctor purchased it for $10 and used it for dissection and teaching medicine. After the doctor's death, young Morehead recalled, a number of boys found what remained of the black man's body and took it out on the street until local authorities removed and buried it. "It then had very much the appearance and characteristics of a mummy." That night, young Morehead slipped into his aunt's room and slept on a sofa beside her bed.[125]

Seldom invoked to save blacks from a death sentence, the pardons issued by state governors sometimes identified and acknowledged gross injustices in the trial, sometimes singled out sentences that had been disproportionate to the crime committed, and often returned prisoners to white employers still eager to work them. In a petition for pardon, the nature of the offense, the petitioner's prison record, and how the petitioner couched his request were of critical importance, as in the appeal of Julius Foster of South Carolina in 1913, praying "that your Excellency will have mercy on a friendless darkey and do something for your servant." To obtain a pardon generally required that some prominent whites intercede and testify to the good character of the prisoner and that he or she posed no danger to the community. The petition signed by "the most reputable citizens" of Ridgeville, South Carolina, requesting a pardon for Arthur Graham, assured the governor that "the petitioner has at all times been an obedient and respectful darkey." Still another successful petition described the applicant as "a hardworking, peaceable, 'white folks' darkey."[126]

Pardons were more readily granted to black prisoners if their victims had been black. In what must have been a clear-cut case, the governor of Mississippi pardoned a black field hand—"a hard working, honest negro, but a white man's friend from rind to core"—who in a domestic dispute had killed a Negro college graduate "so highly educated as to be a full-fledged, good-for-nothing negro bully." A Mississippi planter, in requesting a pardon in 1911 for one of his valued black laborers, assured the governor that "[t]his darkey's reputation is far above the average, in fact he is a white man's negro." The pardon granted Will Dockins in South Carolina in 1913 appeared to be a reward for services he had rendered as a police informer; at least, the chief of police of Aiken, who requested the pardon, testified that Dockins had been "regularly employed by me to do detective work among negroes in this city and county."[127]

Sifting through the large stack of applications for pardons, Governor Cole Blease of South Carolina made his judgments quickly and frequently—a record seventeen hundred pardons during his tenure of office from 1910 to 1914. Some seemed easier than most, none more so than the applications involving blacks and race relations. Like any good politician, Blease had a sense of what the community was willing and unwilling to tolerate in black behavior, and the tolerance level increased perceptibly if the "crime" had not involved whites. A champion of mill workers and poor whites, he used the pardoning power to articulate his views on a range of topics. Whatever his reputation for racial demagoguery, Blease in his often candidly expressed judgments reflected attitudes that would have resonated with whites in much of the South, including the "better sort" who might have chosen to articulate them in a more sophisticated legalese. Blease saw no need to hide his views; he might be accused of crass bigotry, but never of pretense.[128]

Employing the unwritten "negro law," Governor Blease, as did many whites, dismissed certain crimes committed by blacks against other blacks at social gatherings as typical of black behavior. "This is a case of one negro killing another—the old familiar song—'Hot supper; liquor; dead negro.' "[129] In pardoning black or white males convicted of raping black females, Blease made perfectly clear on several occasions why he acted so generously. "I am of the opinion, as I have always been, and have very serious doubt as to whether the crime of rape can be committed upon a negro."[130] In still another pardon, he compared blacks to "the order of the lower animals," claiming that they possessed "absolutely no standard of morality" and that "adultery seems to be their most favorite pastime." In pardoning a white convicted of ravishing a black woman, he refused to believe the person would risk being convicted of rape for "what he could usually get from prices ranging from 25 cents to $1." In a routine case, Blease pardoned Sam Gaskins for the accidental killing of his fiancée; indeed, "if he had been a white man, he would not have been convicted." Having made that point, Blease characteristically used the occasion to add another observation: "It seems to have been a very sad accident; however, after a second thought, possibly it was for the good of humanity, for had they married, no doubt they would have brought forth more negroes to the future detriment of the State." Little wonder the *Chicago Defender*, a black newspaper, chose to preface its story on Blease's pardons with a brief editorial note: "Blease, the degenerate Blease, the Dixey Buffoon, is on another rampage."[131]

The vast majority of black men and women convicted in the courts of law found no refuge in pardons but had to endure the prison and convict lease system. The ordeal they experienced assumed a variety of forms, all of them indelibly impressed on their memories—as they were intended to be.

8

JOE TURNEY ACHIEVED a deserved notoriety in the late nineteenth century. For some years, he assumed the responsibility for escorting black prisoners from Memphis to the Tennessee State Penitentiary in Nashville. Often, however, this prison official made a practice of distributing some of the prisoners to convict farms along the Mississippi River, where employers paid commissions to obtain much-needed laborers. Most of the prisoners had been rounded up for minor infractions, often when police raided a craps game set up by an informer; after a perfunctory court appearance, the blacks were removed, usually the same day, and turned over to Turney. He was reputed to have handcuffed some eighty prisoners to forty links of chain. When a man turned up missing that night in the community, the word quickly spread, "They tell me Joe Turner's come and gone." Family members were left to mourn for the missing.

> He come wid forty links of chain,
>   Oh Lawdy!
> Come wid forty links of chain,
>   Oh Lawdy!
> Got my man and gone.[132]

What "Joe Turner Blues" and other songs described in the late nineteenth and early twentieth centuries was real enough. By the 1890s, the distribution of black prisoners, most of them arrested on minor charges, and their use (and abuse) as convict laborers had become a way of life in the New South—a source of immense profits for the states and employers, and a source of extraordinary suffering for black men who were all too often worked to death.

Peonage made fortunes for employers while keeping blacks in a state of bondage. The law did not sanction it, but whites who benefited from peonage managed to stand above the law. The convict lease system also enriched employers while keeping blacks in a state of bondage. But there was a difference. The law not only sanctioned it but also helped to maintain and expand it by supplying a seemingly endless number of convict laborers.[133]

Under slavery, few if any blacks had been remanded to the South's jails and prisons. If a crime required punishment, plantation justice would prevail, and the slaveowner or overseer would generally administer it. But emancipation altered that relationship, even as it more than doubled the free population and soon overwhelmed the South's penal institutions. With vigorous and selective enforcement of laws and discriminatory sentencing, the jails and prisons came to be filled with unprecedented numbers of blacks. Tens of thousands would be compelled to serve long terms at hard labor, more often than not for petty theft and misdemeanors—for example, up to five years in prison for stealing a farm animal or any property valued at $10 or more. Some labored on chain gangs, still more were leased out as convicts to work: They labored in the coal and iron mines, in the sawmills and turpentine camps; they laid railroad track; they built levees; they grew cotton; and they cleared treacherous, malaria-infested swamplands that few free workers would have tolerated.

The convict lease system emerged as early as Reconstruction, matured in the 1870s and 1880s, and soon became in many states the dominant policy of the penal system. Under convict leasing, private contractors—mostly cotton planters, railroad builders, mine and sawmill operators, and merchants—purchased months or years of the lives of prisoners (almost exclusively black), paying a commission to the state and assuming responsibility for feeding, clothing, and sheltering the convicts during the terms of their sentence. The arrangement conveniently met the needs of employers and the government. State and local officials found a much-welcomed, even profitable alternative to building and maintaining new prisons to house the rapidly growing number of convicts.

But, best of all, employers found a steady source of cheap labor that could be worked anywhere at the most demanding pace. "Why? Because he is a *convict*," a railroad official explained, "and if he dies it is a small loss, and we can make him work there, while we cannot get free men to do the same kind of labor for, say, six times as much as the convict costs." The efficiency of the system was perhaps most vividly dramatized in the ways it copied from industry the dictum that no by-products be wasted. State officials in Tennessee collected the urine of convicts and sold it to local tanneries by the barrel. Students enrolled in a medical school in Nashville practiced on the unclaimed dead bodies of convicts.[134]

What convict labor demanded of blacks physically and emotionally not only resembled slavery but in many instances exceeded its worst abuses and routines. "We go from can't to can't," a Florida convict turpentine worker declared. "Can't see in the morning to can't see at night." Awakened before dawn, the convicts were marched rapidly to the fields in chains, where they worked until dinner (for which they received some forty minutes) and then continued to work until after sundown or "as long as it was light enough for a guard to see how to shoot." The fourteen or more hours they worked each day, the pace demanded of them, the savage beatings meted out to slackers, the dangerous conditions they often confronted, along with the quality of their food, shelter, and medical care, made survival a triumph in itself. "This place is nine kinds of hell," one convict testified. "Am suffering death every day here."[135]

Clearing swampland south of Hattiesburg, Mississippi, for the New Orleans and Northeastern Railroad, convicts were chained in knee-deep pools of muck. The men's thirst drove them "to drink the water in which they were compelled to deposit their excrement." No wonder doctors and health officials were sometimes as occupied with signing death certificates as with treating prisoners, most of the victims suffering from exhaustion, malaria, frostbite, pneumonia, consumption, sunstroke, edema (dropsy), chronic diarrhea, dysentery, scurvy, gunshot wounds, "wounds miscellaneous," and "shackle poisoning" (caused by the chains and leg irons biting into the bare flesh). In many instances, the cause of death was listed as "not stated." The convicts who tried to escape were whipped "till the blood ran down their legs," and some had a metal spur riveted to their feet.[136]

All too often, as the grim mortality rates revealed, employers worked their purchased workers to death. In 1870, a total of 41 percent of Alabama's convicts did not survive; in Tennessee, in 1884, some 148 of every 1,000 prisoners died; in Mississippi in the 1880s, the death rate among convict laborers ranged from 9 to 16 percent annually. Rarely did any of the convict laborers live long enough to serve a sentence of ten years or more. Most investigators agreed that the mortality figures would have been far higher if they had included the broken-down men who obtained pardons and went home to die. For those who found themselves in prison hospitals, the unspeakable horrors of hospitalization suggested a living death. In a surprise visit to the prison hospital in Jackson, Mississippi, the Hinds County grand jury found evidence "of the most brutal and inhuman treatment":

> Most of them have their backs cut in great wales, scars, and blisters, some with the skin peeling off in places as the result of severe beatings. . . . All of them [have] the stamp of manhood blotted out of their faces. . . . They are lying there dying, some of them on bare boards . . . with live vermin crawling over their [bodies].

In Tennessee, where the convict lease system was regarded as relatively benign, conditions in the prison hospital in Nashville were described by one investigator as "too revolting for popular reading."[137]

Unlike slaveowners, employers ran no risk of losing a valuable investment if a convict was worked to death; they had only to replenish the supply with fresh bodies. "Before the war we owned the negroes," an employer explained in 1883. "If a man had a good nigger he could afford to take care of him; if he was sick get a doctor. He might even put gold plugs in his teeth. But these convicts; we don't own 'em. One dies, get another." When the prisons could not fill the demand for laborers, the police simply conducted one of their periodic sweeps, arresting blacks on a variety of trivial offenses—what a black newspaper termed in 1904 "offenses for which the term misdemeanor would be harsh."[138] Most whites seemed indifferent to the fate of convict laborers, at least until the early twentieth century, when the human and economic consequences of convict leasing were widely publicized by government investigations, the press, and organized labor, and became such an embarrassment to the region that reformers began to win public support to abolish the system or reduce its harshness.

Since young black males made up a large proportion of convictions for theft, gambling, assault, disorderly conduct, and vagrancy, they also comprised the bulk of the convict labor supply. From two-thirds to more than three-fourths of the convicts were in their twenties or younger. In 1893, a Savannah newspaper enumerated the juveniles in the penitentiary population. "There are 80 who are below the age of 15, 40 below the age of 14, 27 below the age of 13, 15 below the age of 12, 2 below the age of 11, and one who is only 10 years old." Investigators in Tennessee found the branch prisons "hell holes of rage, cruelty, despair, and vice," containing prisoners of all ages; homosexual assaults on young boys were common and "Gal boys" in considerable demand.[139] In convict labor, the elderly worked alongside the young. Lancaster LeConte, an elderly former slave, asked his former owner, Joseph LeConte, to intervene on his behalf.

> I am hear in prison for the turm of three years for rescving som stolen goods and my helth is so bad that I donnt think I will live to suav them out, so I thought I had done anougf for you in slavery time to ask you to please asist me now in my trubles I hav allways tryd hard to do what I thought was just and rite you no I allwys tryd to do what you asked of me and now I ask you to please send me 65 Dollars to imploy me a lawyer to get me out of hear for I am in hear for nothing . . . I remaine as ever your faith full survnt

The assistance failed to materialize, and Lancaster LeConte lasted fewer than two years in prison, dying in 1889 at age seventy-five.[140]

Prison officials and defenders of the system refuted reports of brutality, but not very persuasively. The same Alabama report that gave glowing accounts of the "good order" of the convict camps included statistical tables that showed that up to 40 percent of the prisoners were dying. Explaining the high mortality rates in the camps, a southern physician told a national convention that one "fact beyond dispute" had to be kept in mind at all times: "as a race, the negro is physically and mentally inferior." The frequency with which black convicts died in the mines demonstrated conclusively to one white woman what she had always assumed: that "the blood of educated people can resist a great deal more than the blood of the uneducated classes."[141]

Convicts who could no longer tolerate their situation resisted as best they could, usually with disastrous results. But they did manage to claim the lives of a number of prison guards before forfeiting their own. Many convicts attempted escape, and some succeeded. Most made the necessary accommodation to convict life. Seeking to establish a sense of community among themselves, they employed a variety of ways to articulate their resentments and to ease the pain of their confinement. The religion many of them embraced in prison provided some escape and solace, even as it often justified and encouraged acts of resistance.

For more than half a century, convict leasing took its toll, breaking men in every conceivable way—and in ways beyond anyone's imagination. Even when the system came under heavy criticism and declined, new or revived methods of punishment proved hardly more humane. Rather than dispatch convicts to plantation farms, they would now be used on county chain gangs for road construction and maintenance. The objective did not change. Both convict lease and the chain gang stood as constant reminders to blacks of their vulnerability and subordination. But even as such punishments impressed blacks with the power exercised by whites, it did nothing to increase respect for the law and law-enforcement officials; on the contrary, the lawlessness of the law was never more vividly revealed.

If convict labor was "nine kinds of hell," confinement in the penitentiary or work on the chain gang easily qualified for the same distinction. Conditions in the penitentiaries were often no better than in the work camps, sometimes even worse, and at both places prison guards meted out their own brands of torture, violence, and humiliation. For the survivors, there was often little life left in them. Jerry Shannan, a veteran of the chain gang in Georgia, was suffering from consumption, a common ailment among prisoners. After treating his condition for several months, authorities chose to send him home, as he was costing the county too much for medical care.

> They got a man to take me up in the buggy and car to my home whether I wanted to go or not. They have not furnished me a doctor or nothing to eat. . . . They worked me in so much water, up above my knees . . . till I am filled with cold and I think they ought to furnish me a doctor so that I can get well.

Rather than provide Shannan with any medical attention, authorities informed him that if he should recover, they expected him to return and finish out his sentence.[142]

Women made up some 7 percent of the black prisoners, most of them incarcerated on minor charges of prostitution and petty theft, some for murders stemming from domestic violence. The conditions they encountered were identical to those of the male prisoners, except that the women were more often the victims of rape and sexual misconduct. At the Huntsville penitentiary in Texas, for example, which housed women prisoners, local citizens complained of the noise emanating from the prison and the nearby labor camps, mostly the screams and groans of the inmates. The prison doctor, a white convict, boasted of his sexual relations with a black female prisoner. After this prisoner gave birth, officials separated her from the child, shaved her head, and placed her in an isolation cell.[143]

For attempting to communicate with state officials about conditions in South Carolina's state penitentiary, Simeon Ellis was subjected to beatings and the application of "a strong electric battery" to his body. "His screams and cries and piteous appeals for mercy could be heard all over the Penitentiary grounds." Perhaps that is what Governor Blease had in mind in 1913 when he commuted the death sentence of a black convicted of murder to life imprisonment at hard labor. "I am not sure but that the present conditions of the Penitentiary would be more punishment than electrocution."[144]

If black men and women did not die in prison, they returned to their homes with battered bodies and minds and vivid memories. The chaplain in South Carolina's penitentiary, who thought it "a great reformatory school," took considerable pride in his accomplishments. "There are now about one hundred men and women who can repeat the Ten Commandments, the Lord's Prayer, the Apostles' Creed, and the whole of Capers' Catechism." But the effects of such instruction, if one listened to the testimony of a guard at the Georgia penitentiary, should have troubled rather than comforted whites, both inside and outside the prison walls. This guard had learned to fear the effects of religion and preaching on black prisoners. "I always double the guard when they begin to pray."[145]

9

IN RICHLAND COUNTY, South Carolina, in the 1920s, a black storyteller reflected about the law and the courts and how they operated half a century after the abolition of slavery. "Dere ain' no use. De courts er dis land is not for niggers. . . . It seems to me when it come to trouble, de law an' a nigger is de white man's sport, an' justice is a stranger in them precincts, an' mercy is unknown." The Bible, he noted, asked people to pray for their enemy, and so he offered up this prayer: "Drap on you' knee, brothers, an' pray to God for all de crackers an' de judges an' de courts an' solicitors, sheriffs an' police in de land. . . ."[146]

As the storyteller suggested, the perversion of justice had become a lasting legacy of the New South. The mechanisms of legal violence— that is, violence sanctioned by the day-to-day workings of the legal system—functioned after Reconstruction as a formidable instrument of social control. In the name of law and justice, whites (including those sworn to uphold and enforce the law) made a mockery of law and justice. The legal system was only one mechanism in the arsenal of white power, but it proved to be a critical and formidable one. Unequal justice interacted with disfranchisement, segregation, economic exploitation, inferior schooling, and violence to remind blacks of all ages and classes of where power rested in this society. By 1907, a newspaper in Yazoo, Mississippi, could observe with satisfaction how the South had become to all intents and purposes a closed society. "With every official in Mississippi a white man, and every jury composed of whites; every judge upon the bench white, and all elections conducted by and only participated in by whites, there can be no possible danger of negro rule."[147]

In communities across the South, blacks came to perceive the law and its enforcers as an outside and alien force, an intrusive and repressive agency against which appeals for fairness and impartiality, humane and just treatment, were all but useless. Even as the United States in the wake of World War I promoted the cause of international justice, blacks demanded some semblance of domestic justice. In the black press and at black meetings, the abuse of the law and the double standard of justice applied to the two races took increasing precedence over other issues. The remark made in a Georgia court that not half of the blacks sentenced would be convicted if properly represented resonated with blacks throughout the South. Addressing a biracial audience in Oklahoma City, a black editor confided to them how black people thought about the legal system:

> I think you ought to know how the black man talks and feels at times when he knows that you are nowhere about, and I want to tell you, if you were to creep up to-night to a place where there are 10,000 Negroes gathered, you would find no division on this one point. I know that they all would say, "WE HAVE NO CONFIDENCE IN WHITE POLICEMEN."

Let there be one hundred or one hundred thousand, they would with one accord all say, "WE HAVE NO CONFIDENCE IN THE WHITE MAN'S COURT." I think you ought to know this, for it is with what men think that we have to deal. They would say in such a meeting that they know before they get into the court what the verdict will be. If their cause is the cause of a black man against a white man they will say that they know that a verdict would be rendered in favor of the white man.[148]

This view of southern justice rested on an abundance of evidence, on tens of thousands of cases tried and not tried. The differences between the courtroom and the lynch mob were not always clear in the New South. Nor in the eyes of black men and women were there discernible differences between a speedy trial and mob justice, between lawless lynchers and lawless judges, sheriffs, constables, policemen, wardens, and prison guards. "The fact is," a black educator noted in 1915, "that lynching has gone on so long in many parts of our country that it is somewhat difficult to draw at this time a sharp line marking off distinctly the point where the lynching spirit stops and the spirit of legal procedure commences. You cannot tell what the most peaceable community will do at any moment under certain conditions."[149]

The most repressive period in the history of race relations in the South also became the most violent. The race chauvinism, the often rabid Negrophobia, the intense feelings and emotions stirred up by the campaigns to disfranchise and segregate blacks expressed themselves simultaneously in an era of unprecedented racial violence. Rather than allay white fears, the campaigns to repress blacks heightened those fears. Rather than provide safe alternatives, the campaigns exacerbated race relations. Once dehumanized, black life was cheapened and made even more expendable. The effort to solidify the subordination of black men and women knew no limits.

> *They got the judges*
> *They got the lawyers*
> *They got the jury-rolls*
> *They got the law*
> *   They don't come by ones*
> *They got the sheriffs*
> *They got the deputies*
> *   They don't come by twos*

They got the shotguns
They got the rope
We git the justice
In the end
   And they come by tens.[150]

CHAPTER SIX

HELLHOUNDS

The scriptures have said, "The things that have been done in the dark will be known on the house tops."

—*Fanny Lou Hamer*[1]

SAM HOSE ASPIRED to be something more than a black laborer in rural Georgia. He learned to read and write, and he impressed people as a bright and able person. Needing to support a nearly invalid mother and a mentally retarded brother, he would have little time to pursue a formal education. He set out for Atlanta in 1898, but settled for a job in nearby Coweta County, where he worked for a planter, Alfred Cranford. Early in April 1899, he asked his employer for an advance in pay (some reported he had tried to collect wages already owed him) and for permission to visit his ill mother. The planter refused, precipitating a harsh exchange of words. On the following day, while Hose chopped wood, Cranford resumed the argument, this time drawing his pistol and threatening to kill Hose. In self-defense, Hose flung the ax, striking Cranford in the head and killing him instantly. A frightened Hose fled to his mother's cabin.

Within two days, newspapers reported an altogether different version. Cranford had been eating dinner when Hose—"a monster in human form"—sneaked up on him and buried the ax in his skull, at the same time kicking him repeatedly in the head. After pillaging the house, he dragged Mrs. Cranford into the room where her husband lay dying. "Within arm's reach of where the brains were oozing out of her husband's head," Hose was said to have raped Mrs. Cranford repeatedly. The newspapers also dutifully reported that Hose suffered from syphilis, for which his employer was having him treated. Before leaving the house, Hose is alleged to have said, "Now I am through with my work, let them kill me if they can."

If versions of Cranford's death varied, the story of Sam Hose's fate did not. Some two thousand men and women witnessed it on Sunday afternoon, April 23, 1899, near Newman, Georgia, some of them arriving from Atlanta on a special excursion train. After stripping Hose of his clothes and chaining him to a tree, the self-appointed executioners stacked kerosene-soaked wood high around him. Before saturating Hose with oil and applying the torch, they cut off his ears, fingers, and genitals, and skinned his face. While some in the crowd plunged knives into the victim's flesh, others watched "with unfeigning satisfaction" (as one reporter noted) the contortions of Sam Hose's body as the flames rose, distorting his features, causing his eyes to bulge out of their sockets, and rupturing his veins. When in Hose's agony he almost managed to unloosen his bonds, the executioners quenched the flames, retied him, and applied more oil to the body before relighting the fire. "Such suffering," reported one newspaper, "has seldom been witnessed." The only sounds that came from the victim's lips, even as his blood sizzled in the fire, were "Oh, my God! Oh, Jesus." Before Hose's body had even cooled, his heart and liver were removed and cut into several pieces and his bones were crushed into small particles. The crowd fought over these souvenirs, and the "more fortunate possessors" made some handsome profits on the sales. (Small pieces of bones went for 25 cents, a piece of the liver "crisply cooked" sold for 10 cents.) Shortly after the lynching, one of the participants reportedly left for the state capitol, hoping to deliver to the governor of Georgia a slice of Sam Hose's heart.[2]

No member of this crowd wore a mask, nor did anyone attempt to conceal the names of the perpetrators. Reporters noted the active participation of some of the region's most prominent citizens in the execution. The next morning, some smoldering ashes and a blackened stake were all that remained. Cranford's wife had been too ill to attend or to identify Hose as the rapist but, as the press reported, her mother provided a positive identification, although she had not witnessed the crime. That more than satisfied the crowd. On the trunk of a tree near the scene, a placard read: "We Must Protect Our Southern Women."

Some southern women rejected such protection. Priding herself on being a native Georgian and a Daughter of the Confederacy, Mrs. P. H. Mell, in a letter to the *Atlanta Constitution*, told of her horror and shame over the savage lynching of Sam Hose and the need for southern women to protest the "unparalleled brutality" committed in their name. Few, however, rallied to her cause, and some expressed shock and bewilderment at her apostasy and ingratitude. "My God how she has degenerated," one Georgian wrote Rebecca Felton, enclosing a clipping of Mrs. Mell's protest. Still another Georgian, in relating the crimes committed by Hose, embroidered even the distorted facts, claiming that the "creature" raped Mrs. Cranford, then "*stripped* her person of every thread and vestige of clothing," and then raped her "twice more and again!" He seemed appalled by the way in which the "outside world" had questioned the lynching. Had Hose possessed ten thousand lives, he wrote, every one of them should have been erased by "the most savage modes" available. The woman to whom he addressed his letter, Rebecca Felton, shared his outrage and made the obligatory observation: "The premeditated outrage on Mrs. Cranford was infinitely more intolerable than the murder of her husband." As for Hose, Felton claimed any "true-hearted husband or father" would have happily dispatched the "beast," with no more concern than if he were shooting down a mad dog; indeed, "[t]he dog is more worthy of sympathy."[3]

The leading newspaper in Atlanta asked only that the crowd be judged by the facts of the case. "The people of Georgia are orderly and conservative, the descendants of ancestors who have been trained in America for 150 years. They are a people intensely religious, homeloving and just. There is among them no foreign or lawless element." The newspaper then provided the details of Hose's alleged offenses—the murder of "an unassuming, industrious and hard working farmer" and the rape of his wife, "swimming in her husband's warm blood" while "the black beast" performed his deed. "Keep the facts in mind," the newspaper urged its readers. "When the picture is printed of the ravisher in flames, go back and view that darker picture of Mrs. Cranford outraged in the blood of her murdered husband."

In visiting their retribution on Sam Hose, whites in this region around Palmetto were acting out their frustration and anger over a series of incendiary and costly fires the previous month. Holding "outlawed negroes" responsible for these acts, authorities had arrested nine men on arson charges (described by a black newspaper as "intelligent, hard working men"). The night of the arrests a masked mob rode into town, lined up the nine suspects, tied them together with ropes, and shot them, killing four (perhaps five). The murder of Cranford a month later fed the same passions and hysteria, and Hose was not the only victim. A reign of terror ensued, in which whites burned down a black church (said to be a "rendezvous for lawless negroes"), forced hundreds of blacks to leave the area, and tortured and lynched a popular black preacher, Lige Strickland, said to have been complicitous in Cranford's murder. The mob also lynched Albert Sewell for allegedly threatening vengeance for the murdered blacks; the *Richmond Planet* thought he had been lynched because he "talked too much."[4]

The governor of Georgia, Allen D. Candler, called Sam Hose's deeds "the most diabolical in the annals of crime," and he immediately made the connection between Hose and the "Palmetto incendiaries," placing principal blame on the "younger generation" of blacks who had never known slavery and on older blacks who misled them. He denounced the entire black community for not having assisted in the apprehension of Hose. "The negroes of that community lost the best opportunity they will ever have to elevate themselves in the estimation of their neighbors." He found it "deplorable" that while "scores of intelligent negroes, leaders of their race" had protested the lynching of Hose, none of them had alluded to "the diabolical crime" that had provoked the lynchers. "I do not believe these men sympathized with Holt [Hose] or the Palmetto incendiaries, but they are blinded by race prejudice, and can see but one side of the question."[5]

In a subsequent investigation, conducted by a white detective, Cranford's wife revealed that Hose had come to the house to pick up his wages and the two men had quarreled. When her husband went for his revolver, Hose in self-defense had picked up and hurled the ax, which killed Cranford instantly. Hose then fled the scene. He never entered the house, she told the detective, nor did he assault her. Still another investigation, conducted by Ida B. Wells, reached the same conclusions. The results of the investigation were of no apparent interest to the white press or presumably to the white public.[6]

Sam Hose . . . Lige Strickland . . . Mary Turner . . . Luther Holbert and his wife . . . Lee Walker . . . Henry Sykes . . . Fred and Jane Sullivan . . . Daniel Barber and his family. All met their deaths in much the same way, as did nearly three thousand black Southerners between 1890 and World War I, with only slight variations in the rituals performed and in the hymns that were sung.

2

A UNITARIAN MINISTER in New York, John H. Holmes, opened his mail one day to find a postcard depicting a crowd in Alabama posing for a photographer next to the body of a black man dangling by a rope—a not uncommon way to memorialize a lynching. Responding to the minister's recent condemnation of lynching, the person who sent the card wrote, "This is the way we do them down here. The last lynching has not been put on card yet. Will put you on our regular mailing list. Expect one a month on the average."[7]

Between 1890 and 1917, to enforce deference and submission to whites, some two to three black Southerners were hanged, burned at the stake, or quietly murdered every week. That estimate is conservative. In the 1890s, lynchings claimed some 139 lives each year, 75 percent of them black; the numbers declined in the next decade, but the percentage of black victims rose to 90 percent. As many if not more blacks were victims of legal lynchings (quick trials and executions) and private white violence and "nigger hunts," murdered by a variety of means in isolated rural sections and dumped into rivers or creeks. The victims tended to be sons or daughters of former slaves, those said by whites to have been born into the false teachings of Reconstruction, who had not yet learned the rituals of deference and submission.

Even an accurate body count of black lynching victims could not possibly reveal how hate and fear transformed ordinary white men and women into mindless murderers and sadistic torturers, or the savagery that, with increasing regularity, characterized assaults on black men and women in the name of restraining their savagery and depravity. Nothing so dramatically or forcefully underscored the cheapness of black life in the South. The way one black Mississippian recalled white violence in the 1930s applied as accurately, and even more pervasively, to the late nineteenth and early twentieth centuries. "Back in those days, to kill a Negro wasn't nothing. It was like killing a chicken or killing a snake. The whites would say, 'Niggers jest supposed to die, ain't no damn good anyway—so jest go on an' kill 'em.'" Whatever their value as laborers, black people were clearly expendable and replaceable. "In those days it was 'Kill a mule, buy another. Kill a nigger, hire another,'" a black Southerner remembered. "They had to have a license to kill anything but a nigger. We was always in season."[8]

The cheapness of black life reflected in turn the degree to which so many whites by the early twentieth century had come to think of black men and women as inherently and permanently inferior, as less than human, as little more than animals. "[W]e Southern people dont care to equal ourselves with animals," a white Floridian told a northern critic. "The people of the South dont think any more of killing the black fellows than you would think of killing a flea . . . and if I was to live 1,000 years that would be my opinion and every other Southern man." A former governor of Georgia, William J. Northen, after canvassing his state in the interest of law and order, found the same disregard for black life. "I was amazed to find scores and hundreds of men who believed the Negro to be a brute, without responsibility to God, and his slaughter nothing more than the killing of a dog."9

Lynching was hardly a new phenomenon. For many decades it had served as a means of extralegal justice in the West, and most of the victims had been white. But in the 1890s, lynching and sadistic torture rapidly became exclusive public rituals of the South, with black men and women as the principal victims. During slavery, blacks had been exposed to violence on the plantations and farms where they worked and from the patrollers if they ventured off those plantations. The financial investment each slave represented had operated to some degree as a protective shield for blacks accused of crimes, but in the event of an insurrection—real or imagined—whites had used murder, decapitation, burning, and lynching to punish suspected rebels and impress on all blacks the dangers of resistance.

The quality of the violence meted out to blacks after emancipation and during Reconstruction, including mob executions designed to emphasize the limits of black freedom, anticipated to a considerable degree the wave of murder and terrorism that would sweep across the South two decades later and become by the turn of the century one of its unmistakable trademarks. "There was another colored man linched," a South Carolinian noted in his diary on September 28, 1893, "they say for having murdered a white man. I tell of these linchings so that if this diary ever comes to light in after years one may see the brutal and unsettled state of the south. One notices that a white man is never linched no matter how cruel he is, and that those who take part in the linchings are never arrested."10

What was strikingly new and different in the late nineteenth and early twentieth centuries was the sadism and exhibitionism that characterized white violence. The ordinary modes of execution and punishment were deemed insufficient; they no longer satisfied the emotional appetite of the crowd. To kill the victim was not enough; the execution needed to be turned into a public ritual, a collective experience, and the victim needed to be subjected to extraordinary torture and mutilation. What had been in the past a usually rapid dispatch of the victim now became part of a voyeuristic spectacle prolonged as long as possible (once for seven hours) for the benefit of the crowd. Nor were whites content after the victim had died; in some instances, they continued to pump bullets into the body, after which they carved it up with knives or burned it to a crisp, or they might permit the body to dangle by the rope for the next several days as a warning to the black community.

The story of a lynching, then, is more than the simple fact of a black man or woman hanged by the neck. It is the story of slow, methodical, sadistic, often highly inventive forms of torture and mutilation. If executed by fire, it is the red-hot poker applied to the eyes and genitals and the stench of burning flesh as the body slowly roasts over the flames and the blood sizzles in the heat. If executed by hanging, it is the convulsive movement of the limbs. Whether by fire or rope, it is the dismemberment and distribution of severed bodily parts as favors and souvenirs to participants and the crowd: teeth, ears, toes, fingers, nails, kneecaps, bits of charred skin and bones. Such human trophies might reappear as watch fobs or be displayed conspicuously for public viewing. The severed knuckles of Sam Hose, for example, would be prominently displayed in the window of a grocery store in Atlanta. A woman in the Mississippi Delta helping to treat an injured lumberjack was shocked when the "strong odor" from his pocket turned out to be a black man's finger. He had participated in a recent lynching and had cut off the finger as a souvenir. "Women and children have got to be protected," he explained. "We treat niggers all right down here as long as they stay in their place, but when they commit the crime that one did, they have to be sent out of the world the quickest way."[11]

Newspaper reporters dutifully reported lynchings and burnings under such lurid headlines as "Colored Man Roasted Alive," describing in graphic detail the agony and death of the victim and devising a vocabulary that would befit the occasion. The public burning of a Negro would soon be known as a "Negro Barbecue," reinforcing the perception of blacks as less than human. Photographers were often on hand to capture the execution, the carnival-like atmosphere, and the expectant mood of the crowd, as in the lynching of Thomas Brooks in Fayette County, Tennessee, in 1915:

> Hundreds of kodaks clicked all morning at the scene of the lynching. People in automobiles and carriages came from miles around to view the corpse dangling from the end of a rope. . . . Picture card photographers installed a portable printing plant at the bridge and reaped a harvest in selling postcards showing a photograph of the lynched Negro. Women and children were there by the score. At a number of

country schools the day's routine was delayed until boy and girl pupils could get back from viewing the lynched man.[12]

During a lynching at Durant, Oklahoma, in 1911, the exuberant and proud lynchers bound their victim to some planks and posed around him while photographers recorded the scene. A black newspaper in Topeka, Kansas, in printing the photograph, wanted every black newspaper to do likewise so that "the world may see and know what semi-barbarous America is doing."[13] Many photographs of lynchings and burnings (such as the burning of Sam Hose) would reappear as popular picture postcards and trade cards to commemorate the event. In Sabine County, Texas, Harkrider Drug Company published a postcard depicting the lynching of five blacks on June 15, 1908. Under the graphic photograph of the blacks dangling from a tree appeared a poetic caption and warning:

THE DOGWOOD TREE

This is only the branch of a Dogwood tree;
An emblem of WHITE SUPREMACY.
A lesson once taught in the Pioneer's school,
That this is a land of WHITE MAN'S RULE.
The Red Man once in an early day,
Was told by the Whites to mend his way.

The negro, now, by eternal grace,
Must learn to stay in the negro's place.
In the Sunny South, the Land of the Free,
Let the WHITE SUPREME forever be.
Let this a warning to all negroes be,
Or they'll suffer the fate of the DOGWOOD TREE.[14]

The mob "execution" of a black man, woman, or family was not only a public spectacle but also public theater, often a festive affair, a participatory ritual of torture and death that many whites preferred to witness rather than read about. Newspapers on a number of occasions announced in advance the time and place of a lynching with such colorful headlines as "Negro Jerky and Sullen as Burning Hour Nears." Special "excursion" trains transported spectators to the scene, employers sometimes released their workers to attend, parents sent notes to school asking teachers to excuse their children for the event, and entire families attended, the children hoisted on their parents' shoulders to miss none of the action and accompanying festivities. Little separated mob lynchings from public executions, neither the rapidity of the "justice" rendered nor the festive mood that often prevailed. "Some ladies were present," a local newspaper said of one such execution attended by three thousand people from all parts of Rankin County, Mississippi, in 1909. "A few were nursing infants who tugged at the mother's breasts, while the mother kept her eyes on the gallows. She didn't want to lose any part of the program she had come miles to see, and to tell to the neighbors at home."[15]

The execution spectacles witnessed by whites would be stamped on the character of the community in a variety of ways. An Alabama black woman working for a white family described the way in which lynching had entered the popular consciousness, affecting young and old alike: "I have seen very small white children hang their black dolls. It is not the child's fault, he is simply an apt pupil." Returning from a lynching, a nine-year-old white youth remained unsatisfied. "I have seen a man hanged," he told his mother; "now I wish I could see one burned." Under the headline "Play of Lynching" and the subheadline "The Leaven Works Among Our Children," a Raleigh newspaper carried the story of Jack McClay, an eleven-year-old white youth who suggested to his companions, all of them white, that they play "lynching" (a game more commonly dubbed "Salisbury"). Securing a piece of rope, he looped it around the neck of one of his playmates, tied the loose end to a nail driven into a wall, and left him hanging with only his toes touching the floor. The injuries he sustained in this mock lynching were slight, but the boy's parents took the matter to court. The judge found Jack McClay guilty and fined him. The defendant's mother "was excited and showed some feeling" when she refused to chastise her son.[16]

The brutalities meted out in these years often exceeded the most vivid of imaginations. After learning of the lynching of her husband, Mary Turner—in her eighth month of pregnancy—vowed to find those responsible, swear out warrants against them, and have them punished in the courts. For making such a threat, a mob of several hundred men and women determined to "teach her a lesson." After tying her ankles together, they hung her from a tree, head downward. Dousing her clothes with gasoline, they burned them from her body. While she was still alive, someone used a knife ordinarily reserved for splitting hogs to cut open the woman's abdomen. The infant fell prematurely from her womb to the ground and cried briefly, whereupon a member of this Valdosta, Georgia, mob crushed the baby's head beneath his heel. Hundreds of bullets were then fired into Mary Turner's body, completing the work of the mob. The Associated Press, in its notice of the affair, observed that Mary Turner had made "unwise remarks" about the execution of her husband, "and the people, in their indignant mood, took exceptions to her remarks, as well as her attitude." In the aftermath of the mob's action, a black Georgian could only ask, "Where are the grand juries? Where are the petit juries? Where are the sheriffs? Where is public opinion?" But he no doubt knew the answers, as did the Toussaint L'Overture Branch of the Red Cross, a black women's organization in Savannah, when it met to record how black women in Georgia were "discouraged and crushed by a spirit of humiliation and dread."[17]

Apprehended for allegedly killing his white employer, Luther Holbert and his wife found themselves subjected to mob justice in Doddsville, Mississippi, in 1904. Some one thousand people stood and watched as the self-appointed executioners went about their business, engaging in the increasingly familiar ritual of torture, mutilation, and murder. A reporter for the *Vicksburg Evening Post* described the execution of the Holberts:

> When the two Negroes were captured, they were tied to trees and while the funeral pyres were being prepared they were forced to suffer the most fiendish tortures. The blacks were forced to hold out their hands while one finger at a time was chopped off. The fingers were distributed as souvenirs. The ears of the murderers were cut off. Holbert was beaten severely, his skull was fractured and one of his eyes, knocked out with a stick, hung by a shred from the socket. . . . The most excruciating form of punishment consisted in the use of a large corkscrew in the hands of some of the mob. This instrument was bored into the flesh of the man and woman, in the arms, legs and body, and then pulled out, the spirals tearing out big pieces of raw, quivering flesh every time it was withdrawn.

Holbert and his employer had quarreled before the murder, but there was no evidence to implicate Holbert's wife. Two blacks, mistaken for Luther Holbert, had already been slain by a posse.[18]

When a mob meted out lynch justice in Fort White, Florida, in 1893, they did so with a ferocity that was becoming all too typical. Trains brought in additional participants and spectators from surrounding cities. After a mock trial, the prolonged execution began. "Every one knew what the crowd meant," a resident noted afterward, "but no one expected such horrible butchery." They sawed at the victim's throat, cut off both his ears, cut out one eye, and stuffed handkerchiefs in his mouth to stifle his "awful screams." Stabbing him repeatedly, the lynchers came close to cutting out his backbone. He was then dragged two blocks before the crowd emptied their guns into his body. One year earlier, near Memphis, the same violence had been inflicted on Lee Walker, removed from the county jail and hanged from a telegraph pole after his skin had been cut to ribbons by the mob. As Walker swung on the pole, blood streaming down his body from the knife wounds, the crowd hurled expletives at him. "The Negro died hard," one observer wrote. "The neck was not broken . . . and death came by strangulation. For fully ten minutes after he was strung up the chest heaved occasionally and there were convulsive movements of the limbs." But the crowd had not finished. Throwing the body into a fire, they watched with "astonishing coolness and nonchalance" as it burned. Finally, the relic hunters moved in to retrieve portions of the rope and what was left of the charred body.[19]

Once having settled on lynch justice, mobs were not overly scrupulous about determining the guilt of the black victim. The idea, after all, as one black observer noted, was to make an example, "knowing full well that one Negro swinging from a tree will serve as well as another to terrorize the community." After a barn burning near Columbus, Mississippi, suspicion fell on the son of Cordelia Stevenson. Not being able to locate him, a mob of whites settled on his mother, seized and tortured her, and left her naked body hanging to the limb of a tree for public viewing. A jury rendered the usual judgment in such cases, deciding she had come to her death at the hands of persons unknown.[20]

Neither women nor entire families escaped the savagery of white mobs. Bessie McCroy, along with her son and daughter, were removed from a jail in Carroll County, Mississippi, and taken to the edge of town, where a crowd of five hundred men hanged them and riddled their bodies with bullets. Members of a mob in Okemah, Oklahoma, entered the local jail to seize Laura Nelson, accused of murdering a sheriff; they then raped the black woman before hanging her along with her teenage son. When a white farmer in Gray, Georgia, was found dead in his home, suspicion fell on Will Green and his seventeen-year-old son. Despite their pleas of innocence, a mob lynched both of them and riddled their bodies with bullets; authorities subsequently determined that neither the father nor the son had anything to do with the farmer's death. Near Albany, Georgia, Felix Lake and his three sons were arrested after the murder of a local sheriff; they were not charged with the crime, but it was thought they might know the identity of the murderer. A mob of fifty men seized the family, hung them to a tree, and riddled their bodies with bullets. Someone thought to commemorate the scene on a postcard.[21]

The way whites in Monticello, Georgia, dealt with a black family in 1915 was no doubt meant as a warning to all blacks who dared to challenge white authority. When the local police chief came to the home of Daniel Barber to arrest him on a bootlegging charge, Barber and his family forcibly resisted the officer. After police subdued and arrested the Barbers, some two hundred enraged whites stormed the jail and dragged Barber, his son, and his two married daughters to a tree in the very center of the black district. The mob chose to hang the entire family, one by one. Daniel Barber had to watch each of his children die before the noose was tightened around his neck.[22]

When permitted to speak before being lynched, some of the victims professed their guilt and asked for atonement, while others protested their innocence. Many simply tried to make peace with their God. Before his burning, Henry Noles of Winchester, Tennessee, confessed his crime and asked his friends to "meet him in glory." He mounted the stump "stolidly" and laughed as he told the mob, "Tell all my sisters and brothers to meet me in glory. I am going to make that my home. Tell my mother to meet me where parting will be no more." Taken from the stump, he was then chained to a tree, his body saturated with oil, and soon "the quivering body was enveloped in flames." A lynch mob in Cuthbert, Georgia, agreed to a victim's request that they take his picture and send it to his sister; she collapsed upon receiving the photo showing him hanging on a tree. Sixteen-year-old Noah Cherry, before the noose was placed around his neck, confessed a crime of revenge and fell on his knees to pray. Observing this "terrible tragedy," an Episcopal minister found only one consolation. "What a comfort to feel that the Almighty is a God of love and mercy as well as Justice." Jesse Washington, a black youth, pleaded his innocence with the lynch mob (he had been retried after a judge had expressed doubt over a guilty verdict), but to no avail. The crowd, made up of "the supposed best citizens of the South," looked on with approval as the flames enveloped the squirming youth; souvenir hunters then proceeded to hack his body with penknives, carrying away their human loot. One white spectator failed to share the carnival mood of the crowd. "I am a white man, but today is one day that I am certainly sorry that I am one," he wrote afterward. "I am disgusted with my country."[23]

The degree to which whites came to accept lynching as justifiable homicide was best revealed in how they learned to differentiate between "good" lynchings and "bad" lynchings. Reporting the execution of Elmer Curl, at Mastadon, Mississippi, in 1910, a newspaper reported it to be "a most orderly affair, conducted by the bankers, lawyers, farmers, and merchants of that county. The best people of the county, as good as there are anywhere, simply met there and hanged Curl without a sign of rowdyism. There was no drinking, no shooting, no yelling, and not even any loud talking." What characterized a "good" lynching appeared to be the quick dispatch of the victim "in a most orderly manner" without prolonging his or her agony for the crowd's benefit. When a mob made up of "prominent citizens," including a member of the South Carolina state legislature, lynched a black man near Charleston, the local newspaper thought it had been done in the "most approved and up-to-date fashion." Still another newspaper attested to the popularity of the lynching when it advised against indicting the lynchers, as it would only make them heroes and "eminently qualify them for public office."[24]

No doubt the mob in Howard, Texas, thought itself orderly, even democratic in its ritualistic execution of a black man. Farmers in the surrounding neighborhood were notified to attend, and some two thousand spectators responded. The victim was given two hours for prayers, and the mob heeded his request that he be able to see his brother and sister before the execution. The question of how he should be executed was submitted to the crowd, and a majority voted for death by burning. Neither the orderliness of the proceedings nor the democratic proclivities of the mob in any way alleviated the agony of the victim. "The negro's moans were pitiful," a reporter noted. "He struggled, his great muscles swelling and throbbing in an effort to break the chains which bound him." Five minutes after the mob applied the match, the victim was dead, and at least one newspaper found the "hellish deed" inexplicable. "The deliberately-planned and calmly-executed spectacle was over. The crowd dispersed." But the legacy of this lynching, the editor insisted, would linger. "That five minutes of a return to primal savagery cannot be wiped out within the course of one brief life time. Five thousand Texans are irremediably debased."[25]

Even some hardened white Mississippians thought the lynching of Lloyd Clay in Vicksburg in 1919 might have been misguided. A twenty-two-year-old day laborer from a respected family, Clay was accused of rape, even though the victim denied he had been her assailant. Overly zealous to remove Clay from the jail, the mob accidentally shot two whites. Still, they carried off the execution, clumsily trying to hang him and finally burning him alive near the center of town. Newspapers called it "hideous" and "horrible," "one of the worst lynchings in history," and at least one newspaper thought Clay was "probably an innocent man, and one wholly out of the classes of the 'bad negro.'" Another newspaper labeled the lynchers rank amateurs who lacked the necessary skills to dispatch their victim. The more than one thousand spectators reportedly remained passive during the execution, though some thought the executioners had been clumsy and inflicted "needless suffering" on Clay. The lynching incurred further criticism for having taken place in a white neighborhood, with at least six white women fainting and still others reporting their "sensibilities" had been "shocked."[26]

Some executions were more spectacular than others, but none was particularly exceptional. If Sam Hose's execution appeared prominently in the southern press, hundreds of lynchings were accorded only a brief mention, particularly as they became routine affairs by the end of the century, requiring no more notice or comment in some newspapers than the daily weather. "Now-a-days," a bishop of the Southern Methodist Church noted, "it seems the killing of Negroes is not so extraordinary an occurrence as to need explanation; it has become so common that it no longer surprises. We read of such things as we read of fires that burn a cabin or a town." Few members of a lynch mob were, in fact, ever apprehended, and only rarely did the leaders or the participants seek to conceal their identity. The confident manner in which they went about their business was matched only by the complacency, the matter-of-factness, and often the good humor with which it was viewed. Occasionally, editorialists and political leaders voiced concern and condemned lynchings, but the public tended to praise the lynchers for fulfilling their responsibilities as white males. A Memphis newspaper chose to judge each lynching according to its merits, basing any verdict on the nature of the victim's crime; it had no problem with lynching a Negro rapist but thought it wrong to lynch a Negro who refused to be vaccinated.[27]

It became convenient for some whites and portions of the press to blame the racial excesses, especially lynching and rioting, on lower-class whites. Although the "best people," like other whites, took for granted the inferiority of blacks, they were said to be more paternalistic and less likely to carry their views to a violent conclusion. "Ravening mobs are not composed of gentlemen," affirmed Atlanta's leading newspaper.[28] But the evidence suggested otherwise. Perhaps "rednecks," "crackers," and "peckerwoods" played a more public role in lynchings, but they often did so with the tacit approval and at times the active and zealous participation of upper- and middle-class whites. Exceptions existed among all classes, but invariably "gentlemen" and "ladies," especially the newer generation of whites who had grown up after the war, were no more sympathetic to black people and their aspirations than were lower-class whites. If they sometimes displayed a greater sympathy, they felt less of a threat to their exalted position in southern society.

Neither crazed fiends nor the dregs of white society, the bulk of the lynchers tended to be ordinary and respectable people, animated by a self-righteousness that justified their atrocities in the name of maintaining the social and racial order and the purity of the Anglo-Saxon race. The mobs who meted out "summary justice" were pronounced by one Georgian as "composed of our best citizens, who are foremost in all works of public and private good." In the same spirit, a Meridian, Mississippi, newspaper concluded, "The men who do the lynchings . . . are not men who flout law but men who sincerely believe they have the best interest of their fellow men and women at heart." The point made by numerous whites, including editors and public officials, was that public opinion counted far more heavily than the law, not only physically but morally. Although a Lexington, Tennessee, editor believed the law should be sustained, "public sentiment is to a law what the ground under a house is to the superstructure. The public sentiment is not a part of the law, the ground is not a part of the house, but neither law nor house can stand on nothing." A patrician senator from Mississippi, John Sharp Williams, although not sympathetic to lynching, understood that on occasion "race is greater than law . . . and protection of woman transcends all law, human and divine."[29]

Drawn from all classes in southern white society, from the "rednecks" to the "best people," lynchers came together in an impressive show of racial and community solidarity. "The crowd seems to consist frequently of well-dressed men and women who . . . were presumably well able to read and write," one observer noted. A newspaper in Edgefield County, South Carolina, bold enough to denounce lynching, made no class distinction in calling for punishment of the lynchers. "It made no difference," said the editor, "if the Culbreath lynchers were some of the most responsible people in Edgefield. . . . The lynching of Culbreath was a barbarous pagan act. They [the lynchers] forfeited all claims to respectability."[30]

But white solidarity almost always prevailed. Townspeople closed ranks to protect their own kind, thereby becoming partners in the crimes committed. Eyewitnesses refused to testify, and grand juries refused to bring indictments against easily identifiable mob participants; even if they had, juries would have refused to convict, whatever the evidence. In the vast majority of reported lynchings, the courts, coroners' juries, or other official bodies chosen to investigate the murders concluded routinely that black victims had met their deaths "at the hands of unknown parties," "at the hands of persons unknown," or "by persons unknown to the jury." Like "the offspring of royalty," a Jackson, Mississippi, newspaper reported in 1899, whites who lynched blacks "feel licensed to do as they please, conscious that they will not be held accountable for their conduct." In an Alabama community, 110 whites examined for a jury that would judge members of a lynch mob were asked, "If you were satisfied from the evidence beyond a reasonable doubt that the defendant took part with or abetted the mob in murdering a Negro, would you favour his conviction?" A total of 76 answered "No," and no doubt the remaining 34 would have weighed very carefully the consequences of rendering a guilty verdict.[31]

After investigating a series of lynchings throughout the South, a federal attorney informed the Department of Justice of "the utter powerlessness of the State Government to punish the criminals who commit these acts."[32] Seldom, in fact, did a state or local political leader choose to condemn or move against a lynching. To do so might jeopardize his political career. James K. Vardaman vowed that "every Negro in the state will be lynched" if necessary to maintain white supremacy. But when as governor he used the militia in 1904 to prevent a double lynching, a Natchez newspaper thought "almost every white man in the state" opposed him. The mayor of Statesboro, Georgia, like some of the more conscientious public officials, deplored lynchings but felt himself helpless to prevent them. "If our grand jury won't indict these lynchers, if our petit juries won't convict, and if our soldiers won't shoot, what are we coming to?"[33]

Not only did distinguished public officials at all levels of government hesitate to condemn lynching, but some also chose to participate in lynch mobs. "I led the mob which lynched Nelse Patton, and I am proud of it," a former U.S. senator from Mississippi, William Van Amberg Sullivan, boasted in 1908. "I directed every movement of the mob and I did everything I could to see that he was lynched." The mob that carried out the grisly dismemberment of Willis Jackson in Honea Path, South Carolina, in 1911 was led by Joshua W. Ashleigh, who represented the district in the state legislature. His son, editor of the local newspaper, also participated in the lynching; indeed, he proudly told his readers that he "went out to see the fun without the least objection to being a party to help lynch the brute." When some shocked South Carolinians demanded a state investigation, Governor Cole Blease demurred. Rather than use his power of office to deter whites from "punishing that nigger brute," he vowed that if necessary he would gladly have resigned as governor "and come to Honea Path and led the mob."[34]

If political leaders failed to act, judges, sheriffs, jailers, and local police often stood by helplessly during a lynching or on occasion actively participated in the ritual. It was not uncommon for members of a lynch mob to pose for news photographers with both the sheriff and the intended victim. Even if a conscientious law enforcement official chose to remain committed to his oath of office, he was likely to encounter insurmountable obstacles, such as the will of the community. That was usually more than sufficient to prompt the official to submit to the seemingly inevitable. "I went into that cell block with every intention of fulfilling my oath and protecting that man," an officer reported, "but when the mob opened the door, the first half a dozen men standing there were leading citizens—businessmen, leaders of their churches and the community—I just couldn't do it." Neither could Sheriff W. M. Waltrip, after apprehending two blacks accused of arson in Franklin County, Alabama, in 1891. He tried to protect the prisoners, but only up to a point. He refused to sacrifice his own life when it would be of no use in any event. "I am heartily opposed to mob law," he informed the governor, "but the hanging of these firefiends has the endorsement of the larger portion of the people, black and white, of this county."[35]

The judicial system often countenanced the denial of justice to blacks accused of crimes. Judge Charles H. Brand of Lawrenceville, Georgia, reflected a prevailing sentiment when on several occasions he refused to order extra protection for accused blacks in imminent danger of being lynched. "I would not imperil the life of one white man to save the lives of a hundred such Negroes"—or, for that matter, "all such Negro criminals in the country." The blacks he refused to defend all lost their lives, but this in no way troubled him. "I am in perfect accord with my conscience and my God." Not all judges shared Brand's equanimity, but they found it easier to condemn lynchings than to prevent them. In his charge to a grand jury in Jasper County, Georgia, Judge J. B. Parke called mob violence a violation of "the traditions that have governed the Anglo-Saxon race from time immemorable." The grand jury was investigating the lynching of a black man, along with his son and two daughters.[36]

Before lynching two men in Morganton, North Carolina, in 1889, the mob held prayer services. That spoke quite eloquently to the degree to which lynchings took place in some of the most churchified communities of the South. If white churches showed a relative indifference to lynching violence, there were some compelling reasons. The lynch mobs often included their parishioners. "The only ways to keep the pro-lynching element in the church," a white Mississippian acknowledged some years later, "is to say nothing which would tend to make them uncomfortable as church members." Some clergymen, however, denounced lynchings, and a few took action. In Bulloch County, Georgia, the Reverend Whitely Langston expelled parishioners who had participated in a lynch mob—a most unpopular action that resulted in the loss of twenty-five members of the congregation. A Baptist minister in South Carolina singled out for condemnation lynchers who sought to justify their actions in the name of defending virtue; in fact, he charged, they made a mockery of virtue, some of them guilty of having relations with black women that helped to provoke "the crime leading to lynchings."[37]

Upon examining the record of 2,585 lynchings in the South from 1885 to 1903, Bishop Warren A. Candler of Atlanta reflected a growing concern over the destabilization of the social order. "Lynching is due to race hatred and not to any horror over any particular crime," the bishop contended, "[and] unless it is checked it may involve anarchy; for men will go from lynching persons of color to lynching persons on account of religion or politics, or their business relations." But a Georgia newspaper in 1897 took issue with clergymen who preached against lynching while ignoring the crime of rape that resulted in extralegal justice. After all, the writer noted, if clergymen examined the Old Testament (Numbers 25, verses 6 through 9), they would find "an account of the first great lynching, seen the Bible condemnation for the gratification of lust, and God's commendation of the lyncher." It was left to Ida B. Wells, a black editor and antilynching activist, to question the relative silence of white churches: "[O]ur American Christians are too busy saving the souls of white Christians from burning in hell-fire to save the lives of black ones from present burning in fires kindled by white Christians."[38]

Statistics of mob violence failed to include the large number of black Southerners executed by "legal lynchings." The need to mete out extralegal justice reflected in the minds of many whites the failure of legal justice to inflict punishment with sufficient speed and severity. The law and the courts were deemed too slow, too cumbersome, and too unreliable. Lawyers and judges, in particular, sometimes found themselves cast as untrustworthy enforcers, susceptible to manipulation by white "patrons" of accused blacks and capable of using technical flaws in criminal judgments to reduce punishment or free the prisoner altogether. "We don't want to lynch anybody," a Macon newspaper insisted, "but if the courts will not punish, society everywhere will protect itself, call it lynching, regulating, or what you will."[39]

If, as many whites agreed, the most effective way to stop lynchings was to ensure "speedy and certain" justice, that might require circumventing the usual constitutional provisions and judicial mechanisms designed to protect the accused. When asked how justice might be meted out more expeditiously, Governor William J. Northen of Georgia suggested the disbarment of lawyers who tried to shield criminals through "bare technicalities and unwarranted delays." In scores of instances, "speedy" justice made "certain" the execution of innocent parties, and frequently the public's need to exact vengeance allowed no patience with a legal process that failed to find sufficient evidence of the guilt of the accused. In Hinds County, Mississippi, a mob broke into a formal inquest and seized and lynched a black man accused of well poisoning. His wife, mother-in-law, and two other blacks were lynched later that day, although the coroner's jury had exonerated them.[40]

Even those who deplored lynching often did so within limits, acknowledging that a higher law might sometimes have to prevail. "There are places and occasions when the natural fury of men cannot be restrained by all the laws in Christendom," the *Atlanta Constitution* contended. The same newspaper recognized as "a hopeful sign" the willingness of courts to handle "crimes of lynching provoking character" with "becoming promptness." That observation prompted a black newspaper to observe that "[t]hose persons oftenest lynched are most

generally such as when given a speedy trial it is so speedy and so completely under the influence of the mob as to impress one that after all it
was a case of lynching by law rather than without."⁴¹

The "better sort" of whites who paid lip service to law and order all
too often found themselves justifying mob violence, mixing their outrage over a lynching with a more compelling sense of justice and retribution. Speaking to an audience at the University of Chicago, John
Temple Graves, the influential Atlanta newspaper publisher, was swept
up in a wave of emotion as he sought to communicate the imminent
peril facing every white female in the South. Under the circumstances,
he likened the lynch mob to an "engine of vengeance, monstrous, lawless, deplorable, but, under the uncured defects of the law the fiery terror of the criminal and the chief defense of woman."⁴² Of course, if
Graves's characterization of the imperiled white female had any merit,
the epidemic of lynchings he condoned had obviously done nothing to
enhance the woman's security. Nor would the eminent publisher have
even contemplated the same mob justice being applied to whites of his
own social class who were guilty of ravishing black women.

The "defects of the law" included more than suspect lawyers, judges,
and cumbersome legal procedures. In cases involving alleged sexual assault, the public recoiled at the idea of the female victim being compelled to relive the assault in the courtroom. "It is too great an ordeal
for the self-respecting white woman to go into court and accuse the
Negro ravisher and withstand a public cross-examination," a Huntsville, Alabama, resident explained to a northern visitor. "It is intolerable. No woman will do it. And, besides, the courts are uncertain.
Lynching is the only remedy." To many whites who considered themselves racial moderates, that was, in fact, the principal excuse for a
lynching. It would spare the victims of sexual assault, who had already
suffered a fate "many times more brutal than death itself," the ultimate
humiliation of a trial—"a second crucifixion, but little less trying to a
modest, virtuous woman than the outrage itself. The one, the act of a
Demon, a Vulture, The other that of a lot of Vultures acting in the
frame of the law."⁴³

Dissatisfaction with the judicial process masked the more overriding
concern that the punishment inflicted by legal justice would fail to
match the magnitude of the "crime." A rapid execution did not satisfy
the emotional hunger of whites who insisted on prolonging and intensifying the taking of a life, not only to inflict a harsher penalty but also to
send a more forceful message to the black community. Various inge-

nious proposals were made for punishments that went beyond lynch-ings. John Temple Graves liked the idea of castration and branding an "R" on each cheek of the offender, but even those did not quite suffice. With the assembled black community looking on, the offender should be compelled to ascend a tower and "pass over a slender bridge into a dark chamber where in utter darkness he perished by a terrible means never known to Negroes."[44]

The assumption persisted that blacks derived some satisfaction from the "pomp and ceremony" of a public trial, not to mention the comfort those sentenced to death or long prison terms found in seeking divine forgiveness. To Benjamin S. Williams, a prominent South Carolina planter, businessman, and politician, that was reason enough to dis-patch the accused as quickly and expeditiously as possible. The argu-ment he conveyed to a Columbia, South Carolina, editor summed up the frustration many whites felt over the inadequacies of the legal ma-chinery and the compelling need to heighten the punishment, to use the terrors and shock of mob violence as an indispensable deterrent.

> Arrest, imprisonment, opportunity for aid of counsel, astute legal ma-neuvering, seizure of technical advantage for prolongation or appeal by counsel for defence, final conviction, sentence and then—days, and weeks perhaps, of loving communion with preachers of the gospel who show to the sinner how the vilest "may return." How his sins, though "scarlet," may be made "white as snow," if he, the guilty con-victed rapist, will only "repent" and ask "forgiveness." Of course he repents and assists in asking forgiveness, and the remainder of his time on earth is a veritable soul love feast, while his victim writhes in an-guish and loving ones suffer the "tortures of the damned." When he takes a seat in the electric chair it is sitting, as it were, in a "chariot of fire" from which he is very soon to land in the great realm of promised eternal glory. The sentence of law is fulfilled. The criminal is dead; but died placidly, in hope, under assurance of eternal happiness in an everlasting paradise.[45]

Of course, the need to send a compelling message to the black commu-nity could be expressed on a number of different levels, as did an At-lanta editor when he suggested in 1906 that whites needed to impress on all blacks their vulnerability. "If necessary, we will double and treble and quadruple the law of Moses, and hang off-hand the criminal, or failing to find that a remedy, we will hang two, three, or four of the Negroes nearest to the crime. . . ."[46]

The crime of rape, when committed by black men on white women, evoked the most vocal and violent response in the white South, conflating as it did racial and sexual fears and tensions. "No crime," one white leader told a regional conference on race problems, "strikes at the integrity of the race or so insults its purity as the crime against women." A Georgia hardware salesman who considered himself "a sober consciencious [sic]" and "representative" southern white man hoped there would never be another lynching, but he had no compunctions about the fate of any black charged with assaulting a white woman. "I say *hang*, if need be *Roast* a thousand a week, until they are convinced that at least that one hellish phase of their nature must be restrained."[47]

Even while condemning lynch law, one editor captured much of the inflated rhetoric that was used throughout the South to justify it. He wanted his readers to appreciate why lynchings occurred. That "nameless and revolting crime," he said of rape, transforms the very life of the victim, forever crushing "peace and joy" out of a young woman's life. No wonder, then, it "starts the pulse of indignant manhood at fever heat, transforms the quiet citizen into the stern avenger, and sets the whole community in arms to rid the earth of the wretch who cumbers it—the fiend whose life is an offense against God and humanity."[48]

Not even the most vitriolic editor could match the rhetorical overkill displayed by an assortment of white political leaders. Whether appealing to readers or voters, whites who helped to shape public opinion also excited it to new heights of racist violence. After a "nigger burning" near Corinth, Mississippi, in 1902, Governor James K. Vardaman conceded that this form of punishment was less than "elevating" and might even contribute to the "moral deterioration" of white civilization. Nevertheless, he thought lynching the only "adequate punishment" for a black "two legged monster" who defiled "the exalted virtue, the vestal purity and superlative qualities of southern woman." Nor did the agrarian radical politician Thomas A. Watson feel any need to temporize his language when it came to justifying mob violence—the need "to lynch him [the Negro] occasionally, and flog him, now and then, to keep him from blaspheming the Almighty, by his conduct, on account of his smell and his color." Lynch law, Watson thought, was actually "a good sign," as it showed "that a sense of justice yet lives among the people." If that language in any way embarrassed some southern whites, it resonated with the people of Georgia, who elevated Watson to the governorship and to the U.S. Senate.[49]

The punishment needed to fit the crime, and no amount of torture and dismemberment suffered by a black person could equal the monstrosity of the deed a black rapist was said to have committed. When a grand jury in Charlotte, North Carolina, empaneled to investigate the death of a black accused of assaulting a white woman, reported that the victim had met "death at the hands of unknown parties," it chose to amplify that familiar judgment. Whatever "party" may have been guilty, the action had been taken "obviously by an outraged public acting in defense of their homes, wives, daughters and children. In view of the enormity of the crime committed . . . we think they would have been recreant to their duty as good citizens had they acted otherwise."[50]

To endorse lynching was to dwell on the sexual depravity of blacks, to raise the specter of the black beast seized by uncontrollable savage sexual passions that were inherent in the race. That is, the inhumanity, depravity, bestiality, and savagery practiced by white participants in lynchings would be justified in the name of humanity, morality, justice, civilization, and Christianity. And there was little reason to question the deep convictions on which whites acted; they came, in fact, to believe in their own rhetoric, much as the defenders of slavery had. The Negro as beast became a fundamental part of the white South's racial imagery at the turn of the century, taking its place alongside the venerated and faithful Sambo retainer, and whites were perfectly capable of drawing on both to sustain their self-image. Blacks, after all, possessed a dual nature: They were docile and amiable when enslaved or severely repressed, but savage, lustful, and capable of murder and mayhem when free and uncontrolled—like those blacks who had grown up since the Civil War. This generation, a Memphis newspaper insisted, had "lost in large measure the traditional and wholesome awe of the white race which kept the Negroes in subjection. . . . There is no longer a restraint upon the brute passion of the Negro."[51]

The imagery of unrestrained bestiality resounded throughout the South, repeated *ad nauseam* by those in political power and by those who aspired to replace them. Ben "Pitchfork" Tillman, who served as governor of South Carolina before being elected to the U.S. Senate, knew how to maintain his political invincibility. On the floor of the U.S. Senate, in 1907, he invoked the images that had come to haunt and obsess his region: white women in the rural South, virtually besieged by black brutes who roamed almost without restraint. Every southern man returning home was fearful of finding his wife or daughter ravished.

> I have three daughters but so help me God, I had rather find either one of them killed by a tiger or a bear and gather up her bones and bury them, conscious that she had died in the purity of her maidenhood, than to have her crawl to me and tell me the horrid story that she had been robbed of the jewel of her womanhood by a black fiend.

Tillman gave that speech many times, not only in the U.S. Senate but also throughout the South and in triumphal speaking tours of the North. Everywhere he was accorded an enthusiastic reception. In South Carolina, as elsewhere, the issue crossed political lines. "Just so long as negro men . . . outrage white women, white men will slay without mercy, judge, or jury negro men," a prominent South Carolinian declared. "Not because Tillman said so; it was not and is not 'Tillmanism.' It is natural. The crime arouses every propensity in man to strike and avenge, instantly, the insult, wrong and outrage."[52]

Concern over black rapists and the compelling need to lynch them sometimes masked the fear that sexual aggression by whites on black women would stimulate in black men the desire for revenge on white women. Although little evidence exists of white rapists of black women being lynched or punished by whites, the issue of lynch justice for alleged rapists did sometimes take an unexpected twist. In South Carolina, three black men were convicted of lynching Manse Waldrop, a white man, after he had raped a thirteen-year-old black girl. Some fifty-two petitions, signed by three thousand to four thousand whites and blacks, including some of the state's leading citizens, were sent to the state capitol—said to have been the largest petition for pardon ever presented a South Carolina governor. Although he did not condone lynching, the governor agreed to pardon the three black men. "These men had seen the law broken and lynchers go free countless times," he observed. A Newberry newspaper caustically praised the governor's decision. "It was the consensus that lynching should prevail, and there had never been a conviction of lynchers for rape. This case was a dirty one. If the lynchers are allowed to go free in other incidents then these ignorant Negroes should not be made to suffer. They were following in the footsteps of their enlightened white neighbors."[53]

In a few reported instances, black mobs meted out extralegal justice to blacks accused of serious offenses. In 1904, Edmund Bell, charged with the murder of a black woman, appeared at a preliminary hearing in Sardis, Alabama. As he was being escorted back to his jail cell in Selma, some ten miles away, a mob of blacks overpowered the constables, took Bell from their custody, and lynched him. A subsequent investigation suggested the probability of collusion between the black lynchers and the white constables.[54]

Reports of sexual assault created a momentum of their own. White women often fed the obsession with black sexuality by depicting themselves as virtually under siege. "I lived in Florida ten years," one woman wrote, "and was never free from fear of the negroe one moment. And if it were only death to be feared, that we could endure. But the thought of outrage is worse than that of a thousand deaths." A white farmer in Decatur County, Georgia, painted an equally grim picture of rural life. "I am an humble farmer surrounded by some brutal negroes. I have a wife and 3 daughters. I fully appreciate the purport and import of your warnings and palsied may become my arm when I refuse to act upon your suggestion."[55]

Playing on such fears and sympathies, Rebecca Felton used every occasion and invoked every conceivable image and stereotype to arouse the white South—and what she perceived to be an indifferent white manhood—over the threat of the black rapist beast. Even if he were "torn by red-hot pincers, or burnt with slow fire, his fate would be elysian" compared to what the woman had been forced to endure. That was why she had no compunctions about the people carrying out proper justice. After all, she asked, "What is this death by the rope, compared to the humiliation, ignominy and life-long suffering of the innocent victim? Any sort of death would be preferred by a pure-hearted Southern girl to this shame and unmerited disgrace! Far better that the brutal beast should kill his victim at one fell stroke than to leave her thus maimed for life—in body, mind and spirit!" From all parts of the South, and from the North as well, whites encouraged Felton to maintain her crusade for the sanctity of white womanhood.[56]

It took little time before a "folk pornography" emerged in the South, playing on themes from the past and adding some new dimensions. Even as whites resisted trials for rapists that would compel the female victims to endure the "glare and stare of public curiosity," newspapers often dwelled in considerable detail on the woman's experience, embellished for public consumption. Fears and phobias about black sexuality produced in the white mind a host of tales and fantasies that came into prominent play with every reported case of rape. "The crowds from here that went over to see [the lynch victim] for themself," a Floridian wrote to a southern critic of mob violence, "said he was so large he could not assault her until he took his knife and cut her, and also had either cut or bit one of her breast [sic] off."[57]

The climate of hysteria would reap a grim harvest, making the South in the estimation of one black observer "the terrified victim of the fears of its own conjuring." Editors and politicians, among many others, depicted a truly frightening South in which no man could leave his family without "the dread that some roving Negro ruffian is watching and waiting" for his opportunity to strike. "You don't know and you can't know," a white Georgian told a northern journalist, "what it means down here to live in constant fear lest your wife or daughter be attacked on the road, or even in her home. Many women in the city of Statesboro dare not go into their backyards after dark. Every white planter knows that there is always danger for his daughters to visit even the nearest neighbor, or for his wife to go to church without a man to protect her."[58] The man who made this observation might have been shocked to learn that black men articulated the same fears about their wives and daughters encountering white males.

The picture of women under siege, especially in the rural South, had the effect of justifying almost any kind of defensive action. Governor William J. Northen of Georgia suggested that homes be turned into "miniature arsenals, at least to the extent of one good winchester and one good pistol; that women be allowed to *carry weapons upon their persons,* concealed, if so desire, and they be taught the use and handling of firearms. . . . An occasional negro lying dead in the bay yard, shot by a brave woman in defense of her honor, will do more to stop this awful crime than all the lynching that may occur in a year." If vigilance and instant justice also resulted in the lynching of innocent blacks, that was a price whites seemed prepared to pay, again testifying to the value placed on black lives. In Rocky Ford, Mississippi, an angry mob chained J. P. Ivy, a black field hand and alleged rapist, to a woodpile, poured gasoline over it, and roasted him to death before a crowd of six hundred spectators. "Oh, God; Oh, God!" the victim shouted as the flames enveloped him. "Have mercy, I didn't do it! I didn't do it!" When he had earlier been brought to a local hospital for identification by the rape victim, a Memphis newspaper reported the young white woman's reaction: "She was not sure, but thought he looked like the one who had attacked her."[59]

White fears were based on the assumption that most lynchings stemmed from sexual assault. But in many cases, reports of sexual assault proved entirely baseless or upon closer examination revealed only that a black male had broken the rules of racial etiquette, had behaved in a manner construed as a racial insult, or had violated the bar on consensual interracial sex. What Walter White would call "the Southern white woman's proneness to hysteria where Negroes are concerned," based on his investigation of scores of lynchings, created situations of imagined rather than actual sexual assaults in which both innocent white and black lives were lost in the name of preserving the sanctity of white womanhood.[60]

While blacks cast their "lustful eyes on white women," a Little Rock newspaper declared, and "as long as any of them seek to break down the barrier that has been between the Negro and white man for a thousand years," whites will be neither "slow or timid" in the methods they employ to mete out an appropriate punishment. "This may be 'Southern brutality' as far as the Boston Negro can see, but in polite circles, we call it Southern chivalry, a Southern virtue that will never die."[61] But chivalry in defense of imperiled white womanhood was only a rationalization, not an explanation of the epidemic of mob murder that consumed the South.

Rape and sexual indiscretion, in actuality, proved to be a relatively minor cause of mob violence. Of the nearly three thousand blacks known to have been lynched between 1889 and 1918, only some 19 percent were accused of rape. But in many cases what the public thought had occurred became much more important than what did occur. The public's perception of lynching, fed by the media and improved means of communication, was invariably that a sex crime by black men had precipitated it. "Having created the Frankenstein monster (and it is no less terrifying because it is largely illusory)," Walter White concluded, "the lyncher lives in constant fear of his own creation. . . ."[62]

The offenses that precipitated mob violence related less to sex crimes (as sensationalized in the press) than to physical assault and murder (the most common charge), theft, arson, violations of the racial code, economic competition, and disputes over crop settlements. Many of the transgressions by blacks would have been regarded as relatively trivial if committed by whites and were not grounds anywhere else for capital punishment: using disrespectful, insulting, slanderous, boastful, threatening, or "incendiary" language; insubordination, impertinence, impudence, or improper demeanor (a sarcastic grin, laughing at the wrong time, a prolonged silence); refusing to take off one's hat to a white person or to give the right-of-way (to step aside) when encountering a white on the sidewalk; resisting assault by whites; "being troublesome generally"; disorderly conduct, petty theft, or drunkenness; writing an improper ("insulting") letter to a white person; paying undue or improper attention to a white female; accusing a white man of writing love letters to a black woman, or living or keeping company with a white woman; turning or refusing to turn state's evidence, testifying or bringing suit against a white person, or being related to a person accused of a crime and already lynched; political activities, union organizing, conjuring, or discussing a lynching; gambling or operating a "house of ill fame"; a personal debt; refusing to accept an employment offer; "jumping" a labor contract; vagrancy; refusing to give up one's farm; conspicuously displaying one's wealth or property; and (in the eyes of whites) trying to act like a white man.[63]

Victims of lynch mobs, more often than not, had challenged or unintentionally violated the prevailing norms of white supremacy, and these ranged from serious offenses (in the eyes of whites) to the trivial. Charles Jones, a youth from Grovetown, Georgia, was lynched by 150 whites for stealing a pair of shoes and "talking big." Henry Sykes was lynched in Okolona, Mississippi, for calling up white girls on the telephone and annoying them. A Texas youth was jailed for writing an insulting letter to a young white woman; a mob broke into the jail and shot him to death. Jeff Brown accidentally brushed against a white girl as he was running to catch a train; a mob hanged him for "attempted rape." For their "utter worthlessness," John Shaw and George Call, two eighteen-year-old youths from Lynchburg, Virginia, were shot to death after the mob's attempt to hang them failed.[64] A South Carolina editor acknowledged in 1917 that some three-fourths of lynchings were for "trivial offenses," and sometimes entirely innocent men were "butchered."[65]

All too often, black Southerners, innocent of any crime or offense, were victims of lynchings or burnings because they were black and in the wrong place at the wrong time. The only evidence against Jim Black, Thomas Ryor, and James Ford, implicated in the murder of the wife of a white farmer of Hendersonville, South Carolina, was that they had been spotted in the neighborhood; the three black youths were quickly lynched. The white farmer later confessed to murdering his wife and concealing her body. Fred and Jane Sullivan were accused of burning a barn; a mob lynched the couple, ignoring their four-year-old child. After emptying their guns into Bob Kennedy for assaulting a white man, a mob discovered he was not the man wanted for the crime and immediately continued their chase for "the guilty one."[66]

Men lynch most readily, a southern critic observed, when the black victim has "offended that intangible something called 'racial superiority.' " That offense, in fact, with no suggestion of sexual impropriety, precipitated scores of brutal lynchings. "When a nigger gets ideas," a federal official in Wilkinson County, Mississippi, declared, "the best thing to do is to get him under ground as quick as possible." Rufus Moncrief made one mistake when on his way home from work he encountered a group of white men: He did not display the expected humble demeanor and seemed reluctant to pull off his hat to them when they spoke to him. The men beat him badly, and soon other whites joined in the attack, some of them severing Moncrief's limbs with a saw; they dragged what remained of him to a nearby tree and strung him up as they continued to mutilate his body. For good measure, they hung Moncrief's dog next to him, and then informed Moncrief's wife that she would find two black puppies hanging to a tree and ordered her to remove them quickly or the farm would be burned to the ground. The eighty-year-old woman cut the bodies down and placed them in a large oats bag for burial. The coroner's inquest decided Moncrief had come to his death at the hands of parties unknown to the jury.[67]

Investigators frequently found no easily ascertainable reason for a lynching, except perhaps white emotional and recreational starvation. For some, "nigger killing" had simply become a sport, like any other amusement or diversion, and its popularity prompted a black newspaper in 1911 to call it "The National Pastime."[68] Like any other amusement or recreational diversion, Walter White said of lynching, it provided whites with a welcome escape from "the endless routine of drab working-hours and more drab home life." In Augusta, Georgia, in 1890, a black man was found one morning in the street, his body riddled with bullets. Suspecting a certain group of men may have been responsible, a white resident asked one of them, "Pat, who killed that nigger?" "Oh, some of the boys," he responded with a grin. "What did they do it for?" the resident asked. "Oh, because he was a nigger," Pat replied, as if that were more than sufficient explanation. "And," Pat added, "he was the best nigger in town. Why, he would even take off his hat to me."[69]

Although seldom cited as the reason for mob violence, the assumption persisted that an occasional lynching, for whatever reason, served a useful purpose, that periodically it became necessary to remind a new generation of blacks of their place in southern society. "You don't understand how we feel down here," a young white Southerner explained to a northern visitor; "when there is a row, we feel like killing a nigger whether he has done anything or not." It was imperative that blacks understand their limits. "A white man ain't a-goin' to be able to live in this country if we let niggers start getting biggity," a white Mississippian said of a black being held for trial. "I wish they'd lemme have him. I'd cut out his black balls and th'ow 'em to the hawgs." Some years later, when the number of lynchings subsided, a white resident of Oxford, Mississippi, told a visitor that lynching still had a reaffirming and cathartic quality that benefited the entire community. "It is about time to have another lynching," he thought. "When the niggers get so that they are not afraid of being lynched, it is time to put the fear in them."[70]

Some lynchings took place for no other apparent reason than to bring down a black person who had managed to achieve a measure of economic success. Anthony P. Crawford, born of slave parents in 1865, had become a substantial landowner and farmer in Abbeville, South Carolina; he had twelve sons and four daughters, most of them living nearby. As secretary of the local A.M.E. Church, he was a pivotal figure in the black community. Few blacks—or whites—had done more to embrace the gospel of self-help. "Anthony Crawford's life and character," one observer noted, "embodied everything that Booker T. Washington held to be virtuous in a Negro." On October 21, 1916, Crawford came to town to sell his cotton. He exchanged harsh words with a local white businessman over the offering price. When a store clerk wielding an ax handle went after Crawford, he backed away, only to be arrested and placed in jail, securing him initially from a white mob angry over his reported insolence. "When a nigger gets impudent we stretch him out and paddle him a bit," the store manager boasted. The president of the National Bank of Abbeville concurred: "Crawford was insolent to a white man and he deserved a thrashing."

Released on bail, Crawford headed toward the gin where his cotton was waiting. The white mob quickly regrouped and attacked him. Crawford resisted, injuring one of the whites, but the men finally overpowered him and kicked him until he had lost consciousness. The sheriff persuaded the mob to permit him to regain custody of Crawford. From his cell, Crawford was heard to say, while spitting blood where they had kicked out his teeth, "I thought I was a good citizen."

By not displaying "the humility becoming a 'nigger,' " however, he had become vulnerable. When a false rumor circulated that Crawford might be moved to another jail, the mob mobilized again and easily entered the jail. After shoving Crawford's broken body down three flights of stairs, they mutilated him, dug their heels into his upturned, quivering face, tied a rope around his neck, and dragged him through the streets of the Negro quarter as a warning. Finally, they hung him to a pine tree and emptied their guns into his body. Dutifully, the coroner convened a jury, which quickly reached the verdict that Anthony P. Crawford had come to his death at the hands of parties unknown. A subsequent citizens' meeting ordered the remainder of the Crawford family to leave town within three weeks.

A leading South Carolina newspaper had little difficulty in ascertaining the principal reason for Crawford's murder. "Crawford was worth around $20,000 and that's more than most white farmers are worth down here. Property ownership always makes the Negro more assertive, more independent, and the cracker can't stand it." But the citizens of Abbeville, regardless of class, demonstrated by their action—and inaction—not only extraordinary cowardice but also their own complicity in the crime. Pointing to the tree where Crawford was hanged, a resident remarked, "I reckon the crowd wouldn't have been so bloodthirsty, only it's been three years since they had any fun with the niggers, and it seems though they jest have to have a lynching every so often."

The governor and many of the state's leading newspapers condemned the Crawford murder. Some expressed concern over the migration of blacks to the North. Some even expressed misgivings about decency and justice in South Carolina.

If Crawford was a "bad Negro," if he had been implicated in murders, assaults or barn burnings it has not been reported. If he was a disturbing factor in his community, if he delivered incendiary speeches, if he stirred his race to animosity towards the whites, if he was in any way notorious or criminal or had been guilty of any offense prior to the day that he was killed, it has not been so reported to the press of Abbeville or of the State.

The only defense set up even by implication, as far as the public is informed, for the lynching of Crawford is that a Negro who uses insulting language to a white man and then fights back when attacked is worthy of death and should be forthwith hanged without process of law, though he is in the custody of the law, in jail, and sorely wounded.

Neither the governor, the newspapers in the state capital, nor the local businessmen who hurriedly met to dissociate themselves from the crime necessarily spoke for the white people of Abbeville—or South Carolina, for that matter. Given the nature of the crime and the absence of any indictments, the sentiments expressed in a local newspaper perhaps came closer to capturing the dominant public mood. "His wealth and coddling from white men desiring his trade, emboldened him to assume an equality that the whites will not tolerate." The "immediate cause" of the lynching was, in fact, irrelevant to the larger issue. "The 'best people' of South Carolina know that when white men cease to whip, or kill negroes who become obnoxious, that they will take advantage of the laxity, and soon make this state untenable for whites of ALL kinds, and that under such conditions the 'best' will be 'like the worst, and the worst like the best.' The point here made is, that no matter who actually killed Crawford, the responsibility for his death rests upon us ALL ALIKE, and because of his own reckless course, due to chest inflation from wealth, it was inevitable and RACIALLY JUSTIFIABLE."[71]

For black South Carolinians, the meaning of the Crawford lynching and its consequences were self-evident. "Our people are restless, more so now, than I have ever known them," a black clergyman informed a white editor. "Their property has been taken from them. In some sections of South Carolina and Georgia, the Negroes have been made to leave their property. Those poor, hardworking men, sons of Anthony Crawford of Abbeville, have only until the 15th of this month to get away. They will leave 50 bales of cotton in the field; the father left 560 acres of land paid for; $300 would have paid all his debts."[72]

When whites condemned lynching, they seemed less concerned over the black victims than over the very real possibility that white civilization itself was on trial. Even as whites could readily agree on the inferiority of blacks and the need to maintain white supremacy, some also perceived and expressed alarm over the descent of their region into barbarism. "The greater peril at this hour where outbreak and lawlessness are at the surface," a southern minister declared, "is not that the negro will lose his skin, but that the Anglo-Saxon will lose his soul." A Greensboro, Georgia, newspaper thought lynching affected the South's position throughout the world. "It ruins the worth of our investments. If it is not stopped then shut the school houses, burn the books, tear down the churches and admit to the world Anglo-Saxon civilization is a failure." Claiming that lynchings feed a "spirit of anarchy," a white Methodist newspaper in South Carolina warned that the entire social order might be in jeopardy. After all, if a Negro could be hanged for some crime, why not a property owner defending his legal rights? "Each such act unpunished but encourages repetition often in a less justifiable and more wanton form. . . . Today the negro, tomorrow the prominent attorney."[73]

Lynchings in the early twentieth century brought into question the very standards of civilized behavior in the South, and the white businessman expressed growing concern over their impact on the economic well-being of the New South. In reporting a lynching of two "apparently inoffensive" Negroes, a Memphis newspaper in 1913 found "no possible motive for the deed" and lamented the loss of "good farm hands, real wealth producers." The average black field hand, in the estimation of the newspaper, spent rather than saved his wages, much to the benefit of local business. "About all he gets goes through his fingers. Commercially, then, he is a very valuable asset. It is not good business to kill them."[74]

If lynchings were calculated to make an impression on the black community and underscore its vulnerability, whites succeeded. But at the same time, it exposed black men and women—in ways they would never forget—to the moral character of the white community. The impression conveyed was not so much the racial superiority of whites as their enormous capacity for savagery and cowardice, the way they inflicted their terror as crowds and mobs, rarely as individuals. "The lynch mob came," a Mississippi woman remembered. "I ain't never heard of no one white man going to get a Negro. They're the most cowardly people I ever heard of."[75]

3

WHEN WHITES TOOK to the streets, as in Wilmington, North Carolina, in 1898, and in Atlanta, Georgia, in 1906, they vented their exasperation over increasing evidence of black aggressiveness and disregard for racial etiquette. The principal targets were blacks "out of their place," and invariably these included leading and propertied blacks. In Wilmington, blacks had used their numerical majority for some years to exercise genuine political power, occupying a number of city offices. In learning the uses of politics, however, they threatened "white supremacy," which had already triumphed throughout most of the South. Wilmington would be "redeemed" comparatively late, in November 1898, as whites used fraud and intimidation to oust black officeholders.

Not content with an electoral triumph, a white mob declared war on black residents. Tensions had been inflamed in recent weeks over rumors of blacks arming themselves and by a provocative editorial in a black newspaper questioning the moral character of white women and charging that some of them used the charge of rape to mask clandestine interracial sexual liaisons when they were detected. The editor, Alex Manly, was responding to an article by Rebecca Felton defending and urging the lynching of black rapists and goading white men to do right by their women. Questioning the basis for the hysteria over rape, Manly found the morals of poor whites "on a par" with those of poor blacks; many white women, he observed, "are not any more particular in the matter of clandestine meetings with colored men than are the white men with colored women." As for the much-vaunted male defense of womanhood, he chided white women of all classes, "Tell your men that it is no worse for a black man to be intimate with a white woman than for a white man to be intimate with a colored woman." And in words that particularly outraged white sensitivities, he denounced white men for raping and seducing black women and warned them of the ultimate consequences of their behavior: "You set yourselves down as a lot of carping hypocrites; in fact you cry aloud for the virtue of your women, when you seek to destroy the morality of ours. Don't think ever that your women will remain pure while you are debauching ours. You sow the seed—the harvest will come in due time."[76]

That was more than most whites could tolerate. After the election, a mob demolished the press and burned down the newspaper office, forcing the editor to flee for his life. Whites then roamed the streets, terrorizing and killing blacks at random, some of them shouting, "We are just shooting to see the niggers run." One black resident, accused of wounding a white man in an exchange of fire, begged the mob for mercy, claiming he had five small children at home. They told him to leave, but he had not gone ten feet before the top of his head was severed by bullets. "It was a horrible sight," a member of the white militia reported. "The negroes are frightened out of their wits."[77]

Long after the riot, black residents found it impossible to forget the scenes they had witnessed. "It come so that we in this town is afraid of a white face," a black mother told a teacher. Still another black resident, in a letter to President William McKinley, asked in the midst of the Spanish-American War, "Is this the land of the free and the home of the brave? How can the Negro sing my country tis of thee?" Alluding to the targets of the white mob, this black woman added a revealing afterthought: "The Negroes that have been banished are all property owners. . . . Had they been worthless Negroes, we would not care." As one of the "mourners in a strange land with no protection near," she chose to remain anonymous. "I cannot sign my name and live."[78]

Nearly fifteen hundred Wilmington blacks, most of them propertied, chose to leave the city; whites moved quickly to confiscate their property for unpaid taxes. From exile in the North, Alex Manly added a footnote: "While the North Carolina negro troops were away fighting for the flag, the white man in the South rose up to drive the colored from the ballot box." Charles Chesnutt had already left his native North Carolina for Cleveland, Ohio, from where he called the massacre "an outbreak of pure, malignant and altogether indefensible race prejudice, which makes me feel personally humiliated, and ashamed for the country and the state." Three years later he would publish the novel *Marrow of Tradition,* based on what had happened in Wilmington. George H. White, reelected to Congress from North Carolina in 1898, the only remaining black member of that body, had had enough. He knew that the violence in Wilmington, along with the successful disfranchisement campaign in the state, had doomed any further black political opportunities. "I can no longer live in North Carolina and be a man."[79] After completing his term, he lived out his remaining years in the North. Nearly three-quarters of a century would elapse before another black person would be elected to the U.S. Congress from the South.

For most white residents, what had triumphed in Wilmington was "the highest sense of honor" over the dark forces of "negroism." The leader of the mob—a lawyer and former congressman who condoned the killing of black voters—became mayor of the city. His wife would become the state president of the United Daughters of the Confederacy. Black residents had been caught off guard by the scope and relentlessness of the white onslaught. John Dancy, an active layman in the A.M.E. Zion Church, an influential editor, and a Republican leader, chose to condemn Manly for remarks he thought calculated to provoke whites. "The manhood of a race that will not defend its womanhood," declared Dancy, "is unworthy of the respect of that womanhood." His remarks may have been designed to placate whites, but they betrayed an ignorance of the historical record. White men who defended white womanhood were hailed as heroes; black men who defended black womanhood were more likely to lose their lives in the effort.[80]

JOURNALISTS, POLITICIANS, and historians defined the outburst in Atlanta in September 1906, much as they described the events in Wilmington in 1898, as "a race riot." The term tends to distort what happened in both places; they were massacres, not riots, and they were inspired, directed, and carried out by members of all classes of white society. The massacre in Wilmington did not compare in scope or ferocity with the savage outburst of racial violence in Atlanta. For much of a week, whites lynched, murdered, assaulted, and plundered black residents.[81]

Racial tensions had been heightened by the vitriolic rhetoric supporting disfranchisement and segregation and by race-baiting white politicians. The continuing influx of young blacks from the countryside, the notoriety (and popularity) of the "Decatur Street dives" that many of them frequented, a rising crime rate, officially sanctioned police terrorism, and reported epidemics of black "impudence" and "presumptuousness," culminating in attacks on white women, created an explosive mixture ("a veritable social tinder box," a visiting journalist called it) that could no longer be contained. Few of the rumored rapes had any basis in fact, but they were enough to create a racial hysteria the press quickly exploited and inflamed, magnifying the scattered incidents into "an intolerable epidemic of rape." Still, whites would perceive the Atlanta Riot much as they perceived Reconstruction, insisting that criminal elements in the black community had brought on the white outrage. Young Margaret Mitchell, who would later achieve fame with her fictional treatment of the Civil War and Reconstruction, remembered as a five-year-old girl seeking refuge under the bed, thinking she was escaping "Negro mobs" seeking to burn down the town.[82]

The "riot" began on September 22. More than ten thousand whites participated (including "members of the best families"); it went on for four days and nights, and much of black Atlanta was laid waste by burning and looting. It left some twenty-six people dead (twenty-five blacks and one white), more than two hundred seriously injured (mostly blacks), and hundreds under arrest (almost all of them blacks); more than a thousand blacks fled the city. None of the dead blacks had been suspected of any crime, and none of them was a vagrant; all of them, a white citizens' committee subsequently reported, were "honest, industrious, and law-abiding citizens," and they had suffered "unspeakable brutality." The city's police chose to make themselves prudently scarce, interceding mostly to disarm blacks trying to protect their homes and families even as gun sales to whites multiplied. The state militia proved equally ineffectual, some of the soldiers preferring to support the mob. "There wuz a gang of soldiers," one black witness recalled, "and I say gang because that is just what I feel they wuz from the way they acted, dressed in uniform of Uncle Sam and sent out because they wuz supposed to keep the law and there they wuz breaking it. They wuz acting like ordinary, revengeful people, pouring out their hatred for the Negro." Down the streets they came, he remembered, shouting and singing,

> We are rough, we are tough,
> We are rough, we are tough,
> We kill niggers and never get enough.[83]

Roving bands of white marauders left an ugly trail of black bodies and demolished homes and shops. They dragged blacks off streetcars and clubbed, slashed, mutilated, and tormented them; they murdered blacks at random ("Burn him! Kill the nigger! Kill the black devil!"); they invaded black business establishments; and they burned down black homes. Lucy Rucker, a child at the time, remembered only spending most of the first night with her mother on the floor in her home, hoping the mob would pass them by; her father and brother had tried to ascertain what was happening and ended up seeking refuge in the post office building. "We didn't know what had happened to them, and we found that they [whites] were butchering people, taking them off streetcars, just killing them, that's all."[84] The assaults on black men, women, and children often degenerated into downright savagery, replete with mutilations and severed limbs; souvenir hunters scrambled for clothes, fingers, and toes. The courageous and risky efforts of some whites to intercede or offer shelter to blacks were mostly ineffectual, as were sporadic and unorganized black attempts at defense and retaliation.

For black Atlantans, and for many southern blacks who lived elsewhere, these four days would forever be etched in their memories. Walter White, then a youth of thirteen, remembered the riot as his racial awakening. "I knew then who I was." He came to learn, too, that intelligence, talent, or virtue made no difference to whites. "A curse like that of Judas was upon us, a mark of degradation fashioned with heavenly authority." He heard the mob outside threatening to burn down his home, shouting, "That's where that nigger mail carrier lives! Let's burn it down! It's too nice for a nigger to live in!" Benjamin Mays, a twelve-year-old boy living in South Carolina, recalled reading about the riot and hearing talk about its causes. He asked his future brother-in-law why white men could do whatever they wished to black women but black men were lynched if they did the same to white women or were merely accused and innocent. "My prospective brother-in-law stopped by the side of the road and gave me a stern lecture. He told me in positive language never to discuss that matter again. It was dangerous talk. . . ." W. E. B. Du Bois, an Atlanta University professor, was out of town when the riot began; he rushed back to the city to be with his wife and six-year-old child, and he knew what he had to do. "I bought a Winchester double-barreled shotgun and two dozen rounds of shells filled with buckshot. If a white mob had stepped on the campus where I lived I would without hesitation have sprayed their guts over the grass. They did not come."[85]

Much of the violence fell on blacks who had succeeded, who had faithfully adhered to the Washingtonian faith—the property-owning blacks, the most industrious, the most respectable, the most law-abiding, the most accommodating, the most educated. The middle-class neighborhoods in which they lived, and where the black colleges were located, became natural targets of the mob, as did the black businesses on Auburn Street. In attacking these areas, the mob proposed to teach the presumptuous, uppity, and "highfalutin niggers"—many of them teachers, physicians, lawyers, clergymen, merchants, and editors—lessons they would never forget. But black men and women placed their own interpretation on the meaning of what they had undergone: Neither a deferential accommodation nor economic success guaranteed them their civil or human rights. In the aftermath of the riot, a young Atlanta black wrote to a friend about the depth of his disillusionment:

How would you feel, if with our history, there came a time when, after speeches and papers and teachings you acquired property and were

educated, and were a fairly good man, it were impossible for you to
walk the street (for whose maintenance you were taxed) with your sister without being in mortal fear of death if you resented any insult
offered to her? How would you feel if you saw a governor, a mayor, a
sheriff, whom you could not oppose at the polls, encourage by deed or
word or both, a mob of "best" and worst citizens to slaughter your
people in the streets and in their own homes and in their places of
business? Do you think that you could resist the same wrath that
caused God to slay the Philistines and the Russians to throw bombs? I
can resist it, but with each new outrage I am less able to resist it.[86]

Noting how the mob singled out for attack "the respectable and law-
abiding coloured person," an English visitor thought the riot "a grimly
ironic comment" on Washington's success formula. So did Charles W.
Chesnutt, who twenty-five years earlier had expressed his conviction
"that as the colored people, as a class, show themselves worthy of respect and recognition, the old prejudice will vanish, or wear away. . . ."
But in 1906 he reminded Washington "that the riot occurred only a few
days after your splendid object lesson of the Negro's progress in business and the other arts of peace." With Washington clearly in mind,
Chesnutt noted "that those best qualified to speak, and whose utter-
ances would carry most weight, have not been in a position to express
themselves fully. I appreciate the difficulty of their situation." He expected it would take "a long time" before "this race problem" could be
resolved peacefully. "The American people will have to swallow the
Negro, in punishment for their sins," he told Washington. "Doubtless
the dose is a bitter one, but there is no other way out. It only remains
for all of us to make the process as little painful as possible to all concerned."[87]

Among the many blacks terrorized and driven from their homes was
Dr. W. F. Penn, a prominent physician, a graduate of Yale, a man who
commanded considerable influence in the community. After the riot, in
many ways reiterating the questions raised by other blacks, he asked a
group of prominent Atlanta whites:

What shall we do? We have been disarmed: how shall we protect our
lives and property? If living a sober, industrious, upright life, accumulating property and educating his children as best he knows how, is not
the standard by which a coloured man can live and be protected in the

South, what is to become of him? If the kind of life I have lived isn't the kind you want, shall I leave and go North?

When we aspire to be decent and industrious we are told that we are bad examples to other coloured men. Tell us what your standards are for coloured men. What are the requirements under which we may live and be protected? What shall we do?

The white citizens of Atlanta had few ready answers, though they went through the motions of reforming the police department and establishing a civic league made up of leading whites to promote interracial harmony.[88] Some deplored the riot, while reasserting traditional paternalistic attitudes. "The negro race is a child-race," one regretful Atlanta lawyer declared. "We are a strong race, their guardians. We have boasted of our superiority, and we have now sunk to this level—we have shed the blood of our helpless wards." Still another white Atlantan claimed to know Dr. Penn, considered him a good man, and vowed that the city would protect such Negroes. "If necessary I will go out and sit on his porch with a rifle."[89] That sentiment at least went beyond that of the president of the United States, Theodore Roosevelt. Although the riot was front-page news across the country, the president made no public condemnation of it.

Like Dr. Penn, most black Atlantans who had fled the city returned gradually and fearfully. Kathleen Redding, a native Atlantan born in 1890, entered Atlanta University one week after the riot. "The campus, of course, was quite hushed . . . the city students were a little wary because we had to cross town to get to the university." Adrienne McNeil Herndon, a graduate of Atlanta University and married to a prominent black businessman, wrote to Booker T. Washington, who had recently selected her for an article on black women. The riot, she told him, had made her feel they could never have a real home "in this ungodly section. Some times I doubt if there is any spot in this country where one with Negro blood can plant a home free from prejudice scorn & molestation. The sanctity of the Negro home is to the majority (the vast majority) of the white race a thing unrecognized." Washington, on the other hand, tried to put the best face on the disaster, calling the post-riot citizens' meetings "the most sane and serious effort that has ever been made in the South by Southern white people to get into touch with the educated and leading colored people."[90]

4

IT SAID MUCH of the desperation many blacks felt in the 1890s and the early twentieth century that they might, like Washington, choose to find in the intensity of white violence and repression a sign of hope and progress. From his extensive investigations, Walter White concluded that "lynching is much more an expression of Southern fear of Negro progress than of Negro crime." Lynching, in this view, did not necessarily succeed in reinforcing racial repression; on the contrary, it suggested the refusal of black men and women to submit with equanimity to that repression. None other than Frederick Douglass suggested in 1892 that the racial violence and lynchings may actually be "a favorable symptom":

> It is proof that the Negro is not standing still. He is not dead, but alive and active. He is not drifting with the current, but manfully resisting it and fighting his way to better conditions than those of the past, and better than those which popular opinion prescribes for him. He is not contented with his surroundings. . . .
>
> A ship rotting at anchor meets with no resistance, but when she sets sail on the sea, she has to buffet opposing billows. The enemies of the Negro see that he is making progress and they naturally wish to stop him and keep him in just what they consider his proper place.
>
> They who aspire to higher grades than those fixed for them by society are scouted and scorned as upstarts for their presumptions.

Embracing that same reassuring posture, John Mitchell, editor of the *Richmond Planet,* urged his people to think more positively about their prospects. "The very oppression which is being forced upon him like a pall is working wonderful results, trying him in the furnace of fire and bringing him out a new race regenerated and redeemed."[91] The extraordinary amount of attention and energy expended on black Southerners, Henry M. Turner argued in 1904, refuted most compellingly the charge of inferiority. "[M]ore laws have been enacted by the different legislatures of the country, and more judicial decisions have been delivered and proclaimed against this piece of inferiority called negro than have been issued against any people since time began." Given the attempts to suppress the race, Turner concluded, "It would appear that the negro is the greatest man on earth."[92]

It was bold talk in the face of harsh realities. How many who underwent the ordeal of fire lived to tell about it? Who can know now what those blacks who lived at the time were prepared to suffer in the name of race regeneration and redemption? Most, after all, found themselves in an impossible situation as they weighed the advice to improve their lives against the realities they faced each day. The contradictions mounted, and few could find ways to reconcile them. How could they be frugal if they found it impossible (even dangerous) to accumulate any savings? How could they maintain a clean appearance and clean homes if denied decent housing and the basic city services whites were accorded—and if whites greeted with derision black efforts to upgrade their appearance and homes? How could they be hardworking and diligent if denied the rewards of their labor? How could they be expected to respect the law if the law and its enforcement agencies denied them minimal respect and protection? How could they be asked to respect contracts if defrauded by employers, landlords, and merchants?

No wonder many blacks who had survived bondage saw little hope for improving their lives or the prospects of their children. "Ah can'[t] see much hope fur de youn' folks," Archie Booker, a former Virginia slave, confessed, and his despondency, like that of many blacks, rested not on his perception of black possibilities but on his insight into white character and behavior. "White folks is too greedy. Looks like de mo a man labors, de mo de othuhs try to git it fum im."[93]

The few self-made black men and women who accumulated property and wealth were social anomalies, though they did keep the aspiration alive for others. Like Booker T. Washington and the black apostles of self-help, they assumed that others could succeed as they had, if only they practiced the necessary virtues and possessed the necessary character, if only they adopted the standard self-help advice and embraced the Washington formula. But the successful, all too often, paid a heavy price if they expected to retain their gains. No one did more to internalize the etiquette of deferential accommodation than those blacks who had the most to lose. "The more a Negro owned," Benjamin Mays perceived, "the more humble he had to act in order to keep in the good graces of the white people."[94]

That was common knowledge, and successful and ambitious blacks found various ways to adapt their day-to-day lives and thoughts to such realities to blunt white suspicions and fears. Explaining his formula for achieving "success" and maintaining his gains, a Mississippi farm owner minced few words: "Hard work, slow saving, and staying in my place, acting humble, that's how I did it." (At the word "humble," he laughed.) When a white Atlanta newspaper featured Cody Bryant, said to be the "richest Negro farmer," and assessed his impressive real-estate and financial worth, it also bestowed on him the ultimate white seal of approval: "Bryant is a splendid type of the old slavery-time negro. Humble, courteous and scrupulously honest, he has the respect and confidence of his white friends and his credit with the mercantile houses and banks . . . is practically unlimited." The newspaper also made a point of noting that Bryant paid no attention to politics, had never attended school, and "has a profound contempt for the latter-day professional negro officeseeker."[95]

For all blacks, the successful and the unsuccessful, the educated and the illiterate, the need to anticipate and to accommodate white expectations took on a critical importance. "The South is gettin to be too dangerous for coloured people," a black waiter in an Atlanta hotel told a northern visitor in the aftermath of the riot. "Do you talk much about these things among yourselves?" the visitor asked him. "We don't talk about much else," he replied. "It's sort of life and death with us."[96]

The waiter had made his point, employing hyperbole to do so. Blacks talked, in fact, about many things, not all of them related to white folks, and by the turn of the century they were sustaining an increasingly separate institutional and cultural life. Whites took notice, and they continued to have misgivings about what they saw.

5

NEITHER THE END of Reconstruction nor the triumph of disfranchisement and Jim Crow brought to white Southerners the racial security they so desperately sought. White supremacy appeared to be firmly in place, sustained by economic coercion, violence, and enforced custom and habit. But a growing uneasiness and restlessness continued to grip the black South, and whites were not oblivious to this development. What a white politician wrote to a friend in South Carolina after the end of Reconstruction seemed no less true at the turn of the century: "We have no enemy in our front. But the negroes are almost as well disciplined in their silence and inactivity as they were before in their aggressiveness."[97]

If disfranchisement, segregation, and violence had an intimidating effect on southern blacks and inhibited their actions, whites somehow seemed no more secure. William H. Skaggs, a prominent Alabama businessman and banker and the former mayor of Talladega, confided his concerns in 1905 to a friend and fellow Alabamian. He had voted for the constitution that disfranchised the Negro, and yet "there is more trouble between the races than there was in 1872." In his recent travels through Mississippi, he had found "the bitterness between the whites and the blacks . . . more pronounced than I had observed before." In his own home counties in Alabama, he confessed, "from all I could see and hear, there was more talk about the 'niggers' and the possible dangers of a conflict between the whites and the blacks than I have heard since I was a small boy." With equal concern, a Memphis newspaper in 1892 noted that the Negro as "a political factor" had been brought under control. "But neither laws nor lynchings can subdue his lusts. Sooner or later it will force a crisis. We do not know in what form it will come."[98]

Nor apparently had the violence and repression visited on black Southerners satisfied the "lusts" of many whites. With a seemingly undiminished fury, whites acted on their fears of black aggression and advancement. Residing on a houseboat on the Mississippi River near New Orleans when they were not working their way up the river, Frank and Alice Thrasher learned to live with the heightened racial tensions. The arrest of three black youths accused of murdering a shrimp fisherman produced a caustic response: "It is hard to tell what will be done with them. The evidence being circumstantial. But Jefferson Parish of which Gretna is the county seat seems to have a great antipathy to the nigger in general and are daily shooting and lynching them without apparent cause. So it would be supposed that they will not let a *guilty* one escape." Although the Thrashers learned to live with these tensions, they could never overcome them. "The longer I live here," Alice Thrasher wrote her brother-in-law, "the more I dread and fear the nigger."[99]

The repression of black Southerners through coercion, fraud, violence, and legal force managed to induce in some whites a false sense of

security. "We are crowing down here like children because we have settled the negro question," John S. Bassett wrote from Durham, North
Carolina, in 1898. But the celebration, thought Bassett, would be short-
lived. "We don't see that we have not settled it by half. At best we have
only postponed it." Five years later, Bassett penned a gloomy analysis of
the "everlasting negro question," concluding that "today there is more
hatred of whites for blacks and blacks for whites than ever before."
Both races, he argued, had been caught "in a torrent of passion which,
I fear, is leading to an end which I dare not name." If blacks had once
acceded to inferior accommodations and treatment, they were becoming, in Bassett's estimation, "too intelligent and too refined" to be satisfied with what their elders had been forced to endure. "Formerly, it did
not hurt his pride to ride in a 'Jim Crow car'; for he had little or no
pride of that kind. Now he considers this law a badge of inferiority, a
mark of intolerance which he will some day wipe out."

But Bassett's warning went unheeded, and he confided to a friend
his intellectual isolation in the New South. "I do not have the honor to
agree with most of my fellow Anglo-Saxons on the negro question."
That proved to be an understatement. In an article that attracted considerable attention, Bassett thought "the only solution to race conflict"
lay in adopting "the children of Africa" into American life. "In spite of
our race feelings, of which the writer has his share, they will win equality some time." Most whites vehemently disagreed. Only a vote by the
faculty and students of Trinity College, expressing their support for the
principles of academic freedom and a free press, saved Bassett from
having to flee his professorship and his residence.[100]

Although black crime rates had supposedly risen sharply, whites
could seldom cite instances of organized black resistance to white controls. But this, too, failed to reassure many whites. The apparent absence of overt black aggression was not so much a source of comfort as
a disturbing confirmation that such aggression was contemplated; the
very appearance of black docility and passivity seemed ominous and
threatening. "The race situation is bad," the editor of the *Charleston
Evening Post* confided to a newspaper colleague in 1919. "We don't know
what is going on among the negroes and explosions may occur at any
time under our feet." Six years earlier, arriving in New Orleans after a
deadly shooting incident involving whites and blacks, a visitor thought
she discerned an atmosphere of racial uncertainty and tension. "Although whites and blacks generally live peaceably together, there is
sometimes a smouldering fire below. . . ."[101]

Even when blacks acted with proper deference, whites seemed no less suspicious. A resident of Conyers, Georgia, thought most Negroes in town were "very peaceable," but that gave him only slight comfort as he viewed the future. "[E]very day I notice they are inching towards the danger line. . . ."[102]

CHAPTER SEVEN

ENDURING

Oh, Lord, I'm troubled in mind!
Oh, Lord, I'm troubled in mind!
Oh, Lord, I'm troubled in mind!
   I want you to ease my troubled in mind.

As I went down the hill to pray,
Met old Satan on my way.
Satan said, "It's no use to pray,
Jesus is dead and God's gone away."

Oh, Lord, I'm troubled in mind!
Oh, Lord, I'm troubled in mind!
Oh, Lord, I'm troubled in mind!
   I want you to ease my troubled in mind.[1]

DURING WORLD WAR I, a visitor came upon a black church near Durham, North Carolina. He listened as the congregation sang a "most weirdly" song, detailing the crucifixion of Christ.

O they took my blessed Lawd,
Blessed Lawd, Blessed Lawd,
O they took my blessed Lawd,
An He never said a mumblin' word,
Not a word, not a word, not a word.

O they bound Him with a purple cord . . .
O they plaited Him a crown o' thorn . . .
O they put it on His head . . .
An' they pierced Him in the side . . .
An' the blood come streamin' down . . .

An' they judged Him all night long . . .
An' they whipped Him up the hill . . .
Then they nailed Him to the cross . . .
An' the blood come tricklin' down . . .
An' He bowed His head and died . . .
An' the stars refused to shine . . .
O wasn't that a pity an' a shame . . .
An' He never said a mumblin' word,
Not a word, not a word, not a word.[2]

The immediacy of the images—as if the singers were themselves witnesses to the event—made the song all the more gripping. In depicting Calvary, the singers combined a faith in salvation with their worldly experiences. Even as they commiserated over Christ's tribulation, they celebrated his triumph and redemption, the way he had made a virtue of his suffering. Within the constraints imposed by segregation, disfranchisement, and lynch violence, black Southerners, much like this congregation, learned how to adapt and endure—and how to transcend. It would not be easy.

2

THE GRATUITOUS INSULTS, the daily reminders of "place," the tensions and dangers black people faced every working day took their inevitable toll, breaking some of the strong-spirited along with the weak. Some were more easily broken than others. For those who had experienced the intimidation and murder that crushed Reconstruction, the repression that came down in the 1890s must have seemed all too familiar. Like Bessie Jones's grandfather, some thought slavery had never really ended but had only taken on a different guise. He recalled feeling no more secure after emancipation than as a slave. "Because we are yet under them white folks' name," he explained to his granddaughter. "We got a slave name. And they know our name."[3]

The white majority tried to define the boundaries within which African Americans could live their lives. Fear of violating those boundaries—unintentionally or as perceived by whites—haunted black men and women in their daily routines, compelling them to act with extreme caution in the presence of whites. That included avoiding any words, gestures, or facial expressions that might be misinterpreted and staying away from whites altogether if possible. Thinking back on her life, Sarah Fitzpatrick described a state of unremitting tension. No matter what one did, she recalled, it proved impossible to escape that tension—"al'ays scaid dat sump'in gonna hap'en all de time; scaid he gwin butt into some white fo'ks an' have trouble, al'ays scaid ya' gwin do sump'in 'rong an' have de white fo'ks beat'cha up." Few articulated as sharply as this former slave the extraordinary burden under which she and her people had tried to survive since emancipation, the exceptional obstacles they had needed to overcome. "See," she explained, "de 'Nigger' ain't got no law, no flag, no nothin. He lives under de white man's law, dat's whut keeps him dis'sad'isfied, an' nuverous all de time."[4]

The slightest deviance from the racial code, no matter how unintended, could produce immediate concern in a black person. A white woman in Atlanta related an incident in which a young black man hurriedly came out of a hallway onto the sidewalk and accidentally brushed against her shoulder. When he turned his head and found he had touched a white woman, she recalled, "such a look of abject terror and fear came into his face as I hope never again to see on a human countenance. He knew what it meant if I was frightened, called for help, and accused him of insulting or attacking me. He stood still a moment, then turned and ran down the street, dodging into the first alley he came to." For this white woman, who sympathized with his plight, it was "a terrible experience." For the black man, it was a part of his daily life. By brushing up against the white woman, he had broken one of the "unwritten rules" of racial etiquette. While a student at Fisk University in the 1880s, W. E. B. Du Bois experienced a similar incident but with a different result. After accidentally jostling a white woman on a Nashville street, he immediately—"in accord with my New England training"—raised his hat and apologized. The woman was furious, leaving Du Bois to brood over the unanswered questions.

> Was it because I showed no submissiveness? Did I fail to debase myself utterly and eat spiritual dirt? Did I act as equal among equals? I do not know. I only sensed scorn and hate; the kind of despising which a dog might incur. Thereafter for at least half a century I avoided the necessity of showing them [whites] courtesy of any sort.[5]

The thoroughness of Jim Crow legislation left little to the imagination. With the newly posted signs designating their "place," blacks went about the task of adapting and enduring. But the new laws failed to cover all aspects of black life. What evolved alongside the statutes and ordinances, with the same purpose in mind, was a racial etiquette enforced as rigidly as the laws themselves. If some customs were enforced more sporadically, that made them no less threatening, as blacks had no way of knowing when or where whites might insist on compliance.

Consistent with deep-seated white resentment of black success or advancement, the prevailing racial code frowned on exhibitions of black accomplishments that suggested an equal capacity and contradicted assumptions about Negro character and indolence. For the Negro to get "out of place" was to aspire to the same goals and possessions whites coveted, and whites often found such aspirations by blacks both distasteful and unnatural. A visitor from South Africa in 1914 thought "one of the saddest features" in the American South to be the fact "that the prejudice of the white man is quickened, and becomes more alert and even bitter, as the Negro or native approaches his standard of life." As a native South African, he found this attitude all too familiar. "In the Southern States a 'nigger in his place' is tolerated, even liked; in South Africa a raw Kaffir is in many cases preferred, and receives kindly consideration, that is not forthcoming when he becomes dressed, educated, and speaks English."[6]

Anticipating white expectations and fearing violence, blacks went out of their way to avoid any behavior that might be interpreted as impertinence or putting on airs. After making her first bale of cotton, Mattie Curtis ginned it and then took it to the market to sell it, all the while trying to suppress the pride she felt over her achievement. To avoid disturbing white sensitivities, she chose to remain as inconspicuous as possible. "De white folks hated de nigger den," she explained, " 'specially de nigger what was makin' somethin' so I dasen't ax nobody whar de market wus."[7]

But blacks did not always succeed in masking their emotions or achievements, and some made no attempt to conceal them. The men and women who comprised the first postemancipation generations found it particularly difficult to make the necessary accommodation. Mamie Fields of Charleston, South Carolina, managed in less than one day to break several times the "unwritten laws" of Jim Crow when she visited her rural relatives near the town of Ehrhardt. The first violation occurred when she insisted over her cousins' objections that they ride into town to shop in the stores. Her aunt's fancy buggy, along with its passengers, immediately attracted the attention of local whites, who were unamused by this display of black achievement. "Those crackers looked at us and got kinda mad," Fields recalled. The second violation was to come to this rural town on a weekday instead of Saturday. "See, in Ehrhardt they even segregated the days of the week. So riding to the store the way we did was almost the same as if we'd walked in the diner and sat down for lunch. Saturday was the day all the black people were supposed to go and shop." The third violation occurred when Fields asked in a local store for a crochet needle, startling the proprietor, who thought such a skill much "too refined" for black people. Claiming she sold no such items, the proprietor could no longer suppress her exasperation as she admonished Fields's cousin, "Don't come down ya in the day and bring her, ridin' in that thing."[8]

The experience underscored an unwritten code of racial etiquette one might encounter anywhere in the South. Ned Cobb recalled having to endure the hostile glances of a white man who "admired my mule and buggy in a way that made it clear he didn't like to see no nigger have a outfit like that." Such conspicuous visibility vexed whites, as it threatened to undermine prevailing notions of both race and class. "Just generally," Mamie Fields reflected, "if you were black, you were not supposed to have either time or money, and if you did, you ought not to show it." For a black person to accumulate even modest wealth and possessions aroused sufficient alarm in white circles to prompt some affluent blacks, as in Natchez, to spread their savings among several banks, including northern establishments. That was also reason enough for many blacks to resort to mail order to acquire possessions that might attract unwanted attention if purchased locally; some also deemed mail order less humiliating, as local stores would not, for example, permit blacks to try on clothes before purchasing them. "Our people used to send off for certain items," Mamie Fields noted. "That way . . . the crackers—or 'the poor buckrah,' as was sometimes said—wouldn't know what you had in your house. Better that way." Even mail order, however, had to be used with discretion, as black families feared reprisals if too many purchases were delivered by express.[9]

In scorning blacks for their shoddy appearance, whites confidently attributed this quality to racial characteristics. But blacks found good reason to avoid calling attention to themselves. To dress ostentatiously (that is, like middle-class whites), especially on weekdays, was to risk attack and derision. It was not uncommon after emancipation, a former Georgia slave recalled, for whites to cut the clothes from the backs of freedmen when they were well dressed. Caroline Smith of Walton County, Georgia, recalled how the Ku Klux Klan in the 1870s had treated blacks who attempted to improve their appearance. "The colored people dare not dress themselves and fix up, like they thought anything of themselves, for fear they would whip us." Traveling by train as a chauffeur with Ringling's Circus in 1915, Taylor Gordon made his first sojourn into the South. In Houston, Texas, he put on his new "Jack Johnson plaid suit" and patent leather shoes and prepared to see the town. As he made his way through the train station, Gordon encountered a white man in a civilian suit wearing "a big star" on his chest and holding a billy club. Grabbing Gordon's lapel, the man demanded to know, "What you doin' in here? You're a Yankee Nigger, ain't cha?" Sensing he was in trouble, Gordon replied, "No, I'm Ringling's Niggah." The words and the deferential tone in which they were expressed struck a responsive chord in the white man. "Oh, you don't say. Well, by God! that saves yah. You sure look like a Yankee Nigger. They're all too damn smart. At any rate you can't come in here with those clothes on. Come here and I'll show you where Niggers belong." He escorted Gordon out the front door and around the corner, thrusting him into a small shed with a few benches along the wall. "That's where you belong in them clothes. If you want to see the sights in that station, put on your uniform." Gordon returned to his railroad car, put on his white coat, duck pants, and red porter's cap, and went out to see the train station—and Houston.[10]

The porter's uniform saved Taylor Gordon because white people associated it with a servile position. Nothing infuriated whites more than the sight of a black man in a military uniform, as during and after the Civil War, the Spanish-American War, and World War I. Not only did the uniform suggest an assertion of authority unwelcomed in blacks, but it also reminded whites of how participation in wars always gave blacks "highfalutin" ideas about commanding a place in American society commensurate with the patriotic services they had rendered on the battlefield. "What did they do to the niggers after this first world war?" Ned Cobb reflected.

> Meet em at these stations where they was gettin off, comin back into the United States, and cut the buttons and armaments off of their clothes, make em get out of them clothes, make em pull them uniforms off and if they didn't have another suit of clothes . . . make em walk in their underwear. I know it was done, I heard too much of it from the ones that come back to this country even. You a damn nigger right on, didn't give you no credit for what you done.[11]

The fear of blacks adopting "highfalutin" ideas about their place in society extended to common social usages. The very terms by which blacks and whites addressed each other and the etiquette governing conversations between them were designed to reinforce the acknowledged superiority of one race and the inferiority of the other. Conventional terms of respect, such as "Mister," "Missus," or "Miss," while demanded at all times of blacks addressing whites, were rarely used by whites in addressing black men and women. It was customary for whites to address blacks, regardless of their age, education, or income, by first names and nicknames, or, if not known to them, as "boy" or "girl," or simply as "nigger." White newspapers adopted these common usages, refusing, for example, to extend to black women the same courtesies extended to white women. A Kentucky newspaper reported as educational news the resignation of "Mrs. Mattie Spring Barr" as a substitute teacher and the election of "Miss Ella Williams," both of them white women; several paragraphs later, it announced the promotion of "Lizzie Brooks" as a regular teacher and "Annie B. Jones" as a substitute, both of them black women. In Bolivar County, Mississippi, as late as the 1930s, postal workers made a point of deleting the term "Mr." on the envelopes of mail sent to black residents.[12]

If whites customarily addressed Negroes in terms of familiarity, no matter how little they knew them, blacks were expected to treat whites of all classes with due respect and deference. Although "massa" would be rarely used after emancipation, some blacks simply substituted "cap'n" or "boss," and these terms found ready acceptance among whites, as they clearly acknowledged the relations of superiors and inferiors. In addressing whites they knew more intimately, such as those for whom they worked, blacks might be permitted to call them by the first name, but only if it was preceded by "Mister," "Missus," or "Miss," as in "Yes, suh, Mister William," or "Yes, ma'am, Miss Caroline."[13]

Racial etiquette demanded of blacks a deference in the presence of whites that they should not expect whites to reciprocate. The chivalry and social courtesies white southern men showed toward white women would rarely if ever be extended by them to black women. The rules of racial etiquette, moreover, frowned on any familiar physical contact, such as shaking hands or a friendly embrace. The same unwritten rules compelled blacks to wait in stores to be served only after all white persons had been accommodated, and commanded blacks to remove their hats in the presence of whites. To make absolutely clear their servile place, black men and women—domestic workers, for example—were to approach and be admitted into the homes of whites only through the back door. "It would have been accepting Negroes as equals if whites had allowed them to enter the front door," one black South Carolinian remembered, and still another recalled "seeing Negroes go to the back door of a white man's house even when the white people were sitting on the front porch."[14]

Any breakdown in linguistic Jim Crow, whether in the terms or the tone blacks used in addressing whites, came to be perceived as "impudence" and "impertinence," symptomatic of a larger breakdown in the deference and subordination demanded and expected of black men and women. Even during "the orgies" of Reconstruction, a North Carolina white man reminded a friend, the old terms of address had remained in common use. "[B]ut now," he lamented around 1913, "these outward signs of deference are nearly always *positively omitted.*" He noted, too, the frequency with which whites referred to blacks as "colored people" and avoided the use of "nigger" as taboo. These changes clearly disturbed him. "Some might insist this is really a very unimportant matter, but it very clearly indicates not only a change in conditions, but what is more important by far, the *direction in which we are drifting. . . .*" Thinking about his own household, William Watts Ball, a South Carolina editor, observed that the servants tended now to use more formal titles, such as "Mrs. Ball," while the "older negroes" still used the permissible "Miss Fay" or "Miss Liza" to address whites for whom they worked. "Does the change," he wondered, "indicate that the negroes are gaining in pride, losing in servility?"[15]

Perhaps nothing blacks said symbolized more the perceived breakdown in race relations at the turn of the century than what they did not say with such regularity—the terms of deference they appeared to be dropping. The fear persisted that permitting blacks such liberties destabilized proper relations between the races and suggested social equality, and whites acted on that fear. A municipal court in Wilmington, North Carolina, fined Christopher Brooks for persistently referring to Negroes with the prefix "Mr.," "Mrs.," and "Miss." Unable to pay the fine, he was committed to the workhouse. When Richard Foster, who enjoyed a reputation as "a man of intelligence and education," wrote a letter to the local merchant from whom he purchased supplies asking that the merchant address him as "Mr. Foster" rather than "Dick," he couched the request in polite terms. But the merchant was so indignant

over this "impudence" that he circulated the letter among local businessmen, all of whom shared his anger. Realizing he was in trouble,
Foster wrote another letter apologizing for his "indiscretion," but the
damage had been done. Faced with violence, Foster chose to leave town
immediately; friends arranged to send his wife and goods. "I know Dick
was a smart nigger," said one resident, "but he was no better than any
other nigger. You Northern people don't understand this matter. If you
would come down here and live six months, you'd see it just as we do."
When James T. Williams, Jr., whose father served as mayor of
Greenville, South Carolina, obtained an interview in Washington,
D.C., with Judson W. Lyons, a Georgian serving as register of the Treasury, he was astonished when a "great big mulatto" advanced to meet
him and introduced himself as "Mr. Lyons." He found him to be "an
awfully polite fellow" and an efficient administrator who wielded considerable power. "However next time I call I will not emphasize so emphatically as I did before the *Mister* in asking for him."[16]

The racial code tolerated—within limits—attaching titles to the
names of black professionals. A black physician, for example, might be
addressed as "Doctor" but never as "Mister." All too often, however, if
whites extended a dignified term to blacks, they did so as a humorous
gesture, designed only to mock their pretensions, as in calling a barely
educated one-room country schoolteacher "Professor," or by adding
"Esquire" to the name of a black lawyer. When it came to a dignitary
such as Booker T. Washington, whites found a convenient way out, particularly after Harvard offered him an honorary degree. "Now I admire
Booker Washington," a white told a northern visitor. "I regard him as a
great man, and yet I couldn't call him Mr. Washington. We were all in a
quandary until a doctor's degree was given him. That saved our lives!
We call him 'Dr.' Washington now." When Joseph W. Holley, a black
college president, sought favors from a prominent local white, he did
not introduce himself as "Mr. Holley" but as "Professor Holley." That
usage posed no problem for whites.[17]

Few aspects of linguistic Jim Crow were more resented than the custom of whites addressing black adults as "boy" and "girl" and older
blacks as "Aunt" and "Uncle." William "Big Bill" Broonzy, born in
1893 in Mississippi, recalled from his youth a thirty-year-old man
whom white people invariably called "boy." When Broonzy went into
the army and returned in 1919, white people were calling the same person "Uncle Mackray." "So he never got to be called a man," Broonzy
reflected; he simply went from "boy" to "Uncle Mackray."[18]

If the ways in which blacks addressed whites took on additional meaning, so did the efforts of blacks to improve their immediate environment. That is, the hostility that greeted black "pretentiousness" in language and clothes might also be visited on black efforts to upgrade their furnishings or the exterior of their homes. Such efforts not only contradicted white assumptions about blacks preferring to live in hovels but also suggested an inferior race getting out of its place, "trying to be white." After building "a nice house," one black owner complied with the advice of local whites that he not paint it; he concluded that such a course of action would be more conducive to his "personal safety." It made perfect sense to a black school principal in Mississippi that a black property owner would think twice before painting or refurbishing his house. "[T]he fact remains," he observed, "that a Negro did not always feel as safe in a neat cottage with attractive surroundings as he did in a tumbling-down shack."[19]

The introduction of automobiles in the early twentieth century made their purchase and use by blacks an immediate problem, as possession of a car set the owners apart from much of the population and placed black drivers on the same roads as whites. Henry Watson, a prosperous black farmer in Georgia, acquired a car and drove with his daughter into the nearest town. Finding this sight too unsettling, local residents forced them at gunpoint to get out of the car, poured gasoline on it, and set it on fire, insulted Watson's daughter, and told both of them, "From now on, you niggers walk into town, or use that ole mule if you want to stay in this city." A Macon, Georgia, newspaper in 1917 reported at least four incidents in which black owners of automobiles were beaten and warned to dispose of their vehicles. After another incident in which a "well-to-do Negro" promptly agreed to white demands that he return the automobile he had recently purchased, a black newspaper in New Orleans protested that in some places blacks were also not permitted to carry hoisted umbrellas or ride in top buggies, presumably because such displays, like the automobile, suggested putting on airs. In Abbeville, South Carolina, three years after the murder of Anthony Crawford for being "prosperous" and "uppity," a mob confronted Mark Smith, a black resident, while he was driving his car with his wife, mother, and children. The mob blocked the road and shot Smith repeatedly as he tried to escape. Seeking to find some motive for the murder, a black resident could only conclude, "[I]t lookes as if they dont want to see the colored people advance or progress to eny extent."[20]

When blacks began to appear as chauffeurs, whites seemed undecided about whether to regard it as a service position they could tolerate. Some regarded such blacks as out of place and providing a bad example. "If Negroes will stick to their plows instead of learning to operate autos," a Superior Court judge in Macon, Georgia, declared, "they and the South will be better off. It depreciates the general efficiency of the Negro race. . . ." His remarks, in refusing to dismiss a warrant against a black driver, elicited a response from a black newspaper in Washington, D.C.: "Yes, the faster the Southern black man rises the more the Southern crackers dislike it."[21]

4

THE DEMANDS OF white supremacy exerted a profound impact on the physical environment in which black men and women lived and on the bodily perils they were forced to endure. Laws, ordinances, and custom, along with an absence of political power, dictated where blacks could reside, the municipal facilities to which they had access, and the quality of health care they could expect.

To find the black neighborhood in almost any town or city, one needed no map or signs. The streets in black districts were seldom if ever paved, and in rainstorms they were certain to turn into quagmires of mud. The housing was the least desirable, sometimes places discarded by whites. Born in "the Bottoms," a section of Knoxville, Tennessee, James Robinson remembered the houses in which blacks lived as "hardly more than rickety shacks clustered on stilts like Daddy Long Legs along the slimy bank of putrid and evil-smelling 'Cripple Creek.'" Encircled by the creek, the tobacco warehouses, a foundry, and slaughter pens, the black neighborhood "was a world set apart and excluded." When the winds blew in its direction, the combined stench of the outhouses and slaughter pens became "unbearable."[22]

Consigned by rigid custom if not by law to deteriorating and disease-ridden neighborhoods, most blacks paid a heavy price in living standards that were far beneath those enjoyed by whites of the same social class. Authorities did little or nothing to provide services such as pavements or sewage to politically powerless blacks. It proved both easy and convenient for whites to explain the substandard and unhealthy structures in which blacks lived as a natural consequence of inherent racial deficiencies. Unlike white immigrants, blacks found it nearly impossible to escape these neighborhoods, even when they could afford to do so. Realtors, if they assisted blacks at all, differentiated between "white property" and "colored property," and those blacks who tried to rent or purchase property in white neighborhoods faced not only social ostracism but also violence.[23]

Even in a relatively modern city such as Atlanta, the showcase of the New South, much of the black population was confined to dilapidated housing in narrow alleyways. Not only did these "cheerless" boxes make for cramped living quarters, but also few of them had running water, forcing the residents to rely on often contaminated well water. The black-populated neighborhoods seldom had sewerage connections, and the wastes (including much of the drainage from the elevated white residential and business sections) piled up in small, stagnant streams and foul-smelling pools in backyards and streets, becoming natural breeding places for malaria-bearing mosquitoes. A small number of urban blacks achieved sufficient success as businessmen and professionals to permit them to purchase more substantial places, but most black people—the working class—had to survive as best they could under circumstances that would have tested the endurance of the most enterprising family. Middle-class blacks, whatever their incomes or occupations, found it difficult to move outside the black urban enclaves. "The result of all this crowding," W. E. B. Du Bois wrote after a thorough study of Atlanta, "is bad health, poor family life, and crime. . . . The high death rate of the Negro is directly traceable to these slum districts."[24]

None of this weighed heavily, if at all, on white consciences. Claiming as they did an intimate knowledge of black people, whites insisted to visitors and persuaded themselves that Negroes preferred to live this way and aspired to nothing better. But even as whites took refuge in such stale arguments, mortality rates revealed disproportionate numbers of blacks dying from diseases—primarily tuberculosis, pneumonia, typhoid fever, and diarrheal diseases—which gained an easy foothold in weakened and undernourished bodies and which had their roots in filth, ignorance, and poverty. The Atlanta Board of Health reported in 1900 that the black death rate exceeded the white death rate by 69 percent. Of 431 black children born that year, some 194, or 45 percent, died before their first birthday, usually from preventable and treatable childhood diseases.[25]

For a time, white indifference and black powerlessness crippled efforts to improve the conditions breeding disease in black enclaves. White officials preferred to view the disproportionate death rates as confirmation of the biological and moral inferiority of blacks. When in 1908 the Atlanta Chamber of Commerce expressed concern over the city's high death rate, the president of the board of health responded that what "appears to be an abnormal death rate" could be easily explained by the large black population, "with their notoriously unhygienic and insanitary modes of living, and their established susceptibility to disease, especially of infant classes." Unlike whites, the official suggested, blacks had little resistance to disease and no natural concern for personal cleanliness; the black race, in his estimation, was marked for extermination by diseases resulting from its contact with civilization.[26]

When whites finally moved to improve sanitary conditions in black Atlanta, they did so for two paramount reasons: concern for the city's reputation and, most important, the fear that unhygienic conditions in black neighborhoods might jeopardize the health of white residents. The *Atlanta Constitution* made as clear as possible why white citizens needed to act:

> Because from that segregated district negro nurses would still emerge from diseased homes, to come into our homes and hold our children in their arms; negro cooks would still bring bacilli from the segregated district into the homes of the poor and the rich white Atlantan; negro chauffeurs, negro butlers, negro laborers would come from within the pale and scatter disease with the same old lavishness; into that district would go the clothes of white families, to be laundered in environments possibly reeking with filth and disease.
>
> The disease germ knows no color or race line. . . .[27]

The compelling need of whites to maintain their supremacy by any means necessary compounded the health hazards incurred by black men and women. Jim Crow virtually dictated inadequate and inferior medical care. Keeping the races apart in hospitals was mandatory, and some excluded blacks altogether. Few black physicians practiced in the South, and most of them were concentrated in the towns and cities, forcing blacks to rely primarily on white doctors willing to treat them. The barriers facing an aspiring black physician helped to explain their scarcity. Of the fourteen black medical colleges founded between 1868 and 1900, only two—Howard University Medical Department in Washington, D.C., and Meharry Medical College in Nashville—survived into the 1920s. Despite the desperate need for black physicians, the notion of blacks training in white medical schools in the South was unthinkable. Surveyed about their policies in the early twentieth century, most such schools replied that no blacks would be admitted. But some went further and made clear their objections. The Baltimore Medical College thought even one black pupil would be "a great injury to our class on entering," while the College of Physicians and Surgeons of Baltimore insisted that it "does not, never has, and never will admit Negroes to its lecture halls and work." The medical school at the University of Georgia vowed, "There are no niggers in this school and there never have been and there never will be as long as one stone of its building remains upon another." And the dean of the Hospital College of Medicine in Louisville boasted that it had "never matriculated a 'coon' in all its history and never will so long as I am Dean."[28]

On the eve of World War I, a race promotion book hailed the increase in black physicians over the past thirty years. But the authors acknowledged a vast racial gulf in the proportion of white and black doctors to their respective populations: one white physician for every three hundred whites, one black physician for every nine thousand blacks. When black medical colleges held their commencements, prominent black citizens from the South's major cities as well as the small hamlets actively courted the new graduates. "This institution and others of similar character," noted the president of the medical college in Raleigh, "cannot begin to meet the calls that are coming constantly for trained physicians and pharmacists." The arrival in any southern community of a black doctor, like a black teacher, often qualified as a major event. "My God, what is dis here town coming to," a black woman in Indianola, Mississippi, exclaimed, about the same time President Theodore Roosevelt chose to appoint a black postmaster. "Dese white foks just now getting ober habing 'er nigger Postmaster and now here comes 'er nigger Doctor—Did Ros'velt send 'm 'ere too?"[29]

Upon securing an education, black graduates needed to find a hospital that would accept them as interns. In some areas, the suspicion persisted, for good reason, that whites discouraged the presence of black professionals, deeming them unwanted competitors and potential troublemakers. Medical examiners in Mississippi had the reputation for routinely failing black dentists and doctors, particularly if they were not native Southerners, and several communities in that state expelled physicians deemed "too prosperous." When an aspiring young black physician proposed to establish a practice in Columbia, Missouri, a local white physician warned him that "the practice among your people is done by white brethren in the profession and it would be a mighty hard thing for a man of your age and most especially your color to wring it from their hands." To discourage any potential clientele for competing black physicians, white doctors might also question their competence. A white doctor in Tennessee explained to a visitor in 1920 "that the negro mind is incapable of any considerable development, and Dr. A, being a colored man, is not to be seriously regarded as a real physician. He is a good negro, but still a negro." Aspiring black physicians also learned to stay away from certain areas where they were clearly unwanted. The president of the medical college in Raleigh had to explain to the residents of a South Carolina town why they would find it difficult to attract a black physician: "The fact is, Colored physicians do not desire to settle in South Carolina. You, of course, understand why without my saying anything further. I wish it were not so."[30]

Upon graduating from medical school, then, black physicians still faced formidable odds. They arrived at their initial post with few possessions and financial means, many of them still paying off debts accrued from their education. They needed to rent an office or work from their homes and establish a following. They found a mostly impoverished clientele, they needed to compete with established white doctors who might resent their competition, and they sensed with good reason that any mistaken diagnosis or treatment would immediately call into question their competence to practice medicine. Of the few whites who patronized them, most were poor; in some communities, however, the black physician developed a reputation for treating venereal diseases, attracting whites of all classes. "When a young fellow of the aristocratic class, and this is an aristocratic town, gets siphilis [sic] or gonorrhea," a pharmacist in Tennessee revealed, "he usually goes to this negro [physician] and so avoids the embarrassment of submitting such a case to a friend of the family."[31]

Not only did black physicians struggle to secure the toleration of whites, they also needed to obtain the confidence of blacks, who, if given the choice, preferred white doctors. "I started my practice here with considerable opposition from my own people," a Meharry graduate said of his first days in Baton Rouge in 1887. Even as many black

Southerners thought they would fare better in the courts with a white lawyer, they were more willing to trust their bodies and lives to white physicians. "The poor colored doctor didn't have a chance," a black Mississippian recalled, "because we wouldn't feel like we had a doctor unless he was white." That also meant that blacks who could afford to pay more tended to single out white doctors, leaving black physicians with the poorest clients.[32]

The preference for white doctors made perfect sense. No doubt blacks knew that white doctors had access to advanced medical procedures and facilities from which black doctors were excluded, and that few white doctors would willingly consult with or assist their black counterparts. Local and state medical societies also barred them, few black hospitals existed, and white hospitals forced black physicians to turn over patients who required hospitalization (usually for surgery) to whites, affording black physicians no opportunity to improve their medical skills or reputations. "We realize that we are put to a great disadvantage when we have cases to operate upon and have no hospital," a North Carolina physician told a black medical convention in 1910. "We are obliged to turn [patients] over to white physicians and when we do this it is hard for our people to have the proper interest and confidence in us."[33]

Sufficient numbers of black physicians prevailed over the odds, survived, and prospered to inspire others to believe they could succeed as well. But the effects of Jim Crow and the demands of white supremacy still took their inevitable toll on the health and physical endurance of black Southerners. Henry Baker, born a slave in Alabama in 1854, summed up in the 1930s the quality of medical care he had found in his lifetime. "When a 'body got sick, 'stead uv all sleepin' wid de sick pusson dey made a pallet on de floor fuh de sick pusson. Whut yuh ast me 'bout horspitals fur? Dere wont no horspitals. De only 'horspitals' 'niggers' had in dem days wuz when dey took dem out o' de house tuh de graveyard yasser dat wuz de next place dey took em. Yuh see de horspitals fer 'niggers' is er brand new field."[34]

5

THE EXACTIONS OF Jim Crow compounded an already difficult and demanding situation for working-class black women. Most of them inhabited a world very much apart from that of middle-class women.

Deprived of the amenities of a middle-class way of life, they could not share most middle-class ideals. Within their neighborhoods they waged a losing battle against filth and disease. Prevailing notions and expectations concerning the "place" of women crossed racial and class lines. Males were expected to demonstrate manly virtues of physical prowess, leadership, and aggressiveness, while females were expected to be deferential, submissive, and dependent, and to be responsive at all times to the needs and demands of men.

If they shared with black men a distinct and inferior place in southern society, black women occupied as well a prescribed place in the black home. When black men moved after emancipation to establish themselves as the center of authority in the family, women were expected to accede to an arrangement already firmly established in white households. The Freedmen's Bureau recognized the dominant position of the black husband and his right to contract on behalf of the family, and that right remained in place long after Reconstruction. Under sharecropping, members of the family tended to divide the labor, and the women assumed as well primary responsibility for the domestic household. Freedmen's Bureau officials, along with black leaders, clergymen, and editors, reinforced such roles in the advice they extended to black women. Like their white counterparts, black women were admonished to learn how to perform their household duties and tend to the needs of their men, even as they made themselves look "as pretty as possible" and reared the children in virtuous habits.[35]

Economic survival and domestic duties were not the only burdens black women had to bear. Even as lurid charges of rape were being leveled at black men, the experience of black women at the turn of the century reflected more than two centuries of white sexual abuse and violence. Compelled to supplement the family income by working in white homes, black women all too often had to deal with the sexual demands of males if they hoped to retain their positions. "I believe nearly all white men take, and expect to take, undue liberties with their colored female servants," a black servant observed in 1912, "not only the fathers, but in many cases the sons also. Those servants who rebel against such familiarity must either leave or expect a mighty hard time if they stay." This woman had already lost a position because she had rejected the advances of the head of the house. "I was young then, and newly married, and didn't know then what has been a burden to my mind and heart ever since: that a colored woman's virtue in this part of the country has no protection."[36]

Women working outside of white homes were by no means immune to the advances and abuse of white men. Since they mostly labored in service positions, they were almost always vulnerable. Working as a waitress and chambermaid in a hotel in Clemson, South Carolina, patronized largely by salesmen and by men who worked at the nearby college, Jane Hunter found herself engaged in "constant battle against unwanted advances." Each day demanded of her the utmost vigilance. She had to learn how to anticipate problems, how to ignore "impudent glances," how to respond to "insulting questions," and how to avoid being in an isolated place. When she entered a room to clean it, she had to exercise the utmost caution: "I pushed the door wide open and looked into every nook and corner to make sure no one was lurking there."[37]

The exploitation of black women by white men for sexual gratification had deep historical roots, and like many aspects of the "peculiar institution" this practice endured long after the Civil War. While black males sought to reassert their authority as head of the family, white males retained and acted on many of the assumptions and attitudes that had sustained their previous relations with black women. More often than not, a sense of powerlessness frustrated the efforts of black Southerners to resist white sexual aggression. The experience could never be expunged from their memories, nor could the conscious failure of legal authorities to bring any action against white male aggressors and abusers.

When whites "courted" black women for sexual pleasure, they sometimes competed with black men for the same woman, raping or humiliating her even if she had a husband or lover. The efforts of black males to check white advances might easily provoke a violent reprisal. Although a married woman with children, a Georgia house servant protested in vain the advances of her employer. When her husband confronted him over his insulting behavior, the angry verbal exchange that followed resulted in the arrest of the black man. After hearing conflicting versions of what had taken place, the police judge fined the black man $25, and he had no difficulty explaining his decision. "This court," he declared, "will never take the word of a nigger against the word of a white man."[38]

White men consciously used charges of rape as a weapon to reinforce the subordination of the black male, to remind him of his powerlessness and inferiority as well as the woman's. It was a way of asserting their power, when they chose to do so, over the entire family. "[I]f one of our men look at a white woman very hard and she complains he is lynched for it," an Alabama black pastor observed; "white men on the high ways and in their stores and on the trains will insult our women and we are powerless to resent it as it would only be an invitation for our lives to be taken."[39]

For a black woman to resist the advances of a white man, and for a black man to intervene in such cases, invited instant retaliation. Still, by the late nineteenth century, the threat of such intervention by black men, the growing numbers who acted on that threat, and the resistance of black women succeeded in diminishing interracial sexual contacts. A growing perception among white males that they ran the risk of contracting venereal disease was also said to have discouraged sexual activity. But a former Tennessee slaveholder insisted in 1900 that it was not so much "fear of disease" as the possibility of black male intervention that inhibited white sexual overtures. "[T]he negro [male] will not let them [white men] have it," he observed. "[I]f a [black] woman comes into a store, and there is a white man standing around, there will be a half a dozen colored men in front of the store waiting for her."[40]

The racial assumptions embraced by whites conveniently exonerated them from complicity in the debasement of black women. The hysteria over rape in the late nineteenth and early twentieth centuries clearly focused on black male aggressors and white female victims. That was the only issue, more than sufficient to justify unspeakable atrocities, as any violence inflicted on the body of a black man paled in comparison to the sexual offense he had allegedly committed. But even as white men venerated their women as the repositories of virtue and purity, some of them saw no contradiction in violating the bodies and minds of black women, in keeping black mistresses, and in patronizing black-run houses of prostitution.

The double standard infuriated blacks, who were quick to sense that many of the foremost defenders of southern virtue and chivalry applied their lofty standards to everyone but themselves. Whites seemed incapable of grasping the fundamental hypocrisy that condemned black rape of white women and condoned or ignored white rape of black women. For a black man, a sexual advance to a white woman was a certain invitation to a tortured death. For a white man, the exploitation of a black woman for his sexual initiation or pleasure enjoyed community toleration. The most expedient way to dispose of the issue was to deny the existence of the white rapist, as black women were said to give themselves willingly, even wantonly, to white men. Not all whites actually believed this argument, however, even if they routinely invoked it for public consumption. While condemning black rape in no uncertain terms, some whites suggested that blacks had been provoked not by white women but by white men taking liberties with black women and thereby inviting retaliation. When T. W. Walker, a Georgia black man, was sentenced to death for killing a wealthy white planter, the first news dispatches could find no reason for the attack; a black newspaper editor, however, charged that the planter had brutally assaulted Walker's wife. Before Walker could be removed from the courtroom, he was shot by the planter's brother; severely wounded, he was then hanged. The planter's brother escaped prosecution but not the black editor, who was immediately arrested for libel.[41]

Most blacks understood that the "rape complex" obsessing whites involved much more than imagined or actual assaults on white women. In the neighborhood in which he grew up, James Robinson remembered street talk about white women who were sexually attracted to black men. Outraged over that attraction, it was said, white men acted out their sexual insecurities when they butchered black men and women. "Negroes were lynched," Robinson heard, "not because they had committed crimes but because white men wanted to put fear in their hearts and keep it there." For making essentially the same argument—that interracial sex might bond consenting white women and black men—Ida B. Wells would be forced into exile in the North. "White men lynch the offending Afro-American," she wrote, "not because he is a despoiler of virtue, but because he succumbs to the smiles of white women."[42]

Within the community, talk also centered around white prostitutes who plied their trade in the black neighborhoods to which they had been ostracized and black women prostitutes who catered to an exclusive white clientele and enjoyed, as a result, some unique privileges. "When I was a boy in the South," a black North Carolinian remembered, "the most popular Negro woman (among the whites) of my town was the courtesan." Not only would the houses of prostitution operated by black women serve white men exclusively, but also the house madams often enjoyed a privileged social position in the community, able as they were to "enter any store and receive more attention than the wife of a Negro legislator." In a few instances, black men concerned over white sexual hypocrisy took matters into their hands; they seized any white men found "in company" with black women and whipped both parties.[43]

In assuming the protection of their women, black and white men asserted a traditional masculine role, essential to their self-esteem and self-respect. The rhetoric underscoring that role often advanced the same rights of exclusive guardianship. When asked what his people wanted, a black carpenter in Montgomery, Alabama, demanded the same right as a white man to protect his wife and daughter against assaults by male predators. "That is what we want, to protect the virtue of our girls. That is the rights I want. I don't want no social equality with the white people, and I don't want them to have none with me."[44] Conservative, accommodationist Alabama educator William Councill, who made a point of not saying anything out of order in the presence of whites, employed his own unique style to address this question. He offered to make a contract with the white race: "We, the Negroes, agree on our part, to hang by the neck until dead, every colored man who violates the seventh commandment with a white woman, if you, the white people, will agree to punish *according to law* every white man who violates the seventh commandment with a colored woman. So help us God." Councill still perpetuated a curious double standard: Black offenders would be lynched, white offenders would be punished *"according to law."* Nor did his eloquent defense of womanhood leave much room for women of his own race:

> We must make the humblest white woman in the remotest and wildest part of our country feel as safe in the presence of a negro, as angelic Eva did alone with Uncle Tom. Let us make the white women of this land and of all lands, feel that our black arms are ever ready—backed by hearts as pure as truth, as guiltless as babes, to defend their honor, that we are willing to throw our black bodies between them and their assailants and shed our blood to the last drop in protecting them, and hunting down and executing these brutes in human form.

Little wonder that his sentiments, when he presented them to a black audience, created such a "long wrangle."[45]

Men of both races found urgent reasons to embellish the image of the woman, placing her even more firmly on the pedestal and asserting the same quality of paternal concern and protection. In rushing to the "defense" of their women, they sought at the same time to reassert their control and domination. The woman they exalted was not the "new," independent, and spirited woman who was questioning her constricted role in society and moving into spheres hitherto the domain of males but the submissive and vulnerable woman who displayed the feminine virtues esteemed in the "weaker sex." The hysteria over black rapists, actively fed and encouraged by leading white politicians and editors, reinforced the dependence of white women on their men. The valor and sacrifice a new generation of white men had been denied by being too young to serve in the Civil War could now be redeemed on a different but no less critical battlefield in defense of southern womanhood.

If whites could rush to the "defense" of their women, so could black men reassure black women. Rather than covet white standards of beauty, men were urged to express pride in the women of their race. William Pickens, a native of South Carolina and an early NAACP organizer, proclaimed the black woman "the most virtuous creature in the United States of America. . . . Her resisting and enduring powers are of the highest order." Rather than seek out white women for companions, black men demanded only that they be given the exclusive right to patrol the behavior and morals of their own women. "What do we want with their daughters and sisters?" asked Henry M. Turner in the aftermath of emancipation. "We have as much beauty as they. Look at our ladies, do you want more beauty than that? *All we ask of the white man is to let our ladies alone,* and they need not fear us. The difficulty has heretofore been, *our ladies were not always at our own disposal.*"[46]

Within the black community, spokesmen advised black men to show the same respect and deference to black women that they showed in public to white women. The term "ladies," they were told, was not reserved for whites only. "When we use the word 'ladies,' " one observer noted, "it is generally understood by colored people to mean white women, only, but they never give any tangible reason for it." That was as unacceptable as greeting white women in public by bowing slightly and doffing one's cap while giving black women only a nod of one's head. "When we make such distinctions ourselves, what can we expect of the white man?" one black etiquette manual advised, even as it admonished black men not to make too conspicuous a display, no matter how well intended, around white women:

Colored men, don't you know that white men don't like too much gallantry from negro men around their women any more than negro men like too much of it from white men around theirs? If you don't know it, I do. Be consistent; if you doff your hat to the one, doff it to the other.[47]

The need to protect the virtue of black women provided the theme for many an editorial, sermon, and lecture. At the same time, black women were expected to reciprocate such protection by policing their appearance and moral behavior. *"She must be kept clean: and she must keep herself clean, at all hazards and at every cost,"* a Methodist clergyman and native of New Orleans insisted in 1892. His "hot African blood" boiled with rage, he added, over the ways in which white men insulted black women, and he urged vigilance on his people. *"We must learn that the purity of woman is the purity of the family; and the purity of the family is the purity of race: and whosoever dares to touch the character of a single girl, or is a foe to the purity of the family, is an enemy of the race and in league with hell."* That "enemy," of course, might be a white man, and the editor of a black newspaper forcefully reminded whites that respect for womanhood was a mutual obligation that crossed racial lines. "We want our ladies respected. . . . White men make us respect white ladies, and they must make white men respect ours."[48]

Whatever the fervent rhetoric on both sides, it could not hide a fundamental truth: No matter how white men chose to rationalize their aberrant sexual behavior, no matter how the white community chose to confine its response to smirks and grins of acknowledgment, black women assumed the greatest risks of sexual abuse, and only black men had to pay the ultimate penalty for interracial sexual relations. Only rarely were any white men convicted of raping a black woman. Even to contemplate meting out such a punishment to white males contradicted a maxim that enjoyed almost universal acceptance in the white South: Black women were naturally licentious, making rape redundant. "A colored woman, however respectable, is lower than the white prostitute," an Alabama black woman observed in 1902, and she thought it highly ironic that southern white women insisted no Negro female was virtuous, yet willingly placed their innocent children in her care.[49] The same set of assumptions that denied that any black woman could be raped asserted that no white woman would voluntarily consent to interracial sex, and hence any white woman who had sexual intercourse with a black man had to be a victim of rape.

Like their male counterparts, most white women embraced the dominant racial values and attitudes. Some of them goaded white men into action against potential black aggressors by shaming them for their negligence and by comparing them unfavorably to their fathers who had fought in the war. The issues that might have bonded women of both races, such as temperance, moral reform, and suffrage gave way to a virulent racial consciousness that made such cooperation sporadic and restrictive. Few white women, in fact, chose to view black women, including those who worked for them, as persons with complex feelings and strong family attachments. Nor did white women differ from men in assuming the natural licentiousness of black women. An Alabama white woman claimed to have known in her lifetime but one black woman she believed to be chaste. "I have always had black servants, and I am ready not only to affirm but to prove that there was not one of them who did not have illegitimate children or was not herself an illegitimate; generally both were true." She professed to see no improvement in the new generation over their slave ancestors—"they are only less excusable." Nor in her estimation could the legacy of slavery explain loose morals among black women. "To this day most of them lack that divine energy of goodness which repels the very suggestion of evil."[50]

But to believe black observers, that "divine energy of goodness" was conspicuously absent in the white community. The daughter of a former slave cited in 1904 as all too typical the "white haired veteran[s] of sin" who—"out of sight of their own women"—preyed on black womanhood. "Yes," she emphasized, "men high in position, whose wives and daughters are leaders of society. I have had a clerk in a store hold my hand as I gave him the money for some purchase and utter some vile request; a shoe man to take liberties, a man in a crowd to place his hands on my person, others to follow me to my very door, a school director to assure me a position if I did his bidding."[51]

Even as black women endured insults and humiliations at the hands of white males, they needed to confront the demands and expectations of black men determined to exercise control. Soon after emancipation, the Freedmen's Bureau recorded, along with newly legalized marriages, the grievances of newly freed black women, most of them examples of white physical abuse, some of them appeals for protection against abuse by husbands and other black men. The same complaints pervaded recollections of former slaves about how they fared after emancipation.

My ole man got so trifling and mean that I quit him and worked for myself.

Dat was the meanest niggah dat ever lived. He would slip up behin' me when I was wukin' in the fiel' an beat me.

He got to runnin around with a ole 'oman. She got all his money. All I ever got was a beating and babies.

I got so I dreaded to see him coming, but I wuz nearly as big as him and I wasnt gonna stand no misabusin. I'd fights him back.[52]

Quarreling, infidelity, spousal abuse, separation, and desertion afflicted white and black families of all social classes. But tensions within working-class black families could be particularly pronounced in an age in which expectations were repeatedly betrayed. Confinement to cramped living quarters and the struggle to eke out a living, compounded by the depredations of whites (both sexual and nonsexual), the exactions of sharecropping, the loss of political power, and the humiliations of Jim Crow strained marriages and made in many instances for a volatile situation. Forced to conceal their anger and wear the mask in the presence of whites, black men found other ways to vent their frustration, and the victims might be those closest to them. When Nathaniel Wright deserted his wife and two children, six-year-old Richard could remember only the pangs of hunger, "and whenever I felt hunger I thought of him with a deep biological bitterness." All too often Ned Cobb had to look on helplessly as his mother and stepmother endured beatings from his father. "If I had a twenty-dollar bill this mornin for every time I seed my daddy beat up my mother and beat up my stepmother I wouldn't be settin here this mornin because I'd have up in the hundreds of dollars. Each one of them women—I didn't see no cause for it. I don't expect it ever come in my daddy's mind what his children thought about it or how they would remember him for it, but that was a poor example, to stamp and beat up children's mothers right before em."[53]

Much like their white counterparts, black males might lash out at women for no reason other than to exercise a male prerogative and to subdue independent spirits. Benjamin Mays recalled his father's hot temperament and the number of times "we children had to hold him to keep him from hurting Mother." If his mother had remained silent during his father's harangues, Benjamin recalled, the arguments might have been fewer. "But Mother had to talk back. Our sympathy was with her." Zora Neale Hurston also came to admire her mother's ability to stand up to threats while asserting her own brand of independence, as when she outraged her husband by telling him that if he did not want to support her and the children, "there was another man over the fence waiting for his job." Louis Armstrong recalled domestic violence, exchanged insults, the bloodied face of his mother, and being shunted from one place to another during marital breakups. "All I had to do was turn my back and a new 'pappy' would appear. Some of them were fine guys, but others were low lives." One day a friend named Cocaine Buddy rushed up to him as he was leaving school to tell him someone was beating his mother; he dropped his books and ran home, hurt the man enough to send him to the hospital, and that was the last time he or his mother saw him.[54]

Many black couples were able to sustain a lasting, loving marriage, with the woman employing various strategies to balance the demands of labor and family. Some did the best they could under adverse conditions that could destabilize the best of relationships. Black women reformers in the late nineteenth century also did what they could to inculcate working-class women with Christian principles of industriousness, sobriety, frugality, and unblemished moral character. But for most such women, the advice, although well-intended, had little relevance to their day-to-day lives. "My ole man, he was a field worker," a South Carolina black woman explained. "He's a good man, but he's rough an' low down. I'm shore married to him though, and I got to make the bes' of a bad bargain."[55]

Upon hearing that some whites proposed erecting statues in memory of the "Old Black Mammies," a Georgia black woman mocked this narrow and distorted view of black womanhood. "What we need," she suggested, was not nostalgia about an invented past but "present help, present sympathy, better wages, better hours, more protection, and a chance to breathe for once while alive as free women." That would not be easy, she acknowledged, as black women bore a disproportionate share of the black burden. "On the one hand, we are assailed by white men, and on the other hand, we are assailed by black men, who should be our natural protectors; and whether in the cook kitchen, at the washtub, over the sewing machine, behind the baby carriage or at the ironing board, we are but little more than pack horses, beasts of burden, slaves!"[56] On the Georgia Sea Islands, women complained of bearing a number of burdens while trying to comply with the expectation that they pick a hundred pounds of cotton each day.

> *Black man beat me—white man cheat me*
> *Won' get my hundud all day*
> *Black man beat me—white man cheat me*
> *Won' get my hundud all day.*[57]

Several decades later, Zora Neale Hurston, who had left Eatonville, Florida, for New York City, had not forgotten her roots in the characters she created for her novels and short stories, such as a former slave revealing to her granddaughter the kind of world she was entering.

> Honey, de white man is de ruler of everything as fur as Ah been able tuh find out. Maybe it's some place way off in de ocean where de black man is in power, but we don't know nothin' but what we see. So de white man throw down de load and tell de nigger man tuh pick it up. He pick it up because he have to, but he don't tote it. He hand it to his womenfolks. De nigger woman is de mule uh de world as fur as Ah can see. Ah been prayin' fuh it tuh be different wid you. Lawd, Lawd, Lawd![58]

For all black Southerners, women and men alike, the operation of the racial system not only exhibited a callous disregard for the sanctity of the family but also consciously diminished their lives, dignity, and aspirations. It could stifle ambition and it could reduce self-esteem, in ways not always easily ascertainable. "The way seems dark, and the future almost hopeless, but let us not despair," a black Alabama woman declared. "Some one will at last arise who will champion our cause and compel the world to see that we deserve justice, as other heroes compelled it to see that we deserved freedom."[59] The year was 1902, but the woman gave no indication if that "champion" might be another resident of Alabama, Booker T. Washington.

6

IF BLACK SOUTHERNERS looked to their "leaders" for guidance on how to endure the assaults on their bodies and minds, they would learn with some exceptions the arts and rhetoric of racial diplomacy and accommodation. As early as 1890, Isaiah Montgomery suggested terms for ending the racial conflict, seizing a critical setting for propounding his views. Although blacks comprised a majority of Mississippi's population, Montgomery was the only black delegate elected in 1890 to the state's constitutional convention, the same convention that would establish the pattern of disfranchisement for the entire South. A prosperous planter, businessman, and conservative accommodationist, Montgomery was best known as the founder of the Negro town of Mound Bayou, in the upper Delta. Whites had come to regard him as a "safe" and "sensible" black leader, no doubt explaining why the dominant faction at the convention chose to seat him over his white rival.[60]

Addressing this assemblage of white men, all of them determined to end black voting, Montgomery made news around the country. In a long and eloquent speech, he supported the convention's efforts. He was willing to sacrifice black voting rights—"a fearful sacrifice laid upon the burning altar of liberty"—in order to end racial conflict, "to bridge a chasm that has been widening and deepening for a generation, to divert the maelstrom that threatens destruction to you and yours, while it promises no enduring prosperity to me and mine." Establishing literacy and property requirements for voting, he acknowledged, would exclude most of his people from the polls. But that exclusion need be only temporary and, in fact, would be ultimately beneficial to the race. The new requirements would encourage blacks to acquire the necessary education and property. Once they did so, Montgomery believed, they would reenter the electorate as intelligent and desirable voters, as a people better able to exercise political responsibility.[61]

Although it required a tactical acceptance of white supremacy, Montgomery's offer promised a truce in the racial conflict. Mississippi whites greeted the speech with "surprised wonder" and understandable enthusiasm, northern whites with unmistakable relief. (A New York newspaper featured it on the first page under the headline "A Noble Speech.") Many blacks were less effusive. What to Montgomery may have been a truce appeared to others nothing less than an unconditional surrender. "No thoughtless, flippant fool," charged a New York black editor, "could have inflicted such a wound upon our cause as Mr. Montgomery has done in this address."[62] The established black leadership in Mississippi, those who had fought the battles of Reconstruction, were adamant in their opposition. Montgomery, on the other hand, felt he had made a pragmatic pact with the state's white citizens, that he had done his best in a difficult situation. After all, he reasoned, black political power had already been nearly eliminated, and those who voted often did so at substantial physical and economic risk. Possessing neither the education, experience, nor wealth to resist whites successfully, blacks needed to create their own opportunities.

The program advanced by Montgomery—accommodation to white

supremacy and withdrawal from politics (which had little to offer blacks) in favor of education, economic advancement, self-help, and racial solidarity—had been articulated by other black spokesmen and gained in popularity in the late nineteenth century. Few articulated the message as compellingly or with the audience and attention Booker T. Washington would command. That was the critical difference. It was not so much what Washington said at the Atlanta Cotton States Exposition in September 1895 but the people—white and black—he subsequently reached, his elevation to the position of national spokesman for the race, and the enormous power and influence (for a black American) he was able to wield from that position.

Like Isaiah Montgomery at the Mississippi Constitutional Convention, Washington also found himself thrust by whites into a position of leadership. Some three decades after emancipation, Washington capitalized in his speeches and writings on the already popular creed of accommodation, self-help, and individual responsibility. He grounded his advice to blacks on familiar themes and promises. In a period of rising racial tensions, he wanted to allay white fears. Rather than talk threateningly about a New Negro, Washington reminded whites of the old Negro, "nursing your children, watching by the sick-bed of your mothers and fathers, and often following them with tear-dimmed eyes to their graves." And he comforted whites by assuring them of black fidelity in the present: "the most patient, faithful, law-abiding, and unresentful people that the world has seen." In a period marked by political repression and enforced separation, Washington made his Faustian bargain: He would acquiesce in disfranchisement and segregation in return for educational and economic opportunities. "In all things that are purely social we can be as separate as the fingers, yet one as the hand in all things essential to mutual progress."[63]

To his own people, Washington offered hope and ultimate redemption in a period of political futility, economic dependence, and betrayed expectations. If they were to survive, prosper, vanquish racial prejudice, and be accepted by whites, they would need to accommodate, "to suffer in silence" and exercise "patience, forbearance, and self-control in the midst of trying conditions"; they would have to place their confidence not in politics, government, or agitation but in the "better sort" of southern whites and, most importantly, in themselves, in their own individual efforts. Like the Jew, the Negro would secure recognition when he had "entwined himself about America in a business and industrial sense."[64]

The death of Frederick Douglass in 1895 and Washington's Atlanta Exposition address that same year marked a critical transition in leadership that was being acted out at several levels of black society. The veterans of the abolitionist and Reconstruction struggles were passing from the scene, replaced by a group whose politics were more grounded in the new realities of race relations, in an appreciation of the possible, in a pragmatism that found no alternative to accommodation other than a racial war blacks could never survive. Even as a new generation of blacks grew more resentful of white repression, their leaders often felt compelled to play the subordinate roles whites expected of them, embracing a practical conservatism designed to advance the interests of the race in a rigidly repressive society that offered few options.

The question of how they became leaders often went to the heart of the dilemma. Most of them commanded influence through positions they held as businessmen, ministers, educators, and lawyers. Whites also played a critical role in creating black leaders. Whether during slavery or in the late nineteenth century, whites often designated certain blacks as intermediaries, not only because these blacks had a standing in the community but because they fulfilled (or at least did not disappoint) white expectations. By directing black frustration and resentment into safe, nonthreatening channels, such leaders helped to stabilize race relations. When the *Atlanta Constitution,* for example, bestowed its blessing on J. C. Price, "an intelligent negro" of Salisbury, North Carolina, it called him "a bright, sensible fellow" who would "never have cause to complain of his white neighbors."[65] On the death of Norris W. Cuney, a moderate black leader in Texas, a newspaper praised the ways in which he had counseled moderation. "He was indeed a safe leader—always alert, looking to his race's interests, but in no sense teaching a false sentiment."[66] The praise heaped on Booker T. Washington invariably stressed the same qualities of humility and practical good sense. The *Atlanta Constitution* proclaimed him "a wise counselor and a safe leader."[67]

Responding to the deterioration of race relations, most black leaders in the Age of Washington appealed for a reconciliation that would ease white fears while affording blacks economic opportunities and the education to make the most of them. They talked about allying themselves with "the best white people of the South," as if "the best" had played no part in the repression of blacks. And not infrequently black leaders scapegoated their own people, castigating black superstitions, emotional religion, and working-class culture, and blaming blacks for their condition. "I would as soon fall into the hands of my white North Carolina friends as my Negro friends," a speaker told a meeting celebrating an anniversary of emancipation in North Carolina, "and I would rather a dozen times over ask a Raleigh white man for a favor than a Raleigh black man."[68]

Trying to explain the race's difficulties and deficiencies by citing white prejudice had its limits. That kind of complaint (or whining), some black spokesmen insisted, diverted the attention of black people from the real problem: themselves. "We are a class of people who represent, comparatively speaking, nothing, and in the business world absolutely nothing," a black critic acknowledged in 1895, as a way of admonishing his people. Making that point even more explicit, a black educator advised a black audience in 1893 that the condition of black people, in the eyes of the civilized world, could be summed up in three negatives: "He *has nothing,* he *knows nothing,* and he *is nobody.*" And having nothing, black people had no real stake in the society; they were both rootless and directionless. The plight of his people reminded one black speaker at a conference on economic uplift of the story of the white man who needed three cents to pay his fare on a ferryboat, only to have a black boatman turn him down. "No, sah," he told the white man, "ah won't let you have it, for a white man who hain't got three cents is just as well off on one side of the river as on the other." That was equally true, the speaker emphasized, of "a negro who hain't got three cents. It don't make much difference which side of the river he's on!"[69]

To be recognized, black people needed to have something to recognize, they needed to be somebody. "So long as we have Jim Crow negroes," a black speaker at the semicentennial celebration of emancipation declared, "we shall need Jim Crow cars." With obvious pride, he described how the discrimination practiced by white insurance companies had driven blacks to organize their own companies. "We are meeting discrimination with organization." The real emancipation, another black leader argued, would come on that day "when we have more bank and railroad stock, fewer high-sounding societies . . . , more landlords and fewer tenants, more owners of plantations and fewer shareworkers, more merchants and fewer dudes, more piety and less religion, more economy and less wastefulness, more confidence and less envy."[70] That would be the way blacks would ultimately win acceptance in white society. One story making the rounds in the black community told of a deacon who arrived late at a white church and found a black man sitting in his pew. He angrily demanded of the usher, "Who put that blasted nigger in my pew?" When informed of the black man's name and that he was worth a hundred thousand dollars, the deacon quickly responded, "Oh, that's all right. Introduce me after service, will you."[71]

The need to become a people worthy of recognition would be repeated incessantly. To bolster that argument, black leaders urged their people to adopt the tactics used so successfully by other immigrant groups to overcome hostility. After all, a Mississippian wrote in 1914, "Jap" was the expression used to disparage Japanese, even as "nig," "nigger," and "coon" were now used to disparage black Americans. But the Japanese overcame these obstacles by exhibiting qualities entitling them to respect and recognition.[72]

More than any other group, however, Jews had come to symbolize for many blacks the ability of a despised minority group to endure repression and to overcome prejudice by virtue of their impressive economic and financial success. Black editors urged their readers, black leaders exhorted their audiences, to look to the Jews for inspiration, to begin, as they did, with the peddler's cart and force their way into the trades and into finance. When Jews were denied access to a place, someone noted, they purchased the property. "By turning their attention entirely to trade," a black writer argued in 1895, "they [Jews] have been enabled to command respect by reason of their money solely. . . ." And yet, he reminded his readers, blacks were "the real producers of the wealth of the country," particularly in the South, giving them a distinct advantage over "the Hebrews," who produce nothing but "strive to control the business of the entire country." In that same spirit, a Savannah black entrepreneur, speaking to the National Negro Business League in 1900, appealed to northern blacks to come South to capitalize on economic opportunities. "[C]ome down and buy and sell to our people . . . and you will make money and have it, instead of the Hebrew having it, as he has it now."[73]

While blacks were asked to emulate the Jews, they remained tied to popular stereotypes of Jews as shrewd and parasitical moneylenders and tricksters, as economic predators who were known to make their fortunes on the backs of other people, and as "Christ-killers." When a rabbi in Norfolk, Virginia, pressed for the prosecution of blacks for violating the Jim Crow laws, the editor of a local black newspaper warned the Jewish community that if they persisted in such tactics, it would redound with "tremendous force" on Jewish merchants "who keep shop upon every corner in the Afro-American residential sections of this city."[74] With equal vehemence, a black newspaper in New Orleans excoriated the Italian immigrant for making every law, custom, and religious teaching subservient "to his greed for money making."[75]

The ambivalence of black Southerners (and black Northerners) toward immigrant groups reflected a growing consternation over how quickly those groups absorbed white racist attitudes and the perceived readiness of native whites to grant them an immediate place in the political and economic order. If nothing else, black spokesmen kept insisting, the "new" immigrants flocking to American shores at the turn of the century should have confirmed for native whites the relative superiority of blacks not only as laborers but also as loyal and patriotic Americans who could be trusted to avoid social disorders and alien ideologies. But the United States, in the estimation of one southern black newspaper, had become so absorbed in the "howl" of whites seeking "to decitizenize and dehumanize" the Negro "that foreigners who are neither in harmony with our government nor in sympathy with our institutions" were simply ignored, even as they spread their "unamerican teachings." To substitute immigrant for black labor, as whites proposed, would mean Romanism, strikes, and anarchy. On the other hand, the paper declared in Washingtonian terms, the South "will never suffer violence at the hand of the Negro" whose "fidelity to trust" withstood "the darkest days of slavery."[76]

The obstacles black men and women had to overcome made their position unique in American society. Although the Irish, the Jews, and other immigrants faced problems of acceptance and discrimination, black Americans were not simply another immigrant group. Alone among those brought to this country against their will, and the only immigrant group to have been enslaved, black Americans confronted a troublesome and unique dilemma in the 1890s and the early twentieth century as they sorted out their prospects and listened to their leaders exhort them to accommodate and lift themselves up by their bootstraps. Even as southern whites reinforced white supremacy, circumscribing black political and civil rights and placing disabling limits on educational and economic opportunities, blacks were expected to play by the same rules whites followed to achieve success. That paradox defied resolution.

The unfairness could not be easily explained away. But the self-help improvement manuals and uplift books that abounded in black communities, as in white, imparted the themes Washington enunciated on so many occasions, as if whites and blacks faced similar obstacles and could overcome them in the same way. Although some of the manuals were written specifically for a black audience, they generally avoided mention of race and repeated the same moral tales and sermons found in their white counterparts, mostly designed to accommodate the young to the modern commercial order. To millions of American youths and adults in the late nineteenth century, black and white, this was the way in which the world was interpreted for them. The manuals instructed them on how to take full advantage of the opportunities always available for the right-thinking and right-acting, presumably regardless of race or color.

In one popular black manual, *Floyd's Flowers or Duty & Beauty for Colored Children,* published in Atlanta in 1905, Silas X. Floyd, the author, noted "the so-called Race Problem" only in closing. He had omitted the discussion deliberately, he explained. "I believe that the less you think about the troubles of the race and the less you talk about them and the more time you spend in hard and honest work, believing in God and trusting him for the future, the better it will be for all concerned." Having said that, he acknowledged "the sufferings" of black people but counseled accommodation and patience. "The white people have all the courts, all the railroads, all the newspapers, all the telegraph wires, all the arms and ammunition and double the men that we have."[77] That in itself had to be a compelling argument, and few blacks (or whites) would have questioned Floyd's grasp of reality.

As accommodationists, most black leaders focused their rhetoric and efforts on how to live and even succeed within the constraints imposed on them, how to pull their punches, how to phrase their appeals to whites, and, most of all, how to maintain at all times a sense of the possible. The idea was to play down white hatred of blacks, pointing up the positive aspects of their historic relationship. That invariably meant invoking the familiar reminder, as Washington did in his Atlanta address, of black faithfulness during slavery and the Civil War, even if such reminders simplified and did violence to the much more complex historical record. In "An Open Address to Our White Friends of the South," a prominent Memphis black dwelled on black service in the past, singling out "the old Confederate Soldier," grateful for how blacks had watched over his wife and children, and "the noble white women of the land," appreciative of how blacks had sought to protect and comfort them during the war. Now that blacks found themselves virtually under siege, he pleaded with whites to reciprocate and "say one word in our behalf."[78]

The appeal was perceived as a way to produce results, in this instance a softening of white repression and violence. Black spokesmen often couched their appeals in reminders not only of loyalty in the past, but also of their peaceful subordination and accommodation in the present. In the face of "terrible conditions," a speaker told an overflowing crowd at an Emancipation Day meeting in Raleigh in 1907, "the Negro has remained almost wholly passive." He has made little effort to assert his constitutional rights. He has tried to avoid "any act or word that might be construed as provocative of race antipathy." He has entrusted his future to "fair-minded and just" whites. "We are impotent. We are helpless. . . . The white race is great and powerful. You can afford to be just. That is all the Negro asks."[79]

Few could match Booker T. Washington in such appeals, and he always made clear his desire to be measured by his concrete accomplishments rather than his rhetoric. After all, he had based his program on what he thought to be possible and where he thought power rested in southern society. When he wrote, for example, in 1895 to Senator Benjamin "Pitchfork" Tillman, a rabid racist demagogue, urging him to use his influence to protect the threatened funding of black schools in South Carolina, Washington employed a style he thought most appropriate for the occasion. "I was born a slave; you a freeman. I am but an humble member of an unfortunate race; you are a member of the greatest legislative body on earth, and of the great, intelligent Caucasian race." Despite these differences, he could not believe that a man as "great and magnanimous" as Tillman would permit the impoverishment of black schools, would reject the appeal of 650,000 "suppliants at your feet," whose "destiny and progress" for another century lay largely in his hands. "I have been told that you are brave and generous, and one too great to harm the weak and dependent; that you represent the chivalry of the South, which has claimed no higher praise than that of protectors of the defenseless."[80]

A classic example of accommodationism, Washington's appeal to Tillman could easily be viewed as groveling before "white massa" for a handout. But Washington would no doubt have argued that his primary concern was with results. If the appeal to white honor and chivalry, no matter how abject and contrived, achieved his objective, the end justified the means. Washington could envision no other strategy better calculated to stop the bleeding of black schools in South Carolina. A New York journalist had urged him to make the open letter "a ringing appeal to the nation," while at the same time conciliating South Carolina whites. No one was better suited to the task than Washington.[81]

A black educator who claimed friendship with both Tillman and Washington used much the same strategy to make an important acquisition for his school. Joseph Winthrop Holley, founder and first president of Albany State College in Georgia, wanted a wealthy white man to give him a cow for his institution. He drove out in his buggy to the man's home. As he approached the house, blacks in the vicinity gathered to see whether he would go to the kitchen like any ordinary black or if as a college president he would go to the front door. In calculating what he would do, Holley kept his eye on the prize: the cow. "I saw the situation and knew just what my people were thinking and saying among themselves." After hitching his horse, he proceeded neither to the front door nor to the kitchen but to the barn, where he asked one of the laborers to tell Judge Putney that Professor Holley (he "did not dare" use the term "Mister") would like to see him when it was convenient. The white maid came out to inform him that as soon as the judge had finished breakfast he would see him in the parlor. They met, the judge referred to him as Professor Holley, and he offered him two cows. "The truth is," Holley reflected, "we colored people can get what we want, if it is within reason, from a white man if we approach him in the right way. He is like the Negro in the minstrel show who says to his companion, 'Don't shove me! You may push me all you want to, but don't *shove* me!' You may push the white man in any reasonable direction you want him to go, but never shove him. This is an all important truth which many impatient reformers should examine."[82]

At every level of society, day in and day out, these racial rituals were played out, though not necessarily with the same results or in the same spirit. Richard Wright, when in Memphis, remembered all too vividly his friend Shorty, who worked as an elevator operator. "Psychologically he was the most amazing specimen of the southern Negro I had ever met." Literate, an avid reader of books and magazines, proud of his race and resentful of white repression, he would nevertheless persist in playing the role of clown in the presence of whites if it helped him obtain the desired end. One day, he promised Wright he would obtain a quarter from the first white man who walked into the elevator. He did so by debasing himself, rolling his eyes, grimacing, clowning, telling the white man repeatedly, "I'm hungry, Mister White Man. I need a quarter for lunch" and "This black sonofabitch sure needs a quarter." Good-naturedly, he threatened not to take the passenger to his floor unless he secured the requested reward. When the white man asked him what he would do for a quarter, Shorty laughed, turned around, and bent over. "You can kick me for a quarter," he told him. The white man laughed and tossed a quarter to the floor. When Shorty stooped to pick it up, the white man kicked him with all his strength, and exclaimed, "Now, open this door, you goddamn black sonofabitch." Shorty complied with a resounding, "Yeeeess, siiiiir," as he picked up the quarter and placed it in his mouth. "This monkey's got the peanuts," he said with a laugh. Wright witnessed the same scene on a number of occasions, and each time he felt "only disgust and loathing." He demanded to know how Shorty could so debase and degrade himself. "I needed a quarter and I got it," Shorty declared without hesitation. "But a quarter can't pay you for what he did to you," Wright said. "Listen, nigger," Shorty replied, "my ass is tough and quarters is scarce."[83]

Within every black community, "leading" black men commanded sufficient influence with "leading" whites to effect arrangements for blacks needing certain kinds of assistance. Such intervention could affect the sentence handed out to a black defendant, the survival of a school, or the ability of a promising black youth to attend a college. The black motorist who has an accident with a white driver, the black traveler desiring Pullman reservations, the black father trying to settle an altercation involving his children, the school principal needing funds to pay his teachers—all came to depend on certain local blacks to help "straighten out things." Albon L. Holsey, born in Georgia around 1890, recalled his own father as such a person. When Albon and a friend once got into trouble with the law, the elder Holsey intervened to save his son; Albon's friend, who had no such intermediary, was sentenced to the chain gang. "A white man of influence has prestige of his own," Albon Holsey came to realize, "but a Negro's influence is measured in terms of his white contacts. So we find Negroes still faced with the necessity of cultivating white folks in order to get by." But such "influence," Albon Holsey reflected, did not come without a price in personal dignity. "This eternal struggle to survive collects its deadly toll of the manhood of the race, for only too often it involves tattling, scheming, selfishness, slanderous whispers, and the blood-bought betrayal of other Negroes."[84]

The "leading" blacks who acted as intermediaries were apt to be conciliatory and accommodationist, but they were not necessarily the willing tools of whites, truckling to their every whim; indeed, if they simply cringed in the presence of whites or served as informers, their credibility among their own people would have been severely compromised, if not nullified altogether. Christia Adair recalled that her father, who ran a hauling business in Edna, Texas, had status in the town among both races. Whites sought his assistance because of the confidence blacks placed in him. "He didn't act like he was better," she said of her father. He "respected" whites, but at the same time he "demanded respect for himself."[85]

For most blacks, the need to placate whites stemmed from the understandable desire to hold on to what they had. Whether in the cities or the countryside, as a young Georgian recalled, many blacks hired as teachers, school principals, and domestics "had to practice deceit and pretend to be happy in order to keep their jobs."[86] But it was at best an uneasy arrangement, and the tensions it produced persisted and festered as a new generation of blacks came to adulthood—a generation deprived of the right to share political power with whites or to effect changes through democratic politics.

7

FIFTEEN-YEAR-OLD Ned Cobb "watched" as whites disfranchised blacks in Alabama in 1901. "I was old enough to look at folks and hear the talk. I didn't like it but nothin I could do." He had in previous years seen his father travel up to nearby Chapel Ridge on election days to cast his ballot, knowing nothing of the candidates, selling his vote to whites willing to buy it. "He was kept out of the knowledge of knowin so that he would *want* to sell his vote because that was the only advantage he could get from votin." White people, Cobb thought, had already made a sham of democratic politics, "[b]ut takin the vote away was worse; if they couldn't just slave the nigger back like he used to be, it was pointin the nigger in that direction. . . . Tellin him he didn't have a right to his thoughts. He just weren't counted to be no more than a dog." To bring this about, Cobb explained, "the rich white man and the poor white man" had collaborated—"the big man and a heap of the little ones." But the "little ones," Cobb sensed, had been badly deceived. "The little ones thought they had a voice, but they only had a voice to this extent: they could speak against the nigger and the big man was happy for em to do it. But they didn't have no more voice than a cat against the big man of their own color."

After 1901, Hayes Cobb stayed home on election day. He never voted again. Nor did Ned Cobb seek to cast a vote when he reached adulthood. "I was right there with my neck under the yoke like the rest of em. I wanted to vote, but I didn't want to vote if my vote weren't no good, weren't worth a doggone. What I goin to vote for? . . . I seed the nigger vote till he'd vote his head off—done him no good at all."[87]

Henry D. Davidson presided over a black industrial school in Bibb County, Alabama, only a short distance from where Ned and Hayes Cobb tried to eke out a living. An active Republican, he resolved to vote, even after the state had moved to eliminate most blacks from the voting rolls. When he appeared before the registration board, he was asked a long list of questions that would have baffled most whites: "What were the Kentucky Resolutions? Who is the Chief Justice of the Supreme Court of Alabama? of the United States? What Alabamian was once Vice President of the United States?" To the dismay of the board, he answered these and other queries about the history of Alabama and the United States, and the chair seemed on the verge of panicking, telling one of the members, "Hurry with more questions; this 'nigger' has answered all the questions you gave us!" Finally, when the questions had been exhausted, the chair told Davidson he would need to find some prominent white men to endorse him if he expected to vote. Rejected by most "prominent" whites, he finally came up with a white lawyer willing to sign an affidavit attesting to his good character, and Davidson retained his right to vote. Less successful, according to a popular story in the black community, was the farmer who answered correctly the "reasonable" questions asked by the voter registrar, forcing the exasperated white man to improvise. "What is a writ of *habeas corpus ad testificandum?*" The aspiring voter replied, "Yassir, boss, I know 'zactly whut dat is, too: dat's jes' a special kinder 'rangement an' device *to keep a Negro f'om votin'!*"[88]

If nothing else, blacks had learned from Reconstruction some of the uses of political power and that it could affect in significant ways their day-to-day lives. By embracing politics, blacks hoped to eliminate the remaining vestiges of slavery, establish public school systems, and construct an activist state that would counterpoise the immemse power wielded by the planter class. Associating the Republican Party with their freedom, they tended to vote the party ticket and rejected the occasional blandishments of the party identified with slavery. The political choices seemed obvious. Born in freedom, Richard R. Wright, Jr. learned at an early age that the Democrats would gladly return black people into slavery, and if unable to achieve that objective would settle for nothing less than depriving blacks of their newly won constitutional rights.[89]

Braving threats and violence, many blacks voted for as long as they could after Reconstruction, clinging to the ballot as an indispensable expression of their freedom. When a white political activist tried to persuade Robert Hill, a former slave, that he should "let them damn Yankees alone" and cast his lot with the Democratic Party in 1880, Hill responded, "Take away all the laws in our favor that them damn Yankees have made, and what would be left?" That same year, Parke Johnston, a Virginian, responded with shock when told to vote Democratic: "You must think I am a d—— fool if you think I am going to vote against the people that set me free." And Bill McNeil of South Carolina vowed to remain a Republican despite the threats on his life ("I sticks out to de end wid de party dat freed me"), as did Betty Brown's stepfather ("[m]y step-daddy say he die 'fore he vote Democrat").[90]

But for most southern blacks, voting and politics spelled trouble, a sign of assertiveness that few whites would tolerate, and that was reason enough to stay away from the polls. It was not that blacks were necessarily averse to casting ballots or failed to understand the issues or candidates. Increasingly, voting and officeholding simply became too risky, possibly fatal. Most blacks were not so much apathetic as pragmatic, placing a higher priority on self-preservation than politics. "Voting makes enemies. I learned that early," recalled Ann Mitchell, who was born in the first years of Reconstruction. When asked about politics and disfranchisement in 1902, a street musician in Greensboro, North Carolina, replied that he tried to ignore politics, and he sang, "I'm gwine live until I die." For many blacks, then, the alternatives were perfectly clear. Elige Davison wanted to vote and thought himself deserving of the privilege, but he was dependent on his employer and landlord. "If he could vote us like he wanted it was all right if not our grub was cut off, or we lost our job."[91]

Not only did intimidation, violence, and economic dependence cut deeply into the black electorate, but disillusionment with post-Reconstruction politics, whatever party won, took a heavy toll on black voters. "I used to vote Republican," recalled Mack Brantley. "They claimed it made times better for my race. I found out better." Berry Smith had voted during Reconstruction, but after its overthrow he "didn' bother wid no politics," as he "didn' want none of 'em." Fewer blacks chose to defy whites in politics, finding the risks far outweighed the benefits. That was why Arch Wesley Nelson never voted in Alabama or Arkansas, before or after disfranchisement. "Never saw no sense in it, myself I couldn't see where it would benefit me. And them that voted didn't get no benefit either."[92]

Politics, in the estimation of growing numbers of blacks in the late nineteenth century, had become the exclusive concern of white folks, and they knew not "to fuss" or "to mix" where white folks "am fussin'." That lesson blacks learned early in life, and many made a point of passing it on to the next generation. Kelly Jackson's father never voted, nor did his son, born in 1894. "I had come up under that atmosphere," the son explained. "I just wasn't going to get in any trouble and have nobody slipping in my house. . . . I never thought about it." Magnolia Gates recalled how her grandparents were tortured and forced off the land they owned when her grandfather, Isaac Turnbow, refused to vote the way whites ordered him to vote; their children must have heeded that lesson, as they made no attempt to vote. "They didn't want to cause any trouble, that's right. A lot of times, you'd want to do these things, but you are afraid. . . . [W]e thought that we didn't have any rights." It simply made no sense to Barney Alford, a Texas farmer, even to attempt to vote. "My time is short on dis earth an' I want to live right an' de white folks kno' how to run deir business an' I is not gwine to git mixed up wid it."[93]

If white folks, on the other hand, wanted their votes and rewarded them in some way, if voting could be turned into a tangible benefit, many blacks—like Hayes Cobb—had no problem with such an arrangement. "I *seed* that," Ned Cobb recalled. "Niggers just fell in there like pigs around their mammy suckin: votin the white man's way. Come time to vote, white man runnin all about the settlement buyin the niggers' votes. Give him meat, flour, sugar, coffee, anything the nigger wanted." In some areas of heavy black concentration, black politicians readily turned out the vote for Democratic candidates in return for minor concessions, perhaps financial compensation, or even a political office. James Boyd, a Texas farmer, took a philosophical view as he resigned himself to voting the straight Democratic ticket "like my white folks did," and many blacks would no doubt have agreed with his assessment. "I didn't seen no use doin' noddin' else, case de white folks goin' do what dey wants anyhow."[94]

Avoiding politics altogether had its distinct advantages. Trying to appease whites by voting their way did not always achieve the desired results. As many blacks came to discover, there was simply no way to win when dealing with white folks. If they acted too obsequiously, they sometimes aroused suspicion, and if they readily agreed to vote the way whites told them to vote, they sometimes aroused suspicion. "The whites knowed when any of us voted the democratic ticket we was lying or doing it to get something," Carrie Campbell recalled of his years in Alabama and Mississippi. In Upson County, Georgia, a black sharecropper found that selling his vote proved costly in the end. His employer, in exchange for the vote, had given him a ham, a sack of flour, and a place to stay on the plantation. But immediately after the election, he ordered the man off his place. "Because," he told him, "if you allow anyone to buy your vote and rob you of your rights as a free citizen, someone could hire you to set my house on fire."[95]

Isaiah Montgomery had set the pattern for acquiescence in disfranchisement with his controversial stand at the Mississippi Constitutional Convention in 1890. The ideas he articulated on that occasion, calling on his people to abandon politics for economic and educational advances, had already resonated with black leaders. When a prominent minister of the African Methodist Episcopal Church in Vicksburg observed in 1886 that "the mass of negroes would do themselves and their country more good if the ballot were out of their reach," he captured the sentiment that constitutional conventions would write into law over the next several decades.[96]

The minister's words perpetuated a myth about recent history that whites had already exploited and that found ready acceptance in many black circles and in Booker T. Washington's catechism: that blacks during Reconstruction were entrusted with political responsibilities they abused out of ignorance and incompetence. For whites, this view of the past had become standard gospel, and too many blacks found it convenient to endorse this badly distorted version of reality. The president of the Colored State Fair in North Carolina compared the vote granted to blacks after the Civil War to a razor his son had wanted to use after watching his father shave. "Our so-called friends of the North after the war gave us a razor, the ballot box, and the result was we cut our throats with it from ear to ear. We are just beginning to learn how to use this razor. We are turning our efforts and thoughts to farming and other industrial pursuits." Booker T. Washington said no less when he regretted how blacks had been entrusted with political responsibility after emancipation without "experience," "preparation," and "ordinary intelligence."[97]

In supporting property and educational qualifications for voting, Montgomery and Washington had insisted that the restrictions be applied equally to both races and assumed that blacks would be encouraged to acquire the necessary literacy and property to qualify as voters. But the argument for equal treatment, while principled, was naive at best, as many blacks realized. What the white South had in mind was not a transition but permanent subordination—political, economic, and social. If Jim Crow translated into separate and unequal facilities, disfranchisement rested on the elimination of most black voters according to laws and constitutional provisions that would be enforced arbitrarily and selectively. Ten years after Montgomery's speech supporting voting restrictions, he appeared before the National Negro Business League to boast of the achievements of Mound Bayou, the town he had helped to found. "Under the prevailing system in Mississippi," he conceded, "we have but little to do with politics, though the precinct ranks among the largest in the county in number of qualified voters under the new constitution." The delegates greeted his acknowledgment with laughter.[98]

The challenge to disfranchisement did not lend itself to any of the dramatic actions employed to protest Jim Crow, but it provoked a comparable reaction. If the right to vote could be denied on racial grounds, how long before black people were denied the right of movement, the right to acquire property, the right to meet in their churches—all the essential accoutrements of a free people, the hallmarks of American citizenship? Whatever the weaknesses of the parties or candidates, the right to vote could still make a difference, whether psychologically or materially. Calling disfranchisement "un-American" and expressing alarm over blacks who "acquiesce so largely" in it, a black newspaper in New Orleans underscored the degree to which politics affected so many areas in which black people had a vital interest. "Robbed of political power, the right to hold property, the right of contract, educational privileges, and the security of life count for but little."[99]

Few blacks might have had any reason to care about presidential or even congressional races, but many knew from personal experience that political power in the New South resided essentially in the local courthouse. What happened there could exert an important influence on their daily lives. "I voted one time in my life," recalled Henry Daniels, who farmed for shares in Georgia and Mississippi, "an' dat was fo' cotton weigher." More than one black person expressed the opinion that since blacks had been disfranchised "they has been more or less under bondage." Nathan Best, who had voted despite threats, found it impossible to overcome legal disfranchisement; he was left to contemplate the "good times" before he lost the vote.[100]

Occupying a range of resentment, sharecroppers, newspaper editors, and black religious and political leaders invoked in various ways the nation's revolutionary heritage and the service of the black soldier. Addressing his appeal to the president of the United States, William H. Gardner of Pool, Alabama, claiming to speak for the "poor & Ignorant," found it inconceivable that those "who protected [the] United States Flag from 61 to 65 . . . are, together with their sons disfranchised." A black newspaper in New Orleans noted the proposal in Virginia to exempt Confederate but not Federal soldiers from the proposed restrictions on voters. That, mocked the editor, would extend the right to "those who fought to destroy the Union, and not those who fought to preserve it."[101]

But much of the appeal to American history rested on the unfairness of a system that exacted taxes from blacks but denied them any influence on government. Although blacks paid taxes on $3 million worth of property in Louisville, a black lawyer noted the absence of blacks at any level of government higher than that of "washing spittoons in the Court House. . . . All municipal offices are in the hands of 'sho' 'nuff white folks,' though they may be Dagos, or Germans, or Slavs." This, he concluded, was a "government of the two races by and for the one race." Although it produced no discernible results, blacks continued to press whites on an issue as old as the republic. Why, asked one black newspaper, should the Negro agree "to do what the Revolutionary sires refused to do—submit to taxation without representation?" If it was wrong to tax white men without permitting them representation, a black speaker told an audience on the anniversary of emancipation in 1912, it was no less oppressive to tax black people and deny them representation.[102]

How to combat disfranchisement resulted in a variety of proposals

and strategies. The most direct appeal was to urge blacks to acquire literacy and property. "Meet the requirements of the Constitution," a
speaker implored an overflowing crowd on Emancipation Day in
Raleigh in 1907, "if you have to burn 'midnight oil' in preparing yourselves to meet them; and when you have met them say to the world
that you can never suffer the boast again that a negro's vote can be had
with a dollar and a drink of whiskey." Booker T. Washington covertly
helped to finance appeals to the courts, and ultimately the legal strategy would attract the support of black activists, particularly the newly
organized National Association for the Advancement of Colored People (NAACP). Some black newspapers urged Congress to enforce the
Fourteenth Amendment, reducing the political power of the South by
reducing its representation and no longer counting the disfranchised
black population.[103]

By the early twentieth century, disfranchisement worked effectively
as part of an intertwining web of repressive apparatuses designed to
keep black people in their "place." Although pockets of black political
participation persisted, mostly in urban areas, for the vast majority of
blacks politics had been deprived of any real meaning. "We have tried
politics," a black Atlantan insisted, "and still we are in our graves."
Wash Hayes, who spent most of his life in Mississippi, remembered his
father voting and he did for several years before he "quit foolin " with
the ballot. "It didn't seem to do no good, or make no difference to no
body who wuz 'lected in de offices an' I jes' quit botherin' wid it." H. C.
Binford, a black schoolteacher, city alderman, and editor in Alabama,
in 1899 informed his readers: "[T]here is nothing in politics for us, it
makes no difference which side wins none of them want the Negro."
Some years later, he conceded, "we have gotten use to being slighted
and have ceased to kick. What's the use?"[104]

To divorce themselves from allegiance to the Republican Party was
no easy task for blacks. Discerning little difference between Democrats
and Republicans, however, many questioned the need to slavishly commit themselves to traditional political loyalties. "Both Republican and
democrat are trying to keep the Negro behind them," an Alabama
black told Washington in 1887. In parts of the South, the Lily-whites, as
they were called, sought to recast the Republican Party and eliminate
black influence. "I was a white man before I was a Republican," a white
Republican proclaimed, and he refused to make any Negro his "ruler."
The inroads made by the Lily-whites simply confirmed for many blacks

what they had suspected for some time: that the Republican Party no longer represented their best interests. "The colored people are consumers," proclaimed the chair of the Colored People's Convention in Richmond in 1890. "The Republicans have deserted them and undertaken to protect the capitalist and manufacturer of the North." Neither party, a black editor agreed, "cares a tinker snap for the poor man. They are run in the interest of capital, monopoly and repression." Why, a black newspaper in Valdosta, Georgia, wondered, should the Negro vote to keep in power a party that did nothing to protect him? "He's lynched every day some where in the South. It should not surprise any body, if *to save his life* and property he goes over to the 3rd party or to the democrats."[105]

For blacks to assert their political independence of both major parties won some measure of support before disfranchisement effectively robbed them of even that electoral strategy. P. B. S. Pinchback, a veteran Republican politician during Reconstruction, reassured his people in 1884 that a Democratic administration in Washington, D.C., would in no way impair their rights and interests. Despairing of both parties, Bishop Henry McNeal Turner advised black voters in 1896 to cast a protest vote. "What time has the fool Negro to bother with the gold or silver side either, while he is lynched, burnt, flayed, imprisoned, etc., two-thirds of the time for nothing. Vote any way in your power to overthrow, destroy, ruin . . . and fragmentize this nation, until it learns to deal justly with the black man." Four years later, Turner announced his intention to vote for William Jennings Bryan, as McKinley had proven himself no friend of black people. "I am willing as a negro to try some other white man." To Turner, however, black people needed to look not to politics for solutions but to themselves, to see themselves as a people.[106]

Disillusionment with the Republican Party in some regions resulted in flirtations in the 1890s with the newly emerging Populist Party. The rhetoric of the Populist movement must have seemed promising. When Populist orators made their appeal to blacks, they talked of bridging their differences and racial animosities for the sake of the economic grievances that united them. They talked boldly of a class alliance along racial lines, of subordinating racial to class grievances, race consciousness to class consciousness. But such moments proved fleeting, the promise was rarely fulfilled, and whites dictated the terms and the degree of black participation.

Within the Populist Party, factions and individuals differed on how to attract black voters. Strategies varied, as did the effectiveness of Populist appeals to black voters. Inconsistencies, contradictions, and ambiguities dominated an always fragile relationship between white and black Populists. Even as Populists sought black votes, they needed to make clear that blacks would remain subordinate within the party, as within society itself. "This is a white man's country and will always be controlled by the whites," a Virginia Populist declared, and few in the party would have dissented from that view. In the end, race consciousness took clear precedence over class consciousness, and Populists proved no more committed to equality for blacks than most other southern white men. Both Populists and Democrats wanted the votes of blacks, but without in any way compromising their commitment to white supremacy. "This is political hypocrisy in the truest sense of the word," a black newspaper in North Carolina said of Populist tactics among blacks, "and a nice little trick to get Negro votes and at the same time degrade and humiliate him."[107]

The presidential election of 1912 summed up the political futility of black Americans, South and North. The Progressive Party rejected a civil rights plank in its platform, and its nominee, Theodore Roosevelt, shared fashionable views of Negro inferiority. He singled out with particular disdain "those very foolish white men who refuse to face facts and refuse to see that the average negro is on a different and far lower level than is the case with the white man." He thought the Negro ought to place his faith in the goodwill and benevolence of southern whites, and he considered the lazy, shiftless, criminal Negro a far greater danger to the race than the deeds of lynchers. The Republican candidate, William Howard Taft, had reassured southern whites that he saw no inconsistency between the Fifteenth Amendment and legal safeguards against "domination by an ignorant electorate" and as president chose to ignore the epidemic of lynch violence.[108] The Democrats nominated Woodrow Wilson, a southern-born Democrat, who assured blacks he wanted to see them treated justly.

Bishop Alexander Walters of the A.M.E. Zion Church endorsed the strategy of blacks' dividing their political loyalties, since the Republican Party had ceased to champion blacks. Walters chose to believe Wilson's campaign rhetoric about racial justice. So did W. E. B. Du Bois. He would have preferred Eugene Debs, the candidate of the Socialist Party, but he cast a pragmatic vote for Wilson. "Woodrow Wilson is a cultivated scholar and he has brains. . . . We have, therefore, a conviction that Mr. Wilson will treat black men and their interests with far-sighted fairness. . . . He will not advance the cause of an oligarchy in the South, he will not seek further means of 'jim crow' insult, he will not dismiss black men wholesale from office, and he will remember that the Negro . . . has a right to be heard and considered."[109]

The Wilson presidency belied those expectations. Black men were dismissed from office, or their positions were downgraded. Jim Crow, already triumphant in Washington, D.C., was now extended to government departments, much to the relief of Wilson's wife, who had expressed shock at seeing black men and white women working in the same room in the Post Office Department. When a delegation of black leaders visited the president to express their outrage over his actions, Wilson told them that segregation was being instituted for their benefit—to reduce racial friction. He was also offended by the manner in which the head of the delegation had expressed black grievances; the next time they come to see him, he told them, they should find a different spokesman. Bishop Walters, like Du Bois, came to recognize the folly of black expectations. Wilson's New Freedom, Walters suggested, "has been all for the white man and little for the Negro."[110]

In the 1860s and 1870s black men and women had glimpsed alternative possibilities in their lives through political participation. Half a century later, politics in the South had become "white folks' business," and so it remained until after World War II. Most blacks maintained their allegiance to the Republican Party until the 1930s, still associating that party with civil rights and public schools. But the Republicans answered few of their needs, and every elected southern politician knew what he owed to white supremacy. That left black activists searching for other outlets. On the eve of World War II, a black Republican stalwart in Mississippi confessed that the party functioned briefly every four years. "We proselytize these few score Negroes to vote . . . and, after pocketing the handouts from the party slush fund . . . we put our committee back in moth balls to await another presidential election." And that was about it. "Hell, naw! We got no local program. We are doctors and preachers and barbers. We make enough money to buy enough liquor to wash the inconveniences of being a nigger out of our brains."[111]

8

EARLY IN HIS LIFE, Blyden Jackson sensed that there were two Americas, separate and unequal. Born in 1910, he grew up in black Louisville, and he soon came to learn the limitations imposed upon him, the places to which he had no access.

> Through a veil I could perceive the forbidden city, the Louisville where white folks lived. It was the Louisville of the downtown hotels, the lower floors of the big movie houses, the high schools I read about in the daily newspapers, the restricted haunts I sometimes passed, like white restaurants and country clubs, the other side of windows in the banks, and, of course, the inner sanctums of offices where I could go only as a humble client or a menial custodian. On my side of the veil everything was black: the homes, the people, the churches, the schools, the Negro park with Negro park police. . . . I knew that there were two Louisvilles and, in America, two Americas. I knew, also, which of the Americas was mine. I knew there were things I was not supposed to do, honors I was not supposed to seek, people . . . to whom I was never supposed to speak, and even thoughts . . . that I was never supposed to think. I was a Negro.[112]

Excluded from the white world, black Southerners drew inward and constructed their own society, with its own institutions and separate social and cultural life. Within these communities, divisions emerged based on class and education, religious affiliation, gradations of color, aspirations and priorities, and perceptions of white people and themselves. Within that increasingly separate world, black men and women tried to deal pragmatically with life as they found it and make the best of their talents.

Driven from politics, black leaders tended to be businessmen, ministers, and educators. The irony of segregation is that it opened up new opportunities for enterprising blacks. A new class of upwardly mobile black entrepreneurs emerged in the late nineteenth and early twentieth centuries to serve an increasingly separate society, to provide services (such as insurance, bank loans, barbering, and burying) that white businessmen or companies refused, and to compete in some places with white retail establishments. The more successful of these entrepreneurs, most of them self-made men, kept the dream alive for others. A. F. Herndon, the wealthiest black in Atlanta, operated the largest barber shop, served as president of an insurance company, and owned and rented some fifty residences.[113] Although few matched Herndon's economic versatility, a growing number capitalized on segregation to achieve their success. Of course, most understood that their position depended on maintaining the good faith and tolerance of local whites and on establishing their credit in local banks.

The social and organizational life of the black community revolved around this emerging middle class. Emulating white society but always exhibiting their own distinctiveness, fraternal, benevolent, and social clubs and organizations fostered race pride and provided the camaraderie and social interaction denied black men and women in the larger society. The rituals, titles, and uniforms that characterized the fraternal orders gave members a welcome respite from their daily routines and made them feel like somebody in a society that insisted they were nobody. Of practical value, the orders and benevolent societies put into practice a mutual self-help ideology that enabled their members to set aside modest savings that would cover the cost of burials and hospitalization and provide some support in hard times.

Even as black men found fellowship and support in their fraternal groups, black women enlisted in a network of organizations, local and national, that provided an opportunity to share cultural, religious, and political interests. The emergence of an active women's movement spoke not only to an intensified interest in temperance, moral reform, and suffrage but to a growing independence, an unprecedented amount of activity in the public sphere, and a recognition of their potential for reshaping their lives and aspirations, along with those less fortunate than themselves. Adopting as its motto "Lifting As We Climb," The National Association of Colored Women (NACW), founded in 1896, provided an important forum for the views of women, and the enhanced consciousness acquired in such organizations encouraged them to act on their views. Accentuating the middle-class makeup of the women's clubs, Mary Church Terrell, the NACW's president, admonished them to address the needs of the less fortunate—the vast majority of black women. "Even though we wish to shun them, and hold ourselves entirely aloof from them, we cannot escape the consequences of their acts." Not only duty but also self-preservation, Terrell declared, "demand that we go down among the lowly, the illiterate, and even the vicious to whom we are bound by the ties of race and sex, and put forth every possible effort to uplift and re-claim them."[114]

The Independent Order of Saint Luke, a mutual benefit society or-ganized in Richmond, stood as a model for what local organizing could accomplish. Under the leadership of Maggie Lena Walker, the order adopted an activist agenda aimed at improving economic opportunities for black women and eliminating segregation and disfranchisement. Many of the mutual aid societies evolved into banks and insurance companies, and in 1903, Walker, the daughter of a washerwoman, be-came the first woman bank president in the United States, founding the Saint Luke Penny Savings Bank in Richmond. Washerwomen, includ-ing Walker's mother, were among its important supporters.[115]

Few black enterprises were as ambitious or as audacious as the town of Mound Bayou, in the very heart of the Mississippi Delta. Disdaining politics and agitation, Isaiah Montgomery opted for separation, envi-sioning and founding in 1887 this self-sufficient, self-governing, all-black community. "Everything here was Negro," a native of the town recalled, "from the symbols of law and authority and the man who ran the bank down to the fellow who drove the road scraper. That gave us kids a sense of security and power and pride that colored kids didn't get anywhere else." Mound Bayou was to have been a living embodiment of Washington's gospel of uplift and economic independence, and resi-dents took pride in the fact that no white person owned property within the city limits. For a time the community of four thousand people thrived, but fluctuating cotton prices, bank failures, and the need for credit soon compromised its independence, and by the early 1920s many of its once-independent farmers had been forced back into ten-antry.[116]

Businessmen, ministers, professionals, and teachers tended to oc-cupy the top of the black pyramid in the cities that were attracting in-creasing numbers of rural blacks in the late nineteenth and early twentieth centuries. Before long, they had managed to establish the nu-cleus of a black middle class. They acquired property, educated their children, and improved their homes, though with cautious ostentation. They belonged to clubs and churches, and in many communities pro-duced a social season, complete with coming-out parties for black debutantes. The "leading colored citizens" in each community aspired to as much autonomy as they could enjoy and afford. "All I want is to be protected and let alone, so that I can build up this business," an Atlanta proprietor declared. To be "protected," he explained, meant only the

right to equal justice. "That doesn't mean social equality. We have a society of our own, and that is all we want. If we can have justice in the
courts, and fair protection, we can learn to compete with the white
stores and get along all right."[117]

For the majority of blacks in the rural and urban South, however,
this may well have been another world altogether. Black women reformers might argue that the virtues of thrift, cleanliness, and education crossed class lines, but a black woman forced to work in a white
home, in a factory, or in the fields might find such advice of little relevance to her life. Comparatively few blacks could share in the affairs
and rituals of the black elite, and some thought middle- and upper-
class blacks were all too bent on aping white society, to the exclusion of
most of their own people.

> *Niggers gettin' mo' like white fo'ks,*
> *Mo' like white fo'ks eve'y day.*
> *Niggers learnin' Greek an' Latin,*
> *Niggers wearin' silk an' satin,*
> *Niggers gettin' mo' like white fo'ks eve'y day.*[118]

Black entrepreneurs, professionals, and editors often employed the
rhetoric of racial solidarity and race pride in urging their people to patronize their own race. But even the discrimination they shared with all
blacks could not overcome class tensions and biases. In the 1930s, an
unemployed black man in Natchez, speaking to a group of unemployed workers, articulated an anger and frustration familiar to an earlier generation of black Southerners, directing his attack at the very
people he was urged to emulate:

An' de Negro who got somethin' is jus' as bad! Those Negroes up on
Water Street [black business section], an' dose doctuhs don't keer uh
goddam about *eny'* of you! All dey keer about is yo' money! When my
mothuh or my sistuh gits sick, dey ask me ef I've got money to pay
them befo' they'll come. An' if I ain't got the money, them - - - will let
her die, first. They jus' as bad as them pecks [peckerwoods, or white
people].[119]

Two ways of life coexisted, sometimes uneasily, in every substantial
black community: "colored society" and the black working class, themselves differentiated into subgroups. There was the community of black

businesses, newspapers, and social organizations, and there was the community of menial labor, unemployment, and inferior public services. And in the countryside, where most blacks resided, there remained the tenant farmers and sharecroppers, burdened with debt, tied to a land that barely sustained them and their families. For all the talk about a New Negro, there were many New Negroes, often with different needs, strategies, and views of the possible.

The options remained constricted. For the inner resources that enabled them to endure the worst of times, black Southerners at the turn of the century turned of necessity to their own institutions, no matter how limited the sustenance those institutions could afford them. None loomed larger and played a more central role in their lives than the places where they gathered to seek divine guidance.

9

THE CHURCH STOOD in the woods on the bank of the Suwanee River, only a short distance from the Georgia-Florida border. This structure was but a larger version of the shabby, crudely floored, and crudely furnished cabins that punctuated this region and housed most of its black population. Overhead, bits of the sky were visible through the crevices in the church roof. The glassless window openings were closed by heavy wooden shutters that swung back to admit the light. A large, broken circular saw, suspended between two trees, was used as the bell to summon the parishioners for church and the children for Sunday school. The furnishings were as bleak as the structure itself. The seats consisted of benches, some of them broken, almost all of them backless. Perched on a low platform, the pulpit was little more than a shelf covered with a cloth.

Two preachers presided, one of them sitting on the platform bench waiting his turn while the other exhorted the small congregation. The exhorter developed a certain rhythmic quality, speaking in explosive shouts of four or five words, then inhaling with a rasping snort that accentuated his words. Adding to the fervor of the sermon, the preacher's voice at times became so hoarse that the words were barely distinguishable. Occasionally he would break his delivery with a wail or by singing a line of a hymn. Striding back and forth on the platform, waving his arms frantically and distorting his body movements, he might have appeared like a wild man to the uninitiated. He seemed to cherish his dra-

matic role, sometimes crouching behind the pulpit, virtually hidden
from the congregation, or suddenly leaning back on the stage and making a frenzied appeal to God overhead.

Throughout the service, while defending themselves from swarming
mosquitoes, the congregation accentuated his preaching with cries of
"Amen," "Glory be," and "Yes, indeed," and sometimes provided a
humming chorus for his hymns. The main theme of the preacher's ex-
hortation was the miserable condition of man, but that cry of misery
would at the end be transformed into a joyous and ecstatic affirmation,
"I'm goin' to Jesus now." No sooner did he take his seat on the bench
than the other preacher was on his feet, starting a song in which everyone joined vigorously, and still more exhortations, prayers, and singing
would follow.[120]

It was a familiar scene repeated in thousands of similar structures
across the rural South. If it lacked the decorum of the established
church bodies, it more than made up for it in the spiritual enthusiasm
that gripped the congregation. If the minister lacked the requisite education for the more austere and learned urban ministry, he more than
made up for it with his charisma and spiritual eloquence. This scene
acted out in Suwanee country exemplified the appeal of the black
church, the still pervasive influence of the folk preachers, and the ways
in which black people since their arrival in the seventeenth century had
adapted Christianity to their own needs and worldview.

WHILE FULFILLING ITS role as a spiritual agency, the church took
on broader responsibilities as the traditional center and unifying institution in the black community. Viewed by many of its members as an
extension of the family, the church served as a school, a lecture hall, a
social and recreational center, a meeting place for an assortment of
groups, and a source of information. On a number of levels, as a
preacher in the Georgia Black Belt observed, the church served the
needs of the parishioner. "He turns to it not only for his spiritual wants,
but looks toward it as the center of his civilization. Here he learns the
price of cotton or the date of the next circus; here is given the latest
fashion plates or the announcement for candidates for justice of the
peace." Lucy Miller Mitchell recalled the church as central to the social
life of the community. "You were president of the missionary society, or
you taught in the Sunday school; your friends were people with whom
you came in contact in that context." But perhaps most of all, as Ben-

jamin Mays recalled of the church he attended in rural South Carolina, "This was the one place where the Negroes in my community could be free and relax from the toil and oppression of the week. Among themselves they were free to show off and feel important."[121]

Spiritual guide, moral leader, teacher, and disciplinarian, the preacher emerged as the most visible, the most influential, and often the most powerful leader in virtually any black community in the New South. Mirroring that community, he brought to it a range of qualities, depending on his education and training, his family background and economic status, and his life experiences. When W. E. B. Du Bois described the preacher as "the most unique personality developed by the Negro on American soil," he had in mind "a leader, a politician, an orator, a 'boss,' an intriguer, an idealist," a combination of "adroitness with deep-seated earnestness, of tact with consummate ability." But, as he also noted, the "type" varied considerably according to time and place, "from the West Indies in the sixteenth century to New England in the nineteenth, and from the Mississippi bottoms to cities like New Orleans or New York."[122]

Communicating directly and regularly with their constituents, the clergy preached the gospel to them and played a pivotal role in shaping their lives, thoughts, and expectations as well as their religious and moral character. Although the sermons often invoked visions of the afterworld, most ministers were very much a part of this world, serving in many instances as teachers, perhaps working in the fields or town to supplement their meager ministerial salaries, and assuming leading positions in the benevolent and fraternal organizations. By no means confined to religious concerns, some of them sat on the boards of black-owned companies or were themselves owners or part owners.[123] Saving souls was part of their business, but they might also be asked to save lives, acting in certain crises as intermediaries with the white community.

The rituals of the church imparted spiritual comfort and lasting memories. Baptized in 1912 at age fifteen, Roberta Bowman of Macon, Georgia, some seventy years later could still vividly recall the details of the ceremony and most of the names of the twenty-five candidates who were initiated with her that day. Not all the memories of such rituals, however, were positive. For some, the revelations that came out of their church experiences were less than the church elders intended. Richard Wright recalled the vivid biblical tales to which he was exposed as a youth in Mississippi—"a gospel clogged with images of vast lakes of eternal fire, of seas vanishing, of valleys of dry bones, of the sun burning to ashes, of the moon turning to blood, of stars falling to the earth . . . a cosmic tale that began before time and ended with the clouds of the sky rolling away at the Second Coming of Christ; chronicles that concluded with the Armageddon; dramas thronged with all the billions of human beings who had ever lived or died as God judged the quick and the dead. . . ." For an impressionable youth, it was almost more than he could absorb, and Wright felt himself emotionally affected by the experience and prepared to believe—at least until he realized that the stories had little if anything to do with the world he knew and experienced daily.[124] For scores of blacks, young and old, however, the vivid word images persisted, the doubts were resolved, and repentance and salvation took on lives of their own.

If baptisms took on a special meaning in the black community, so, too, did the funerals. For the black community, death often demanded a shared grief, and funerals could attract large crowds, even if few knew the person being buried. "My people like funerals," a black friend said of the open-coffin funeral of a fourteen-year-old girl who had died of tuberculosis. A funeral provided the preacher with the opportunity to render judgment, and in that role he could "preach the dead 'smack into heaven' or into hell, according to the life he or she had lived." No wonder, as Benjamin Mays observed, the church would be crowded if the deceased had been a prominent citizen, but it would be overflowing if the deceased had a bad reputation, as everyone came eager to hear the preacher's verdict.[125]

Few of the postemancipation triumphs enjoyed by black Southerners could match the enthusiasm with which most of them greeted separation from the white churches. To be able to worship in their own churches and listen to their own ministers not only lent substance to their notions of freedom but also permitted them to enjoy a distinctive version of Christian worship that made them feel much closer to God. In proclaiming the "indispensable necessity" of the Negro to the growth and progress of civilization, a black school principal in Raleigh needed only to single out the unique virtues of black Christianity. Without the Negro, he told an Emancipation Day audience in 1917, Christianity would be lacking in soul, "for while the white man gives it system logic and abstraction, the negro is necessary to impart feeling, sanctioned emotions, heart throes and ecstasy."[126]

Even the hymns sounded different in the black churches. When some white women visited the school in which Zora Neale Hurston was a student, they were impressed by her recitations and awarded her an Episcopal hymnbook bound in white leather with a golden cross embossed on the front cover. The book contained only the words, not the music, and young Zora committed the words of the songs to memory. But they seemed to her dull and lifeless. "If white people liked trashy singing like that, there must be something funny about them that I had not noticed before. I stuck to the pretty ones where the words marched to a throb I could feel."[127]

The minister assumed a wide range of responsibilities in the lives of black Southerners. Winfield Henri Mixon had not reached his fortieth birthday when in the 1890s he labored as the presiding elder of the African Methodist Episcopal Church in five counties in Alabama's Black Belt. The activities in which he participated spoke to the range and diversity of duties and responsibilities assumed by a minister and his expanded role in the community. Between 1892 and 1895, in recording his activities, the Reverend Mixon noted he had organized 13 missions, attended 193 love feasts and prayer meetings, attended 42 funerals, performed 21 marriage ceremonies, visited 116 sick families, licensed 26 to exhort and preach, baptized 115 adults and 128 children, delivered 1,152 sermons and lectures, administered the Holy Sacrament to 14,910, and traveled 24,000 miles. "We have been carrying the blaze of christianity. We have been watching the dancing rays of wealth. We have been driving the shining steel of education through the head of ignorance." Mixon concerned himself with day-to-day problems of survival blacks confronted ("[m]any people are without money, wood, coal and comforts of life"), their moral condition (the evil traffic in alcohol and the number of "sons and daughters of Ham" in the convict farm), the Masonic Lodge to which he belonged ("[w]e believe in the church first; masonry second"), and the black college (Payne) he helped to found and administer. He offered spiritual and moral guidance, but also advice on staying out of debt and avoiding lawsuits and unnecessary indulgences ("excursions"), and admonitions to his people to place more confidence in themselves.[128]

Drawing from history, life experiences, and theology, ministers preached both a biblical and a pragmatic gospel. The sermon often revolved around depictions of the afterlife, proximity to God, atonement on the cross, and the duties and responsibilities that fell to parishioners to examine and reform their lives and stay "in the straight path." Since emancipation, black clergymen had defined as a principal role the need to undo the moral depravity, self-debasement, and dependence that slavery had encouraged in its victims. That need persisted, as did the obligation to instruct a new postslavery generation in the practical lessons of daily life; in the virtues of temperance, marital fidelity, chastity, and domestic economy; and in the evils of gambling, lying, cheating, and blasphemy.[129]

Although the emphasis varied from church to church, much of the impassioned oratory from the pulpit was reserved for examining prospects in the afterlife. Having heard the minister's rhapsodic descriptions of the joys of heaven, few cared to contemplate the alternative. "I am sure," Benjamin Mays recalled, "that a burning hell and a golden-streeted heaven were as real as their farms to a majority of the people in Mount Zion and in the community at large." If an educated minister made these differences clear, they were underscored with even more devastating effect and unforgettable images and fervor by the mostly uneducated but still popular folk preachers. Through their voices and bodily contortions, the "beautifulness" of heaven and the "horrifulness" of hell stood in striking contrast, and every member of the audience could be made to feel

> dat awful region where de sun never shines, and where the thermometer stands fifty degrees below zero on de Fourth of July. Oh my bretheren, and sisteren, I beseeches you to beware of dat awful place where hell is friz over all de year round; and where de devil am gwine to roll you in de snow throughout de countless ages of eternity. . . . De very breath of your nostrils am gwine to freeze and beat you in de face like a snow storm; and hail and sleet am gwine to blow and beat on dat old leaky roof of hell continuously.

With that as their certain destiny in the absence of repentance, the parishioners in the Mount Ever Rest Colored Church in rural Mississippi were even more receptive to the minister's admonition to quit their "cussin; lyin; stealin; crap shootin; whisky drinkin, and backbiting one another to de white folks." After the sermon, the minister explained to a visitor why he had chosen those particular images to describe hell. He understood the Bible talked of fire and brimstone, but he knew better than to try to frighten any of his parishioners with hot weather: "if you wants to git next to him, you got to threaten him wid cold."[130]

How to measure the success of a sermon became an increasingly divisive issue within the church, mostly pitting the trained against the untrained preachers. The more impassioned exhorters measured success by the number of lost souls they rescued who confessed their sins and became candidates for baptism. Despite efforts to root out the uneducated, excessively emotional preachers, they continued to exert a powerful appeal in the rural South. They commanded a loyal following but often had to work outside the church to eke out a living. "Everybody owes me, everybody knows me, nobody pays me," one such preacher recalled, but he still took pride in his ecclesiastical talents. "My grandfather was a preacher and didn't know *A* from *B*. He could preach. I had a uncle and he was a preacher and didn't know *A* from *B*. . . . I am no mathematician, no biologist, neither grammarian, but when it comes to handling the Bible I knocks down verbs, break up prepositions and jumps over adjectives. Now I tell you something—I am a God sent man." But even "a God sent man," if not properly educated, encountered a mixed reception. "We used to listen," one churchgoer confessed, "to those whooping and hollering preachers who snort so you could hear them over three hundred yards, and we would come home and say, 'that's the greatest sermon I ever heard.' But now we want men who can teach us something."[131] Even in some of the more fashionable urban black churches, visitors found what they deemed appalling evidence of emotional extravagance and survivals of paganism.[132]

Charles Chesnutt learned from Elder Davis, black pastor of the A.M.E. Zion Church in Fayetteville, North Carolina, the trade secrets of a successful minister. He accommodated his style of preaching, Davis explained, to the three classes of people he needed to reach: the educated class (who "know what preaching is"), the less intelligent ("with very little learning"), and the "ignorant" and "unlettered" (who could not be reached except by "excitement and extravagance"). For the first class, he employed "regular pulpit style," mixed some Latin and Greek into the discourse, organized the sermon under subtopics, and read for a time from manuscript. For the next class, he used a more colloquial style and paid less attention to grammar but still maintained his dignity. For the lowest and easily the largest class, nothing less than a gospel bombardment would suffice.

> I shut up the Bible; rumple up my hair; shove up my coat-sleeves;— have taken my coat clean off in country churches; I leave the text altogether, and fall back on my imagination! I first go down to the depths of hell and depict all the horrors of dark damnation; the flames, the

anguish, the shrieks and groans of the tortured souls. Then I appeal to sinners to look at this that they are coming to. I forget all about grammar, and come down to plain "niggerisms."

Then leaving hell, I transport the audience to heaven, and paint the glories of that blessed place. I point to the long white robe, the starry crown, the golden slippers. I use up the Revelation and the older prophets who attempted to describe Heaven, and then fall back on my imagination. About this time, the audience being worked up to the right pitch, I bring my fist down on the Bible, knock the water pitcher off the pulpit, and by a final burst of extravagance, bring down the house.

Visiting one of Elder Davis's gospel performances, Chesnutt encountered mourners writhing and shrieking, hysterically laughing and weeping, nearly suffocating each other in their enthusiastic hugs, sometimes violently throwing themselves back on the benches, and some tearing off their clothes. It was a truly frightening scene, Chesnutt thought, "such as I never witnessed before, and never wish to see again."[133]

Chesnutt had brought his own intellectual and class biases to this scene, visiting on the parishioners some of the same disdain and impatience he had displayed in teaching poor rural children in North and South Carolina. What he and other critics described in the black church was actually a familiar cultural struggle in which the "better class" admonished their people to abandon the emotional religion of slavery for the rational religion that one found in the educated ministry of the more established churches. It simply made no sense to Chesnutt that so many black churchgoers would continue to prefer, if not insist on, a spiritual experience and inspiration that "rational" religion seemed incapable of supplying, at least not with the same depth of feeling and conviction.

Although often poorly paid, the preacher impressed some observers as more of a businessman than a religious leader. Like Elder Davis, he accommodated the gospel to the people to whom he was speaking and the compensation to which he aspired. "As the audience became more incoherent, he became more coherent," an observer noted of a minister whose rhythm and vocal velocity varied according to the contributions he received and who once refused to permit a coffin to be brought into the church for the funeral service until the salary owed him had been paid. Saddened over the decline of religion among his people, a farmer attending a conference at Tuskegee shook his head at the number of "hypocrites" filling the pulpits. "You let a man preach de true Gospel and he won't git many nickels in his pocket; but if he hollers and jumps he gits all the nickels he can hold and chickens besides." A newly installed pastor in Raleigh, North Carolina, Franklin P. Mallard, in requesting a father's permission to marry his daughter, conceded that preaching was not a "money making" profession but he still felt the field to be "promising" and he fully expected to be "a hit" once he had established himself "in this needy field." He first needed to marry as soon as possible, however, as the congregation expected it of him and treated a single minister with suspicion. "One cannot make Pastoral calls unless being exposed to criticisms."[134]

Within the black community, the mostly rural folk preachers were subjected to a barrage of criticism as misleaders, if not at times outright frauds. The more established clergy, along with many of their constituents, expressed dismay over the persistent sway of the uneducated preachers and their crude theology. Leaders of black Baptist women's groups singled out for criticism in 1915 those who bellowed "like an untamed animal of the Balaam specie while their thousands of followers scream like they are being stung by wasps, and shout until the building rocks in self-defense." The "dilapidated, ramshackle, greasy" buildings in which the services were held, the women charged, resembled the preachers themselves, appalling parodies of the churches where respectable black folk communicated with God. A missionary of the National Baptist Convention, after canvassing Baptist churches in rural Alabama in 1903, thought they symbolized "all that is miserable, backward, ignorant and uninviting."[135]

The foremost black leaders lent their support to efforts to reform the church and make it less of a racial embarrassment and affront to God. When Booker T. Washington declared in 1890 that "three-fourths of the Baptist ministers and two-thirds of the Methodists are unfit, either mentally or morally, or both, to preach the Gospel to any one or to attempt to lead any one," he addressed directly the most persistent questions plaguing the black church: the formally educated versus the folk clergy, proper decorum versus excessive emotionalism, and the responsibility of ministers to uplift their people in this world. The church, critics insisted, needed to reorder its priorities. That meant spending less time on the afterworld to the neglect or exclusion of this world, spending less time on preparing black people to die and more time on providing desperately needed guidance on how to live. "The trouble with us," Washington once declared, "is that we are always preparing to die." For more than a decade, Washington exerted his influence over the black church, treating it as a vital community institution to control. He appreciated the large constituency the church reached, and he thought it critical to align the church with his own creed: that work and the acquisition of wealth were moral activities, the precondition for genuine moral and religious sentiment. A delegate to the National Negro Business League meeting in 1900 captured that spirit. "I am one of those who believe the Negro must do something besides praying all the time. [Applause.] We started out directly after the surrender praying, 'Lord, give me Jesus and you can have all the world.' The white man in the South took us at our word and we got all the Jesus and he got all the world. [Laughter and applause]."[136]

Although Washington claimed to admire enterprising and successful black men, he obviously found distasteful the notion of men enriching themselves through the church by exploiting the gullibility of black parishioners. More than once he illustrated his criticism of the church by telling of the laborer in a cotton field in mid-July who suddenly stopped, looked upward, and exclaimed, "O Lord, de work is so hard, de cotton is so grassy, and de sun am *so* hot, I bleave dis darkey am called to preach." The preacher who measured his success by how many of his congregants were "groaning, uttering wild screams, and jumping" before going into a trance had, in Washington's estimation, abdicated his position as a spiritual leader. Such preachers, critics charged, exploited the gullibility of their people and used visions of the next world to acquire riches in this world.[137]

As one of the leading agencies of capital accumulation in the black South, the church had no objections to the acquisition of wealth. Like Washington, the many ministers who advanced their version of the Gospel of Success shared the belief that the church spent too much time preparing people to die when they should be uplifting them to live nobly and grandly and to find their "place" in this world. A black minister in 1898 advised his pupils to accommodate their sermons to the modern age—to teach their parishioners "how to vote, how to bargain, how to plan, how to do any work he is called to." What the black clergy often articulated were the same bourgeois self-help shibboleths that could be heard enunciated in white pulpits across the country. The idea

was to inspire their constituents to reach beyond their present circumstances and difficulties, to recognize their deficiencies but also their potential as a people.

> Show our people the paramount importance of acquisitiveness. . . .
> Teach that frugality and economy should be handmaids of industry.
> Teach the people the sacredness of an obligation. Teach the impor-
> tance of promptness in filling engagements. Teach the desirability of
> system in affairs. Teach the harmfulness of baleful habits. Teach these
> basal religious fundamentals.[138]

Avoiding the unique problems black men and women faced in an increasingly repressive South, preachers embraced the common assumption in the American success creed that the individual was responsible
for his own success or failure. Often blaming their own people for their
condition, ministers suggested that poverty and hard times resulted not
so much from white racial practices as from sinful ways and the absence
of individual discipline. Material accumulation and spiritual growth,
they argued, went hand in hand, and there was no necessary conflict
between godliness and wealth. Those who achieved success demonstrated through hard work, perseverance, and self-denial that they deserved not only a high station in this life but salvation in the next. The
few self-made black men who obtained property and wealth, among
them some of the very ministers articulating the Gospel of Success, assumed that because they had succeeded, others could also, providing
they possessed the same qualities. Combining the roles of minister and
president of a coaling company in Birmingham, Alabama, T. W.
Walker told the National Negro Business League in 1900 that "when
you teach a people to be frugal, industrious and saving, you have done
much toward making them moral and religious and useful citizens."[139]

The advice failed to heed the painful lesson that evidence of economic success might as easily intensify racial tensions and violence.
Much of the clergy, like other black leaders, preferred to believe otherwise, and many embraced the more optimistic view that the violent repression of blacks only underscored the impressive progress of the
race. The Negro needed to experience trials and persecutions in order
to overcome them; although blatantly unfair, white repression had the
desired effect of inspiring the race to advance itself. The disfranchisement laws, insisted a black Baptist divine, were a "scourge with which
God is whipping the Negro to acquire property and education."[140] Ar-

ticulated in various ways, this theme became a mainstay of Washingtonian accommodation, as it could foster hope and inspiration even in the worst of times.

Compared to his white counterpart, the black preacher exerted a greater authority within his community. That authority, however, rested on precarious grounds, dependent as it often was on white whims and toleration. As a pragmatic matter, at times a question of life or death, the black minister in the South viewed himself as a necessary agent of social control. He had to find ways to navigate the conflicting roles assigned him, that of pleasing constituents while not alienating necessary white tolerance and support. Even as he encouraged the aspirations of his people, he needed to disabuse their minds of extravagant pride and unrealisic ambitions. That delicate balance was not always easy to maintain.

The role of the black church as a restraining influence or as a mobilizing and provocative force could never be satisfactorily resolved. That half a century later it would serve as an organizing base for the civil rights movement had its roots in earlier times, as did its accommodationist side. The ability of the church to impose restraint, to channel frustration and anger, and to divert people from their own grievances and oppression made it a potentially conservative force with a mixed legacy in the community. Not long after the Civil War, Matilda Carter recalled all too vividly how the black preacher in the First Baptist Church, "de mos' powerful colored man in town," collaborated with "de rebels" to return property to the original owners, who then charged the same people rent for living on the land. "Rev'en Taylor was dar to help make folks sign. What he said to a Negro was law." As a restraining influence, the minister might also hope to check black resentment directed at the whites who circumscribed their lives. In the community in South Carolina where he grew up, Benjamin Mays recalled, the typical minister (including his own) "accepted the system and made no effort to change it." Of the 118 people in that community who could recall the sermons they heard around the turn of the century, 59 (50 percent) reported that their ministers taught them nothing about white people; 20 (17 percent) were instructed to obey white people and be submissive and deferential; 21 were taught to be respectful to whites; and some chose not to respond to the question. Only 4 respondents recalled ministers who urged them to demand their rights. During the agitation in North Carolina over disfranchisement, rumors circulated of an imminent black uprising. But, as a white magistrate reported, the "white niggers . . . got their colored preacher to try to calm down his folks and persuade 'em out o' their plot to try to get back the vote."[141]

Conflicting expectations by whites and blacks often made the role of the minister difficult. Even as whites welcomed black churchmen as a conservative and accommodationist influence, they remained sensitive to anything that smacked of racial heresy and subversion. Not only was excessive emotionalism a source of some concern, but also the lessons taught in sermons and Sunday school came in for special attention. Some white churchmen thought they had a responsibility to teach blacks in the proper ways of Christianity. "What he needs is a higher ideal . . . the Negro masses will never rise above the Negro preachers; and the Negro preachers will never get far above the level of the masses until they acquire the white man's ideals directly from the white man." But having acquired those ideals, they needed to understand the "place" assigned them by God—a useful, but lower, place than the superior Anglo-Saxon. What black ministers ought to be teaching their parishioners, a white North Carolina Baptist minister insisted, was that "the average Negro must serve . . . the white race or die. This is his mission in America, and will be until all people now living shall be dead and forgotten."[142] This was the quality of thinking every black minister had to consider seriously as he went about the business of proselytizing.

But accommodation had its limits. Even as preachers tried to ease the path to heaven, many of them struggled in various ways to make life less hellish on earth. The many churches burned to the ground since emancipation and the number of preachers beaten, intimidated, and murdered provided grim testimony to the price paid by blacks to wage such a struggle. How could the church stand apart from politics, a black journal asked soon after emancipation, when the issues in question were civil rights, suffrage, education, and equal protection under the law? That question took on even greater urgency in the late nineteenth century, as blacks witnessed the dismantling of the gains they had made during Reconstruction. Without hesitation, a black minister in Charlottesville told a Baptist conclave in 1880 that "it is as much the minister's duty to teach politics from the pulpit as to teach Christ."[143]

The politics of the clergy varied considerably. During Reconstruction, political and religious leaders were often the same men, and black churches housed political meetings. But the effects of disfranchisement and violence in the late nineteenth century severely dampened political involvement. For some, the retreat from politics was pragmatic and a necessary means of preserving themselves and their churches, for others, a reflection of their deep disillusionment with both parties and all candidates. Neither party deserved black votes, a Baptist minister argued in 1908, and racial problems would not be resolved through politics, at least not favorably. "The political condition of the Negro in the South could not be worse; the blame rests alone upon the States; the remedy is righteousness. The election of Mr. Taft or Mr. Bryan will not produce the millennium dawn." Black ministers in the South who chose to reject the two major political parties turned not toward the Populist but to the temperance movement. In announcing his support of Bryan in 1900, Henry M. Turner proclaimed himself neither a Democrat nor a Republican but a Prohibitionist.[144]

Disfranchisement did not necessarily end ministerial involvement in politics. Alternating between accommodation and protest, ministers chose their issues cautiously, as they acknowledged the limitations of either strategy. As a caretaker of their people, some clergymen felt themselves compelled to participate in the campaigns against lynching, segregation, and disfranchisement, and willingly employed the pulpit to denounce racial repression. Winfield Henri Mixon, while striking an accommodationist stance in his relations with whites, confided to his diary the rage he felt over the violence and injustices being visited on his people: "the wicked, ill-gotten, squint-eyed, blood suckers" who "hang, lynch, shoot, burn, or flay" black men and women. "My pen shall never stand, my voice shall never stop, my tongue shall never cease."[145]

Perhaps the most positive role the minister might play in a time of retreat, violence, and repression was to instill in his people the spiritual resources that would enable them to survive. As an institution managed and owned by black people, the church by its very existence and democratic structure imparted racial pride and dignity, providing parishioners of all classes the opportunity to participate in its meetings and rituals and to exercise roles denied them in the larger society. In their sermons, ministers often imparted a message that resonated with hope and confidence in ultimate redemption, in the ability of black men and women not only to endure but also to overcome. Addressing students in the Memorial Chapel at Hampton Institute in Virginia, a black clergyman told them how as a teacher he had examined current textbooks in history. "They said nothing about my people." That is because, he explained, "the people who do something are the ones who make history." But he believed God was preparing black people to redeem themselves as a people. "He isn't going to take all peoples and make one composite race here [but] he will make of us one distinct race, able to do something by ourselves." Historically, he noted, peoples who have been oppressed have managed to reach a higher and better civilization. "It was so with the Jews; it was so with the Puritans." And, he reassured them, God was welding black people together "so that we may realize our work and our mission." After telling his congregation the story of the liberation of the Jews, a clergyman in Washington, D.C., alluded to the emancipation of blacks and the confident prediction of whites that the race as a free people would die out. The preacher paused at this moment, laughed loudly, and shouted to his parishioners, "But we don't die out so easy!" Grins, laughter, and shouts greeted his observation.[146]

Few black clerics matched Bishop Henry M. Turner of the A.M.E. Church in the zeal with which he sanctioned a new role and attitude for black people. On one occasion, he was presiding at a church conference when the pastor of the church in which the meeting was held announced as the next hymn "Wash Me and I Shall Be Whiter Than Snow." Turner leaped to his feet, and holding his hand high above his head, ordered the organist not to proceed. "That's the trouble with you colored folks now," he declared. "You just want to be white. Quit singing that song and quit trying to be white. The time has come when we must be proud that we are black and proud of our race." For nearly an hour, Turner built on that theme, stirring his audience, including an impressionable teenage black Georgian, Albon Holsey. "I shall always cherish the memory of that meeting."[147]

By the 1880s, the betrayal of the achievements and promise of Reconstruction had embittered Turner. The betrayal took on additional meaning for him when in 1883 the U.S. Supreme Court invalidated the Civil Rights Act of 1875 that outlawed discrimination in public accommodations. That "barbarous" decision, he declared, "absolves the allegiance of the Negro to the United States." He remained confident, however, that God would still guide the race to a higher purpose. "It may be that the Supreme Court's decision was designed by Providence to arouse the negro to a sense of his responsibility." Ten years later, at a national black convention, Turner insisted that "the Negro cannot remain here in his present condition and be a man . . . for at the present rate his extermination is only a question of time." Disillusioned with politics and with the United States, Turner embraced emigration to Africa for black Americans.[148]

Although his emigration scheme never materialized, Turner,

through his sermons, speeches, and editorials, exposed large numbers of black people to a different conception of themselves. Convinced that the church should play a leading role in transforming the black psyche, he constructed a theology designed to improve the self-image of the race. It asked black people to reject any of the teachings and practices of white Christianity that reinforced feelings of inferiority. Since the God they worshiped had created them the equal of all other human beings, Turner in his indictment of white theology focused on the significance assigned to "whiteness." No longer should black people have to gaze on a blond-haired, blue-eyed, Caucasian Jesus. Only the white man's presumptuousness and distortion of Christianity depicted God and Jesus in his image. God is a Negro, Bishop Turner boldly proclaimed. When that statement provoked both ridicule and criticism from whites and blacks alike, Turner patiently explained what he meant. God was actually neither white nor black, but whites had insisted on seeing him through their spectacles. Throughout history, Turner observed, every race of people tended to portray God in its own image, even the heathen in Africa. He mocked the whites and "fool Negroes" who embraced as God "a white-skinned, blue-eyed, projecting-nosed, compressed-lipped and finely-robed *white* gentleman, sitting upon a throne somewhere in the heavens." Such notions were not only foolish and contradicted by history, but they were also counterproductive. "As long as we remain among the whites, the Negro will believe that the devil is black . . . and that he [the Negro] was the devil . . . and the effect of such sentiment is contemptuous and degrading." Besides, he noted, "the devil is white and never was black."[149]

Many if not most southern blacks who worshiped in the late nineteenth and early twentieth centuries needed the church not so much to politicize or mobilize them as to comfort them, to enable them to escape daily hardships and an inhospitable world. The decorum and formalities of the established churches, like many of the sermons, left many parishioners unsatisfied; they were not so ready to give up the religious practices and fervor that had sustained them through so many trials. It was not that they were unwilling to learn new ways but that they wanted to remain within easy reach of God's presence. "Some of them couldn't read or write good," Minnie Whitney said of the ministers she left behind in Virginia, "but, they was called by God. All they would tell you was where to find the text and close the Bible up and preach a sermon out of this world."[150]

To many rural folk, what outsiders called "miserable, backward, ignorant, and uninviting" were precisely the qualities they wanted to maintain and that attracted them to church. Some who clung to the "old time religion" found that it sustained them in ways that the more decorous and intellectualized forms of worship could not. W. E. B. Du Bois thought the church needed to purge itself of "the noisy and unclean leaders of the thoughtless mob" and substitute for them "clean" and educated "apostles of service and sacrifice." But his admonition fell on unreceptive ears in much of the rural South. To Du Bois, "men of scholarship" and "men of affairs" in the pulpits would inspire black men and women to improve the race rather than subscribe to "unimportant dogmas and ancient and outworn creeds." But to a North Carolinian who still clung to those dogmas and creeds, "All the D.D.s in the world" could not alter his admittedly "old fogy" belief in "the plain teaching of the Bible."[51]

Even educated ministers sometimes found themselves compelled to accommodate their preaching to the expectations of their constituents. It proved to be no easy task, as Frederick Jones, a young minister and graduate of a theological seminary, discovered when he assumed a pastorate in Frogtown, North Carolina. He appeared for his first sermon clad in the latest fashion, all of the finery, including his standing collar and gloves, calculated to make an impression on his congregation. As he delivered his sermon, based on sound doctrine he had learned at the seminary, the congregation sat perfectly still, not a single voice shouting an "amen," nobody nodding a head in approval. At the end of the sermon he announced the time for the next preaching. But at this point one of the veteran parishioners stood up and declared, "We ain't had no preach dis' mornin' yit. We want brudder Sam to preach for us," referring to an older black man sitting behind the minister. The congregation shouted their assent, and the new minister turned to Sam: "Say something to them; they don't seem to be satisfied." After limping across the platform several times, "Brudder Sam" pounded the Bible with his fist, and to an excited chorus of "Amen! Amen!" he shook the church building to its foundations. "Dese fellers comes out heah wid dere starched shirts, and dey' beaver hats, and dere kid gloves, but dey don't know nuffin b[o]ut 'ligion." And the parishioners roared back, "Dat's so! Amen! No, dey don't!" The preacher went on for another hour and a half in his singsong style, punctuated with groans and hoarse inhalings. Frederick Jones learned from the experience. He obtained a new wardrobe, purchased a pair of work shoes, and at the next

and succeeding sermons tried his best to approximate the emotional
fervor of "Brudder Sam."[152]

Dissatisfaction with conventional theology and the repression that
came down with such extraordinary and violent force in the 1890s demanded for some a new or reinvigorated spiritual medicine. When
blacks complained, as did a Jackson, Mississippi, observer in the early
twentieth century, that "church-going has degenerated into a fashion,"
they had in mind churches that were losing their spiritual vitality, suc-
cumbing to biblical scholarship and decorous services, and beginning
to resemble their austere and pretentious white counterparts. Such
churches had lost touch with many black worshipers, as they had allegedly lost touch with the very essence of Christianity, and had very
little to offer to the most disaffected, the most desperate in search of relief.

> *I wonder what de matter wid Zion, O my Lord,*
> *I wonder what de matter wid Zion, good Lord,*
>   *Rolling in Zion, Jubalee!*
>
> *My preacher don' preach a like a used to, O my Lord, . . .*
> *My sister don' shout like she used to, O my Lord, . . .*
> *My mou'ner don' mou'n like a used to, O my Lord, . . .*
> *My leader don' lead like a used to, O my Lord, . . .*
> *My deacon don' pray like a used to, O my Lord, . . .*
>
> *Oh, the people don't sing like they used to sing,*
> *The mourners don't moan like they used to moan,*
> *The preachers don't pray like they used to pray,*
> *That's what's the matter with the church today.*[153]

The Holiness movement, initially a split in the Methodist Church,
swept through the South in the 1890s, attracting both black and white
followers but soon branching off into separate racial organizations. The
Holiness preachers rejected worldly materialism, stressed a second
"blessing" of sanctification, deplored unrighteous living, and demanded adherence to a rigid, moralistic code of behavior. The largest
of the Holiness churches, the Church of God in Christ, was established
at Lexington, Mississippi, in 1897 "in an old gin on the bank of a little
creek." The Reverend Charles Price Jones, a cofounder, claimed to
have been yearning for "spiritual assurance, heart peace, rest of soul,

the joy of salvation." Such commodities were extremely rare for black folk in Mississippi, where Jones had his vision of "the beauty of holiness and the advantages of righteousness." If this world could not offer his people any reassurances, they would need to renounce it and seek salvation elsewhere. His church, where "neither form nor fashion" prevailed, offered salvation and hope to a people who found neither in this life, whether in the fields they plowed or in the regular churches some of them had attended, and it offered them the redemptive power of healing, a closer companionship with God, and a much-welcomed change and excitement in their working lives. Underscoring the ecstatic dimension of worship, services employed musical instruments and featured secular song (including ragtime, blues, and jazz) and dance as a part of the ritual. It brought theological entertainment to a new level.[154]

> Oh, Jesus (Oh, Jesus), my rock
> In a weary land (Yes),
> Our shelter
> In a time of storm.
> Please have mercy tonight (Yes)
> Oh, Lord [more high-pitched agony; shriller], Lord (Lord),
> Lord (Lord), Lord Jesus [scream] (Howdy) [woman shouts]
> I know you heard me one Sunday morning
> When I was in sin.
> [First strong responses from women, as shouting fervor begins]
> You got on my side.
> You cut loose my stammering tongue,
> Set my heart on fire.
> [Long pause, filled by the clear-voiced "oo-oo" of women][155]

Whatever the absence of decorum in the folk or Holiness churches, they were places of refuge that filled an emptiness in black lives, that raised people out of despair. The shouts, the rhythmic chanting, the foot stomps, the preaching, the singing, the hand claps, the degree of personal participation made for an intense emotional experience. It could not be intellectualized; it had to be felt. The same could be said for the revivals that periodically swept through both black and white communities in the South. Even regular churchgoers who preferred more decorous forms of worship and frowned on the excessive emotionalism and frenzy of the folk preachers often succumbed to the revival—that extraordinary and unforgettable moment when a parishioner claimed to enter into immediate communion with the Holy Spirit. A young W. E. B. Du Bois witnessed in Tennessee his first southern black revival, "a scene of human passion such as I had never conceived before." Olivia A. Davidson, whom Booker T. Washington would marry in 1885, was at a loss for words after witnessing a revival near Tuskegee; the costumes, services, songs, and shoutings "made up a scene which, having once seen one can never forget but which is utterly indescribable." Zora Neale Hurston retained equally vivid memories of the revival she attended as a young girl. After rhapsodizing in considerable detail about the "scenery of heaven," the revival minister descended into the "furnaces of Hell." Everybody within the reach of his voice knew that those who failed to "get religion" would reap nightmarish results, with "hellhounds" pursuing "their ever dying souls." Weeks after a revival, Jesse Thomas recalled how his neighborhood would still be reverberating with discussions of what had happened and assessing its success based on the number of new converts or reaffirmations of faith. For most believers, the revival brought personal liberation, but for some the terror made it memorable. "I would come home from the revival meetings," Lucy Miller recalled, "and lay in my bed looking up at the ceiling, hoping that the devil would not break through to come and take me away."[156]

Even as Washington and Du Bois deplored the excesses, tens of thousands of mostly working-class blacks embraced those excesses because it helped to enrich their lives. Perhaps, Benjamin Mays concluded, the exuberant Gospel and frenzied extravagance he heard preached as a child was in many ways "an opiate," but that was no reason to condemn it. "They believed the trials and tribulations of the world would all be over when one got to heaven. Beaten down at every turn by the white man, as they were, Negroes could perhaps not have survived without this kind of religion. . . . Sometimes an opiate is good in medicine. Sometimes it may be good in religion."[157]

Whatever could bring people to imagine a different world had its champions, particularly among the dawn-to-dusk laborers who saw no contradiction between spending Saturday night in a "juke joint" and Sunday morning in church. To Anne Bell, who spent her childhood in slavery, freedom had brought little but hard work and struggle. "Does I believe in 'ligion?" she asked aloud. "What else good for colored folks? I ask you if dere ain't a heaven, what's colored folks got to look forward to? They can't git anywhere down here." For young James Robinson, as he came to understand the meaning of blackness in a repressive South, the Sunday school teacher offered him the welcome assurance that "it wouldn't be like this always." For the old, those who had managed to survive that repression, there were also consolations and assurances. The question of who would be admitted to heaven had permitted them to share thoughts about the world as they had experienced it. The idea that white people would encounter difficulties at the Pearly Gates seemed obvious enough. "Everybody talks about heaven ain't goin' there," an old slave song proclaimed, and in the estimation of a Georgia black, "It was the general opinion of our old people that there would be no white people in heaven."

> *Po' man goin' to heaven,*
> *Rich man goin' to hell;*
> *For po' man got his starry crown,*
> *Rich man got his wealth.*

In Louisiana an elderly black preacher drew large audiences, eager to hear her testify that she had visited heaven, found Jesus Christ to be a Negro, and while there never saw a single white person.[158]

With or without whites, black believers knew it would be different, not another version of earth. Years of hard labor and tribulation in this world would finally be rewarded.

> *Dere's no rain to wet you,*
> *O, yes, I want to go home [repeated after each line]*
> *Dere's no sun to burn you,*
> *O, push along, believers,*
> *Dere's no hard trials,*
> *Dere's no whip a-crackin',*
> *My brudder on de wayside,*
> *O, push along, believers,*
> *Where dere's no stormy weather.*
> *Ev'y day will be Sunday in heaven.*

Emaline spent her life in South Carolina, where she and her family could never get out of debt to their landlord and employer no matter how hard they labored. "De plain Gawd's truth is dat Mister Stores done stole mos' ev'vything he niggers meck caze we is ignunt an' cain't figger wid him." As certain as she was that "Mister Stores" cheated them, she knew that the Lord would consign him to "de bottomless pit!" And that thought both consoled and elated her. "Ho, hit'll be a glorious day, dat hit will! . . . Thank Gawd, dere won't be no landlawds up dere before Jesus' seat, and dat's what will meck hit heaben! Yassuh! Dat hit sho' will!"[159]

The assurance that racial distinctions would have no place in the next world sustained many a believer in this world. An old Georgia cotton picker fully expected to be buried in the segregated cemetery, but he knew, too, that "on de Day ob Judgment dere be no camps. No, sir— only black an' white souls." Over several generations, moreover, blacks had heard the popular story of a white preacher telling a group of slaves about how white folks would walk through heaven on streets of silver and gold, while God had "some mighty good asphalt streets and some cement streets" reserved for the "darkies." After the white preacher had finished, a black preacher stood up to lead the congregation in prayer, but he first alluded to the streets of heaven. "Lord, I done come up like de bulrushes wid my head bowed down, like de rushes covered wid de morning dew. Lawd, I know dat I's your child and when I get to heaven I's gonna walk any damn where I please." Still other black believers anticipated a heaven where color would play no role at all.

> For by the laws of de just,
> And de laws of de right,
> We'll all be white in Heben's delight,
> Dar'll be no distinction dar.[160]

Whatever the enthusiasm for an afterworld free of racial distinctions and white oppressors, black people had not given up all hope for their condition on earth. The way they read and interpreted the Bible sustained their belief in the ultimate redemption of black folk in this world. "I may never live to see it," Sarah Fitzpatrick conceded, "but I do b'lieve dat de 'Nigger' will have mo' power dan whut he's got now. De Lawd says so in de Bible. It may take a long time but it sho' will come, you watch whut I tell you." In the meantime, her faith permitted her to contemplate some heavenly rewards. "Hebben is a good place but everbody ain't goin to it," she knew. A Methodist, she had mostly confined her family's prayers to Sundays. "At home I didn't have prayer ever'night, me an' de chillun wuz so tired at de end uv' de day dat we didn't worry 'bout prayer fo' we went to bed." But after a lifetime of hard work and struggle, she had few doubts about her destiny—"a better place, whar I kin git some res' whar every day will be Sun'dy."[161]

Whether attending the established or the folk churches, whether one listened to sermons extolling the acquisition of wealth or vivid depictions of hell and heaven, not all blacks were persuaded of the relevance of the church to their daily lives. Not all blacks could find the same degree of comfort, encouragement, and escape, if any at all. Not all blacks could find meaning in the offerings of the preacher or hope in the reading of the Bible. Some viewed the church as a relic of bondage, using God to keep black people down and reinforce their submission and dependence. A former slave who had been beaten many times in his life, and in whose house "hatred was as visible as swamp mist," rejected his wife's religion because he vowed he would never kneel again to anybody or anything. "How can I save him from Hell if he won't kneel?" she pleaded.[162]

Whether by observing their elders in prayer or from their own religious experiences, some young blacks professed to have no illusions. For young Richard Wright the vivid depictions of heaven and hell and the biblical tales lasted only as long as he remained in the church and within reach of the minister's voice. "[B]ut as soon as I went out of the church and saw the bright sunshine and felt the throbbing life of the people in the streets I knew that none of it was true and that nothing would happen." He still found the church useful, however, not as a place to learn about God but to meet school friends.

> Some of the Bible stories were interesting in themselves, but we always twisted them, secularized them to the level of our street life, rejecting all meanings that did not fit into our environment. And we did the same to the beautiful hymns. When the preacher intoned:
>
> *Amazing grace, how sweet it sounds*
>
> we would wink at one another and hum under our breath:
>
> *A bulldog ran my grandma down.*

Zora Neale Hurston as a child listened to her father ("known to thousands as 'Reverend Jno' ") preach. "Everything was known and settled," she remembered. She went to the revivals, watched the sinners on the mourner's bench, listened to the hymns, heard the testimonials, the shouts, and the ecstatic cries, and she witnessed the baptisms in the lake. It was "high drama," and she had fond memories of bearing witness. "But of the inner thing, I was right where I was when I first began to seek answers." And she remained skeptical. After hearing people in her father's church talk about actually seeing the sights and scenes around God's throne, she wondered why such people did not look and act differently after such a profound experience. "[T]hese people looked and acted like everybody else," she noted. "They plowed, chopped wood, went possum-hunting, washed clothes, raked up back yards and cooked collard greens like anybody else. . . . It mystified me. There were so many things they neglected to look after while they were right there in the presence of All-Power. I made up my mind to do better than that if ever I made the trip."[163]

Disillusionment with the church often translated into doubts about those entrusted with their religious uplift, perceiving them as hustlers and moral hypocrites rather than holy men. Even as black preachers made judgments about who would be permitted inside the Pearly Gates, some blacks wondered aloud if the preachers themselves would qualify. A story that made the rounds told of a black couple killed on the way to their wedding. Although admitted to heaven, the couple remained frustrated in their wedding plans, as for twenty-five years no preachers had been allowed to enter. That story would have resonated with Sarah Fitzpatrick, who found preachers to be "all right in deir place, but some ob dem sho' do git out ob deir place an' dey can't tell me nothin' 'bout doin' right les' dey is right demselves." Louisiana blacks reiterated those sentiments in song:

> *I wouldn't trust a preacher out o' my sight,*
> *Say I wouldn't trust a preacher out o' my sight,*
> *'Cause they believes in doin' too many things far in de night.*[164]

The degree of violence and repression sustained during the late nineteenth and early twentieth centuries no doubt intensified prayers throughout the South. But it also brought into question the efficacy of prayer. "Why didn't you ask God to give us some coal and some wood?" James Robinson's mother asked her husband. "You're always praying to Him. You've got your head stuck in a Bible and you're always down at that durn tabernacle whooping and hollering and shouting. You do so much for God, why doesn't He do something for you?"

Some years later, young Robinson, who grew up in Knoxville, Tennessee, realized why whites encouraged black preachers. "They were a cheap and useful tool with their soothing talk—'they that wait on the Lord'; 'You may have all this world but give me Jesus.' "[165]

The preacher offered salvation in the next world, but to many blacks he could not explain this world satisfactorily. Fewer found themselves persuaded by the standard response that the Lord works in mysterious ways. That was not good enough. Ida B. Wells worshiped in the A.M.E. Church in Memphis, she listened to the scholarly and saintly bishops, but she wondered why they did not give the people "practical talks." The people needed guidance about this life, but the preachers dwelled on the afterlife. Born in 1894, John Montgomery, Jr., worked as a common laborer and a chimney sweep in New Orleans. His father had been a chimney sweep, his mother a washerwoman. He had worked as a chimney sweep for eighteen years, preferring it to anything else he had done. He liked the independence, and he earned enough to more than survive. It was dirty work, and each night he needed to take a bath in kerosene. He knew little of religion, except that he had no intention of becoming a Christian. "That's the trouble with niggers," he exclaimed. "They pray too damn much. Every time you look around you see some nigger on his knees and the white man figurin' at his desk. What in the world is they prayin' fo'? Tryin' to get to heaven? They is goin' to get there anyhow. There ain't no other hell but this one down here."[166] Many a bluesman articulated the same sentiments, anticipating death as a grim but welcome escape from the realities of this world:

> Well the grave-yard must be an awful place,
> Lay a man on his back an' throw dirt in his face.
> Honey, how long have I got to wait,
> Honey, how long must I hesitate?[167]

A century after emancipation, Ernest J. Gaines, born on a Louisiana plantation in 1933, told a story in which a young black man confronted a preacher in the waiting room of a dentist's office in Bayonne, Louisiana. When the youth asked the preacher to demonstrate the existence of God, the preacher replied that his heart made him a believer. That was not good enough for the young skeptic. "As long as you listen to what your heart tells you," he declared, "you will have only what the white man gives you and nothing more." The preacher expressed his regrets over the youth's theological delinquency, but that only fed the young man's impatience. "You're sorry for me," he persisted, "you're sorry for me because I rock that pillar you're leaning on. . . . You believe in God because a man told you to believe in God. A white man told you to believe in God. And why? To keep you ignorant so he can keep his feet on your neck." That was more than the preacher could tolerate. After hitting the youth in the head, the preacher hurriedly left the room, declaring, "I never felt so sorry for a man before." One of the women in the room still found it difficult to believe that the young man really did not believe in God and expressed the hope that others of his age did not share such heresy. "Yes ma'am," he replied, "I hope they aren't all like me. Unfortunately, I was born too late to believe in your God. Let's hope that the ones who come after will have your faith—if not in your God, then in something else, something definitely that they can lean on. I haven't anything. For me, the wind is pink, the grass is black."[168]

CHAPTER EIGHT

CROSSROADS

Well, I drink to keep from worrying and I laugh to keep from crying
Well, I drink to keep from worrying and I laugh to keep from crying
I keep a smile on my face so the public won't know my mind.

Some people thinks I'm happy but they sure don't know my mind,
Some people thinks I'm happy but they sure don't know my mind,
They see this smile on my face, but my heart is bleeding all the time.[1]

W E. B. DU BOIS PREPARED "a careful and reasoned statement"
on the Sam Hose case for the *Atlanta Constitution*. Armed with a letter of
introduction to Associate Editor Joel Chandler Harris, Du Bois chose
to deliver the article in person. On his way downtown, he learned of
the lynching of Hose and that some of the victim's knuckles were on
display at a grocery store he would pass on the way to the newspaper's
office. "I turned about and went home. I never met Joel Chandler Harris. Something died in me that day."[2]

The night after the lynching, Booker T. Washington drafted a letter
of protest he proposed to send to the governor of Georgia. Before
doing so, however, he showed it to his friend T. Thomas Fortune, who
fluctuated in his embrace of agitation and accommodation as the most
effective way to combat racial injustice. Fortune read the letter and tore
it up. "Washington," he told him, "you are the only man that now
stands between the white and colored man as a bond of sympathy.
Don't send that letter. It will destroy the power we have." To newspaper
reporters, Washington refused to comment on the brutal lynching, feeling the need "to keep silent and not engage in any controversy that
might react on the work to which I am now lending my efforts."[3]

Addie and William Hunton were establishing a home for themselves
in Atlanta in 1899 when they learned of the lynching of Hose and the
subsequent distribution of his body parts as souvenirs. It had a devas-

tating effect on the couple. "In consternation my husband and I drew apart from our friends to consider what to do," Addie Hunton recalled. "The wisdom of having our expected child born to us in such an environment seemed quite doubtful, but after prayer and deep thought, we decided to remain." Seven years later, however, after the white riot that devastated black Atlanta, the Huntons had seen enough, and they chose to leave for the North.[4]

News of the Hose lynching reached overseas. Edward W. Blyden, a black Presbyterian minister who had moved to Liberia but often returned to the United States for visits, read about the Hose burning in a New York newspaper. He shared the story with a group of African natives, most of whom found it impossible to believe or absorb. "Their imagination had never pictured any tragedy so frightful or revolting," he said of his audience. "Nothing in their experience or their traditions could afford any parallel to such hideous barbarities practiced as they were by people supposed to be Christian and highly civilized."[5]

While two thousand white spectators watched the dismemberment of Hose, American soldiers were engaged in combat in the Philippine Islands, seeking to suppress Filipino insurgents under the command of Emilio Aguinaldo who were fighting for independence. The war itself had come under sharp criticism in the black community, as it underscored the contradiction between the proclaimed American mission abroad and the virulence of racism at home. None other than Aguinaldo made the most devastating comparison between American actions in the Philippines and white repression in the South. He invoked the image of Sam Hose. In a printed appeal, "To the Colored American Soldier," the insurgents told black troops that they were spilling their blood "without honor" and that their real fight was in America. "Your friends, the Filipinos, give you this good warning. You must consider your situation and your history, and take charge that the blood . . . of Sam Hose proclaims vengeance."[6]

Robert Charles exacted his own "vengeance." He was a recent arrival in New Orleans, and news of the burning and dismemberment of Hose infuriated him. Friends testified they had never seen him express such anger, that he was "beside himself with fury," declaring it to be the duty of every Negro to own a rifle and to prepare to use it in unison to defend themselves. For Charles, the Hose lynching and growing racial tensions reinforced his growing separation from a South he found increasingly incorrigible in the ways white people acted on their racial views. He listened to the ideas propagated by the African Emigration

Society, which promoted the emigration of blacks from Mississippi and Louisiana to Africa. Shortly after the Hose lynching, Charles chose to become a subscription agent for the *Voice of Missions,* a paper published by Henry M. Turner, a bishop of the African Methodist Episcopal Church and a leading advocate of emigration to Africa.[7]

The circumstances that brought Charles to New Orleans had become familiar to a new generation of southern blacks. Born in freedom, in late 1865 or early 1866, Charles personified the worst fears of white Southerners in the late nineteenth century—a New Negro, footloose and restive, undisciplined by slavery, unschooled in the obsequiousness and demeanor whites expected of black men and women. He was raised in Copiah County, Mississippi, southeast of Vicksburg, where his parents worked as sharecroppers. Unwilling to resign himself to his parents' way of life, Charles left the tenant farm in the hope of improving his economic prospects. He came to New Orleans around 1894, where he spent much of his time with others who had migrated from Copiah County. In 1900 he was thirty-four and literate, moving his residence frequently and working as a laborer in a variety of jobs— on street labor gangs, as a roustabout on the levee, a helper at the sugar works and saw mill, an engine-room coal shoveler in a local hotel. Like many of his young contemporaries, he was living precariously, trying somehow to survive and to suck some joy and meaning out of his life. To believe the press, he was but one of many blacks "driven out of the parishes" who had made New Orleans "the refuge of all the bad negroes in the Southwest."

On July 23, 1900, Charles and a friend were waiting for two women who had agreed to meet them after work; one was a close acquaintance employed in the city as a domestic servant. While the two men sat outside her home, a police sergeant and two of his patrolmen approached them, having been told of some "suspicious-looking negroes" loitering in the neighborhood. They exchanged angry words, and when Charles rose, one of the policemen felt threatened, grabbed him, and then began to beat him with a billy club. Charles and the policeman both drew and fired their pistols, wounding each other slightly. Charles fled to his room. When the police (including the captain of the precinct) came to get him, Charles opened fire, this time with his Winchester rapid-firing rifle.

After the initial shootings, Charles eluded an intensified police manhunt. Meanwhile, his exploits prompted white mobs to take to the streets of New Orleans, attacking black men and women they encountered. The police finally tracked down Charles to his hideout, whereupon he opened fire from a window with his Winchester and proved to be a remarkably accurate shot. Surrounded by more than a thousand men, who were spraying the building with gunfire, Charles continued to blast his pursuers, inflicting additional casualties. "His aim was deadly," one newspaper reported, "his coolness must have been something phenomenal." Finally, the by now exasperated police, urged on by an expectant and furious crowd estimated at from ten thousand to twenty thousand men, set fire to the building in the hope of smoking out Charles. As he fled the flames, Charles was hit. Dragging him into the street, the police and members of the crowd fired repeatedly into the prostrate body. The son of one of the slain policemen stomped on the face of the corpse until it had become almost unrecognizable. "Everybody," a reporter wrote, "wanted to show his contempt for the corpse."

The quick death of Charles only embittered the crowd and encouraged them to find other blacks upon whom they could wreak their vengeance. For four days, mobs surged through New Orleans, seizing control of downtown sections, killing at least a dozen black people and injuring many more, and destroying black property, including a noted school. Blacks withdrew into their homes, workers stayed away from their jobs. "Africa had gone into eclipse," a reporter noted. Meanwhile, whites were left to brood over what Charles had accomplished. He had managed to shoot twenty-seven whites, killing seven of them, including four police officers. His feat almost immediately assumed legendary proportions. Even in death, one newspaper observed, he "inspired horror" for those who came to gaze at his body: "In the expression of his closely locked jaws there lingered . . . a suggestion of that terrible hatred of the whites which seems to have been his one dominating trait through life." No wonder the police chose to bury him hurriedly and secretly, before dawn, under military guard, in an unmarked grave in potter's field.

Like Sam Hose, Robert Charles fed white fears based on perceptions of an increasingly unrecognizable race, of a generation all too rapidly casting off more of the vestiges and demeanor of enslavement. But Charles elevated those fears to a new level. Few blacks had dared to give such full vent to their frustrations and bitterness, to make open war on whites. "No one man," a newspaper declared, "has ever before so profoundly aroused the anger and indignation of its citizens." The newspapers immediately proclaimed Charles a "monster," a "brute,"

"a black butcher," "a bad nigger," a "Negro beast," and a "bloodthirsty
champion of African supremacy." (When Charles was still at large,
newspapers described his physical features and added, "Fond of talking
about race wrongs and Liberian emigration project.") The mayor speculated that Charles had wanted to incite an insurrection. One newspaper predicted "race war," another reported increasing "complaints of
the impudent if not threatening manner of negroes in the public
squares, in the streets, and even in the cars," and several papers suggested that the literature of the African Emigration Society and the
preachings of Bishop Henry Turner had "inspired" Charles to shoot
white people. Pamphlets found in his room argued that the oppression
of blacks had reached a point "where further endurance is almost unbearable." Some whites found it convenient to dismiss Charles as a
crazed fanatic or anarchist, making it unnecessary to consider the
frightening implications of his deeds. Still others, however, warned
whites to heed the lesson of Charles and to maintain vigilance. "The
average negro is, after all, little else than a tamed savage," one newspaper editorialized. "Several hundred years of slavery and forty years of
freedom, under the most enlightened circumstances, have not taken the
savage out of his nature."

The "better class of the race" took pains to denounce and dissociate
itself from the actions of Charles. A state convention of black Baptists,
meeting in New Orleans, condemned "all acts of lawlessness perpe-
trated by the lawless element of our race" and pledged their efforts to
assist authorities in bringing such people to justice; at the same time, it
urged authorities "to use the strong arm of the law with equal justice to
all alike." A black New Orleans newspaper conceded that the literature
of emigration had a tendency to agitate some blacks, making them
"restless and unsettled . . . to no good purpose." But it also noted
Charles's origins: "bloody Copiah," the county where "mob violence
and slaughter" were commonplace and where Charles's "education in
race hatred and bloodshed first began." The newspaper estimated that
"a large percentage" of the black population of New Orleans had, like
Charles, come from "such terror stricken districts." These individuals
were not necessarily "bad people," the newspaper advised, but they
were "exceedingly nervous and are constantly fearing for the worst."
The editor praised "the better element of our white citizens" who opposed mob law. And he admonished local blacks never to forget the
principal lesson of the riot: that their only hope was to cast their lot on

"the right side" and identify themselves with "the best white citizens" of the city, those who understood the Negro and valued him as "a laborer and a well behaved citizen." If blacks heeded that lesson, they would not be held responsible for the acts of the "lower and criminal classes." Finally, the editor singled out as an affront to the "peace and dignity" of the community the black family who had harbored Charles in their home after he had murdered two police officers. "However much they may have sympathized with him in his troubles, surely they knew the case had gone too far to do him any good."[8]

Although welcoming black condemnation of Charles, whites were not altogether persuaded. Noting that "deceit and deception" were characteristic of Negroes, one local newspaper found the recent denunciations of Charles in the black community to be "utterly worthless," articulated by the same men who might on other occasions preach "the bitterest incendiarisms and fierce resentment against the whites to a negro meeting in a secret den." Still another local newspaper, while welcoming black pledges of law and order, noted that "as a class" blacks did nothing to punish "the outlaws" of their race; "on the contrary, they show every disposition to shield and shelter them."[9]

Black people did not soon forget Robert Charles. But they did not necessarily share and few probably read the admonitions of the local black newspaper. The aftershocks would continue for months. In southwestern Louisiana, a black man fretted over the riot and sometimes had alcoholic nightmares that he was being lynched. While riding on a train, he dreamed a white mob was hanging him and he began shouting, struggling all the while with an imaginary rope around his neck. When the white conductor came down the aisle and demanded quiet, the man shot him. He was removed from the train at the next station and lynched from a telegraph pole. In New Orleans, memories of Charles's deed lingered, despite the efforts to expunge him from history. Five weeks after the burial of Charles, a black man walked across the street to where his neighbor, Fred Clark, also black, sat in a chair, reading. The man pulled out a revolver, put it to Clark's head, and killed him. Fred Clark had informed the police where to find Charles on the day he died.

The exploits of Robert Charles inspired a song that, in the words of Jelly Roll Morton, "never did get very far." It was deemed too subversive to sing, even to recall. "I once knew the Robert Charles song, but I found out it was best for me to forget it and that I did in order to go along with the world on the peaceful side." That song, Morton remembered, was "a trouble breeder." He conveniently forgot the song. He never forgot Robert Charles.[10]

2

ALTHOUGH OF DIFFERENT generations, Robert Charles and Robert Johnson shared a common heritage. Both grew up in Copiah County, Mississippi. Neither was able to make peace with his society. Both gave up on it, and became a new breed of interior exile, trying to find ways to give expression to their deepest feelings. Both drifted from place to place, and both died violent deaths, Charles at thirty-four, Johnson from poisoning at twenty-seven. But both left behind them a legacy that would endure. Charles made his mark with a Winchester rifle, Johnson with his demonic songs and guitar licks. Some thirty years after the New Orleans "riot," Robert Johnson conveyed in his music a sense of terror that would no doubt have resonated deeply with Robert Charles and his generation.

In "Cross Road Blues," Robert Johnson underscored the predicament every black youth was taught to avoid. Night is approaching, and he finds himself at a rural crossroads desperately trying to flag a ride. He is in a strange place where no one knows him and where the warning "Nigger, don't let the sun go down on you here" was understood and vigorously enforced. He is uncertain in which direction he should head, and he suspects it will make no difference.

> *I went to the crossroad, fell down on my knees.*
> *I went to the crossroad, fell down on my knees.*
> *Asked the Lord above, "Have mercy save poor Bob, if you please."*
> *Mmmmm, standin' at the crossroad I tried to flag a ride.*
> *Didn't nobody seems to know me, everybody pass me by.*
>
> *Mmm, the sun goin' down, boy, dark gon' catch me here.*
> *Oooo ooee eeee, boy, dark gon' catch me here.*
> *I haven't got no lovin' sweet woman that love and feel my care.*
> *You can run, you can run, tell my friend poor Willie Brown.*
> *You can run, tell my friend, poor Willie Brown*
> *Lord, that I'm standing at the crossroad, babe,*
> *I believe I'm sinkin' down.*[11]

The song spoke to only one aspect of an elaborate apparatus that circumscribed the actions of black Southerners. But it underscored the precariousness and vulnerability of black life in the Age of Jim Crow. To describe what was happening around them, black observers, as well as whites, increasingly employed the language of war, suggesting a region on a virtual wartime footing. Some twenty-five years after emancipation, a Georgia black leader described his people as essentially under siege, occupying a steadily deteriorating position. In much of the South, he reported, "a system of terrorism and guerrilla warfare exists, to which open war, with two contending armies in the field, governed by the usages of Christian nations, would be an improvement." By 1910, in the estimation of a visitor, race relations in the South had become a "state of war."[12]

This "war" black men and women were clearly losing; indeed, it had become a virtual rout. The other side owned the land, the law, the police, the courts, the government, the armed forces, and the press. The political system denied blacks a voice; the educational system denied them equal access and adequate resources; popular culture mocked their lives and aspirations; the economic system left them little room for ambition or hope; and the law and the courts functioned effectively at every level to protect, reinforce, and deepen their political powerlessness, economic dependence, and social degradation. Those were formidable odds. "You know what it was like for the Indians, surrounded by fifty whites with rifles?" a black Mississippian asked. "Then you know what it was like in the Delta."[13]

The terror inflicted by white mobs was far more spectacular, but scores of blacks who had never witnessed a lynching or a riot fell victim to the quiet violence practiced by whites who rigidly controlled their daily lives. From their personal experiences, most blacks knew how the landlord, the merchant, the banker, the judge, the sheriff, and the local politicians interacted to make certain the machinery of domination functioned effectively. This kind of violence devastated lives by depriving people of choices, dramatizing how little black men and women could do to make changes in their lives. The exasperation expressed by a sharecropper who spent his working days in Mississippi and Arkansas in the early twentieth century suggested how little had changed since Reconstruction. "De landlord is landlord [i.e., white], de politicians is landlord, de judge is landlord, de shurf [sheriff] is landlord, ever' body is landlord, en we ain't got nothin'."[14]

But if blacks learned to fear whites, and although many were economically dependent on them, that did not necessarily translate into respect or admiration. Nor did they necessarily view whites as "superior." Imposing their own interpretations on race relations and standards of civilized behavior, blacks speculated on why white people thought and acted as they did. Looking back on a lifetime of coexistence with whites, a former house servant thought white people were indifferent to the feelings of blacks because they refused to believe that blacks were capable of harboring genuine feelings. "Ya' know when white fo'ks treat 'Niggers' mean hit ain't cause dey think its right, dey jes' think dat de 'Niggers' is nothin' mo' dan a brute. Dey don't want'cha to say yas an' naw to dem needda. Ef ya do, they think ya crazy." Given the people he encountered in the Black Belt in the early 1890s, a white visitor concluded that blacks seriously questioned white pretensions toward civilized behavior and viewed the white man "as a person of alien and, upon the whole, objectionable character from surface to core."[15]

The confidence southern whites exuded in the unique knowledge they possessed of the Negro lay in the assumption that black lives and emotions lacked any real depth or complexity, that Negroes were transparent in their behavior and expression. It seemed to David L. Cohn, a native Southerner who spent his boyhood in the Mississippi Delta, that "nearly all white Southerners" shared "a genial delusion" about Negroes: that because they lived among them, employed them as cooks, maids, nurses, and washerwomen, they intimately understood Negro life. But Cohn himself readily conceded that he possessed no such knowledge, and he believed few of his white neighbors did, no matter what they said to the contrary. "The truth is," he observed, "most Southern whites have only the faintest comprehension of the inner lives of Negroes which remain forever secret and alien to them." Some of the whites who "knew" the Negro and claimed a fondness for the race, in the estimation of a black educator, exhibited the kind of love usually reserved for a pet pony or a dog. "Whites would have the most intimate contacts and share their most sacred secrets, but the moment a black began to act human, he was put 'in his place.' "[16]

Whatever whites said about their unique gift of comprehending Negroes, many came to realize that they knew only what blacks chose to reveal—and that was remarkably little. To get at "the real feeling of a Negro," to know what went on in their cabins, clubs, churches, and "innumerable societies," many whites confessed, had always been difficult but was now virtually impossible. The very circumstances of their enslavement had made blacks "defensively secretive," in the estimation of one observer of southern society, but that defensiveness had become heightened since emancipation. "In the past, the instinct was passive and defensive; but with growing education and intelligent leadership it is rapidly becoming conscious, self-directive and offensive."[17]

The most remarkable revelation was that the very blacks they thought they knew best—those who worked in their homes—they often knew least of all. That discovery had stunned many families during and after the Civil War, and it persisted well into the twentieth century. One white woman told of a cook who had been in the family's service for nineteen years; the family loved her, they submitted to her "many small tyrannies," they made her a confidante "in the most intimate private and family matters," the daughters had even shared with her their love affairs. "But do you know," the woman remarked in obvious exasperation, "Susie never tells us a thing about her life or her friends, and we couldn't, if we tried, make her tell what goes on in the society she belongs to."[18] To reveal that they actually knew little or nothing about the women who worked for them had to be a difficult admission, as it lessened considerably the confidence with which they could govern black lives and anticipate black behavior. If whites refused to give up notions of superiority, that did not necessarily make them feel more secure in the presence of their "inferiors."

The difference between how much each race knew the other could, of course, be easily understood. For black men and women to know white folks—their whims, expectations, moods, and moves—was more than a matter of curiosity; their very survival depended on such knowledge, and they had every opportunity to acquire it. "By long and close association with the white man," one observer noted, "the negro has learned all of his ways, and can read at a glance his innermost thoughts, and can now size him up and classify him just as accurate as a cotton buyer does the different grades of cotton, and can do it much quicker." Ned Cobb learned from his experience in the Alabama Black Belt to anticipate by tone of voice and movement white expectations. "I've had to play dumb sometimes—I knowed not to go too far and let them know what I knowed, because they taken exception of it too quick. . . . They'd have dealins with you, furnish you what you needed to make a crop, but you had to come under their rulins. They'd give you a good name if you was obedient to em, acted nice when you met em and didn't question em bout what they said they had against you. You begin to cry about your rights and the mistreatin of you and they'd murder you."[19] The bluesman said as much when he sang:

You better be smart, you better not cry,
You sure have trouble with the man.[20]

If blacks found it impossible to respect many of the whites they encountered and for whom they worked, that was because they knew
them so well (including the "better sort") and that few whites actually
lived by the values they publicly embraced. "I knows 'em," insisted a
Tennessee black woman, "I knows white folks from their birth; only difference is I ain't birthed one, that's the only difference. The sight of 'em
don't excite me one bit, I tell you, 'cause I know white folks from the
cradle up." Among themselves, blacks mocked white pretensions to superiority, dismissing them as mostly specious nonsense, along with
white notions of honor, civility, and chivalry. A popular folk wisdom, no
doubt reinforced by generations of blacks working in white homes,
most effectively disposed of white pretensions to racial superiority:

These white folk think
That they so fine,
But their dirty linen stinks
Just like mine!

Richard Wright's boyhood friend imparted with delight his own varia-
tion of that folk wisdom:

All these white folks dressed so fine
Their ass-holes smell just like mine. . . .[21]

Not all whites looked alike, nor did they necessarily think alike about
matters of race. But many blacks found it difficult to find meaningful
differences between "good" whites and "bad" whites. It had been customary to do so on the basis of class. The notion that "the better sort"
of whites had more compassion for black people had long been a staple
in black rhetoric. Booker T. Washington had repeatedly expressed his
confidence in the friendship and patronization of upper-class whites,
and most black leaders and editors voiced similar sentiments. But based
on their experiences, many blacks found no reason to share that confidence. Charles Chesnutt, although he fraternized with educated whites
in his native North Carolina, greeted with disdain blacks who spoke
proudly of their "white friends." He claimed to have no white friends.
"I could not degrade the sacred name of 'Friendship' by associating it

with any man who feels himself too good to sit at table with me, or to sleep at the same hotel. True friendship can only exist between men who have something in common—between equals in something, if not in everything; and where there is respect as well as admiration. I hope yet to have a friend."[22]

For the bulk of black Southerners, the distinction in motive and method between, for example, paternalistic racial conservatives and the more rabid and demagogic racists may have been too subtle to be fully understood or to be meaningful. Neither industriousness nor accommodation brought white respect, and neither disfranchisement nor segregation brought racial peace. The "better sort," if more enlightened in their racial views, were no more inclined to treat blacks as equals. Some of them participated in (if they did not lead) lynch mobs, and they did little or nothing to ameliorate the oppressive conditions under which most black people lived. "[T]he white folks down here," an Alabama black man confided in 1910, "all dey cares fer in de nigger is what dey kin make outer him. Dey says, 'We alls is glad you is gettin' homes.' Dey don' like it at all. Dey likes we niggers fer all de corn dey kin get out er us, an' all de cotton dey kin git out er us, an' den dey's done."[23]

3

THE MECHANISMS and pervasiveness of white repression, both the ritualized and institutionalized subordination demanded of black men and women, exacted a psychological and a physical toll, shaping to an extraordinary degree day-to-day behavior and demeanor, affecting even speech and body movements. A black South Carolinian thought the effects of accommodation to be readily discernible in the "subdued" manner of his people, in how they moved on the sidewalks, and in "the servile way" they acted when trading in the stores. The stories of lynchings, burnings, and beatings, as they were intended to do, permanently entered black consciousness. Richard Wright remembered most vividly the "paralysis of will and impulse" induced by the fear of making the wrong move, the "sustained expectation of violence" that forced him to curb his impulses, speech, movements, manner, and expression. "The penalty of death awaited me if I made a false move and I wondered if it was worth-while to make any move at all. The things that influenced my conduct as a Negro did not have to happen to me directly; I needed but to hear of them to feel their full effects in the deepest layers of my consciousness. Indeed, the white brutality that I had not seen was a more effective control of my behavior than that which I knew."[24]

Circumspect and self-effacing in the presence of whites, employing if necessary an exaggerated deference, avoiding whites when possible, black men and women went about their business, adopting a variety of responses to the world about them. The "life" experience of an Alabama black farmer persuaded him to remain as inoffensive as possible. "Them was awful times," he recalled. Since the days of the Ku Klux Klan, his life had become one of resignation. "I knowed what side to get on, and that's the side I stayed on, the white folks." For many blacks, the ideal strategy (and a way to maintain one's self-respect) was to avoid any contact with white people, verbal or physical. Closely resembling the strategy of avoidance, some blacks opted for maximizing their personal welfare (and survival) by not becoming involved in the problems of others. Joseph Sutton knew that it "don't pay to talk about" lynchings, and he heeded the advice of older folk who told him, "Praise the bridge that carries you over," no matter what happens to the next person who comes along to cross that bridge.[25]

For every black seething with frustration and resentment, others accommodated as best they could, and most experienced both moods—resentment and accommodation—at various times in their lives, often simultaneously. The imperative was to find ways to circumvent the system without seeming to do so. When asked how he had survived, Charley Thomas of Tunica County, Mississippi, glared at his questioner. "*You* know the answer to that. This is Mississippi. You see me? I learned to live here. I learned *how* to live here." A traveler in the Mississippi Valley in 1906 found that nearly every black person he encountered had thoughts and opinions on the issues of the day, especially those affecting race, but they recognized the need to be cautious and evasive in the presence of whites, even to play dumb if necessary. "Hit doan' do to talk much," one black remarked, "or we git into a heap er trouble. We low-born, an' the white folks are not likin' us to say anything."[26]

Whatever the limits of permissible dissent and behavior in the New South, the accommodations black men and women made to white expectations came to be increasingly a grinless and restless accommodation, subversive of the racially harmonious relationships envisioned by the "better sort" of whites and by most black leaders. The emergence of a New Negro evoked a mixed response in the black community, often reflecting different conceptions of the meaning of the term. Some older blacks, particularly when speaking to whites, professed to be dismayed over the assertiveness of the young, what some called the "new issue free niggers." But others took a certain pride in the audacity of young blacks and the degree to which they ignored or chose to drop some of the old customs. "These niggers ain't gonna take nothing off these white folks," a former Tennessee slave recalled with admiration. "They ain't scared of white folks. . . ."[27]

The term "New Negro," as used by whites, generally revisited old fears and described Negroes undisciplined by slavery who did not know their place. The same term, as employed by blacks, suggested a generation better educated, more inclined to cast off the vestiges of enslavement, and determined to break the degrading and humiliating dependence on whites. "We have no sympathy with the idea of the 'good old darkey,' " a black newspaper in New Orleans declared in 1898, as it pronounced the imminent demise of this relic of slavery. "One generation more, and the Negro that can be kicked, fed on promises, and called by any name, will be gone and a new Negro will come to the front." No less excited at the prospect, Ida B. Wells, who in many ways personified what a white woman derisively described as "these new-fangled Niggers," warned whites of a new mood in the black South:

> The old southern voice that made the Negroes jump and run to their holes like rats, is told to shut up, for the Negro of today is not the same as Negroes were thirty years ago. So it is no use talking about Negroes ought to be kept at the bottom where God intended them to stay; the Negro is not expected to stay at the bottom.[28]

That view would be articulated in a variety of ways, with the rhetorical flourish of a Wells or with the uncompromising matter-of-factness of the bluesman who while suggesting a new mood retained a firm grasp of reality:

> *Goin' no higher,*
> *Goin' no lower down.*
> *Goin' no higher,*
> *Goin' no lower down.*

Gonna stay right here,
Gonna stay right here,
'Til they close me down.[29]

No doubt a Robert Charles summed up the fears many whites har-bored of the New Negro. He had grown up during Reconstruction. He was part of a generation that had learned its lessons about civics and the law in the white man's school of civilization, and, as a New Orleans black newspaper noted, "our experience as pupils has been so sad and expensive that we could not forget some things if we would." They had come of age as whites plunged the South into savage violence and re-pression, in total contempt of constitutional and human rights. "Law-lessness was its inheritance, and the red splotch of violence its birthmark," one black observer said of the new generation.[30] Mostly reared in the countryside, they were quicker than their parents to give up unrewarding agricultural labor and take their chances in the towns and cities. Educated to respect the law, they learned that no law was strong enough to protect blacks in their rights or property or freedom. Educated to be humble and contrite in the presence of whites, they were less able to tolerate the indignities of Jim Crow and contain their resentments. Educated to respect authority, they found it difficult to do so when authority itself bore the largest responsibility for the violence and repression. Educated in patriotic values, they saw that these had lit-tle meaning for their circumscribed lives. Taught to respect their par-ents, they found it increasingly difficult to tolerate the way their parents acted in the presence of whites. Taught to respect their leaders, they re-alized that the leaders themselves depended on the patronage and tol-eration of the dominant white authority.

4

MEN LIKE Booker T. Washington thought themselves to be represen-tative race leaders. It was in many ways a most unenviable position, as they had to play a complicated role. Isolated by class and position from most of their people, they took on the burden of representing them. For most blacks, after all, the advice about individual responsibility, about lifting themselves up by their bootstraps, about making it ulti-mately into the middle-class mainstream seemed contradicted by the relentlessness of white hostility. If the advice became increasingly less credible, so did the leaders who enunciated it. The black press, though overwhelmingly friendly to Washington if not controlled by him altogether, voiced a growing skepticism over leaders who, in their estimation, deceived rather than led. Terming them "Beggar Leaders," one newspaper described such blacks as "miserable hypocrites" who "throw around them an orphan home cloak, or a church cloak, or a purposed industrial Negro school cloak, where girls are to be taught cooking and the boys farming."[31]

The contradiction seemed obvious, and W. E. B. Du Bois would underscore it when he made his break with Washington in 1903. Black leaders admonished their people to respect themselves and to be proud of their race, but they espoused an accommodation that made self-respect and race pride almost impossible. "Do not show us how to be men and then blame us for being men," a Mobile black newspaper pointedly demanded of Washington ("the white man's ideal Negro"). Washington's self-help creed won him recognition and fame in both white and black America, and Du Bois himself had initially welcomed the uplift message. But no matter how warmly a much-relieved white South greeted that message, some blacks suspected that white people had their own agenda. "I very much fear," Charles Chesnutt wrote to Washington in 1908, "that the South does not mean, if it can prevent it, to permit education or business or anything else to make of the Negro anything more than an agricultural serf."[32]

Living not too far from each other, Ned Cobb and Washington never actually met, although Cobb recalled going to Tuskegee for some of the commencement exercises and seeing Washington. Cobb would have been thirty years old when Washington died in 1915. Some years later, Cobb tried to sort out his thoughts about the school principal who had achieved fame among both whites and blacks and exerted an influence rare for a black man:

> He was a nigger of this state and well known and everything, but here's what his trouble was, to a great extent: he didn't feel for and didn't respect his race of people enough to go rock bottom with em. He leaned too much to the white people that controlled the money—lookin out for what was his worth, that's what he was lookin for. He was a big man, he had authority, he had pull in life, he had a political pull any way he turned and he was pullin for Booker Washington. He wanted his people to do this, that, and the other, but he never did get to the roots of our troubles. He had a lot of friends, he had a lot of courage,

but it was all his way. He had a lot of anything a man needed for his-self, but the right main thing, he weren't down with that. Yet and still the veil was over the nigger's eyes. Booker Washington didn't try to pull that veil away like he shoulda done. . . . Wrong-spirited, Booker Washington was—quite natural, there's nobody on earth perfect, but Booker Washington was a man got down with his country in the wrong way.[33]

Although appreciating the compelling reasons behind the accommodation made by their leaders and elders, growing numbers of young blacks found it difficult if not impossible to adopt the same code of racial behavior. What a new generation found particularly troubling were the indignities inflicted by whites on their elders, ranging from Jim Crow insults and the names by which they were identified to their being cheated out of wages they had earned through hard labor. The experience of L. C. Dorsey, born in the early 1930s on a plantation in the Mississippi Delta, spoke to generations of abuse and exploitation in the past. She sensed early on that most of the workers remained poor because, like her father, they were illiterate and could not read the accounts. Young Dorsey acquired enough knowledge at school to begin to keep records, and she told her father precisely how much he had cleared. After the "settlement," however, her father had been paid only "a token" of what he had earned. And for young Dorsey, as for many who had found themselves in similar situations, this constituted a forceful initiation into the realities of the New South. If her father could tolerate this kind of abuse, young Dorsey could not.

When I got home and found out what the settlement had really been, there was another coming of age—people were locked into this system, and the fear and lack of control made them take that. There was no protest. There was no saying I'm not going to take that. There was nobody else you could appeal to. *Nobody else.* That did something for my whole life from that point on. Maybe if I was white I would have become a Klansman. But what it made me was a very angry person who spent the next twenty years using that anger against unfair systems.[34]

As young blacks found it increasingly difficult to contain their feelings and emotions, the ways in which their parents acted and spoke in the presence of whites sometimes became major sources of embarrassment and humiliation, culminating in conflicts within the family. Ned Cobb, for one, consciously rejected the "slavery ways" of his father, refusing to be "disrecognized." Richard Wright had nothing but contempt for his uncle's attempts to teach him "to grin, hang my head, and mumble apologetically when I was spoken to." Frances Mary Albrier thought it impossible to share her grandmother's professed affection for the white family she had once served: "My grandmother loved her master, and I never would have. She always found excuses." Nor could Sadie Gray understand her father's continuing adoration of his white father, particularly after he had turned over his entire estate to Mercer University to educate white boys and left him nothing. "Daughter," he had replied, with tears in his eyes, "you do not understand. My father was a good man. I was a slave in the system, and he was a slave to the system." Benjamin Davis, Jr., the son of a prominent Georgia black politician and entrepreneur, was at odds with his father's accommodationist stance. "This question of blind respect for authority remained a matter of cleavage between my father and me, the dividing line between our philosophies of life."[35]

The generational conflict showed every indication of deepening. Some years later, James Farmer recalled a father born in 1886 of ex-slave parents who became the first black Ph.D. in Texas and taught in Holly Springs, Mississippi, at Rust College, and in Austin, Texas, at Sam Houston College. The black community looked up to him as a scholar and wise counselor; the white community considered him "a 'good' Negro, compromising if not subservient, who knew his place." Although proud of his father's achievements, James felt it impossible to admire the quality of his father's "accommodation to a system that made him less than a man. I despised that within him that would not fight, perhaps because I saw the same survival instinct in myself. But I swore that when I grew up, scared or not, I'd never kowtow to meanness. . . . They'll have to kill me."[36]

In the face of relentless white hostility, blacks acknowledged the importance of generational differences and the difficulties young blacks confronted in trying to adapt to a humiliating and repressive system their elders had learned through harsh experience. Nor did it escape the attention of blacks that whites, too, were changing, that fewer invoked the language of paternalism or pretended to have a special compassion for black people. The student newspaper at Fisk University singled out in 1889 a new generation of whites "who are even more hostile and bitter than the older ones," comparing them with a new generation of blacks, a generation "ignorant of the so-called instinctive fear of their fathers," "prone to brood in bitterness and suppressed rage over their wrongs," and "more sensitive to injustice and quick to resent." That same paper, when it posed the question "Who Are We?" spoke both to the hopes of many young blacks and to the worst fears of white Southerners: "We are not the Negro from whom the chains of slavery fell a quarter of a century ago, most assuredly not."[37]

A white man visiting a black college in Atlanta came face-to-face with that new mood and spirit in the black South. Addressing some five hundred students, he told them not to be "bitter." Every race, he explained, had its mission in life. The Anglo-Saxons were identified with "strength," "enterprise," and "aggression"; the Negro race's peculiar mission had been "submission." He then paused nervously, looked at his unreceptive audience, and managed to stammer nervously, "At least, your fathers and mothers—I don't know about you all."[38]

5

THE BLACK WOMAN contemplated her next move. Some white men had seized and killed her husband. Determined to avenge his murder, she took a shotgun, wrapped it in a sheet, and proceeded to the place where he had been shot. The white assailants were still there. She humbly pleaded with them that she be permitted to recover her husband's body for burial. After they agreed, she knelt by the side of her husband and prayed. The white men, silent and armed, watched her. Before they realized what was happening, she unwrapped the sheet and, shooting from her knees, killed four of them instantly. Apocryphal or not, the story impressed young Richard Wright as "emotionally true" and it inspired him to believe that if he should ever have to face a white mob, he would be able to muster the same fury and courageous resolve that had moved this black woman. The fantasy comforted him, even as it reinforced the tensions within him.[39]

Lynchings were intended to send a message to the entire black community. But blacks read and responded to the message in a variety of ways, not always in the spirit whites expected. That some were intimidated into sullen and helpless resignation is hardly surprising. "If God does not help us vain is the help of man," a black minister in South Carolina confided to his journal after hearing of still another lynching in Barnwell County. "This thing is becoming unbearable, O' heaven where shall it end?"[40] Far more noteworthy and ominous, however, was the talk of limits. It seemed to J. H. Coleman, writing in desperation to Booker T. Washington in 1897, that "as men" they could no longer tolerate white atrocities. Failure to act, he thought, would only encourage whites to wage an even more brutal war on black men and women.

> I think it Wood be a good idear for our Peple now to be taugh How to unite an Protect life an Propety an Protect our femeals if some of us have to looze our life. Mr. Washington if we do not Protest against this Why after While tha Will come to our Schools an take our Teachers out an mob Them an also come to our Homes an take our Wives an Daughters out an male treat them.[41]

As the assaults on black lives increased and grew more savage, talk of self-defense was heard more frequently, and those who resisted took on heroic proportions. When whites in Lonoke, Arkansas, tried to expel the town's black population in 1898, a black resident admonished his people to defend themselves. "The law is in the hands of the men who perpetrate these crimes. Arm yourselves and protect your lives and your homes. When the Negroes of Lonoke County kill about twenty-five of these lawless white men the outrages against the Negro race will stop, and not until then." In precisely that spirit, a black newspaper in New Orleans described a number of incidents in various parts of the South in which blacks had employed violence in self-defense. The stories appeared under the headline "Risking Life That Others May Live," and the editor's preface suggested with obvious satisfaction "that the Negro has determined to protect himself and his home at all hazards."[42]

Perhaps the most ominous sign in the call to arms was the openness with which blacks urged it. In Montgomery, Alabama, the black editor of the *Weekly News* suggested that blacks "die like men [and] . . . take two or three white devils along . . . and stop being shot up and killed . . . like dogs." The *Richmond Planet,* among the leading black newspapers in the South, itemized black lynchings in each issue and called on blacks to defend their homes and women. Gun advertisements reinforced this editorial advice: "there is no use talking, a Winchester rifle in your house and a man there who knows how to use it will bring respect from white folks and the colored ones too, for that matter. Great is the Winchester rifle." Ida B. Wells would not have confined the ownership and use of the weapon to black men. The investigation she conducted of

lynchings persuaded her "that a Winchester rifle should have a place of
honor in every black home, and it should be used for that protection
which the law refuses to give." Citing incidents in Jacksonville, Florida,
and Paducah, Kentucky, among other places, the lesson she drew was
abundantly clear:

> The only times an Afro-American who was assaulted got away has
> been when he had a gun and used it in self-defense. . . . When the
> white man who is always the aggressor knows he runs as great [a] risk
> of biting the dust every time his Afro-American victim does, he will
> have greater respect for Afro-American life. The more the Afro-
> American yields and cringes and begs, the more he has to do so, the
> more he is insulted, outraged and lynched.

Fearing for her life, Wells began to carry a gun soon after the lynching
of her friend Tom Moss. "I had already determined to sell my life as
dearly as possible if attacked. I felt if I could take one lyncher with me,
this would even up the score a little bit." Benjamin Mays did not carry
a pistol, but his brothers did "and most of the boys in the county," including those who called on his sisters. "Since the firearms were a little
heavy, they would put them on the table while visiting my sisters."[43]

The ultimate price of resistance, even in self-defense, was loss of life,
often accompanied by torture and dismemberment. But this threat did
not altogether stifle retaliatory violence, neither the rhetoric nor the
deed itself. Nor did it necessarily deter blacks from challenging those
entrusted with enforcement of the law. The individual response of
Robert Charles to police harassment in New Orleans in 1900 had more
dramatic and far-reaching consequences than most but was by no
means unique. Across the South in the late nineteenth and early twentieth centuries, blacks in increasing numbers mobilized to protect members of the community from arresting officers, abusive railroad and
streetcar conductors, exploitative employers (who refused to pay
promised wages or held workers in peonage), lynch mobs, and police violence. And, increasingly, blacks—acting alone or in groups—demonstrated a willingness to employ armed violence, both defensive and
retaliatory. "If you must die, take one with you," was heard with greater
frequency, and more than one aggrieved black acted on the advice.[44]

Georgia enjoyed the distinction of leading the nation in recorded
lynchings, but that apparently failed to achieve its desired effect. More
than a dozen sheriffs and town marshals, along with a number of po-

licemen and constables, lost their lives at the hands of blacks in the early twentieth century, most of them while trying to make arrests. Earlier incidents of blacks seeking to block arresting officers had prompted Atlanta's police chief to warn that black obstructionism "is becoming too common. Almost every day something of the kind occurs." But such "obstructionism" some blacks considered minimal resistance. After listing grievances against the police, the editor of a black newspaper in Atlanta—appropriately titled *Weekly Defiance*—demanded to know how much longer blacks would tolerate police violence. "Are we going to be murdered like dogs right here in this community and not open our mouths?"[45]

In what came to be known as the Darien "insurrection," blacks in McIntosh County, Georgia, mobilized in 1899 to protect Henry Delegale, a prominent black resident who had been arrested on a highly dubious rape charge. Fearing Delegale would be lynched, armed blacks surrounded the jail to prevent the sheriff (or anyone else) from removing the prisoner. As word spread of an imminent "race war," the governor ordered the state militia into Darien. Once blacks were assured the militia would escort the prisoner to Savannah for safekeeping and not to a lynching, they felt they had scored a triumph. But whites had been so shaken by the black mobilization that they determined to round up and place on trial the organizers, deeming them "rioters." Meanwhile, members of the Delegale family forcibly resisted attempts by some temporary deputies to arrest them for having incited an "insurrection," killing one of the deputies. In the resulting trials, twenty-three of the "rioters" were found guilty and given heavy fines and prison terms, and two of Delegale's sons, charged with murder, were sentenced to life imprisonment. A jury, in the meantime, found Henry Delegale not guilty of the rape charge that had precipitated the outbreak.[46]

Although black violence against whites remained exceptional, in Georgia and elsewhere, that seemed less important than the fact that it occurred at all. When armed blacks in Wiggins, Mississippi, in 1906 tried to prevent a lynching, they exchanged shots with a white mob shaken and enraged over this unexpected show of force; both sides suffered casualties. That same year, in the Atlanta Riot, whites had little difficulty in seizing the downtown sections and wreaking havoc, but when they invaded the black neighborhoods they encountered armed resistance. When a white mob formed in Stanford, Kentucky, to lynch two blacks jailed on charges of assaulting three white tobacco growers, local blacks resolved to protect the prisoners. After assuming positions

in the rear of the courthouse, they built bonfires, tied white handkerchiefs on their arms, and announced they would fight any mob that appeared. Upon finding both blacks and county officials ready to defend
the jail, the mob failed to appear. After a fight involving a black and a
white railroad worker in Jackson, Tennessee, a lynch mob of more than
one hundred whites assembled, only to be confronted by blacks armed
with Winchester rifles and revolvers. Four militia companies had to be
called out in 1906 to reinforce the police in Chattanooga, where more
than one thousand blacks stopped work in several industrial plants and
where house servants walked off their jobs to protest the lynching of a
black resident whose conviction was being appealed.[47]

Verbal confrontations, along with occasional outbreaks of violence,
accompanied enforcement of the Jim Crow laws. Although most black
travelers accommodated to the restrictions, some found it impossible to
tolerate humiliation at the hands of particularly abusive conductors,
and numbers of blacks took their cases to the courts. When twenty-
two-year-old Ida B. Wells was ordered into a segregated railroad car in
1884, she refused to move and had to be forcibly removed from her
seat. She chose to leave the train at the next station and successfully
sued the railroad for damages. "Darky Damsel Gets Damages," a
Memphis newspaper headline declared, but an appeals court later
overturned the verdict, charging that Wells had intended "to harass
with a view to this suit, and that her persistence was not in good faith to
obtain a comfortable seat for the short ride." In Uniontown, Alabama,
a train conductor forcibly ejected a black traveler for failing to provide
adequate room for white passengers disembarking. The next time the
train came through town, the aggrieved black traveler appeared, this
time with five friends, and shot the conductor. The group was captured
and placed in jail, and a white resident anticipated their fate. "The
white people here intend to kill all the 5 negroes secretly to-night or tomorrow. . . . I am not satisfied this is a very safe Country for white people, too many negroes." White fears of social equality and
indiscriminate race mixing in public places had fueled the campaign
for segregation. But blacks charged that whites molested and insulted
black women, particularly when they were placed together in the smoking cars. A Muskogee, Oklahoma, newspaper reported the arrest of a
prominent black man for objecting to "the familiarity of white men
with colored women on the street car."[48]

To listen to whites, the very homes in which blacks were employed as
domestics sometimes became battlegrounds. The wife of Richard

Pines struck Sarah Barnett, a household servant, with a stick. Barnett retaliated, using her hands. No doubt shocked at this response, Richard Pines seized his revolver and shot Barnett through the shoulder. Whatever the nature of the offense, the court focused only on the provocative defensive behavior of Sarah Barnett, who was convicted of assaulting a white woman and fined. Unable to pay, she was confined in the county jail. Still another mistress of the house did not fare as well. "Goaded beyond endurance," Ann Beston, a servant in a Rome, Georgia, household, stabbed and killed her abusive mistress; she was then overpowered and lynched. "But all should be grateful," a northern black newspaper commented, "that she removed thc cause of the trouble in this one instance at least."[49]

When blacks translated militant rhetoric into action, they invariably paid the same price Robert Charles paid, even if they acted in self-defense. Much like Charles's short-lived stand, black "uprisings" were mostly spontaneous, unorganized, individualistic, and quickly and ruthlessly suppressed. But they were symptomatic of a growing inclination by young blacks to challenge the conditions they had inherited. Attempts by groups of young blacks to vote and to gain access to segregated trains and streetcars, the growing resistance to police officers making arrests in black communities, controversial editorials in black college newspapers (even a critical obituary of Jefferson Davis), and demands by students to exert a greater control over their education—all of these demonstrated a rising confidence among some blacks in their ability to effect changes in their lives without catering to white sensibilities.

Although violent resistance remained newsworthy, black protests were mostly nonviolent and dignified, such as the boycotts of segregated facilities, often conducted by college-educated young blacks who wanted to suggest a new mood and determination in the community. But any kind of resistance confounded and frightened whites. Rumors quickly inflated the number and actions of black protesters until they assumed revolutionary proportions. That was more than enough (as during slavery) to mobilize the entire white community, and the terms the white press applied to such outbreaks conveniently rationalized the disproportionate force used to suppress them. A "mass meeting" of blacks held to protest a lynching, as in East Point, Georgia, could be easily magnified into a potentially insurrectionary situation demanding forcible white intervention. A one-sided "slaughter" of blacks in St. Charles, Arkansas, in 1903, could be transformed into a "riot." "Thir-

teen have been killed, and if the newspaper reports are to be relied
upon not a single white man," a black editor observed, "and yet it's
[called] a race riot." And more than half a century after Nat Turner's
rebellion, "intense excitement" swept through Southampton County,
Virginia, "especially amongst the women, about a negro insurrection."
The nearby military was placed on alert, three of the "leaders" were
captured and jailed, "and the question of lynching them was excitedly
discussed."[50]

Neither the end of slavery nor the triumph of white supremacy
some thirty years later dissolved the racial tensions that kept many
whites and blacks on a virtual warlike footing. The growing number
of confrontations suggested a black population not always ready to
bend to the will and whims of whites. The outbreaks of violence,
rumors of insurrection, and blacks obstructing enforcement of the
law reinforced white concerns about a gun-toting New Negro threatening to subvert the very foundations of southern society. States and lo-
calities responded with overwhelming force, not only to suppress black
resistance but also to disarm black communities, and white mobs often
made official intervention unnecessary. Whatever the proportion of
blacks in a particular community or county, whites always commanded
the preponderance of firepower. "Had to walk a quiet life," James
Plunkett came to realize. "The least little thing you would do, they
would kill ya."[51]

6

ALTHOUGH THE BLACK press questioned the rationale and the
practices of white supremacy, dissent had proven to be a risky enterprise in the New South. Some editors were outspoken in their support
of civil rights and managed to survive. Most of them made a pragmatic
accommodation and tried to be as circumspect as possible in expressing
their views on race relations. Editors largely sided with the Washingtonian creed, advocating economic uplift over agitation and tempering
their opposition to Jim Crow with appeals for racial harmony. Some
black journalists edited "black papers" owned and controlled by white
businessmen, and several resembled the editor described by a native
white Mississippian: "There was nothing biggity about him like there is
about some educated Nigras, and he got the cooperation of the better

element of the white people when they saw he wasn't smart-alecky and started printing the right kind of editorials."[52]

But some black editors took enormous risks. A prominent Mississippi planter found ominous a black editor who praised the deeds of Robert Charles while recalling with pride the marksmanship of his own father. "Everybody in Jackson County not only knew that he was a dead shot, but that he would shoot," the editor had said. "That is not a bad reputation for an Afro-American to have in the South even at this time." Such statements, the planter lamented, were by no means exceptional but "might be indefinitely multiplied." He cited as another example a "prominent mulatto editor" who had declared that he was "tired hearing about good niggers, that what he wanted was to see bad niggers, with guns in their hands."[53]

In the absence of a local press that met their needs, some blacks turned to black newspapers in the North. By World War I the favorite had become the *Chicago Defender,* virtually smuggled into the region, often by Pullman porters working the North–South lines. In Mississippi a prominent black observed that "negroes grab the *Defender* like a hungry mule grabs fodder," and in its pages they would find not only a graphic description of white atrocities in the South but also news of opportunities awaiting them in the North.[54]

The few black editors in the South who became confrontational often paid a price, as did other black dissenters. Jesse C. Duke, editor of the *Montgomery Herald,* urged his people to exhibit "race pride . . . and manhood" and to stop degrading themselves by "crawling on your belly to lick white men's boots." That was threatening enough, but he then made the fatal mistake of openly discussing in his articles on lynching what most blacks confined to furtive street conversations: "the growing appreciation of the white Juliet for the colored Romeo." He was forced to flee Montgomery, and several leading blacks in the city were threatened for having spoken out in his defense.[55] Eugene N. Bryant, editor of the *Brookhaven People's Relief* in Mississippi, was ousted in 1910 for "stirring up race hatred" and "dabbling in politics," mostly by reprinting editorials from northern "race" papers. Not content with expelling him from the community, a mob commanded by members of the local police burned his home and five of his rental houses, destroyed his press, and had him arrested in Jackson for "criminal libel."[56]

Ida B. Wells chose to call the newspaper she edited in Memphis *Free Speech,* and it became an important dissenting voice in the late-nineteenth-century South. Whether protesting conditions in the black schools, disfranchisement, segregation, or lynching, her editorials gave full voice to the unfairness and brutality of white repression. Criticism of the school board had cost her a teaching position she had held for seven years. Her advice to blacks to leave Memphis, as it "will neither protect our lives and property, nor give us a fair trial in the courts," infuriated whites dependent on black labor and patronage. Her call for blacks to avenge lynchings, even if they had "to burn up whole towns," placed her press in jeopardy. Finally, an editorial challenging allegations of rape against black men and questioning the "moral reputation" of white women ended Wells's journalistic career in Memphis. Assuming a man had written the "incendiary" editorial on white women, one newspaper thought it a duty "to tie the wretch who utters these calumnies to a stake at the intersection of Main and Madison Sts., brand him in the forehead with a hot iron and perform upon him a surgical operation with a pair of tailor's shears." *Free Speech*—the press and furnishings—perished at the hands of a mob, and with her life threatened Wells became, in her words, "an exile from home for hinting at the truth."[57]

Duke, Bryant, and Wells were but three of an impressive coterie of black dissenters driven into exile—vivid testimony to the fact that for black men and women, speech and expression were no freer in the South than the ballot. The same restraints placed on editors extended to other black dissenters, making life exceedingly difficult if not perilous for them if they remained in the South. Charles Chesnutt moved North in the 1880s, after several years of teaching school, having despaired of realizing his ambitions and of exercising his civil rights. "I have no faith in the Southern people's sense of justice so far as the Negro's rights are concerned," he would write to Booker T. Washington from "exile" in the North.[58]

7

IN SPEAKING OF "the Black World beyond the Veil," W. E. B. Du Bois suggested in 1903 a world beyond the reach of whites and of which they were essentially ignorant. Some eight years earlier, Paul Laurence Dunbar briefly departed from his mostly comforting themes and dialect style to suggest as powerfully as any contemporary black leader or writer a people compelled to mask their inner feelings:

We wear the mask that grins and lies,
It hides our cheeks and shades our eyes,—
This debt we pay to human guile;
With torn and bleeding hearts we smile,
And mouth with myriad subtleties.

Why should the world be over-wise,
In counting all our tears and sighs?
Nay, let them only see us, while
We wear the mask.[59]

The bluesman translated these sentiments into a classic bit of folk wisdom:

Got one mind for white folks to see,
'Nother for what I know is me;
He don't know, he don't know my mind,
When he see me laughing
Just laughing to keep from crying.[60]

To survive was to accommodate, to wear the mask, to watch every word and action in the presence of whites, to veil inner feelings. Ralph Ellison once called southern life the most dramatic form of life in the United States, because it was so full of actors, white and black.[61] For black Southerners, however, experience taught them that misreading or misplaying a role might cost them their lives; they could afford neither garbled lines nor ad-libs. Few blacks chose open rebellion or violent resistance and agitation. Whether or not they adopted Washington's strategy, they sensed that blacks were bound to lose if any protracted racial conflict broke out. Most blacks, then, made their peace with the ruling race. But even as they learned to accommodate, even as they learned *"how* to live," even as they accepted the reality of subordination, even as they learned to wear the mask, many found ways to impart some meaning and dignity to their lives.

If most black Southerners accommodated, they did so from a sense of limited options, not because they placed any credence in the tenets of white superiority. But they did not necessarily submit. Nor did they necessarily internalize the white man's image of them and accept subordination as a permanent condition. The difference between accommodation and submission may have been quite subtle, but it marked the line black people drew between themselves and white people, and for many blacks defined the terms of survival. Like many others, young Richard Wright learned to curb his impulses, speech, expression, and manner. But there had to be limits, he came to realize, if he was to retain any semblance of self-respect. Whatever the expectations of the whites he encountered, whatever the requirements of the occasion, he confessed his inability to accommodate to every white whim. "I could not help it. I could not grin."[62]

If many whites misread black accommodation for total submission and failed to recognize the difference, the intensity of the repression and violence in the late nineteenth and early twentieth centuries strongly suggested that not all whites were as easily persuaded. Whatever their repeated expressions of racial self-confidence, some whites readily suspected that large numbers of blacks chose to mask their anger and resentment behind a self-effacing demeanor. One young white visitor came away from Mississippi in 1910 persuaded that nearly every black had two personae: "two distinct social selves, the one he reveals to his own people, the other he assumes among the whites." Thomas Bailey, in his often astute assessment of black behavior, noted with both distaste and distrust the Negro's "exaggerated" courtesy, use of "pseudo-humble words," and "demeanor of pretended servility." He suspected that even a black person thought to be "the white man's nigger" demonstrated something less than "real humility":

> I doubt whether the negro that always has the word "Boss" on his lips is either especially polite or especially humble; rather he is habituated to the use of servile words, or else cunning enough to know that they serve as a convenient mask. . . . "Playing 'possum" seems to be a device of natural selection in the interests of survival.[63]

Ned Cobb spelled out in his life the critical difference between accommodation and submission. He readily conceded that he had played a sometimes dangerous and disingenuous game in which whites dictated the rules and arbitrarily meted out the penalties. To "get along" and to obtain what he wanted from white people, he acquired the necessary demeanor and verbal skills. He learned "to humble down and play shut-mouthed" in many instances. He knew to play dumb when the situation demanded it. And although he "got tired of it," he learned "to fall back," to take "every kind of insult." But there were limits, and these assumed a growing importance in his life. He refused to submit passively to the whims of every white man. "In my years past, I'd accommodate anybody; but I didn't believe in this way of bowin to my knees and doin what *any* white man said do. Still, I always knowed to give the white man his time of day or else he's ready to knock me in the head. I just aint goin to go nobody's way against my own self. First thing of all—I care for myself and respect myself." That determination to maintain his self-respect, to draw a line between himself and whites, ultimately cost him twelve years in a state prison, where he could contemplate the difference between the life of a black convict and the life of a black sharecropper. "Outside, they raised figures against me in place of wire."[64]

Where and how black men and women drew the line between accommodation and submission would be part of their legacy. Adopting a variety of responses, often intricate and not always easily ascertainable, they tried to circumvent the system and maintain their self-respect. For some, it was nothing less than a matter of common courtesy, an insistence that white people recognize them as visible and mature men and women. A Tennessee woman had no desire to "mess with" white folks. But, as she insisted, "when the white folks steps in this house, especially the men, I demand respect. I always says, 'Won't you rest your hat?' Yes-sir, just as I feel." Still another black woman, an elderly domestic, often walked the streets, muttering to herself, "I ain't nobody's aunt. They call me aunt, and I ain't nobody's aunt."[65]

Reflecting some years later over the predicament southern blacks confronted in the early twentieth century, Ralph Ellison thought Richard Wright's generation had three choices available to them: "They could accept the role created for them by the whites and perpetually resolve the resulting conflicts through the hope and emotional catharsis of Negro religion; they could repress their dislike of Jim Crow social relations while striving for a middle way of respectability, becoming—consciously or unconsciously—the accomplices of the whites in oppressing their brothers; or they could reject the situation, adopt a criminal attitude, and carry on an unceasing psychological scrimmage with the whites, which often flared forth into physical violence."[66]

The choices were never easy, the risks were always great. Within rigidly prescribed boundaries, black men and women improvised strategies. Some (like Robert Charles) could no longer contain their feelings and opted for a direct confrontation; some preferred a quieter subversion of the system. But still others, who were rapidly drawing attention at the turn of the century, became essentially interior exiles, falling away from society altogether. None of them had access to the more privileged functions and organizations of black society. None of the traditional institutions and outlets offered any solace: not the family, the school, or the church. Aliens in their own land, empty of belief or hope, volatile, they chose to live by their wits on the fringes of society. Operating in a kind of underworld emerging in the 1890s, mostly in the cities and towns, young blacks tested the limits of permissible dissent and misconduct, sometimes outside the law, and found alternative ways to survive and to circumvent the system, being "as much a criminal" as they dared to be. Within their enclaves and neighborhoods, in the saloons, roadhouses, juke joints, and pool halls they frequented, they created and sustained a culture of their own, with its distinctive language, rituals, and modes of expression, and its distinctive ways of grappling with their condition and prospects.

The idea was to avoid a suicidal confrontation, to adopt the necessary deference in the presence of whites and use that deference to allay suspicion. Having learned the futility of hard labor, having experienced or watched others experience the pitfalls of ambition and self-assertion, they might assume an existential attitude toward their lives, value diversions and escape (gambling, drinking, drugs, sexual activity) over labor, and improvisation and spontaneity over order and decorum. Since many employers deemed them troublesome and unemployable, they would fulfill those expectations and "make a career of natural badness," turning white rejection and stereotypes to their advantage. "A nigger is a nigger," they would say, "he lives in the basement . . . no use to run upstairs." Some years later, in the 1930s, a black songster would give voice to precisely this attitude:

> 'Cause white folks expect nigger to be lazy
> Ain't no cause to worry
> I wouldn't disappoints him for the world
> That's why I never hurry.[67]

Few found any reason to place their faith in a political system that denied them a voice, in a work ethic that denied them the rewards of their labor, or in the laws and courts that denied them a semblance of justice. Since they felt powerless to change society, they would do whatever they could to heighten their own lives, to savor every kind of personal experience. Cocaine and opium could induce religious experiences few preachers could even envision, provide a kind of instant liberation. That blacks should be attracted to narcotics did not surprise a New Orleans newspaper: "To them cocaine is a merciful friend," it observed only two weeks after the Robert Charles disturbance, "and little wonder is it that they will go to any length or make any sacrifice that will enable them to enjoy a few hours of forgetfulness"; cocaine was capable of making "unhappy victims of misfortune" feel momentarily youthful and strong, spreading a "golden cloud over a wretched past and hopeless future" and evoking "visions of wealth, contentment and happiness."[68]

The cost was minimal. Ten cents, an observer wrote from Atlanta in 1906, will purchase more than enough cocaine "to make a man wholly irresponsible for his acts," and it was often readily available in various forms at a nickel or a dime from a druggist. A Memphis newspaper estimated around the turn of the century that as many as 80 percent of the city's blacks—a highly inflated figure—used cocaine:[69]

> *Well, the cocaine habit is mighty bad,*
> *It kill ev'ybody I know it to have had,*
> *O my babe!*

> *Well, I wake in de mornin' by the city-clock bell,*
> *An' the niggers up town givin' cocaine hell.*
> *O my babe, O my babe!*

> *I went to the drug-store, I went in a lope;*
> *Sign on the door: "There's no mo' coke."*
> *O my babe, O my babe, O my babe!*[70]

After complaining in 1913 of how cocaine and opium were "causing so much trouble among the negroes," Senator Ben Tillman of South Carolina called attention to two mulatto youths in Harriston, Mississippi, who "got crazed on cocaine and went on the war path," killing eight people and wounding many others.[71]

Both whites and blacks had much to deplore about the mostly young blacks who adopted what appeared to be a dissolute, undisciplined, and criminal way of life. "They are lazy and thriftless, and want to frolic rather than work," a white Presbyterian minister said of the young blacks he observed, as if work and frugality were rewarding alternatives for the descendants of slaves and sharecroppers who had given their lives to hard labor. A former attorney for the Commonwealth of Virginia simply referred to them as "masterless men," most of them drifters, many of them with a propensity toward crime.[72]

Within the black community, editors, clergymen, and "leading" citizens wanted to make clear the distinction between themselves—the class that "everywhere commands respect"—and "the reverse element":

> It is among the latter class that most of the race troubles have their foundation; among the class that comes and goes aimlessly, having no home, no employment, no respect for themselves or for those about them. These people care for neither church nor school, and are ever ready to defy the law at every opportunity.

These were the blacks, warned Kelly Miller, a black college professor, who were "giving the whole race an evil reputation." Calling attention to "a widening chasm" within the community, Miller in 1899 cited the "hundreds and thousands" of young blacks in the slums, alleys, and highways "who are no more influenced by the churches and schools than if they were located in the continent of Asia." Few Emancipation Day orations in the early twentieth century did not include a condemnation of how such blacks preyed on the community; indeed, reports circulated of white streetcar conductors (previously notorious for intimidating black passengers) being compelled to protect black women against black "ruffians."[73]

Responding to the epidemic of lynchings, some black leaders and preachers sought to place the blame on the "criminal" class among them who provoked the outrage, fears, and violence of whites. They wanted to make clear that black rapists and criminals formed a very small, unacceptable part of the community, many of them outsiders. "[T]here never was a respectable colored man lynched in the south," a black Montgomery minister observed; most of the victims of lynching, he contended, "came out from the slums at night, like the raccoon, and stole back again."[74]

With the continuing migration of rural blacks into the cities and towns in the twentieth century, the consternation among blacks (and whites) extended to unwanted cultural manifestations of "the young element of our race." The urban saloons and "honky-tonks," as well as the rural roadhouses that catered to them, came under particular scrutiny, as did the happenings within them. Leila Holmes, a Holiness preacher in South Carolina, sounded the alarm over what was happening to their children. "The younger generation in Columbia is just ruined. The songs they sing are plumb outlandish. They dance somethin' scandalous, day and night, by these nickelos [nickelodeons]. Instead of being in school tryin' to learn how to be decent, they out cuttin' the buck day in and day out, steppin' in every trap the devils got set for 'em."[75]

Few whites or blacks drew a grimmer portrait of this class of blacks than Sutton Griggs, a black Baptist minister in Tennessee for three decades. His fame rested mostly on the numerous books he published, several of which used fictional characters to invoke racial pride and to condemn white racial practices. His heroes and heroines rejected violence as a way of overthrowing those practices, preferring exile abroad or placing their faith in the church, the law, and the ultimate triumph of interracial democracy. But in a tract he published in 1909, Griggs focused attention on the "bad Negro" and his "demoralizing influence" on the black community. Not only does he refuse to work, but as a thief he also preys on the earnings of others. By his very presence, he reduces real-estate values in the neighborhoods in which he lives. And when he travels, as he changes homes frequently, he spreads his "viciousness" elsewhere. To Griggs—and many shared this view—the "bad Negro" carried in himself the germs that would destroy society. "He is the lighted torch blazing over a powder magazine."[76]

The term "bad Negro" or "bad nigger" came into more frequent use by both whites and blacks. For many whites, Robert Charles had epitomized the "bad nigger," as did many black victims of lynchings. Bluesmen and blueswomen would add different dimensions to the reputation of the "bad nigger," as would black folklore, until the term took on a more complex meaning than simply badness or goodness, depending on who used the term and in what context. The stories of his extraordinary, often superhuman exploits would regale generations of black Americans. From the 1890s, in fact, black folklore and song accorded an increasingly prominent place to the black outlaw and desperado, usually a loner who chose to violate all of the moral and legal precepts of society, who wielded his own brand of justice.[77]

Went up town wid my hat in my han';
"Good mornin', jedge, done kill my man.
Didn't quite kill him, but I fixed him so
He won't bodder wid me no mo'.[78]

The "bad nigger" came to be celebrated in black lore and song for his cunning, boldness, coolness, and wit, often in the face of overwhelming odds, and for the uncanny ability and imaginative powers he displayed in outwitting his enemies. Unlike his counterparts in white folklore, he did not rob from the rich and give to the poor. He preyed on his own people as well as whites, terrorizing both blacks and whites, the innocent and the guilty, the wealthy and the poor. Rather than show any remorse for his depredations, he mocked piety and expressed indifference about his fate.

> *I'm so bad, I don't ever want to be good, uh, huh;*
> *I'm going to de devil and I wouldn't go to heaven, uh, huh,*
> *No I wouldn't go to heaven if I could.*[79]

The legends surrounding Railroad Bill were based on the life of Morris Slater in the 1890s. A black turpentine worker in Alabama, Slater shot and killed a police officer, escaped, and then roamed southwestern Alabama robbing trains, eluding pursuers by transforming himself into a variety of animals. Reversing the Robin Hood image, he would steal canned food and sell it to poor blacks who lived along the railroad tracks, threatening to kill them if they refused. He shot and killed a sheriff who had vowed to capture him, and he was said to have robbed a train knowing that it carried a posse sent to hunt him down.[80]

> *Well, the policemen all dressed in blue*
> *Comin' down sidewalk two by two,*
> *   Wus lookin' fer Railroad Bill.*
>
> *Standin' on de corner, didn't mean no harm,*
> *Policeman grab me by de arm,*
> *   Wus lookin' for Railroad Bill.*[81]

Of equal renown, John Hardy, a black West Virginia steel driver, killed a man in a crap game and became an outlaw. Aaron Harris achieved a reputation as a ruthless killer, claiming among his victims gamblers who won money from him, prostitutes who withheld money from him, and policemen who challenged him.

> *Aaron Harris was a bad, bad man,*
> *Baddest man ever was in this land.*

The exploits of Stagolee (with variations on that name) would be sung by black vagrants and in labor camps across the South.

> *Stagolee, he went a-walkin' with his .40 gun in his hand;*
> *He said, "I feel mistreated this mornin', I could kill most any man."*

And there were others, whose experiences were similar, whose prowess and contempt for authority would be well known, many of them legends in their own time.[82]

In the end, such men paid a heavy price for their arrogance and boldness, most of them dying the way they had lived, but remaining to the very end tough and defiant. Railroad Bill walked into a store in Atmore, Alabama, in March 1896, whereupon two men blew his head off to collect the $1,200 reward; many kept insisting that he had transformed himself and was still watching his pursuers with amusement. John Hardy, about to be hanged, was asked if he wanted to pray. He replied, "Just give me time to kill another man, Lord, Lord, / Just give me time to kill another man." Aaron Harris met his death in July 1915, when another outlaw, George Robertson (Boar Hog), ambushed him.

> *Aaron pawned his pistol one night to play in a gambling game,*
> *He pawned his pistol one night to play in a gambling game,*
> *Then old Boar Hog shot him and blotted out his name.[83]*

In real life, as in lore and song, the few who chose open defiance forfeited their lives for their contempt of authority. And black men and women reacted to them, much as they did to the legendary outlaws, with a certain ambivalence, an admiration of some of their exploits mixed with doubts about the ultimate meaning of those exploits. As a child in Mississippi, Richard Wright watched with awe black men who sneered at the customs and taboos, who cursed and violated the laws, who rode the Jim Crow streetcars without paying and sat where they pleased, who mimicked the antics of white folks and conspired to get what they wanted out of them, and who were happiest when they had outwitted their foes and saddest when they brooded over the impossibility of ever becoming free. All of these men, Wright confessed, left "a marked impression" on him, some of them because he had wanted to emulate their actions. But eventually, Wright observed, they paid a terrible price for their feats. "They were shot, hanged, maimed, lynched, and generally hounded until they were either dead or their spirits broken."[84]

In an age of "bad niggers," many whites and blacks thought the boxer Jack Johnson the "baddest" of them all, suggesting how "bad" or "ba-ad" took on some strikingly different meanings in white and black communities. To blacks, Johnson became a folk legend; to whites, a reminder of the uppity, menacing, lustful black male they had come to fear. Born in Galveston in 1878, he worked at a variety of jobs while acquiring and honing his boxing skills. He shocked the sports world in 1908 when he defeated Tommy Burns, a white man, to become the first black world's heavyweight boxing champion, and the way he did it provoked even more consternation. Johnson not only defeated Burns, he taunted and humiliated him in the ring. One story making the rounds in black communities related how the two fighters met in the center of the ring for the referee's instructions. After eyeing his opponent, Burns is said to have warned him, "Boy, I'm gonna whip you good. I was *born* with boxing gloves on." Jack Johnson smiled and replied, "I have news for you, white man. You're about to die the same way!" Apocryphal or not, the story summed up the match. A black newspaper in Richmond headlined the event in bold type, "A Southern Negro Is Heavyweight Champion of the World," and it thought "no event in forty years has given more genuine satisfaction to the colored people of this country."[85]

The burden of being "the hope of the white race" fell on Jim Jeffries, a former champion persuaded to come out of retirement despite his vow never to step into a ring with a black man. Billed as "the fight of the century," the Johnson-Jeffries bout attracted national attention. And its implications in a racially conscious if not racially obsessed America were made abundantly clear. "That portion of the white race that has been looking to me to defend its athletic superiority," said Jeffries, "may feel assured that I am fit to do my very best." Johnson, too, realized that more was at stake than the crown: "[I]t was my own honor, and in a degree the honor of my race."[86] But Reverdy Ransom, a prominent A.M.E. Church leader, tried to place the forthcoming bout in its proper historical context:

> The darker races of mankind, and the black race in particular, will keep the white race busy for the next few hundred years . . . in defending the interests of white supremacy. The black singer is coming with his song, the poet with his dreams, the sculptor with his conception of some form of beauty and of awe . . . and the scholar with his truth—in every domain of thought. The greatest marathon race of the ages is about to begin between the white race and the darker races of

mankind. What Jack Johnson seeks to do to Jeffries in the roped arena will be more the ambition of Negroes in every domain of human endeavor.[87]

When Johnson entered the ring, a brass band played and some twenty thousand rabidly partisan Jeffries fans sang the popular hit "All Coons Look Alike to Me." They did not sing for very long. Johnson demolished the heavily favored and previously unbeaten Jeffries. And, as in the Burns fight, he did so with a derisive smile and a taunting commentary that few whites or blacks could ever shake from their memory. "Come on now, Mr. Jeff. Let me see what you got," Johnson reportedly shouted. "Do something, man. This is for the champ*peenship*. . . . I can go on like this all afternoon, Mr. Jeff." Jeffries could not, and he suffered a devastating and humiliating defeat—as did, many acknowledged (or boasted), the entire white race.[88]

To blacks, Jack Johnson's feats took on added symbolic importance. Even if some identified with him surreptitiously, so as not to provoke whites, Johnson gave them an outlet. When he brought a white man to his knees, humbling and humiliating him in the process, he brought the entire white race to its knees, acting out the frustrations and bitterness of tens of thousands of blacks based on a lifetime of insults and betrayals. It was a rare triumph in an era of devastating and often humiliating setbacks.

News of Johnson's spectacular victory spread rapidly. Ten-year-old Louis Armstrong was on his way to pick up the newspapers he delivered when he encountered a crowd of black youths running toward him on Canal Street in New Orleans. "You better get started, black boy," one of them said, pulling him along. "Jack Johnson has just knocked out Jim Jeffries. The white boys are sore about it and they're going to take it out on us." Richard Wright recalled Jack Johnson as one of a number of topics one should not raise in the presence of southern white men. Fourteen-year-old Benjamin Mays remembered "vividly" the impact of the fight and the need to avoid discussing the subject with whites. "White men in my county could not take it. A few Negroes were beaten up because a Negro had beaten a white man in far-away Nevada."[89]

Overjoyed, blacks in some places dropped their masks, if momentarily, to give full voice to an impressive racial triumph. Dismayed whites reacted to Johnson's beating up on Jeffries by beating up indiscriminately on blacks in their vicinity. Racial skirmishes, sometimes violent

riots, broke out in every southern state and in much of the country. A
Richmond black newspaper advised its readers that "a colored man
who imagines himself Jack Johnson, will get an awful beating." And a
white newspaper in the same city, in warning blacks not to be misled,
expressed concern that "all over the country a simple-minded race is
getting into its head a false pride, a foolish impression, a disastrous ambition."[90] After Johnson's earlier triumph over Burns, a judge in Birmingham, Alabama, expressed a similar alarm in ruling on a homicide
case. A prominent white Baptist deacon, resenting the impudent tone
of a black carriage driver, had shot and killed him during an argument
about his fee. The judge released the assailant after lecturing the victim's friends:

> You Niggers are getting beside yourselves since Jack Johnson won the
> fight from a white man. I want you to mind what you do in this town.
> Remember, you are in the South, and remember further that when
> you speak to white gentlemen you should speak in a way that is best be-
> coming a Nigger. This act will be repeated daily by the white gentle-
> men of this city if you Niggers don't find your places.[91]

The rage of white America centered on more than the reality of a
black heavyweight champion. No sooner had whites suffered through
Jeffries's humiliation in the ring than they had to watch Jack Johnson
embrace his wife. She was white. "Jack Johnson committed two grave
blunders as far as whites were concerned," Benjamin Mays recalled:
"He beat up a white man and he was socializing with a white woman—
both deadly sins in 1908."[92] But Johnson was no ordinary black man.
He did not know his place, he refused to acknowledge racial barriers.
Violating nearly every racial code and custom, making no effort to
mask his feelings, he flaunted his lifestyle, his fashionable clothes, his
expensive jewelry, his shaved head, his fast automobiles, and the white
women he escorted and, in three instances, married.

The stories of his prowess, in and out of the ring, entered fully into
black folklore. The veracity of these tales made little difference; blacks
perceived them as true, and for good reason. After Johnson's spectacular achievements in the ring, they could believe anything of him.

> It was on a hot day in Georgia when Jack Johnson drove into town. He
> was really flying: Zoooom! Behind his fine car was a cloud of red

Georgia dust as far as the eye could see. The sheriff flagged him down and said, "Where do you think you're going, boy, speeding like that? That'll cost you $50.00!" Jack Johnson never looked up; he just reached in his pocket and handed the sheriff a $100.00 bill and started to gun the motor; ruuummm, ruuummm. Just before Jack pulled off the sheriff shouted, "Don't you want your change?" And Jack replied, "Keep it, 'cause I'm coming back the same way I'm going!" Zooooooom.[93]

Booker T. Washington, among others, was not amused. Whatever pride Johnson brought to the race, his unconventional behavior poisoned race relations. The division within the black community tended to be along class lines, with many middle-class blacks perceiving him as an embarrassment, a setback to those who wanted to cultivate a different kind of image. Emmett J. Scott, Washington's private secretary at Tuskegee, tried through an intermediary to persuade Johnson not to grant interviews and to refrain from boasting about his triumphs; he hoped a strong manager might subdue Johnson, "because I do not like white men to feel that Negroes cannot stand large prosperity."[94]

When the motion picture *Birth of a Nation* took the country by storm in 1915, the audience focused much of its attention on the black villain, Silas Lynch, who summed up the Black Peril in his impudence, venality, and lust for white women. Johnson had much the same effect on white America, and his boxing achievements and lifestyle resulted in a host of bills restricting and punishing interracial marriage. Congress outlawed the importation and interstate transportation of films or other visual representations of prizefights. "No man descended from the old Saxon race," one congressman declared, "can look upon that kind of contest without abhorrence and disgust."[95]

But to working-class blacks, in particular, Jack Johnson remained a "ba-ad" man who commanded enormous admiration. No other black person in their memory had displayed so impressively the ability to outwit, outthink, and outfight white folks. The myth of white invincibility had been shattered, at least for a moment.

> *Amaze an' Grace, how sweet it sounds,*
> *Jack Johnson knocked Jim Jeffries down.*
> *Jim Jeffries jumped up an' hit Jack on the chin,*
> *An' then Jack knocked him down again.*

The Yankees hold the play,
The white man pulls the trigger;
But it make no difference what the white man say,
The world champion's still a nigger.[96]

8

CRIME AMONG BLACKS, W. E. B. Du Bois conceded in 1904, had increased dramatically over the past thirty years, and in the cities "a distinct criminal class" had emerged. He found nothing surprising about this development. It did not prove any innate propensity of blacks to commit crimes, nor did it simply grow out of black ignorance and destitution. What emerged after the Civil War was "a double system of justice" that dealt with black violations, no matter how trivial, with extreme severity, while treating white offenses with leniency or ignoring them altogether. Color, not the crime, determined a person's guilt on virtually any charge. With justification, then, Du Bois suggested, "Negroes came to look upon courts as instruments of injustice and oppression, and upon those convicted in them as martyrs and victims." When in the late nineteenth century "the real Negro criminal" made his appearance and committed far more serious crimes, black people refused to give any credence to the evidence of white witnesses or the fairness of white juries. "[T]he greatest deterrent to crime, the public opinion of one's own social caste, was lost, and the criminal was looked upon as crucified rather than hanged."[97]

What whites came to notice by the 1880s was the appearance of "a double system of judgment" in the black community. If blacks were victimized by blacks, they condemned the guilty. But in the estimation of Philip A. Bruce, a young Virginia aristocrat and influential writer, no such judgment fell on a black person "guilty of a violation of the law, however gross, from which white people alone suffer." Rather than seek out such criminals for prosecution, blacks exercised, he thought, a "curious freemasonry" that rallied around the accused and sought to protect them; indeed, it tended to unite "a whole community of plantation negroes," old and young alike. An exasperated Mississippi planter noted in his diary the difficulty encountered in arresting a suspected black murderer. One black reported the suspect had come to his house asking for food, another placed him at a different location asking for water. "I'm of the opinion that these reports are simply lies made up by negroes to mislead the posse in search."[98]

Many observers, white and black, agreed that a certain distinction attached itself to the black criminal. He returned to his community without stigma; in fact, he stood as high if not higher in the estimation of many, especially if his crime had claimed only whites as victims. This elevated status caused no end of frustration and dismay to white observers. "A convict whose term of service has expired stands as high in the estimation of the colored masses as if no charge of crime had ever been preferred against him," a Georgia prison official noted. "Indeed, in some instances, he is lionized by his race, who seem unable or unwilling to discover the clear distinction between unwarranted persecution and the just enforcement of the just penalties." Upon returning from prison, he might even be greeted as a hero, with festive music, prayer, and a warm reception. In condemning the tolerance said to be afforded black criminals, an Atlanta newspaper noted that in the pursuit and arrest of a white criminal, law officers met with the support and cooperation of the black public. But such support and cooperation quickly evaporated if the suspect being sought was a black person.

> The moment that a negro steals, or robs, or commits some other crime, his person seems to become sacred in the eyes of his race, and he is harbored, protected and deified. If he is captured, resists an officer and is shot, as he should be, and as a white criminal would be, immediately the leading negroes drum up a mass meeting and proceed to pass a string of senseless but sympathetic resolutions, after a series of harangues that would be a disgrace to the Zulus.

The Atlanta paper did not seem to consider the amount of white criminal activity deemed immune from prosecution if the victims were black, or the instances in which coroners' juries returned verdicts of "We find that the deceased came to his death at the hands of persons unknown to us."[99]

That the white and black public might differ in their response to law enforcement officers was hardly surprising. To assist police in apprehending a suspect, blacks feared, was to deliver an individual to be lynched or to be judged exclusively by prejudiced whites. Not only were sheriffs, police, and jailers often "passive spectators" at lynchings, but they also sometimes actively collaborated with the lynchers. The leader of the Atlanta Civic League, organized after the Atlanta Riot in 1906, conceded that blacks often refused to cooperate with law enforcement officials. "One reason for that is that the Negro has too little confidence in our courts. We must give him that, above all things."[100]

The "celebration" of the criminal proved inseparable from black perceptions of the quality of justice available to black men and women. Those able to circumvent the system, to outwit whites, to get the most out of the system might command considerable admiration within the black community as long as their actions did not violate the property and lives of their own people. What whites defined as criminal behavior, moreover, some blacks viewed as nothing less than compensation for the unpunished crimes of whites, as partial payment for what whites over several centuries had expropriated for themselves from black bodies. Commenting on the growing number of black crimes reported in the white press, a black newspaper in Savannah estimated that if white crimes against blacks were punished with equal vigor, "they would doubly offset that of the colored people." And a black newspaper in Richmond invoked history to respond in the strongest possible terms to allegations of black criminality. "All of the hog, sheep, cow and chicken stealing by the dishonest members of [our] race since the world began will not begin to equal one hundreth part of the amount of money which has been stolen by members of the white race, who lay claim to all of the intelligence, religion and learning."[101]

The power wielded by whites in the courts and prisons, although claiming its share of victims, did not necessarily convert the survivors into law-abiding citizens. Characterizing the chain gang system in Georgia "an epitomized hell," a white critic noted that none of those who returned to their communities did so with any enhanced respect for the law. "They came back hating law, despising the restraints of law, enemies of society, the enemies of white people with hatred and malignity in their hearts." A visitor to the United States in 1909 noted the growing class of "criminal negroes" in the South. But after observing the workings of the judicial system, along with the entire apparatus of white repression, he found the statistics of black crime altogether plausible. If anything, he had expected a larger number of black offenders. "When we consider in how many respects the race is outlawed, it seems wonderful that more of them should not fall into habits of outlawry." Richard Wright as a youth in Mississippi had not yet committed a crime, but he had witnessed firsthand the men who made and enforced the law. "I had seen how they acted, how they regarded black people, how they regarded me; and I no longer felt bound by the laws which white and black were supposed to obey in common. I was outside those laws; the white people had told me so."[102]

Even as the outlaw and "bad man" became a distinctive folk figure of the new generation of black Southerners, a new form of music took root in the same generation, mostly among the young men and women who had disengaged themselves from the norms and values of conventional black and white society.

> *I got the blues, but too damn mean to cry,*
> *Oh, I got the blues but I'm too damn mean to cry.*[103]

9

ASKED TO DIRECT a black Knights of Pythias band in Clarksdale, Mississippi, thirty-year-old W. C. Handy came there in 1903. Born in Florence, Alabama, the son of freed slaves, Handy acquired an interest in music early in his life, drifted from place to place and from job to job, finally playing and traveling with various minstrel troupes and brass bands before accepting the position in Mississippi. The band he formed there played the Delta circuit, at "affairs of every description," until Handy came to know intimately "every foot of the Delta."

One night, Handy was in the railroad station at Tutwiler, waiting for a train that was some nine hours late. It proved to be an unforgettable night. A lean, shabbily clothed black man had started playing his guitar, sliding a knife on the strings as he sang some strange song. He repeated three times in succession the line "Goin' where the Southern cross' the Dog," accompanying himself on the guitar with what Handy recalled as "the weirdest music I had ever heard." Not understanding the lyrics, Handy leaned over and asked him what they meant. The man seemed mildly amused. "Perhaps I should have known," Handy thought, "but he didn't mind explaining. At Moorhead the eastbound and the westbound met and crossed the north and southbound trains four times a day. This fellow was going where the Southern cross' the Dog, and he didn't care who knew it." That is, he was headed for Moorhead, where the Southern Railroad crossed the Yazoo Delta Railroad, known to locals as the Yellow Dog. If the music seemed "weird," the explanation did not, at least as Handy recalled it some years later. "Southern Negroes sang about everything. Trains, steamboats, steam whistles, sledge hammers, fast women, mean bosses, stubborn mules—all become subjects for their songs. They accompany themselves on anything from which they can extract a musical sound or rhythmical effect, anything from a harmonica to a washboard."

Recalling his experience in Tutwiler, Handy thought he had come face-to-face with something called "blues," and the experience would be heightened shortly afterward when in Cleveland, a Delta town, he was leading his orchestra in a dance program. A member of the audience requested that the local band be permitted to play a few dance numbers. Led by "a long-legged chocolate boy," the musicians consisted of "a battered guitar, a mandolin, and a worn-out bass," and the music they played, Handy recalled, "was pretty well in keeping with their looks." It had no clear beginning or end, the strumming took on a "disturbing monotony," and as the musicians played, their eyes rolled and their shoulders swayed. Handy found it "haunting," but he wondered how long an audience could tolerate it. The answer came soon enough. "A rain of silver dollars began to fall around the outlandish, stomping feet. The dancers went wild." In a few minutes, more money lay on the floor than Handy's musicians were being paid for their entire engagement. That was when Handy began to appreciate "the beauty of primitive music." If it needed polishing, it was unquestionably "the stuff the people wanted. It touched the spot." The "old conventional music" still had its place, Handy concluded, "but there was no virtue in being blind when you had good eyes."[104]

The year before Handy heard those "weird" and "haunting" sounds in Tutwiler and Cleveland, sixteen-year-old Gertrude Rainey of Columbus, Georgia, was touring as a performer with a musical tent show. In a small town in Missouri, "a girl from the town" came to the tent and sang a "strange and poignant" song that attracted such a response that Rainey incorporated it into her act. When asked to describe the song, Rainey replied, "It's the *Blues.*"[105]

Sidney Bechet, born in New Orleans in the late nineteenth century, played as a teenager with a number of professional bands, including Buck Johnson's. For a short time Bechet performed in Texas, only to find himself in the Galveston jail on the familiar charge of being in the wrong neighborhood. In the cell he shared, a fellow prisoner sang a song that differed from anything Bechet had ever heard, "that took every thought I had out of my mind until it had me so close inside it I could *taste* how it felt." The man who sang it, Bechet thought, "was more than just a man. He was like every man that's been done a wrong. Inside him he'd got the memory of all the wrong that's been done to all my people. That's what the memory is . . . when I remember that man, I'm remembering myself, a feeling I've always had. When a blues is good, that kind of memory just grows up inside it. . . . There's nothing about that night I could ever forget."[106]

Several years before Handy heard the blues in Tutwiler, Bill and Annie Patton moved onto Dockery Farms, a large plantation in Sunflower County, in the upper Delta. Making the most of his opportunities, the hardworking Bill Patton achieved a measure of independence for a tenant farmer; his son Charlie, born between 1887 and 1891, soon became one of the best-known and most accomplished of the Delta bluesmen. He preferred honing his musical skills to working with his father on the farm. "Charlie hated work like God hates sin," fellow bluesman Son House said of him, and a neighbor recalled how Charlie prided himself on being too "smart" to work. Charlie himself sang, "I ain't gonna have no job mama, rollin' through this world."[107]

Like most of the bluesmen, Charlie Patton relished his freedom, the life of a masterless man. By 1910 he had already built up an impressive repertoire. The perceived difficulty of blacks in taking charge of their own lives and destinies would weigh heavily in his songs, along with the need to find ways to live with fear and uncertainty.

> *I'm goin' away, to where I don't know*
> *I'm worried now, but I won't be worried long*
> *My rider got somethin', she's tryin' to keep it hid*
> *My rider got somethin', she try to keep it hid*
> *Lord I got somethin' to find that somethin' with.*
>
> *Every day seem like murder here*
> *(My God I'm gonna stay around)*
> *Every day seem like murder here*
> *I'm gonna leave tomorrow, I know you don't bit more care.*
>
> *Can't go down this dirt road by myself*
> *Can't go down this dirt road by myself*
> *(My God who you gonna carry?)*
> *I don't carry my rider, gonna carry me someone else.*[108]

He used his freedom to roam the Delta, playing for house parties and frequenting the rapidly proliferating roadhouses and saloons. "He used to play out on the plantations," bluesman Howlin' Wolf remembered of Patton, "at different one's homes out there. They'd give a supper—call it a Saturday night hop or something like that. . . . He'd play different spots—he'd be playing here tonight and somewhere else the next night, and so on." His nephew recalled the concerts Patton gave at Dockery Farms, where he still often resided but seldom worked:

> It'd be hundreds of people at these places. Couldn't half of them get in the house. They had these here juke houses. They'd be so crowded till you couldn't even stir around in there. He played on the inside. Just like on a Saturday a whole bunch would get together, and he'd play at Dockery's at the big store. There used to be a big brick store there at Dockery's. He'd sit out there on the store porch. People all from Lula, Cleveland, everywhere. . . .[109]

Will Dockery liked to think of himself as a paternalistic planter, and he enjoyed a relatively good reputation for honest dealings among his tenants and laborers. But in the winter of 1921, Patton had finally outlived his welcome and Dockery had him banished from the plantation, ostensibly because of his effect on the female sharecroppers: They "wouldn't half-work; theyd be sleepy all day on account of listenin' him to play at night at different parties."[110] Perhaps Patton's lifestyle had become too much for the moralistic Dockery to tolerate, as Patton in his own way had come to personify the "bad nigger," even if whites and blacks in Coahoma County in the early 1900s differed as to the ultimate meaning of the term.

> *I like to fuss and fight*
> *I like to fuss and fight*
> *Lord, and get sloppy drink off a bottle and ball*
> *And walk the streets all night.*[111]

No single person could be crowned "King of the Delta Blues," but Charlie Patton qualified for a distinctive place in the blues subculture that was emerging in the South. Of the distinctive forms of expression that came out of Patton's generation, none was more compelling and more intense than the music they created. It was in these years, in the Mississippi Delta, where blacks outnumbered whites three to one, in places such as Ruleville, Drew, Cleveland, Leland, Dockery Farms, Friar Point, and Stovall's Plantation, but also in East Texas, Arkansas,

Louisiana, Georgia, Alabama, and the Carolinas, and in urban New Orleans, Helena, Memphis, and St. Louis, that a new musical form appeared. Blues, as it was called, distinguished by its three-line verse, with an AAB rhyme scheme (the pattern often varied), could be heard on street corners and in storefronts, barbershops, train stations, cafés, and brothels, at house "frolics," country dances, and Saturday night fish fries, in the boardinghouses, the turpentine and lumber work camps, and the crossroads stores—wherever the performers worked, and if they had no work, wherever they could find people ready to part with some of their loose change.

Bluesmen and blueswomen made the rounds of the country joints, barrelhouses, cabarets, honky-tonks, roadhouses, stores, and cafés that dotted the plantation and urban landscape. Dubbed by some the "all-night clubs," they opened Friday evening and ran continuously until Sunday night. Featuring a bar, a dance floor, and a small stage for the musicians, these places might function simultaneously as saloons, gambling dens, dance halls, and brothels, as Charlie Patton suggested.

> *There's a house over yonder, painted all over green*
> *Some of the finest young women Lord a man most ever seen.*[112]

Some of these places may have originated in the barrelhouses and "chock-houses" maintained by the sawmills and the larger lumber companies in Mississippi, Louisiana, Arkansas, and Texas to provide diversions for the loggers. Some rural blacks turned their homes into "clubs" on certain nights, selling homemade liquor and home-cooked food, and employing local musicians who performed "jump-ups" and blues, intended for both dancing and listening. Known by various names, such places at some point would be dubbed "juke houses" and "juke joints." Many cafés by day were transformed into "juke joints" at night. (The term "juke" has been traced to similar-sounding words in West African languages having to do with "partying," and to the Gullah "joog," which translated into "disorderly" in the Georgia Sea Islands.) Whatever the various names by which these places came to be known, they often existed only at the tolerance of the plantation owner or local sheriff, who received a share of the "house" profits. Within a decade, before the players reached larger audiences with their recorded songs, the place of the "juke joint" in the distinctive culture of the black South had been set. If America's foremost jazz musicians often started by playing at rent parties in Harlem and Chicago, bluesmen and blueswomen invariably started by performing at the house parties and "joints" in the rural South before making it to the "chitlin' circuit."[113]

The men and women who played and sang the blues were mostly poor, propertyless, disreputable itinerants, many of them illiterate, many of them loners, many of them living on the edge. Rejecting the static lives of their parents, almost always on the move, they felt freer than most, and prided themselves on being masterless, on being able to enjoy a freedom of movement and expression denied many of their people, on being free of a labor system that tied others (including their families) to the land through violence, coercion, and the law. Patton's niece said of her uncle, "He just left when he got ready, because he didn't make no crops. . . . He was a *free man.*"[114]

Wherever they performed, the bluesmen and blueswomen had an impact. The format and content both bewildered and dismayed some listeners. It was unlike anything anyone had experienced before, and not everyone wanted to listen to it again. Some thought it unearthly, terrifying, threatening, and subversive. Middle-class blacks had expended considerable energy trying to escape primitive stereotypes reinforced by the blues, and many churchgoing blacks thought the blues to be downright blasphemous—the devil's music. It was an identity they resented and resisted. After purchasing his first guitar with money he had saved from work, W. C. Handy came home overjoyed, only to find his parents furious. "One of the devil's playthings," his father shouted. "Take it away. Take it away, I tell you. Get it out of your hands. Whatever possessed you to bring a sinful thing like that into our Christian home? Take it back where it came from." At his father's insistence, a stunned Handy turned in his guitar for a new *Webster's Unabridged Dictionary.* That transaction no doubt met with the approval of his teacher at school, who had already made clear her distaste for musicians: They were "idlers, dissipated characters, whisky drinkers and . . . social pariahs." Charlie Patton's father was said to have initially hit his son with a bullwhip for his musical interest, only to relent and eventually buy him a guitar when he came to appreciate his son's determination and talent. "I can't do nothing with him," his mother said with a sigh. "I reckon he was called to pick that guitar." Some years later, a young Robert Johnson took several beatings from his stepfather for avoiding field work. "He'd tell him to go out there and work," a neighbor recalled; "well, he'd get that old guitar, and go off somewheres else." This was not the music of "respectable" folks, and what a black-authored etiquette manual said of blacks partaking of the popular "cakewalk" dance craze would have applied with much greater force to anyone dancing to the blues: "That certain muscles of the trunk and limbs are developed and beautified, is not denied. Yet they are developed at great expense to the laws of ethics and refinement."[115]

Even if the instruments could be momentarily denied aspiring musicians, the impulses and feelings that gave birth to the music in the first place overcame every obstacle. "It didn't make any difference," Lonnie Johnson recalled, " 'cause the feelin' was there and that's all you needed, to get started anyway." Raised in Clarksdale, McKinley Morganfield (Muddy Waters) remembered singing from the moment he began chopping cotton as a young boy in the 1920s and the feelings he was trying to articulate. "I do remember I was always singin', 'I cain't be satisfied, I be all troubled in mind.' Seems to me like I was always singin' that, because I was always singin' jest the way I felt, and maybe I didn't exactly *know* it, but I jest didn't like the way things were down there—in Mississippi."[116]

The feelings were hardly new, but the ways in which they were expressed had assumed different forms. The musical roots of the blues may be found in the religious music of black Americans, in their chants, work songs, field hollers, ring shouts, and country breakdowns, each of them leaving a mark on the new music, drawing from a common stock of expression and feelings. But the blues was at the same time strikingly different, far deeper, more immediate, more gripping, more painful. Ishman Bracey, born in 1901 in Hinds County, Mississippi, sang, "I've been down so long, Lawd, down don't worry me."[117] Like the religious and work songs, much of the blues was improvised, and blues singers invariably employed a variety of vocal devices— moaning, shouting, falsetto—to enhance their presentation, to convey their innermost feelings.

Blues had long been around as a state of mind if not as a musical format. In a New Orleans newspaper in 1839, a "Sam Jonsing" explained the blues in terms of a man who looks to the future as though he has just drawn a blank in the big lottery.

> Wen he gets [up] in de mornin' he feels bad, and wen [he] goes to bed at night he feels wusser. He tinks dat his body is made ob ice cream, all 'cept his heart, and dat—dat's a piece ob lead in de middle. All sorts ob sights are hubbering around, and red monkeys is buzzing about his ears. . . . [D]em's what I calls de bloos.[118]

As a feeling, the blues is capable of tearing a person apart inside; blues music is able to inflict the same painful sensation, as Willie Brown made clear.

> *The blues ain't nothin' but a lowdown shakin' chill*
> *If you ain't had 'em, I hope you never will.*[119]

And some years later, Robert Johnson, as he did so often, raised the stakes and defined the blues in starker and more frightening tones.

> *The blues is a low down aching old heart disease*
> *And like consumption, killing me by degrees.*[120]

Often personalized, the blues examined through daily experiences many of the subjects that preoccupied black Southerners. Travel (whether by foot or rail), the pain of loneliness and loss, faithlessness in love, sexual prowess, the meager rewards of labor, natural disasters (boll weevils and floods), dislocation, poverty, hypocritical preachers, escape through drink and drugs, the inequities of justice, the pervasiveness of color, the satisfaction of vanquishing an adversary, the betrayal of expectations, the imminence of violence and death—these only begin to suggest the range of themes on which bluesmen and blueswomen reflected and philosophized. They felt bound to their audience by a common history and by shared experiences. "There's lots of trouble here, and more on down the road," a black Texan sang in 1915. "You will always find trouble, no matter where you go."[121]

In relating their experiences, their hopes and despair, their betrayals and triumphs, bluesmen and blueswomen did so in the certainty that many people in their audience would understand and share their blues.

> *Ef you ever been down, you know jes how I feel—*
> *Lak a broken-down engine got no drivin' wheel,*
> *Lak a po' sojer boy lef' on de battle-fiel'.*[122]

Through their songs, blues performers could express themselves with a directness, a matter-of-factness, that whites rarely tolerated from blacks in public; they could convey emotions and feelings many whites had thought them incapable of possessing. Bluesmen and blueswomen had a way of using humor and wit, images and metaphors, to unmask the society around them, to explore forbidden subjects, to subvert prevailing values and faiths, and to suggest ways of working out difficulties. The best of them had a liberating effect on their audiences, if only because they echoed shared concerns, questions, and sensibilities. "Because people in general they takes the song as an explanation for *themselves*," Henry Townsend observed, "they believe this song is expressing *their* feelin's instead of the one that singin' it. They feel that maybe I have just hit upon somethin' that's in their lives, and yet at the same time it was some of the things that went wrong with me too."[123]

Not exclusively the music of the "bad man," though it might celebrate his feats, the blues addressed experiences that were familiar to the lives of many working-class black men and women. It was living history that also drew on the experiences of previous generations. Gertrude "Ma" Rainey, born in 1886, had grown up in Georgia, where she witnessed the human wreckage produced by the chain gang and the judicial system.

> *It was early this mornin' that I had my trial,*
> *It was early this mornin' that I had my trial,*
> *Ninety days on the country road, and the judge didn't even smile.*[124]

Neither "protest music" nor political commentary, blues defied the usual categories. It seldom if ever addressed directly such issues as disfranchisement or segregation, but neither did it avoid race relations and white duplicity. One bluesman found his own way to mock the employer who insisted on treating him as a child by repeatedly calling him "son."

> *Woh, you ain't got no black child.*[125]

Although conditions of deprivation, repression, and violence helped to shape and sustain the blues, so did the need to confront and transcend those conditions, to recall both good times and bad times, the triumphs along with the defeats. Blues had a language of its own, and to a remarkable degree it enabled black Southerners to confront betrayed expectations and an accumulation of frustrations, bitterness, and troubles. It could be heard in the defiance articulated by an anonymous Memphis bluesman,

I feel my hell a-risin', a-risin' every day;
I feel my hell a-risin', a-risin' every day;
Someday it'll burst this levee and wash the whole wide world away.

or in the chilling fantasy described by Furry Lewis, born in 1900 and raised in the Delta at Greenwood,

I believe I'll buy me a graveyard of my own.
I believe I'll buy me a graveyard of my own.
I'm goin' kill everybody that have done me wrong.[126]

or in a different kind of fantasy in which black Southerners turn segregation on its head,

Well, I'm goin' to buy me a little railroad of my own;
Ain't goin' to let nobody ride but the chocolate to the bone.
Well, I goin' to buy me a hotel of my own;
Ain't goin' to let nobody eat but the chocolate to the bone.[127]

or in the terrifying imagery and mesmerizing sounds communicated by Robert Johnson as he roamed the Delta,

I got stones in my passway and my road seems dark as night
I got stones in my passway and my road seems dark as night
I have pains in my heart, they have taken my appetite.[128]

or in the outburst underscoring the frustration felt by those denied the fruits of their labor,

I asked that boss-man for to gimme my time;
Sez he, "Ole Nigger, you're a day behin'."

I asked him once, I asked him twaist;
Ef I ask him again, I'll take his life.[129]

And few could match the emotional depths plumbed by Bertha "Chippie" Hill in her plaintive, chilling lament,

I'm gonna lay my head on a lonesome railroad line
And let the 2:19 pacify my mind.[130]

Eloquent and evocative black spokesmen and spokeswomen in their own right—Charlie Patton, Tommy Johnson, Son House, Ma Rainey, Willie Brown, Blind Lemon Jefferson, Henry Thomas, Memphis Minnie, and Robert Johnson, among many others. None of them would achieve recognition in the dictionaries of American and black biography, or in anthologies of American literature. But to listen to them is to feel—more vividly and more intensely than any mere poet, novelist, or historian could convey—the despair, the thoughts, the passions, the aspirations, the anxieties, the deferred dreams, the frightening honesty of a new generation of black Southerners and their efforts to grapple with day-to-day life, to make it somehow more bearable, perhaps even transcend it.[131]

10

THE YEAR Woodrow Wilson was inaugurated president of the United States, black Americans celebrated the fiftieth anniversary of emancipation. That same year, some forty-five black Southerners were lynched. Wilson made no mention in his inaugural address of the anniversary or of race relations, underscoring the indifference of both the president and the nation to the ongoing racial crisis in the South. But black Southerners had a great deal to say. Since the Civil War, blacks had used each anniversary of emancipation to assess their progress. Invariably these proved to be optimistic celebrations of black people on the threshold of a progressive age in which color and race would lose their significance. The fiftieth anniversary produced more than its share of such prophecies.

Throughout the South in 1913, the "Year of Jubilee," black speakers recited the extraordinary progress blacks had made over the past half century in farm and home ownership, in business enterprise and the professions, in the accumulation of wealth, in the dramatic reduction of illiteracy (from 90 percent in 1865 to some 30 percent in 1913), and in the number of newspapers published and books written.[132] For some blacks (and whites), the progress made since the Civil War had more than vindicated emancipation and validated the black potential. White Southerners were less certain; some denied the evidence of black progress, some welcomed it, some feared it, most remained insistent on the need to subordinate blacks—the unsuccessful and the successful— to a white-dominated and white-managed social and economic order.

W. E. B. Du Bois, writing in *The Crisis* on the semicentennial of emancipation, enumerated the major obstacles southern blacks still confronted: disfranchisement, segregation, curtailed educational opportunities, the subjugation of black women, the prohibition of legal marriage between the races, and the expulsion of blacks from the land by disease, starvation, or mob violence. Urging blacks to reject "apologetic and explanatory" statements "based on temporary philanthropic relief," Du Bois used this occasion to demand that blacks organize around a militant opposition to white repression. "Abraham Lincoln began the emancipation of the Negro-American. The National Association for the Advancement of Colored People proposes to complete it." (The NAACP had been founded in 1909.) Booker T. Washington, on the other hand, chose to use the semicentennial to focus on the gains in education, comparing the "social experiment" in the South over the past fifty years to the first Christian missionaries dispatched from Rome to Christianize and civilize the people of western Europe.[133] The comparison might have seemed ironic to some blacks, as the question had been raised as to whether missionaries might be sent to the American South to civilize the white people who lived there.

The semicentennial prompted black Southerners not only to assess their progress over the past fifty years but also to contemplate the issues of racial identity and pride that Du Bois had voiced so eloquently a decade earlier. The Negro, as he viewed him, had been "born with a veil, and gifted with second-sight in this American world." Forced to view himself through the eyes of white men, to calculate his every move and word in terms of white expectations and demands, the Negro came to be exposed to a myriad of conflicting images.

> It is a peculiar sensation, this double-consciousness, this sense of always looking at one's self through the eyes of others, of measuring one's soul by the tape of a world that looks on in amused contempt and pity. One ever feels his two-ness,—an American, a Negro; two souls, two thoughts, two unreconciled strivings; two warring ideals in one dark body, whose dogged strength alone keeps it from being torn asunder.

The history of Negro Americans, Du Bois contended, revolved around this perennial conflict—"this longing to attain self-conscious manhood, to merge his double self into a better and truer self." What seemed critical was the need for black people, even as they sought admission to white society, to retain their racial heritage and individuality.

> He would not bleach his Negro soul in a flood of white Americanism, for he knows that Negro blood has a message for the world. He simply wishes to make it possible for a man to be both a Negro and an American, without being cursed and spit upon by his fellows, without having the doors of Opportunity closed roughly in his face.[134]

But it would not be easy. What blacks confronted was a white society intent on maintaining its supremacy in every sphere of activity. That made it all the more imperative for blacks to define who they were and to counter the self-debasing images with which they were constantly bombarded. By the turn of the century, within the black community, the very name by which they preferred to be known collectively provoked divisions. Colored people, black people, Negroes, Afro-Americans—each commanded popularity, often simultaneously. After emancipation, many freed blacks had taken new surnames to mark their new status, and that development in turn raised questions about a collective name that would emphasize their independence of white domination. The ensuing debate persisted into the next century, reflecting as it did shifts in racial consciousness, the ways in which whites employed the various terms depicting blacks, uncertainty among blacks about their relation to Africa, and still unresolved questions about black identity in a hostile white society.

In the early nineteenth century, "Colored American" had come into increasing popularity among blacks as a way to assert racial pride while affirming their Americanization at a time when some whites wanted to deport them to Africa. The terms "black" and "Negro" were disdained after emancipation if only because their former owners preferred them and whites had often used them as words of derision; the terms also suggested unmixed ancestry and hence excluded large numbers of colored people. "African" seemed even less attractive at a time when black leaders emphasized assimilation and American identity. For a brief time, "Afro-American" flourished, a term popularized by T. Thomas Fortune, a black editor in New York. Bishop Alexander Walters of the A.M.E. Zion Church gave the term his blessing, believing it to be comparable to "Anglo-Saxon" and a positive shift from a racial description to a cultural and historical identity. "Why should this whole race be designated by a term which defines color alone? Men and races are designated by the term which defines the country, the race to which they belong, and not by the color which distinguishes them from the rest of mankind. We are Afro-Americans—not colored Americans or Negro Americans."[135]

Whatever the force of Walters's argument, the usage proved short-lived, perhaps reflecting a continuing black ambivalence toward Africa. Robert H. Terrell, a prominent lawyer in Washington who married Mary E. Church in 1891, thought the designation "meaningless" if not "ridiculous" and counterproductive. "If by being called an Afro-American I could get a single opportunity or privilege that I do not already possess I shouldn't mind the hyphenated name. . . . So far as I am concerned I am satisfied to be known as a Negro American or a Colored American. I don't want to dodge either name." With equal fervor, Alexander Crummell, a prominent black academic with strong ties to Africa, thought "Afro-American" a "bastard, milk and water term" that most Negroes by 1898 had repudiated.[136]

Shortly after the end of Reconstruction, a Louisiana black newspaper indicated a preference for "Negro" as long as it was capitalized, like any other nationality. "The French, German, Irish, Dutch, Japanese and other nationalities, are honored with a capital letter but the poor sons of Ham must bear the burden of a small *n*." The problem with "colored," some argued, was the implication that whites were not colored, that white represented the standard to which other colors have been added; it also failed to differentiate blacks from other "colored" peoples, such as Asians and Indians. The founding in 1896 of the National Association of Colored Women prompted a response from Sarah Dudley Pettey, a woman activist in North Carolina and a columnist for the weekly newspaper of the A.M.E. Zion Church. Disapproving of the term "colored" in the name of the association, she thought it little more than a "softening" of the word "nigger" to "you colored people." And she noted, too, that all people were colored, "from the fairest blonde to the darkest hue of humanity." She preferred "Afro-American," as it designated "both the races and countries from whence we, the amalgamated race, came."[137]

By the late nineteenth century, "Negro" had become the preferred term in the black community, and the "New Negro" came to be used frequently to depict a new generation of proud and self-assertive black Southerners. Washington and Du Bois both embraced "Negro," insisting only that it be capitalized. So did Edward A. Johnson in *A School*

History of the Negro Race in America, published in 1891. He admonished "fellow teachers" to make certain "Negro" was capitalized. "It deserves to be so enlarged, and will help, perhaps, to magnify the race it stands for in the minds of those who see it." And George Washington Williams, whose two-volume *History of the Negro Race in America* (1883) was the first scholarly history of black Americans, thought it unwise for Negroes to drop the term. "It is a good, strong and healthy word, and ought to live. It should be covered with glory; let Negroes do it."[138]

When Roland Barton, a high school sophomore, questioned the use of the term "Negro," calling it "a white man's word to make us feel inferior," Du Bois chose to respond in full in the pages of *Crisis.* He found "Negro" to be "etymologically and phonetically . . . much better and more logical than 'African' or 'colored' or any of the various hyphenated circumlocutions." But Du Bois went further in his response, asking essentially what was in a name:

> If a thing is despised, either because of ignorance or because it is despicable, you will not alter matters by changing its name. If men despise Negroes, they will not despise them less if Negroes are called "colored" or Afro-Americans. . . . The feeling of inferiority is in you, not in any name. The name merely evokes what is already there. Exorcise the hateful complex and no name can ever make you hang your head. . . . Get this then, Roland, and get it straight even if it pierces your soul; a Negro by any other name would be just as black and just as white; just as ashamed of himself and just as shamed by others, as today. . . . It is not the name—it's the Thing that counts.[139]

What compounded the problem of identity was the way an oppressive racial system sometimes forced blacks to embrace the values of their oppressors and the lengths to which some blacks would go in their desire to identify with and be accepted by the "superior race." From childhood, blacks had learned the premium placed on whiteness and Western standards of beauty, and that revelation became part of their daily lives well into adulthood. Whatever blacks chose to call themselves collectively, some seemed intent on looking, acting, and sounding as little Negro, colored, black, or Afro-American as possible. Advertisements in black newspapers and periodicals sought to place a fair skin and soft, silky, and glossy hair within easy reach of anyone able to afford the preparations, enabling black women to alter their appearance and even "excel the famed beauty of the Caucasians." Such products as Straightine and Kink-ine promised to transform knotty, kinky, and curly hair, while a number of face bleach preparations guaranteed various degrees of whiteness. "This preparation will not make you white, but will make your complexion fair," Dixie Liquid Bleach advertised, while Black Skin Remover went a step further, promising to make the skin of a black or brown person "four or five shades lighter, and a mulatto person perfectly white."[140]

The implicit message conveyed by much of the advertising seemed clear enough: White features are beautiful, black features are ugly; white is pure, black is dirty; white is desirable, black is undesirable. Some blacks found themselves in effect embracing the standards and priorities of those who sought to keep them down and diminish their capacity for improvement. Even as Helen Lee, a schoolteacher in Virginia, sought to develop in her black students "a positive viewpoint toward being black," familiarizing them with their history and achievements, she acknowledged the pervasiveness of whiteness. "All of us—teachers and parents alike—were trying so hard to make our children conform to the white world."[141]

To some blacks, however, it made no sense. Why model themselves after a people who mocked, degraded, and repressed them and whose own standards of civilized behavior were suspect? To deny their race, heritage, and history, to whitewash their culture (or facial features), to ape the ways of white people, in the expectation that they could gain the respect and recognition of such people, was an exercise in futility that could produce only self-hatred and self-deprecation. Henry M. Turner, among others, challenged his people to look to themselves, not to whites, for inspiration and emancipation. "A man must believe he is somebody before he is acknowledged to be somebody. . . . Neither the Republican nor Democratic party can do for the colored race what they can do for themselves. Respect Black." No less insistent, Sutton E. Griggs, a southern clergyman and writer, thought it only a matter of time before the Negro came onto "the center of the stage." What he feared was that the race might lose its distinctiveness through assimilation. "With the loss of color might go the loss of special feeling of kinship. Feeling all this in every fibre of our soul, we cannot view with equanimity the forces at work tending to whiten the race."[142]

Rather than view their color as a badge of degradation, black spokesmen urged their people to embrace it as a symbol of strength and beauty, superior in most respects to the pale, pasty-complexioned

Caucasians. Only the presumptuousness and arrogance of whites elevated their color. *"Black is no mark* of reproach to people who do not worship white," Edward A. Johnson wrote in his *School History of the Negro Race in America.* West Indians, he noted, depicted the devil as white, and Indians and Africans mocked whites as palefaces. "People in this country have been educated to believe in white because all that is good has been ascribed to the white race both in pictures and words. God, the angels and all the prophets are pictured white and the Devil is represented as black."[143]

11

NOTHING SO DRAMATICALLY underscored the contradictions in the black experience in America than the spectacle of a people denied the rights and privileges accorded to white citizens responding to the call to defend those rights and privileges on the battlefield. When asked to provide the necessary support in time of war, blacks invariably responded with the same enthusiasm as their white compatriots. And the language of their support rarely wavered: This was an opportunity to affirm their patriotism with their lives.

To demonstrate the ardor of their national loyalty and to disprove theories of racial inferiority, black spokesmen claimed a patriotism second to none and superior to most recent arrivals from Europe. Not only would blacks fight foreign enemies, but they would also oppose those within the nation who threatened to make class war on the economic system. "We have never been numbered among our country's enemies," a black attorney told the Colored Bar Association of Mississippi. "We have never been found in the ranks of the Socialists and Anarchists in their attack upon social order and our free institutions."[144] And, sensing no apparent paradox, black spokesmen spoke with pride of the exploits of black troops in the Indian wars of the late nineteenth century. The "loyalty and bravery" shown by black troops, declared H. C. Bruce, had turned the tide for the United States at Wounded Knee, among other places.[145]

The Spanish-American War initially attracted black sympathy as the effort to assist a colored people—Cubans—achieve their freedom from colonial rule. Booker T. Washington set the proper tone when he vowed to recruit "at least ten thousand loyal, brave, strong black men in the south who crave an opportunity to show their loyalty to our land and would gladly take this method of showing their gratitude for the lives laid down and the sacrifices made that the Negro might have his freedom and rights." Shortly before the declaration of hostilities, a black religious journal in New Orleans reiterated the traditional basis for black support in America's wars: "It will give them an opportunity to show to the world that they are loyal and true citizens to their country . . . notwithstanding the fact that so many people are pleased to say this is a white man's country." And some optimistic black spokesmen went so far as to suggest that an impressive display of black patriotism might be the means to "end our race troubles."[146]

But there was also a strong dissent. The black press reflected deep divisions within its public, many of whom thought it more critical to defend freedom in the United States than in Cuba or the Philippines. A black newspaper in Charlotte asked how blacks could offer their services to a government that had proven itself powerless to protect the right of black families in the South to life, liberty, and the pursuit of happiness.[147]

Few spokesmen were quite as blunt as John Mitchell, Jr., the influential editor of the *Richmond Planet*, in articulating the paradox of black participation in a war for Cuban and Filipino freedom. "A race of people who, denied the right of suffrage, outraged, butchered, with their rights ruthlessly trampled upon . . . that would kiss the hand that smites [it] and begs the privilege of dying for their oppressors is degenerate indeed." If black men were not deemed "good enough to exercise the right of franchise," they were not "good enough to exercise the right to enlist in the service of the United States." The financial and military resources that were being mobilized to liberate the Cubans from Spanish tyranny, Mitchell believed, ought to be expended instead on liberating southern blacks from white-imposed tyranny and poverty. Although Mitchell would give some grudging support to the war in Cuba, once hostilities were declared, he campaigned relentlessly for black officers for black regiments, ultimately adopting a slogan that would win considerable support in the black community: "no officers, no fight."[148]

Not only did some blacks question why they should offer their services to a government unable or unwilling to protect their basic civil rights, but they also expressed a certain camaraderie with Cubans and Filipinos. Would the fate of these colored peoples under American rule or tutelage be the same as that of blacks in the South and Indians in the

West? Would they not be cursed with "color-phobia, jimcrow cars, dis-franchisement, lynchers and everything that prejudice can do to blight the manhood of the darker races"? Many blacks thought so, and re-sented being asked to fight against a people very much like their own who were also struggling and dying for their freedom.[149]

When President McKinley spoke of Filipinos, he expressed a pater-nalistic attitude toward a people many Americans regarded as racial in-feriors. But when some blacks identified with the struggles of "our colored cousins," they were asserting a kinship that spanned the Pacific Ocean. No wonder, then, when in 1899 the United States dispatched two black regiments to help put down the Filipino insurgents, some black spokesmen were outraged. Whites talked about taking up the "White Man's Burden"; blacks responded with alarm over the "Black Man's Burden." Lewis H. Douglass, the son of the black leader who had died in 1895, echoed other critics when he observed "that wherever this government controls, injustice to dark races prevails." The many references to Filipinos as "niggers" only reinforced Douglass's convic-tion that American imperialism meant "the extension of race hate and cruelty, barbarous lynchings and gross injustice" to the colored peoples of Asia. John Mitchell simply labeled McKinley's moves against the in-surgents a "cruel and imperialist war," and the *Richmond Planet* singled out for praise a former black officer in the 6th Virginia Infantry Regi-ment who refused a commission in one of the regiments being re-cruited to fight in the Philippines. He chose instead to teach in the public schools—a position, the *Planet* noted, that would permit him to contribute to the uplift of colored people rather than to their extermi-nation.[150]

The deeper implications of American actions in Cuba and the Philippines were not lost on black soldiers fighting the war. "The U.S. has no right to subjugate these people," a sergeant wrote from Cuba. "American rule in the Philippines would be only a repetition of White rule in the south and American rule on this island today. The sole aim and cry would be to 'Keep the nigger down!' " Those who found them-selves helping to suppress Filipino insurgents noted how the white sol-diers referred contemptuously to Filipinos as "niggers" and abused and humiliated them as inferiors. "I feel sorry for these people," a black sol-dier wrote home from the Philippines in 1899, shortly before he was killed in action. "You have no idea the way these people are treated by the Americans here. I know their feeling towards them as they speak their opinions in my presence, thinking I am white." A graduate of Tuskegee Institute stationed in the Philippines confided to Booker T. Washington that "any man who has any humanity about him at all will make a mistake to fight against such a cause as this. I believe these people are right and *we* are wrong and terribly wrong."[51]

What some blacks viewed as an opportunity to display their military prowess and secure their rights, many white Southerners saw as black men dangerously out of place. The language employed by whites to express their anxiety over black soldiers in the Civil War would be revived. The arming of black troops was "a dangerous experiment," "a step towards quasi-social equality." The uniform would transform the Negro "from a docile, tractable and peaceable individual into an offensive, insolent creature," and the military experience acquired by blacks would "have a demoralizing effect on them when they return." The sight of uniformed black men carrying rifles or sidearms terrified many whites, and reports that whites might be compelled to salute black officers infuriated them. A South Carolina colonel who commanded a volunteer regiment vowed to court-martial and remove any of his men who dared to salute a black officer. "We have enlisted to fight for our country and not to practice social equality with an inferior race whom our fathers held in bondage." Throughout the South, municipal authorities made every effort to enforce Jim Crow and to make certain that military service in no way misled blacks about changes in race relations. During the trial of a black noncommissioned officer in Macon, Georgia, the city prosecutor began his case with a warning that might have been echoed throughout the white South: "I am going to show a nigger soldier that he is the same as any other nigger."[52]

Even as some blacks thought that Jim Crow could not survive this war, whites insisted on reinforcing the machinery of their supremacy. From the outset, as black troops (some of them from the North) moved into various military encampments in the South en route to Cuba, skirmishes broke out, both in the camps and in the nearby towns, several of them claiming both black and white lives. The insults hurled at black soldiers, the Jim Crow statutes relentlessly enforced, the cafés, saloons, hotels, and railroad restaurants that turned them away provoked F. J. Loudin of Fisk University to share with a friend one of his fantasies: "to hear that the Spanish fleet has cast anchor off Charleston, New Orleans, Savannah and a few more of those hell holes and is pouring in lead and iron so they [whites] will know that the great day of His wrath is upon them." The soldiers of one black regiment—the 6th Virginia Infantry—took matters into their own hands. Stationed at Camp Haskell, near Macon, they had been informed of a nearby persimmon tree, known as the hanging tree, which had claimed a number of lives. The most recent victim had been hanged, riddled with bullets, and castrated; his testicles were displayed in a jar of alcohol in a local white saloon. Infuriated by this information, black soldiers chopped the tree down and split it into firewood. From there they proceeded to a public park on the outskirts of Macon, where they tore down a sign reading "No Dogs and Niggers Allowed," and some went into the city and demanded service in "white only" saloons and restaurants. That ended the brief rebellion, as military authorities quickly herded the men back to the camp, disarmed the entire regiment, and placed them under arrest for twenty days.[153]

With the conclusion of the war, many black spokesmen expressed pride in the recruitment and conduct of black troops.[154] Not only had they fought gallantly in both Cuba and the Philippines, but in the much-celebrated battle of San Juan Hill they had "saved the day" for Theodore Roosevelt and his Rough Riders. Without their help, one black veteran recalled, Roosevelt would never have survived. Although Roosevelt some years later contested this version, probably because it compromised perceptions of his military prowess, he could never quite overcome his initial praise of black troops and his admission during the 1900 campaign that they had saved his life in Cuba. Roosevelt's attempt to rewrite history came as no surprise to one black soldier in Cuba who had previously thought of him as a friend of the Negro. "[B]ut he has proved himself to be just like most other white men, none too high to stoop to do the black man a mean trick."[155]

The steady increase in the number of lynchings, along with the treatment accorded returning black troops, made it abundantly clear that the war had changed nothing in race relations. On the contrary, the war seemed to have exacerbated racial tensions and violence by raising simultaneously black expectations and white anxieties. Bishop Henry M. Turner thought black soldiers had died "for nothing," for a country where enough of his people had been "lynched to death to reach a mile high if laid one upon the other, and enough women and children to form the head and foot slab if they should be arranged to stand upon the head of each other." Known primarily for his dialect poetry, Paul Laurence Dunbar composed some tributes to the heroism of black soldiers. But in the aftermath of the war, he expressed concern over "a new attitude" in the nation, in which the American people told its black citizens, "You may fight for us but you may not vote for us. You may prove a strong bulwark when the bullets are flying but you must stand from the line when the ballots are in the air. You may be heroes in war but you must be cravens in peace."[156]

More than three decades after the Civil War, the sectional wounds were healing. The Spanish-American War bound the country together in a shared patriotism based on military victory abroad. But for black Americans, the reunion had a depressing side, as it rested essentially on a perceived Anglo-Saxon mission in the world and white supremacy at home. Race "riots," which had become a euphemism for attacks on urban blacks, affected both North and South. At the same time, popular science and university-trained specialists fed and rationalized—even as popular culture (the newspaper and magazine caricatures, vaudeville and minstrelsy, and household artifacts) reflected and reinforced—white perceptions of black inferiority. It seemed clear to a black Georgian that as the North and South celebrated their reunification, black Americans suffered a "deeper humiliation and degradation." The Negro's white friends were "silent and indifferent," the Georgian observed, while "his enemies have grown bolder and more defiant. It looks as though annihilation is what is desired, and the Christian public fold their arms and say, 'Let him die' he is not Anglo-Saxon."[157]

Having seen their expectations disappointed, blacks made clear their disillusionment, even some who had been the most optimistic about the opportunities the war afforded. "The millennium that is to be has not dawned," conceded a black editor who had supported the war in the Philippines. Booker T. Washington, after reciting in October 1898 the patriotic services of blacks during the recent war and throughout history, acknowledged that one victory continued to elude this nation—the battle to conquer racial prejudice, and he viewed this cause "as far reaching and important as any that has occupied our army and navy." Despite the victory abroad, a "cancer" still gnawed at the heart of the nation, "that shall one day prove as dangerous as an attack from an army without or within."[158]

For many black veterans, participation in the war and travel abroad gave them a new perspective on the provincial nature of their segregated and repressive society at home. Observing firsthand the conduct of U.S. troops and officers in Cuba and the Philippine Islands, they also witnessed the consequences of home-grown American racism. Theophilus G. Steward served as a chaplain to the black 25th Infantry, and shortly after the war broke out he experienced the South's racial customs. "A glorious dilemma that will be for the Cuban negro," he thought, "to usher him into the condition of the American negro." In the Philippines, he served as chaplain and as government supervisor of schools for Filipinos in Luzon Province; he also authored a book commemorating the service of black troops. Steward came to appreciate the larger implications of the war and the Western quest for empire. He proposed to place the condition of black people in the United States in a much larger context, to internationalize their struggle for freedom. "We are accustomed to think the color question an American question," he wrote, "and to regard the Negro race as the only race affected disadvantageously by it." But his experience in Asia had taught him differently, and he now came to view what had always been a domestic problem as part of a much larger problem, bound up with the destinies of other peoples. "Nothing is clearer than the great color question is dividing the world. Just as it is wicked to be black in America I fear the day will dawn when it will be wicked to be white. Three fourths of mankind are surely awakening. . . . The coming people are those of Asia and Africa. . . . The color line is an awful fact and on it the world's great battle is to come, either economically or with the sword. It is a most happy thing for the American Negro that he has been kicked, cuffed and shot out of the white race. This excludes him from the destiny of that race and allots him a position with the age to come."[59]

But for most black Southerners, the international implications of the war took on little meaning for their day-to-day lives. If they thought about the war at all, it was only to reflect once again over expectations raised only to be betrayed. "In reality de 'nigger' ain't got no business gwine tuh war," thought Henry Baker. Born into slavery in 1854, he spent a lifetime in Alabama working as a sharecropper, a renter, and a laborer, always striving to own his own place. "All de wahs I know 'bout wuz started by de white folks en dey asked de 'niggers' tuh come in en he'p finish hit. En de 'niggers' bein' obedient tuh God, dey go en do what de white folks say. En aftuh he does hit, hit is a pow'rful mo'nful time wid him 'cause he don't git much outta hit."[160]

Ned Cobb, born thirty-one years after Henry Baker, shared with him the experience of trying to eke out a living in rural Alabama. A teenager during the Spanish-American War, Cobb, like Baker, could only shake his head in dismay when he thought about black involvement in America's wars. "I've had white people to tell me, 'This is a white man's country, white man's country.' They don't sing that to the colored man when it comes to war. Then it's all *our* country, go fight for the country. Go over there and risk his life for the country and come back, he aint a bit more thought of than he was before he left." The treatment accorded black soldiers on their return particularly infuriated Cobb. "[A]fter the battle is fought and the victory is won—I'm forced to say it—it all goes over to the whites. . . . The colored man goin over there fightin, the white man goin over there fightin, well, the white man holds his ground over here when he comes back, he's the same; nigger come back, he aint recognized more than a dog."[161]

12

BORN IN THE mid-1890s in the upper Mississippi Delta, bluesman Willie Brown lived and worked mostly on Jim Yeager's plantation, not far from Dockery Farms. He played music with Charlie Patton and Son House, and helped to teach and inspire a younger Robert Johnson, who followed Brown from job to job. In one of his songs, "Future Blues," Brown used "apocalyptic imagery" to convey some of the feelings of impermanence that pervaded the black South in the early twentieth century.

> Can't tell my future, I can't tell my past.
> Lord, it seems like every minute sure gon' be my last.
> Oh, minutes seems like hours, and hours seems like days.
> Yes, minutes seems like hours, hours seems like days.[162]

Whatever the exertions made by black Southerners, no matter how fervently they embraced the work ethic, no matter how bravely they fought as U.S. soldiers, the future seemed all too bleak and unredeeming, much like the present and the past. Even as black leaders, editors, and preachers thrashed about with their programs, manifestos, and sermons, many black men and women sensed they had been done in. The semicentennial recitals of race progress, the optimism and confidence expressed by a Booker T. Washington, the achievements of a new black middle class, the impressive strides made in education, could not overcome the realities most blacks faced a half century after emancipation.

When common rural black folk, most of them born around the time of emancipation, came to assess their lives, few of their testimonials would have been considered fit reading for the success primers. The rhetoric about racial progress, the impressive statistics, and the rags-to-riches stories seemed not to touch or reflect their lives. What Langston Hughes suggested some years later in his bluesy reflection, the lives of the vast majority of black Southerners in the late nineteenth and early twentieth centuries documented all too vividly:

> *Where I come from*
> *folks work hard*
> *all their lives*
> *until they die*
> *and never own no parts*
> *of earth or sky.*[163]

No matter how "progress" might be measured—by their homes, their income, or their future prospects—large numbers of black men and women lived in a grim and unpromising world. A lifetime spent in hard and continuous labor had done little or nothing to improve the quality of their lives. Unlike the popular tales of success dominating the black press and uplift literature, their life experiences could be compressed into a few sentences.

> When I got big enough to work, after freedom, I washed and ironed, three days of the week, for the white folks, and worked in the field three days. That is what I is done all my life.

> I lived in the quarters and chopped cotton and corn in the field. . . . Nothing ever happened in my life.

> Worked around white folks all my life, cooking, sewing, and washing.

> I wish I could have me one acre o' land dat I could call mine. I'd be willin' to eat dry bread de rest o' my life if I had a place I could settle down on and nobody could tell me I had to move no more. I hates movin'.

> I jest tends to the wants of white folks. Colored folks is made to give a hand to white folks. And I does it.

I worked in these white people's homes. . . . Well, I worked for one
family for over fifty years. It happens like that—you just keep on with
them. . . . I worked all the time, till I got too old. I didn't have no hours
there, 'cause anytime I went, they wouldn't even let nobody else work
but me. Such is life!

All my life, ain't never had a pay day in my life. I ain't never worked
and been able to draw down no money at all in a week or no time in
my life. Never! Never had no money in my life. All I ever done was to
farm. . . . I worked so hard. My children—I had nothing but girls—
and I had to work hard. I wanted them to do a little better than I did. I
didn't want them to come up like me.[164]

Resignation to a life with such limited options and such bleak
prospects did not come easily, mixed as it was with a sense of betrayal.
The alternatives had been all but exhausted—politics, rebellion, organization, protest, alliances with whites, participation in America's wars.
The Washingtonian strategy underestimated, if it did not misread altogether, the depth and permanence of white hostility to black aspirations. The Du Boisian strategy of protest and agitation had its obvious
risks and limits in a violent and repressive society where whites owned
the machinery and arsenals of power. Both strategies, both policies—
accommodation and radical agitation—demanded far-reaching and
often complex sacrifices and commitments. The tenacious racism in
the South, the indifference of most whites in the North, and the silence,
treachery, and moral bankruptcy of the "Progressive" presidents
(Theodore Roosevelt, William Howard Taft, and Woodrow Wilson)
hardly suggest an atmosphere in which black militancy or radicalism
would have made much difference; the more likely outcome would
have been a race war blacks were certain to lose.

Few whites, on the other hand, could have thought they had resolved
the "race problem." Neither black accommodation nor resignation
translated into contentment or into respect for the white world; blacks
did not expect in their dealings with whites any demonstration of fairness or a sense of justice. "It's stamped in me, in my mind, the way I
been treated," Ned Cobb said of his life as a tenant farmer and sharecropper in Alabama, "the way I have seed other colored people
treated—couldn't never go by what you think or say, had to come up to
the white man's orders. . . . Well, that's disrecognizin me, and then he

slippin around to see that I doin like he say do, and if I don't he don't think it's on account of I got my own way of doin, but he calls it igno- rant and disobeyin his orders. Just disrecognized, discounted in every walk of life. . . . That's the way they worked it, and there's niggers in this country believed that shit. . . . I've studied and studied these white men close."[165]

Whatever their demeanor in the presence of whites, black Southern- ers found ways to temper and survive their repression. In the spirit they often evinced, in the modes of expression they adopted, and in the ways they chose to confront and ameliorate the mechanisms of race control, they exhibited a growing restlessness. The only question re- mained how much longer they could contain their resentment and anger. For the black newspaper in Selma, Alabama, edited by Mans- field Edward Bryant, the break came as early as 1889. The South had become two Souths, Bryant suggested, and the black South would ulti- mately prevail.

> Were you [the whites] to leave this Southland, in twenty years it would be one of the grandest sections of the globe. We would show you mossback-crackers how to run a country. You would never see con- victs, half-starved, depriving honest working-men of an honest living. It is only a matter of time when throughout this whole State affairs will be changed, and, I hope, to your sorrow. We were never destined to be always servants, but, like all other races, will and must have our day. You now have yours. You have had your revolutionary and civil wars, and we here predict that at no very distant day we will have our war, and we hope, as God intends, that we will be strong enough to wipe you out of existence, or hardly leave enough of you to tell the story.[166]

If few knew Bryant, most blacks were familiar with Bishop Henry M. Turner, whose popularity in the late nineteenth century was proba- bly exceeded only by that of Douglass and Washington. Profoundly disillusioned with the abrogation of civil rights and the lynchings, Turner advocated emigration to Africa and urged blacks to take up arms to defend their homes and leaders. In an editorial in his newspa- per, "Negro, Get Guns," Turner wrote: "Let every Negro in this coun- try who has a spark of manhood in him supply his house with one, two, or three guns . . . and when your domicile is invaded by the bloody lynchers or any mob . . . turn loose your missiles of death and blow the

fiendish wretches into a thousand giblets." Critics immediately charged
Turner with trying to foment a race war, and indeed Robert Charles
had worked as a subscription agent for Turner's newspaper before
doing battle in New Orleans. Turner sensed he lacked the support of
most blacks for his more radical positions, and he would reconcile himself to the role of a vocal maverick. As early as 1877, however, responding to the violent overthrow of Reconstruction, he thought it only a
matter of time before his people would begin to see things differently.
"They are sullen, despondent and discontented and sooner or later
these feelings will lead to trouble. The Southern whites rely upon the
strong arm of power to produce submission, but they are resting upon
a slumbering volcano, which sooner or later will cause a fearful erup-
tion."[167]

With the upheavals accompanying World War I, both the invincibility and the superiority of Anglo-Saxon civilization came into question.
After serving in the Philippines at the turn of the century, Theophilus
G. Steward had written that the great battles of the twentieth century
would be fought along the color line. Nearly a quarter of a century
later, he echoed that sentiment, questioning how long Anglo-Saxons
would continue to rule. "We have got to drop the white fetish," he advised his son in 1923; "the whites have failed—completely failed; and
their overthrow is nigh. . . . Europe is going to the bow-wows; and
America will follow. . . . Negroes are fast taking front places in the more
refined parts of civilization. They are yet worshipping whites under the
delusion of white superiority, but that will pass before long."[168]

The notion of a black millennium took on a life of its own, by no
means confined to bishops, educators, and editors; it found expression
at various levels of the black South. In 1887 a group of one hundred
"uneducated and hard working" black men in Montgomery, Alabama,
addressed a letter to the governor urging that blacks be treated "as hu-
mans and as cittisons." The wording of the appeal no doubt attracted
considerable attention:

> We have made up our minds to go down for the Race. We expect to
> carrie down a goodly [number of whites] with us. . . . Revenge we will
> have one way or another. Fires will burn and that you know, and this
> town can be sent down to ashes very soon.

Unless the governor did something, "eather by fare means or by fould,"
the petitioners warned, they would subscribe to "the indians rule."

that is when a indian gos down by the hands of a white man their must be a white man to follow him. It don't make any difrance wheather its the man that did the killing or not just so its a white man between the ages of 16 and 150 years old. . . . We don't care who get kill.[169]

Based on her faith in God and a new generation of blacks, Sarah Fitzpatrick also sensed a new era in race relations. Born a slave in Alabama, she had spent her entire life in the South, working as a house servant and living under "de white man's law." She knew that most whites treated blacks "mean" not because they thought it right but because they did not really think about it at all—"dey jes' think dat de 'Nigger' is nothin' mo' dan a brute." But if her generation had feared whites, she sensed that the generations born after emancipation feared them much less. "De ole 'Niggers' is natch'u'ly scaid uv de white man, but young ed'jucated 'Niggers' ain't scaid of de white man lack de ole 'uns. . . ." For that very reason, among others, she held out hopes for a better future for her children and grandchildren. After all, she reflected at age ninety, "dere's very little I don' understand 'bout life, I been through it all an' its putty clear to me now." Nothing was clearer but that the future lay with black people. "[D]e Lawd's got a han' in wurkin' dis thing out, 'cause ya know it says in de Bible, 'Dat de bottom rail will *become de top one fo' de end uv times.'* That was a time she could easily envision. "Ef de 'Niggers' wuz in power today like de white man is in charge uv dem, de white man would sho' have a hard time 'mong some uv de 'Niggers,' but I looks at it lack dis, I'd say, 'Well ya been hard on me Mr. White-man but I ain't gonna treat ya bad, cause god is always 'bove de deb'el.' I may never live to see it but I do b'lieve dat de 'Nigger' will have mo' power dan whut he's got now. De Lawd says so in de Bible. It may take a long time but it sho' will come, you watch whut I tell you."[170]

Writing from the battlefront in 1899, a black sergeant in Cuba confided to a New York black journalist that he now considered himself "a man without a country, a mere soldier of fortune serving a flag I may be destined to hate." As he weighed the prospects of his people, he could no longer restrain his bitterness and discouragement. He had enlisted as a private in the belief that the achievements of the black soldier would advance the cause of his people. But persistent reports of lynchings, the silence of the federal government, and the attempts to rob black soldiers of the fruits of victory had drained him of "every spark of patriotism, every vestige of loyalty which I once possessed."

He was left only with his "old dream of a great Negro republic built up out of the ruins of certain southern states, where Negroes make their own laws, sit as judge and jurors in their own courts, levy their own taxes, build their own schools, and raise and officer their own armies." Why not organize to make this "dreamland" a reality? The two races, he thought, would never live in harmony together, the avowed friends of the Negro were rapidly diminishing, every act of government was designed to keep them down, and whites refused to tolerate any black ambitions above those of the most menial occupations. He acknowledged the unlikelihood of realizing this "dreamland" in his lifetime. "[B]ut would it not be better to leave to our posterity the legacy of names made great by their association with freedom's battles than to leave to them a fortune gained by cringing and truckling to white men?" The sergeant inked out his name and regiment, cautioning the journalist about the need for confidentiality, "as it would hurt me a great deal should it ever come under the eyes of the authorities."[171]

But even as they contemplated a life beyond repression, black Southerners had to face the harsh realities of the present. In certain respects they faced more formidable odds in 1913 than in 1863. Once a symbol of sectional strife, the Negro fifty years later had become a symbol of national reconciliation on the basis of white supremacy, a symbol around which white Northerners and white Southerners could rally with equal fervor and conviction. Race riots at the turn of the century attested not only to a heightening of racial tensions but also to a nationalization of racial attitudes. When President Theodore Roosevelt wrote in 1906 "that as a race and in the mass they [Negroes] are altogether inferior to the whites," he articulated a belief embraced by most Americans, a belief that was being acted out not only in Alabama, Georgia, and Mississippi but also in Latin America and Asia.[172] Nor did most Americans question the insistence of Woodrow Wilson that segregation would work to improve the lot of black Americans by easing racial tensions.

It was precisely that nationalization of racial attitudes that alarmed men such as Charles Chesnutt, who had exiled himself from North Carolina to Cleveland. The descent of the South into the depths of racial demagoguery and violence could be expected, he wrote to Booker T. Washington in 1904, but when the president of Harvard University "comes out with his curious speech in New York, justifying by inference the rigid caste system of the South which is the real thing that is holding the colored people down, I feel the foundations falling."

Based on what was happening around the country, Chesnutt questioned Washington's insistent emphasis on the power of education, wondering "if we do not underestimate the power of race prejudice to obscure the finer feelings of humanity."[173]

Even the most committed accommodationists came to be deeply troubled by the rising tide of racist legislation and violence. In a national publication in 1899, W. H. Councill concluded with unusual bluntness that everything the Negro had was at the sufferance of whites and there was no future for black people in the United States. Washington, too, gave way to bouts of despair and disillusionment. Responding to the threat that Mississippi might deprive blacks of educational opportunities, he thought if the move succeeded "there will be but one more step: the reduction of the race to a system of industrial slavery, or peonage." He could only ponder over the ways in which white mobs and lynchers made a travesty of his program and promises. "Within the last fortnight," he wrote in 1904, "three members of my race have been burned at the stake; of these one was a woman. Not one of the three was charged with any crime even remotely connected with the abuse of a white woman. . . . The custom of burning human beings has become so common as scarcely to excite interest or attract unusual attention."[174] The same year he commemorated the fiftieth anniversary of emancipation, Washington had to record still more lynchings, including two black farmers near Germantown, Kentucky, who, according to a white newspaper, were "apparently inoffensive Negroes, good farm hands, real wealth producers. . . . No motive was assigned for the deed." And yet, Washington eagerly grasped at any reason for encouragement. That year some forty-five blacks had been lynched, four fewer than the previous year. That decline, he concluded, "though small, means something in the way of a higher civilization."[175]

On the eve of World War I, most of the black population lived in the South, concentrated in rural regions. Few of them could maintain a faith in progress, trapped as they were in a web of controls that encouraged neither initiative nor hope. If some still clung to a belief in self-help, even as they were denied the tools by which to help themselves, most maintained a familiar struggle, tried to realize whatever joy they could out of a bad situation, resigned themselves to a hard life in a sharply circumscribed world, and raised a new generation, many of whom would choose to look elsewhere for the chance to realize dreams and aspirations denied their parents and grandparents. Steadily increasing numbers of blacks, especially young blacks, searched for a way out, for a chance to live their lives more fully and more freely. "The North symbolized to me," remembered Richard Wright, "all that I had not felt and seen; it had no relation whatever to what actually existed. Yet, by imagining a place where everything was possible, I kept hope alive in me."[176]

13

ALIUS BROWN, the high sheriff of Jefferson County, Alabama, achieved a reputation in the late nineteenth century for ruthlessness and efficiency. His claim to distinction rested largely on the remarkable white horse he rode, and the stories about that horse's powers reverberated through black Birmingham and in the countryside. The sheriff reportedly never had to shoot at a fleeing black man. He only needed to get down from the horse and let this extraordinary animal pursue him. It would set out after the black fugitive "like a hound dog after a rabbit" and quickly overtake him, then clasp the fugitive's arm in his teeth and return him to Sheriff Brown. In the early 1890s, at the pipe works at Bessemer, only a few miles from Birmingham, black laborers sang,

> *Here comes Alius Brown, baby,*
> *Ridin' after me,*
> *Ridin' after me, baby*
> *Ridin' after me.*
> *Here comes Alius Brown*
> *Ridin' after me;*
> *I'm goin' back to "Birn-in-ham."*[177]

Some forty years later, from the Mississippi Delta, as if to suggest how little had changed, bluesman Robert Johnson articulated a lonely and terrifying sense of personal betrayal and anguish that transcended both time and location. With a chilling and relentless matter-of-factness, he suggested a society impossible to change or overcome. He suggested, too, a new generation of interior exiles like himself, exiles in their own land. Even as the black Southerner struggled to achieve some semblance of dignity, to hang on to his self-esteem, the dominant society seemed intent on denying him his very identity, his very humanity. And, like Alius Brown's remarkable white horse, it pursued him relentlessly, latched on to him, and refused to let go.

I got to keep moving, I got to keep moving
blues falling down like hail
blues falling down like hail
Uumh, blues falling down like hail
blues falling down like hail
and the days keeps on worryin' me
there's a hellhound on my trail,
hellhound on my trail,
hellhound on my trail.[178]

EPILOGUE

I got the blues, but I haven't got the fare,
I got the blues, but I haven't got the fare,
I got the blues, but I am too damn'd mean to cry.
                                            —*Anonymous bluesman*[1]

Every day seem like murder here,
Every day seem like murder here,
I'm gonna leave tomorrow, I know you don't bit more care.
                                            —*Charlie Patton*[2]

I'm tired of being Jim Crowed, gonna leave this Jim Crow town,
Doggone my black soul, I'm sweet Chicago bound,
Yes, Sir, I'm leavin' here, from this ole Jim Crow town.
                                            —*Cow Cow Davenport*[3]

ON THE EVE of World War I, a black country preacher in Mississippi recalled his life in the South. He talked about three generations of his family. His father had been born and raised a slave. "He never knew anything else until after I was born. He was taught his place and was content to keep it. But when he brought me up he let some of the old customs slip by." The preacher conceded that in his own life, more often than not, he had accommodated to the requirements of the prevailing racial etiquette. "I know there are certain things that I must do, and I do them, and it doesn't worry me; yet in bringing up my own son, I let some more of the old customs slip by."

The son attended school through the eighth grade, acquiring more education than any previous member of the family. He had been helping his father on the farm. But over the last year he had grown increasingly restless and discontent. This was the last crop he would make, he told his father; once the crop had been completed, he intended to leave for Chicago. "When a young white man talks rough to me, I can't talk rough to him. You can stand that; I can't. I have some education, and inside I has the feelin's of a white man. I'm goin'."[4]

AMONG THEMSELVES, Blacks assessed their prospects and options. And in the late nineteenth and early twentieth centuries, in an increasingly repressive South, a persistent and overriding theme in their conversations (as in their songs) was movement—away from where they were living and working if not always toward a clearly defined destination.

> *Times is gittin' might ha'd,*
> *Money gittin' might scace;*
> *Soon's I sell my cot'n 'n co'n,*
> *I'se gwine tuh leave dis place.*[5]

As conditions deteriorated, the discussions took on a greater urgency. "There is a feeling of unrest, insecurity, almost panic," an Alabama woman observed. "In our homes, in our churches, wherever two or three are gathered together, there is a discussion of what is best to do. Must we remain in the South or go elsewhere? Where can we go to feel that security which other people feel? Is it best to go in great numbers or only in several families? These and many other things are discussed over and over."[6]

Nine of ten black Americans still lived in the South in 1917, some three of four of them in rural sections. Half a century later, black Americans had become primarily urban (75 percent), and fewer than half of them (45 percent) lived in the South. Such statistics only begin to suggest the extraordinary dimensions of the migrations that transformed the racial map of the United States in the twentieth century. None of this migratory activity was new, only its size and destination. After the Civil War, scores of newly freed slaves viewed movement as a vital expression of their emancipation, a way to define and act on their new status. Economic and family considerations influenced where blacks moved, as did the vision embraced by many former slaves in the 1860s and 1870s of a Reconstruction based on a new, racially egalitarian South in which blacks and whites shared power and economic resources.

The story of black migration is the story of many migrations, some of them confined to the South, all of them responding to the determination to make changes that would immediately or ultimately improve the quality of their lives. In testing their freedom after the Civil War, most blacks limited their movement to the same region, often to the same locality; some moved no further than down the road to the next plantation, replacing one landlord with another, and some would be drawn to opportunities in the newly developed and fertile cotton lands in the Southwest, including a substantial movement in the 1890s into the Mississippi Delta and Oklahoma. That complex pattern of movement within the South would persist into the twentieth century.

The popular idea that "freedom was free-er" in the towns and cities stimulated an ongoing movement, as it had since emancipation. In abandoning agricultural labor for urban ways and work, blacks found neither escape from Jim Crow restrictions nor security of employment; many simply replaced unrewarding field labor with equally unrewarding menial and unskilled work at poverty wages. But the city provided blacks more personal freedom, more opportunities, and a sense of community difficult to realize in the rural districts; it gave them not only a welcome relief from the never-ending cycle of rural indebtedness but also greater access to schools, churches, and benevolent societies. "In the country," William Pickens recalled, "my father worked while another man reckoned." In the town to which the family moved in South Carolina, on the other hand, "Wages were small but paid promptly, and there was no binding debt." At the very least, Pickens said of his family, "They went, as one instinctively moves from a greater toward a lesser pain. There was one certain advantage; the children obtained six months instead of six weeks of schooling."[7] Some men (such as Richard Wright's father) deserted their families for a new life in the cities, while others hoped to find employment that would ultimately enable them to move the entire family.

> *I'm just from the country, never been in your town before,*
> *I'm just from the country, never been in your town before,*
> *Lord, I'm broke and hungry, ain't got no place to go.*
>
> *I was raised in the country, I been there all my life,*
> *I was raised in the country, I been there all my life,*
> *Lord, I had to run off and leave my children and my wife.*[8]

Much of the movement of black Southerners in the late nineteenth century responded to economic considerations. But movement came to be at the same time an important outlet, an expression of dissatisfaction in which disfranchised and alienated black people voted with their feet. Not long after Reconstruction had been violently ended in Mississippi, a Starkville black expressed the wish to leave "this God forsaken country," even if it meant selling his property at half of its value; many blacks in the vicinity, he insisted, were contemplating migration to New Mexico or Arizona.⁹ Between 1865 and 1880 nearly forty thousand blacks settled in Kansas. Some six thousand of them had participated in the Exodus of 1879, migrating from rural Texas, Louisiana, Mississippi, and Tennessee, many of them riding on riverboats up the Mississippi River to St. Louis, then moving overland to Kansas, where in a number of instances they established exclusively black towns. Although described as migrants, many of them were, in fact, refugees from poverty and terrorism, breaking with a way of life they found increasingly unbearable. A Louisiana black leader found the banks of the Mississippi "literally covered with colored people and their little store of worldly goods." What united them, he reported, was the belief that *"anywhere* is better than here."¹⁰

No single person emerged to guide the Kansas Exodus. "We have found no leader to trust but God overhead of us," declared a group of Exodusters, as members of this movement would be described. "Every Black man is his own Moses now," a prospective migrant observed, and still another Exoduster invoked biblical imagery to reassure the hesitant and uncertain among them.

> Moses . . . took 'em out o' bondage, and wen dey was all a-waverin' an' mighty feared he took em' 'cross de Red Sea an' den dey was safe. . . . Dis is our Red Sea, right hyah in St. Louis, atween home an' Kansas, an' if we sticks togeder an' keeps up our faith we'll get to Kansas and be out o' bondage for shuah. . . . Dem as is a-waverin' an' is a'feared is goin' to sink in dis hyah Red Sea.¹¹

As interest in the Exodus mounted, so did the obstacles. Opposition was by no means limited to whites fearful of losing valuable laborers. The divisions among black leaders raised legitimate questions about whether they understood the desperation driving the migrants. Much like Booker T. Washington some years later, Frederick Douglass placed his confidence in a regenerated South based on a productive black laboring class. "Not only is the South the best locality for the Negro on the ground of his political powers and possibilities," he declared in 1879, "but it is best for him as a field of labor. He is there, as he is nowhere else, an absolute necessity." Douglass thought the Exodus "premature," "hurtful," and a "disheartening surrender," as "it would make freedom and free institutions depend upon migration rather than protection; by flight, rather than by right; by going into a strange land, rather than by staying in one's own." Even as Douglass's assessment underestimated the repression and obstacles southern blacks confronted (he called the setbacks "exceptional and transient"), it dramatized the degree to which black Southerners in the late nineteenth and early twentieth centuries would often need to unlearn their trust in their leaders in order to learn the truth about their situation and the options open to them.[12]

The Exoduster Movement proved to be short-lived. Many of the refugees found themselves stranded on the banks of the Mississippi after the riverboats refused to stop for them. Their plight discouraged others from joining them, and in the end only about one in a thousand southern blacks participated. But the Exodus nonetheless suggested the determination of some blacks to respond to their situation by abandoning the South, making it clear that, in the words of a Louisiana black leader, "there is a point, beyond which, even Negro endurance cannot last."[13] That spirit, although it wavered, never abated altogether. If anything, the desperation that underscored it only became more intense, as in this appeal from a group of blacks in Winona, Mississippi, to the governor in 1875:

> [W]e the colored people of Montgomery County are in a bad fix for we have no rights in the county and we want to know of you if there is any way for us to get out of the county and go to some place where we can get homes . . . so you will please let us know if we can go to Africa. If any emigrants to Africa for the black man. If so please let us know.[14]

Some twenty years later, expressing a similar urgency, E. B. Brown of Birmingham, Alabama, writing a barely literate note for a number of her people, contacted an organization seeking to move blacks from the United States to Africa.

> Please tell me if you know any way that we can go to Africa. Please. Let me know. . . . Write to me at once if you Please. We want to go to

Africa about 350 People or 400 we negro want to go to Africa so bad
untill we Look that way. Write to East Birmingham, Ala.[15]

Henry McNeil Turner claimed to have received many such letters expressing the same feelings, the same urgency, the same desperation.
"Every man that has the sense of an animal must see there is no future
in this country for the Negro," Turner observed in 1900. "[W]e are
taken out and burned, shot, hanged, unjointed and murdered in every
way. Our civil rights are taken from us by force, our political rights are a
farce."[16]

The organized efforts to find a haven in Africa persisted but yielded
few results. Most blacks deemed themselves Americans and could see
no way in which a return to Africa would improve their lives. Alfred
Charles Sam—known to his followers as "Chief"—convinced numbers
of cotton farmers in eastern Oklahoma in the early twentieth century
that Africa offered an alternative to disfranchisement, violence, and
falling cotton prices. But nothing came of the movement except dashed
hopes and one British merchant vessel with sixty emigrants aboard
headed for a disastrous journey to the Gold Coast Colony in British
West Africa.[17] Although Henry M. Turner still propounded a back-to-
Africa solution, and despite periodic revivals of interest, culminating in
the Marcus Garvey movement in the 1920s, the vast majority of southern blacks expressed little interest or enthusiasm. "Africa ain't did me
nothin'," observed Marguerite Jonas, who worked as a cook in New
Orleans. "I don't see why I got to go back to Africa. I'm doin' all right
here. I don't need nothin' in Africa."[18]

The merits of migration remained a theme of discussion within the
black community, and the growing repression that set in after 1890 only
raised the stakes in the debate. In a public meeting in Charlotte, North
Carolina, in 1901, two young women—Addie Sagers and Laura
Arnold—debated the topic "Is the South the Best Home for the
Negro?" Reiterating Booker T. Washington's position, Sagers warned
of a hostile North in which public attitudes and trade unions relegated
blacks to menial and service employment. "Even the drudgery work is
done by foreigners." And in the spirit of Isaiah Montgomery a decade
earlier, she embraced disfranchisement as an opportunity to advance
literacy and education among blacks. But Sagers's views of a promising
South failed to impress her opponent in the debate, who summarily dismissed the notion that southern blacks might aspire to the American
Dream by remaining where they were. That dream, Arnold suggested,

was for white folks only. "The South may be a 'land of flowers' for the Anglo-Saxon, but for the Negro—at his touch, the flowers fold their petals and wither away, and he finds himself, with bleeding hands grasping the prickly thorns." All too many blacks, she noted, had placed their confidence in the security of property, only to be devastated without notice or reason. "Displease by look, word, or deed a white man, and if he so desires, before nightfall, your property is likely to be reduced to ashes, and the owner a mangled corpse." Whatever the risks of moving to an unknown North, she insisted, the chances for survival would be vastly improved. The South had become a "crucible" and "many of us . . . will be burned to cinders. . . . You sleep over a volcano, which may erupt at any moment, and only your lifeless bodies will attest that you believed the South to be the best home for the Negro." Two weeks later, Laura Arnold left North Carolina for Washington, D.C. Some ten years earlier, using much the same imagery, a black clergyman in Charleston had warned his people that coexistence with whites could prove fatal. "I am somewhat of a believer in the tale about the Lord's fire. The fire will not burn the people, but it will be so warm that our people will have to move on or get burnt; and I rather believe that they will move on."[19]

Debates on the merits of migration soon gave way to black men and women consciously acting on their perceptions of reality. Since the 1890s, the number of black Southerners heading northward had increased dramatically. That movement culminated during and after World War I in what came to be known as the Great Migration. The sheer magnitude and direction of this movement, along with the spirit and determination that pervaded it, eclipsed all previous movements out of the South and made it strikingly different. Some half a million black Southerners departed between 1916 and 1919, and nearly a million more would follow in the 1920s, almost all of them heading for the large cities and industrial centers in the Northeast and Midwest. Some towns in the South lost most of their black residents, and some states (most notably Louisiana and Mississippi) recorded the first decline in their black population.[20]

The attraction of the North was hardly new. Since slavery, when the North Star had symbolized freedom for runaways, black Southerners perceived the North as different. What resonated in their perceptions was not only the possibility of earning more and retaining it but also the chance to maintain some semblance of dignity and self-respect. "Up Norf dey's kin', down Souf de beat you" was the way a Norfolk resident summed up the two sections. "People is kinder up dere," an Alabama black woman thought, and that was why her people called it "God's Country."

> Ain't no Mistrus's an' Marster's up dere, say yes an' no up dere. . . . No gwin in de back door. White fo'ks an' "Niggers" go in an' out de same door up dere. . . . Ya' know it makes a heep o' diff'rense when er "Nigger" is in a country wha' he's not al'ays scaid dat sump'in gonna hapen all de time. . . .

Whatever the new challenges they would encounter, migrants speculated, the North at least promised to be a place "where a negro man can appreshate being a man. . . ."[21]

Not all blacks subscribed to such optimistic visions of the North. Some preferred a South in which the terms of accommodation were clearly understood to a North in which a black person never knew what to expect and where acts of aggression and discrimination were likely to be more arbitrary. Insisting that blacks faced "disadvantages" everywhere ("[i]n the North you have Jim Crow work, in the South we have Jim Crow cars"), Booker T. Washington claimed as late as 1914 that he had "never seen any part of the world where it seemed to me the masses of the Negro people would be better off than right here in these southern states." Washington's disciple Robert R. Moton had no hesitation in choosing the South, with its "old paternal feeling," over an alien and unreceptive North, with its "strong foreign element. . . . I should feel safer in a race riot at Atlanta, Georgia, than I would be in New York."[22] A black man in Arkansas who had spent his childhood enslaved in Kentucky and Tennessee believed the higher wages offered in the North would ultimately prove to be the "ruin" of the black migrant. "The foreigner there is his enemy & there will eventually be a great massacre or bloody riot & race war."[23] For the early migrants, expectations about the North were often disappointed, and some felt isolated from their old friends and community. "[Y]ou'd be astonished to see just how high race prejudice runs in the North," a domestic servant in New York informed a southern friend in 1904. "It is fearful. . . . I'm the only colored servant anywhere around this Avenue. It is either white servants or none. . . . I feel very lonely here. I have no associates at all. I know lots of colored people here but they are not the kind I feel interested in."[24]

For many southern blacks, the attachment to their homes, familiarity with their work tasks, and skepticism about the quality of freedom they might enjoy elsewhere reinforced a continuing belief that they could ultimately overcome the obstacles placed before them. "I didn't pay no attention to leavin," Ned Cobb recalled. "I wanted to stay and work for better conditions. I knowed I was in a bad way of life here but I didn't intend to get out—*that* never come in my mind. I thought somehow, some way, I'd overcome it. I was a farmin man at that time and I knowed more about this country than I knowed about the northern states." A Savannah clergyman, in explaining his decision to remain, looked at the alternatives in 1908, as proposed by various black and white leaders—emigration, expatriation, colonization, amalgamation, and extermination. "My doctrine is, if you let me coin a word, *"stayhere-ation"* and when I say that, I mean stay here as a separate and distinct race, and the God that has brought us thus far can carry us on." Phyllis Carter, like so many, weighed the attractions of the North. Her husband pleaded with her to join him there with the children but she remained skeptical. To Carter, "up North" suggested the unknown, and she needed to consider her responsibility to the children. She had no desire to depend on anyone but herself. "He left and I stayed. He wasn't there two months before they sent his body back." She was to learn nothing more about his fate in the North, only that he was "alive when he left and dead when they brought him back."[25]

Whatever the persistent doubts about the Promised Land to the North, a radical shift in black thinking and acting occurred around 1915. Extraordinary economic opportunities previously unavailable to blacks were suddenly open. With the outbreak of war in Europe, a virtual halt in the flow of European immigrants, and the demands of military preparedness in the United States, major industrial employers broke the color line to acquire needed laborers. Working for set wages unheard of in the South, even if industrial employment introduced new demands, work rhythms, and chains of command, had distinct advantages over being subject to the whims of landlords and storekeepers and fluctuating cotton prices. The hard times that followed the ravages of the boll weevil, along with the devastating floods in Mississippi in 1912 and 1913, only accelerated a movement already under way. Even those who chose to remain used the threat of migration as a lever to improve their position.

> *The time is coming and it won't be long,*
> *You'll get up some morning, and you'll find me gone.*

So treat me right and jolly me along
If you want this nigger to sing the old home song.[26]

The migrants moved individually and in families and groups. They came in horse-drawn carts, by automobile, in car caravans, in buses, on boats, and (until they reached the Mason-Dixon line) in Jim Crow rail coaches. To listen to them, a complex of factors influenced the decision to leave, to give up the struggle to make something of the land in favor of urban living and factory work. News of newly opened opportunities in the North meshed with a grim assessment of conditions and prospects at home. Expressed in a variety of ways—in songs, letters, and conversations—black Southerners of all classes articulated an overwhelming sense of uneasiness, urgency, and despair. Nothing would get better in the long run; conditions were bound to deteriorate, not improve. The white South offered only more of the same: exploitative labor, political and social subordination, corrupted justice, separate and inferior educational facilities, and extraordinary levels of lethal violence. "The Slogan down here is: 'To hell with the South,' " a resident of Texarkana, Texas, wrote in 1917. As much as they might revere the places where they and their ancestors were born and raised, coexistence with whites had taken a toll that was no longer deemed acceptable. While that conclusion might be grasped only reluctantly by some, it could no longer be avoided. "The Negro loves the South," a Vicksburg resident insisted, "but he does not love the white man's South."[27]

Rather than cite a specific grievance, many prospective migrants ascribed their decision to the totality of their experience in the South. With every lynching, with every reported act of terrorism, with every setback, the conception of the South as less than civilized came to be further corroborated. The desire to preserve one's existence was more than enough reason to leave—and that desire resonated through the testimony of those who chose to give up on the South. "After twenty years of seeing my people lynched for any offense from spitting on the sidewalk to stealing a mule," a migrant informed the *Chicago Defender*, "I made up my mind that I would turn the prow of my ship toward the part of the country where the people at least made a pretense at being civilized." For the Reverend D. J. Johnson, on the other hand, there was little time to reflect over his decision to migrate:

I was drivin' this team for this old man. He paid me $5.00 a week and previous to that I had worked for another one for $2.00 a week. And I left and worked for this one for $5.00 a week, and this old man's boys, they threatened me. If I didn't come back and work for the $2.00, I was in danger, see? So they even set the time that they were gonna come and get me. And they were gonna get me on Monday and I left Sunday night.[28]

The desperation sounded by blacks in their appeals for help in moving revolved around the acknowledgment that life had become cheap and expendable. To remain in the South was to be treated as less than human. "I am so sick I am so tired of such conditions," a resident of Lexington, Mississippi, confessed, "that I sometime think that life for me is not worth while. . . ." A Texan explained to a Detroit organization assisting migrants that he longed to come North and make a "man" of himself. "I am Sick of the South and allways has been, but the opertunity has just come our way so by God healp and you I will soon be out of the South. I was just reading in the morning Beaumont Enterprise Paper where thay Burn one of the Racc to Stake for God sack please help to get me out of the South." An Alabamian who claimed to live "in the darkness of the south" thought he was "counted no more thin a dog," and a Greenville, Mississippi, man wanted to remove his family from "this cursed south land" where "a negro man is not good as a white man's dog." From Palestine, Texas, a man who was "afraid to walke the streets after night" was "sure ancious to make it in the north because these southern white people are so mean and they seems to be getting worse." Some prospective migrants, in appealing for help, enclosed a clipping of a lynching, noting that it "speaks for itself."[29]

The migration went to the very heart of the dilemma black leaders had never been able to surmount—the penalty blacks had to pay for success and ambition. After half a century of "hoping against hope," a black religious journal observed in 1917, black Southerners had learned that "neither character, the accumulation of property, the fostering of the Church, the schools and a better and higher standard of the home" had resulted in either respect or the opportunity for substantial mobility. "Confidence in the sense of justice, humanity and fair play of the white South is gone." Numerous individuals fleshed out the journal's conclusion. For a fifty-year-old "hardworking farmer" in Alpharetta, Georgia, the urge to leave the South and "be free" resulted from whites constantly thwarting his ambitions: "Better not accumulate much, no matter how hard and honest you work for it, as they—well, you can't enjoy it." And a Mississippian described the latest casualty of success in his community and the impact it had:

> Just a few months ago they hung Widow Bagage's husband from Hirshbery bridge because he talked back to a white man. He was a prosperous farmer owning about 80 acres. They killed another man because he dared to sell his cotton "off the place." These things have got us sore. Before the North opened up with work all we could do was to move from one plantation to another in hope of finding something better.[30]

The contrast migrants made between a civilized and "freer" North and a brutalizing and unfree South helped to fuel the migration. Few if any meetings needed to be called to mobilize migrants. Few if any leaders or promoters emerged, and, if anything, leaders often became followers. The "Great Northern Drive," as some blacks called it, evolved into a self-conscious, independent movement, generating a momentum of its own that the best efforts of white Southerners and various black "leaders" could not check. Alarmed over a migration that threatened to deplete the black labor supply, whites resorted to the familiar tactics of repressive ordinances, intimidation, and terrorism. Police arrested blacks in railroad stations as vagrants, they hauled passengers off northern-bound trains, they imposed heavy fines on labor agents, and they sought to suppress black newspapers such as the *Chicago Defender* that were circulated throughout the South and advertised the glories and opportunities awaiting southern blacks in a free North.[31]

For every barrier whites erected to migration, blacks developed procedures and tactics to circumvent them. Entire families slipped away in the middle of the night, without informing employers, landlords, or church and community leaders; some gave every indication of remaining and suddenly disappeared. "You could see a man today and he would be calling the people who were leaving all kinds of names; he could even beat you when it came to calling them fools for going north. The next day when you met him he wouldn't talk so loud and the next day he wouldn't let you see him. That would be the last of him, because, unless you went to the depot, you wouldn't see him again."[32]

In making their move, blacks paid little attention to their own leaders and suspected some of them of being in the pay of whites when they advised them to remain in the South. "Confidentially," one prominent black conceded, any black leader who argued against migration invited serious doubts about his leadership; a businessman he knew wrote an article opposing the migration, "and his business has not paid expenses since, I am reliably informed." Clergymen who preached against the migration saw their congregations dwindle. To retain their clientele and congregations, many businessmen, professionals, and clergymen chose to follow them northward. "The colored people are migrating from here so rapidly," a funeral director and embalmer wrote from Rome, Georgia, "that it will be necessary for me to find another field, and in view of that fact I have about decided to try Detroit."[33]

If anything, the desperate efforts of southern whites to keep blacks from leaving only encouraged blacks to think they could improve their lives by leaving. That was why Richard Wright was trying to save his earnings, and when he finally told his employer he was leaving for Chicago, he found himself questioned sharply.

> "The North's no good for your people, boy."
> "I'll try to get along, sir."
> "Don't believe all the stories you hear about the North."
> "No, sir. I don't."
> "You'll come back here where your friends are."
> "Well, sir. I don't know."
> "How're you going to act up there?"
> "Just like I act down here, sir."
> "Would you speak to a white girl up there?"
> "Oh, no, sir. I'll act there just like I act here."
> "Aw, no, you won't. You'll change. Niggers change when they go North."
>
> I wanted to tell him that I was going north precisely to change, but I did not.
>
> "I'll be the same," I said, trying to indicate that I had no imagination whatever.[34]

For tens of thousands of black Southerners, the reasons for leaving the South had become so compelling that the actual destination mattered less than what they left behind. "Anywhere north will do us," a prospective migrant declared, "and I suppose the worst place there is better than the best place here." For the first generations of black Southerners born in freedom, the migration took on a particular significance. Unable to make the same accommodation their parents and grandparents had made to the racial order, they had found it impossible to contain their restlessness, disillusionment, and anger. Many of them had not yet assumed family responsibilities; they were in a position to make the most of new opportunities; they might aspire to jobs unavailable to older blacks; and, if nothing else, they could satisfy their curiosity about what lay outside the South. Perhaps America would prove to be larger than a Mississippi, a Georgia, an Alabama, or a South Carolina. More aggressive, less constrained by the old customs and etiquette, they were better equipped to make the transition to urban and industrial ways of living and working. A seventeen-year-old girl from Alexandria, Louisiana, had finished schooling and was ready to work, but not at the conditions that prevailed in Louisiana. "I am tired of down hear in this . . . I am afraid to say. Father seem to care and then again dont seem to but Mother and I am tired of all of this."[35]

Contemplating his situation, Richard Wright reviewed his "chances" if he were to remain in the South. He could resist by organizing blacks to fight whites, as his grandfather had done during Reconstruction. But he sensed that there was no way to win a racial war. Not only did whites outnumber them, but they were also too strong. "If I fought openly I would die and I did not want to die." He could subordinate himself to the racial order and live as "a genial slave." But he realized that was no longer possible. "All of my life had shaped me to live by my own feelings and thoughts." He could find an outlet by fighting other blacks, solving "the problem of being black," as others had, "by transferring their hatred of themselves to others with a black skin and fighting them." But he found such a course "cold" and unacceptable. He could, of course, simply forget about whites and everything he had read, and find release in sex and liquor. But that course he found "repugnant." "If I did not want others to violate my life, how could I voluntarily violate it myself?"

How to resolve the dilemma tormented him. "My days and nights were one long, quiet, continuously contained dream of terror, tension, and anxiety. I wondered how long I could bear it." In 1927, nineteen-year-old Richard Wright, a second-generation freeborn black, headed for Chicago. On the train taking him there, he thought over the youth he had spent in Mississippi, Arkansas, and Tennessee:

> The face of the South that I had known was hostile and forbidding, and yet out of all the conflicts and the curses, the blows and the anger, the tension and the terror, I had somehow gotten the idea that life

could be different, could be lived in a fuller and richer manner. As had happened when I had fled from the orphan home, I was now running more away from something than toward something. But that did not matter to me. My mood was: I've got to get away; I can't stay here.

Southern whites, Wright insisted, had never known him, whatever their claims to the contrary. His "deepest instincts," he realized, had always rejected the "place" whites tried to assign him, along with any admission of his inferiority:

[N]o word that I had ever heard fall from the lips of southern white men had ever made me really doubt the worth of my own humanity. True, I had lied. I had stolen. I had struggled to contain my seething anger. I had fought. And it was perhaps a mere accident that I had never killed. . . . But in what other ways had the South allowed me to be natural, to be real, to be myself except in rejection, rebellion, and aggression?

Wright would never return to the South. But he sensed that the South would always remain with him; his feelings had been formed there, and the culture of the South had been instilled into his personality and consciousness. He was taking with him on this journey "into the unknown" a part of the South "to transplant in alien soil, to see if it could grow differently."[36]

For Richard Wright, as for tens of thousands like him, the move northward exceeded economics or politics. "We'd heard all about how the North was freer," Sidney Bechet remembered, "and we were wanting to go real bad." It was a place where black men and women could breathe easier and "live with a little less fear," where the tensions, anxieties, and burdens of daily living might be lessened. These were, at least, the expectations: some kind of redemption through migration. "I headed North," Wright recalled, "full of a hazy notion that life could be lived with dignity, that the personalities of others should not be violated, that men should be able to confront other men without fear or shame, and that if men were lucky in their living on earth they might win some redeeming meaning for their having struggled and suffered here beneath the stars."[37]

What black migrants found in the North exceeded the expectations of many, even as urban living and working introduced new tensions, anxieties, and betrayals. In places such as Chicago and New York, Pittsburgh and Detroit, Cleveland and Philadelphia, black migrants came to learn that racial privilege knew no Mason-Dixon line. Nor did racial privilege always manifest itself in lynchings, Jim Crow, disfranchisement, and peonage. It was all very different, and it was very much the same. It was a different America, and it was a familiar America.

NOTES

CHAPTER ONE

1. Theodore Rosengarten, *All God's Dangers: The Life of Nate Shaw* (New York, 1974), 8.

2. "(What Did I Do to Be So) Black and Blue," in *Louis Armstrong: Portrait of the Artist as a Young Man, 1923–1934* (Columbia Legacy CD 57176). The song was written by Andy Razaf.

3. "Tech 'Er Off, Charlie," in Tom E. Terrill and Jerrold Hirsch, eds., *Such as Us: Southern Voices of the Thirties* (Chapel Hill, N.C., 1978), 254–59.

4. Ruth E. Hill, ed., *The Black Women Oral History Project* (10 vols.; Westport, Conn., 1991), V, 23.

5. Benjamin E. Mays, *Born to Rebel: An Autobiography* (New York, 1971), 22.

6. A Southern Colored Woman, "The Race Problem: An Autobiography," *The Independent*, LVI (March 17, 1904), 589; Robert Russa Moton, *Finding a Way Out: An Autobiography* (New York, 1922), 32–34.

7. *These Are Our Lives: As Told by the People and Written by Members of the Federal Writers' Project of the Works Progress Administration in North Carolina, Tennessee, and Georgia* (Chapel Hill, N.C., 1939), 73; Charles L. Perdue, Jr., Thomas E. Barden, and Robert K. Phillips, *Weevils in the Wheat: Interviews with Virginia Ex-Slaves* (Charlottesville, Va., 1976), 109.

8. Jacob Reddix, *A Voice Crying in the Wilderness: The Memoirs of Jacob L. Reddix* (Jackson, Miss., 1974), 71–72.

9. Mary Church Terrell, *A Colored Woman in a White World* (Washington, D.C., 1940), 15–16; Louis Armstrong, *Satchmo: My Life in New Orleans* (New York, 1954), 14–15; Richard Wright, *Black Boy: A Record of Childhood and Youth* (New York, 1945), 41.

10. James Weldon Johnson, *Along This Way: The Autobiography of James Weldon Johnson* (New York, 1933), 84–86; Alfreda M. Duster, ed., *Crusade for Justice: The Autobiography of Ida B. Wells* (Chicago, 1970), 18–19.

11. James H. Robinson, *Road Without Turning: The Story of Reverend James H. Robinson: An Autobiography* (New York, 1950), 41–43.

12. Jane Maguire, *On Shares: Ed Brown's Story* (New York, 1975), 28.

13. Richard Wright, "Black Boy (American Hunger)," in *Richard Wright: Later Works* (New York, 1991; Library of America Edition, ed. Arnold Rampersad), 180.

The new edition restored the cuts made in the 1945 edition, among them this story. Where the texts in the two editions are identical, footnotes will refer to the 1945 edition.

14. Robinson, *Road Without Turning*, 42; Mays, *Born to Rebel*, 18.

15. Wright, *Black Boy*, 64, 65.

16. Mays, *Born to Rebel*, 26.

17. Mays, *Born to Rebel*, 1; Martin Luther King, Sr., with Clayton Riley, *Daddy King: An Autobiography* (New York, 1980), 29–31; Pauli Murray, *Proud Shoes: The Story of an American Family* (New York, 1956), 262–65. The term "white death" is used by Richard Wright in *Black Boy*, 150.

18. Hill, ed., *Black Women Oral History Project*, VIII, 14; Benjamin J. Davis, *Communist Councilman from Harlem: Autobiographical Notes Written in a Federal Penitentiary* (New York, 1969), 26.

19. Richard R. Wright, Jr., *87 Years Behind the Black Curtain: An Autobiography* (Philadelphia, 1965), 69–70; Hill, ed., *Black Women Oral History Project*, VIII, 123. Some years later, Marcus Garvey would awaken in Audley (Queen Mother) Moore "a deep consciousness" of her race and history.

20. Murray, *Proud Shoes*, 268; Wright, *87 Years Behind the Black Curtain*, 26; Albon L. Holsey, "Learning How to Be Black," *American Mercury*, XVI (April 1929), 423.

21. Hosea Hudson, *Black Worker in the Deep South: A Personal Account* (New York, 1972), 4–5.

22. Wright, *87 Years Behind the Black Curtain*, 64.

23. Holsey, "Learning How to Be Black," 424; Hill, ed., *Black Women Oral History Project*, II, 45.

24. Wright, *87 Years Behind the Black Curtain*, 69, 71; Charles Evers, *Evers* (New York, 1971), 22–23, 29.

25. Margaret Walker, "Growing Out of Shadow," *Common Ground*, IV (Autumn 1943), 42; James Yates, *Mississippi to Madrid: Memoir of a Black American in the Abraham Lincoln Brigade* (Seattle, 1989), 22.

26. Lura Beam, *He Called Them by the Lightning: A Teacher's Odyssey in the Negro South, 1908–1919* (Indianapolis, 1967), 14–15.

27. William H. Holtzclaw, *The Black Man's Burden* (New York, 1915), 18; William J. Edwards, *Twenty-five Years in the Black Belt* (Boston, 1918), 4–5.

28. Hill, ed., *Black Women Oral History Project*, VIII, 344; Wright, *Black Boy*, 13, 17, 60, 89–90; Holtzclaw, *Black Man's Burden*, 18; Holsey, "Learning How to Be Black," 422; Edwards, *Twenty-five Years in the Black Belt*, 15.

29. Harry Oster, *Living Country Blues* (Detroit, 1969), 8.

30. Holsey, "Learning How to Be Black," 424; Walker, "Growing Out of Shadow," 42, 43.

31. Ely Green, *Ely: An Autobiography* (New York, 1966), 13–17, 24.

32. Zora Neale Hurston, *Dust Tracks on a Road: An Autobiography* (Philadelphia, 1942), 49–51.

33. Beam, *He Called Them by the Lightning*, 15. "Sheeney" (or "Sheeny"), "Chink," and "Dago" were disparaging terms applied to Jews, Chinese, and Italians, respectively.

34. Wayne F. Urban, *Black Scholar: Horace Mann Bond, 1904–1972* (Athens, Ga., 1992), 10; Wright, *Black Boy*, 53–54. For a former slave's recollections of a song in which "De Jews done kill po' Jesus," see George P. Rawick, ed., *The American Slave: A Composite Autobiography: Supplementary Series 2* (10 vols.; Westport, Conn., 1979), II: Texas Narr. (Part 1), 411.

35. Hill, ed., *Black Women Oral History Project*, VIII, 250; Wright, *Black Boy*, 143–44; Robinson, *Road Without Turning*, 35–36.

36. Hill, ed., *Black Women Oral History Project*, V, 22, VIII, 333–34; Wright, *Black Boy*, 19, 20–21, 41–43.

37. Evers, *Evers*, 29, 39; Martin Luther King, Jr., "Letter from Birmingham Jail," in *Why We Can't Wait* (New York, 1964), 83.

38. Hill, ed., *Black Women Oral History Project*, VIII, 122.

39. Chester Himes, *The Quality of Hurt: The Autobiography of Chester Himes* (New York, 1972), 11–12.

40. Maguire, *On Shares: Ed Brown's Story*, 31.

41. Mays, *Born to Rebel*, 2; Evers, *Evers*, 29.

42. Robinson, *Road Without Turning*, 21; Hurston, *Dust Tracks on a Road*, 69–72. On the country store as a "social center" on Saturdays see Holtzclaw, *Black Man's Burden*, 17; on the community pumps as "congregating places" see Wright, *87 Years Behind the Black Curtain*, 60.

43. Wright, *Black Boy*, 68–71, 200.

44. A Southern Colored Woman, "The Race Problem: An Autobiography," *The Independent*, LVI (March 17, 1904), 589.

45. Hurston, *Dust Tracks on a Road*, 46; Mays, *Born to Rebel*, 45–46.

46. Hill, ed., *Black Women Oral History Project*, VII, 221–22.

47. Wright, *Black Boy*, 47–48.

48. Wright, *87 Years Behind the Black Curtain*, 69; Evers, *Evers*, 28, 29; Davis, *Communist Councilman from Harlem*, 29.

49. Murray, *Proud Shoes*, 270.

50. Charles W. Chesnutt, Manuscript Journal and Note-Book III, 1881–82, entry for Jan. 3, 1881, Fisk University Library, Nashville; published in Richard Brodhead, ed., *The Journals of Charles W. Chesnutt* (Durham, N.C., 1993), 157–58; Green, *Ely*, 3.

51. Hurston, *Dust Tracks on a Road*, 20–24.

52. Alice Allison Dunnigan, *A Black Woman's Experience: From Schoolhouse to White House* (Philadelphia, 1974), 16; Hill, ed., *Black Women Oral History Project*, VIII, 120. See also I, 48.

53. Hill, ed., *Black Women Oral History Project*, VII, 181, VI, 330; Robinson, *Road Without Turning*, 34–35.

54. Susan Tucker, *Telling Memories Among Southern Women: Domestic Workers and Their Employers in the Segregated South* (Baton Rouge, La., 1988), 113; Kathryn L. Morgan, *Children of Strangers: The Stories of a Black Family* (Philadelphia, 1980), 19.

55. Leon F. Litwack, *Been in the Storm So Long* (New York, 1979), 223–24; Fannie Lou Hamer, "To Praise Our Bridges," in Dorothy Abbott, ed., *Mississippi Writers: Reflections of Childhood and Youth* (5 vols.; Jackson, Miss., 1985–91), II, 328.

56. Thomas W. Talley, *Negro Folk Rhymes* (New York, 1922), 10–11; Newman I. White, *American Negro Folk-Songs* (Cambridge, Mass., 1928), 326, 320. See also Lawrence W. Levine, *Black Culture and Black Consciousness* (New York, 1977), 284–93.

57. E. M. Woods, *The Negro in Etiquette* (St. Louis, 1899), 83; Murray, *Proud Shoes*, 233; Morgan, *Children of Strangers*, 30.

58. Wright, *Black Boy*, 204; Mary E. Mebane, *Mary: An Autobiography* (New York, 1981), 5.

59. Ralph Ellison, *Shadow and Act* (New York, 1964), 90.

60. Mays, *Born to Rebel*, 46–47. For the racial etiquette governing terms of address see Chapter 7, 332–34.

61. Robinson, *Road Without Turning*, 35; Green, *Ely*, 55.

62. Mays, *Born to Rebel*, 26, 29; Neil R. McMillen, *Dark Journey: Black Mississippians in the Age of Jim Crow* (Urbana, Ill., 1989), 16.

63. Hill, ed., *Black Women Oral History Project*, V, 22; Septima Poinsette Clark with LeGette Blythe, *Echo in My Soul* (New York, 1962), 28–29; Mays, *Born to Rebel*, 28.

64. Mays, *Born to Rebel*, 30; Bessie Jones, *For the Ancestors: Autobiographical Memories* (Urbana, Ill., 1983), 40.

65. Oster, *Living Country Blues*, 141–42.

66. Mays, *Born to Rebel*, 22–23; Wright, *Black Boy*, 171.

67. On the ritual of deference in the South, see Allison Davis, Burleigh B. Gardner, and Mary R. Gardner, *Deep South: A Social Anthropological Study of Caste and Class* (Chicago, 1941), 22–24.

68. Wright, *Black Boy*, 175.

69. Hurston, *Dust Tracks on a Road*, 28–29.

70. Morgan, *Children of Strangers*, 27, 51.

71. Robinson, *Road Without Turning*, 43–49. See also "How Caddy Taught William Not to Be a Coward" and "How Caddy Made Marjorie Find a Way to Walk over the Bridge" in Morgan, *Children of Strangers*, 29–31.

72. Hill, ed., *Black Women Oral History Project*, VII, 181.

73. Wright, *Black Boy*, 138, 158–59, 160–61, 172; Richard Wright, "The Ethics of Living Jim Crow," in *Uncle Tom's Children* (New York, 1938), xiii.

74. Rosengarten, *All God's Dangers*, 23; Wright, *Black Boy*, 6, 38–39, 92–95.

75. Carole Merritt, *Homecoming: African-American Family History in Georgia* (Atlanta, 1982), 32.

76. Holtzclaw, *Black Man's Burden*, 21–24.

77. George P. Rawick, ed., *The American Slave: A Composite Autobiography* (19 vols.; Westport, Conn., 1972), II: S. C. Narr. (Part 2), 23, 149–50.

78. Morgan, *Children of Strangers*, 11, 15–19, 31–32. Some parents chose to shelter their children as much as possible from stories of slavery. "They wouldn't let us hear much," Mary Jane Breland recalled of the conversations between her freeborn parents and her grandparents, who had been slaves; "they wouldn't let the children be around." Interview with Mary Jane Breland (born in 1884), in *Hattiesburg American*, Feb. 17, 1985.

79. Green, *Ely*, 31; Davis, *Communist Councilman from Harlem*, 23–24.

80. Terrell, *A Colored Woman in a White World*, 11; Billie Holiday, *Lady Sings the Blues* (New York, 1956), 8.

81. Jones, *For the Ancestors*, 61.

82. Interview with Janet Johnson at Gibbs Elementary School, Bentonia, Miss., Jan. 28, 1980, Yazoo County Scholar-in-Residence Oral History Program, Yazoo City Public Library, Yazoo City, Miss.

83. Hill, ed., *Black Women Oral History Project*, I, 245; Jones, *For the Ancestors*, 50.

84. *Southern Workman*, XXII (Jan. 1893), 15–16.

85. The term "shocks of childhood" is used by Richard Wright in *Black Boy*, 33.

86. Mays, *Born to Rebel*, 22, 23, 35, 49.

87. W. C. Handy, *Father of the Blues: An Autobiography* (New York, 1941), 81.

88. Wright, *Black Boy*, 87–88, 147–48, 220, 222.

89. Charles W. Chesnutt, Manuscript Journal and Note-Book II, 1877–81, entries for Oct. 16, 1878, May 29, 1880, Fisk University; published in Brodhead, ed., *Journals of Charles W. Chesnutt*, 93, 139–40.

90. Interview with Mary Tuck, 1974, Mississippi Department of Archives and History and the Yazoo County Library System Oral History Project, Yazoo City Public Library, Yazoo City, Miss.

91. Rosengarten, *All God's Dangers*, 26–27, 33, 48, 49–52, 303.

92. *Charley Patton: Founder of the Delta Blues* (CD: Yazoo 1020); Robert Palmer, *Deep Blues* (New York, 1981), 48–54; Stephen Calt and Gayle Wardlow, *King of the Delta Blues: The Life and Music of Charlie Patton* (Newton, N.J., 1988).

CHAPTER TWO

1. Levine, *Black Culture and Black Consciousness*, 254.

2. Rawick, ed., *American Slave*, XVIII: Unwritten History of Slavery, 45.

3. Rawick, ed., *American Slave*, XVIII: Unwritten History of Slavery, 184; Suppl. Ser. 2, II: Tex. Narr. (Part 1), 255. See also *American Slave*, II: S.C. Narr. (Part 2), 50; Suppl. Ser. 2, I: Ala. et al. Narr., 14; Perdue et al., eds., *Weevils in the Wheat*, 230; interviews with Kelly Jackson, Bentonia, Miss., Aug. 19, 1975, and Dec. 10, 1979, Yazoo Scholar-in-Residence Oral History Project, Yazoo City Public Library, Yazoo City, Miss.

4. Litwack, *Been in the Storm So Long*, 472.

5. Perdue et al., eds., *Weevils in the Wheat*, 295; Moton, *Finding a Way Out*, 20–21.

6. Litwack, *Been in the Storm So Long*, 472–73; Booker T. Washington, *The Story of the Negro: The Rise of the Race from Slavery* (2 vols.; New York, 1909), II, 115–16; Booker T. Washington, *Up from Slavery: An Autobiography* (New York, 1901), 6–7, 26–32, 37; Mary McLeod Bethune, "Faith That Moved a Dump Heap," in Gerda Lerner, ed., *Black Women in White America: A Documentary History* (New York, 1972), 136.

7. Litwack, *Been in the Storm So Long*, 473.

8. Federal Writers' Project, *These Are Our Lives*, 53; Hill, ed., *Black Women Oral History Project*, VII, 220–24; Sydney Nathans, " 'Gotta Mind to Move, a Mind to Settle Down': African Americans and the Plantation Frontier," in William J. Cooper, Jr., Michael F. Holt, and John McCardell, eds., *A Master's Due: Essays in Honor of David Herbert Donald* (Baton Rouge, La., 1985), 215.

9. Litwack, *Been in the Storm So Long*, 473; M. F. Armstrong and Helen W. Ludlow, *Hampton and Its Students* (New York, 1874), 99; William H. Heard, *From Slavery to Bishopric in the A.M.E. Church: An Autobiography* (Philadelphia, 1924), 34.

10. Charles W. Chesnutt, Manuscript Journal and Note-Book I, 1874–75, entry for June 7, 1875, Fisk University Library; published in Brodhead, ed., *Journals of Charles W. Chesnutt*, 61–62.

11. Federal Writers' Project, *These Are Our Lives*, 337–38.

12. Ray Stannard Baker, *Following the Colour Line* (New York, 1908), 53; Hill, ed., *Black Women Oral History Project*, I, 209; Perdue et al., eds., *Weevils in the Wheat*, 69; Litwack, *Been in the Storm So Long*, 472.

13. Hill, ed., *Black Women Oral History Project*, X, 7; Davis, *Communist Councilman from Harlem*, 25–26; Henry Hugh Proctor, *Between Black and White: Autobiographical Sketches* (Boston, 1925), 15.

14. Green, *Ely*, 31–32.

15. Louis R. Harlan and Raymond W. Smock, eds., *The Booker T. Washington Papers* (14 vols.; New York, 1972–89), II, 101–2. The first four volumes were edited by Harlan, the remaining volumes by Harlan and Smock.

16. Terrill and Hirsch, eds., *Such As Us*, 92; interview with Mary Tuck, Sept. 3, 1974, Mississippi Department of Archives and History and the Yazoo County Library System Oral History Project, Yazoo City Public Library, Yazoo City, Miss. See also Rawick, ed., *American Slave*, XIV: N.C. Narr. (Part I), 277, XVI: Tenn. Narr., 29, 44; James Nunn, *The Oral History of James Nunn: A Unique North Carolinian* (Chapel Hill, N.C., 1977), 31.

17. Sam Gadsden, *An Oral History of Edisto Island: Sam Gadsden Tells the Story* (Goshen, Ind., 1974), 46; Virginia Pounds Brown and Laurella Owens, *Toting the Lead Row: Ruby Pickens Tartt, Alabama Folklorist* (University, Ala., 1981), 72; *Crisis*, II (Oct. 1911), 230.

18. Rawick, ed., *American Slave*, XVI: Tenn. Narr., 29; Federal Writers' Project, *These Are Our Lives*, 71; Terrill and Hirsch, eds., *Such As Us*, 229.

19. Federal Writers' Project, *These Are Our Lives*, 356; Charles S. Johnson, *Growing Up in the Black Belt: Negro Youth in the Rural South* (Washington, D.C., 1941), 119; Mays, *Born to Rebel*, 35–36.

20. Davis, *Deep South*, 420.

21. Terrill and Hirsch, eds., *Such As Us*, 258; Rosengarten, *All God's Dangers*, 29.

22. Oster, *Living Country Blues*, 55.

23. Beam, *He Called Them by the Lightning*, 96.

24. Louis R. Harlan, *Separate and Unequal: Public School Campaigns and Racism in the Southern Seaboard States, 1901–1915* (Chapel Hill, N.C., 1958), 18.

25. Moton, *Finding a Way Out*, 13–14; Perdue et al., eds., *Weevils in the Wheat*, 331.

26. Baker, *Following the Colour Line*, 54; W. T. B. Williams, "Report on the Atlanta Public Schools," April 15, 1905, and "Report on the Schools in Clayton County, Georgia," March 18, 1905, Rockefeller Archive Center, Tarrytown, N.Y.; Clark, *Echo in My Soul*, 17; *Crisis*, III (November 1911), 20.

27. Hill, ed., *Black Women Oral History Project*, VIII, 4, 13, 14; Baker, *Following the Colour Line*, 53; W. T. B. Williams, "Report on Negro Schools of Charleston, S.C.,"

April 1, 1904, Rockefeller Archive Center; Clark, *Echo in My Soul,* 16–18; Julian Street, *American Adventures* (New York, 1917), 386–87.

28. For descriptions of schools see, for example, Johnson, *Along This Way,* 109–12; Murray, *Proud Shoes,* 234; Proctor, *Between Black and White,* 7; Clifton Johnson, *Highways and Byways of the South* (New York, 1904), 42–43; Davis, *Communist Council-man from Harlem,* 25; Perdue et al., eds., *Weevils in the Wheat,* 126; Clark, *Echo in My Soul,* 36–38; Mays, *Born to Rebel,* 11; Yates, *Mississippi to Madrid,* 17–19; Henry D. Davidson, *"Inching Along" or The Life and Work of an Alabama Farm Boy: An Autobiography* (Nashville, 1944), 40; Edwards, *Twenty-five Years in the Black Belt,* 35; *Crisis,* III (November 1911), 20; Beam, *He Called Them by the Lightning,* 77; Hill, ed., *Black Women Oral History Project,* VII, 219, VIII, 245, 250.

29. Harlan, *Separate and Unequal,* 22–23; Lerner, ed., *Black Women in White America,* 138; Murray, *Proud Shoes,* 179.

30. Clark, *Echo in My Soul,* 39; John J. Morant, *Mississippi Minister* (New York, 1958), 11; interviews with Kelly Jackson, Bentonia, Miss., Aug. 19, 1975, and Dec. 10, 1979, Yazoo Scholar-in-Residence Oral History Project, Yazoo City Public Library, Yazoo City, Miss. On the length of the school term see, for example, W. T. B. Williams, "Report on the Schools in Clayton County, Georgia," March 18, 1905, Rockefeller Archive Center; Hill, ed., *Black Women Oral History Project,* VII, 219, VIII, 13; Mays, *Born to Rebel,* 3; Clark, *Echo in My Soul,* 36, 39; Johnson, *Highways and Byways of the South,* 42; Nunn, *The Oral History of James Nunn,* 33; Davidson, *Inching Along,* 24; Holtzclaw, *Black Man's Burden,* 26; Rawick, ed., *American Slave,* Suppl. Ser. 2, I: Ala. Narr., 289; interview with E. B. Roberts, Dec. 11, 1979, Yazoo County Scholar-in-Residence Oral History Project, Yazoo City Public Library, Yazoo City, Miss.

31. Clark, *Echo in My Soul,* 36; Spencer R. Crew, *Field to Factory: Afro-American Migration, 1915–1940* (Washington, D.C., 1987), 18; John W. Blassingame, ed., *Slave Testimony: Two Centuries of Letters, Speeches, Interviews, and Autobiographies* (Baton Rouge, La., 1977), 667.

32. Washington, *Up from Slavery,* 30–31; Mays, *Born to Rebel,* 7, 38; Holtzclaw, *Black Man's Burden,* 30.

33. W. E. B. Du Bois, *The Souls of Black Folk: Essays and Sketches* (Chicago, 1903), 63–64; *The Autobiography of W. E. B. Du Bois: A Soliloquy on Viewing My Life from the Last Decade of Its First Century* (New York, 1968), 116–17.

34. W. T. B. Williams, "Report on Atlanta Public Schools," April 15, 1905, Rockefeller Archive Center; Baker, *Following the Colour Line,* 54; Clark, *Echo in My Soul,* 38–39.

35. Jesse O. Thomas, *My Story in Black and White: The Autobiography of Jesse O. Thomas* (New York, 1967), 12. See also Crew, *Field to Factory,* 18; Hill, *Black Women Oral History Project,* VII, 219.

36. W. T. B. Williams, "Report on Schools in Burke County, Georgia," March 25, 1905, Rockefeller Archive Center; Edwards, *Twenty-five Years in the Black Belt,* 100.

37. Holtzclaw, *Black Man's Burden,* 53–54, 102; Wright, *87 Years Behind the Black Curtain,* 22; Proctor, *Between Black and White,* 18.

38. W. T. B. Williams, "Report on the Atlanta Public Schools," April 15, 1905, Rockefeller Archive Center.

39. Thomas, *My Story in Black and White*, 12; Holtzclaw, *Black Man's Burden*, 14–15, 52; W. T. B. Williams, "Report on the Schools in Burke County, Georgia," March 25, 1905, Rockefeller Archive Center.

40. Letter from Mrs. Jacob Moorer, Orangeburg, S.C., describing her sixteen years as a public school teacher, *Southwestern Christian Advocate* (New Orleans), April 5, 1900.

41. For use of these texts see, for example, Rawick, ed., *American Slave*, II: S.C. Narr. (Part 1), 55; Suppl. Ser. 2, I: Ark. Narr., 110, 250, II: Tex. Narr. (Part 1), 78, 252, IV: Tex. Narr. (Part 3), 1327–28; Davidson, *Inching Along*, 25; Emily Herring Wilson, *Hope and Dignity: Older Black Women of the South* (Philadelphia, 1983), 38.

42. Wright, *87 Years Behind the Black Curtain*, 31–32; Charles W. Chesnutt, Manuscript Journal and Note-Book I, entry for July 13, 1875, Fisk University Library; published in Brodhead, ed., *Journals of Charles W. Chesnutt*, 71.

43. *Southern Workman*, XXVIII (Feb. 1899), 63–64.

44. William Archer, *Through Afro-America: An English Reading of the Race Problem* (London, 1910), 107.

45. Wright, *Black Boy*, 143–44.

46. Lawrence D. Reddick, "Racial Attitudes in American History Textbooks of the South," *Journal of Negro History*, 19 (July 1934), 225–65; Ruth Miller Elson, *Guardians of Tradition: American Schoolbooks of the Nineteenth Century* (Lincoln, Neb., 1964), 87–100; Marie E. Carpenter, *The Treatment of the Negro in American History School Textbooks* (Menasha, Wis., 1941).

47. Archer, *Through Afro-America*, 174; Mamie Garvin Fields with Karen Fields, *Lemon Swamp and Other Places: A Carolina Memoir* (New York, 1983), 45.

48. Rawick, ed., *American Slave*, XVIII: Unwritten History of Slavery, 45–46; Shepard Krech III, *Praise the Bridge That Carries You Over: The Life of Joseph L. Sutton* (Cambridge, Mass., 1981), 10; Wright, *Black Boy*, 123. On the stories passed down from elders concerning slavery see Chapter 1, 43–46.

49. Mays, *Born to Rebel*, 2.

50. Mays, *Born to Rebel*, 2; Hamer, "To Praise Our Bridges," in Abbott, ed., *Mississippi Writers: Reflections of Childhood and Youth*, II, 326; Murray, *Proud Shoes*, 271; Beam, *He Called Them by the Lightning*, 17.

51. James A. Atkins, *The Age of Jim Crow* (New York, 1964), 56; Holtzclaw, *Black Man's Burden*, 31–32.

52. Yates, *Mississippi to Madrid*, 19.

53. Charles N. Hunter quoted in Joel Williamson, *The Crucible of Race: Black-White Relations in the American South Since Emancipation* (New York, 1984), 67; David A. Straker, *The New South Investigated* (Detroit, 1888), 207.

54. *The Morning Post* (Raleigh, N.C.), June 14, 1903, in Hunter Scrapbooks, Box 17, 1902–27, Charles N. Hunter Papers, Duke University Library, Durham.

55. Testimony of Richard R. Wright, Sr., Nov. 23, 1883, U.S. Senate, 48th Cong., Committee on Education and Labor, Report of the Committee of the Senate upon the Relations Between Labor and Capital, and Testimony Taken by the Committee (4 vols.; Washington, D.C., 1883), IV, 813. Richard R. Wright, Sr., was the father of Richard R. Wright, Jr., who wrote *87 Years Behind the Black Curtain*.

56. Harlan, ed., *Booker T. Washington Papers*, III, 121; Robert Smalls, Beaufort, S.C., to John E. Bruce, April 7, 1910, John E. Bruce Papers, Schomburg Center for Research in Black Culture of the New York Public Library, New York.

57. Handy, *Father of the Blues*, 60–61; Rev. J. G. Merrill to Dr. Wallace Buttrick, May 29, 1902, Rockefeller Archive Center. For a critical observation of ragtime music played at Tuskegee Institute see Garfield McCaster to "My dear Principal [Booker T. Washington]," Jan. 30, 1914, in Harlan and Smock, eds., *Booker T. Washington Papers*, XII, 429.

58. Moton, *Finding a Way Out*, 56–62.

59. Wright, *87 Years Behind the Black Curtain*, 36; Charles W. Chesnutt, Manuscript Journal and Note-Book II, 1877–81, entry for Oct. 16, 1878, Fisk University Library; published in Brodhead, ed., *Journals of Charles W. Chesnutt*, 93.

60. On Armstrong and Hampton Institute see Washington, *Up from Slavery*, 50–62, and Louis R. Harlan, *Booker T. Washington: The Making of a Black Leader 1856–1901* (New York, 1972), 56–69.

61. Harlan, *Booker T. Washington: The Making of a Black Leader*, 66, 72; J. W. Gibson and W. H. Crogman, *Progress of a Race or The Remarkable Advancement of the Colored American*, rev. ed. (Naperville, Ill., 1912), 355; Sheldon Hackney, *Populism to Progressivism in Alabama* (Princeton, N.J., 1969), 163.

62. *Southern Workman*, XVIII (Oct. 1899), 403. On the operations of the Southern Education Board and the General Education Board see Harlan, *Separate and Unequal*, and James D. Anderson, *The Education of Blacks in the South, 1860–1935* (Chapel Hill, N.C., 1988).

63. Davidson, *Inching Along*, 40, 47, 87–94.

64. *The Bulletin* (Samuel Houston College, Austin, Tex.), Jan. 17, 1908, Rockefeller Archive Center; *The College Journal* (Georgia State Industrial College, College, Ga.), Jan. 1901, Smith-Shivery Family Papers, Schomburg Center for Research in Black Culture of the New York Public Library; Elias B. Holloway, "Memories of Clark University, Atlanta, Ga. During the Years of 1884–85–86–87," Elias B. Holloway Papers, South Caroliniana Library, University of South Carolina, Columbia.

65. Woods, *Negro in Etiquette*, 17–19, 22–24, 29, 76–77, 83, 126.

66. Joseph Winthrop Holley, *You Can't Build a Chimney from the Top* (New York, 1948), 59; W. J. Edwards to "Dear Friend," March 25, 1902, Rockefeller Archive Center. The letter was an appeal for funds.

67. Joseph A. Booker to Rev. T. J. Morgan, Jan. 21, 1901, Rockefeller Archive Center.

68. Edwards, *Twenty-five Years in the Black Belt*, 36.

69. Charlotte R. Thorn, Principal, Calhoun Colored School, Calhoun, Lowndes County, Alabama, to Forrester B. Washington, Director, Detroit League on Urban Conditions Among Negroes, April 12, 1918, Carter G. Woodson Papers, Library of Congress, Washington, D.C.

70. David E. Cloyd to Dr. Wallace Buttrick, April 11, 1903, Rockefeller Archive Center.

71. Seth Low, Committee on Investment of Endowment Fund, Tuskegee Institute, to Booker T. Washington, Dec. 12, 1906; Samuel T. Dutton, Teachers College,

Columbia University, New York, to Robert C. Ogden, Committee on Investment of Endowment Fund, Tuskegee Institute, April 16, 1906, Rockefeller Archive Center.

72. Henry E. Fries, President of the Board of Trustees and Chairman of the Board of Managers, Slater Industrial and State Normal School, Salem, N.C., to Alex. Purves, May 16, 1902; S. G. Atkins, President of the Faculty, Slater Industrial and State Normal School, to Alex. Purves, May 19, 1902, Rockefeller Archive Center.

73. Mays, *Born to Rebel*, 42–43; McMillen, *Dark Journey*, 103.

74. *The Bulletin* (Samuel Houston College, Austin, Texas), Jan. 17, 1908, Rockefeller Archive Center; Handy, *Father of the Blues*, 59–61; Hackney, *From Populism to Progressivism in Alabama*, 186–87.

75. Gustavus A. Steward, "Journal of Happenings," St. Paul School, Lawrenceville, Virginia, entries for Feb. 23, Mar. 18, 1913, Theophilus G. Steward Papers, Schomburg Center for Research in Black Culture of the New York Public Library.

76. *Crisis,* I (April 1911), 29.

77. McMillen, *Dark Journey*, 93.

78. Ralph Ellison, *Invisible Man* (New York, 1952), 28. On erecting and raising funds for the monument see William H. Hughes and Frederick D. Patterson, eds., *Robert Russa Moton of Hampton and Tuskegee* (Chapel Hill, N.C.), 93–94.

79. Johnson, *Highways and Byways of the South*, 358.

80. Litwack, *Been in the Storm So Long*, 487–88; Murray, *Proud Shoes*, 222–23; Diary and Notes of Nimrod Porter, Maury Co., Tennessee, Vol. 3, Southern Historical Collection, University of North Carolina.

81. Clark, *Echo in My Soul*, 17; U.S. 42d Cong., 2d sess., House Report 22, *Report of the Joint Select Committee to Inquire into the Condition of Affairs in the Late Insurrectionary States* (13 vols.; Washington, D.C., 1872), VI: Georgia (Part 1), 402; Wilson, *Hope and Dignity*, 135.

82. David Macrae, *America Revisited and Men I Have Met* (Glasgow, 1908), 60; Archer, *Through Afro-America*, 106; George P. Rawick, ed., *American Slave: Supplementary Series 1* (12 vols.; Westport, Conn., 1977), VI: Miss. Narr. (Part 1), 18; VIII: Miss. Narr. (Part 3), 954, Suppl. Ser. 2, IV: Tex. Narr. (Part 3), 957; Blassingame, ed., *Slave Testimony*, 743; F. J. Robinson, Lexington, Ga., to Governor R. B. Bullock, April 9, 1869, Georgia State Archives, Atlanta; Martha Bates Dunlap, Indian Creek, W. Va., to Mrs. James Bates [c. 1872], Dunlap Family Papers, Tulane University Library, New Orleans; *Weekly Louisianian*, March 6, 1875; Litwack, *Been in the Storm So Long*, 487.

83. Beam, *He Called Them by the Lightning*, 28–30, 34.

84. W. T. B. Williams, "Report on Negro Schools of Charleston, S.C.," April 1, 1904, Rockefeller Archive Center; Clark, *Echo in My Soul*, 60–61; A Southern Colored Woman, "The Race Problem: An Autobiography," *Independent*, LVI (Mar. 17, 1904), 587.

85. Handy, *Father of the Blues*, 80–82.

86. F. M. Fitch, The Slater Industrial and State Normal School for Colored Youth of Both Sexes, Winston-Salem, N.C., to the Secretary and Members of the General Education Board, May 14, 1902, Rockefeller Archive Center; Wright, *87 Years Behind the Black Curtain*, 35.

87. *Easton (Md.) Gazette*, Nov. 19, 1898, and July 26, 1902, quoted in Krech, *Praise the Bridge That Carries You Over*, 174–75.

88. Archer, *Through Afro-America*, 43.

89. Wright, *Black Boy*, 129; Mays, *Born to Rebel*, 34; Macrae, *America Revisited*, 52; Matthew C. Butler to Harry Hammond, March 12, 1890, Hammond, Bryan, Cumming Families Papers, South Caroliniana Library, University of South Carolina.

90. C. B. Berry, *The Other Side: How It Struck Us* (London, 1880), 85; Archer, *Through Afro-America*, 129. Similar arguments are made in J. W. Williams to Francis G. Ruffin, Dec. 12, 1888, Francis G. Ruffin Papers, Southern Historical Collection, University of North Carolina, and in George Campbell, *White and Black: The Outcome of a Visit to the United States* (London, 1879), 293.

91. *Raleigh News and Observer*, Jan. 14, 1903, Hunter Scrapbooks, Charles N. Hunter Papers, Duke University Library; Hilary A. Herbert, "The Problems That Present Themselves," in Southern Society for the Promotion of the Study of Race Conditions and Problems in the South, *Race Problems of the South: Proceedings of the First Annual Conference at Montgomery, Alabama, May 8, 9, 10, A.D. 1900* (Richmond, Va., 1900), 31. Henceforth cited as *Race Problems of the South* (Montgomery Conference, 1900).

92. Richard H. Edmonds, "Burden of the Negro Problem," in *The Possibilities of the Negro in Symposium* (Atlanta, 1904), 123; Claude H. Nolen, *The Negro's Image in the South: The Anatomy of White Supremacy* (Lexington, Ky., 1967), 127–28; Williamson, *Crucible of Race*, 333.

93. McMillen, *Dark Journey*, 72; Hackney, *Populism to Progressivism in Alabama*, 205.

94. A. D. Candler, State of Georgia, Executive Office, to Mrs. W. H. [Rebecca] Felton, Dec. 12, 1901, Rebecca Felton Papers, University of Georgia, Athens; W. Laird Clowes, *Black America: A Study of the Ex-Slave and His Late Master* (London, 1891), 165.

95. Charles W. Chesnutt, Manuscript Journal and Note-Book III, entry for Jan. 21, 1881, Fisk University Library; published in Brodhead, ed., *Journals of Charles W. Chesnutt*, 160–61.

96. *Crisis*, III (Jan. 1912), 95, 107.

97. *Raleigh News and Observer*, Nov. 17, 1906, Hunter Scrapbooks, Box 13: 1871–1928, Charles N. Hunter Papers, Duke University Library.

98. Macrae, *America Revisited*, 60; *Memphis Evening Scimitar*, June 4, 1892, in Ida B. Wells, *Southern Horrors* (New York, 1892), 18.

99. Baker, *Following the Colour Line*, 85; Archer, *Through Afro-America*, 17.

100. Col. T. L. Preston, University of Virginia, to F. G. Ruffin, November 2, 1888, Francis G. Ruffin Papers, Southern Historical Collection, University of North Carolina.

101. Bennet Civis Puryear, *The Public School in Its Relations to the Negro* (Richmond, Va., 1877), 4, 9–11, 16–17.

102. W. T. B. Williams to Dr. Wallace Buttrick, Jan. 15, 1904, Rockefeller Archive Center; Alice May [Lucile Whitehurst], "What A Southern Woman Has To Say On the Negro Question" (1902), with a request that it be published as an article, Rebecca Felton Papers, University of Georgia; Nathan C. Munroe, Jr., to Julia Blanche (Munroe) Kell, Kell Collection, Duke University Library.

103. Johnson, *Highways and Byways of the South*, 82–83.

104. Baker, *Following the Colour Line*, 59.

105. Holtzclaw, *Black Man's Burden*, 75–76, 84; Thomas Dixon, Jr., *The Leopard's Spots: A Romance of the White Man's Burden, 1865–1900* (New York, 1902), 459; William R. Richards to Charles W. Chesnutt, June 11, 1900, Charles W. Chesnutt Papers, Fisk University Library.

106. *The Caucasian* (Clinton, Sampson County, North Carolina), Feb. 1, 1883, Hunter Scrapbooks, Box 14, Charles N. Hunter Papers, Duke University Library.

107. *Greenwood Commonwealth*, quoted in *Southwestern Christian Advocate*, Jan. 13, 1898; *Crisis*, III (Dec. 1911), 63; Puryear, *The Public School in Its Relations to the Negro*, 13–14.

108. Willis B. Parks, "A Solution of the Negro Problem Psychologically Considered; The Negro Not a Beast," and John Temple Graves, "The Problem of the Races," in *The Possibilities of the Negro in Symposium*, 20–21, 145, 149. On the charge that the New Negro was largely responsible for the increase of rapes against white women see Chapter 4, 212–13.

109. Hilary A. Herbert to President Theodore Roosevelt, Nov. 12, 1904, Hilary A. Herbert Papers, Southern Historical Collection, University of North Carolina; Mrs. W. H. [Rebecca] Felton, "The Race Problem in the United States" (1898), manuscript article; Mary Lalome Allen to Mrs. W. H. Felton (1898), Rebecca Felton Papers, University of Georgia Library.

110. *Raleigh Times*, Dec. 18, 1915, *Raleigh News and Observer*, Nov. 17, 1906, Hunter Scrapbooks, Box 13: 1871–1928, Charles N. Hunter Papers, Duke University Library; Bruce J. Dierenfield, *Keeper of the Rules: Congressman Howard W. Smith of Virginia* (Charlottesville, 1987), 7. See also letter from William Cowart, Newberry, Fla., to Oswald Garrison Villard, April 1, 1911, in *Crisis*, II (May 1911), 32.

111. Baker, *Following the Colour Line*, 242; "What Has the Negro Meant to the South? What Has the South Meant to the Negro," in Mildred Lewis Rutherford, ed., *Miss Rutherford's Scrap Book: Valuable Information About the South* (10 vols.; Athens, Ga., 1925), III, 7.

112. W. E. B. Du Bois, "Religion in the South," in Booker T. Washington and W. E. B. Du Bois, *The Negro in the South: His Economic Progress in Relation to His Moral and Religious Development* (Philadelphia, 1907), 180. Frederick Douglass made a similar argument, and it may be found in Philip Foner, ed., *The Life and Writings of Frederick Douglass* (4 vols.; New York, 1950–55), IV, 194–95, 378.

113. Thomas P. Bailey, *Race Orthodoxy in the South* (New York, 1914), 278–79.

114. Levine, *Black Culture and Black Consciousness*, 318.

115. Thomas F. Gossett, *Race: The History of an Idea in America* (Dallas, 1963), 274–75.

116. Williamson, *Crucible of Race*, 95; *Crisis*, I (Feb. 1911), 10.

117. Baker, *Following the Colour Line*, 55–56.

118. Daniel W. Hollis, *University of South Carolina* (2 vols.; Columbia, S.C., 1956), II, 61–79; Joel Williamson, *After Slavery: The Negro in South Carolina During Reconstruction, 1861–1877* (Chapel Hill, N.C., 1965), 223, 232–33, 236; Rawick, ed., *American Slave*, III: S.C. Narr. (Part 3), 46; Elias J. Meynardie to Prof. William James Rivers,

July 5, 1877, William James Rivers Papers, South Caroliniana Library, University of South Carolina.

119. Dr. E. E. Ellis, draft proposal, local school system, after Oct. 10, 1881, Ellis Family Papers, South Caroliniana Library, University of South Carolina.

120. Wright, *87 Years Behind the Black Curtain*, 35–36.

121. The *Afro-American* (Baltimore), Oct. 19, 1895.

122. *The New Era* (Washington, D.C.), Jan. 27, 1870; Richard H. Edmonds, "Burden of the Negro Problem," in *Possibilities of the Negro in Symposium*, 124.

123. Yates, *Mississippi to Madrid*, 17–18.

124. Du Bois, "The Economic Revolution in the South," in Washington and Du Bois, *Negro in the South*, 102; Beam, *He Called Them by the Lightning*, 77.

125. *Southern Workman*, XXVIII (March 1899), 114; Rosengarten, *All God's Dangers*, 25, 216–18.

126. McMillen, *Dark Journey*, 72, 78–79; Harlan, *Separate and Unequal*, 95.

127. Johnson, *Highways and Byways of the South*, 44; Anderson, *Education of Blacks in the South*, 183.

128. Mays, *Born to Rebel*, 44.

129. McMillen, *Dark Journey*, 72–75; *Chicago Defender*, Oct. 24, 1914.

130. Murray, *Proud Shoes*, 269–70.

131. Hill, ed., *Black Women Oral History Project*, VIII, 249.

132. Beam, *He Called Them by the Lightning*, 73–74.

133. Norris W. Cuney, "Commencement Address" (1893). (The same address apparently was given to commemorate the thirtieth anniversary of emancipation. Norris W. Cuney Papers, Bennett College, Greensboro, N.C.); "Thirty-first Anniversary of Hampton Institute," *Southern Workman*, XXVIII (July 1899), 244–45; *Cong. Record*, 51 Cong., 1st sess., 2151.

134. Harlan, ed., *Booker T. Washington Papers*, II, 51.

135. Mays, *Born to Rebel*, 43; Du Bois, *Autobiography*, 126; Atkins, *Age of Jim Crow*, 95–96.

136. Wright, *Black Boy*, 152–56.

137. *Southern Workman*, XVIII (Feb. 1899), 68; C. Vann Woodward, *Origins of the New South, 1877–1913* (Baton Rouge, La., 1951), 218; Edwards, *Twenty-five Years in the Black Belt*, 127; Letter to the Editor, *Chicago Defender*, April 28, 1917.

138. Brown and Owens, *Toting the Lead Row*, 103.

CHAPTER THREE

1. Richard Wright used the passage from Job as the prologue for *Black Boy*. The other quotes are from Wright, "Bright and Morning Star," in *Uncle Tom's Children*, 322, and Howard W. Odum and Guy B. Johnson, *The Negro and His Songs: A Study of Typical Negro Songs in the South* (Chapel Hill, N. C., 1925), 255.

2. Du Bois, *Souls of Black Folk*, 110–62.

3. Howard W. Odum and Guy B. Johnson, *Negro Workaday Songs* (Chapel Hill, N.C., 1926), 115.

4. Rawick, ed., *American Slave*, Suppl. Ser. 1, Vol. 8: Miss. (Part 3), 1130. See also Suppl. Ser. 2, Vol. 2: Tex. Narr. (Part 1), 451.

5. Johnson, *Highways and Byways of the South*, 333.

6. David Katzman, *Seven Days a Week: Women and Domestic Service in Industrializing America* (New York, 1978), 192; Orra Langhorne, *Southern Sketches from Virginia 1881–1901*, ed. Charles E. Wynes (Charlottesville, Va., 1964), 37; Johnson, *Highways and Byways of the South*, 343.

7. Rawick, ed., *American Slave*, Vol. 8: Ark. Narr. (Part 1), 248.

8. Langhorne, *Southern Sketches from Virginia*, 36–37; Johnson, *Highways and Byways of the South*, 337. See also Van Woodward, *Origins of the New South*, 208.

9. William Pickens, *American Aesop: Negro and Other Humor* (Boston, 1926), 71–72.

10. Johnson, *Highways and Byways of the South*, 337; E[ustace] C. Moncure to St. Leger Landon Moncure, Jan. 16, 1878, St. Leger Landon Moncure Papers, Duke University Library; Baker, *Following the Colour Line*, 78. "A Po White Man," born in the South but writing from New York, explained to Tom Watson in 1907 that employers in the South "want a nigger and they will tell you so—they say they would rather have a nigger because they can not treat a white man like they want to. . . ." "A Po White Man" to Tom Watson, May 22, 1907, Thomas E. Watson Papers, Southern Historical Collection, University of North Carolina.

11. *An Oral History of Edisto Island: Sam Gadsden Tells the Story*, 46. See also Baker, *Following the Colour Line*, 84.

12. Rawick, ed., *American Slave*, Suppl. Ser. 2, Vol. 3: Tex. Narr. (Part 2), 853. For an almost identical observation see Perdue et al., eds., *Weevils in the Wheat*, 95.

13. Lacy Ford, "Labor and Ideology in the South Carolina Upcountry: The Transition to Free-Labor Agriculture," in Walter J. Fraser, Jr., and Winfred B. Moore, Jr., *The Southern Enigma: Essays on Race, Class, and Folk Culture* (Westport, Conn., 1983), 34; Baker, *Following the Colour Line*, 76–77.

14. Joe M. Richardson, *Negro in the Reconstruction of Florida 1865–1877* (Tallahassee, Fla., 1965), 53.

15. Eugene Marshall, Manchester, Tenn., to his sister in Brockton, Mass., Eugene Marshall Papers, Mississippi Department of Archives and History, Jackson, Miss; Davis, *Deep South*, 356.

16. Campbell, *White and Black*, 260; Rawick, ed., *American Slave*, IV: Texas Narr. (Part 2), 134.

17. Loren Schweninger, "A Vanishing Breed: Black Farm Owners in the South," *Agricultural History*, 63 (Summer 1989), 48–50; Woodward, *Origins of the New South*, 205–6. On an emerging rural black middle class see Manning Marable, "The Politics of Black Land Tenure, 1877–1915," in *Agricultural History*, LIII (1979), 142–52.

18. McMillen, *Dark Journey*, 112–13, 116–17.

19. Rosengarten, *All God's Dangers*, 108.

20. E[ustace] C. Moncure to St. Leger Landon Moncure, Jan. 16, 1878, St. Leger Landon Moncure Papers; William White, Newbern, Ala., to Henry Watson, Sept. 17, 1870, Henry Watson, Jr., Papers, Duke University Library.

21. C. Meriwether, "The Southern Farm Since the Civil War," *The Nation*, 57 (Oct. 12, 1893), 265.

22. Baker, *Following the Colour Line*, 59; Mays, *Born to Rebel*, 6; Tom Amis, Duck Pond, Madison Parish, La., to Julia Amis, April 5, 1870, Elizabeth A. C. (Hooper) Blanchard Papers, Southern Historical Collection, University of North Carolina. A planter who lived some one hundred miles south of Memphis expressed exasperation in 1904 over the refusal of black women to perform domestic labor; he had to send his family wash weekly by rail to a laundry in Memphis. Hilary A. Herbert to President Theodore Roosevelt, Nov. 12, 1904, Herbert Papers, Southern Historical Collection, University of North Carolina. (Herbert was relating a conversation he had with this planter in the summer of 1904.) On the postemancipation withdrawal of women from domestic and field work see, for example, Litwack, *Been in the Storm So Long*, 244–45, and R. W. Wallace to Mary A. Wallace, Nov. 30, 1868, Wallace, Rice, Duncan Papers, Louisiana State University Library, Baton Rouge.

23. Rosengarten, *All God's Dangers*, 9, 121.

24. Jacqueline Jones, *Labor of Love, Labor of Sorrow: Black Women, Work, and the Family from Slavery to the Present* (New York, 1985), 63; Dolores Janiewski, "Sisters under Their Skins: Southern Working Women, 1880–1950," in Joanne V. Hawks and Sheila L. Skemp, eds.,*Sex, Race, and the Role of Women in the South* (Jackson, Miss., 1983), 13–35, esp. 16.

25. Dorothy Sterling, ed., *We Are Your Sisters: Black Women in the Nineteenth Century* (New York, 1984), 322; Rawick, ed., *American Slave*, XVIII: Unwritten History of Slavery, 115.

26. Martha Robb Montgomery (wife of Isaiah T. Montgomery), quoted in McMillen, *Dark Journey*, 129; Hurston, *Dust Tracks on a Road*, 24; Wilson, *Hope and Dignity*, 42; Rawick, ed., *American Slave*, Suppl. Ser. 2, V: Texas Narr. (Part 4), 1736, 1737. See also Sterling, *We Are Your Sisters*, 325–26.

27. Rawick, ed., *American Slave*, XVIII: Unwritten History of Slavery, 143; Harold Courlander, "Introduction, Notes and Texts," *Negro Folk Music of Alabama*, Vols. III and IV: Rich Amerson (New York, Folkways Records Albums No. FE 4471 and FE 4472, 1956 and 1960), 2; Rawick, ed., *American Slave*, Suppl. Ser. 1, I: Ala. Narr., 4; Brown and Owens, *Toting the Lead Row*, 108, 111. The quotes are based on a composite of these sources, and the wording varies slightly with each version.

28. Wilson, *Hope and Dignity*, 42.

29. Nathans, "Gotta Mind to Move, a Mind to Settle Down," 215n.

30. Charles Nordhoff, *The Cotton States in the Spring and Summer of 1875* (New York, 1876), 99.

31. Mays, *Born to Rebel*, 4–6; Jones, *For the Ancestors*, 16; Blassingame, ed., *Slave Testimony*, 665. On renting and sharecropping see also Nathans, "Gotta Mind to Move, a Mind to Settle Down," 216.

32. Peter R. Davis to Elizabeth Amis, March 25, 1867, Elizabeth A. C. (Hooper) Blanchard Papers; Elizabeth Oakes Smith to Mr. & Mrs. Spence, June 30, 1874, Appleton Oaksmith Papers; Diary of William Porcher Miles, 1886–87, Vol. 21, Jan. 3, 10, 1887, Southern Historical Collection, University of North Carolina; *An Oral History of Edisto Island: Sam Gadsden Tells the Story*, 50; David Evans, "Charley Patton: The Conscience of the Delta," in Robert Sacre, ed., *The Voice of the Delta: Charley Patton* (Liège, Belg., 1987), 134. On different arrangements, see also Camp-

bell, *White and Black in the United States,* 307, 314, 337, 396, 372–73, and WPA, *These Are Our Lives,* 48–51.

33. Charles Jones Jenkins to Harry Hammond, Feb. 28, 1880, Hammond, Bryan, Cumming Families Papers, South Caroliniana Library, University of South Carolina.

34. Rawick, ed., *American Slave,* III: S.C. Narr. (Part 4), 173.

35. John A. and Alan Lomax, *American Ballads and Folk Songs* (New York, 1934), 233–34.

36. Interview with Kelly Jackson, Aug. 19, 1975, Yazoo Scholar-in-Residence Oral History Project, Yazoo City Public Library, Yazoo City, Miss.; Laurence C. Jones, *The Bottom Rail: Addresses and Papers on the Negro in the Lowlands of Mississippi and on Inter-Racial Relations in the South During Twenty-five Years* (New York, 1935), 26. For additional testimony on the unfairness of settlements see *Southern Workman,* 28 (May 1899), 183; Edwards, *Twenty-five Years in the Black Belt,* xiv–xv; *Southwestern Christian Advocate,* April 16, 1903; Rosengarten, *All God's Dangers,* 286; Blassingame, *Slave Testimony,* 648; Rawick, ed., *American Slave,* Suppl. Ser. 2, II: Tex. Narr. (Part 1), 203, 204, V: Tex. Narr. (Part 4), 1566, 1568, 1612; interview with E. B. Roberts, Dec. 11, 1979, Yazoo County Scholar-in-Residence Oral History Project, Yazoo City Public Library, Yazoo City, Miss.; Oster, *Living Blues,* 58; Hill, ed., *Black Women: Oral History Project,* V, 10. Benjamin Mays (b. 1894) polled 118 of his black contemporaries in rural South Carolina: 101 (85.6 percent) were certain, based on their experiences and observations, that blacks had been cheated badly by their white "bosses." (One declared, "Whites didn't cheat Negroes—they robbed them!") Seven disagreed. Mays, *Born to Rebel,* 6.

37. Holley, *You Can't Build a Chimney from the Top,* 161.

38. Terrill and Hirsch, eds., *Such As Us,* 88–89. See also WPA, *These Are Our Lives,* 21.

39. Hurston, *Dust Tracks on a Road,* 20; Rawick, ed., *American Slave,* Suppl. Ser. 2, I: Ala. et al. Narr., 71, 91; *An Oral History of Edisto Island: Sam Gadsden Tells the Story,* 48–49; Rosengarten, *All God's Dangers,* 190. On the way the system stifled black ambition see also Edwards, *Twenty-five Years in the Black Belt,* xiv–xv, and Rawick, ed., *American Slave,* Suppl. Ser. 2, II: Tex. Narr. (Part 1), 204 ("I never did anything but farm and it got to where the white man he wouldn't allow the negro anything but jest a get by").

40. William Pickens, *Bursting Bonds* (Boston, 1923), 25–26, 28–29. For other versions or renditions of the rhyme see Holley, *You Can't Build a Chimney from the Top,* 161, and Terrill and Hirsch, eds., *Such As Us,* 42.

41. Crew, *Field to Factory,* 17; Paul Oliver, *Conversation with the Blues* (New York, 1965), 72.

42. Johnson, *Highways and Byways of the South,* 340.

43. Frederic Trautmann, ed., *Travels on the Lower Mississippi, 1879–1880: A Memoir by Ernst von Hesse-Wartegg* (Columbia, Mo., 1990), 101–2; Nell Irvin Painter, *Exodusters: Black Migration to Kansas After Reconstruction* (New York, 1977), 3; *Southwestern Christian Advocate,* April 16, 1903.

44. Nathans, "Gotta Mind to Move, a Mind to Settle Down," 218; Frederick Douglass, *My Bondage and My Freedom* (New York, 1855), 252–53.

45. McMillen, *Dark Journey*, 132. Thomas Doyle decided one year not to run an account at the store. "It sure opened my eyes when I seen how much cheaper you could buy things for cash. That yeah I cleared two hundred dollars." WPA, *These Are Our Lives*, 49.

46. Perdue et al., eds., *Weevils in the Wheat*, 53. "It's all hard, slavery and freedom, both bad when you can't eat," Andrew Boone recalled. "The ole bees makes de honey comb, the young bee makes de honey, niggers makes de cotton an' corn an' de white folks gets de money. Dis wus de case in Slavery times an' its de case now." Rawick, ed., *American Slave*, XIV: NC. Narr. (Part 1), 137.

47. Johnson, *Highways and Byways of the South*, 341; Woodward, *Origins of the New South*, 208.

48. Thomas, *My Story in Black and White*, 11–12.

49. Holtzclaw, *Black Man's Burden*, 148–50.

50. Rosengarten, *All God's Dangers*, 32.

51. Gen. P. Bunguyn, Jackson, North Carolina, to M. W. Ransom, Jr., April 14, 1890, Matt Whitaker Ransom Papers, Southern Historical Collection, University of North Carolina.

52. Rosengarten, *All God's Dangers*, 32–33.

53. Pete Daniel, *The Shadow of Slavery: Peonage in the South, 1901–1969* (Urbana, Ill., 1972), 22. Consult this work for the full details and complexities of peonage, as well as the efforts to challenge and end the system. For a detailed description and indictment of the system see W. S. Reese, Jr., Office of the United States Attorney, Middle District of Alabama, Montgomery, June 15, 1903, File 5280-03, Department of Justice Records (Record Group 60), National Archives.

54. Baker, *Following the Colour Line*, 97.

55. Alexander Akerman, Office of United States Attorney, Southern District of Georgia, Macon, Department of Justice, to Attorney General of the United States, July 20, Aug. 10, 1903, File 3098-1902, Department of Justice Records (Record Group 60), National Archives.

56. Daniel, *Shadow of Slavery*, 41.

57. Rosengarten, *All God's Dangers*, 337; C. E. Mathews [Mathers?] to Attorney General of the United States, May 27, 1908, File 5280-03, Department of Justice Records (Record Group 60), National Archives.

58. Rawick, ed., *American Slave*, Suppl. Ser. 1, IV: Ga. Narr. (Part 2), 404–5; Norris W. Cuney, "Notes on Black Labor," n.d., but most likely early 1890s, Norris W. Cuney Papers, Bennett College, Greensboro, N.C.

59. Wright, *Black Boy*, 164; George Washington Lovejoy to Booker T. Washington, May 12, 1890, in Harlan, ed., *The Booker T. Washington Papers*, III, 57.

60. Howard N. Rabinowitz, *Race Relations in the Urban South, 1865–1890* (New York, 1978), 85–86, 196.

61. On black lawyers see Chapter 5, 249–52; on black physicians see Chapter 7, 338–41.

62. See Woodward, *Origins of the New South*, 142–74, 205–34, 291–320.

63. Du Bois, *Souls of Black Folk*, 5.

64. Quoted in *National Monitor*, reprinted with approval by the *Weekly Louisianian*, Jan. 25, 1879.

65. *The College Journal* (Georgia State Industrial College, College, Georgia), January, 1901, Smith-Shivery Family Papers, Schomburg Center for Research in Black Culture of the New York Public Library; Edward A. Johnson, *A School History of the Negro Race in America* (Raleigh, N.C., 1891), 442–43.

66. *Christian Recorder,* Aug. 18, 1866, Sept. 30, 1865.

67. *Richmond Planet,* July 27, 1889, July 12, 1890.

68. *Raleigh Times,* Jan. 1, 1907, *Raleigh News and Observer,* Jan. 2, 1907, Hunter Scrapbooks, Box 13, 1871–1928, Hunter Papers, Duke University Library. See also "Address Delivered on the Occasion of the Celebration of Emancipation Day, Raleigh, N.C., Jan. 1, 1912," manuscript copy, Hunter Papers, pp. 10–12, 23; *Raleigh News and Observer,* Jan. 2, 1917, Hunter Scrapbooks, Box 14, 1877–1924, Hunter Papers.

69. William H. Councill, *The Negro Laborer: A Word to Him* (Huntsville, Ala. [1887]), 5–7, 9–12.

70. *The Black Republican* (New Orleans), April 29, 1865; Harlan and Smock, eds., *The Booker T. Washington Papers,* V, 335.

71. Washington, *Up from Slavery,* 220; "An Address Before the National Afro-American Council," July 2, 1903, "An Address Before the National Negro Business League," August 19, 1914, in Harlan and Smock, eds., *Booker T. Washington Papers,* VII, 191, XIII, 121–23; Victoria E. Matthews, ed., *Black-Belt Diamonds: Gems from the Speeches, Addresses, and Talks to Students of Booker T. Washington* (New York, 1898).

72. Booker T. Washington, Tuskegee, to Charles Chesnutt, July 7, 1903. Private and Confidential. Chesnutt Papers, Fisk University Library, Box 2, Folder 14.

73. Gibson and Crogman, *Progress of a Race,* 359; Booker T. Washington, *The Future of the American Negro* (Boston, 1899), 176; Robert L. Factor, *The Black Response to America* (Reading, Mass., 1970), 253. See also Harlan and Smock, eds., *Booker T. Washington Papers,* V, 387–88.

74. Francis L. Broderick, *W. E. B. Du Bois: Negro Leader in a Time of Crisis* (Stanford, Calif., 1955), 66.

75. Sterling Brown, "Negro Folk Expression: Spirituals, Seculars, Ballads, and Work Songs," *Phylon,* XIV (1st Quarter 1953), 52. For another version see Talley, *Negro Folk Rhymes,* 122.

76. Loyle Hairston, "Growing Up in Mississippi," in Abbott, ed., *Mississippi Writers: Reflections of Childhood and Youth,* II, 313.

77. *Christian Recorder,* May 21, 1864.

78. Quoted in a letter to the editor from Charles N. Hunter, Raleigh, January 13, 1904, in response to a published interview with former governor Daniel L. Russell that appeared in the *Washington Post* and was reprinted in the *Raleigh News and Observer,* Jan. 14, 1904, Hunter Scrapbooks, Box 16, 1888–1905, Duke University Library. The usually cautious and accommodationist Hunter replied with considerable anger to Russell's comments, finding them to be "a horrible and horrifying empalement of the white race. . . . If what Governor Russell says is true our religion is a fetich, a farce, a fraud, and the white man's boasted civilization and refinement are but the gildings of moral depravity complete and monstrous." For an additional critique see C. N. Hunter to Governor T. J. Jones, Jan. 19, 1904, Hunter Papers.

79. R. C. Anthony, Freedmen's Bureau, Warrenton, Ga., Nov. 2, 7, 1868, to Col. J. R. Lewis, endorsement by Lewis to Governor R. B. Bullock, Nov. 7, 10, 1868;

affidavit of Daniel Lee, Oct. 1, 1869, R. B. Bullock Correspondence, Governor's Papers, Georgia State Archives.

80. Rawick, ed., *American Slave,* Suppl. Ser. 1, I: Ala. Narr., 58; Brown and Owens, *Toting the Lead Row,* 135; Rawick, ed., *American Slave,* Suppl. Ser. 1, III: Ga. Narr. (Part 1), 117; Rawick, ed., *American Slave,* V: Tex. Narr. (Part 4), 1648.

81. Gadsen, *An Oral History of Edisto Island: Sam Gadsden Tells the Story,* 57.

82. James Roberts Gilmore ("Edmund Kirke"), "On the French Broad," in *Here and There in Our Own Country, Embracing Sketches of Travel and Descriptions of Places, Etc., Etc.* (Philadelphia, 1885), 15.

83. Isaiah T. Montgomery, "The Negro in Business," *The Outlook,* Nov. 16, 1901, 733.

84. Montgomery to Washington, Sep. 6, 1904, in Harlan and Smock, eds., *Booker T. Washington Papers,* VIII, 61–63.

85. Simon Peter Smith to Rev. Edward Franklin Williams, Oct. 17, 1879, May 20, 1908, Edward Franklin Williams Papers, Amistad Research Center, Tulane University, New Orleans.

86. *Savannah Tribune* and *Louisville News* in Robert T. Kerlin, *The Voice of the Negro 1919* (New York, 1920), 95, 131; *Southwestern Christian Advocate,* March 9, 1899.

87. Hill, ed., *Black Women Oral History Project,* VII, 221, VIII, 121, IV, 265; Wright, *Black Boy,* 47–48; Hamer, "To Praise Our Bridges," in Abbott, ed., *Mississippi Writers: Reflections of Childhood and Youth,* II, 321. Similar examples abound in the black press, government documents, autobiographies, and oral histories; see, for example, *Chicago Defender,* April 7, 1917 (The correspondent—a black farmer in Alpharetta, Georgia—wrote to the *Defender* to inquire into employment opportunities in the North. "Don't publish my name; it might reach here. Write me as soon as you can."); Victoria Byerly, *Hard Times Cotton Mill Girls: Personal Histories of Womanhood and Poverty in the South* (Ithaca, N.Y., 1986), 31; and *A Statement from Governor Hugh M. Dorsey as to the Negro in Georgia* (Atlanta, Ga., April 22, 1921), Section D: County No. 21, n.p.

88. "The Negro Problem," *Independent,* LIV (Sep. 18, 1902), 2223; *Southwestern Christian Advocate,* Jan. 28, 1904.

89. Oster, *Living Blues,* 44, 145; Odum and Johnson, *The Negro and His Songs,* 7, 255.

90. Blassingame, *Slave Testimony,* 664; interview with Mrs. Magnolia Gates, Aug. 19, 1975, Yazoo County Bicentennial Oral History Project, Yazoo City, Miss.; Rosengarten, *All God's Dangers,* 149–52.

91. McMillen, *Dark Journey,* 171. For threats by white property owners in Jackson to use violence to keep a black physician from moving into their neighborhood see p. 13.

92. Terrell, *A Colored Woman in a White World,* 105–6; Ida B. Wells, *A Red Record: Tabulated Statistics and Alleged Causes of Lynchings in the United States, 1892–1893–1894* (Chicago, [1895]), 73–74.

93. Richard Wormser, "Behind the Veil," Videoline Productions.

94. Wells, *Crusade for Justice,* 47–55, 64–65. See also Terrell, *A Colored Woman in a White World,* 105–6.

95. *Crisis,* I (December 1910), 27. White raiding parties in a number of instances ordered the removal of families from lands they rented, giving them only a few days

to gather their belongings (but not their crops) before moving, and threatened the white landlords if the black tenants did not move. See, for example, *Chicago Defender,* Jan. 22, 1916.

96. *Crisis,* III (January 1912), 101.

97. Lillie Stokes to J. J. Stokes, Feb. 6, 1893, Joel A. Stokes and Family Papers, Merritt M. Shilg Memorial Collection, Louisiana State University; McMillen, *Dark Journey,* 120; Rawick, ed., *American Slave,* Suppl. Ser. 1, VI: Miss. Narr. (Part 1), 253–54; *Crisis,* I (March 1911), 9; *Chicago Defender,* Jan. 22, 1916.

98. *Report of the Joint Select Committee to Inquire into the Condition of Affairs in the Late Insurrectionary States,* 12: Mississippi (Part 2), 891–92.

99. Jacqueline Dowd Hall, *Revolt Against Chivalry: Jessie Daniel Ames and the Women's Campaign Against Lynching* (New York, 1979), 140. For examples of whitecap violence, see W. S. Reese, Jr., U.S. Attorney, Dept. of Justice, Montgomery, Ala., to Attorney General of the United States, Feb. 25, 1905; William Hanson, U.S. Marshal, Galveston, Tex., to Attorney General of the United States, Nov. 10, 1904; T. Brady, Jr., Special Assistant to the U.S. Attorney, Brookhaven, Miss., to Attorney General of the United States, May 9, 1906; George Randolph, U.S. Attorney, Memphis, Tenn., to Attorney General of the United States, Nov. 3, 1904 (with enclosure), May 9, 1905; J. M. Humphreys, Atoka, Okla., to Hon. Frank Lee, Aug. 16, 1911 (with accompanying "Notice to Negro Residents of Atoka"), Records of the Attorney General of the U.S. and the Department of Justice Records (Record Group 60), National Archives; *A Statement from Governor Hugh M. Dorsey as to the Negro in Georgia* (Atlanta, Ga., April 22, 1921), Section C: County No. 10 to County No. 20, n.p. For a full treatment of the whitecaps in Mississippi see William F. Holmes, "Whitecapping: Agrarian Violence in Mississippi, 1902–1906," *The Journal of Southern History,* XXXV (May 1969), 165–85. The depredations of "Regulators" and "Whitecaps" in Louisiana were reported in, for example, *New York Age,* April 5, 19, 1890, and *Southwestern Christian Advocate,* March 2, 1899.

100. McMillen, *Dark Journey,* 120, 121; William H. Holtzclaw, *Black Man's Burden,* 174–75.

101. Rosengarten, *All God's Dangers,* 544, 192.

102. Rosengarten, *All God's Dangers,* 193, 264.

103. Rosengarten, *All God's Dangers,* xxi, 27.

104. Baker, *Following the Colour Line,* 44; Archer, *Through Afro-America,* 32–33. For similar testimony see Bishop Lucius H. Holsey in *The Possibilities of the Negro in Symposium,* 108–9.

105. Committee (John Milton Waldron, J. Anderson Taylor, W. J. Howard, et al.) to President William H. Taft, August 13, 1910, Department of Justice Records, National Archives. In responding to the appeal, the acting attorney general reminded the committee that the protection of life and property "is generally a duty devolving upon the state authorities" unless a right secured by the U.S. Constitution or federal law has been violated. "Your letter and petition deal with the subject of the treatment of colored persons generally and therefore furnish no facts which would warrant this Department in taking any steps to redress the wrongs complained of."

106. P. L. Carmouche to Booker T. Washington, Nov. 30, 1912, in Harlan and Smock, eds., *Booker T. Washington Papers,* XII, 62–63.

107. *Louisville News,* October 18, 1919, quoted in Kerlin, *Voice of the Negro,* 131.

108. Quoted in *London Daily Chronicle,* July 28, 1911, the clipping contained in a letter from R. R. Moton, The Hampton Normal and Agricultural Institute, Hampton, Va., to Major J. C. Hemphill, Editor, *Richmond Times Dispatch,* Aug. 12, 1911, Hemphill Family Papers, Duke University Library.

109. Rabinowitz, *Race Relations in the Urban South,* 27; Alfred Maurice Low, *America at Home* (London, 1908), 190; Eric Anderson, *Race and Politics in North Carolina, 1872–1901: The Black Second* (Baton Rouge, La., 1981), 242–45. On the assassination of a black postmaster in Lake City, South Carolina, see, Williamson, *Crucible of Race,* 190.

110. Clifton Johnson, *Highways and Byways of the Mississippi Valley* (New York, 1906), 57; Thomas H. Baker, *The Memphis Commercial Appeal: The History of a Southern Newspaper* (Baton Rouge, La., 1971), 206.

111. McMillen, *Dark Journey,* 61; *Southwestern Christian Advocate,* Jan. 8, 1903; Rawick, ed., *American Slave,* Suppl. Ser. 1, III: Ga. Narr. (Part 1), 286–90.

112. *Crisis,* I (Dec. 1910), 14.

113. Robert Russa Moton, *What the Negro Thinks* (New York, 1929), 212.

114. C. Vann Woodward and Elisabeth Muhlenfeld, *The Private Mary Chesnut: The Unpublished Civil War Diaries* (New York, 1984), 261; Stephen Graham, "Marching Through Georgia: Following Sherman's Footsteps To-Day, Part II," *Harper's Magazine,* CXL (May 1920), 818; H. S. Bell, "Plantation Life of the Negro in the Lower Mississippi Valley," *Southern Workman,* XXVIII (August 1899), 313–14; Wright, *Black Boy,* 120.

115. Crew, *Field to Factory,* 14; Davis et al., *Deep South,* 372–73.

116. *Southwestern Christian Advocate,* June 8, 1899; Johnson, *Highways and Byways of the South,* 359; Mayor J. J. Pierpont of Savannah, Ga., as quoted in *Chicago Defender,* Jan. 29, 1916.

117. C. De Rochel, Houma, La., to Mr. J. A. [Joseph A.] Humphreys, June 14, 1882, Gibson-Humphreys Papers, South Caroliniana Library, University of South Carolina; Donelson Caffery, Franklin, La., to My Dear Son [Earl], Nov. 11, 1887, Caffery, Donelson Papers, Louisiana State University Library; Alice Louisa Fripp, Diary, Beaufort County. South Caroliniana Library, University of South Carolina.

118. Jack Chalaron, Oakland Plantation, Pointe Coupee Parish, to J. A. Chalaron, Aug. 11, 1878, Chalaron Papers, Tulane University Library, New Orleans; A. T. Montgomery, Belmont, Claiborne County, Miss., Manuscript Diary, Mississippi Department of Archives and History, Jackson; Hugh Lide Law, Hartsville, S.C., Manuscript Plantation Diary, entry for Nov. 1, 1907, South Caroliniana Library, University of South Carolina; J. E. Ransom to Matt Ransom, Jan. 5, 11, 1897, Matt Whitaker Ransom Papers, Southern Historical Collection, University of North Carolina.

119. Archer, *Through Afro-America,* 95. On black workers and organized labor see, for example, Paul B. Worthman, "Black Workers and Labor Unions in Birmingham, Alabama, 1897–1904," *Labor History,* 10 (Summer 1969), 375–407; Herbert Gutman, "The Negro and the United Mine Workers of America: The Career and Letters of Richard L. Davis and Something of Their Meaning: 1890–1900," in *Work, Culture and Society in Industrializing America* (New York, 1976), 121–208; Melton A.

McLaurin, *The Knights of Labor in the South* (Westport, Conn., 1978); Peter J. Rachleff, *Black Labor in the South: Richmond, Virginia, 1865–1890* (Philadelphia, 1984); Melvyn Dubofsky, *We Shall Be All: A History of the Industrial Workers of the World* (Chicago, 1969), 212–20; and Eric Arnesen, *Waterfront Workers of New Orleans: Race, Class and Politics, 1863–1923* (New York, 1991).

120. Gunnar Myrdal, *An American Dilemma: The Negro Problem and Modern Democracy* (2 vols.; New York, 1944), I, 509.

121. Conversation between Charles Chesnutt and George Haigh in Fayetteville, N.C., in Charles Chesnutt, Manuscript Journal and Note-Book II, 1877–81, entry for March 16, 1880, Fisk University Library; published in Brodhead, ed., *Journals of Charles W. Chesnutt*, 126; Wilbur Fisk Tillett, "Southern Womanhood As Affected by the War," *Century Magazine*, New Series, XLIII (1891), 11; W. H. Hidell to Mrs. Rebecca Felton, Dec. 18, 1883, Rebecca Felton Papers, University of Georgia Library.

122. Langhorne, *Southern Sketches from Virginia*, 108, 134–35.

123. Katzman, *Seven Days a Week*, 189; William R. Pope to Mrs. William R. Pope, March 29, 1919, Pope-Carter Family Papers, Duke University Library.

124. Odum and Johnson, *Negro Workaday Songs*, 117.

125. "More Slavery at the South," *Independent*, LXXII (Jan. 25, 1912), 196–97. See also Tucker, *Telling Memories Among Southern Women*, 76–78, and Hill, ed., *Black Women Oral History Project*, VIII, 353. "All the time," Esther Mae Scott recalled, "I'm trying to tell you, we didn't have no weeks. The world go round, and the weeks go round from can to can't, when you could see until you couldn't see. We called it from can to can't. Nobody give you no time off."

126. "More Slavery at the South," *Independent*, LXXII (Jan. 25, 1912), 198.

127. Charles A. Le Guin, ed., *A Home-Concealed Woman: The Diaries of Magnolia Wynn Le Guin, 1901–1913* (Athens, Ga., 1990), 183, 255–56, 314.

128. "Keeping Servants" and "The Domestic" in Woods, *The Negro in Etiquette*, 84, 112–14.

129. Tucker, *Telling Memories Among Southern Women*, 88, 89.

130. Murray, *Proud Shoes*, 159–60; Woods, *Negro in Etiquette*, 114.

131. U.S. Senate, 48th Cong., *Report of the Committee of the Senate upon the Relations Between Labor and Capital* (5 vols.; Washington, D.C., 1885), IV, 328, 343. On "troubles" with black help, particularly the "new issue," see, for example, Tillett, "Southern Womanhood As Affected by the War," 9–16; John Sedgwick Billings, Jr., to Katharine H. Billings, June 2, 1900, Julia Hammond Richards to Katie Katharine Hammond Billings, Aug. 23, 1906, Hammond, Bryan, Cumming Families Papers; Addie to Emmie, Feb. 15, 1883, Carrie to Emmie, Dec. 20, 1890, Julia to Emmie, Oct. 23, 1906, Mannie to Emmie, May 7, 1907, S. J. [?] Sams to Emma, Oct. 30, 1919, Sams Family Papers, South Caroliniana Library, University of South Carolina; W. H. Hidell to Rebecca Felton, Dec. 18, 1883, Rebecca Felton Papers, University of Georgia Library; Eugene Marshall, Manchester, Tenn., to his sister in Brockton, Mass., Feb. 24, 1904, Eugene Marshall Papers; Mrs. C. P. Poppenheim, Charleston, S.C., to her daughter, Louisa Bouknight Poppenheim and Mary Barnett Poppenheim Papers, Duke University Library; conversation between George Haigh and Charles Chesnutt, Charles Chesnutt Journal and Note-Book II, 1877–81,

entry for March 16, 1880, Fisk University Library; published in Brodhead, ed., *Journals of Charles W. Chesnutt,* 126, 127.

132. Eugene Marshall, Manchester, Tenn., to his sister in Brockton, Mass., Feb. 24, 1904, Eugene Marshall Papers, Duke University Library; Archer, *Through Afro-America,* 18.

133. "More Slavery at the South," *The Independent,* LXXII (Jan. 25, 1912), 199; "The Negro Problem: How It Appeals to a Southern White Woman," *Independent,* LIV (Sep. 18, 1902), 2227; Woods, *Negro in Etiquette,* 84. On the "service pan" see also Charles Chesnutt Manuscript Journal and Note-Book II, 1877–81, entry for March 16, 1880, Fisk University Library; published in Brodhead, ed., *Journals of Charles W. Chesnutt,* 127; Terrill and Hirsch, eds., *Such As Us,* 223–24; and Archer, *Through Afro-America,* 18.

134. Levine, *Black Culture and Black Consciousness,* 253, 336.

135. Rawick, ed., *American Slave,* Suppl. Ser. 1, VIII: Miss. Narr. (Part 3), 903, 905–6.

136. Harlan and Smock, eds., *Booker T. Washington Papers,* XI, 266–67.

137. Rabinowitz, *Race Relations in the Urban South,* 73–76; Sterling, ed., *We Are Your Sisters,* 357–58.

138. Edward L. Ayers, *The Promise of the New South: Life After Reconstruction* (New York, 1992), 235–37, 256–59.

139. Woodward, *Origins of the New South,* 410; Rosengarten, *All God's Dangers,* 144, 221–22.

140. White, *American Negro Folk Songs,* 352.

141. Rosengarten, *All God's Dangers,* 223–24.

142. Rosengarten, *All God's Dangers,* 226; Levine, *Black Culture and Black Consciousness,* 241.

143. For several versions of the song see Newman Ivey White, ed., *The Frank C. Brown Collection of North Carolina Folklore* (7 vols; Durham, N.C., 1952–64), III, 245–47.

144. Paul Oliver, *Blues Fell This Morning: The Meaning of the Blues* (New York, 1961), 19. See also Handy, *Father of the Blues,* 75; Oster, *Living Country Blues,* 116–23; and Levine, *Black Culture and Black Consciousness,* 240–41.

145. White, ed., *Frank C. Brown Collection of North Carolina Folklore,* III, 246.

146. Rosengarten, *All God's Dangers,* 228; Randy Finley, "Black Arkansans and World War I," *Arkansas Historical Quarterly,* XLIX (Autumn 1990), 253.

CHAPTER FOUR

1. Ellison, *Shadow and Act,* 116.
2. Baker, *Following the Colour Line,* 26.
3. *Shreveport [La.] Times,* quoted in Kerlin, *Voice of the Negro,* 128.
4. Louisiana Narratives, Federal Writers' Project of the Works Progress Administration for the State of Louisiana, unpublished, State Library of Louisiana, Baton Rouge.
5. Bailey, *Race Orthodoxy in the South,* 92–93.

6. Carl Holliday, "The Young Southerner and the Negro," *South Atlantic Quarterly*, 8 (1909), 17–31.

7. Du Bois, *Souls of Black Folk*, 68; McMillen, *Dark Journey*, 6; Archer, *Through Afro-America*, 209; *The Possibilities of the Negro in Symposium*, 10; Leonidas F. Scott to Mrs. William H. Felton [Rebecca Felton], May 30, 1894, Rebecca Felton Papers, University of Georgia. On the perceived deterioration of race relations see also Maurice S. Evans, *Black and White in the Southern States: A Study of the Race Problem in the United States from a South African Point of View* (London, 1915), 71–74, and E. Y. McMorries, Ph.D., Principal, University School, Plantersville, Ala., Dec. 3, 1902, to John W. DuBose. DuBose Papers, Alabama State Archives.

8. Archer, *Through Afro-America*, 142–43.

9. *The Possibilities of the Negro in Symposium*, 30.

10. *The Possibilities of the Negro in Symposium*, 30. See also the observations of Iza Duffus Hardy, *Between Two Oceans: Or, Sketches of American Travel* (London, 1884), 298–301, who found no evidence of racial antagonism in his journey through the South, only tributes to wartime slave loyalty and kindly feelings for "old Sambo." Howard Rabinowitz discusses this phenomenon in *Race Relations in the Urban South*, 29.

11. Belle Kearney, *A Slaveholder's Daughter*, 5th ed. (New York, 1900), 105–6.

12. *Race Problems of the South* (Montgomery conference, 1900), 36.

13. Mrs. Nicholas Ware Eppes, *The Negro of the Old South* (Chicago, 1925), x; *Manufacturers Record* (Baltimore), n.d., Hunter Scrapbooks, Box 15, 1887–1929, Charles N. Hunter Papers, Duke University.

14. Thomas Nelson Page, *The Negro: The Southerner's Problem* (New York, 1904), 163–204; Sterling Brown, *The Negro in American Fiction* (Washington, D.C., 1937), 51–53.

15. For analyses of Harris's work see Brown, *Negro in American Fiction*, 53–58; Bernard Wolfe, "Uncle Remus and the Malevolent Rabbit," *Commentary*, VIII (July 1949), 31–41; Darwin T. Turner, "Daddy Joel Harris and His Old-Time Darkies," *Southern Literary Journal*, I (Fall 1968), 20–41; Lawrence W. Levine, " 'Some Go Up and Some Go Down': The Meaning of the Slave Trickster," in Stanley Elkins and Eric McKitrick, eds., *The Hofstadter Aegis: A Memorial* (New York, 1974), 94–124; Levine, *Black Culture and Black Consciousness*, 82–83; and Wayne Mixon, "The Ultimate Irrelevance of Race: Joel Chandler Harris and Uncle Remus in Their Time," *Journal of Southern History*, LVI (August 1990), 457–80.

16. Martha S. Gielow, *Mammy's Reminiscences and Other Sketches* (New York, 1898). The inscription is in my personal copy. See also, for example, Howard Weeden, *Bandanna Ballads* (New York, 1904) and *Songs of the Old South* (New York, 1901), Irwin Russell, *Christmas-Night in the Quarters* (New York, 1917), and Essie Collins Matthews and Leigh Richmond Miner, *Ben King's Southland Melodies* (Chicago, 1911).

17. *Washington Herald*, Oct. 23, 1913, newspaper clipping in Vardaman file, Mississippi State Archives. Vardaman was speaking before the meeting of the State Society of Mississippi of the District of Columbia. For similar remarks see also a clipping in the same file, *The Issue* (Jackson, Miss.), Aug. 21, 1913.

18. Robert W. Winston, Raleigh, N.C., to Moorfield Storey, Boston, July 31, 1919, Robert W. Winston Papers, North Carolina State Archives, Raleigh.

19. Francis Butler Simkins, *Pitchfork Ben Tillman: South Carolinian* (Baton Rouge, La., 1944), 403–4, 398–99.

20. *The Possibilities of the Negro in Symposium,* 69–73. On the fiftieth anniversary of the Emancipation Proclamation, Hunter arranged for a Negro state fair in North Carolina to feature an "Old Slaves dinner." To finance the affair, he solicited contributions from surviving slaveholders and their families. Joel Williamson, *Crucible of Race,* 68. For a reunion of ex-slaves and descendants see also Hill, ed., *Black Women Oral History Project,* III, 6.

21. Charles N. Hunter to the Editor, *Fayetteville Observer,* Jan. 31, 1927, Hunter Scrapbooks, Box 15, 1887–1928; Hunter to the Editor, *Raleigh Times,* Dec. 14, 1915, Hunter Scrapbooks, Box 13, 1871–1928, Charles N. Hunter Papers, Duke University Library. "The feeling that existed between us in the old days has not disappeared," the president of the Ex-Slaves' Association declared in extending an invitation to whites and blacks to meet on October 29, 1913. *Negro Fair Bulletin,* Sept. 16, 1913, Hunter Scrapbooks, Box 16, 1886–1921. See also *Raleigh Times,* Sept. 22, 1913, and *Raleigh News and Observer,* Oct. 29, 1914, for descriptions of ex-slave dinners at the annual Negro Fair. Hunter Scrapbooks, Box 13, 1871–1928, and Box 16, 1891–1911, Hunter Papers.

22. *Atlanta Constitution,* Dec. 5, 24, 1932, Federal Writers' Project of the Works Progress Administration, Negro Studies, Georgia Project, A879, Manuscript Division, Library of Congress. For similar reports see *Raleigh Times,* Oct. 27, 1916, Hunter Scrapbooks, Box 13, 1871–1928. For other activities of the Georgia Ex-Slaves' Association, see *Atlanta Constitution,* Dec. 25, 1917, Dec. 12, 1920 (with photograph).

23. John Mickie, Holly Springs, Miss., to Dr. Edward H. Moren, Aug. 2, Feb. 23, 1873; Joseph H. Davidson, Mount Meigs, Ala., Sept. 13, 1880, to Dr. Edward H. Moren. Edward H. Moren Papers, Alabama State Archives, Montgomery. For additional letters see Mickie to Moren, Sept. 29, 1873; Davidson to Moren, Nov. 7, 1878, Mar. 6, Apr. 14, Sept. 28, 1880, Jan. 18, 1883, Jan. 26, 1884. For a tribute by an ex-slave in memory of his former mistress see Joseph H. Davidson, "Tribute by an Ex-Slave in Memory of Mrs. M. F. Moren," *Centreville Press* [1927], Moren Papers, Alabama State Archives.

24. Mrs. Lucy Worth Jackson, Pittsboro, Chatham County, N.C., to Henry Mauger London, [Jan. 27], 190[3], George London Collection, North Carolina Historical Archives, Raleigh.

25. *New York Age,* May 13, 1915.

26. McDonald Furman [Ramsey, S.C.] to [Miss Ann E. Furman, Yemassee], [1893], Richard [Furman], Privateer, Sumter County, S.C., to Sudie [Furman], Oct. 5, 1903, Miller-Furman-Dabbs Families Papers, South Caroliniana Library, University of South Carolina; Rawick, ed., *American Slave,* Suppl. Ser. 1, VI: Miss. Narr. (Part 1), 68–72; VII: Miss. Narr. (Part 2), 532–33.

27. Rabinowitz, *Race Relations in the Urban South,* 29; clipping (newspaper not identified), [October 2, 1910], Richard S. Andrews Papers, Duke University. For obituary notices see *Charlottesville Progress,* quoted in J. Nelson Fraser, *America, Old and New: Impressions of Six Months in the States* (London, 1912), 273. See also *McComb Enterprise,* 1932, quoted in Rawick, ed., *American Slave,* Suppl. Ser. 1, X: Miss. Narr.

(Part 5), 2144–45, on the death of Harriet, who had completed "sixty years of continuous and unbroken service" to a single family. Her employers made the funeral arrangements, many whites and blacks attended, and the *Enterprise* concluded its report with the observation that "certainly no colored person has been held in greater respect by the white people than Harriet." For discussion and examples of these tributes see also Blassingame, ed., *Slave Testimony,* 447–48.

28. Rawick, ed., *American Slave,* Suppl. Ser. 1, VII: Miss. Narr. (Part 2), 660–61; Litwack, *Been in the Storm So Long,* 19; Levine, *Black Culture and Black Consciousness,* 193.

29. Will, San Antonio, Tex., to Lou, May 19, 1897. Edmunds-Dawkins-Battise Families (Columbia and St. Matthews, S.C.). South Caroliniana Library, University of South Carolina.

30. "What Has the Negro Meant to the South? What Has the South Meant to the Negro," in Rutherford, ed., *Miss Rutherford's Scrap Book,* III, 17; *Manufacturers Record* (Baltimore), n.d., Hunter Scrapbooks, Box 15, 1887–1929, Charles N. Hunter Papers, Duke University Library.

31. "Tribute to a Servant, Faithful to the Last," 1906, Preston H. Turner Papers, Southern Historical Collection, University of North Carolina. "In all his career, since the war up to the Suffrage Amendment he invariably voted the Democratic ticket."

32. File on James Lynch, Mississippi State Archives, Jackson. It includes an excerpt from the *Times-Democrat (New Orleans),* March 7, 1900, indicating that Governor Longino had approved a bill making an appropriation to remove the remains and monument of Lynch from Jackson's white cemetery to the Negro cemetery. He had been the only black person interred in the cemetery. A typed report in this file declared that a check of the cemetery records of Greenwood Cemetery, compiled in 1940, did not list Lynch, and concluded that the body and the monument must have been removed to the Negro cemetery. But a penciled notation, dated November 16, 1972, indicated the monument was still there.

33. Testimony of Jim Polk Hightower, a former slave, in Rawick, ed., *American Slave,* Suppl. Ser. 1, VIII: Miss. Narr. (Part 3), 1013; James Lane Allen, *The Blue Grass Region of Kentucky and Other Kentucky Articles* (New York, 1907), 82; *Raleigh News and Observer,* Nov. 17, 1906, Feb. 3, 1907, Charles N. Hunter Scrapbooks, Box 16, 1886–1921, Box 13, 1871–1928, Duke University Library. On proposals to reward "faithful service" in the Confederate Army with pensions, see also, for example, *Raleigh News and Observer,* Nov. 17, 1906, Feb. 3, 1907, Hunter Scrapbooks, Charles N. Hunter Papers, Duke University Library.

34. Eppes, *Negro of the Old South,* 114; Mrs. W. H. Felton, "The Race Problem in the United States" [1898?], Rebecca Felton Papers, University of Georgia Library.

35. Freeman H. M. Murray, "Emancipation and the Freed in American Sculpture," Negro Studies Project, South Carolina (A888), Federal Writers' Project of the Works Progress Administration, Manuscript Division, Library of Congress, and also quoted in Leon F. Litwack, "Many Thousands Gone: Black Southerners and the Confederacy," in Harry P. Owens and James J. Cooke, eds., *The Old South in the Crucible of War* (Jackson, Miss., 1983), 49–50. See also Myrta L. Avary, *Dixie After the War* (New York, 1906), 401.

36. *Jacksonville Times Union,* repr. in the *New York Age,* June 18, 1914, Hunter Scrapbooks, Box 17, 1902–27, Charles N. Hunter Papers, Duke University Library. The *New York Age,* a black newspaper, praised the resolution as "significant evidence of the arrival of the day of better things in their relations between black and white men in the South." Several months later, noting the Jacksonville meeting, the Omer R. Weaver Camp of the United Confederate Veterans, meeting in Little Rock, Arkansas, adopted a virtually identical resolution. *Durham Reformer,* Aug. 20, 1914, Hunter Scrapbooks, Box 15, 1885–1929. For earlier efforts to erect monuments to the former slaves see Rev. I. E. Lowery, *Life on the Old Plantation in Ante-Bellum Days or A Story Based on Facts* (Columbia, S.C., 1911), 11–12.

37. U.S. Senate, 67th Cong., 4th sess., S. 4119, December 8, 1922, Senate Report No. 1072, January 29, 1923; *Washington Star,* Feb. 3, 7, 1923; Ethel Leach Carpenter, Birmingham, Ala., to the Commission of Fine Arts, Washington, D.C., July 9, 1923, October 25, 1929; Elise Towson Coble, Eskridge Family Association, July 12, 1939, in General Files, 1910–1954, Records of the Commission of Fine Arts (Record Group 66), National Archives, Washington, D.C. For a report of the speech by Representative Stedman see *Raleigh News and Observer,* Jan. 10, 1923, in Hunter Scrapbooks, Box 15, 1885–1929, Charles N. Hunter Papers, Duke University Library.

38. Rebecca Felton, Palmer House, Chicago, to William H. Felton, March 15, 1893, Rebecca Felton Papers, University of Georgia Library, Athens.

39. Edgar G. Murphy, *The Basis of Ascendancy* (New York, 1911), 11.

40. *Memphis Daily Commercial,* May 17, 1892, in Wells, *Southern Horrors,* 16–17. See also, e.g., *Memphis Evening Scimitar,* June 4, 1892, quoted on 17–18.

41. *Southwestern Christian Advocate* (New Orleans), Dec. 18, 1902; Rabinowitz, *Race Relations in the Urban South,* 28; Macrae, *America Revisited,* 54.

42. Mannie, Newborn, Ga., to Emmie [Sams], Aug. 14, 1906, Sams Family Papers, South Caroliniana Library, University of South Carolina; testimony of J. H. Hale, *Report of the Industrial Commission on Agriculture and Agricultural Labor,* 59th Cong., 1st sess., Document No. 179 (Washington, D.C., 1901), X, 400.

43. Lawrence J. Friedman, *The White Savage: Racial Fantasies in the Postbellum South* (Englewood Cliffs, N.J., 1970), 167; Langhorne, *Southern Sketches from Virginia,* 123–24.

44. Arthur Krock, ed., *The Editorials of Henry Watterson* (New York, 1923), 314; Baker, *Following the Colour Line,* 28; *The Southern Workman,* 28 (October 1899), 392. Soon after the Civil War, a Tuscaloosa, Alabama, newspaper was already lamenting the unfortunate impact of emancipation on the former slaves, particularly their diminished capacity to laugh and make music. "Negroes, as bondsmen, were happier, more sleek and greasy-looking, and better clothed, than they are now. We never hear the ringing horse-laughs, the picking of banjoes, beating of tamborines, and knocking of feet against puncheon-floors, that formerly marked their *sans souci* existence. Instead . . . they may be heard to grumble, in squads, collected in fence-corners; and may be seen with ashy faces, grum [grim?] countenances, and squalid appearance generally." Quoted in Allen W. Trelease, *White Terror: The Ku Klux Klan Conspiracy and Southern Reconstruction* (New York, 1971), 253–54.

45. Avary, *Dixie After the War,* 401–2.

46. Baker, *Following the Colour Line,* 37–38.

47. Baker, *Following the Colour Line,* 44.

48. J. R. Sparkman, "The Negro: His *past*—as slave—and his *present* as Freedman with a view of determining his future as citizen" (1889), J. R. Sparkman Papers, South Caroliniana Library, University of South Carolina. The reference to "the eternal, insoluble Negro question" that continues to "vex, perplex, and demoralize" the white South may be found in Jabez M. Curry, Asheville, N.C., to his son [Manly Bowie Curry], St. Paul, Minn., Sept. 16, 1889, J. M. Curry Papers, Duke University Library. He advised his son, who was residing in Minnesota, "Being away from the negroes, I pray that you may keep away." For the English traveler's observations see Archer, *Through Afro-America,* 42.

49. Beam, *He Called Them by the Lightning,* 26.

50. J. M. Curry, Richmond, to his son [Manly Bowie Curry], Feb. 13, 1885, Feb. 1, 1890, Jabez Lamar Monroe Curry Papers; Paul H. Hayne, "Copse Hill," Groveton (near Augusta), Ga., to Rev. A. A. Lipscomb, Athens, Ga., Jan. 9, 1886, Paul Hamilton Hayne Papers, Duke University Library.

51. Robert W. Winston, Raleigh, N.C., to Moorfield Storey, July 31, Aug. 23, Sept. 20, Oct. 2, 1919, Robert W. Winston Papers. North Carolina State Archives, Raleigh.

52. Archer, *Through Afro-America,* 142; Alfred H. Stone, *Studies in the American Race Problem* (New York, 1908), 428–29.

53. W. W. Ball, Diary 1, 1916, entry for April 25. W. W. Ball Papers, Duke University Library.

54. *Race Problems of the South* (Montgomery conference, 1900), 50. For the need to maintain white supremacy, see also *Possibilities of the Negro in Symposium,* 14–15; Evans, *Black and White in the Southern States,* 70–71.

55. Clowes, *Black America,* 15. W. Laird Clowes was commissioned in the autumn of 1890 by *The Times* to visit the American South to study race relations. The same sentiment may be found in John L. Weber, *Charleston News & Courier,* Dec. 22, 1888, to Prof. W. J. Rivers, Chesterton, Md., President of West Chester University, William James Rivers Papers, South Caroliniana Library, University of South Carolina; J. J. Pringle Smith, Charleston, S.C., to Frank G. Ruffin, Dec. 2, 1888, Francis G. Ruffin Papers, Southern Historical Collection, University of North Carolina.

56. Bailey, *Race Orthodoxy in the South,* 29–30.

57. Robert W. Winston, Raleigh, N.C., to Moorfield Storey, Oct. 2, 1919, Robert W. Winston Papers, North Carolina State Archives, Raleigh; Hugo Munsterberg, *The Americans* (New York, 1904), 177–78.

58. Robert W. Winston, Raleigh, N.C., to Moorfield Storey, Sept. 20, Oct. 2, 1919, Robert W. Winston Papers, North Carolina State Archives, Raleigh; Charles P. Moncure, Woodville, Va., May 30, 1883, to R. A. Brock, Brock Collection, Huntington Library, San Marino, Calif. Typical was the observation of James Lane Allen in *The Blue-Grass Region of Kentucky and Other Kentucky Articles:* "The kind, affectionate relations of the races under the old regime have continued with so little interruption that the blacks remain content with their inferiority, and lazily drift through life" (83).

59. *Possibilities of the Negro in Symposium,* 34, 12–14.

60. Thomas Dixon, N.Y., May 9 [1905], to the Editor of the *News & Courier,* May 9 [1905], Hemphill Family Papers, Duke University Library; Col. T. L. Pres-

ton, University of Virginia, Nov. 2, 1888, to F. S.[?] Ruffin, Nov. 2, 1888, Francis G. Ruffin Papers, Southern Historical Collection, University of North Carolina.

61. Gossett, *Race,* 279–80.

62. W. W. Ball, Diary 3, 1916–18, entry for June 3, 1917, W. W. Ball Papers, Duke University Library.

63. Macrae, *America Revisited,* 75; Guion Griffis Johnson, "The Ideology of White Supremacy, 1876–1910," in Fletcher Green, ed., *Essays in Southern History* (Chapel Hill, N.C., 1949), 152.

64. Robert W. Winston, Raleigh, N.C., Oct. 2, 1919, to Moorfield Storey, Robert W. Winston Papers, North Carolina State Archives, Raleigh; Evans, *Black and White in the Southern States,* 70.

65. Macrae, *America Revisited,* 54; Edward L. Ayers, *Vengeance and Justice: Crime and Punishment in the 19th Century American South* (New York, 1984), 236.

66. R. L. Gibson, U.S. Senate, Washington, D.C., to John Marsh Avery, May 24, 1890, Avery Family Papers (Gibson was describing a letter he had received from Jabez M. Curry. "This of course is confidential," he added); Hilary A. Herbert to President Theodore Roosevelt, Nov. 12, 1904 (Personal), Hilary A. Herbert Papers, Southern Historical Collection, University of North Carolina; Bailey, *Race Orthodoxy in the South,* 369–70.

67. Robert W. Winston, Raleigh, N.C., to Moorfield Storey, Sept. 20, 1919, Robert W. Winston Papers, North Carolina State Archives; McMillen, *Dark Journey,* 29; Archer, *Through Afro-America,* 21, 22.

68. Rev. Quincy Ewing, Rector, Church of Advent, Birmingham, Ala., to Francis J. Garrison, Oct. 12, 1905, Booker T. Washington Papers, Schomburg Center for Research in Black Culture of the New York Public Library.

69. Johnson, *Highways and Byways of the South,* 346.

70. Johnson, *Highways and Byways of the South,* 347.

71. Nathan C. Munroe, Jr., Washington, D.C., April 19, 1904, to his sister Julia Blanche (Munroe) Kell, Sunnyside PO, Spalding Co., Ga., Kell Collection, Duke University Library; [Mary Allan-Olney], *The New Virginians* (2 vols.; Edinburgh & London, 1880), II, 43, 261–62.

72. Clowes, *Black America,* 93.

73. Charles Trotter Lassiter, Petersburg, Va., to Joseph B. Earnest, Jr., Feb. 5, 1914, Daniel William Lassiter, Francis Rives Lassiter, and Charles Trotter Lassiter Papers, Duke University Library.

74. Harry Johnston, *The Negro in the New World* (London, 1910), 447; T. U. Dudley, "How Shall We Help the Negro?" *Century Magazine,* XXX (1885), 278.

75. Philip A. Bruce, *The Plantation Negro as Freeman* (New York, 1889), 129–30, 261, 256.

76. Johnston, *Negro in the New World,* 446–47.

77. Hilary A. Herbert to President Roosevelt, Nov. 12, 1904 (Personal), Hilary A. Herbert Papers, Southern Historical Collection, University of North Carolina. See also Herbert in *Race Problems of the South* (Montgomery conference, 1900), 28, 29; Page, *The Negro,* 94–97.

78. *Possibilities of the Negro in Symposium,* 149, 152–53; *Race Problems of the South* (Montgomery conference, 1900), 162–63.

79. Bruce, *Plantation Negro as a Freeman*, 83–84, 129–30.

80. Newspaper clipping, c. 1894, in which Rebecca Felton responds to an editorial in the *Boston Transcript*, Rebecca Felton Papers, University of Georgia Library.

81. *Possibilities of the Negro in Symposium*, 161.

82. Rabinowitz, *Race Relations in the Urban South*, 28.

83. Friedman, *White Savage*, 84; Mrs. Mary C. Bryan, in "How Should the Women and Girls in Country Districts be Protected: A Symposium Secured by Mrs. Loulie M. Gordon," April 23, 1899, and Leonidas F. Scott, Conyers, Ga., to Mrs. W. H. Felton, May 30, 1894, Rebecca Felton Papers, University of Georgia Library.

84. Robert W. Winston, Raleigh, N.C., to Moorfield Storey, Sep. 20, 1919, Robert W. Winston Papers, North Carolina State Archives, Raleigh; John L. Weber to Prof. W. J. Rivers, Dec. 22, 1888, William James Rivers Papers, South Caroliniana Library, University of South Carolina.

85. Simkins, *Pitchfork Ben Tillman*, 399; Frank E. Anderson to F. Ruffin, Sep. 29, 1888, Francis G. Ruffin Papers, Southern Historical Collection, University of North Carolina; Stuart Galishoff, "Germs Know No Color Line: Black Health and Public Policy in Atlanta, 1900–1918," *Journal of the History of Medicine*, 40 (Jan. 1985), 27; Archer, *Through Afro-America*, 60.

86. Albert D. Kirwan, *Revolt of the Rednecks: Mississippi Politics, 1876–1925* (New York, 1951), 146–47.

87. Macrae, *America Revisited*, 74. "Is it possible for Anglo-Saxons to live in this . . . country on terms of political equality with an inferior race? If history repeats itself, there must be submission, or extermination." E. Y. McMorries, Principal, University School, Plantersville, Ala., to John W. DuBose, Dec. 3, 1902, DuBose Papers, Alabama State Archives. For similar sentiments, and for proposals to colonize blacks in a separate territory within the United States, see Macrae, *America Revisited*, 74–75; John L. Weber, *The News & Courier*, Charleston, S.C., to Prof. W. J. Rivers, South Caroliniana Library, University of South Carolina.

CHAPTER FIVE

1. Murray, *Proud Shoes*, 269–70.

2. Oliver, *Blues Fell This Morning*, 208. Another version, "Death Cell Blues," sung by Blind Willie McTell, may be found in *The Definitive Blind Willie McTell* (Columbia Legacy C2K 53234).

3. "The Race Problem: An Autobiography," *The Independent*, LVI (March 17, 1904), 587–89.

4. Gossett, *Race*, 264.

5. Munsterberg, *The Americans*, 178; Stone, *Studies in the American Race Problem*, 224.

6. Langhorne, *Southern Sketches from Virginia*, 37; Johnson, "The Ideology of White Supremacy," 136.

7. Jane Bobo Springs to Mary Elizabeth Springs, Nov. 4, 1880, Childs Family Papers, South Caroliniana Library, University of South Carolina.

8. William F. Holmes, *The White Chief: James Kimble Vardaman* (Baton Rouge, La., 1970), 199.

9. Ayers, *Vengeance and Justice*, 239; *Augusta (Ga.) Chronicle*, quoted in *Chicago Defender*, June 6, 1914.

10. Walter White, *A Man Called White* (New York, 1948), 8. For similar sentiments, expressed in 1877, see Puryear, *The Public School in Its Relations to the Negro*, 13–14. "Equality is equality. If the negro is fit, as the law in question declares he is, to make laws for the control of our conduct and property; to give orders as a colonel or general, which we must implicitly obey; to sit in senatorial robes; to wear the spotless ermine; to occupy the chair of Washington, he is certainly fit to eat with us at our tables, to sleep in our beds, to be invited into our parlors, and to do all acts and things which a white man may do."

11. Page, *The Negro*, 112–13; Rebecca Felton, Letter to the Editor of the *Telegraph*, n.d., Felton to the *Atlanta Constitution*, Dec. 19, 1898, Rebecca Felton Papers, University of Georgia.

12. See, e.g., Georgia Chilton (Bowdon) [Mrs. Mark] McElderry, Talladega, Ala., to J. W. DuBose, March 17, 1897, DuBose Papers. Alabama State Archives, Montgomery. On blacks and the Populist Party see also Chapter 7, 371–72.

13. *Race Problems of the South* (Montgomery conference, 1900), 162.

14. See Anderson, *Race and Politics in North Carolina*, Chaps. 12–16. For a vivid depiction of how black political participation disrupted the social order, see Alfred Moore Waddell's speech to the Montgomery conference in 1900 in *Race Problems of the South* (Montgomery conference, 1900), 42–43.

15. Paul Lewinson, *Race, Class, and Party: A History of Negro Suffrage and White Politics in the South* (New York, 1932), 84–85; Vernon Wharton, *The Negro in Mississippi, 1865–1890* (Chapel Hill, N.C., 1947), 210.

16. McMillen, *Dark Journey*, 43.

17. McMillen, *Dark Journey*, 41. On disfranchisement in Mississippi see Wharton, *Negro in Mississippi*, 206–15, and McMillen, *Dark Journey*, 35–71.

18. McMillen, *Dark Journey*, 46; Levine, *Black Culture and Black Consciousness*, 319.

19. Montgomery Family Papers, South Caroliniana Library, University of South Carolina. I am appreciative to Allen H. Stokes, Jr., manuscripts librarian, for calling this collection to my attention. On the workings of disfranchisement in South Carolina see, for example, Diary of Frederik Holmes Christensen, Beaufort, July 7, 1908, South Caroliniana Library.

20. Van Woodward, *Origins of the New South*, 342–43; Hackney, *Populism to Progressivism in Alabama*, 206. On disfranchisement in the South see Woodward, *Origins of the New South*, 321–49, and J. Morgan Kousser, *The Shaping of Southern Politics: Suffrage Restriction and the Establishment of the One-Party South, 1880–1910* (New Haven, Conn., 1974).

21. Terrill and Hirsch, eds., *Such As Us*, 262–64. For implementation of the "educational clause" in South Carolina see *Crisis*, II (June 1911), 58–59.

22. McMillen, *Dark Journey*, 45.

23. McMillen, *Dark Journey*, 43; Hackney, *Populism to Progressivism in Alabama*, 191; Street, *American Adventures*, 423.

24. *Race Problems of the South* (Montgomery conference, 1900), 37; Hackney, *Populism to Progressivism*, 177; *Southwestern Christian Advocate*, Feb. 24, 1898.

25. Hackney, *Populism to Progressivism in Alabama*, 177, 181.

26. Hackney, *Populism to Progressivism in Alabama*, 202.

27. Quoted in Field to Factory: An Exhibition at the National Museum of American History, Smithsonian Institution; Wharton, *Negro in Mississippi*, 210–11.

28. *Greenwood Commonwealth*, quoted in *Southwestern Christian Advocate*, Jan. 13, 1898.

29. *New Orleans Times-Democrat*, July 9, 1890, quoted in Otto H. Olsen, ed., *The Thin Disguise: Turning Point in Negro History, Plessy* versus *Ferguson: A Documentary Presentation* (New York, 1967), 53; Montgomery Family Papers, South Caroliniana Library, University of South Carolina.

30. On the term "Jim Crow," see Preface, xiv–xv.

31. Howard N. Rabinowitz, "From Exclusion to Segregation: Southern Race Relations, 1865–1890," *Journal of American History*, 63 (Sept. 1976), 325–50, and *Race Relations in the Urban South*, 197.

32. Gadsden, *Oral History of Edisto Island: Sam Gadsden Tells the Story*, 46.

33. Baker, *Following the Colour Line*, 30; Ayers, *Promise of the New South*, 139; Archer, *Through Afro-America*, 70–71.

34. Linda Matthews, "Keeping Down Jim Crow: The Railroads and the Separate Coach Bills in South Carolina," *South Atlantic Quarterly*, 73:1 (1974), 127–28.

35. *New York Times*, Nov. 6, 1902.

36. Baker, *Following the Colour Line*, 31; Street, *American Adventures*, 422.

37. Baker, *Following the Colour Line*, 31; *Southwestern Christian Advocate*, Sept. 29, 1904. On "separate but equal" facilities on trains and streetcars, see also *Southwest Christian Advocate*, Nov. 6, 1902, Mar. 26, 1903, June 8, 1905; Archer, *Through Afro-America*, 93, 176; Baker, *Following the Colour Line*, 30–34; Dr. Sudhindra Bose, *Fifteen Years in America* (Calcutta, 1920), 358; W. L. George, *Hail Columbia! Random Impressions of a Conservative English Radical* (New York, 1921), 185.

38. Archer, *Through Afro-America*, 127; *Southwestern Christian Advocate*, June 22, 1905, April 20, 1899.

39. Bertram Doyle, *The Etiquette of Race Relations in the South: A Study in Social Control* (Chicago, 1937), 147; Wright, *87 Years Behind the Black Curtain*, 71; Hill, ed., *Black Women Oral History Project*, X, 23.

40. C. Vann Woodward, *The Strange Career of Jim Crow*, 3d rev. ed. (New York, 1974), 98.

41. Doyle, *Etiquette of Race Relations*, 147; Rabinowitz, *Race Relations in the Urban South*, 189–90; *Crisis*, I (March 1911), 28, II (June 1911), 77; W. Owens King, Atlanta, Ga., to John E. Bruce, Aug. 26, 1891, John E. Bruce Papers, Schomburg Center for Research in Black Culture of the New York Public Library. The black visitor to Atlanta was an entertainer from the North on tour in the South.

42. Eliza A. Gleason, *The Southern Negro and the Public Library* (Chicago, 1941), 19–24; Archer, *Through Afro-America*, 40–41; Rabinowitz, *Race Relations in the Urban South*, 239.

43. Sm. Cowart, Newberry, Fla., to Oswald Villard, April 1, 1911, repr. *Crisis*, II (May 1911), 32; Lillie B. Chace Wyman, "A Southern Study," *New England Magazine*, IV (June 1891), 524.

44. Archer, *Through Afro-America*, 127; *Southwestern Christian Advocate*, April 14, 1898.

45. Atkins, *Age of Jim Crow*, 95–96; *Crisis*, I (Nov. 1910), 8, (April 1911), 6.

46. Mays, *Born to Rebel*, 26. On the etiquette associated with automobiles see also McMillen, *Dark Journey*, 11.

47. *Chicago Defender*, March 6, 1915.

48. Ayers, *The Promise of the New South*, 67–68. See also *Crisis*, I (Nov. 1910), 6, 7, 11, (Dec. 1910), 9, (Jan. 1911), 12, (April 1911), 8–9, II (May 1911), 5 (Aug. 1911), 140; III (Nov. 1911), 27–30.

49. McMillen, *Dark Journey*, 12–13; *Norfolk Journal & Guide*, March 27, 1915, Hunter Scrapbooks, Box 13 (1871–1928), Charles N. Hunter Papers, Duke University Library; Bailey, *Race Orthodoxy in the South*, 79; Donald L. Grant, *The Way It Was in the South: The Black Experience in Georgia* (New York, 1993), 170.

50. Woodward, *Strange Career of Jim Crow*, 86–87; *Southwestern Christian Advocate*, April 2, 1903; Rabinowitz, *Race Relations in the Urban South*, 189; Baker, *Following the Colour Line*, 36.

51. *Birmingham Age-Herald*, January 16, 1902, quoted in Hackney, *Populism to Progressivism in Alabama*, 182; *New York Star*, Jan. 7, 1890, quoted in Clowes, *Black America*, 96.

52. Johnson, *Highways and Byways of the South*, 90; Rawick, ed., *American Slave*, Suppl. Ser. 2, I (Ala. Narr.), 91–92.

53. Archer, *Through Afro-America*, 72; *Richmond Leader*, quoted in *Crisis*, I (March 1911), 13; Ayers, *Promise of the New South*, 17; McMillen, *Dark Journey*, 12.

54. "More Slavery at the South" and "The Negro Problem," *The Independent*, LXXII (Jan. 25, 1912), 198–99 and LIV (Sep. 18, 1902), 2221; *Crisis*, I (Nov. 1910), 14.

55. Quincy Ewing, "The Heart of the Race Problem," *Atlantic Monthly*, 103 (March 1909), quoted in Charles E. Wynes, ed., *Forgotten Voices: Dissenting Southerners in an Age of Conformity* (Baton Rouge, La., 1967), p. 132.

56. Murray, *Proud Shoes*, 268.

57. Tucker, *Telling Memories*, 79.

58. *Orangeburg Plain Speaker*, Dec. 4, 1889, quoted in Clowes, *Black America*, 98.

59. "The Negro Problem," *The Independent*, LIV (Sept. 18, 1902), 2221; Hackney, *Populism to Progressivism in Alabama*, 188.

60. Du Bois, *Souls of Black Folk*, 152–53; Howard N. Rabinowitz, "The Conflict Between Blacks and the Police in the Urban South, 1865–1900," *Historian*, XXXIX (Nov. 1976), 68; Taylor Gordon, *Born to Be* (New York, 1929), 119; Handy, *Father of the Blues*, 86.

61. Levine, *Black Culture and Black Consciousness*, 311–12; Pickens, *American Aesop*, 80.

62. Levine, *Black Culture and Black Consciousness*, 315.

63. *Southwestern Christian Advocate*, March 10, 1904.

64. Ayers, *Promise of the New South*, 138, 139.

65. August Meier and Elliott Rudwick, "The Boycott Movement Against Jim Crow Streetcars in the South, 1900–1906," *Journal of American History*, 55 (March 1969), 756–75.

66. For incidents in which blacks were forcibly ejected, jailed, and fined, see *Chicago Defender*, Feb. 26, Nov. 11, 1916, and *The Reason Why the Colored American Is Not in the World's Columbian Exposition* [Chicago] [1893], 17. For Rucker's recollection, see Hill, ed., *Black Women Oral History Project*, VIII, 282, 287.

67. *Plessy v. Ferguson* (1896), 163 U.S. 537, 543, 544, 551, 552.

68. Gossett, *Race*, 275.

69. *New Orleans Times-Democrat*, quoted in *Crisis*, I (Dec. 1910), 15; Clarence Poe to the Editor, March 22, 1915, *Norfolk Journal & Guide*, March 27, 1915, Hunter Scrapbooks, Box 13 (1871–1928), Charles N. Hunter Papers, Duke University Library; *Knoxville Sentinel*, quoted in *Crisis*, II (May 1911), 12.

70. R. H. Battle, Raleigh, N.C., to Hon. H. G. Connor, Nov. 10, 1898, Henry Groves Connor Papers, Southern Historical Collection, University of North Carolina; Charles B. Aycock to Charles N. Hunter, Jan. 10, 1905, Charles N. Hunter Papers, Duke University Library; Charles E. Rice, Birmingham, Ala., to J. W. DuBose, Feb. 18, 1905, DuBose Papers, Alabama State Archives, Montgomery; Archer, *Through Afro-America*, 139.

71. Puryear, *The Public School in Its Relations to the Negro*, 4, 5.

72. Johnson, *Highways and Byways of the South*, 352.

73. Philip A. Bruce, *The Rise of the New South* (Philadelphia, 1905), 448; Kirwan, *Revolt of the Rednecks*, 146, 180–81.

74. *Raleigh Evening Times*, March 29, 1906, in Hunter Scrapbooks, Box 13, 1871–1928, Charles N. Hunter Papers, Duke University Library.

75. Gilmore (Kirke), *Here and There in Our Own Country*, 15; Mays, *Born to Rebel*, 7, 17.

76. Kenneth M. Stampp, *Peculiar Institution* (New York, 1956), 141; Rawick, ed., *American Slave*, VIII: Ark. Narr. (Part 1), 105.

77. Williamson, *After Slavery*, 334.

78. Campbell, *White and Black in the United States*, 300–301; Sterling, *We Are Your Sisters*, 377.

79. John William De Forest, *A Union Officer in the Reconstruction* (New Haven, Conn., 1948), 101.

80. Terrill and Hirsch, eds., *Such As Us*, 263.

81. "The Negro Problem," *The Independent*, LIV (Sep. 18, 1902), 2223.

82. Gibson and Crogman, *Progress of a Race*, 556–57.

83. Johnson, *Along This Way*, 143–44.

84. Irvin C. Mollison, "Negro Lawyers in Mississippi," *Journal of Negro History*, XV (Jan. 1930), 53.

85. Mollison, "Negro Lawyers in Mississippi," 52–59. See also Archer, *Through Afro-America*, 98.

86. Mollison, "Negro Lawyers in Mississippi," 53–56; John Hope Franklin, *Race and History: Selected Essays, 1938–1988* (Baton Rouge, La., 1989), 278. It was in Rentiesville, in 1915, that Buck Franklin's son, John Hope, was born; he would go on to become a prominent historian of the South and African Americans. For additional examples of black attorneys expelled or excluded from courts see J. Clay Smith, Jr., *Emancipation: The Making of the Black Lawyer, 1844–1944* (Philadelphia, 1993), 228, 272–73.

87. Mollison, "Negro Lawyers in Mississippi," 57.

88. *The Emmanuel Magazine,* July 3, 1909, quoted in Gilbert T. Stephenson, *Race Distinctions in American Law* (New York, 1911), 240–41; *Charleston News and Courier,* April 2, 1895, quoted in J. L. Oldfield, "A High and Honorable Calling: Black Lawyers in South Carolina, 1868–1910," *Journal of American Studies,* 23 (Dec. 1989), 405.

89. W. A. Pledger to Senator Oliver P. Morton, Feb. 19, 1876, W. A. Pledger Letter Book, Duke University Library.

90. Baker, *Following the Colour Line,* 49; John Dittmer, *Black Georgia in the Progressive Era, 1900–1920* (Urbana, Ill., 1977), 83; W. A. Pledger to Senator Oliver P. Morton, Feb. 19, 1876, W. A. Pledger Letter Book, Duke University Library; Litwack, *Been in the Storm So Long,* 286.

91. *Augusta (Ga.) Chronicle,* Jan. 5, 1890, in Clowes, *Black America,* 128; *Crisis,* 2 (July 1911), 99; White, *American Negro Folk Songs,* 382.

92. Elliott G. Rockarby, U.S. Commissioner, Jan. 29, 1904, to P. C. Knox, Attorney General of the United States. U.S. Department of Justice, Records of the Attorney General's Office (5280-03: 27070); Rosengarten, *All God's Dangers,* 340.

93. A. M. Salley, Sheriff, Orangeburg County, S.C., to his son [student at The Citadel), Jan. 26, 1889, Alexander Samuel Salley, Jr., Papers; Henry Hammond [Waynesboro, Ga.] to Emily Cumming Hammond, Oct. 11, 1907, Hammond, Bryan, Cumming Families Papers, South Caroliniana Library, University of South Carolina; *Crisis,* 2 (July 1911), 96.

94. Jeffrey S. Brand, "The Supreme Court, Equal Protection, and Jury Selection: Denying That Race Still Matters," *Wisconsin Law Review,* Vol. 1994, No. 3, 538–44.

95. Brand, "The Supreme Court, Equal Protection, and Jury Selection," 542; Stephenson, *Race Distinctions in American Law,* 253–71.

96. "The Negro Problem," *The Independent,* LIV (Sep. 18, 1902), 2222.

97. McMillen, *Dark Journey,* 205.

98. *Crisis,* 1 (March 1911), 28.

99. Archer, *Through Afro-America,* 96–97; Laura F. Edwards, "Sexual Violence, Gender, Reconstruction, and the Extension of Patriarchy in Granville County, North Carolina," *The North Carolina Historical Review,* LXVIII (July 1991), 244–45.

100. *New York Times,* July 24, 1908; *Baltimore Afro-American,* Jan. 5, 1918.

101. Street, *American Adventures,* 243.

102. McMillen, *Dark Journey,* 210–11. See also David M. Oshinsky, *"Worse Than Slavery": Parchman Farm and the Ordeal of Jim Crow Justice* (New York, 1996), 104–5.

103. Krech, *Praise the Bridge That Carries You Over,* 89–90.

104. The material that follows on "negro law" is drawn from "The Negro Law of Mississippi," in S. F. Davis, *Mississippi Negro Lore* (Indianola, Miss., 1914), 21–28.

105. Russell Ames, "Protest and Irony in Negro Folksong," *Science and Society,* XIV (Summer 1950), 210.

106. Sidney Bechet, *Treat It Gentle* (New York, 1960), 107.

107. Oster, *Living Country Blues,* 52–53, 308–11. On Stagolee see Levine, *Black Culture and Black Consciousness,* 413–15.

108. Levine, *Black Culture and Black Consciousness,* 307, 318–19; Pickens, *American Aesop,* 82.

109. Diary of Frederik Holmes Christensen, Beaufort, entry for Oct. 30, 1896, South Caroliniana Library, University of South Carolina; Washington correspondent of the *Pittsburgh Dispatch*, Jan. 11, 1890, quoted in Clowes, *Black America*, 94–95.

110. *Crisis*, 1 (Dec. 1910), 7; *Southwestern Christian Advocate*, May 26, 1898.

111. *Southwestern Christian Advocate*, July 7, 1904. On sentencing black violators of municipal ordinances to chain gangs and work farms, see e.g., W. S. Reese, Jr., U.S. Attorney, to W. H. Moody, March 27, 1905, U.S. Department of Justice, Records of the Attorney General's Office.

112. W. W. Ball, editor of *The State*, Columbia, S.C., to Frederick Calvin Norton, *The Courant*, Hartford, Conn., Dec. 1, 1917. W. W. Ball Papers, Duke University Library. For an example of blacks obtaining justice see the details of a trial in Abbeville, S.C., in which an all-white jury acquitted the black defendant of murdering a white man. William P. Greene to W. W. Ball, editor of *The State*, Feb. 26, 1919. W. W. Ball Papers, Duke University Library.

113. Records of the Attorney General's Office, U.S. Department of Justice, dealing with peonage cases, contain descriptions of black men and women rounded up by police and sentenced for minor violations of municipal ordinances. The men were sent to the chain gang, the women to work on the farms. See, for example, W. S. Reese, Jr., Montgomery, to W. H. Moody, March 27, 1905, Department of Justice. See also Urban, *Black Scholar: Horace Mann Bond*, 10; *Crisis*, 1 (March 1911), 6. For isolated examples of black police see Rabinowitz, "The Conflict Between Blacks and the Police in the Urban South," 65–68.

114. Holsey, "Learning How to Be Black," 424.

115. Ayers, *Vengeance and Justice*, 229–30.

116. Ayers, *Vengeance and Justice*, 231.

117. David L. Cohn, *God Shakes Creation* (New York, 1935), 155–56.

118. McMillen, *Dark Journey*, 205.

119. *Statement of Pardons, Paroles and Commutations Granted by Cole L. Blease, Governor of South Carolina, 1913* (Columbia, S.C., 1914), 474.

120. Memphis Slim, Big Bill Broonzy, and Sonny Boy Williamson, *Blues in the Mississippi Night: As Told to and Recorded by Alan Lomax* (Rykodisc RCD90155, 1990).

121. Blassingame, ed., *Slave Testimony*, 650; Henney Moton, Woodville, Miss., to J. Stewart McGehee, July 19, 1893, J. Burruss McGehee Papers, Louisiana State University Library.

122. McMillen, *Dark Journey*, 203; Mollison, "Negro Lawyers in Mississippi," 66; Smith, *Emancipation: The Making of the Black Lawyer*, 292–93.

123. Henry Hammond, Superior Court, Thomson, Ga., to Mrs. Henry Hammond, Sept. 3, 1906, Hammond, Bryan, Cumming Families Papers, South Caroliniana Library, University of South Carolina; McMillen, *Dark Journey*, 203.

124. Oshinsky, *"Worse Than Slavery,"* 215; Diary of Frederik Holmes Christensen, Beaufort, entry for Oct. 15, 1897, South Caroliniana Library, University of South Carolina.

125. John Motley Morehead, July 19, 1934, to A. B. Andrews, Raleigh, N.C., Alexander B. Andrews, Jr., Papers, North Carolina Historical Archives, Raleigh.

126. *Statement of Pardons, South Carolina, 1913*, 273, 288–89, 333. The discussion of Governor Blease's pardons is based on an examination of *Statement of Pardons, Paroles*

and Commutations Granted by Cole L. Blease, 1913 (Columbia, 1914), contained in *Reports and Resolutions of the General Assembly of the State of South Carolina . . . January 13, 1914,* III (Columbia, 1914). Cited as *Statement of Pardons, South Carolina, 1913.* I am grateful to Trenton E. Hizer and Lacy K. Ford, Jr., for their assistance in locating this document.

127. Oshinsky, *"Worse Than Slavery",* 182–83; *Statement of Pardons, South Carolina, 1913,* 164–66.

128. On Cole Blease's racial views see *Statement of Pardons, South Carolina, 1913,* and David L. Carlton, *Mill and Town in South Carolina, 1880–1920* (Baton Rouge, La., 1982), esp. 243–48.

129. *Statement of Pardons, South Carolina, 1913,* 339, 292–93, 420; see also for pardons in black-on-black homicides, 205, 210–12, 222, 223–24, 237–38, 245–46, 282–85, 288–89, 303.

130. *Statement of Pardons, South Carolina, 1913,* 236, 384.

131. *Statement of Pardons, South Carolina, 1913,* 305, 279–80; *Chicago Defender,* Feb. 14, 1914.

132. Somehow, in the song, Turney came to be called Turner. For various versions of the "Joe Turner Blues," the song and its origins, see Handy, *Father of the Blues,* 145–47; Oster, *Living Country Blues,* 306–7; Odum, *Negro and His Songs,* 206–7; Dorothy Scarborough, *On the Trail of Negro Folk-Songs* (Cambridge, Mass., 1925), 265–66; William Broonzy, *Big Bill Blues: William Broonzy's Story* (London, 1955), 27–33.

133. On peonage and the convict lease system see Daniel, *Shadow of Slavery;* Oshinsky, *"Worse Than Slavery";* Ayers, *Vengeance and Justice;* Matthew J. Mancini, *One Dies, Get Another: Convict Leasing in the American South, 1866–1928* (Columbia, S.C., 1996).

134. Oshinsky, *"Worse Than Slavery,"* 58, 59.

135. Oshinsky, *"Worse Than Slavery,"* 70; Ayers, *Vengeance and Justice,* 193, 200; George W. Cable, *The Silent South* (New York, 1885), 126–71.

136. Oshinsky, *"Worse Than Slavery,"* 44–45.

137. Oshinsky, *"Worse Than Slavery,"* 46; Ayers, *Vengeance and Justice,* 200–201; Cable, *Silent South,* 131.

138. Oshinsky, *"Worse Than Slavery,"* 55; *Southwestern Christian Advocate,* July 7, 1904.

139. Ayers, *Vengeance and Justice,* 199. By 1880, in Mississippi, one of every four convicts was an adolescent or a child, and that ratio would persist. Oshinsky, *"Worse Than Slavery,"* 46–47.

140. Lester D. Stephens, "A Former Slave and the Georgia Convict Lease System," *Negro History Bulletin,* 39 (Jan. 1976), 505.

141. Ayers, *Vengeance and Justice,* 220.

142. Jerry Shannan, Cabaniss, Ga., to The Governor of the City of Washington, D.C. [presumably intended for the president], May 24, 1903, Department of Justice, Records of the Attorney General, File No. 3098-02 (8588), National Archives, Washington, D.C.

143. Anne M. Butler, "Still in Chains: Black Women in Western Prisons, 1865–1910," *The Western Historical Quarterly,* XX (Feb. 1989), 27–29.

144. *Statement of Pardons, South Carolina, 1913,* 254–55, 474.

145. Cable, *Silent South,* 149; Ayers, *Vengeance and Justice,* 201–2.

146. E. C. L. Adams, *Nigger to Nigger* (New York, 1928), 108–9.

147. McMillen, *Dark Journey,* 198.

148. Kerlin, *Voice of the Negro,* 62–65.

149. Holtzclaw, *Black Man's Burden,* 156–57.

150. Sterling Brown, "Old Lem," in *The Collected Poems of Sterling A. Brown* (New York, 1980), 170.

CHAPTER SIX

1. Hamer, "To Praise Our Bridges," in Abbott, ed., *Mississippi Writers,* II, 326.

2. The account of the Hose lynching is based on the *Richmond Planet,* Oct. 14, 1899, which reprinted the extensive investigation conducted by a detective sent by Ida B. Wells, and on the *Savannah Tribune,* April 29, May 6, 13, 1899; *Atlanta Constitution,* April 14–25, 1899; *Atlanta Journal,* April 24, 1899; *New York Tribune,* April 24, 1899; *New York Times,* April 24, 25, 1899; *Boston Evening Transcript,* April 24, 1899; *Kissimmee Valley (Florida) Gazette,* April 28, 1899; *Springfield (Massachusetts) Weekly Republican,* April 28, 1899, in Ralph Ginzburg, *100 Years of Lynchings* (Baltimore, 1961, 1988), 10–21; Thomas D. Clark, *Southern Country Editor* (Indianapolis, Ind., 1948), 229–31; W. Fitzhugh Brundage, *Lynching in the New South: Georgia and Virginia, 1880–1930* (Urbana, Ill., 1993), 82–84; Grant, *The Way It Was in the South,* 162–64. Much of the press referred to him as Sam Holt. Only the *New York Times* (April 25, 1899) published the story of a lyncher procuring a slice of Hose's heart for the governor.

3. J. C. Clarke to Mrs. W. H. Felton, May 2, 1899, Wells B. Whitemore [Whitman?], Marietta, Ga., to Rebecca Felton, April 25, 1899, and "How Should the Women and Girls in Country Districts Be Protected: A Symposium Secured by Mrs. Loulie M. Gordon," Rebecca Felton Papers, University of Georgia Library.

4. On the Palmetto violence see *Atlanta Journal,* March 16, 1899; *Atlanta Constitution,* March 17, 18, 21. Most of the newspapers reporting the Hose execution also reported the subsequent lynching of Strickland and Sewall.

5. On Governor Candler's message see *Savannah Tribune,* April 29, 1899; *Atlanta Journal,* April 24, 1899; *Atlanta Constitution,* April 24, 1899. In his 1899 annual message, Candler, without any evidence to support his position, attributed the rising black crime rate to education, estimating that some 90 percent of black crimes were committed by individuals who had had some exposure to schooling. Dittmer, *Black Georgia,* 117.

6. Grant, *The Way It Was in the South,* 163–64; *Richmond Planet,* Oct. 14, 1899.

7. Postcard in NAACP, Administrative File, Lynching, etc., 1885–1916, NAACP Papers, C371, Library of Congress; *Crisis,* 3 (Jan. 1912), 110.

8. Evers, *Evers,* 23; McMillen, *Dark Journey,* 224.

9. *Crisis,* 2 (May 1911), 32; 3 (Jan. 1912), 108.

10. Diary of Frederik Holmes Christensen, entry for Sept. 28, 1893. South Caroliniana Library, University of South Carolina.

11. Helen Dick Davis, ed., *Trials of the Earth: The Autobiography of Mary Hamilton* (Jackson, 1992), 98–99. For the reference to the Atlanta butcher shop see W. E. B. Du Bois, "My Evolving Program for Negro Freedom," in Rayford W. Logan, *What The Negro Wants* (Chapel Hill, N.C., 1944), 53.

12. *Crisis*, 10 (June 1915), 71.

13. *Topeka Plaindealer*, quoted in *Crisis*, 3 (Dec. 1911), 60.

14. Postcard, "The Dogwood Tree," published by Harkrider Drug Co., Center, Texas, in NAACP Papers, C336, Manuscript Division, Library of Congress.

15. McMillen, *Dark Journey*, 245; Ayers, *Vengeance and Justice*, 247–48; Oshinsky, *"Worse Than Slavery,"* 105.

16. "The Negro Problem," *Independent*, LIV (Sept. 18, 1902), 2224; Booker T. Washington to Editor of the *New Orleans Times-Democrat*, June 19, 1899, in *Southern Workman*, XXVIII (Oct. 1899), 375; *Raleigh News and Observer*, Aug. 10, 1906, in Hunter Scrapbooks, Box 16, 1886–1921, Charles N. Hunter Papers, Duke University Library.

17. *Savannah Tribune*, May 25, 1918; Walter F. White, "The Work of a Mob," *Crisis*, 16 (Sept. 17, 1918), 221–22.

18. *Vicksburg Evening Post*, Feb. 13, 1904, quoted in Walter White, *Rope and Faggot: A Biography of Judge Lynch* (New York, 1929), 35–36.

19. Emily K. . . . , Fort White, Florida, to M. Du Bois, Nov. 30, 1893, Egbert Du Bois Papers, Duke University Library; *Memphis Commercial*, July 23, 1892[?], quoted in Ida B. Wells, "Lynch Law," in *The Reason Why the Colored American Is Not in the World's Columbian Exposition*, 30–33.

20. Kelly Miller, "Possible Remedies for Lynching," *Southern Workman*, XXVIII (Nov. 1899), 419; *Chicago Defender*, Dec. 18, 1915.

21. Clark, *Southern Country Editor*, 239; *Crisis*, 2 (July 1911), 99–100; *Chicago Defender*, July 10, 1915, Jan. 29, 1916.

22. *Crisis*, 9 (March 1915), 225–28; Dittmer, *Black Georgia*, 139. The same issue of *Crisis* reprints editorial opinion from around the country. In the South, the savage lynching elicited some negative reactions. The *Atlanta Journal* pronounced it "savage lawlessness," and a meeting of some two hundred Monticello residents, with the mayor presiding, voiced its disapproval.

23. *Baltimore Afro-American Ledger*, Aug. 31, 1901; Jones, *For the Ancestors*, 42; Willie [William R. Savage], Norfolk, Va., to My Dear Mamma [Elizabeth Rutherford Savage], Nov. 17, 1885, William R. Savage Papers, Southern Historical Collection, University of North Carolina; *Chicago Defender*, May 20, 1916.

24. Fraser, *America, Old and New*, 277n; *Crisis*, 3 (Dec. 1911), 61–62.

25. *The State* (Columbia, S.C.), Sept. 10, 1905, NAACP Files, C343, Manuscript Division, Library of Congress.

26. McMillen, *Dark Journey*, 241.

27. T. Thomas Stanford, *The Tragedy of the Negro in America* (North Cambridge, Mass., 1897), 198; *Memphis Commercial Appeal*, Jan. 22, 1900, quoted in Baker, *Memphis Commercial Appeal*, 206.

28. Kearney, *A Slaveholder's Daughter*, 95.

29. *Savannah Morning News*, quoted in Ayers, *Vengeance and Justice*, 244–45; McMillen, *Dark Journey*, 239; Lexington *Whig and Tribune*, quoted in Clark, *Southern*

Country Editor, 234–35; George B. Tindall, *The Emergence of the New South* (Baton Rouge, La., 1967), 170–71. After investigating scores of lynchings at the turn of the century, James E. Cutler concluded that whites felt very much at peace with their actions. In a democracy with a republican form of government, he noted, "the people consider themselves a law unto themselves. They make the laws; therefore they can unmake them. Since they say what a judge can do, they entertain the idea that they may do this thing themselves. To execute a criminal deserving of death is to act merely in their sovereign capacity, temporarily dispensing with their agents, the legal administrators of the law." James E. Cutler, *Lynch-Law: An Investigation into the History of Lynching in the United States* (New York, 1905), 269.

30. Johnston, *Negro in the New World,* 465; Clark, *Southern Country Editor,* 241.

31. McMillen, *Dark Journey,* 245; Baker, *Following the Colour Line,* 198.

32. W. S. Reese, Jr., Department of Justice, Montgomery, Ala., to Attorney General of the United States, Oct. 6, 1904, U.S. Department of Justice Records, RG 60, Central Files, Straight Numerical Files, #44182, National Archives, Washington, D.C.

33. McMillen, *Dark Journey,* 224, 246–47; Rebecca Felton, "Governor Candler's Address to the People of Georgia on the Lynching Question," manuscript letter to the editor of the *Atlanta Journal,* Rebecca Felton Papers, University of Georgia Library; Baker, *Following the Colour Line,* 190.

34. McMillen, *Dark Journey,* 224; *Crisis,* 3 (Dec. 1911), 56–57.

35. Hall, *Revolt Against Chivalry,* 140; W. M. Waltrip, Sheriff, Franklin County, Belgreen, Alabama, to Governor Thomas G. Jones, April 3, 1891. Governor's Papers. Alabama State Archives, Montgomery.

36. *Crisis,* 2 (Aug. 1911), 143; *Chicago Defender,* Feb. 27, 1915.

37. Clark, *Southern Country Editor,* 243; McMillen, *Dark Journey,* 246; Baker, *Following the Colour Line,* 189; *Crisis,* 3 (Dec. 1911), 61.

38. Clark, *Southern Country Editor,* 227; Ayers, *Vengeance and Justice,* 247; Wells, *Crusade for Justice,* 154–55.

39. *Macon Daily Telegraph,* April 1, 1916, in NAACP Papers (C343), Manuscript Division, Library of Congress.

40. Governor Northen, in "How Shall the Women and Girls in Country Districts Be Protected: A Symposium Secured by Mrs. Loulie M. Gordon," Rebecca Felton Papers, University of Georgia Library; McMillen, *Dark Journey,* 208. On criticism of the legal machinery see also Clark, *Southern Country Editor,* 235–36; Williamson, *Crucible of Race,* 186–87; Ayers, *Vengeance and Justice,* 246–47; Anna to Mama, Jan. 12, 1890, Sams Family Papers, South Caroliniana Library, University of South Carolina; *Race Problems of the South* (Montgomery conference, 1900), 30–31; Trautmann, *Travels on the Lower Mississippi,* 80–82.

41. *Southwestern Christian Advocate,* July 17, 1902.

42. *Possibilities of the Negro in Symposium,* 15.

43. Baker, *Following the Colour Line,* 198–99; P. Hale, Sandersville, Ga., to Dr. J. B. Hawthorne, Dec. 27, 1898, Rebecca Felton Papers, University of Georgia Library; Hall, *Revolt Against Chivalry,* 146.

44. Williamson, *Crucible of Race,* 214.

45. Benjamin S. Williams, Brunson (Hampton County), South Carolina, to W. E. Gonzalez, editor of *The State,* December 17, 1912, Benjamin S. Williams Papers, Duke University Library. A Georgia newspaper, the *Waycross Herald,* made the same argument: "The Negro, arrested for outrage, kept in jail, tried by jury and sentenced to be hung with all the honors of war and the law, becomes a hero and goes straight to heaven from the gallows, thus setting an example which some of those witnessing the scene will afterwards emulate."

46. *Atlanta Evening News,* Dec. 12, 1906, quoted in Baker, *Following the Colour Line,* 25.

47. *Race Problems of the South* (Montgomery conference, 1900), 164; D. P. Hale, Sandersville, Ga., to Dr. J. B. Hawthorne, Dec. 27, 1898, Rebecca Felton Papers, University of Georgia Library.

48. Clark, *Southern Country Editor,* 242.

49. McMillen, *Dark Journey,* 235; C. Vann Woodward, *Tom Watson: Agrarian Rebel* (New York, 1938), 432.

50. Clark, *Southern Country Editor,* 235.

51. *Memphis Daily Commercial,* May 17, quoted in Wells, *Southern Horrors,* 17.

52. Simkins, *Pitchfork Ben Tillman,* 397; Benjamin S. Williams, Brunson (Hampton County), South Carolina, to W. E. Gonzalez, Editor of *The State,* Dec. 17, 1912, Benjamin S. Williams Papers, Duke University Library. For a critical response see W. E. Gonzalez to Benjamin S. Williams, Dec. 26, 1912. "You are supporting lawlessness against everything for which civilization stands."

53. Clark, *Southern Country Editor,* 241.

54. W. S. Reese, Jr., Office of the U.S. Attorney, Montgomery, Ala., to Hon. W. H. Moody, U.S. Department of Justice, Feb. 1, 1905; Reese, Feb. 3, 1905, to Attorney General of the United States, Feb. 3, 1905, Department of Justice Files, National Archives.

55. J. M. Guilliams, Holbrook Normal College, Fountain City, Tenn., to Mrs. W. H. [Rebecca] Felton, Nov. 18, 1898; T. A. Cunningham to Rebecca Felton, Jan. 1, 1899, Rebecca Felton Papers, University of Georgia Library.

56. "How Should the Women and Girls in Country Districts Be Protected: A Symposium Secured by Mrs. Loulie M. Gordon"; Rebecca Felton to the Editor of the *Telegraph,* n.d.; Rebecca Felton to the *Atlanta Constitution,* Dec. 19, 1898, Rebecca Felton Papers. The Rebecca Felton Papers at the University of Georgia contain a large number of letters from northern as well as southern whites applauding her call for the severe repression of blacks, including limitations on their education, as a way to curb lynching. See Leonidas F. Scott, Conyers, Ga., to Felton, May 30, 1894; Charles E. Felton, Chicago, to Felton, Nov. 17, 1898; Ulla G. Hardeman, Atlanta, Ga., to Felton, Dec. 22, 1898; J. W. Renfroe, Atlanta, Ga., to Felton, July 5, 1902; Lily Johnson, Oxford, Ga., to Felton, Aug. 6, 1902; George T. Smith, Covington, Ga., Aug. 4, 1902, to Felton, and Felton, "The Race Problem in the United States," ms. article or letter (1898); "Governor Candler's Address to the People of Georgia, On the Lynching Question," ms. letter to the *Atlanta Journal.*

57. Hall, *Revolt Against Chivalry,* 150–51. The term "folk pornography" was used by Hall in her insightful chapter on lynching and rape.

58. White, *Rope and Faggot*, 56; *Memphis Daily Commercial*, May 17, quoted in Wells, *Southern Horrors*, 16; Baker, *Following the Colour Line*, 179–80.

59. "How Shall the Women and Girls in Country Districts Be Protected: A Symposium Secured by Mrs. Loulie M. Gordon," Rebecca Felton Papers, University of Georgia Library; White, *Rope and Faggot*, 25–26.

60. White, *Rope and Faggot*, 57–58; *Crisis*, 3 (Nov. 1911), 11. For instances in which both whites and blacks suffered from the hysteria over sexual assaults, see, for example, Ayers, *Vengeance and Justice*, 241–42.

61. *Little Rock Daily News*, quoted in *Crisis*, 15 (April 1918), 288–89.

62. NAACP, *Thirty Years of Lynching in the United States, 1889–1918* (New York, 1919), 36; White, *Rope and Faggot*, 56–57. See also Monroe N. Work, ed., *Negro Year Book: An Annual Encyclopedia of the Negro, 1937–1938* (Tuskegee, Ala., 1937), 156–58.

63. *An Analysis of 3,216 Lynchings in Thirteen States for the Period 1889 to March 1935* [NAACP]; NAACP, *Thirty Years of Lynching*; *Lynch List As Published in the Richmond Planet* (Richmond, [1889?]); Clowes, *Black America*, 95; *Arkansas Weekly Mansion* (Little Rock), June 23, 1883; Johnston, *Negro in the New World*, 466; *Chicago Defender*, Jan. 10, 1910; Kerlin, *Voice of the Negro*, 100–101; McMillen, *Dark Journey*, 236. "It is said the negro gets justice in the State courts, and yet to be 'impolite,' 'indolent,' or 'impertinent' are capital offenses in the South, for which the negro is mercilessly shot down, and in all the Court Records since the war not a single white man has been hung for wantonly killing a colored man, much less for murdering an 'indolent' or 'impertinent' 'nigger.' " From speech of W. A. Pledger of Georgia, *Official Compilation of Proceedings of the Afro-American League National Convention Held at Chicago, January 15, 16, 17, 1890* (Chicago, 1890), 23.

64. Articles from a variety of newspapers and periodicals, in Group 1 Administrative File Subject File (C371), NAACP Papers, Manuscript Division, Library of Congress.

65. W. W. Ball, editor of *The State*, Columbia, S.C., to Frederick Calvin Norton, Dec. 1, 1917, W. W. Ball Papers, Duke University Library.

66. *New York Tribune*, March 3, 1904, Dec. 2, 1905, in Group 1, Administrative File Subject File (C371), NAACP Files, Division of Manuscripts, Library of Congress.

67. Hall, *Revolt Against Chivalry*, 141–42; Allison Davis, *Leadership, Love and Aggression* (New York, 1983), 160; *Chicago Defender*, Sept. 22, 1917. Of the 4,715 blacks known to have been lynched between 1882 and 1946, some 26 percent were accused of a minor infraction or of no crime at all.

68. *Crisis*, 1 (Jan. 1911), 18–19. The term appeared above a two-page cartoon depicting a lynching, and the caption read, "Seventy-five percent of the Negroes lynched have not even been accused of rape."

69. White, *Rope and Faggot*, 9; *Pittsburgh Dispatch*, Jan. 11, 1890, quoted in Clowes, *Black America*, 94–95. On "nigger killing" as a recreational diversion see also Johnston, *Negro in the New World*, 463.

70. Albert Bushnell Hart, "The Outcome of the Southern Race Question," *The North American Review*, 188 (July 1908), 56; David L. Cohn, *Where I Was Born and Raised* (Boston, 1948), 74; McMillen, *Dark Journey*, 236–37.

71. [Roy Nash], "The Lynching of Anthony Crawford" (1916); W. T. Andrews, Attorney-at-Law, Sumter, S.C., to W. E. B. Du Bois, Oct. 26, 1916; *Scimitar (Abbeville, S.C.)*, February 1, 15, 1917, *New York Evening Post*, Nov. 23, 1916, NAACP Papers (C343,364), Manuscript Division, Library of Congress.

72. Richard Carroll, Columbia, S.C., to W. W. Ball, managing editor, *The State*, Nov. 9, 1916. W. W. Ball Papers, Duke University Library. See also W. W. Ball, Ms. Diary 2, 1916, entry for November 3, in which he recounts a visit from one of Crawford's sons to seek advice about leaving and protection. "I could only advise him to employ a lawyer of courage and intelligence and to follow the lawyer's direction. I expressed, though, the opinion that the family, failing to leave November 15, would not be molested."

73. Rev. John E. White, "The Need of a Southern Program on the Negro," *South Atlantic Quarterly*, 6 (1907), 184–85; Clark, *Southern Country Editor*, 226; Carlton, *Mill and Town in South Carolina*, 246. Walter Hines Page wrote in 1893: "The gravest significance of this whole matter lies not in the first violation of the law, nor in the crime of lynching, but in the danger that Southern public sentiment itself under the stress of this new and horrible phase of the race-problem will lose the true perspective of civilization." Gossett, *Race*, 272.

74. *Memphis Commercial Appeal*, July 19, 1913, in *Chicago Defender*, Aug. 16, 1913.

75. Hamer, "To Praise Our Bridges," in Abbott, ed., *Mississippi Writers*, II, 323.

76. The editorial in *The Record* was attributed to editor Alex Manly, but William L. Jeffries, associate editor, later claimed credit. It is reprinted in Thomas W. Clawson, "The Wilmington Race Riot of 1898," ms., Thomas Clawson Papers, Southern Historical Collection, University of North Carolina. On authorship of the editorial see Helen G. Edmonds, *The Negro and Fusion Politics in North Carolina, 1894–1901* (Chapel Hill, N.C., 1951), 173. A Committee of Colored Citizens disclaimed any responsibility for "the obnoxious article" and agreed to cooperate with whites in expelling the editor from the community. The Committee of Colored Citizens to Hon. A. M. Waddell, Chairman, Citizens Committee, Wilmington, n.d., Alfred Waddell Papers, Southern Historical Collection, University of North Carolina.

77. Cronly Family Papers; Jack Metauer Winfree, Wilmington, N.C., to Elizabeth Hinsdale, Nov. 12, 1898, Hinsdale Family Papers, Duke University Library.

78. Glenda Elizabeth Gilmore, *Gender and Jim Crow: Women and the Politics of White Supremacy in North Carolina, 1896–1920* (Chapel Hill, N.C., 1996), 113.

79. Gilmore, *Gender and Jim Crow*, 114–15, 117; *New York Times*, Aug. 26, 1900; Charles Chesnutt to Walter Hines Page, Nov. 10, 1898, in Helen Chesnutt, *Charles Waddell Chesnutt: Pioneer of the Color Line* (Chapel Hill, N.C., 1952), 104.

80. John C. Dancy, *Sand Against the Wind: The Memoirs of John C. Dancy* (Detroit, 1966), 66–70; Gilmore, *Gender and Jim Crow*, 115–16; Alfred V. Wood and others to Hon. Alfred Moore Waddell, Dec. 21, 1898, Alfred Waddell Papers, Southern Historical Collection, University of North Carolina. The Waddell Papers also contain many congratulatory letters from around the country on the "salvation" and "deliverance" of Wilmington. For descriptions of the riot and its meaning see also Gilmore, *Gender and Jim Crow*, 91–118; Edmonds, *The Negro and Fusion Politics in North*

Carolina, 158–77; Williamson, *Crucible of Race,* 195–201; H. Leon Prather, *We Have Taken a City: Wilmington Racial Massacre and Coup of 1898* (Rutherford, N.J., 1984); Jack Metauer Winfree, Wilmington, N.C., Nov. 12, 1898, to Elizabeth Christophers, Hinsdale Family Papers; J. S. Bassett, Durham, N.C., to Dr. Herbert Baxter Adams, Nov. 15, 1898, Herbert Baxter Adams Papers; Cronly Family Papers, Duke University Library. I am grateful to Cita Cook for bringing the Cronly Family Papers to my attention.

81. In addition to the footnoted quotations from sources, the account of the riot is based on Charles Crowe, "Racial Violence and Social Reform—Origins of the Atlanta Riot in 1906," and "Racial Massacre in Atlanta, September 22, 1906," *Journal of Negro History,* 53 (July 1968), 234–56, and 54 (April 1969), 150–73; Ray Stannard Baker, *Following the Color Line,* 3–21; White, *A Man Called White,* 5–12; Williamson, *Crucible of Race,* 209–22.

82. Darden A. Pyron, *Southern Daughter: The Life of Margaret Mitchell* (New York, 1991), 31–32.

83. Baker, *Following the Colour Line,* 15–16; Rawick, ed., *American Slave,* Suppl. Ser. 1, IV: Ga. Narr. (Part 2), 407–8.

84. Hill, ed., *Black Women Oral History Project,* VIII, 284. See also X, 11.

85. White, *A Man Called White,* 8–11; Mays, *Born to Rebel,* 18; Du Bois, *Autobiography,* 286.

86. Baker, *Following the Colour Line,* 16–17.

87. Archer, *Through Afro-America,* 209–10; Charles W. Chesnutt to Booker T. Washington, Nov. 3, 1906, Box 2, Folder 15, Oct. 9, 1906, Box 1, Folder 10, Charles W. Chesnutt Papers, Fisk University Library.

88. Baker, *Following the Colour Line,* 19–21.

89. Lowery, *Life on the Old Plantation,* 166–67.

90. Hill, ed., *Black Women Oral History Project,* I, 135; Adrienne McNeil Herndon, Atlanta, to Booker T. Washington, Feb. 12, 1907, in Harlan and Smock, eds., *Booker T. Washington Papers,* IX; 216–17; Booker T. Washington to Frances J. Garrison, Dec. 3, 1906. Washington Papers, Schomburg Center for Research in Black Culture of the New York Public Library; Booker T. Washington to Charles Chesnutt, Oct. 29, 1906, Charles W. Chesnutt Papers, Fisk University Library.

91. White, *Rope and Faggot,* 11; Introduction to *The Reason Why the Colored American Is Not in the World's Columbian Exposition,* in Foner, ed., *Life and Writings of Frederick Douglass,* IV, 476; Rabinowitz, *Race Relations in the Urban South,* 234–35. For a similar argument see the *Chicago Defender,* March 28, 1914, in which Ralph W. Tyler writes from Jackson, Mississippi, "Race prejudice in this state is now more largely because of the wonderful, rapid material and educational advancement of the race than because of inborn race hatred." The white editor of *Southern Workman,* organ of Hampton Institute, concurred. Responding to news of racial troubles in Georgia, he wrote, "It is not strange that with the elevation of the black man race hatred should increase. . . . No race has won its way without passing through just such troublous times." *Southern Workman,* XXVIII (June 1899), 203.

92. Henry M. Turner, "Races Must Separate," in *The Possibilities of the Negro in Symposium,* 94.

93. Perdue et al., eds., *Weevils in the Wheat,* 54.

94. Mays, *Born to Rebel*, 9.

95. Hortense Powdermaker, *After Freedom: The Portrait of a Community in the Deep South* (New York, 1939), 106; *Atlanta Constitution*, April 8, 1906.

96. Baker, *Following the Colour Line*, 27.

97. L. Q. C. Lamar, Oxford, Miss., to William Henry Trescott, July 24, 1877, William Henry Trescott Papers, South Caroliniana Library, University of South Carolina.

98. William H. Skaggs to Col. John W. Du Bose, Birmingham, Jan. 2, 1905, Du Bose Papers. Alabama State Archives, Montgomery; Ayers, *Vengeance and Justice*, 239.

99. Alice Thrasher to Arthur P. Thrasher, Sep. 28, 1896, Thrasher Papers, Louisiana State University Library.

100. John S. Bassett, Durham, N.C., to Dr. Herbert Baxter Adams, Nov. 15, 1898, Herbert Baxter Adams Papers, Duke University Library; John S. Bassett, "Stirring Up the Fires of Race Antipathy," *South Atlantic Quarterly*, 7 (1908), 301, 304, 305.

101. T. R. Waring, editor of the *Charleston Evening Post*, to William W. Ball, Oct. 10, 1919, W. W. Ball Papers, Duke University Library; Mrs. Alec Tweedle, *America As I Saw It or America Revisited* (London, 1913), 301. See also Munsterberg, *The Americans*, 169. "[O]pposition between whites and blacks has never been in the history of America so sharp and bitter and full of hatred as it is to-day. Just in the last few years the hatred has grown on both sides, so that no friend of the country can look into the future without misgivings."

102. Leonidas F. Scott, Conyers, Ga., to Mrs. William H. Felton [Rebecca Felton], May 30, 1894, Rebecca Felton Papers, University of Georgia Library.

CHAPTER SEVEN

1. Federal Writers' Project, Works Progress Administration, Folklore Subjects, Folder 31 (Songs), Arkansas State Archives, Little Rock, Ark.

2. R. Emmet Kennedy, *Mellows: Negro Work Songs, Street Cries, and Spirituals* (New York, 1925), 126–28; Henry M. Belden and Arthur Palmer Hudson, eds., *Folk Songs from North Carolina*, in Newman Ivey White, ed., *The Frank C. Brown Collection of North Carolina Folklore* (7 vols.; Durham, N.C., 1952–64), III, 626–27; Sterling Brown, "Negro Folk Expression: Spirituals, Seculars, Ballads and Work Songs," in *Phylon*, XIV (First Quarter 1953), 48.

3. Jones, *For the Ancestors*, 51.

4. Blassingame, ed., *Slave Testimony*, 653.

5. Baker, *Following the Colour Line*, 8; Du Bois, *Autobiography*, 121.

6. Evans, *Black and White in Southern States*, 32.

7. Rawick, ed., *American Slave*, XIV: N.C. Narr. (Part 1), 221.

8. Fields, *Lemon Swamp*, 71–73.

9. Rosengarten, *All God's Dangers*, 193; Fields, *Lemon Swamp*, 72, 73; McMillen, *Dark Journey*, 259.

10. Rawick, ed., *American Slave*, XII: Ga. Narr. (Part 1), 325; Sterling, *We Are Your Sisters*, 350; Gordon, *Born to Be*, 117.

11. Rosengarten, *All God's Dangers*, 161.

12. Doyle, *Etiquette of Race Relations*, 142–44; *Crisis*, 1 (Jan. 1911), 26; Charles S. Johnson, *Patterns of Negro Segregation* (New York, 1943), 39. When blacks protested that such tampering with mail was illegal, the practice stopped. "They don't like to mess with Uncle Sam," a local insurance agent noted.

13. Doyle, *Etiquette of Race Relations*, 142; Baker, *Following the Colour Line*, 64.

14. Mays, *Born to Rebel*, 8.

15. Bailey, *Race Orthodoxy in the South*, 368–69; W. W. Ball, Diary 1, 1916, W. W. Ball Papers, Duke University Library.

16. *New York Times*, July 24, 1908; Johnson, *Highways and Byways of the South*, 332–33; James T. Williams, Jr., Washington, D.C., to James T. Williams, Jan. 18, 1902, Greenville, S.C., James Thomas Williams Papers, South Caroliniana Library, University of South Carolina. The same hostility greeted whites who chose to use a term winning some support from black professionals in the late nineteenth century—"a colored person." "Why, the very idea of calling a nigger a colored man!" one furious white retorted, "if that does not beat all! The nigger is a nigger. He has got to keep his place." Bose, *Fifteen Years in America*, 357.

17. McMillen, *Dark Journey*, 23–24; Baker, *Following the Colour Line*, 63–64; Doyle, *Etiquette of Race Relations in the South*, 145; Holley, *You Can't Build a Chimney from the Top*, 61.

18. Some ten years later, Broonzy used the experience as the theme of a new song, "When Will I Get to Be Called a Man?" *Big Bill Blues: William Broonzy's Story*, 44–45.

19. Ayers, *Promise of the New South*, 210; McMillen, *Dark Journey*, 25.

20. *Chicago Defender*, Nov. 3, 1917; *Macon Daily Telegraph*, n.d., in NAACP Collections, Group 1, C-371 (although the date of the newspaper was not listed, the date of the NAACP report was October 24, 1917); *Southwestern Christian Advocate*, June 22, 1905; Howard Jones to "My dear Brother" [Horace Jones], June 14, 1919, Horace Jones to James Weldon Johnson, June 14, 1919, NAACP Papers (C364), Manuscript Division, Library of Congress.

21. *Chicago Defender*, May 11, 1912.

22. Robinson, *Road Without Turning*, 18.

23. See, for example, the experience of an Alabama black family in "The Negro Problem," *The Independent*, LIV (Sept. 18, 1902), 2221–22.

24. The material on Atlanta in this section is based on Stuart Galishoff, "Germs Know No Color Line: Black Health and Public Policy in Atlanta, 1900–1918," *Journal of the History of Medicine*, 40 (Jan. 1985), 22–41.

25. Galishoff, "Germs Know No Color Line," 23.

26. Galishoff, "Germs Know No Color Line," 26–27.

27. Galishoff, "Germs Know No Color Line," 29.

28. W. E. B. Du Bois, ed., *The Health and Physique of the Negro American* (Atlanta, 1906), 98. On the problems facing black medical colleges, see Todd L. Savitt, "The Education of Black Physicians at Shaw University, 1882–1918," in Jeffrey Crow and Flora J. Hatley, eds., *Black Americans in North Carolina and the South* (Chapel Hill, N.C., 1984), 160–88, and "Abraham Flexner and the Black Medical Schools" in Barbara

Barzansky and Norman Gevitz, *Beyond Flexner: Medical Education in the Twentieth Century* (New York, 1992), 65–80.

29. Gibson and Crogman, *Progress of a Race,* 582; Todd L. Savitt, "Entering a White Profession: Black Physicians in the New South, 1880–1920," *Bulletin of the History of Medicine,* 61 (1987), 513, 520–21; McMillen, *Dark Journey,* 170.

30. McMillen, *Dark Journey,* 170, 171; Savitt, "Entering a White Profession," 521, 522.

31. Savitt, "Entering a White Profession," 515, 529–30.

32. Savitt, "Entering a White Profession," 517; McMillen, *Dark Journey,* 171; Gibson and Crogman, *Progress of a Race,* 582–83.

33. Savitt, "Entering a White Profession," 522–27.

34. Blassingame, *Slave Testimony,* 669. On the varying success of black physicians see Savitt, "Entering a White Profession," 507, 530–32.

35. Litwack, *Been in the Storm So Long,* 245–46.

36. "More Slavery at the South," *The Independent,* LXXII (Jan. 25, 1912), 198.

37. Jane Edna Hunter, *A Nickel and a Prayer* (Cleveland, 1940), 32.

38. "More Slavery at the South," *The Independent,* LXXII (Jan. 25, 1912), 197–98. For an example of a black youth murdered for trying to defend his sister see Sutton E. Griggs, *The Race Question in a New Light* (Nashville, Tenn., 1909), 19.

39. Ayers, *Promise of the New South,* 153.

40. Ayers, *Promise of the New South,* 152; U.S. 57th Cong., 1st sess., Document 179, *Report of the Industrial Commission on Agriculture and Agricultural Labor* (Washington, D.C., 1901), X, 514.

41. *Crisis,* 3 (Jan. 1912), 101.

42. Robinson, *Road Without Turning,* 21; Wells, *Southern Horrors,* 6.

43. Gilmore, *Gender and Jim Crow,* 70–71.

44. Testimony of J. K. Green, *Report of the Committee of the Senate Upon the Relations Between Labor and Capital,* IV, 454, quoted in Walter L. Fleming, *Documentary History of Reconstruction* (2 vols.; Cleveland, 1907), II, 446.

45. Councill, *Negro Laborer,* 26; Rebecca Felton to *Post,* "Lynching and Its Causes," n.d., in Rebecca Felton Papers, University of Georgia Library.

46. Friedman, *White Savage,* 141; *The Colored American,* Jan. 13, 1866 (also in *Christian Recorder,* Feb. 24, 1866).

47. Woods, *Negro in Etiquette,* 22–24, 58.

48. Rev. J. W. E. Bowen, *What Shall the Harvest Be? A National Sermon; or, A Series of Plain Talks to the Colored People of America, on Their Problems . . .* (Washington, D.C., [1892]), 67–68: Gilmore, *Gender and Jim Crow,* 75.

49. "The Negro Problem," *The Independent,* LIV (Sept. 18, 1902), 2222.

50. "The Negro Problem," *The Independent,* LIV (Sept. 18, 1902), 2226.

51. "The Race Problem: An Autobiography," *The Independent,* LVI (Mar. 17, 1904), 587. See also Darlene Clark Hine, "Rape and the Inner Lives of Black Women in the Middle West," *Signs,* 14 (Spring 1989), 912–20.

52. Rawick, ed., *American Slave,* Suppl. Ser. 2, II: Texas Narr. (Part 1), 302; Suppl. Ser. 1, VII: Miss. Narr. (Part 2), 444; Odel Jackson, La Fuche Parish, WPA manuscript narratives, Louisiana State Library, Baton Rouge; "Fight a Going to

Heaven," WPA Records, 60, Vol. 151, "Our Lives," Mississippi State Archives, Jackson.

53. Wright, *Black Boy*, 14; Rosengarten, *All God's Dangers*, 10.

54. Mays, *Born to Rebel*, 9–10; Hurston, *Dust Tracks on a Road*, 24–25; Armstrong, *Satchmo*, 8, 12, 26, 27–28.

55. Johnson, *Highways and Byways of the South*, 274.

56. "More Slavery at the South," *The Independent*, LXXII (Jan. 25, 1912), 200.

57. Lydia Parrish, *Slave Songs of the Georgia Sea Islands* (New York, 1942), 247. The "hundud" referred to the one hundred pounds of cotton she was expected to pick each day.

58. Zora Neale Hurston, *Their Eyes Were Watching God* (Philadelphia, 1937), 29.

59. "The Negro Problem," *The Independent*, LIV (Sept. 18, 1902), 2224.

60. McMillen, *Dark Journey*, 48.

61. *The World (New York)*, Sept. 27, 1890, reprinted the entire speech, along with a reporter's reaction, editorial comment, and an account of Montgomery's life. Montgomery Papers, Southern Historical Collection, University of North Carolina. For an appreciation of Montgomery and his work by a white Mississippi politician see Subject File, Mississippi State Historical Society, Jackson.

62. *The World (New York)*, Sept. 27, 1890; August Meier, *Negro Thought in America, 1880–1915: Racial Ideologies in the Age of Booker T. Washington* (Ann Arbor, 1963), 38.

63. Washington, *Up from Slavery*, 221–22.

64. Washington, *Future of the American Negro*, 65–66.

65. *Atlanta Constitution*, Jan. 9, 1890.

66. *Wharton Elevator*, March 26, 1898, Cuney Papers, Bennett College, Greensboro, N.C. Cuney had his limits, as he indicated on a number of occasions in his career. "While we send missionaries to Asia, Africa and the rest of the world to carry civilization," he wrote in 1889, "we are overlooking the growth of a brute force in our own country which overrides law and order and settles by lynch law and mob violence those questions which ought to be settled by the Courts of the land." Cuney to R. B. Rentfro, Oct. 17, 1889, Cuney Papers, Bennett College.

67. Harlan, *Booker T. Washington: The Making of a Black Leader*, 222.

68. William Pickens to Isaac Carper, April 11, 1915, William Pickens Papers, Schomburg Center for Research in Black Culture of the New York Public Library; *Raleigh News and Observer*, Jan. 2, 1913, Hunter Scrapbooks, Box 13, 1871–1928, Charles N. Hunter Papers, Duke University Library.

69. H. C. Bruce, *The New Man: Twenty-nine Years a Slave. Twenty-nine Years a Free Man* (York, Pa., 1895), 146; *Southern Workman*, XXVIII (January 1899), 6; Low, *America at Home*, 199. The story of the boatman is also related in Pickens, *American Aesop*, 59.

70. *Raleigh News and Observer*, Jan. 2, 1913, Hunter Scrapbooks, Box 13, 1871–1928, Charles N. Hunter Papers, Duke University Library; Mifflin W. Gibbs, *Shadow and Light: An Autobiography* (Washington, D.C., 1902), 200. For similar sentiments see Norris W. Cuney, "Oration on the 30th Anniversary of Negro Freedom," n.d., Cuney Papers, Bennett College, Greensboro.

71. Edward F. Jones to Booker T. Washington, Dec. 5, 1898, Washington Papers, Manuscript Division, Library of Congress.

72. Dispatch from Belzonia, Mississippi, to the *Chicago Defender*, Dec. 12, 1914.

73. Bruce, *The New Man*, 143–44; *Proceedings of the National Negro Business League . . . 1900* (Boston, 1901), 125.

74. *Norfolk Journal and Guide*, reprinted in a dispatch from Norfolk to the *Chicago Defender*, Dec. 19, 1914. In Negro humor, as historian Lawrence Levine has suggested, the penny-pinching Jewish materialist, along with the numskull Irish, figured prominently. He found black humor concerning Jews often played on both Jewish and Negro stereotypes. Although most jokes depicted Jews taking advantage of blacks, the two groups shared on occasion a certain empathy for the plight of the other. Levine, *Black Culture and Black Consciousness*, 305–6.

75. *Southwestern Christian Advocate*, July 19, 1900.

76. *Southwestern Christian Advocate*, Apr. 3, 1903, Dec. 8, 1904.

77. Silas X. Floyd, *Floyd's Flowers or Duty and Beauty for Colored Children* (Atlanta, 1905), 321–22.

78. Dr. T. O. Fuller to the editor of the *Memphis Evening Striker*, Dec. 27, 1902, Hunter Scrapbooks, Box 17, 1902–27, Charles N. Hunter Papers, Duke University Library.

79. *Raleigh News and Observer*, Jan. 2, 1907, Hunter Scrapbooks, Box 13, 1871–1928, Charles N. Hunter Papers, Duke University Library. For a slightly different wording of the same address see *Raleigh Times*, Jan. 1, 1907.

80. Booker T. Washington to Benjamin Ryan Tillman, Nov. 4, 1895, in Harlan and Smock, eds., *Booker T. Washington Papers*, IV, 71–73.

81. Harlan and Smock, eds., *Booker T. Washington Papers*, IV, 73n.

82. Holley, *You Can't Build a Chimney from the Top*, 60–61. In recalling the story, Holley makes no reference to which door he used to enter the house. Presumably that was less important than where the judge agreed to meet him.

83. Wright, *Black Boy*, 198–200.

84. Holsey, "Learning How to Be Black," 425.

85. Hill, ed., *Black Women Oral History Project*, I, 54.

86. Wright, *87 Years Behind the Black Curtain*, 71.

87. Rosengarten, *All God's Dangers*, 34–36.

88. Davidson, *Inching Along*, 73–76; Pickens, *American Aesop*, 61–62.

89. Wright, *87 Years Behind the Black Curtain*, 70.

90. Charles Chesnutt, Manuscript Journal and Note-Book III, 1881–82, entry for January 21, 1881, Fisk University Library; published in Brodhead, ed., *Journals of Charles W. Chesnutt*, 160; Blassingame, ed., *Slave Testimony*, 489; Rawick, ed., *American Slave*, III: S.C. Narr. (Part 3), 165; XI: Mo. Narr., 54. On voting despite intimidation see also Suppl. Ser. 2, IV: Tex. Narr. (Part 2), 724, 782, (Part 3), 1268.

91. Rawick, ed., *American Slave*, Suppl. Ser. 2, I: Ala. Narr., 103; Gilmore, *Gender and Jim Crow*, 130–31; Rawick, ed., *American Slave*, Suppl. Ser. 2, IV: Tex. Narr. (Part 3), 1117. See also Suppl. Ser. 1, V: Tex. Narr. (Part 4), 1456, IX: Miss. Narr. (Part 4), 1400; Testimony of W. E. B. Du Bois, U.S. 57th Cong., 1st sess., *Reports of the Industrial Commission on Immigration* (Washington, D.C., 1901), XV, 168.

92. Rawick, ed., *American Slave*, VIII: Ark. Narr. (Part 1), 244, VII: Miss. Narr., 132., Suppl. Ser. 2, I: Ala. Narr., 110.

93. Rawick, ed., *American Slave,* Suppl. Ser. 1, VI: Miss. Narr. (Part 1), 44, Suppl. Ser. 2, IV: Texas Narr. (Part 3), 1086; Kelly Jackson, Bentonia, Miss., interviewed Aug. 19, 1975, and Mrs. Magnolia Gates, interviewed Sept. 1974 and Aug. 19, 1975, Oral History Project, Yazoo City Public Library, Yazoo, Miss. Magnolia Gates's mother was born about 1874.

94. Rosengarten, *All God's Dangers,* 34–35; Rawick, ed., *American Slave,* Suppl. Ser. 2, II: Tex. Narr. (Part 1), 368.

95. Rawick, ed., *American Slave,* XIII: Ga. Narr. (Part 3), 170, Suppl. Ser. 1, VIII: Miss. Narr. (Part 3), 1089.

96. Clowes, *Black America,* 86.

97. *Raleigh News and Observer,* Oct. 29, 1909, in Hunter Scrapbooks, Box 15, 1885–1929, Charles N. Hunter Papers, Duke University Library; Washington, *Future of the American Negro,* 11.

98. *Proceedings of the National Negro Business League, 1900,* 102.

99. *Southwestern Christian Advocate,* April 5, 1906.

100. Rawick, ed., *American Slave,* Suppl. Ser. 1, VII: Miss. Narr. (Part 2), 552; Supp. Ser. 2, II: Tex. Narr. (Part 1), 59; Suppl. Ser. 1, VI: Miss. Narr. (Part 1), 134.

101. William H. Gardner, Pool, Alabama, to the Hon. President of the United States, July 16, 1904, and an accompanying letter from the Office of the U.S. Attorney, Northern District of Alabama, Birmingham, to the Attorney General of the United States, Aug. 1, 1904, urging court action, Records of the Office of the Attorney General, 38697 (39212), National Archives; *Southwestern Christian Advocate,* April 10, 1902.

102. Archer, *Through Afro-America,* 34–35; *Southwestern Christian Advocate,* March 16, 1899; "Address Delivered on the Occasion of the Celebration of Emancipation Day, Raleigh, N.C., Jan. 1, 1912, ms. copy, Charles N. Hunter Papers, Duke University Library. See also *Georgia Baptist,* repr. *Crisis,* I (Nov. 1910), 8; Rawick, ed., *American Slave,* Suppl. Ser. 1, III: Tex. Narr. (Part 2), 854; Suppl. Ser. 2, I: Ala. Narr., 73–74, III: Tex. Narr. (Part 2), 763.

103. *Raleigh News and Observer,* Jan. 2, 1907, Hunter Scrapbooks, Box 13, 1871–1928, Charles N. Hunter Papers, Duke University Library; *Southwestern Christian Advocate,* Jan. 9, 1902.

104. E. R. Carter, *Black Side: A Partial History of the Business, Religious, and Educational Side of The Negro in Atlanta* (Atlanta, 1894), 289–90; Rawick, ed., *American Slave,* Suppl. Ser. 1, VIII: Miss Narr. (Part 3), 967; Hackney, *Populism to Progressivism in Alabama,* 186.

105. E. J. Carter to Booker T. Washington, July 3, 1887, in Harlan, ed., *Booker T. Washington Papers,* II, 366; Woodward, *Origins of the New South,* 218–19; S. H. Blocker, Editor of *Black and White,* to J. E. Bruce, Oct. 21, 1892, John E. Bruce Papers, Schomburg Center for Research in Black Culture of the New York Public Library.

106. P. B. S. Pinchback to My Dear Doctor, Nov. 25, 1884, Pinchback Papers, Howard University Library; Edwin Redkey, ed., *Respect Black: The Writings and Speeches of Henry McNeal Turner* (New York, 1971), 175; Clarence A. Bacote, "Negro Proscriptions, Protests, and Proposed Solutions in Georgia, 1880–1908," *Journal of Southern History,* XXV (Nov. 1959), 481; Edwin S. Redkey, "Bishop Turner's African Dream," *Journal of American History,* 54 (Sept. 1967), 284.

107. Woodward, *Origins of the New South*, 258; *The True Reformer* (Littleton, N.C.), July 25, 1900.

108. Theodore Roosevelt to Francis Warrington Dawson, Oct. 20, 1911, Francis W. Dawson Papers, Duke University Library. On Taft and lynching violence, see *Crisis*, I (March 1911), 6.

109. Meier, *Negro Thought in America*, 187–88.

110. Alexander Walters, *My Life and Work* (New York, 1917), 184, 195–96. On Woodrow Wilson and black America, see Williamson, *Crucible of Race*, 364–95.

111. McMillen, *Dark Journey*, 58.

112. Blyden Jackson, *The Waiting Years: Essays on American Negro Literature* (Baton Rouge, La., 1976), 3–4. For a study of black Louisville, see George C. Wright, *Life Behind a Veil: Blacks in Louisville, Kentucky, 1865–1930* (Baton Rouge, La., 1985).

113. Baker, *Following the Colour Line*, 41.

114. Mary Church Terrell, "The Duty of the National Association of Colored Women to the Race," in Beverly Washington Jones, *Quest for Equality: The Life and Writings of Mary Eliza Church Terrell, 1863–1954* (Brooklyn, 1990), 144. See also [Elizabeth Lindsay Davis], *Lifting As They Climb: National Association of Colored Women* (Washington, D.C., 1933); Mrs. N. F. Mossell, *The Work of the Afro-American Woman* (Philadelphia, 1908); Cynthia Neverdon-Morton, *Afro-American Women of the South and the Advancement of the Race, 1895–1925* (Knoxville, Tenn., 1989).

115. Elsa Barkley Brown, "Maggie Lena Walker and the Independent Order of Saint Luke: Advancing Women, Race, and Community in Turn-of-the-Century Richmond," in Linda K. Kerber and Jane Sherron De Hart, *Women's America*, 4th ed. (New York, 1995), 231–39.

116. McMillen, *Dark Journey*, 186–90.

117. Baker, *Following the Colour Line*, 40.

118. *Nation*, 105 (Aug. 9, 1917), 144, quoted in Levine, *Black Culture and Black Consciousness*, 245.

119. Davis, *Deep South*, 472.

120. Johnson, *Highways and Byways of the South*, 56–59.

121. W. E. B. Du Bois, ed., *The Negro Church* (Atlanta University Publications No. 8; Atlanta, 1903), 57; Hill, ed., *Black Women Oral History Project*, VIII, 13; Mays, *Born to Rebel*, 11. On the role of women in the church see also Evelyn Brooks Higginbotham, *Righteous Discontent: The Women's Movement in the Black Baptist Church, 1880–1920* (Cambridge, Mass., 1993).

122. Du Bois, *Souls of Black Folk*, 190–91.

123. See, for example, Edward L. Wheeler, *Uplifting the Race: The Black Minister in the New South, 1865–1902* (Lanham, Md., 1986), 17–22.

124. Merritt, *Homecoming*, 51; Wright, *Black Boy*, 113.

125. Beam, *He Called Them by the Lightning*, 31–32; Mays, *Born to Rebel*, 14–15.

126. *Raleigh News and Observer*, Jan. 2, 1917, Hunter Scrapbooks, Charles N. Hunter Papers, Duke University Library.

127. Hurston, *Dust Tracks on a Road*, 60.

128. Winfield Henri Mixon, Diary, entries for Feb. 16, 17, 1903, "Record of Church Activities and Report to Bishop for the Years 1892–1895," Mixon Papers, Duke University Library.

129. Litwack, *Been in the Storm So Long*, 457.

130. Mays, *Born to Rebel*, 15; Davis, *Mississippi Negro Lore*, 16–20.

131. Rawick, ed., *American Slave*, XVIII: Unwritten History of Slavery (Fisk University), 46, 48 (see also Benjamin Mays's impressions of his pastor in *Born to Rebel*, 14–17); Stanford, *Tragedy of the Negro in America*, 135.

132. See, for example, William Wells Brown, *My Southern Home; or, the South and Its People* (Boston, 1880), 191–93.

133. Charles W. Chesnutt, "A Novel Idea in Preaching," in Manuscript Journal and Note-Book II, 1877–81, entry for March 25, 1880, Fisk University Library; published in Brodhead, ed., *Journals of Charles W. Chesnutt*, 129–31. For the fate of Elder Davis see Journal, III, Jan. 15, 1881 (Brodhead, ed., *Journals of Charles W. Chesnutt*, 158–59).

134. Beam, *He Called Them by the Lightning*, 31–32; Gibson and Crogman, *Progress of a Race*, 447; Franklin B. Mallard, Raleigh, N.C., to Charles Smith, Savannah, Ga., May 23, 1906, Smith-Shivery Family Papers, Schomburg Center for Research in Black Culture of the New York Public Library.

135. Paul W. Harvey, "Southern Baptists and Southern Culture, 1865–1920" (Ph.D. diss., University of California, Berkeley, 1992), 344, 352–53. Published as *Redeeming the South: Religious Cultures and Racial Identities Among Southern Baptists, 1865–1925* (Chapel Hill, N.C., 1997).

136. "The Colored Ministry: Its Defects and Needs" in Harlan, ed., *Booker T. Washington Papers*, III, 72–73; *Proceedings of the National Negro Business League, 1900*, 209.

137. "The Colored Ministry: Its Defects and Needs" in Harlan, ed., *Booker T. Washington Papers*, III, 71–75. The article appeared in *Christian Union*, 42 (Aug. 14, 1890), 199–200, and Washington also gave a speech on the same subject at the Fisk commencement in June 1890. For responses to Washington's article see III, 97–98 (Daniel A. Payne, a bishop of the A.M.E. Church); 114–15 (Frances J. Grimke); and 116–17, 119–20, and a defense by Washington of his position, 101–3. For similar sentiments see also *Southern Workman*, 18 (1899), 329–30 (Frances J. Grimke).

138. Harvey, "Southern Baptists and Southern Culture," 387, 394.

139. *Proceedings of the National Negro Business League, 1900*, 106.

140. Harvey, "Southern Baptists and Southern Culture," 387–89.

141. Perdue et al., eds., *Weevils in the Wheat*, 69; Mays, *Born to Rebel*, 16; Terrill and Hirsch, eds., *Such As Us*, 263.

142. Harvey, "Southern Baptists and Southern Culture," 396–97, 398.

143. Litwack, *Been in the Storm So Long*, 470; Harvey, "Southern Baptists and Southern Culture," 370.

144. Harvey, "Southern Baptists and Southern Culture," 370–71, 374–75; Wheeler, *Uplifting the Race*, 80–83; Bacote, "Negro Proscriptons, Protests, and Proposed Solutions in Georgia," 481.

145. Winfield Henri Mixon, Ms. Diary, Jan. 22, 1895, Mixon Papers, Duke University Library. On accommodation and protest in the church see also Rabinowitz, *Race Relations in the Urban South*, 217–20.

146. *Southern Workman*, 28 (1899), 34; Leon Paul Blouet ("Max O'Rell"), *A Frenchman in America (the Anglo-Saxon race revisited)* (Bristol and London, 1891?), 309.

147. Holsey, "Learning How to Be Black," 425.

148. John Dittmer, "The Education of Henry McNeal Turner, in Leon Litwack and August Meier, eds., *Black Leaders of the Nineteenth Century* (Urbana, 1988), 261, 265.

149. Dittmer, "The Education of Henry McNeal Turner," in Litwack and Meier, eds., *Black Leaders of the Nineteenth Century*, 260–61; *Baltimore American*, May 12, 1884, in *The North Carolina Republican and Civil Rights Advocate* (Weldon, N.C.), May 22, 1884.

150. Crew, *From Field to Factory*, 26.

151. James A. Whitted to Charles N. Hunter, Nov. 24, 1890, Charles N. Hunter Papers, Duke University Library.

152. Charles W. Chesnutt, Manuscript Journal and Note-Book, II, 1877–81, entry for March 25, 1880, Fisk University Library; published in Brodhead, ed., *Journals of Charles W. Chesnutt*, 131–32.

153. Du Bois, ed., *The Negro Church*, 161; Levine, *Black Culture and Black Consciousness*, 161–62.

154. Daniel Wolff et al., *You Send Me: The Life and Times of Sam Cooke* (New York, 1995), 7–17; Anthony Heilbut, *The Gospel Sound* (New York, 1975), 174–75.

155. Wolff, *You Send Me*, 12–13.

156. Du Bois, *Autobiography*, 120; Olivia A. Davidson to Mary Berry, Sept. 12, 1881, in Harlan, ed., *Booker T. Washington Papers*, II, 148; Hurston, *Dust Tracks on a Road*, 277–82; Thomas, *My Story in Black and White*, 16; Hill, ed., *Black Women Oral History Project*, VIII, 16. On experiencing revivals see also Wright, *Black Boy*, 167–71.

157. Mays, *Born to Rebel*, 15–16.

158. Rawick, ed., *American Slave*, II: S.C. Narr. (Part 1), 53; Robinson, *Road Without Turning*, 35; Wright, *87 Years Behind the Black Curtain*, 71; Odum and Johnson, *Negro and His Songs*, 109; Tom Amis, Duck Pond, Madison Parish, La., to Bettie, Feb. 24, 1870. Elizabeth A. C. (Hooper) Blanchard Papers, Southern Historical Collection, University of North Carolina.

159. Karl Lemmermann, "Improvized Negro Songs," *The New Republic*, XIII (Dec. 22, 1917), 214; Odum and Johnson, *Negro and His Songs*, 49; Terrill and Hirsch, eds., *Such As Us*, 80, 84–85.

160. Stephen Graham, "Marching Through Georgia: Following Sherman's Footsteps To-Day," *Harper's Magazine*, CXL (April 1920), 616; J. Mason Brewer, *Worser Days and Better Times: The Folklore of the North Carolina Negro* (Chicago, 1965), 103; Belden and Hudson, eds., *Folk Songs from North Carolina*, in White, ed., *Frank C. Brown Collection of North Carolina Folklore*, III, 617.

161. Blassingame, ed., *Slave Testimony*, 646, 655.

162. Beam, *He Called Them by the Lightning*, 63–64.

163. Wright, *Black Boy*, 113; Hurston, *Dust Tracks on a Road*, 274–83.

164. Levine, *Black Culture and Black Consciousness*, 326; Blassingame, ed., *Slave Testimony*, 646.

165. Robinson, *Road Without Turning*, 27, 49.

166. Wells, *Crusade for Justice*, 22; Terrill and Hirsch, eds., *Such As Us*, 232.

167. White, *American Negro Folk Songs*, 391.

168. Ernest J. Gaines, "The Sky Is Gray," in *Bloodline* (New York, 1968), 95–102.

CHAPTER EIGHT

1. Oliver, *Blues Fell This Morning*, 23.
2. W.E.B. Du Bois, *Dusk of Dawn: The Autobiography of W.E.B. Du Bois* (New York, 1940), 67; "My Evolving Program for Negro Freedom," in Logan, *What The Negro Wants*, 53; Du Bois, *Autobiography*, 222.
3. Harlan, *Booker T. Washington: Making of a Black Leader*, 262–63.
4. Addie W. Hunton, *William Alphaeus Hunton: A Pioneer Prophet of Young Men* (New York, 1938), 132–33.
5. Timothy E. Fulop, " 'The Future Golden Day of the Race': Millennialism and Black Americans in the Nadir, 1877–1901," *Harvard Theological Review*, 84 (1991), 75–76.
6. Gatewood, *Black Americans and the White Man's Burden*, 287.
7. The material on Robert Charles and the New Orleans riot is based on William Ivy Hair, *Carnival of Fury: Robert Charles and the New Orleans Race Riot of 1900* (Baton Rouge, 1976); in addition, I have examined three of the leading newspapers, the *Daily Picayune*, the *Times-Democrat*, and the *Daily States*, for the period from July 24 to August 10, 1900. I have also read the black newspaper *Southwestern Christian Advocate* for the period 1890 to 1917. Except for some editorial admonishments, it had little to say about Robert Charles.
8. On black reactions to Charles, see the *Times-Democrat (New Orleans)*, July 25, 26, 1900, and *Southwestern Christian Advocate*, Aug. 2, 16, 1900.
9. *Daily States*, Aug. 7, 1900; *Times-Democrat*, July 25, 1900.
10. Alan Lomax, *Mister Jelly Roll: The Fortunes of Jelly Roll Morton, New Orleans Creole and "Inventor of Jazz"* (New York, 1950), 56–57.
11. "Cross Road Blues," *Robert Johnson: The Complete Recordings* (C2K 46222 Columbia). More than once in his travels, W. C. Handy recalled, he encountered a sign saying, "Nigger don't let the sun go down on you here." Handy, *Father of the Blues*, 86.
12. *Official Compilation of Proceedings of the Afro-American League National Convention, Held at Chicago, January 15, 16, 17, 1890* (Chicago, 1890), 24; Archer, *Through Afro-America*, 234. On the floor of the House of Representatives, George H. White, the last of the post-Reconstruction black congressmen, declared on February 23, 1900, "Possibly at no time in the history of our freedom has the effort been made to mould public sentiment against us and our progress so strongly as it is now being done." *Congressional Record*, 51st Cong., 1st sess., 2152.
13. Nathans, "Gotta Mind to Move, a Mind to Settle Down," 220.
14. Terrill and Hirsch, eds., *Such As Us*, 56.
15. Blassingame, ed., *Slave Testimony*, 653; Clowes, *Black America*, 11.
16. Cohn, *Where I Was Born and Raised*, 276–77; Wright, *87 Years Behind the Black Curtain*, 74. Some years later, Louisiana native Walker Percy conceded that a white Southerner looks at a Negro twice in his life: "[O]nce when he is a child and sees his nurse for the first time; second, when he is dying and there is a Negro with him to

change his bedclothes." During the intervening years, although he sees blacks every day, they remain essentially invisible to him. *The Last Gentleman* (New York, 1966), 195.

17. Baker, *Following the Colour Line*, 39.

18. Baker, *Following the Colour Line*, 38–39.

19. Davis, *Mississippi Negro Lore*, 8–9; Rosengarten, *All God's Dangers*, 545.

20. Oster, *Living Country Blues*, 44.

21. Rawick, ed., *The American Slave*, XVIII: Unwritten History of Slavery, 22; Ralph Ellison, *Going to the Territory* (New York, 1986), 99; Wright, *Black Boy*, 162.

22. Charles W. Chesnutt, Manuscript Journal and Note-Book III, 1881–82, entry for March 7, 1882, Fisk University Library; published in Brodhead, ed., *Journals of Charles W. Chesnutt*, 172.

23. Blassingame, ed., *Slave Testimony*, 535.

24. Mays, *Born to Rebel*, 33; Wright, *Black Boy*, 150–51, 171.

25. Brown and Owens, *Toting the Lead Row*, 85; McMillen, *Dark Journey*, 49; Krech, *Praise the Bridge That Carries You Over*, xxi. For other examples of blacks adopting a policy of caution, circumspection, and resignation, see Rawick, ed., *American Slave*, II: S.C. Narr. (Part 2), 151; Suppl. Ser. 1, VIII: Miss. Narr. (Part 3), 806; Suppl. Ser. 2, III: Tex. Narr. (Part 2), 650–51.

26. Nathans, "Gotta Mind to Move, a Mind to Settle Down," 220; Johnson, *Highways and Byways of the Mississippi Valley*, 86.

27. Blassingame, ed., *Slave Testimony*, 488; Rawick, ed., *American Slave*, XVIII: *Unwritten History of Slavery*, 118.

28. *Southwestern Christian Advocate*, July 21, Dec. 18, 1902. The same newspaper on December 18 quoted a white woman in Atlanta who felt annoyed at seeing so many well-dressed young blacks in the city. But the paper placed their own interpretation on her description of "new-fangled Niggers," calling it "a designation of honor." "She must have been impressed that they looked and acted differently from the Negro to which she was accustomed. To her they were new in their appearance and new in their conduct; not the Negro she had seen in her kitchen and not the one she had seen lounging about the street corner; not the one she had read of in the daily papers, nor was it he of whom she had heard as frequenting the dives and crowding the courtrooms. No indeed, it was an entirely new individual."

29. David Evans, *Big Road Blues: Tradition and Creativity in the Folk Blues* (Berkeley, Calif., 1982), 19.

30. *Southwestern Christian Advocate*, March 23, 1899; Archibald H. Grimke, *The Ultimate Criminal*. Occasional Papers, No. 17, The American Negro Academy (Washington, D.C., 1915), 6.

31. *Fort Worth Hornet*, October 25, 1919, in Kerlin, *Voice of the Negro*, 27.

32. *Mobile Southern Watchman*, June 1, 8, 1901, quoted in Hackney, *Populism to Progressivism in Alabama*, 197; Charles W. Chesnutt to Booker T. Washington, Oct. 19, 1908, Charles W. Chesnutt Papers, Fisk University Library.

33. Rosengarten, *All God's Dangers*, 542–43.

34. L. C. Dorsey, "Harder Times Than These," in Abbott, ed., *Mississippi Writers: Reflections of Childhood and Youth*, II, 168.

35. Rosengarten, *All God's Dangers,* 27–28, 116; Wright, *Black Boy,* 138; Hill, ed., *Black Women Oral History Project,* I, 212; Mays, *Born to Rebel,* 33; Davis, *Communist Councilman from Harlem,* 38, 42.

36. James Farmer, *Lay Bare the Heart: An Autobiography of the Civil Rights Movement* (New York, 1985), 58, 65. For generational conflicts see also Hosea Hudson, *Black Worker in the Deep South,* 6–7.

37. *Fisk Herald,* VII (October 1889), 11–12, VII (March 1889), 12, quoted in Rabinowitz, *Race Relations in the Urban South,* 335. On white-black relations becoming "less intimate and friendly" see also Kelly Miller in *Southern Workman,* XXVIII (July 1899), 247.

38. *Crisis,* 8 (Aug. 1916), 180.

39. Wright, *Black Boy,* 64–65. Some two decades later, Wright would weave the essentials of this incident into a story depicting a black mother using the same tactic to avenge the torture of her son, a Communist Party organizer in the South. "Bright and Morning Star" in *Uncle Tom's Children,* expanded ed. (New York, 1938), 321–84.

40. Abraham Middleton, Manuscript Diary, South Caroliniana Library, University of South Carolina. Middleton was a black A.M.E. minister and conference official serving churches principally in the Pee Dee and Summerville regions.

41. J. H. Coleman, St. Louis, Mo., to Booker T. Washington, July 12, 1897, in Harlan and Smock, eds., *Booker T. Washington Papers,* IV, 314.

42. *Southwestern Christian Advocate,* Feb. 10, Dec. 15, 1898.

43. Allen W. Jones, "The Black Press in the 'New South': Jesse C. Duke's Struggle for Justice and Equality," *Journal of Negro History,* LXIV (Summer 1979), 215–28; Rabinowitz, *Race Relations in the Urban South,* 234; Wells, *Southern Horrors,* 23; Wells, *Crusade for Justice,* 62; Mays, *Born to Rebel,* 12.

44. Almost every issue of *Crisis* between 1910 and World War I reported some violent clash between armed whites and blacks, most of them stemming from the efforts of blacks to protect their people from arrest and lynchings. See, e.g., *Crisis,* I (Dec. 1910), 10; 2 (Oct. 1911), 233; 3 (Nov. 1911), 12, (Dec. 1911), 56; 11 (April 1916), 293–96. The *Chicago Defender* also reported such clashes with increasing frequency. See, e.g., Mar. 7, May 16, 1914, May 8, June 19, 1915. See also *Southwestern Christian Advocate,* Dec. 1, 15, 1898, Mar. 31, 1904; Clowes, *Black America,* 135–36, 137; [J. R. Coffey] (name deleted from letter), Wewoka, Okla., to Chapin Brinsmmade, Nov. 29, 1913, NAACP Papers, Manuscript Division, Library of Congress. For narrative tales of blacks defending their rights see also Levine, *Black Culture and Black Consciousness,* 398–99.

45. Dittmer, *Black Georgia,* 138; Rabinowitz, "The Conflict Between Blacks and the Police in the Urban South," 72.

46. W. Fitzhugh Brundage, "The Darien Insurrection of 1889," *Georgia Historical Quarterly,* 74 (Summer 1990), 234–53; *Southwestern Christian Advocate,* Aug. 31, Sept. 14, 1899.

47. McMillen, *Dark Journey,* 225–26; *Crisis,* 1 (March 1911), 10; *Chicago Defender,* Oct. 28, 1916; *Atlanta Constitution,* Mar. 22, 1906.

48. Wells, *Crusade for Justice,* 18–20; R. [Rosalie] Du Bose to John W. Du Bose, June 6, 1911, John W. Du Bose Papers, Alabama State Archives, Montgomery (for a similar incident, see *Chicago Defender,* Nov. 29, 1913); *Crisis,* 7 (March 1914), 222.

49. Edwards, "Sexual Violence, Gender, Reconstruction, and the Extension of Patriarchy in Granville County, North Carolina," 5; *Chicago Defender,* June 29, 1912.

50. Clowes, *Black America,* 104; *Southwestern Christian Advocate,* March 31, 1904; J. D. McConnico, Winton, Hertford County, N.C., to James L. Anderson, Feb. 27, 1889, James L. Anderson Papers. North Carolina Historical Archives, Raleigh. A graphic description of an insurrection panic in North Carolina may be found in the recollection of Roger T. Stevenson in Terrill and Hirsch, eds., *Such As Us,* 263.

51. Interview with James Plunkett, a former resident of Virginia, in Crew, *Field to Factory,* 12.

52. McMillen, *Dark Journey,* 175–76.

53. Stone, *Studies in the American Race Problem,* 434, 435.

54. Emmett J. Scott, *Negro Migration During the War* (New York, 1920), 30–33.

55. Clowes, *Black America,* 141–42; Wells, *Southern Horrors,* 5–6; I. Garland Penn, *The Afro-American Press and Its Editors* (Springfield, Mass., 1891), 302; Harlan, ed., *Booker T. Washington Papers,* II, 325–26. See also Jones, "The Black Press in the 'New South,'" 215–28. In his editorial, Duke concluded, "If something is not done to break up these lynchings it will be so that after a while they will lynch every coloured man that looks at a white woman with a twinkle in his eye."

56. McMillen, *Dark Journey,* 176.

57. Wells, *Southern Horrors,* 4–5; *Crusade for Justice,* 35–69.

58. Charles W. Chesnutt to Booker T. Washington, June 27, 1903, Charles W. Chesnutt Papers, Fisk University Library.

59. Paul Laurence Dunbar, *Lyrics of Lowly Life* (New York, 1896), 167.

60. "Me And My Captain," in Lawrence Gellert, ed., *"Me and My Captain": Negro Songs of Protest* (New York, 1939), 5.

61. Ellison, *Going to the Territory,* 100–101.

62. Wright, *Black Boy,* 172.

63. McMillen, *Dark Journey,* 283; Bailey, *Race Orthodoxy in the South,* 296.

64. Rosengarten, *All God's Dangers,* 390, 545.

65. Rawick, ed., *American Slave,* XVIII: *Unwritten History of Slavery,* 71; Tucker, *Telling Memories,* 173.

66. Ellison, *Shadow and Act,* 83. More than likely, Ellison thought, the last attitude came the closest to reflecting Wright's position, although he failed to act on it and found comfort instead in the thought of leaving the South altogether.

67. Beam, *He Called Them by the Lightning,* 45; Levine, *Black Culture and Black Consciousness,* 253.

68. *New Orleans Daily States,* Aug. 8, 1900.

69. Baker, *Following the Colour Line,* 47; Calt and Wardlow, *King of the Delta Blues,* 95.

70. "Cocaine Habit" in Odum and Johnson, *The Negro and His Songs,* 218.

71. Williamson, *Crucible of Race,* 210.

72. Macrae, *America Revisited,* 54; Charles Trotter Lassiter, Petersburg, Va., to Joseph B. Earnest, Jr., Feb. 5, 1914, Daniel William Lassiter, Francis Rives Lassiter, and Charles Trotter Lassiter Papers, Duke University Library.

73. "Negro Class Distinctions," *Southern Workman,* XXVIII (October 1899), 372; "Possible Remedies for Lynching," *Southern Workman,* XXVIII (November 1899),

421; *Raleigh News and Observer,* Jan. 2, 1917, Hunter Scrapbooks, "Address Delivered on the Occasion of the Celebration of Emancipation Day, Raleigh, North Carolina, January 1, 1912," manuscript copy, Charles N. Hunter Papers, Duke University Library.

74. Ayers, *Vengeance and Justice,* 244.

75. "Life History of Leila Holmes, Columbia, South Carolina," Federal Writers' Project, Works Progress Administration, South Carolina, South Caroliniana Library, University of South Carolina. For critical observations by blacks on the "younger generation" see also Johnson, *Highways and Byways of the Mississippi Valley,* 64–65. For descriptions of black "low life" in the urban South see Paul De Rousiers, *American Life* (Paris and New York, 1892), 141; Johnston, *The Negro in the New World,* 457–60; Baker, *Following the Colour Line,* 56–57, 60–61; Atkins, *Age of Jim Crow,* 42.

76. Griggs, *Race Question in a New Light,* 23–25.

77. For the best discussion of this subject, see "Bad Men and Bandits," in Levine, *Black Culture and Black Consciousness,* 407–26.

78. Odum and Johnson, *Negro and His Songs,* 164.

79. Levine, *Black Culture and Black Consciousness,* 408.

80. Levine, *Black Culture and Black Consciousness,* 410–11.

81. Odum and Johnson, *Negro and His Songs,* 201, 286.

82. Levine, *Black Culture and Black Consciousness,* 412–14; Lomax, *Mister Jelly Roll,* 55.

83. Levine, *Black Culture and Black Consciousness,* 410–12, 414–15.

84. Richard Wright, *How "Bigger" Was Born* (New York, 1940), 3–6.

85. Henry D. Spalding, *Encyclopedia of Black Folklore and Humor* (Middle Village, N.Y., 1972), 368–69; Al-Tony Gilmore, *Bad Nigger! The National Impact of Jack Johnson* (Port Washington, N.Y., 1975), 29, 32. The best account of the life and times of Johnson is Randy Roberts, *Papa Jack: Jack Johnson and the Era of White Hopes* (New York, 1983). For the Johnson-Burns bout, see Jack Johnson, *Jack Johnson—In the Ring—And Out* (Chicago, 1927), 155–68; Nat Fleischer, *Black Dynamite* (5 vols.; New York, 1938–1947), IV: "Fighting Furies": Story of the Golden Era of Jack Johnson, Sam Langford, and Their Negro Contemporaries, 68–73; Finis Farr, *Black Champion: The Life and Times of Jack Johnson* (London, 1964), 34–62; and Roberts, *Papa Jack,* 54–66.

86. Farr, *Black Champion,* 107; Johnson, *Jack Johnson,* 183.

87. Gilmore, *Bad Nigger!,* 38.

88. For the Johnson-Jeffries bout see Johnson, *Jack Johnson,* 169–87; Fleischer, *Black Dynamite,* IV: "Fighting Furies": Story of the Golden Era of Jack Johnson, Sam Langford, and Their Negro Contemporaries, 75–97; Farr, *Black Champion,* 63–114; Roberts, *Papa Jack,* 85–86, 89–107; Fraser, *America, Old and New,* 218–19.

89. Armstrong, *Satchmo,* 36; Wright, *Black Boy,* 253; Mays, *Born to Rebel,* 19.

90. Gilmore, *Bad Nigger!,* 19, 44, 59–72.

91. *Chicago Defender,* July 30, 1910.

92. Mays, *Born to Rebel,* 19.

93. Levine, *Black Culture and Black Consciousness,* 433.

94. Emmet Jay Scott to J. Frank Wheaton, March 23, 1909, in Harlan and Smock, eds., *Booker T. Washington Papers,* X, 75–76.

95. Gilmore, *Bad Nigger!*, 89–90.

96. "Jack Johnson and Jim Jeffries," in Brewer, *Worser Days and Better Times*, 178.

97. Du Bois, *Souls of Black Folk*, 177–79.

98. Bruce, *Plantation Negro as a Freeman*, 90–91; A. T. Montgomery, Diary, entry for April 27, 1908, Mississippi State Archives, Jackson.

99. Ayers, *Vengeance and Justice*, 209, 210; Rabinowitz, "The Conflict Between Blacks and the Police in the Urban South," 73; "Does Anyone Else Conceal Crime," an editorial in *Southwestern Christian Advocate*, July 16, 1903.

100. Baker, *Following the Colour Line*, 49. On black perceptions of law enforcement officials collaborating in lynchings see *Savannah Tribune*, Jan. 2, 1892, quoted in Ayers, *Vengeance and Justice*, 245–46.

101. Ayers, *Vengeance and Justice*, 228.

102. William H. Felton, "An Epitomized Hell," in Mrs. William H. [Rebecca] Felton, *"My Memoirs of Georgia Politics"* (Atlanta, 1911), 587, 589–90; Archer, *Through Afro-America*, 100–101; Wright, *Black Boy*, 176.

103. Odum and Johnson, *Negro Workaday Songs*, 18; Odum and Johnson, *The Negro and His Songs*, 5, 164, 173; W. H. Thomas, *Some Current Folk-Songs of the Negro* (Folk-Lore Society of Texas, 1912), 9.

104. Handy, *Father of the Blues*, 72–74, 76–77.

105. Sandra Lieb, *Mother of the Blues: A Study of Ma Rainey* (Amherst, Mass., 1981), 3.

106. Bechet, *Treat It Gentle*, 106–8.

107. Calt and Wardlow, *King of the Delta Blues*, 110. On the life and work of Patton, see also Palmer, *Deep Blues*, 48–54, 56–79, 82–89, and David Evans, "Charley Patton: The Conscience of the Delta," in Sacre, ed., *Voice of the Delta*, 109–214.

108. Various versions of this song, said to have been part of his repertoire by 1910, may be found in Evans, "Charley Patton: The Conscience of the Delta," in Sacre, ed., *Voice of the Delta*, 181–82; Michael Taft, ed., *Blues Lyric Poetry: An Anthology* (New York, 1983), 211, and *Charley Patton: Founder of the Delta Blues* (Yazoo Records CD 1020).

109. Giles Oakley, *The Devil's Music: A History of the Blues* (New York, 1977), 55; Evans, "Charley Patton: The Conscience of the Delta," in Sacre, ed., *The Voice of the Delta*, 145.

110. Calt and Wardlow, *King of the Delta Blues*, 110, 144–45.

111. "Elder Greene Blues," *King of the Delta Blues: The Music of Charlie Patton* (Yazoo CD 2001).

112. "Moon Going Down," *Charley Patton: Founder of the Delta Blues* (Yazoo CD 1020); Calt and Wardlow, *King of the Delta Blues*, 60.

113. Paul Oliver, *Savannah Syncopators: African Retentions in the Blues* (London, 1970), 93; John S. Otto and Augustus M. Burns, "Roadhouses," in Charles Reagan Wilson and William Ferris, eds., *Encyclopedia of Southern Culture* (Chapel Hill, N.C., 1989), 1238–39; Paul Oliver, liner notes for *Juke Joint Blues* (Blues Classics BC23), repr. Paul Oliver, *Blues Off the Record: Thirty Years of Blues Commentary* (New York, 1984), 45–47. The term "honky-tonk" appeared as early as 1894 in an Ardmore, Oklahoma, newspaper, referring to an event "well attended by ball-heads, bachelors, and leading citizens."

114. Evans, "Charley Patton: The Conscience of the Delta," in Sacre, ed., *Voice of the Delta*, 143.

115. Handy, *Father of the Blues*, 10–11; Calt and Wardlow, *King of the Delta Blues*, 109–10; Evans, "Charley Patton: The Conscience of the Delta," in Sacre, ed., *Voice of the Delta*, 141; Woods, *Negro in Etiquette*, 131–33.

116. Mark Thomas, "I'm a Roamin' Rambler," *Jazz Quarterly*, II, No. 4 (1944), 18; Paul Oliver, *Conversation with the Blues* (New York, 1965), 30.

117. Ishman Bracey, "Trouble-Hearted Blues," in Taft, *Blues Lyric Poetry*, 38.

118. *New Orleans Picayune*, quoted in *Boston Morning Post*, January 1, 1840. I am grateful to Dale Cockrell and Randall Burkett for calling this item to my attention.

119. Calt and Wardlow, *King of the Delta Blues*, 143.

120. "Preaching Blues," *Robert Johnson: The Complete Recordings* (Disc 2, Columbia CD C2K 46222). W. C. Handy wrote a song copyrighted in 1915, "Shoeboot's Serenade," which included these lines:

I woke up this morning with the Blues all 'round my bed

Thinking about what you, my baby, said.

Do say the word and give my poor heart ease,

The Blues ain't nothing but a fatal heart disease. . . .

Handy, *Father of the Blues*, 144–45.

121. Levine, *Black Culture and Black Consciousness*, 256.

122. Sterling Brown, "The Blues As Folk Poetry," in Langston Hughes and Arna Bontemps, eds., *The Book of Negro Folklore* (New York, 1965), 385.

123. Oliver, *Conversation with the Blues*, 165.

124. Oakley, *Devil's Music*, 92.

125. Oster, *Living Blues*, 43.

126. Levine, *Black Culture and Black Consciousness*, 418.

127. Odum and Johnson, *Negro and His Songs*, 188.

128. Robert Johnson, "Stones in My Passway," in *The Blues Line: A Collection of Blues Lyrics*, comp. Eric Sackheim (New York, 1969), 219, and *Robert Johnson: King of the Delta Blues Singers* (Columbia Records, CL 1654).

129. Levine, *Black Culture and Black Consciousness*, 252; Odum and Johnson, *Negro and His Songs*, 164.

130. For "Chippie" Hill's rendition of the song, see "Trouble in Mind," in *Bertha "Chippie" Hill: Complete Recorded Works, 1925–1929* (Document Records: DOCD-5330).

131. Recently published literary anthologies have begun to correct the omission of blues lyrics. See, for example, Henry Louis Gates, Jr., and Nellie Y. McKay, eds., *The Norton Anthology of African American Literature* (New York, 1997), 22–36.

132. Woodward, *Origins of the New South*, 368. See, for example, *Raleigh News and Observer*, Jan. 2, 1913, reporting a semicentennial emancipation celebration in which the main speaker addressed the progress of the race since 1863. For a more scholarly contemporary assessment see American Academy of Political and Social Science, *The Negro's Progress in Fifty Years* (Philadelphia, 1913).

133. *Crisis*, 5 (Jan. 1913), 128–29; Booker T. Washington, "Industrial Education and the Public Schools" in American Academy of Political and Social Science, *The Negro's Progress in Fifty Years*, 219–32.

134. Du Bois, *Souls of Black Folk*, 3–4.

135. Litwack, *Been in the Storm So Long*, 540–41; Emma Lou Thornbrough, *T. Thomas Fortune: Militant Journalist* (Chicago, 1972), 131–35; Walters, *My Life and Work*, 201.

136. Robert H. Terrell to J. E. Bruce, Sept. 29, 1896, Alexander Crummell to J. E. Bruce, March 22, 1898, John E. Bruce Papers, Schomburg Center for Research in Black Culture of the New York Public Library.

137. "Spell It with a Capital," in *Weekly Louisianan*, Dec. 7, 1878; Walters, *My Life and Work*, 200; Gilmore, *Gender and Jim Crow*, 15. For a defense of "colored" as the preferred term see, for example, Bruce, *The New Man*, 128–29.

138. Booker T. Washington to Hamilton Holt, May 31, 1907, Booker T. Washington Papers, Schomburg Center for Research in Black Culture of the New York Public Library. ("I very much hope that the *Independent* will soon get to the point where it will use a capital "N" in printing the word "Negro."); Johnson, *A School History of the Negro Race in America*, rev. ed. (1897), v; Crogman, *Progress of a Race*, 20.

139. *Crisis*, 35 (March 1928), 96–97. For a similar endorsement of "Negro" see "By What Name Shall We Be Called?" in *Southwestern Christian Advocate*, April 13, 1905.

140. *The New Era*, Feb. 3, 1870; *Richmond Planet*, Jan. 13, 1900 (Straightine); *Washington Bee*, June 9, 1909 (Kink-ine), Dec. 19, 1909 (Dixie Liquid Bleach); *New Orleans Southern Republican* (Black Skin Remover). For similar ads see *Washington Bee* (Nelson's Hair Dressing); *Baltimore Afro-American Ledger*, Aug. 10, 1901 (Ozono Hair Tonic), Nov. 9, 1901 (Miro Hair Invigorator and Straightener); *Indianapolis Freeman*, Nov. 11, 1893 (Mme. Turner's Mystic Face Bleach); *New Orleans Crusader* (Monesia Hair Invigorator and Magic Balm).

141. Helen Jackson Lee, *Nigger in the Window* (New York, 1978), 84, 89.

142. "The Democratic Victory" in Redkey, ed., *Respect Black*, 72; Griggs, *The Race Question in a New Light*, 15–16.

143. Johnson, *A School History of the Negro Race in America* (1891 ed.), 16.

144. Crogman, *Progress of a Race*, 559–60. For similar sentiments see Bruce, *The New Man*, 132–33, and Campbell, *White and Black in the United States*, 296–97.

145. Charles Steward, "Colored American Soldiers," *Southern Workman*, XXVIII (August 1899), 290–91; Bruce, *The New Man*, 132.

146. Gatewood, *Black Americans and the White Man's Burden*, 24, 26; *Southwestern Christian Advocate*, April 14, 1898.

147. George P. Marks III, "Opposition of Negro Newspapers to American Philippine Policy, 1899–1900," *The Midwest Journal*, IV (Winter 1951–52), 15. See also George P. Marks III, ed., *The Black Press Views American Imperialism (1898–1900)* (New York, 1971).

148. Gatewood, *Black Americans and the White Man's Burden*, 85, 34, 31, 82–83. On the mobilization of blacks, including the campaign for black officers, see Gatewood, *Black Americans and the White Man's Burden*, 64–101; *Southwestern Christian Advocate*, April 27, 1899.

149. Marks, "Opposition of Negro Newspapers to American Philippine Policy," 17, and the entire article and Marks, *The Black Press Views American Imperialism*, for similar expressions of opinion.

150. Gatewood, *Black Americans and the White Man's Burden*, 184, 212, 219, 220; Marks, "Opposition of Negro Newspapers to American Philippine Policy," 17. The story about the black officer was also given prominent mention in a black newspaper in Washington, D.C., edited by Alexander L. Manly. He had only recently edited a newspaper in Wilmington, North Carolina, but his "incendiary" article on white womanhood so outraged whites that they forced him to flee into exile in the North.

151. Sgt. [inked out], Troop [inked out], Cavalry, Gibara, Cuba, to John E. Bruce, June 22, 1899, John E. Bruce Papers, Schomburg Center for Research in Black Culture of the New York Public Library; Marks, "Opposition of Negro Newspapers to American Philippine Policy," 21; Robert Leon Campbell to Booker T. Washington, Christmas Eve 1900, in Harlan and Smock, eds., *Booker T. Washington Papers*, V, 695. See also Gatewood, *Black Americans and the White Man's Burden*, 130–31, 220, 278, 282, 284–85.

152. Mrs. W. H. [Rebecca] Felton, "The Race Problem in the United States" [1898?], Rebecca Felton Papers, University of Georgia Library; Gatewood, *Black Americans and the White Man's Burden*, 73–74, 130, 136, 142; Col. R. C. Croxton, Camp Haskell, Macon, Ga., to Francis R. Lassiter, Jan. 2, 1899, Daniel William Lassiter, Francis Rives Lassiter, and Charles Trotter Lassiter Papers, Duke University Library. On treatment of black nurses returning after the war see *Southwestern Christian Advocate*, Sept. 29, 1898.

153. *Southwestern Christian Advocate*, Aug. 25, Dec. 8, 1898; Gatewood, *Black Americans and the White Man's Burden*, 45–55, 116–18, 129–53.

154. Crogman, *Progress of a Race*, 131–46; *Southern Workman*, XXVIII (Aug. 1899), 292–94; Edward A. Johnson, *History of Negro Soldiers in the Spanish-American War* (Raleigh, N.C., 1899); Theophilus G. Steward, *The Colored Regulars in the United States Army* (Philadelphia, 1904); and *Southwestern Christian Advocate*, Dec. 8, 1898, responding to criticism of the conduct of black soldiers.

155. Perdue et al., eds., *Weevils in the Wheat*, 57; *Raleigh News and Observer*, Jan. 2, 1913, Hunter Scrapbooks, Box 13, 1871–1928, Charles N. Hunter Papers, Duke University Library; Willard B. Gatewood, Jr., *Smoked Yankees and the Struggle for Empire: Letters from Negro Soldiers, 1898–1902* (Urbana, Ill., 1971), 44–45, 49–50; Gatewood, *Black Americans and the White Man's Burden*, 106–7, 201–3, 241–43; Sgt. [name inked out], Troop [inked out], Cavalry, Gibara, Cuba, to John E. Bruce, June 22, 1899. John E. Bruce Papers, the Schomburg Center for Research in Black Culture of the New York Public Library.

156. "The Quarrel with Spain," in Redkey, ed., *Respect Black*, 173–74; Gatewood, *Black Americans and the White Man's Burden*, 110.

157. Gatewood, *Black Americans and the White Man's Burden*, 197.

158. Gatewood, *Black Americans and the White Man's Burden*, 110; "An Address at the National Peace Jubilee," Oct. 16, 1898, in Harlan, ed., *Booker T. Washington Papers*, IV, 490–92.

159. *Nation*, LXVI (May 5, 1898), 335; manuscript journal kept by Theophilus G. Steward, Luzon, Philippine Islands, 1900; manuscript, "The Color Problem World Wide," Theophilus G. Steward Papers, Schomburg Center for Research in Black Culture of the New York Public Library.

160. Blassingame, ed., *Slave Testimony*, 675.

161. Rosengarten, *All God's Dangers*, 161.

162. Willie Brown, "Future Blues," in *Masters of the Delta Blues: The Friends of Charlie Patton* (Yazoo CD 2002). Robert Palmer used the term "apocalyptic imagery" in his review of the album in *Rolling Stone*, March 5, 1992.

163. Langston Hughes, *Montage of a Dream Deferred* (New York, 1951), 11.

164. Rawick, ed., *American Slave*, Suppl. Ser. 1, VII: Miss. Narr. (Part 2), 672, VI: Miss. Narr. (Part 1), 198–99; Odel Jackson, Federal Writers' Project Works Progress Administration, Louisiana State Library, Baton Rouge; *These Are Our Lives*, 21, 356; Tucker, *Telling Memories*, 77–78; interview with Kelly Jackson, Aug. 19, 1975, Dec. 10, 1979. Yazoo County Oral History Project, Yazoo City, Miss.

165. Rosengarten, *All God's Dangers*, 109–10.

166. *Selma Southern Independent*, quoted in Clowes, *Black America*, 138–39. For a slightly different version, as quoted in the *Tuscaloosa Times*, Aug. 21, 1889, and *Tuscaloosa Gazette*, Aug. 15, 1889, see Jones, "The Black Press in the 'New South,' " 220.

167. Dittmer, "The Education of Henry McNeal Turner" in Litwack and Meier, eds., *Black Leaders of the Nineteenth Century*, 270; *Christian Recorder*, Dec. 20, 1877. In an interview with Turner in 1884 he repeated his conviction that "it is only a question of time when they will awake from their slumber and see things in a different light." *Baltimore American*, May 12, 1884, repr. *The North Carolina Republican and Civil Rights Advocate* (Weldon, N.C., May 22, 1884).

168. Theophilus G. Steward to Frank Steward, March 3, 1923, Theophilus G. Steward Papers, Schomburg Center for Research in Black Culture of the New York Public Library.

169. Jones, "The Black Press in the 'New South,' " 220.

170. Blassingame, ed., *Slave Testimony*, 653–55.

171. Sgt. [inked out], Troop [inked out], Cavalry, Gibara, Cuba, to John E. Bruce, June 22, 1899, John E. Bruce Papers, Schomburg Center for Research in Black Culture of the New York Public Library.

172. Theodore Roosevelt to Owen Wister, April 27, 1906, in Elting E. Morison et al., eds., *The Letters of Theodore Roosevelt* (8 vols.; Cambridge, Mass., 1951–54), V, 226.

173. Charles Chesnutt to Booker T. Washington, March 5, 1904. Charles W. Chesnutt Papers, Fisk University Library.

174. Hackney, *Populism to Progressivism in Alabama*, 186; Booker T. Washington to Frances J. Garrison, Aug. 31, 1903, Booker T. Washington Papers, Schomburg Center for Research in Black Culture of the New York Public Library (He sent a similar letter that day to Oswald Garrison Villard, repr. Harlan and Smock, eds., *Booker T. Washington Papers*, VII, 273); Harlan and Smock, eds., *Booker T. Washington Papers*, VII, 447.

175. Booker T. Washington to Editor of the *Portland (Me.) Eastern Argus*, Nov. 19, 1913, clipping, Booker T. Washington Papers, Manuscript Division, Library of Congress. A similar letter was sent to the *Boston Transcript*, Nov. 19, 1913, in Harlan and Smock, eds., *Booker T. Washington Papers*, XII, 340–41.

176. Wright, *Black Boy*, 147.

177. Handy, *Father of the Blues*, 140–41.

178. "Hellhound on My Trail," *Robert Johnson: The Complete Recordings* (Disc 2, Columbia CD C2K 46222).

EPILOGUE

1. Thomas, *Some Current Folk Songs of the Negro*, 9.

2. Evans, "Charley Patton: The Conscience of the Delta," in Sacre, ed., V*oice of the Delta*, 181.

3. Charles "Cow Cow" Davenport, "Jim Crow Blues," in Oliver, *Blues Fell This Morning*, 46.

4. U.S. Department of Labor, Division of Negro Economics, *Negro Migration in 1916–17* (Washington, D.C., 1919), 33.

5. Levine, *Black Culture and Black Consciousness*, 264.

6. "The Negro Problem," *Independent*, LIV (Sept. 18, 1902), 2221.

7. Pickens, *Bursting Bonds*, 13.

8. Oliver, *Blues Fell This Morning*, 23.

9. L. A. Sullivan to Blanche K. Bruce, Oct. 1, 1877, Blanche K. Bruce Papers, Howard University Library, Washington, D.C.

10. *Weekly Louisianian*, March 15, 1879. On the Exodus Movement see Nell Painter, *Exodusters: Black Migration to Kansas After Reconstruction* (New York, 1977). For additional material see Chapter 3, p. 135.

11. Painter, *Exodusters*, 188; Fulop, " 'The Future Golden Day of the Race', 83.

12. Foner, ed., *Life and Writings of Frederick Douglass*, IV, 340, 334, 336. On black leadership and the Exodus see also Painter, *Exodusters*, 247–50.

13. *Weekly Louisianian*, March 15, 1879.

14. [Colored people], Winona, Mississippi, Nov. 3, 1875, to Governor Adelbert Ames. Governor Adelbert Ames Papers, Mississippi State Archives, Jackson. Simon Peter Smith, a black teacher and preacher, described in 1877 "a very enthusiastick" black meeting in Columbia, South Carolina, on behalf of migration to Africa. "You have no idea how much the people are oppressed in the South," Williams added. Simon Peter Smith to Rev. Edward Franklin Williams, Aug. 21, 1877, Edward Franklin Williams Papers, Amistad Research Center, Tulane University, New Orleans, La.

15. E. B. Brown to Charles T. Geyer (secretary of the New York State Colonization Society), Aug. 30, 1896, Phelps-Stokes Collection, Schomburg Center for Research in Black Culture of the New York Public Library.

16. Edwin S. Redkey, *Black Exodus: Black Nationalist and Back-to-Africa Movements, 1890–1910* (New Haven, Conn., 1969), 24–46, 170–251; Henry M. Turner, "The Negro Has Not Sense Enough," *Voice of Missions*, July 1, 1900, repr. John H. Bracey, Jr., August Meier, and Elliott Rudwick, eds., *Black Nationalism in America* (Indianapolis, Ind., 1970), 173. For a memorial signed by a number of black residents of Williamsburg, South Carolina, petitioning Congress to appropriate funds to send them to Liberia, see U.S. 51st Cong., 1889–1891, Petitions for Emigration to Liberia, Records of the U.S. Senate, National Archives.

17. See William E. Bittle and Gilbert L. Geis, "Alfred Charles Sam and an African Return: A Case Study in Negro Despair," *Phylon*, 23 (Second Quarter 1962), 178–94, and *The Longest Way Home: Chief Alfred C. Sam's Back-to-Africa Movement* (Detroit, 1964).

18. Terrill and Hirsch, eds., *Such As Us*, 221.

19. Gilmore, *Gender and Jim Crow*, 132–33; Clowes, *Black America*, 187–88.

20. On the Great Migration see U.S. Department of Labor, Division of Negro Economics, *Negro Migration in 1916–17* (Washington, D.C., 1919); Emmett J. Scott, *Negro Migration During the War* (New York, 1920); Thomas J. Woofter, Jr., *Negro Migration* (New York, 1920); Clyde V. Kiser, *Sea Island to City: A Study of St. Helena Islanders in Harlem and Other Urban Centers* (New York, 1932); Florette Henri, *Black Migration: Movement North, 1900–1920* (New York, 1976); William Cohen, *At Freedom's Edge: Black Mobility and the Southern White Quest for Racial Control, 1861–1915* (Baton Rouge, La., 1991); James R. Grossman, *Land of Hope: Chicago, Black Southerners, and the Great Migration* (Chicago, 1989); and Peter Gottlieb, *Making Their Own Way: Southern Blacks' Migration to Pittsburgh, 1916–30* (Urbana, Ill., 1987).

21. Perdue et al., eds., *Weevils in the Wheat*, 115; Blassingame, ed., *Slave Testimony*, 653; Emmett J. Scott, ed., "Additional Letters of Negro Migrants of 1916–1918," *Journal of Negro History*, IV (Oct. 1919), 444.

22. Booker T. Washington to Charles W. Chesnutt, July 7, 1903, Booker T. Washington Papers, Fisk University, Nashville, Tenn.; Grossman, *Land of Hope*, 59; R. R. Moton to J. C. Hemphill, Aug. 12, 1911, Hemphill Family Papers, Duke University Library.

23. Blassingame, ed., *Slave Testimony*, 633.

24. Clarisa Sledge to Charles N. Hunter, May 22, 1904, Charles N. Hunter Papers, Duke University Library.

25. Rosengarten, *All God's Dangers*, 295–96; Bacote, "Negro Proscriptions, Protests, and the Proposed Solutions in Georgia, 1880–1908," 498; Beverly J. Robinson, *Aunt [ānt] Phyllis* (Washington, D.C., 1982), 14.

26. Levine, *Black Culture and Black Consciousness*, 266.

27. W. A. Plant to Detroit League on Urban Conditions Among Negroes, May 20, 1917, Carter G. Woodson Collection, Manuscript Division, Library of Congress; "Vicksburg," Migration Study, Mississippi, Summary, National Urban League Papers, Manuscript Division, Library of Congress.

28. Henri, *Black Migration*, 130; Crew, *From Field to Factory*, 31. Based on investigations of blacks deserting the farming districts, a Savannah black newspaper reported that "the most universal reason given has been the terror of physical violence, this even outweighing the insecurity of property and the failure of justice in the courts."

29. Emmett J. Scott, comp., "Additional Letters of Negro Migrants of 1916–1918," *Journal of Negro History*, 4 (Oct. 1919), 440, 443, 452; "Letters of Negro Migrants of 1916–1918," *Journal of Negro History*, 4 (July 1919), 304; C. J. Young, Port Arthur, Texas, to Detroit League on Urban Conditions Among Negroes, May 24, 1917, Carter G. Woodson Collection, Manuscript Division, Library of Congress. For similar sentiments in letters to the Detroit League see, for example, William Harper, Jr., Memphis, Tenn., May 14, 1917 ("i am tired of this place"); G. William

Palmer, Charleston, S.C., April 28, 1917 ("It is my sole desire to leave the South for the betterment of my Condition"); William H. Carter, Dawson, Ga., May 7, 1917 ("It is my desire to go North where I can have a better opportunity and good treatment"); Monk Daniel, Cordelle, Ga., April 30, 1917 ("men here wants to come so bad until they dont know what to do"); Mattie Effie Simon, Atlanta, Ga., April 29, 1918 ("I would like to make a change at wonce please").

30. Grossman, *Land of Hope*, 18, 34; Letter to the Editor, *Chicago Defender*, April 7, 1917.

31. See for examples of white alarm and intimidation *Chicago Defender*, Aug. 19, Nov. 11, 1916; Scott, *Negro Migration During the War*, 72–94. The *Defender* christened the exodus "The Great Northern Drive."

32. Scott, *Negro Migration During the War*, 39.

33. Scott, *Negro Migration During the War*, 39–40; U.S. Department of Labor, *Negro Migration in 1916–17*, 31; O. W. Curtis to Thomas A. Cole [Detroit League on Urban Conditions Among Negroes], May 8, 1917, Carter G. Woodson Collection, Manuscript Division, Library of Congress.

34. Wright, *Black Boy*, 224–25.

35. Scott, comp., "Additional Letters of Negro Migrants of 1916–1918," 413, 442.

36. Wright, *Black Boy*, 221–22, 226, 227–28.

37. Bechet, *Treat It Gentle*, 96; Wright, *Black Boy*, 228.

SELECTED BIBLIOGRAPHY

BOOKS, ARTICLES, AND GOVERNMENT DOCUMENTS CITED MORE THAN ONCE IN THE NOTES

Afro-American League. *Official Compilation of Proceedings of the Afro-American League National Convention Held at Chicago, January 15, 17, 1890*. Chicago, 1890.

Allen, James Lane. *The Blue Grass Region of Kentucky and Other Kentucky Articles*. New York, 1907.

American Academy of Political and Social Science. *The Negro's Progress in Fifty Years*. Philadelphia, 1913.

Anderson, Eric. *Race and Politics in North Carolina, 1872–1901: The Black Second*. Baton Rouge, La., 1981.

Anderson, James D. *The Education of Blacks in the South, 1860–1935*. Chapel Hill, N.C., 1988.

Archer, William. *Through Afro-America: An English Reading of the Race Problem*. London, 1910.

Armstrong, Louis. *Satchmo: My Life in New Orleans*. New York, 1954.

Atkins, James A. *The Age of Jim Crow*. New York, 1964.

Avary, Myrta L. *Dixie After the War*. New York, 1906.

Ayers, Edward L. *The Promise of the New South: Life After Reconstruction*. New York, 1984.

———. *Vengeance and Justice: Crime and Punishment in the 19th Century American South*. New York, 1984.

Bacote, Clarence A. "Negro Proscriptions, Protests, and Proposed Solutions in Georgia, 1800–1908." *Journal of Southern History XXV (Nov. 1959): 471–98*.

Bailey, Thomas. *Race Orthodoxy in the South*. New York, 1914.

Baker, Ray Stannard. *Following the Colour Line*. New York, 1908.

Baker, Thomas H. *The Memphis Commercial Appeal: The History of a Southern Newspaper*. Baton Rouge, La., 1971.

Beam, Lura. *He Called Them by the Lightning: A Teacher's Odyssey in the Negro South, 1908–1919*. Indianapolis, 1967.

Bechet, Sidney. *Treat It Gentle*. New York, 1960.

Blassingame, John, ed. *Slave Testimony: Two Centuries of Letters, Speeches, Interviews, and Autobiographies*. Baton Rouge, La., 1977.

Blease, Cole L. *Statement of Pardons, Paroles and Commutations Granted by Cole L. Blease, Governor of South Carolina, 1913.* Columbia, S.C., 1914.

Bose, Sudhindra. *Fifteen Years in America.* Calcutta, 1920.

Brand, Jeffrey S. "The Supreme Court, Equal Protection, and Jury Selection: Denying That Race Still Matters." *Wisconsin Law Review* 3 (1994): 511–630.

Brewer, J. Mason. *Worser Days and Better Times: The Folklore of the North Carolina Negro.* Chicago, 1965.

Broonzy, William. *Big Bill Blues: William Broonzy's Story.* London, 1955.

Brown, Sterling. "Negro Folk Expression: Spirituals, Seculars, Ballads and Work Songs." *Phylon* XIV (1st Quarter 1953): 45–61.

———. *The Negro in American Fiction.* Washington, D.C., 1937.

Brown, Virginia Pounds, and Laurella Owens. *Toting the Lead Row: Ruby Pickens Tartt, Alabama Folklorist.* University, Ala., 1981.

Bruce, H. C. *The New Man: Twenty-nine Years a Slave, Twenty-Nine Years a Free Man.* York, Pa., 1895.

Bruce, Philip A. *The Plantation Negro as Freeman.* New York, 1889.

Cable, George W. *The Silent South.* New York, 1885.

Calt, Stephen, and Gayle Wardlow. *King of the Delta Blues: The Life and Music of Charlie Patton.* Newton, N.J., 1988.

Campbell, George. *White and Black: The Outcome of a Visit to the United States.* London, 1879.

Carlton, David L. *Mill and Town in South Carolina, 1880–1920.* Baton Rouge, La., 1982.

Chesnutt, Charles W. *The Journals of Charles W. Chesnutt,* ed. Richard Brodhead. Durham, N.C., 1993.

Clark, Septima, with LeGette Blythe. *Echo in My Soul.* New York, 1962.

Clark, Thomas D. *Southern Country Editor.* Indianapolis, Ind., 1948.

Clowes, W. Laird. *Black America: A Study of the Ex-Slave and His Late Master.* London, 1891.

Cohn, David L. *Where I Was Born and Raised.* Boston, 1948.

Councill, William H. *The Negro Laborer: A Word to Him.* Huntsville, Ala., 1887.

Crew, Spencer. *Field to Factory: Afro-American Migration, 1915–1940.* Washington, D.C., 1987.

Daniel, Pete. *The Shadow of Slavery: Peonage in the South, 1901–1969.* Urbana, Ill., 1972.

Davidson, Henry D. *"Inching Along" or The Life and Work of an Alabama Farm Boy: An Autobiography.* Nashville, Tenn., 1944.

Davis, Allison, Burleigh B. Gardner, and Mary R. Gardner. *Deep South: A Social Anthropological Study of Caste and Class.* Chicago, 1941.

Davis, Benjamin. *Communist Councilman from Harlem: Autobiographical Notes Written in a Federal Penitentiary.* New York, 1969.

Davis, S. F. *Mississippi Negro Lore.* Indianola, Miss., 1914.

Dittmer, John. *Black Georgia in the Progressive Era, 1900–1920.* Urbana, Ill., 1977.

———. "The Education of Henry McNeal Turner." In Leon Litwack and August Meier, eds., *Black Leaders of the Nineteenth Century.* Urbana, Ill., 1988.

Dorsey, Hugh M. *A Statement from Governor Hugh M. Dorsey as to the Negro in Georgia.* Atlanta, Ga., April 22, 1921.

Doyle, Bertram. *The Etiquette of Race Relations in the South: A Study in Social Control.* Chicago, 1937.

Du Bois, W. E. B. *The Autobiography of W. E. B. Du Bois: A Soliloquy on Viewing My Life from the Last Decade of Its First Century.* New York, 1968.

―――. "My Evolving Program for Negro Freedom." In Rayford W. Logan, ed., *What the Negro Wants.* Chapel Hill, N.C., 1944.

―――. *The Negro Church.* Atlanta, 1903.

―――. *The Souls of Black Folk: Essays and Sketches.* Chicago, 1903.

Du Bois, W. E. B., ed. *The Health and Physique of the Negro American.* Atlanta, 1906.

Edmonds, Helen G. *The Negro and Fusion Politics in North Carolina, 1894–1901.* Chapel Hill, N.C., 1951.

Edwards, Laura F. "Sexual Violence, Gender, Reconstruction, and the Extension of Patriarchy in Granville County, North Carolina." *The North Carolina Historical Review* LXVIII (July 1991): 237–60.

Edwards, William J. *Twenty-five Years in the Black Belt.* Boston, 1918.

Ellison, Ralph. *Going to the Territory.* New York, 1986.

―――. *Invisible Man.* New York, 1952.

―――. *Shadow and Act.* New York, 1964.

Eppes, Mrs. Nicholas Ware. *The Negro of the Old South.* Chicago, 1925.

Evans, David. "Charley Patton: The Conscience of the Delta." In Robert Sacre, ed., *The Voice of the Delta: Charley Patton.* Liège, Belg., 1987.

Evans, Maurice S. *Black and White in the Southern States: A Study of the Race Problem in the United States from a South African Point of View.* London, 1915.

Evers, Charles. *Evers.* New York, 1971.

Farr, Finis. *Black Champion: The Life and Times of Jack Johnson.* London, 1964.

Federal Writers' Project of the Works Progress Administration in North Carolina, Tennessee, and Georgia. *These Are Our Lives.* Chapel Hill, N.C., 1939.

Fields, Mamie Garvin, with Karen Fields. *Lemon Swamp and Other Places: A Carolina Memoir.* New York, 1983.

Fleischer, Nat. " 'Fighting Furies' "—Story of the Golden Era of Jack Johnson, Sam Langford, and Their Negro Contemporaries," Vol. 4 in *Black Dynamite,* 5 vols. New York, 1938–47.

Floyd, Silas X. *Floyd's Flowers or Duty and Beauty for Colored Children.* Atlanta, 1905.

Foner, Philip, ed. *The Life and Writings of Frederick Douglass,* 4 vols. New York, 1950–55.

Fraser, J. Nelson. *America, Old and New: Impressions of Six Months in the States.* London, 1912.

Friedman, Lawrence J. *The White Savage: Racial Fantasies in the Postbellum South.* Englewood Cliffs, N.J., 1970.

Fulop, Timothy E. "The Future Golden Day of the Race": Millennialism and Black Americans in the Nadir, 1877–1901." *Harvard Theological Review* 84 (1991): 75–99.

Gadsden, Sam. *An Oral History of Edisto Island: Sam Gadsden Tells the Story.* Goshen, Ind., 1974.

Galishoff, Stuart. "Germs Know No Color Line: Black Health and Public Policy in Atlanta, 1900–1918." *Journal of the History of Medicine and Allied Sciences* 40 (Jan. 1985): 22–41.

Gatewood, Willard B., Jr. *Black Americans and the White Man's Burden, 1898–1903*. Urbana, Ill., 1975.

Gibson, J. W., and W. H. Crogman. *Progress of a Race or The Remarkable Advancement of the Colored American*, rev. ed. Naperville, Ill., 1912.

Gilmore, Al-Tony. *Bad Nigger! The National Impact of Jack Johnson*. Port Washington, N.Y., 1975.

Gilmore, Glenda Elizabeth. *Gender and Jim Crow: Women and the Politics of White Supremacy in North Carolina, 1896–1920*. Chapel Hill, N.C., 1996.

Gilmore, James Roberts ("Edmund Kirke"). *Here and There in Our Own Country, Embracing Sketches of Travel and Descriptions of Places*. Philadelphia, 1885.

Gordon, Taylor. *Born to Be*. New York, 1929.

Gossett, Thomas F. *Race: The History of an Idea in America*. Dallas, 1963.

Graham, Stephen. "Marching Through Georgia: Following Sherman's Footsteps Today, Part II." *Harper's Magazine* CXL (May 1920): 813–23.

Grant, Donald L. *The Way It Was in the South: The Black Experience in Georgia*. New York, 1993.

Green, Ely. *Ely: An Autobiography*. New York, 1966.

Griggs, Sutton E. *The Race Question in a New Light*. Nashville, 1909.

Grossman, James R. *Land of Hope: Chicago, Black Southerners, and the Great Migration*. Chicago, 1989.

Hackney, Sheldon. *Populism to Progressivism in Alabama*. Princeton, N.J., 1969.

Hair, William Ivy. *Carnival of Fury: Robert Charles and the New Orleans Race Riot of 1900*. Baton Rouge, 1976.

Hall, Jacqueline Dowd. *Revolt Against Chivalry: Jessie Daniel Ames and the Women's Campaign Against Lynching*. New York, 1979.

Hamer, Fanny Lou. "To Praise Our Bridges." In Dorothy Abbott, ed., *Mississippi Writers: Reflections of Childhood and Youth*, 5 vols. Jackson, Miss., 1985–91.

Handy, W. C. *Father of the Blues: An Autobiography*. New York, 1941.

Harlan, Louis. *Booker T. Washington: The Making of a Black Leader, 1856–1901*. New York, 1972.

————. *Separate and Unequal: Public School Campaigns and Racism in the Southern Seaboard States, 1901–1915*. Chapel Hill, N.C., 1958.

Harlan, Louis R., and Raymond W. Smock, eds. *The Booker T. Washington Papers*, 14 vols. New York, 1972–89.

Harvey, Paul W. "Southern Baptists and Southern Culture, 1865–1920." Ph.D. diss., University of California, Berkeley, 1992. Revised and published as *Redeeming the South: Religious Cultures and Racial Identities Among Southern Baptists, 1865–1925*. Chapel Hill, N.C., 1997.

Henri, Florette. *Black Migration: Movement North, 1900–1920*. New York, 1976.

Higginbotham, Evelyn Brooks. *Righteous Discontent: The Women's Movement in the Black Baptist Church, 1880–1920*. Cambridge, Mass., 1993.

Hill, Ruth, ed. *The Black Women Oral History Project*, 10 vols. Westport, Conn., 1991.

Holiday, Billie. *Lady Sings the Blues*. New York, 1956.

Holley, Joseph Winthrop. *You Can't Build a Chimney from the Top*. New York, 1948.

Holmes, William F. *The White Chief: James Kimble Vardaman*. Baton Rouge, La., 1970.

Holsey, Albon L. "Learning How to Be Black." *American Mercury* XVI (Apr. 1929): 421–25.

Holtzclaw, William H. *The Black Man's Burden*. New York, 1915.

Hudson, Hosea. *Black Worker in the Deep South: A Personal Account*. New York, 1972.

Hurston, Zora Neale. *Dust Tracks on a Road: An Autobiography*. Philadelphia, 1942.

Johnson, Clifton. *Highways and Byways of the Mississippi Valley*. New York, 1906.

———. *Highways and Byways of the South*. New York, 1904.

Johnson, Edward. *A School History of the Negro Race in America*. Raleigh, N.C., 1891; rev. ed., 1897.

Johnson, Guion Griffis. "The Ideology of White Supremacy, 1876–1910." In Fletcher Green, ed., *Essays in Southern History*. Chapel Hill, N.C., 1949.

Johnson, Jack. *Jack Johnson—in the Ring—and Out*. Chicago, 1927.

Johnson, James Weldon. *Along This Way: The Autobiography of James Weldon Johnson*. New York, 1933.

Johnston, Harry. *The Negro in the New World*. London, 1910.

Jones, Allen W. "The Black Press in the 'New South': Jesse C. Duke's Struggle for Justice and Equality." *Journal of Negro History* LXIV (Summer 1979): 215–28.

Jones, Bessie. *For the Ancestors: Autobiographical Memories*. Urbana, Ill., 1983.

Katzman, David. *Seven Days a Week: Women and Domestic Service in Industrializing America*. New York, 1978.

Kearney, Belle. *A Slaveholder's Daughter*, 5th ed. New York, 1900.

Kerlin, Robert T. *The Voice of the Negro 1919*. New York, 1920.

Kirwan, Albert D. *Revolt of the Rednecks: Mississippi Politics, 1876–1925*. New York, 1951.

Krech, Shepard III. *Praise the Bridge That Carries You Over: The Life of Joseph L. Sutton*. Cambridge, Mass., 1981.

Langhorne, Orra. *Southern Sketches from Virginia, 1881–1901,* ed. Charles E. Wynes. Charlottesville, Va., 1964.

Lerner, Gerda, ed. *Black Women in White America: A Documentary History*. New York, 1972.

Levine, Lawrence W. *Black Culture and Black Consciousness*. New York, 1977.

Litwack, Leon F. *Been in the Storm So Long: The Aftermath of Slavery*. New York, 1979.

Lomax, Alan. *Mister Jelly Roll: The Fortunes of Jelly Roll Morton, New Orleans Creole and "Inventor of Jazz."* New York, 1950.

Low, Alfred Maurice. *America at Home*. London, 1908.

Lowery, Rev. I. E. *Life on the Old Plantation in Ante-Bellum Days or A Story Based on Facts*. Columbia, S.C., 1911.

Macrae, David. *America Revisited and Men I Have Met*. Glasgow, 1908.

Maguire, Jane. *On Shares: Ed Brown's Story*. New York, 1975.

Marks, George P. III. "Opposition of Negro Newspapers to American Philippine Policy, 1899–1900." *The Midwest Journal* IV (Winter 1951–52): 1–25.

———, ed. *The Black Press Views American Imperialism (1898–1900)*. New York, 1971.

Mays, Benjamin E. *Born to Rebel: An Autobiography.* New York, 1971.

McMillen, Neil R. *Dark Journey: Black Mississippians in the Age of Jim Crow.* Urbana, Ill., 1989.

Meier, August. *Negro Thought in America, 1880–1915: Racial Ideologies in the Age of Booker T. Washington.* Ann Arbor, Mich., 1963.

Merritt, Carole. *Homecoming: African-American Family History in Georgia.* Atlanta, 1982.

Mollison, Irvin C. "Negro Lawyers in Mississippi." *Journal of Negro History* XV (Jan. 1930): 38–71.

Morgan, Kathryn L. *Children of Strangers: The Stories of a Black Family.* Philadelphia, 1980.

Moton, Robert Russa. *Finding a Way Out: An Autobiography.* New York, 1922.

Munsterberg, Hugo. *The Americans.* New York, 1904.

Murray, Pauli. *Proud Shoes: The Story of an American Family.* New York, 1956.

Nathans, Sydney. " 'Gotta Mind to Move, A Mind to Settle Down': African Americans and the Plantation Frontier." In William J. Cooper, Jr., Michael F. Holt, and John McCardell, eds., *A Master's Due: Essays in Honor of David Herbert Donald.* Baton Rouge, La., 1985.

National Association for the Advancement of Colored People (NAACP). *Thirty Years of Lynching in the United States, 1889–1918.* New York, 1919.

National Negro Business League. *Proceedings of the National Negro Business League . . . 1900.* Boston, 1901.

A Negro Nurse. "More Slavery at the South." *The Independent* 72 (Jan. 25, 1912): 196–200.

"The Negro Problem: How It Appeals to a Southern Colored Woman." *The Independent* 54 (Sept. 18, 1902): 2221–24.

"The Negro Problem: How It Appeals to a Southern White Woman." *The Independent* 54 (Sept. 18, 1902): 2224–28.

Nunn, James. *The Oral History of James Nunn: A Unique North Carolinian.* Chapel Hill, N.C., 1977.

Oakley, Giles. *The Devil's Music: A History of the Blues.* New York, 1977.

Odum, Howard W., and Guy B. Johnson. *The Negro and His Songs: A Study of Typical Negro Songs in the South.* Chapel Hill, N.C., 1925.

———. *Negro Workaday Songs.* Chapel Hill, N.C., 1926.

Oliver, Paul. *Blues Fell This Morning: The Meaning of the Blues.* New York, 1961.

———. *Conversation with the Blues.* New York, 1965.

Oshinsky, David M. *"Worse Than Slavery": Parchman Farm and the Ordeal of Jim Crow Justice.* New York, 1996.

Oster, Harry. *Living Country Blues.* Detroit, 1969.

Page, Thomas Nelson. *The Negro: The Southerner's Problem.* New York, 1904.

Painter, Nell. *Exodusters: Black Migration to Kansas After Reconstruction.* New York, 1977.

Palmer, Robert. *Deep Blues.* New York, 1981.

Perdue, Charles L., Jr., Thomas E. Barden, and Robert K. Phillips, eds. *Weevils in the Wheat: Interviews with Virginia Ex-Slaves.* Charlottesville, Va., 1976.

Pickens, William. *American Aesop: Negro and Other Humor.* Boston, 1926.

————. *Bursting Bonds.* Boston, 1923.

The Possibilities of the Negro in Symposium. Atlanta, 1904.

Proctor, Henry Hugh. *Between Black and White: Autobiographical Sketches.* Boston, 1925.

Puryear, Bennet [Civis]. *The Public School in Its Relations to the Negro.* Richmond, Va., 1877.

Rabinowitz, Howard N. "The Conflict Between Blacks and the Police in the Urban South, 1865–1900." *Historian* XXXIX (Nov. 1976): 62–76.

————. *Race Relations in the Urban South, 1865–1890.* New York, 1978.

Race Problems of the South: Report of the Proceedings of the First Annual Conference Held Under the Auspices of the Southern Society for the Promotion of the Study of Race Conditions and Problems in the South at Montgomery, Alabama, May 8, 9, 10, A.D. 1900. Richmond, Va., 1900.

Rawick, George P., ed. *The American Slave: A Composite Autobiography,* 19 vols. Westport, Conn., 1972.

————. *The American Slave: A Composite Autobiography.* Supplement, Series 1, 12 vols. Westport, Conn., 1977.

————. *The American Slave: A Composite Autobiography.* Supplement, Series 2, 9 vols. Westport, Conn., 1979.

The Reason Why the Colored American Is Not in the World's Columbian Exposition. Chicago, 1893.

Redkey, Edwin S. "Bishop Turner's African Dream." *Journal of American History* 54 (Sept. 1967): 271–90.

Roberts, Randy. *Papa Jack: Jack Johnson and the Era of White Hopes.* New York, 1983.

Robinson, James H. *Road Without Turning: The Story of Reverend James H. Robinson: An Autobiography.* New York, 1950.

Rosengarten, Theodore. *All God's Dangers: The Life of Nate Shaw.* New York, 1974.

Rutherford, Mildred Lewis, ed. *Miss Rutherford's Scrap Book: Valuable Information About the South,* 10 vols. Athens, Ga., 1925.

Savitt, Todd L. "Entering a White Profession: Black Physicians in the New South, 1880–1920." *Bulletin of the History of Medicine* 61 (1987): 507–40.

Scott, Emmett J. *Negro Migration During the War.* New York, 1920.

————, ed. "Additional Letters of Negro Migrants of 1916–1918." *Journal of Negro History* IV (October 1919): 412–65.

————. "Letters of Negro Migrants of 1916–1918." *Journal of Negro History* IV (July 1919): 290–340.

Simkins, Francis Butler. *Pitchfork Ben Tillman: South Carolinian.* Baton Rouge, La., 1944.

Smith, Jay Clay, Jr. *Emancipation: The Making of the Black Lawyer, 1844–1944.* Philadelphia, 1993.

A Southern Colored Woman. "The Race Problem—An Autobiography." *The Independent* 56 (March 17, 1904): 586–89.

Stanford, T. Thomas. *The Tragedy of the Negro in America.* North Cambridge, Mass., 1897.

Stephenson, Gilbert T. *Race Distinctions in American Law.* New York, 1911.

Sterling, Dorothy, ed. *We Are Your Sisters: Black Women in the Nineteenth Century.* New York, 1984.

Stone, Alfred H. *Studies in the American Race Problem.* New York, 1908.

Street, Julian. *American Adventures.* New York, 1917.

Taft, Michael, ed. *Blues Lyric Poetry: An Anthology.* New York, 1983.

Talley, Thomas W. *Negro Folk Rhymes.* New York, 1922.

Terrell, Mary Church. *A Colored Woman in a White World.* Washington, D.C., 1940.

Terrill, Tom E., and Jerrold Hirsch, eds. *Such As Us: Southern Voices of the Thirties.* Chapel Hill, N.C., 1978.

Thomas, Jesse O. *My Story in Black and White: The Autobiography of Jesse O. Thomas.* New York, 1967.

Thomas, W. H. *Some Current Folk-Songs of the Negro.* The Folk-Lore Society of Texas, 1912.

Tillett, Wilbur Fisk. "Southern Womanhood as Affected by the War." *Century Magazine,* New Series XLIII (1891): 9–16.

Trautmann, Frederic, ed. *Travels on the Lower Mississippi, 1879–1880: A Memoir by Ernst von Hesse-Wartegg.* Columbia, Mo., 1990.

Tucker, Susan. *Telling Memories Among Southern Women: Domestic Workers and Their Employers in the Segregated South.* Baton Rouge, La., 1988.

Urban, Wayne F. *Black Scholar: Horace Mann Bond, 1904–1972.* Athens, Ga., 1992.

U.S. Department of Labor, Division of Negro Economics. *Negro Migration in 1916–17.* Washington, D.C., 1919.

U.S. 42d Cong., 2d sess., House Report 22. *Report of the Joint Select Committee to Inquire into the Condition of Affairs in the Late Insurrectionary States,* 13 vols. Washington, D.C., 1872.

U.S. 48th Cong., Senate, Committee on Education and Labor. *Report of the Committee of the Senate upon the Relations Between Labor and Capital, and Testimony Taken by the Committee,* 4 vols. Washington, D.C., 1883.

U.S. 59th Cong., 1st sess., Document No. 179. *Report of the Industrial Commission on Agriculture and Agricultural Labor.* Washington, D.C., 1901.

Walker, Margaret. "Growing Out of Shadow." *Common Ground* IV (Autumn 1943): 42–46.

Walters, Alexander. *My Life and Work.* New York, 1917.

Washington, Booker T. *Future of the American Negro.* Boston, 1899.

———. *Up from Slavery: An Autobiography.* New York, 1901.

Washington, Booker T., and W. E. B. Du Bois. *The Negro in the South: His Economic Progress in Relation to His Moral and Religious Development.* Philadelphia, 1907.

Wells, Ida B. *Crusade for Justice: The Autobiography of Ida B. Wells,* ed. Alfreda M. Duster. Chicago, 1970.

———. *A Red Record: Tabulated Statistics and Alleged Causes of Lynchings in the United States, 1892–1893–1894.* Chicago, 1895.

———. *Southern Horrors.* New York, 1892.

Wheeler, Edward L. *Uplifting the Race: The Black Minister in the New South, 1865–1902.* Lanham, Md., 1986.

White, Newman. *American Negro Folk-Songs.* Cambridge, Mass., 1928.

White, Newman, ed. *The Frank C. Brown Collection of North Carolina Folklore,* 7 vols. Durham, N.C., 1952–64.

White, Walter. *A Man Called White.* New York, 1948.

———. *Rope and Faggot: A Biography of Judge Lynch.* New York, 1929.

Williamson, Joel. *After Slavery: The Negro in South Carolina During Reconstruction, 1861–1877.* Chapel Hill, N.C., 1965.

———. *The Crucible of Race: Black-White Relations in the American South Since Emancipation.* New York, 1984.

Wilson, Emily Herring. *Hope and Dignity: Older Black Women of the South.* Philadelphia, 1983.

Wolff, Daniel, et al. *You Send Me: The Life and Times of Sam Cooke.* New York, 1995.

Woods, E. M. *The Negro in Etiquette.* St. Louis, 1899.

Woodward, C. Vann. *Origins of the New South, 1877–1913.* Baton Rouge, La., 1951.

———. *The Strange Career of Jim Crow,* 3d rev. ed. New York, 1974.

Wright, Richard. *Black Boy: A Record of Childhood and Youth.* New York, 1945.

———. *Uncle Tom's Children.* New York, 1938.

Wright, Richard R., Jr. *87 Years Behind the Black Curtain: An Autobiography.* Philadelphia, 1965.

Yates, James. *Mississippi to Madrid: Memoir of a Black American in the Abraham Lincoln Brigade.* Seattle, 1989.

MANUSCRIPT SOURCES FROM COLLECTIONS CITED IN THE NOTES

Alabama State Archives, Montgomery
John W. DuBose Papers
Edward H. Moren Papers

Amistad Research Center, Tulane University Library, New Orleans
Edward Franklin Williams Papers

Arkansas State Archives, Little Rock
Federal Writers' Project, WPA, Folklore Subjects

Bennett College, Greensboro, North Carolina
Norris W. Cuney Papers

Manuscript Department, Duke University Library, Durham, North Carolina
Herbert Baxter Adams Papers
Richard S. Andrews Papers
W. W. Ball Papers
Cronly Family Papers
Jabez Lamar Monroe Curry papers
Francis W. Dawson Papers
Egbert Du Bois Papers
Paul Hamilton Hayne Papers
Hemphill Family Papers
Hinsdale Family Papers

Charles N. Hunter Papers
Kell Collection
Daniel William Lassiter, Francis Rives Lassiter, and Charles Trotter Lassiter
  Papers
Eugene Marshall Papers
Winfield Henri Mixon Papers
St. Leger Landon Moncure Papers
W. A. Pledger Letter Book
Pope-Carter Family Papers
Louisa Bouknight Poppenheim and Mary Barnett Poppenheim Papers
Henry Watson, Jr., Papers
Benjamin S. Williams Papers

Special Collections, Fisk University Library, Nashville, Tennessee
  Charles W. Chesnutt Papers
  Booker T. Washington Papers

Georgia State Archives, Atlanta
  Governor's Papers

Special Collections Department, University of Georgia Library, Athens
  Rebecca Felton Papers

Manuscripts Division, Howard University Library, Washington, D.C.
  Blanche K. Bruce Papers
  P. B. S. Pinchback Papers

Manuscripts Division, Library of Congress, Washington, D.C.
  Federal Writers' Project, WPA, Negro Studies Projects
  National Association for the Advancement of Colored People (NAACP) Papers
  National Urban League Papers
  Booker T. Washington Papers
  Carter G. Woodson Collection

Louisiana State Library, Baton Rouge
  Federal Writers' Project, WPA, Manuscript Narratives

Department of Archives and History, Louisiana State University Library, Baton
Rouge
  Caffery, Donelson Papers
  Joel A. Stokes and Family Papers, Merritt M. Shilg Memorial Collection
  Thrasher Papers
  Wallace, Rice, Duncan Papers

Mississippi Department of Archives and History
  Governor's Papers
  James Lynch File
  Eugene Marshall Papers
  A. T. Montgomery Diary
  Isaiah Montgomery in Subject File

James K. Vardaman File
WPA Records ("Our Lives")

National Archives, Washington, D.C.
    Records of the Commission of Fine Arts
    Department of Justice Records (Record Group 60)

North Carolina State Department of Archives and History, Raleigh
    James L. Anderson Papers
    Alexander Boyd Andrews, Jr., Papers
    George E. London Collection
    Robert W. Winston Papers

Southern Historical Collection, University of North Carolina, Chapel Hill
    Avery Family Papers
    Elizabeth A. C. (Hooper) Blanchard Papers
    Thomas Clawson Papers
    Henry Groves Connor Papers
    Hilary A. Herbert Papers
    William Porcher Miles Diary
    Montgomery Papers
    Appleton Oaksmith Papers
    Nimrod Porter, Diary and Notes
    Matt Whitaker Ransom Papers
    Francis G. Ruffin Papers
    William R. Savage Papers
    Preston H. Turner Papers
    Alfred Waddell Papers
    Thomas E. Watson Papers

Rockefeller Archive Center, Pocantico Hills, Tarrytown, New York
    General Education Board Papers
    John F. Slater Fund Papers

Schomburg Center for Research in Black Culture, New York Public Library
    John E. Bruce Papers
    New York Colonization Society Records
    Phelps-Stokes Fund Collection
    William Pickens Papers
    Smith-Shivery Family Papers
    Theophilus G. Steward Papers
    Booker T. Washington Papers

South Caroliniana Library, University of South Carolina, Columbia
    Childs Family Papers
    Frederik Holmes Christensen Diary
    Edmunds-Dawkins-Battise Families Papers
    Ellis Family Papers
    Federal Writers' Project, WPA, Life Histories

Alice Louisa Fripp Diary
Gibson-Humphreys Papers
Hammond, Bryan, Cumming Families Papers
Elias B. Holloway Papers
Hugh Lide Law Diary
Miller-Furman-Dabbs Families Papers
Montgomery Family Papers
William James Rivers Papers
Alexander Samuel Salley, Jr., Papers
Sams Family Papers
J. R. Sparkman Papers
William Henry Trescott Papers
James Thomas Williams Papers

Tulane University Library, New Orleans, La.
Chalaron Papers
Dunlap Family Papers

Yazoo City Public Library, Yazoo City, Mississippi
Yazoo County Bicentennial Oral History Project
Yazoo County Library System Oral History Project
Yazoo County Scholar-in-Residence Oral History Program

DISCOGRAPHY OF ARTISTS AND ALBUMS
CITED IN THE TEXT OR NOTES

Louis Armstrong: Portrait of the Artist as a Young Man, 1923–1934. Columbia Legacy CD 57176.

Blues in the Mississippi Night: As Told to and Recorded by Alan Lomax. Memphis Slim, Big Bill Broonzy, and Sonny Boy Williamson. Rykodisc RCD90155.

The Blues: A Smithsonian Collection of Classic Blues Singers. Smithsonian Collection of Recordings RD 101: 1–4.

Juke Joint Blues. Blues Classics BC23.

Ishman Bracey and Charley Taylor, 1928–1929. Document Records DOCD-5049.

Willie Brown. *Masters of the Delta Blues: The Friends of Charlie Patton.* Yazoo CD2002.

Bertha "Chippie" Hill: Complete Recorded Works, 1925–1929. Document Records DOCD-5330.

Eddie "Son" House. *The Complete Library of Congress Sessions.* Travelin' Man CD02.

Robert Johnson: The Complete Recordings. Columbia C2K 46222.

Furry Lewis in His Prime, 1927–1928. Yazoo Records 1050.

The Definitive Blind Willie McTell. Columbia C2K 5323.

Charley Patton: Founder of the Delta Blues. Yazoo Records 1020.

King of the Delta Blues: The Music of Charlie Patton. Yazoo Records 2001.

The Voice of the Delta: The Complete Paramount Recordings of Charley Patton. Black Swan HCD 21–22.

Ma Rainey's Black Bottom. Yazoo Records 1071.

The Complete Plantation Recordings: Muddy Waters. Library of Congress Field Recordings CHD 9344.

INDEX

Abbeville, S.C., 309–11, 335
accommodation, black, 404, 415–17,
    481, 488, 493; in churches, 387–91;
    generational conflicts over, 420–2, 493;
    in politics, 354–63, 366–8; press, 428–30;
    and submission, difference between,
    430–4; Washingtonian, 146–50, 151, 160,
    309, 317–18, 321, 387–91, 404, 428, 431,
    458, 471–2, 476–7; see also etiquette, racial;
    subordination, black
accounting, black literacy in, 54–5, 57, 60,
    131–2, 158, 420
Adair, Christia, 363
Africa, 31, 71, 75, 329, 405, 459, 469;
    American black heritage in, 75–6, 210–13,
    459–63, 486; emigration to, 392, 405–6,
    408, 473, 485–6, 489; proposed
    deportation to, 118, 211, 459
"African," use of term, xvii, 459, 461
African Emigration Society, 405–6, 408
African Methodist Episcopal Church, 145,
    309, 314, 367, 372, 382, 384, 392, 402,
    406, 440, 459, 460
African Methodist Episcopal Zion Church,
    384–5, 460
"Afro-American," use of term, xvii, 459–60
Aggrey, Abna, 32, 41
agriculture, 18, 50; black success in, 115, 122,
    130, 132, 137–9, 143–4, 147, 150–60,
    309–12, 329, 492; boll weevil problem,
    175–8, 489; crop lien, 136; disputes over
    crop settlements, 3–7, 54, 55, 60, 115, 129,
    131–6, 139–40, 155, 164, 180, 306, 309–10,
    420; vs. education, 54, 57–8, 59, 64–6,
    95–8, 125–7; indebtedness cycle, 115,
    130–42, 155, 163–7, 175, 311, 378, 483;
    industrial training, 58, 67, 78–86; labor,
    3–7, 18, 29, 36–7, 49, 54, 57–9, 64–5, 98,
    114–42, 150–60, 163–5, 175–8, 210, 280,
    306, 342, 351, 358, 418, 420, 450, 452,
    469, 472, 481, 483, 489; New Negro
    disinterest in, 210, 211, 481, 489; "paying
    out," 155, 159; peonage, 15, 140–2, 165;
    "settlin' time," 131–6; sharecropping,
    114–23, 125, 127–42, 143, 163–5, 210, 342,
    350, 378, 406, 411; tenant farms, 3–7, 55,
    114–23, 127–42, 143, 163–5, 210, 378, 406;
    wage labor, 115, 124, 128–30, 139, 165;
    "whitecap" violence, 157–8; see also specific
    crops
Aguinaldo, Emilio, 405
Alabama, 19, 23, 31, 33, 48, 49, 186, 415,
    416, 429, 438, 439, 442, 451, 469, 472–4,
    476, 478, 482, 485, 491; black churches,
    382, 386, 388; black education, 60, 68,
    70, 79–86, 88, 92, 101, 106, 108, 109;
    black labor, 118, 119, 123, 124, 127, 137,
    140, 141, 143, 155, 158–9, 164, 171–2; black
    vote and disfranchisement, 225, 227, 228,
    244, 323, 363–70; black women, 346–9,
    352; boll weevil, 175; criminal justice
    system, 249, 255, 256–7, 264, 272, 274,
    295; Jim Crow segregation, 217–18, 232,
    235–9, 256, 257, 426; lynchings, 283–4,
    288, 295, 296, 299, 346, 394, 423; New
    Negro, 207, 212, 227
Alabama Black Belt, 227, 382, 413
Alabama Constitutional Convention (1901),
    93, 227, 228
Albrier, Frances, 46, 421
alcohol, forced drinking of, 10–11
Alford, Barney, 366
Alger, Horatio, 48
ambition, black, 27–9, 49, 59, 150–5, 219,
    321–2, 491; curbing of, 7, 23, 27–8, 59–60,
    79, 91–100, 112, 115, 143–4, 150, 153–63,

A NOTE ABOUT THE AUTHOR

Leon F. Litwack was born in Santa Barbara, California. He received his B.A., M.A., and Ph.D. from the University of California, Berkeley, where he is currently the Alexander F. and May T. Morrison Professor of American History. Mr. Litwack has also taught at the University of Wisconsin, as the Ford Foundation Professor of Southern Studies at the University of Mississippi, and as a visiting Fulbright professor of American history at Moscow State University, Beijing University, the University of Helsinki, and the University of Sydney. For *Been in the Storm So Long: The Aftermath of Slavery,* he received in 1980 the Pulitzer Prize in History and the Parkman Prize awarded by the Society of American Historians. He has been the recipient of two Distinguished Teaching Awards at Berkeley, a Guggenheim Fellowship, and a National Endowment for the Humanities Film Grant, with which he produced *To Look for America* in 1971. In 1986–87 he was President of the Organization of American Historians, and in 1987 he was elected to the American Academy of Arts and Sciences. He is coeditor of the forthcoming *Harvard Guide to African American History.*

A NOTE ON THE TYPE

This book was set in a type called Baskerville. The face itself is a facsimile reproduction of types cast from the molds made for John Baskerville (1706–1775) from his designs. Baskerville's original face was one of the forerunners of the type style known to printers as "modern face"—a "modern" of the period A.D. 1800.

Composed by ComCom, Allentown, Pennsylvania
Printed and bound by Quebecor Printing, Martinsburg, West Virginia
Designed by Robert C. Olsson